IF YOU THINK YOU'VE HEARD IT ALL, YOU PROBABLY HAVEN'T HEARD . . .

The most expensive species in captivity is the giant panda, for which four U.S. zoos each pay an annual fee of $1 million to China to lease a pair.

The most bungee jumps in 24 hours was accomplished by fitness coach Colin Phillips (UK), who recorded 151 jumps from a 328-foot-tall crane.

The most consecutive rolls by an aircraft was achieved by Kingsley Just, who rolled his Pitts Special biplane 987 times for just under an hour without any break.

Betty White holds the title of longest-running TV career by a female entertainer, having made her television debut in 1939, just after graduating high school, and still making us laugh at the age of 92 years.

The most expensive diamond sold at auction was the "Pink Star," which was sold to an anonymous bidder for more than $76 million on November 12, 2013, in Geneva, Switzerland. The oval 59.60-carat diamond took two years to cut.

The smallest dog is a female Chihuahua called Milly, who measured 3.8 in. tall on February 21, 2013. As a puppy, she was fed using an eyedropper and was small enough to fit on a teaspoon.

Accreditation

Guinness World Records Limited has a very thorough accreditation system for records verification. However, while every effort is made to ensure accuracy, Guinness World Records Limited cannot be held responsible for any errors contained in this work. Feedback from our readers on any point of accuracy is always welcomed.

Abbreviations & Measurements

Guinness World Records Limited uses both metric and imperial measurements. The sole exceptions are for some scientific data where metric measurements only are universally accepted, and for some sports data. Where a specific date is given, the exchange rate is calculated according to the currency values that were in operation at the time. Where only a year date is given, the exchange rate is calculated from December 31 of that year. "One billion" is taken to mean one thousand million.

General Warning

Appropriate advice should always be taken when attempting to break or set records. Participants undertake records entirely at their own risk. Guinness World Records Limited has complete discretion over whether or not to include any particular record attempts in any of its publications. Being a Guinness World Records record holder does not guarantee you a place in any Guinness World Records publication.

GUINNESS WORLD RECORDS 2015

BANTAM BOOKS
NEW YORK

2015 Bantam Books Mass Market Edition

GUINNESS WORLD RECORDS™ 2015
Copyright © 2014 by Guinness World Records Limited.
Published under license.

GUINNESS WORLD RECORDS is a trademark of Guinness World Records Limited and is reproduced under license by Bantam Books, an imprint of Random House, a division of Random House, LLC, a Penguin Random House Company, New York.

Revised American editions copyright © 2014, 2013, 2012, 2011, 2010, 2009, 2008, 2007, 2006, 2005, 2004, 2003, 2002, 2001, 2000, 1999, 1998, 1997, 1996, 1995, 1994, 1993, 1992, 1991, 1990, 1989, 1988, 1987, 1986, 1985, 1984, 1983, 1982, 1981, 1980, 1979, 1978, 1977, 1976, 1975, 1974, 1973, 1972, 1971, 1970, 1969, 1968, 1966, 1965, 1964, 1963, 1962, 1961, 1960 by Guinness World Records Limited

For more information address: Guinness World Records Limited

Bantam Books and the House colophon are registered trademarks of Random House LLC.

ISBN 978-1-101-88380-8

Printed in the United States of America

www.bantamdell.com

2 4 6 8 9 7 5 3 1

Bantam Books mass market edition: March 2015

GUINNESS
WORLD
RECORDS

2015

EDITOR-IN-CHIEF
Craig Glenday

CONTENTS

Check out related and cross-referenced pages of records.

QUOTE "When one thinks of Guinness World Records, automatically 'extraordinary' and 'remarkable' comes to mind. So for me to win, I am truly honored and delighted." **Usain Bolt**

INTRODUCTION

EDITOR'S LETTER

Welcome to this special diamond anniversary edition of the world's **biggest-selling annual book**. We may be entering our 60th year, but we're not looking to retire just yet! While this year's book revisits six ever-changing decades of record breaking, we've still squeezed in every major new and updated record from the last year, so expect the usual mix of unrivaled sporting achievements, talented pets, cutting-edge scientific discoveries, and the most remarkable human beings on the planet . . .

MOST CONSECUTIVE DAILY PERSONAL VIDEO BLOGS ON YOUTUBE As of May 6, 2014, Charles Trippy (U.S.A.) had posted 1,831 daily "vlogs" on his YouTube channel, "Internet Killed Television." During Apr. 2014, Charles documented his separation from wife and fellow vlogger Alli, shown left, who had vlogged with him.

MOST SUCCESSFUL REALITY TELEVISION FORMAT *Got Talent* (Fremantle Media/Syco) has been sold to 58 countries since Jun. 2007. Second left is *America's Got Talent* host Nick Cannon, with judges (from left) Howard Stern, Howie Mandel, Heidi Klum, and Mel B. Learn more about the show and other TV records on pp. 381–386.

FACT: In 2013 alone, the *Got Talent* family grew with editions in Afghanistan, Brazil, Iceland, Kazakhstan, and Moldova.

Globally, **only 7.6% of claims** became official world records last year.

There's been no letup in the demand for record breaking, with around 50,000 new claims, inquiries, and updates filling our inboxes and mail trays over the past 12 months. We've had correspondence and claims from around the world, from Afghanistan (**longest chain of paper dolls**: a successful attempt, at 4.09 mi., or 6.5 km) to Zimbabwe (**longest live DJ set**: TBC, but the current record of 168 hr. will be hard to beat!), alongside inquiries from as far afield as East Timor, Tongo, and Tajikistan.

The U.S.A. remains the no. 1 country for record claims, with 13,352 applications registered. Thanks and congratulations to everyone who has made it into our database as an official GWR record holder and gone on to receive their official Guinness World Records certificate as evidence of their efforts.

LONGEST TV CAREER BY A FEMALE ENTERTAINER Betty White (U.S.A.) made her TV debut in 1939, just after graduating from high school, and is still making us laugh at the age of 92 years 39 days (as of Feb. 25, 2014). Betty took time out from her busy schedule to accept her GWR certificate marking more than 75 years on TV, radio, stage, and in movies. Thanks, Betty!

SHORTEST LIVING WOMAN We'd like to say a big thank you to 2-ft. 0.7-in.-tall (62.8-cm) Jyoti Amge of India for helping us launch our last book in New York. Jyoti—who's shorter than a fire hydrant—headed straight for Times Square, where she was celebrated at a huge size on the famous billboard.

As ever, record breaking in the U.S.A. extended from coast to coast:

- New York: Publishing giant HarperCollins and cartoonist Lincoln Peirce (U.S.A.) unveiled the **longest cartoon strip by a team** at 3,983 ft. 2 in. (1,214 m) on the set of NBC's *Today* on Apr. 11, 2014.
- Ohio: Eric Walter (U.S.A.) achieved the **fastest 400 m joggling with three objects**, taking 55.81 sec. at Bowling Green State University in Bowling Green on Jul. 20, 2013.
- Missouri: David Babcock (U.S.A.) took home a GWR certificate for the **longest scarf knitted while running a marathon**, thanks to his 12-ft. 1.75-in. (3.70-m) neckwear, knocked up during the Kansas City Marathon on Oct. 19, 2013.
- Colorado: Caboose Hobbies in Denver was confirmed as the world's **largest model train store**, with 18,600 sq. ft. (1,728 m²) of floor space open to the public and more than 100,000 items on display.
- California: 16-year-old Leo Howard (b. Jul. 13, 1997) became the **youngest person to direct a TV episode** when he helmed the "Fight at the Museum" episode of Disney's *Kickin' It* series in L.A. between Feb. 12 and 19, 2014.

YOUTUBE GOES IN ONE DIRECTION One Direction (UK) spent part of 1D Day (a seven-hr. streaming marathon on Nov. 23, 2013) attempting to break some Guinness World Records titles. None succeeded, but dry that tear 1D fans: the boys still hold several records, including **first UK group to enter the U.S. albums chart at No. 1 with their debut**—a feat The Beatles never managed. Music records start on p. 362.

MOST TV STAND-UP SPECIALS Since debuting with *HBO Comedy Half-Hour* in Oct. 1996, actress and comedian Kathy Griffin (U.S.A.) had hosted 20 stand-up specials on TV as of Dec. 18, 2013. In 2011, she became the first comedian to host four televised specials in a calendar year. Here, she is accepting her official certificate from GWR's Stuart Claxton.

LOUDEST CROWD ROAR AT AN INDOOR SPORTS STADIUM Fans of the NBA's Sacramento Kings cheered at an ear-splitting 126 dBA at Sleep Train Arena in Sacramento, California, on Nov. 15, 2013. Despite the vocal fans, the Kings lost that night's game to the Detroit Pistons by 97–90. Find all the sporting winners in this year's sports section starting on p. 465.

SPRING BREAKS ON NBC'S *TODAY* Morning show *Today* hosted Spring Breakers week from Apr. 7 to 11, 2014, and raised more than $150,000 for charity. Daily record attempts included the **highest trampoline bounce by a team** (22 ft. 1 in.; 6.73 m, main picture) with extreme trampolining brothers Sean, Eric, and T.J. Kennedy. Geronimo set the **most double-dutch skips by a dog in one minute** at 128, making owner Samantha Valle (U.S.A.) skip with delight. The **largest exercise ball class** was held by trainer Michelle Bridges (AUS), with 353 aching participants. And then there was the demon barber— David Alexander (U.S.A.) set the record for the **most heads shaved in one hour** (73), with just 11 sec. to spare. Dare we say it was a close shave?

RECORD STARS

Record holders come from all walks of life. We've had successful attempts from school kids, such as the 1,463 students from Lexington Catholic High School and area middle schools in Kentucky, who took part in the **largest game of Secret Santa** on Dec. 4, 2013. In the professional world, we've had the likes of the staff at the Something Sweet Bake Shop in Daphne, Alabama, who baked the **largest brownie**: a titanic treat that tipped the scales at 234 lb. 3 oz. (106.2 kg)—the weight of nearly three teenagers!— on Sep. 12, 2013. And athletes have broken records, too, such as Corey "Thunder" Law of the Harlem Globetrotters, who made the **longest basketball shot**—109 ft. 9 in. (33.45 m)—at U.S. Airways Center in Phoenix, Arizona, on Nov. 11, 2013. And TV star Rob Dyrdek has been breaking records again—find out more on page xvii.

As well as all these new records, because it's our 60th birthday, we've traced the evolution of some of your favorite record categories. You'll find "Flashback" features at the beginning of each chapter. Each one explores a record-breaking topic—including 60 years of space travel (pp. 4–9), new discoveries in the animal world (pp. 69–73), and advances in telecommunications technology (pp. 393–398)—and traces how the records have evolved in the years since our first book was published in 1955. We've also dipped into our earlier editions to bring you bite-size Flashbacks throughout the book, comparing records from the past to those of today. It's fascinating to see how much has changed since the 1950s . . . and how much has stayed the same!

One of the reasons for the success of GWR over the past 60 years is that we've embraced any new habits, fashions, and technology. We're not a dusty reference book—we reflect what's happening around us.

This year is no exception, which is why you'll find new categories for topics such as 3D printing (p. 462), Instagram and Twitter (pp. 297–298), alternative transport (pp. 419–424), and digital piracy (p. 381). Look out, too, for some 2013 "neologies" (new words), such as "bitcoin" (p. 287), "twerking" (pp. xvii and 244), and "selfies" (p. 297).

FIRST ACT TO PLAY A CONCERT ON EVERY CONTINENT

Congratulations to music legends Metallica—from left: Kirk Hammett, Lars Ulrich, James Hetfield, and Robert Trujillo—who finally secured a world record that has eluded bands for years: the first to play a gig on every continent. Find out more on p. 365.

LARGEST PILLOW FIGHT Exuberant dance duo Dada Life (Olle Corneer and Stefan Engblom, both SWE) organized a mid-concert pillow fight for fans at the Aragon Ballroom in Chicago, Illinois, on Oct. 27, 2013. With the clock striking midnight, lasers lighting the room and the duo's beats providing the soundtrack, 3,813 pillow-wielding participants proved themselves "Born to Rage."

MOST PEOPLE TWERKING SIMULTANEOUSLY Big Freedia, aka Freddie Ross (U.S.A.), led a 358-strong crowd in twerking on Sep. 25, 2013. The booty-shaking dance exploded into the mainstream in 2013, thanks to Miley Cyrus, but Big Freedia is a legend in the hip-hop genre that inspired it: New Orleans Bounce. Check out mass participation records on pp. 241–246.

GWR IN GATLINBURG Visitors to the GWR museum in Gatlinburg, Tennessee, above, were able to try their hand at setting world records live on site. New interactive elements and 100 live shows were introduced in 2013 and, with GWR adjudicators on hand, 88 visitors walked out as new record holders over the summer. In 2014, visitors to GWR museums in Hollywood and San Antonio will also be able to try their hand at world record attempts.

FARTHEST REVERSE RAMP JUMP BY CAR Rob Dyrdek (U.S.A.) added to his portfolio of 18 skateboarding records with a car jump performed by driving and launching his Chevrolet Sonic RS Turbo *backward* over 89 ft. 3.25 in. (27.2 m). His great leap took place at Six Flags Magic Mountain in California on Feb. 13, 2014. More conventional motor sports action is to be found on pp. 528–532.

CHALLENGERS

While you're online, be sure to check out the Challengers section of our website, too. This gives wannabe record holders fast access to an official Guinness World Records adjudicator for a series of do-try-this-at-home record categories, such as Food & Drink, Sports & Fitness, and Video Games. You'll find out how this unique service works at www.guinnessworldrecords.com/challengers.

FACT: Broc assumes the record of **tallest teen** previously held by Brenden Adams of Washington. Brenden, who's now 19 years old, took the record at 13 years old at the height of 7 ft. 4.6 in.!

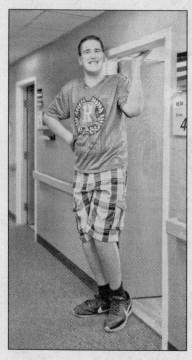

TALLEST TEENAGER Broc Brown (U.S.A., b. Apr. 15, 1997) measured 7 ft. 1.5 in. (217.17 cm) tall in Apr. 2014. A student at Vandercook Lake High School in Jackson, Michigan, Broc was diagnosed with Sotos syndrome (cerebral gigantism). Although he can dunk, he's too big for basketball, and Nike has supplied him with size 24 athletic shoes—bigger than those worn by Shaquille O'Neal.

We're indebted, as always, to our countless record claimants and fans. Of course, we try to answer every e-mail and letter, although we can't find room for every single new record—our annual book features only about 10% of all the superlatives we have on file, and includes those classic records that have stood the test of time. So if you've achieved a record and you haven't been selected, better luck next time.

If you haven't yet set a record and you want a chance to see your name in the *Guinness World Records* book, why not apply now? Record breaking is free and open to absolutely everyone—you'll find out how to do it on p. xxix.

We need the public to keep on breaking those records, because we're nothing without our record holders. We also need to keep on documenting the world. Sixty years ago, it wasn't possible to make a transatlantic phone call (p. 394), no human had set foot on the Moon (p. 6), no one had ever rowed across an ocean, and no one had ever heard of twerking. Just imagine where we might be in 60 years' time . . .

Craig Glenday
Editor-in-Chief

MOST GAME-SHOW EPISODES HOSTED BY THE SAME PRESENTER
If the answer is "The host of the quiz show *Jeopardy!* since Sep. 10, 1984," then the question must be "Who is Canada's Alex Trebek?" As of Apr. 17, 2014, he has missed only one of 6,830 episodes, when he switched with Pat Sajak of *Wheel of Fortune* on April Fool's Day 1997.

LONGEST ABDOMINAL PLANK
Gabi Ury (U.S.A.) had just turned 16 when she rested her whole body weight on her forearms and toes for 1 hr. 20 min. 2 sec. on Apr. 19, 2014. As if setting a record in the female category for the grueling plank position wasn't enough on its own, she has a condition called VATER syndrome that has led to 14 major surgeries. She raised money in her attempt for the Children's Hospital Colorado and received her certificate on the set of ABC's *Good Morning America*.

DIAMONDS

Largest diamond in the universe BPM 37093 is a white dwarf star 50 light-years from Earth in the constellation of Centaurus. In 2004, astronomers from the Harvard-Smithsonian Center for Astrophysics in Massachusetts, U.S.A., deduced that the carbon white dwarf had crystallized into a diamond some 2,500 mi. (4,000 km) across. The star has been nicknamed "Lucy," after The Beatles' song "Lucy in the Sky with Diamonds." Assuming the cost of $1,600 per carat, Lucy would set you back $16,000,000,000,000,000,000,000,000,000,000,000,000 ($16 undecillion).

Largest brilliant-cut diamond A 545.67-carat brilliant diamond known as the "Golden Jubilee Diamond" was purchased from the diamond specialty group De Beers by a syndicate of Thai businessmen and was presented to the King of Thailand in 1995 to commemorate his golden jubilee. It is now mounted in the Thai royal scepter.

All the diamonds ever polished in history would fill just **one double-decker bus**.

Largest cut fancy black diamond An unnamed fancy black diamond containing small red diamond crystals was polished into 55 facets over several years and finished in Jun. 2004. It weighs 555.55 carats—the repetitive use of the number five is culturally significant in the Islamic world—and was inspired by Ran Gorenstein (BEL), who also commissioned it.

Most diamonds in one ring The "Tsarevna Swan" ring, which was created by the Lobortas Classic Jewelry House (UKR), is white gold set with 2,525 diamonds. Fully wearable, it was presented and measured in Kiev, Ukraine, on Jul. 21, 2011.

Most expensive diamond per carat The diamond price record per carat is $1,375,938 for a 7.03-carat fancy vivid blue modified rectangular brilliant-cut diamond sold by Sotheby's on May 12, 2009. It was cut from an original stone that weighed 26.58 carats.

Most valuable boots A pair of size-8.5 women's ankle boots made with 167 oz. (4,738 g) of gold and covered in 39,083 natural fancy colored diamonds weighing 1,550 carats was unveiled by Diarough/UNI-Design and A. F. Vandevorst (BEL) in Hong Kong in Dec. 2013. The boots were valued at $3.1 m.

MOST VALUABLE SNOOPY
On Nov. 13, 2009, to celebrate the 60th anniversary of Charles Schulz's cartoon-strip canine Snoopy, Tse Sui Luen Jewellery of Hong Kong, China, created a 5.5-in.-tall (14-cm) "Diamond Snoopy" encrusted with 9,917 diamonds. Also known as "The Ever-Shining Star," the 207-carat creation went on sale with a price tag of HK$2,888,880 ($372,750).

FACT: This scintillating Snoopy also features 783 black diamonds and a collar made from 415 red ruby gemstones!

LARGEST DIAMOND PENDANT The largest nonreligious pendant is "Crunk Ain't Dead," owned by hip-hop artist Lil' Jon (U.S.A.). With 3,576 white diamonds, it weighs 2 lb. 2.4 oz. (977.6 g) without its chain.

FIRST 100% DIAMOND RING On Mar. 8, 2012, the jewelers Shawish (CHE) unveiled the first ring to be made entirely from a diamond. The 150-carat creation is reportedly worth a whopping $70 m.

MOST VALUABLE CASINO CHIP A casino chip designed by Gerald N. Lewy (CAN) was valued at CAN$450,000 ($436,500) on May 30, 2013. The 22-carat pink gold chip is set with 173 round brilliant-cut diamonds (17 of them around the rim) and 64 natural pink diamonds.

Most expensive diamond sold at auction On Nov. 12, 2013, the "Pink Star"—a flawless pink diamond—was sold to an anonymous bidder for 76,325,000 Swiss francs ($83.01 m) at Christie's in Geneva, Switzerland. The oval 59.60-carat diamond is mounted on a ring and measures 1.06 x 0.81 in. (2.69 x 2.06 cm). It took two years to cut.

Most faceted diamond Diamonds are cut with varying numbers of facets to enhance their sparkle (see below), the most common being the 57 or 58 facets of the "brilliant" cut found in most engagement rings. The "Brilliant Lady 21" cut, which was created by Louis Verelst (BEL), has 221 facets, producing a large number of reflections and resulting in increased brilliance.

First manmade diamond In 1955, scientists in GE's laboratory in Schenectady, New York, U.S.A., built an ultrahigh-pressure apparatus called the "Diamond Press." The press produced pressure of over 1.5 million lb./sq. in. (1 billion kg/m^2) and up to 5,000°F (2,760°C). Metal and carbon were melted together, using an electrical current, and then cooled. The result: perfectly formed manmade diamonds up to 1/10th carat in weight.

The **largest manmade cut diamond** is a 2.16-carat synthetic marquis-cut diamond created by the Scio Diamond Technology Corporation (U.S.A.). The 0.5-in. (13.42-mm) diamond was tested in Apr. 2013 by the Gemological Institute of America.

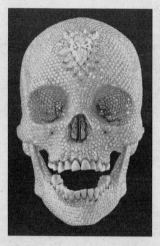

MOST VALUABLE MATERIALS IN A WORK OF ART *For the Love of God* by Damien Hirst (UK) is a human skull encrusted with 8,601 flawless diamonds, including a 52.4-carat pink diamond in the forehead. The total 1,106.18 carats of diamonds were reported to cost a dazzling £12 m ($23.7 m).

MOST VALUABLE NECKLACE "The Incomparable" contains a 407.48-carat flawless diamond and 102 "satellite" diamonds. Manufactured by the jewelers Mouawad, based in Switzerland, it was valued on Feb. 13, 2013 at an incredible $55 m. The flawless diamond was discovered in the Congo some 30 years ago in a pile of kimberlite, a by-product of diamond mining.

FACT: The Incomparable appeared on eBay in 2002 with a starting price of $22.5 m but failed to sell.

LARGEST UNCUT DIAMOND

The largest ever single, rough, uncut diamond was the "Cullinan," which weighed 3,106.75 carats when found in 1905 in South Africa. It was cut into nine smaller diamonds, the largest of which, the "Great Star of Africa," weighs 530.2 carats and tops the royal scepter (far left) wielded by the UK's Queen Elizabeth II. The next largest fragment—the "Second Star of Africa"—sits in the Queen's Imperial State Crown.

"BABY" WILLIAMS

The latest fashion accessory for any self-respecting rapper is "grillz"—i.e., diamond dentures. The king of bling is undoubtedly Bryan "Baby" Williams (U.S.A.), who reportedly spent a record $500,000 on having his teeth permanently fitted with 18-carat white gold and platinum crowns set with asher-cut diamonds.

ROCK STARS: DIAMONDS DEFINED

Diamond—the world's **hardest natural substance**—is a mineral formed 85–125 mi. down in Earth's mantle. It is a form (allotrope) of the chemical element carbon (C) in which the atoms are arranged in a tetrahedral crystalline formation. Diamonds are measured in carats, with one carat equal to 200 mg. For each carat of diamond mined, 550,000 lb. of earth is excavated.

LARGEST HEIST: *The 90-second Break-in*

At lunchtime on Jul. 28, 2013, an armed man entered the Carlton International hotel (above left) in Cannes, France. His target: jewelry worth 103 m euros ($136.7 m). He single-handedly pulled off the biggest diamond heist ever in just one-and-a-half minutes. The diamond-encrusted watches, rings, and earrings he stole (above right) belonged to Lev Leviev—a Soviet-born Israeli diamond and property mogul—and had been on display in an exhibition at the hotel.

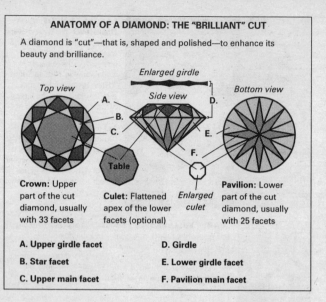

ANATOMY OF A DIAMOND: THE "BRILLIANT" CUT

A diamond is "cut"—that is, shaped and polished—to enhance its beauty and brilliance.

Enlarged girdle

Top view

Side view

Bottom view

A.
B.
C.
D.
E.
F.

Table

Crown: Upper part of the cut diamond, usually with 33 facets

Culet: Flattened apex of the lower facets (optional)

Enlarged culet

Pavilion: Lower part of the cut diamond, usually with 25 facets

A. Upper girdle facet
B. Star facet
C. Upper main facet

D. Girdle
E. Lower girdle facet
F. Pavilion main facet

OFFICIALLY AMAZING!

CELEBRATING THE 60-YEAR STORY OF THE BIGGEST-SELLING ANNUAL

"Turn the heat of argument into the light of knowledge." This was the remit of the first-ever edition of *The Guinness Book of Records*, which itself had its origins in an argument. On Nov. 10, 1951, during a shooting party at North Slob, by the Slaney River in County Wexford, Ireland, Sir Hugh Beaver (1890–1967)—MD of the Guinness Brewery—and his fellow fowl hunters failed to bag some golden plovers flying overhead. Could the plover be the fastest game bird in Europe? A debate ensued, but no answer could be found, not even in the well-stocked library of Sir Hugh's host later that evening.

It occurred to Sir Hugh that people across the UK and Ireland would be arguing over all kinds of topics, and that perhaps a book should be published to settle those debates. If he could create such a book, he could even give it away to some of the 80,000 or so pubs in the UK as part of a promotion to sell more Guinness stout. To help him with his plan, he needed to locate a fact-finding agency, and, luckily, an underbrewer at the Guinness Brewery in Park Royal, London, had the answer: the McWhirter twins.

In the 1950s, Sir Hugh Beaver (left)—Managing Director of the Guinness Brewery—had the idea for a book of world records that might help settle arguments in pubs. Sixty years on, the idea of superlatives continues to fascinate and excite . . . and inspires millions of people to strive for immortality by becoming record holders themselves.

That underbrewer was Chris Chataway (1931–2014), an amateur athlete who acted as pacemaker for Roger Bannister, who on May 6, 1954 had broken the four-minute mile—a feat once thought to be impossible. The timekeeper for the race was Norris McWhirter (1925–2004), who, along with his identical twin Ross (1925–75), had recently set up a fact-finding agency in London.

Sir Hugh commissioned the McWhirters to create his book of superlatives, and in 1954 the twins set up an office in a disused gym at 107 Fleet Street in London. Under the name Guinness Superlatives, they spent an intense few months researching and collating the first edition of *The Guinness Book of Records*, which was bound on Aug. 27, 1955.

While it was initially intended as a promotional item, the book had a life beyond the bars, and when *The Guinness Book of Records* was offered up for the public to buy (minus the beer-proof coating!) in October of that year, it became an instant best-seller, and it has remained at the top of the charts ever since. Within a year, it had launched in the U.S.A.—as *The Guinness Book of World Records*—and today is available in more than 100 countries in up to 20 languages.

In the years since its debut, the book has had a change of owner—it was sold by the Guinness Brewery in 1999—and a change of name to its current title *Guinness World Records*, reflecting the fact that it's more than just a book; it also has TV shows, museums, websites, digital apps, e-books, and, most recently, live events.

RECORD ADJUDICATION

As the accepted global arbiter of record-breaking achievement, Guinness World Records now processes around 50,000 claims a year, and has sent adjudicators as far afield as the bottom of the ocean and the top of the Burj Khalifa, the world's **tallest building**. We've expanded into larger premises in London, and opened new offices in New York (U.S.A.), Tokyo (JPN), Beijing (CHN), and Dubai (UAE), with more record representatives and editorial consultants dotted all around the world.

As you'll see in this year's edition, we continue to evolve and adapt, reflecting the ever-shifting modern landscape and providing a snapshot of the universe in which we live. As long as humans continue to push the limits of what's possible, we'll be there with our stopwatches and counters, documenting and ratifying the achievements. And the next 60 years will undoubtedly be as fascinating and record breaking as the last.

1954 Sir Hugh Beaver invites the McWhirter twins to start work on a book of superlatives

1955 Twins Ross (left) and Norris McWhirter publish the first edition of *The Guinness Book of Records* for the Guinness Brewery.

1956 The first U.S. edition is published

1962 First French edition

1963 First German edition

1967 First Japanese, Danish, and Norwegian editions

1968 First Swedish, Finnish, and Italian editions

1971 First Dutch edition

1972 In the UK, the BBC produce a spin-off of TV show *Blue Peter* called *Record Breakers*, hosted by Roy Castle (right) and the McWhirter twins; it runs for nearly 30 years.

1973 Broadcaster David Frost (second on left) acquires TV rights for GWR specials. The *Hall of Fame* special seen at right appeared in 1986.

1975 First GWR museum opens in the Empire State Building, New York, U.S.A.

1976 First Czech edition

1977 First Hebrew, Serbo-Croat, and Icelandic editions

1978 First Slovenian edition

1996 GWR opens an office in New York, U.S.A.

1998 *Guinness World Records Primetime* debuts on Fox TV on Jul. 27, 1998, hosted by Mark Thompson, and runs for 53 episodes.

1999 GWR launches its first UK TV show, named simply *Guinness World Records*, hosted by UK soccer star Ian Wright.

2000 guinnessworldrecords.com launches

2003 The 100-millionth copy of the book is sold

2005 First annual Guinness World Records Day

Officially Amazing!

2005 Her Majesty, Queen Elizabeth II, receives a copy of our 50th anniversary edition from GWR President Alistair Richards.

2006 Editor-in-Chief Craig Glenday welcomes the King of Pop, Michael Jackson, to the London offices on the eve of the 2006 World Music Awards, where Jackson's *Thriller* album is acknowledged as the **biggest-selling album of all time**.

2010 GWR app launches; office opened in Tokyo, Japan

2012 Office opened in Beijing, China

2013 Office opened in Dubai, UAE

2013 Hong Kong actor Jackie Chan accepts his two GWR certificates, for **most stunts by a living actor** (more than 100 movies) and **most credits in one movie** (15).

2015 GWR celebrates its 60th anniversary

EXPERIENCE GWR LIVE
Look out for the exciting new Guinness World Records Attractions, the first of which is scheduled to open in 2015. See records come to life using cutting-edge digital technology, and attempt your own records in front of official GWR adjudicators.

BE A RECORD-BREAKER

HAVE YOU GOT A RECORD-BREAKING TALENT TO SHARE?

Anyone can set a record and there are more ways of doing it now than ever before. It's free of charge and you can apply right away at **www.guinness worldrecords.com**. When we started in 1955, record holders could only appear in the book—now you can get on TV, appear at live events, or get your attempt on our website.

DO YOU KNOW WHICH RECORD YOU WANT TO ATTEMPT?

If you think you've got what it takes to tackle an existing record, we want to hear from you. Want to try something new? We are equally excited by new ideas, so let us know right away.

YES

REGISTER ONLINE Head on over to **www.guinnessworldrecords.com** and click on "Register" at the top of the screen. It's a matter of minutes to set up your account and you're almost set.

COLLECT EVIDENCE Make sure you give yourself plenty of time to practice your record attempt. When you're ready to go, you'll have to be careful to collect all the evidence we need to ensure your best chance of a successful attempt.

NO

READ, WATCH, BROWSE Keep reading the book! You'll find ideas there and in our TV shows and you can check out the latest action on the website at **www.guinnessworldrecords .com**. This will give you a sense of the records that we usually accept.

HAVE YOU GOT THE GUIDELINES YET?

YES

JUST THE FACTS Gather your evidence and send it to us. Depending on the record, we'll need independent eyewitness statements, photos, video, and other proof outlined in the guidelines. Now just wait to hear . . .

NO

RECORD RULES If your chosen record already exists (or we like your idea), we'll send you the guidelines that anyone must follow when making an attempt. If you've submitted an idea and we don't accept it, we will tell you why.

DID YOU BREAK YOUR RECORD?

YES

YOU'RE A RECORD-BREAKER! If you've followed the rules and beaten an existing record or even set a new one, you'll receive a letter of confirmation. You will also be sent your official Guinness World Records certificate welcoming you into the family of record holders. Congratulations! If you're very lucky, you may even make it into next year's book.

NO

BETTER LUCK NEXT TIME You may not be successful, but don't give up! Come back and try again or choose a different record for another chance to receive that world-famous certificate.

FACT: You can attempt a world record right now by visiting **www.guinnessworldrecords.com/challengers** and, once you get the green light, you can upload a video of your attempt. You'll soon hear—GWR adjudicate every week.

SPACE

CONTENTS

This **gallery of galaxies** illustrates the beauty of our Universe . . .
not shown to scale!

1. NEAREST ACTIVE GALAXY Galaxies that contain a compact highly luminous core emitting intense radiation are known as "active" galaxies. At just 11 million light-years away, the enormous elliptical galaxy Centaurus A is the closest of these active galaxies to our own.

2. MOST COMMON TYPE OF GALAXY Spiral galaxies, such as Messier 101—pictured here by the *Hubble* space telescope—account for 77% of all galaxies. Our Milky Way is also a spiral galaxy, characterized by spiral arms wound around a brighter core.

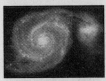

3. FIRST DISCOVERED SPIRAL GALAXY William Parsons, 3rd Earl of Rosse (IRL), identified M51 (the "Whirlpool Galaxy") as a spiral in 1845. He used the *Leviathan*, then the world's **largest telescope**, at Birr Castle, County Offaly, Ireland.

4. CLOSEST GALAXY TO THE MILKY WAY The Canis Major dwarf galaxy lies an average of 42,000 light-years from the center of our galaxy. It was only found in 2003 because it was difficult to detect behind the plane of our own spiral galaxy as seen from Earth.

5. MOST REMOTE OBJECT VISIBLE TO THE NAKED EYE The Andromeda galaxy, known as Messier 31, is about 2.5 million light-years from Earth. Runner-up in this category is Messier 33, a spiral galaxy that can be glimpsed at a distance of 2.53 million light-years.

6. DENSEST GALAXIES Ultra Compact Dwarf (UCD) galaxies, such as M60-UCD1 (pictured), contain around a hundred million stars squashed into a space measuring 200 light-years across.

7. LARGEST SATELLITE GALAXY Of the 15 minor satellite galaxies orbiting the Milky Way, the largest and brightest is the Large Magellanic Cloud, some 160,000 light-years from the center of the Milky Way.

8. FASTEST APPROACHING GALAXY The Universe might be expanding, but M86, a lenticular galaxy around 52 million light-years away in the Virgo Cluster, is moving toward us at a rate of 260 mi./s (419 km/s).

9. LARGEST GALAXY IC 1101, in the Abell 2029 cluster, has a major diameter of 5.6 million light-years—80 times the diameter of the Milky Way—and a light output equivalent to 2 trillion times that of the Sun. It may be the result of many smaller galaxies merging.

10. LARGEST DISTANT GALAXY "El Gordo" is the nickname of a galaxy cluster 7 billion light-years away. Discovered via a disturbance in the cosmic microwave background, El Gordo is actually two clusters colliding at a rate of several million mph.

MILESTONES IN SPACE

No human had crossed the edge of space when GWR started in 1955. It wasn't until 1961 that the milestone was reached, but the pioneers of space exploration went on to rack up achievements at a blistering pace—visiting the Moon, building space stations, and sending rovers to Mars and a probe beyond our Solar System.

NASA's five Space Shuttles spent some **1,320 days** in space.

FACT: Chris says there have been musical instruments in space since a U.S. Project Mercury astronaut brought a harmonica—and the Russians had a guitar on a *Salyut* space station.

CHRIS HADFIELD On May 12, 2013, Commander Chris Hadfield (CAN) posted the **first music video filmed in space**, David Bowie's "Space Oddity," recorded on board the *ISS*. In an interview with GWR, Chris revealed that he had fronted bands for years but never covered Bowie, much less "Space Oddity." "The astronaut dies in it!" laughed Chris. "Why would I play that song, of all things?" Chris agreed—once his son Evan altered the words—and recorded vocals on his iPad. "It sounded way better than I thought it would, as if the track had soaked up a sense of place." Chord changes in zero gravity were a challenge because his guitar would float away when strummed, when it would sit in his hands on Earth. Other tracks were added and the video was mixed on Earth. For a father-son project, Chris was delighted at the song's success. "It bridged science fiction and science fact."

It is testament to the power of human imagination that space flight quickly became an accepted part of everyday thought and discussion. Our concept of an expanding future for space exploration occupies much of our science fiction movies and television, and even cash-strapped nations compete to send probes to our sister planets.

The conquest of space was kick-started as part of the increasingly bitter Cold War in the 1950s between the U.S.A. and the USSR. In 1955, both powers announced their intention to launch satellites, and the Soviets were the first to achieve the **first artificial satellite** with *Sputnik 1* in 1957. They were again the first to launch a man into space in 1961. Eager to catch up, U.S. President Kennedy promised that the U.S.A. would be the first to get humans on the Moon. "We choose to go to the Moon in this decade," he said in 1962, ". . . because that challenge is one that we are willing to accept, one we are unwilling to postpone."

With that bold declaration, the space race became hotter than ever and the brightest and bravest ensured it changed humanity and the way we saw our planet and our place in the Solar System.

1961 FIRST MANNED SPACE FLIGHT: Russian cosmonaut, Flight Major Yuri Gagarin, achieves an altitude of 203 mi. in *Vostok 1* on Apr. 12, 1961. Gagarin completes a single orbit of the Earth (still the **shortest orbital flight**) and ejects 108 min. into the flight as planned.

1969 FIRST MEN ON THE MOON: Neil Armstrong (U.S.A.), commander of the *Apollo 11* mission, takes his first small step at 2:56 a.m. GMT on Jul. 21, 1969, followed onto the surface of the Moon by Edwin "Buzz" Aldrin Jr. (U.S.A.).

1970 FARTHEST DISTANCE FROM EARTH REACHED BY HUMANS: The crew of *Apollo 13* reach 248,654 mi. above the Earth's surface on the "dark" (far) side of the Moon at 1:21 a.m. BST on Apr. 15, 1970. They are 157.8 mi. above the lunar surface.

1973 FARTHEST DISTANCE TRAVELED ON ANOTHER WORLD: The unmanned Soviet *Lunokhod 2* rover travels 26 mi. on the Moon between Jan. 16 and Jun. 23, 1973.

1981 FIRST MANNED MAIDEN SPACE FLIGHT: John Young and Robert Crippen (both U.S.A.) launch the inaugural orbital mission of the Space Shuttle *Columbia* on Apr. 12, 1981. It is the first time a new spacecraft system is piloted in space without a prior unmanned flight.

1984 FIRST UNTETHERED SPACEWALK: U.S. astronaut Bruce McCandless II tests the Manned Maneuvering Unit (MMU) from the Space Shuttle *Challenger* on Feb. 7, 1984.

1986 FIRST FLIGHT BETWEEN SPACE STATIONS: Mir EO-1 is the first expedition to the Soviet *Mir* space station. Its crew, Leonid Kizim and Vladimir Solovyov, launch from Earth on Mar. 13, 1986, reach *Mir* two days later, and remain docked for six weeks. *Mir* deorbits some 15 years later on Mar. 23, 2001. More than 100 people visit over its lifespan.

1995 FIRST SHUTTLE DOCKING: On Jun. 29, 1995, the Space Shuttle *Atlantis* connects with *Mir* as part of the Shuttle–*Mir* Program. This marks the 100th space flight launched by the U.S.A. as *Atlantis* brings Anatoly Solovyev and Nikolai Budarin to *Mir* and returns Vladimir Dezhurov, Gennady Strekalov (all RUS), and Norman Thagard (U.S.A.) to Earth.

1997 FIRST MARS ROVER: The 1997 *Sojourner* (U.S.A.) vehicle is landed by NASA's *Mars Pathfinder* spacecraft on Jul. 4. A small mobile laboratory, *Sojourner* travels an approximate total of 328 ft. and conducts such experiments as measuring the chemical composition of rocks.

1998 LARGEST SPACE STATION: The *International Space Station* (*ISS*) is a modular structure that launches in 1998. On Feb. 24, 2011, the STS-133 Shuttle mission launches to dock the Leonardo Permanent Multipurpose Module with the *ISS*, bringing it to its current mass of 924,739 lb.

2004 FIRST PRIVATELY FUNDED MANNED SPACE FLIGHT: On Jun. 21, 2004, *SpaceShipOne* reaches 328,490 ft., piloted by Mike Melvill (ZAF), built by Scaled Composites, and funded by Paul Allen (both U.S.A.).

2004 LAND SPEED RECORD ON MARS: Twin NASA Mars exploration rovers *Opportunity* (shown right) and *Spirit*, landing in Jan. 2004, are each capable of speeds up to 2 in. per sec.

2005 MOST REMOTE PLANETARY LANDING: *Huygens* lands on Saturn's largest moon, Titan, in Jan. 2005. Data and images are sent back by the European Space Agency (ESA) probe from the Moon that is at an average distance of 888 million mi. from the Sun.

2008 CLOSEST FLYBY OF MERCURY: On Jan. 14, 2008, NASA's *MESSENGER* spacecraft performs a gravity-assist flyby to just 123.7 mi. above the surface at closest approach.

2014 FIRST HUMAN-MADE OBJECT TO TRAVEL IN INTERSTELLAR SPACE: On Sep. 12, 2013, NASA announces that *Voyager 1* has crossed the heliopause, the boundary between the Solar System and interstellar space. As of Apr. 9, 2014, it is 11.84 billion mi. from the Sun on a mission begun in 1977 (see p. 27).

SPACE PIONEERS

1961: Yuri Gagarin: First man in space
Gagarin's flight of Apr. 12 (see p. 5) hit a speed of 25,394.5 mi. and made him a Soviet hero. Tragically, he was killed in a jet flight in 1968 at the age of just 34.

1963: Valentina Tereshkova: First woman in space
Launched in *Vostok 6* from Kazakhstan on Jun. 16, Tereshkova (USSR) flew for 2 days 22 hr. 50 min. She went on to be politically prominent in the USSR.

1965: Alexey Leonov: First spacewalk
Leonov (USSR) conducted the first ever extra-vehicular activity (EVA)—aka spacewalk—when he exited the *Voskhod 2* craft for 12 min. on Mar. 18, 1965.

1969: Neil Armstrong: First men on the Moon
The commander of the *Apollo 11* mission was the first to walk on the surface of the Moon. He had learned to fly at 15 years old, before he got his driving license.

1969: "Buzz" Aldrin: First men on the Moon
In 2013, Aldrin (U.S.A.) looked back: "Neil had an optimistic way of using the word 'beautiful.' But when I looked out, it wasn't beautiful. It was desolate."

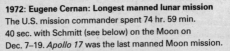

1972: Eugene Cernan: Longest manned lunar mission
The U.S. mission commander spent 74 hr. 59 min. 40 sec. with Schmitt (see below) on the Moon on Dec. 7–19. *Apollo 17* was the last manned Moon mission.

1972: Harrison Schmitt: Longest Moon walk
Along with Cernan (see above), the U.S. geologist spent 7 hr. 37 min. on the Moon on Dec. 12, the pair covering 12.6 mi. and taking extensive samples.

1994–95: Valeri Polyakov: Longest manned space flight
The USSR-born doctor was sent to the *Mir* space station on Jan. 8, 1994 and, after a space flight lasting 437 days 17 hr. 58 min., landed—in full health—on Mar. 22, 1995.

1998: John Glenn: Oldest astronaut
The war hero, senator, and first American to orbit Earth (U.S.A., b. Jul. 18, 1921) made a 1998 space comeback on Oct. 29 on the Space Shuttle, at 77 years 103 days old.

2004: Mike Melvill: First commercial astronaut
After piloting *SpaceShipOne* in 2004 (see p. 7), the pioneer was awarded the first commercial astronaut wings by the U.S. Federal Aviation Administration.

2005: Sergei Krikalev: Most time spent in space
The USSR-born cosmonaut notched up 803 days 9 hr. in space, including stints on *Mir*, Space Shuttles, and the *ISS*. He retired from active space flight in 2007.

2007: Sunita Williams: Most spacewalk time (female)
The U.S. astronaut has spent a total of 50 hr. 40 min. on spacewalks. In Sep. 2012, she carried out external repairs to the power supply unit of the *ISS*.

UNIVERSE

Largest cloud of primordial hydrogen First discovered in 2000, LAB-1 is an astronomical object known as a Lyman-alpha blob. Measuring ca. 300,000 light-years across and 11.5 billion light-years from Earth, LAB-1 is a cloud of hydrogen gas that has yet to coalesce into galaxies. The blob is glowing—possibly due to the light from galaxies within that have already formed. Owing to its distance, we see LAB-1 as it was when the Universe was only around 15% of its current age.

Largest void The Giant Void is a very large region of space with an abnormally low density of galaxies and other matter within the constellation Canes Venatici. Also known as the "Giant Void in NGH (Northern Galactic Hemisphere)," the "Canes Venatici Supervoid," or its more scientific designation AR-Lp 36, is the largest confirmed void to date in the visible Universe. With an estimated diameter of 300–400 Mpc (1–1.3 billion light-years), its geometric center is approximately 1.5 billion light-years away.

FIRST SIGHTING OF AN EXTRAGALACTIC PLANET In 2009, astronomers announced that they had seen a planet in the Andromeda galaxy, 2.2 million light-years away. It became visible when it passed in front of a star, an event known as "microlensing," when the light of a star is magnified by an object passing in front. The Andromeda event was first seen in 2004, when it was believed to be owing to a binary star.

MOST MASSIVE BLACK HOLE On Dec. 5, 2011, astronomers using the *Gemini North*, *Keck II*, and *Hubble* observatories reported a supermassive black hole in the center of elliptical galaxy NGC 4889, some 336 million light-years away. The black hole's mass is estimated at 20 billion times that of the Sun.

Twin sunsets: the planet **Kepler-47b** is lit by two stars.

HIGHEST-ENERGY GAMMA RAYS FROM A GAMMA-RAY BURST
In May 2013, NASA announced that its *Fermi* gamma-ray space telescope had detected a burst measuring at least 94 billion electron volts (35 billion times the energy of normal, visible light). This explosion, known as GRB 130427A, came from a galaxy 3.6 billion light-years away.

MOST DISTANT BLACK HOLE
A supermassive black hole resides in the center of quasar ULAS J112001.48+064124.3. In terms of redshift (a light measurement—higher than 1.4 means the source is receding at more than the speed of light), it measures 7.085. This black hole was announced in Jun. 2011 and emits radiation from superheated matter that surrounded it less than 770 million years after the Big Bang.

Densest known galaxy
M60-UCD1, announced in Sep. 2013, is a type of galaxy called an Ultra-Compact Dwarf (UCD). This class was discovered in 1999 by astrophysicists led by Dr. Michael Drinkwater (UK). These galaxies are potentially leftover building blocks that once formed much larger galaxies. Half of the mass of M60-UCD1 is found within a radius of only 80 light-years, making the density of stars 15,000 times greater than our area of the Milky Way.

Most distant dwarf galaxy
In 2012, astronomers led by Dr. Simona Vegetti of the Massachusetts Institute of Technology announced the discovery of a dwarf galaxy orbiting a large elliptical galaxy some 10 billion light-years away. Undetectable by telescope, its gravity causes light distortion that gives it away. It's possible the galaxy is composed exclusively of dark matter, or it may contain stars that are too dim to be visible at this distance.

WE ARE ALL STARDUST

You're older than you might think—most of the elements in your body include atoms that arose during the Big Bang, 13.82 billion years ago.

The astronomer and influential science communicator Carl Sagan (U.S.A., 1934–96), host of the original *Cosmos* TV show in 1980, famously wrote: "The nitrogen in our DNA, the calcium in our teeth, the iron in our blood, the carbon in our apple pies were made in the interiors of collapsing stars. We are made of star-stuff."

Highest electrical current Scientists at the University of Toronto, Canada, have made the "shocking" discovery of the highest known electrical current in the Universe. Generated by a cosmic jet more than 2 billion light-years away in a galaxy known as 3C303, the electrical current is measured at 1E18 amps (1 followed by 18 zeros). The scientists used the effect of the current on radio waves coming from the galaxy to measure this tremendous amount of electrical energy, which is most likely generated by magnetic fields from a black hole at the center of the galaxy. The resulting jet of matter extends into space to around 150,000 light-years—possibly the largest bolt of lightning ever seen.

LARGEST STRUCTURE The Hercules-Corona Borealis Great Wall consists of a staggeringly huge cluster of galaxies and other normal matter measuring 10 billion light-years across and about 10 billion light-years from Earth. Superclusters are bound by gravity; this one was announced in Nov. 2013 by astronomers who mapped it by charting gamma-ray bursts (pictured) in the region.

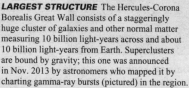

MOST MAGNETIC OBJECT If a magnetar flew within 100,000 mi. (161,000 km) of Earth, it could strip the data off every credit card. Fortunately, there have been fewer than a dozen identified examples of these neutron stars (which come from the dead core of collapsed stars densely packed to the size of a city). Magnetars, thought to originate from the supernovae of massive stars, have magnetic fields that are up to a trillion times the size of, for example, a hospital MRI machine.

DEEPEST NOTE The Universe's lowest note is caused by acoustic waves generated by a supermassive black hole. It is in the center of the Perseus cluster of galaxies (left), 250 million light-years away. The sound—a B-flat note, 57 octaves below middle C—propagates through thin gas surrounding the black hole.

See Earth from space on pp. 48–50.

LONGEST GALACTIC JET An energetic jet of matter emitted from a supermassive black hole in the center of galaxy CGCG 049-033 measures 1.5 million light-years long. Life on any planets in the path of the jet stream would be extinguished.

Most distant supernova A Type IIn supernova some 11 billion light-years away was located using data from the Canada-France-Hawaii Telescope. In 2009, astronomers announced they had seen a galaxy that brightened momentarily with a spectrum characterized by a narrow color band of emitted light from hydrogen as it burns.

Oldest light The Cosmic Microwave Background (CMB) is radiation that formed 380,000 years after the Big Bang. When the Universe was born, a tremendous amount of light was generated that remains all pervasive. The CMB can be seen as photons coming from all directions. The 2013 *Planck* map of CMB showed, among other things, that the Universe is older than thought, at 13.82 billion years.

Smallest extrasolar planet Kepler-37b is a planet only slightly larger than the Moon. It orbits the star Kepler-37, around 210 light-years from Earth in the constellation of Lyra. Its discovery by NASA's *Kepler* space observatory—the mission launched to carry out research into habitable planets—was announced on Feb. 20, 2013. Kepler-37b is only 1,199 mi. (1,930 km) across, making it smaller than the planet Mercury.

NOTHING TO SEE HERE: Dark Matter Astronomers in the 1970s, particularly Vera Rubin (near left), measured the velocities of stars in other galaxies and noticed that the stars at the galaxies' edges moved faster than predicted. To reconcile the observations with the law of gravity, scientists proposed that there is matter we can't see and called it "dark matter." This, the most common form of matter, neither emits nor absorbs light and radiation as stars and planets do. Measuring the effect of dark matter in gravitational terms, scientists have proposed that together with dark energy it makes up 95% of the Universe.

FACT: Light travels at 186,400 mi./s and a light-year measures how far light travels in a year.

COSMOLOGICAL COMPOSITION

Astronomers once thought that the Universe was composed largely of "stuff"—i.e., stars and planets made of atoms and heavy elements. However, observations of how galaxies move suggest that most of the total mass of the Universe is invisible. It is currently understood that the majority of the Universe is "dark" energy and matter; the stars and planets, plus the interstellar hydrogen and other gases and dust, account for just ca. 5%.

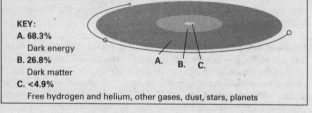

KEY:

A. 68.3%
Dark energy

B. 26.8%
Dark matter

C. <4.9%
Free hydrogen and helium, other gases, dust, stars, planets

SOLAR SYSTEM

MERCURY

Largest impact basin on Mercury The Caloris Basin has a diameter of ca. 950 mi. (1,550 km) and is surrounded by 1.2-mi.-high (2-km) mountains. It was formed 3.8–3.9 billion years ago when a 60-mi.-wide (100-km) object struck.

Fastest planet Mercury takes 87.96 days to orbit the Sun at an average distance of 35.9 million mi. (57.9 million km), giving an average speed of 107,030 mph (172,248 km/h)—almost twice as fast as Earth.

VENUS

Brightest planet With a maximum magnitude of -4.4, Venus is the brightest planet visible from Earth with the naked eye.

First thunder heard on another planet On Dec. 25, 1978, the USSR's *Venera 11* lander touched down on Venus. Among its instruments was an acoustic detector, which heard an 82-dB sound of unknown origin. A Venusian thunderclap is the most probable explanation.

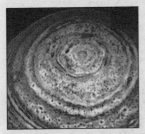

LARGEST HEXAGON The largest hexagon in our Solar System is on Saturn's North Pole, where a massive pattern of hexagonal clouds, with sides measuring around 8,500 mi. (13,800 km) in length, is located. It was first seen by the *Voyager* in the early 1980s and has since been studied in more detail, proving that it has lasted for at least 30 years.

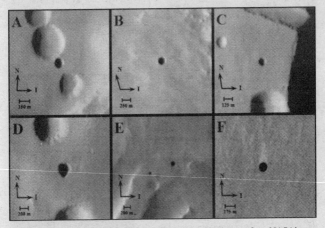

FIRST CAVES ON ANOTHER PLANET In Mar. 2007, images from NASA's *Mars Odyssey* showed the discovery of what appeared to be seven circular pits on Mars' surface with entrances to underground caverns. In only one of the seven pits does a floor appear to be visible, at least 426 ft. (130 m) below the surface.

The word "planet" derives from the ancient Greek for **"wandering star."**

SIZE MATTERS

In our 1955 edition, the most remote planet was assumed to be Pluto, with a mean distance from the Sun of 3.6×10^9 mi. Pluto was discovered on Feb. 18, 1930 by Clyde Tombaugh, an astronomer working at the Lowell Observatory in the U.S.A. Today, Pluto no longer holds the record, because over the years astronomers raised doubts over its planetary status, citing its diminutive size and erratic orbit. In 2006, the International Astronomical Union offered a new definition of a planet; Pluto didn't qualify, and its status was revised to "dwarf planet."

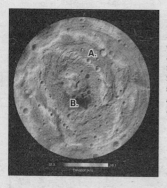

TALLEST CENTRAL PEAK FOR AN IMPACT CRATER Rheasilvia is a 313-mi.-wide (505-km) impact crater on asteroid 4Vesta between Mars and Jupiter. At its center is a peak rising a record 12 mi. (20 km) above the crater floor (the central red feature seen on the satellite image left).
A. Crater walls
B. Central peak

MOST TAILS FOR AN ASTEROID On Sep. 10, 2013, the *Hubble* telescope found a bizarre asteroid with six distinct tails like a comet. The 1,570-ft.-wide (480-m) asteroid P/2013 P5 probably has the tails due to the pressure of solar radiation, which has increased the asteroid's spin so much that mass is lost from its own rotation.

BEYOND THE SOLAR SYSTEM

Voyager I, the **most remote manmade object**, is, as of 3:26 p.m. GMT on Feb. 6, 2014, a distance of 11,827,492,990 mi. from Earth. Having left the Solar System in Aug. 2012, it is now traveling through interstellar space.

EARTH

Densest planet Earth is the densest planet, with an average density of 5.517 times that of water.

Deepest crater Earth's Moon is home to the largest and deepest known crater in the Solar System. The South Pole–Aitken impact basin on the far side of the Moon is 1,400 mi. (2,250 km) in diameter and has an average depth of 39,000 ft. (12,000 m).

LARGEST PLANET Our Solar System's mightiest body is Jupiter, with an equatorial diameter of 89,405 mi. (143,884 km) and a polar diameter of 83,082 mi. (133,708 km). Its mass and volume are around 317 and 1,323 times that of Earth respectively. Jupiter also has the **shortest day of any planet in the Solar System**, at just 9 hr. 55 min. 29.69 sec.

A. Jupiter   E. Mars
B. Saturn   F. Mercury
C. Uranus   G. Earth
D. Neptune   H. Venus

GLOSSARY

Dwarf planet: a body with enough mass to form a spherical shape, but not enough gravitational attraction to clear its orbit of debris as it orbits the Sun.

Light-year: the distance that light travels in one year in a vacuum: some 5.87 trillion mi. (5.87×10^{12} mi.).

Mass: a measure of the quantity of matter in a body as well as its inertia.

Weight: the force of an object due to gravity.

FACT: Saturn has the largest ring system: billions of tiny, orbiting particles of dust and ice, equivalent in mass to 30 million Mount Everests.

For more on measuring mountains, see p. 51.

MAGNIFICENT MOUNTAINS: OLYMPUS, KEA, AND EVEREST

Olympus Mons on Mars is the **highest mountain in the Solar System**, with an elevation (peak height) of 15.5 mi.—nearly three times that of Everest. However, Everest isn't Earth's highest mountain when Mauna Kea on Hawaii is measured from base to peak.

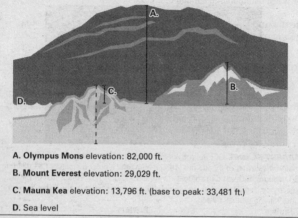

A. **Olympus Mons** elevation: 82,000 ft.

B. **Mount Everest** elevation: 29,029 ft.

C. **Mauna Kea** elevation: 13,796 ft. (base to peak: 33,481 ft.)

D. Sea level

MARS

Highest clouds In Aug. 2006, European scientists reported their discovery of clouds some 55–62 mi. (90–100 km) above the surface of Mars. Detected by an instrument onboard the European Space Agency's *Mars Express* orbiter, the clouds are composed of carbon dioxide ice crystals. If the density of this upper atmosphere is greater than thought, it will mean more aerobraking for landing ships.

Largest area of surface ice Almost all of the ice on Mars's surface is in the poles. The southern cap is the largest at around 260 mi. (420 km) across, and contains enough water to cover the entire planet in a layer 36 ft. (11 m) deep.

JUPITER

Most moons to a planet As of 2013, 67 natural satellites of Jupiter have been discovered. Most are small, irregularly shaped bodies of ice and rock, and many are almost certainly captured asteroids.

One of the Jovian moons, Ganymede, has the **greatest mass of a moon in the Solar System**. It is twice as heavy as Earth's Moon and has a width of 3,273 mi. (5,267 km).

SATURN

Least dense planet Saturn is mainly composed of hydrogen and helium, the two lightest elements in the Universe. It would float on water if there was a bathtub large enough to hold it.

Tallest clouds A massive vortex of clouds, about five times higher than Earth's hurricanes, was discovered to be at Saturn's south pole in 2006.

NEPTUNE

Farthest planet in the Solar System Since Pluto's demotion from "planet" status in 2006 (see p. 16), Neptune is the farthest planet from the Sun. At a distance of 2.8 billion mi. (4.5 billion km) away, it orbits at 3.38 mi./s (5.45 km/s) and takes 164.79 years to complete each orbit.

Fastest winds There are no faster winds in our Solar System than those on Neptune. NASA's *Voyager 2* probe measured winds of around 1,500 mph (2,400 km/h) in 1989.

SCALED UP: the Sweden Solar System When the Stockholm (now Ericsson) Globe Arena opened in Sweden in Feb. 1989 as the world's **largest hemispherical building**, it gave two Swedish academics an idea. If the 360-ft.-wide building was considered a scaled-down Sun, how far away would the planets lie, and what size would they be? Nils Brenning and Gösta Gahm went on to champion the **largest representation of the Solar System**—a 1:20-million-scale "model" that stretches 590 mi. across the country, with planets, minor planets, and comets represented by scaled globes or artworks at their relative distances apart.
A. Sun (360 ft. wide)
B. Mercury (9.8 in. wide), 1.8 mi. away
C. Earth (2 ft. 1.5 in. wide), 4.7 mi. away

FASTEST TRIP TO THE *ISS*
The fastest time to reach the *International Space Station* (*ISS*) from launch to dock is 5 hr. 39 min., achieved on May 29, 2013 UTC by the crew of Expedition 36 onboard the *Soyuz TMA-09M* (inset). They launched from Baikonur in Kazakhstan at 8:31 p.m. UTC and docked with the *ISS*'s "Rassvet" module at 2:10 a.m. UTC on May 30.

COMETS

Largest source of comets Beyond Neptune's orbit lie the Kuiper Belt, the Scattered Disk, and the Oort Cloud, collectively known as Trans-Neptunian Objects. The Oort Cloud contains trillions of cometary nuclei. It surrounds the Sun at a distance of ca. 50,000 Astronomical Units (1 AU = distance from Earth to the Sun), around 1,000 times the distance from the Sun to Pluto. Scientists believe the cloud to be the source of most of the comets that visit the inner Solar System.

Longest comet tail The tail of comet Hyakutake measured 350 million mi. (570 million km) long—more than 3 AU. The tail was discovered by Geraint Jones of Imperial College, London, UK, on Sep. 13, 1999, using data gathered by the ESA/NASA spacecraft *Ulysses* on a chance encounter with the comet on May 1, 1996.

MOST RECENT GREAT COMET Great Comets are those that become extremely bright in the night sky. The most recent Great Comet was Comet McNaught, first discovered by Robert McNaught (AUS) in 2006. At its peak brightness, on Jan. 12, 2007, its tail measured a maximum of 35 degrees long in the sky.

FIRST COMETARY SOFT LANDER Launched on Mar. 2, 2004, the European Space Agency's (ESA) Rosetta mission will rendezvous with comet 67P/Churyumov-Gerasimenko in 2014. The spacecraft will study and map the comet then release the *Philae* lander, which will anchor itself to the surface of the 2.4-mi.-wide (4-km) comet with harpoons and will survive for at least a week.

Halley's Comet should make its next appearance in **2061**.

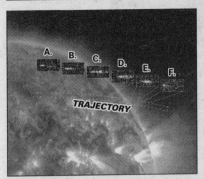

TRAJECTORY

FIRST COMET OBSERVED BEING DESTROYED BY THE SUN On Jul. 6, 2011, NASA's Solar Dynamics Observatory captured images of comet C/2011 N3's demise. The comet had a nucleus 29–147 ft. (9–45 m) wide and got within 62,100 mi. (100,000 km) of the Sun's surface, moving at about 1.3 million mph (2.1 million km/h), before breaking up and being vaporized. Pictured here are snapshots from the last 10 min. in the life of comet C/2011 N3 as it breaks apart and is vaporized by the Sun

A. 00:01:12	**D.** 11:56:00
B. 11:59:36	**E.** 11:51:36
C. 11:57:00	**F.** 11:49:48

FIRST ANTICOMET MEDICATION Halley's Comet visited the inner Solar System in 1910. Earth passed through its tail, which included the toxic gas cyanogen. Needless panic buying of gas masks, "anticomet umbrellas," and "anti-comet pills" followed.

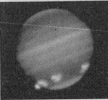

LARGEST RECORDED IMPACT IN THE SOLAR SYSTEM From Jul. 16 to 22, 1994, more than 20 fragments of comet Shoemaker-Levy 9 collided with Jupiter. The greatest impact was of the "G" fragment, which exploded with the energy of roughly 600 times the nuclear arsenal of the world, equivalent to 6 million megatons of TNT.

LARGER THAN WE THOUGHT . . .

In 1955, *The Guinness Book of Records* said that it was estimated that no comet head contains "mass in excess of 20 miles in diameter" and that the longest tail "may trail out to 200 million miles." The **largest comet** now known is Chiron, which has a diameter of 113 mi. and a tail that has measured up to 791 million mi. long.

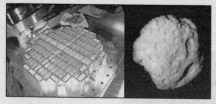

FIRST COMET SAMPLE RETURNED

Encountering the comet Wild 2 (near left) in early 2004, the *Stardust* spacecraft swept up tiny samples of cometary dust in an aerogel collector (far left) and returned the material to Earth on Jan. 15, 2006. Its ongoing analysis is providing insights into the chemical makeup of this icy, primordial body.

FIRST COMET DISCOVERED TO BE PERIODIC

Halley's Comet, aka 1P/Halley, orbits the Sun every 75.32 years. Sightings of this comet go back to at least 240 B.C., but it was English astronomer Edmond Halley who, in 1705, first realized that observations of this comet were of the same object and predicted its return for the year 1758. The main picture (above left) shows a Babylonian clay tablet from ca. 164 B.C. that mentions the comet. Above right, the Bayeux Tapestry (made ca. 1100) depicts the comet along with Latin text stating: "These [people] are looking in wonder at the star."

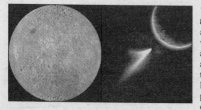

TAIL END: What Happens to Comets?

The "death" of a comet can come about in a variety of different ways. Not all comets are tied to an orbit around the Sun, and some of them simply fly out of the Solar System. Each time a comet passes the Sun, it loses samples of dust and ice; if all of the ice is lost, the comet can become an inactive, asteroid-like structure. Alternatively, complete loss of ice can result in the comet breaking up into dust clouds. Finally, comets can meet a violent end when their orbit results in them crashing into a moon or planet. Our own Moon (above left) is pockmarked with impact craters caused by comets and asteroids crashing into its surface.

COMET WATCH

Closest comet flyby by a spacecraft: *Giotto* flew within 124 mi. of Grigg-Skjellerup on Jul. 10, 1992.

Most comet tails met by a spacecraft: *Ulysses* flew through the tails of Hyakutake (1996), McNaught-Hartley (2004), and McNaught (2007).

Most comets discovered by a spacecraft: *SOHO* (Solar and Heliospheric Observatory) had discovered 2,574 comets by Dec. 2013.

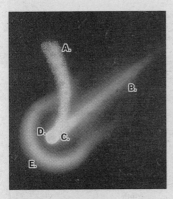

COMET UP CLOSE
NUCLEUS: Dust, rocky debris, and frozen gas
COMA: Cloud of evaporated gases and dust around nucleus
HYDROGEN ENVELOPE: Gets larger as comet nears the Sun
DUST TAIL: Follows comet's orbit; may be 93 million mi. long
ION TAIL: Made up of ionized gases flowing along the magnetic field lines of the plasma of the solar wind

A. Dust tail
B. Ion tail
C. Coma
D. Nucleus
E. Hydrogen envelope

FIRST IMPACT ON A COMET On Jul. 4, 2005, a 770-lb. (350-kg) copper "bullet" from NASA's *Deep Impact* craft hit comet Tempel 1 at 6.4 mi./s (10.3 km/s). The impact—equivalent to that of 10,360 lb. (4.7 metric tons) of TNT—created a crater 330 ft. (100 m) wide and 100 ft. (30 m) deep.

Closest approach to Earth by a comet On Jul. 1, 1770, traveling at 86,100 mph (138,600 km/h), Lexell's Comet came within 1,360,000 mi. (2,200,000 km)—or just 0.015 AU—of Earth.

Smallest comet visited by a spacecraft NASA's *Deep Impact* spacecraft, launched on Jan. 12, 2005, was retasked as the EPOXI mission on Jul. 3, 2007 with the goal of studying extrasolar planets and performing a flyby of comet 103P/Hartley. The flyby occurred on Nov. 4, 2010, as *Deep Impact* passed within 430 mi. (700 km) of the nucleus. The comet is around 1.4 mi. (2.25 km) long and has a mass of around 590 billion lb. (300 million tonnes).

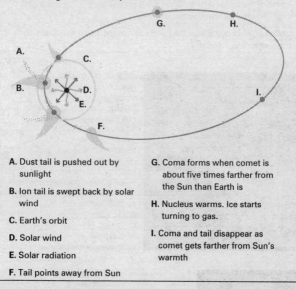

COSMIC PATH: A COMET'S JOURNEY THROUGH SPACE

A comet's coma and tails form during its journey around the Sun. One tail is composed of dust; the other is an ion (gas) tail. Solar wind and radiation angle the tails away from the comet

A. Dust tail is pushed out by sunlight

B. Ion tail is swept back by solar wind

C. Earth's orbit

D. Solar wind

E. Solar radiation

F. Tail points away from Sun

G. Coma forms when comet is about five times farther from the Sun than Earth is

H. Nucleus warms. Ice starts turning to gas.

I. Coma and tail disappear as comet gets farther from Sun's warmth

Most distant observations of a comet On Sep. 3, 2003, the European Southern Observatory in Paranal, Chile, released an image of Halley's Comet at 2,600 million mi. (4,200 million km) from the Sun. It shows Halley as a fuzzy dot with a brightness of magnitude of 28.2, nearly a billion times fainter than the faintest objects visible with the naked eye.

Largest observed coma The coma of the Great Comet of 1811—discovered on Mar. 25, 1811 by French astronomer Honoré Flaugergues—had a diameter of about 1.2 million mi. (2 million km).

SETI

SETI stands for the **Search for Extraterrestrial Intelligence**.

First known pulsar On Nov. 28, 1967, British astronomers Jocelyn Bell Burnell and Antony Hewish spotted a radio signal from another star. All stars emit radio signals, but this turned on and off with perfect regularity: one pulse lasting 0.04 sec. every 1.3373 sec. The pair playfully named the phenomenon "LGM-1" ("Little Green Men 1"). In fact, they had found what would be called a pulsar—a portmanteau of "pulsating star." Pulsars are the rapidly rotating remnants left by a supernova—and their behavior is entirely natural, if very precise. The first was later named CP 1919.

MOST POWERFUL RADIO SIGNAL AIMED INTO SPACE On Nov. 16, 1974, scientists at the Arecibo radio telescope in Puerto Rico sent a message containing basic data on humanity (far left). The binary radio signal was broadcast to the M13 globular cluster in the constellation of Hercules and lasted 169 sec. It will arrive in 25,000 years at a strength 10 million times that of radio signals from our Sun. Any reply will take another 25,000 years to return to Earth.

FIRST EQUATION ESTIMATING INTELLIGENT LIFE IN OUR GALAXY In 1961, U.S. astronomer Frank Drake devised an equation to give estimates of the number of planets inhabited by intelligent life:

$$N = R_* \, F_p \, N_e \, F_l \, F_i \, F_c \, L$$

While many of these variables (see glossary below) are extremely speculative, Drake himself estimated the number of advanced civilizations in our galaxy to be as high as 10,000.

THE DRAKE EQUATION

N	Number of civilizations for possible radio communication
R_*	Average star formation rate in our galaxy
F_p	Fraction of those stars with planets
N_e	Average of planets that might support life
F_l	Fraction of those planets that develop life
F_i	Fraction of those planets that develop civilizations
F_c	Fraction of civilizations that develop detectable technology
L	Length of broadcast time of such civilizations

LISTENING TIME

The amount of radio telescope capacity used for SETI is much less than is popularly assumed. Project Phoenix was given the **largest allocation for a single SETI project** at Arecibo to analyze patterns in radio signals. It used about 5% of the total observatory time (2,400 hr.) from Sep. 1998 to Mar. 2004. Worldwide, just 30 or so scientists and engineers work full-time in SETI.

Largest planet-hunter space telescope NASA's Kepler space telescope was launched on Mar. 7, 2009 on a Delta II rocket from Cape Canaveral, U.S.A. The spacecraft measures 8 ft. 10 in. x 15 ft. 5 in. (2.7 x 4.7 m) and follows an Earth-trailing heliocentric orbit. It can capture images of

planets outside the Solar System, called exoplanets or extrasolar planets, using a mirror 4 ft. 7 in. (1.4 m) in diameter and a 95-megapixel camera. As of Feb. 2014, it has identified 961 exoplanets—over half of the total discoveries of the past 20 years—and 2,903 unconfirmed candidates.

FIRST INSURANCE AGAINST ALIEN ABDUCTION The UFO Abduction Insurance Co. (U.S.A.) offers an insurance policy costing $19.95 that pays out $10 m to abductees. Proof of abduction is all that the insurance company requires—an extraterrestrial signature will suffice.

FIRST EARTHLIKE PLANET On Dec. 5, 2011, Kepler-22b was announced as the first of more than 700 planets thought to reside within the habitable zone of its star, some 600 light-years away. At 2.4 times the size of Earth, the planet orbits its Sun-like star in around 290 days. If the planet has an Earth-like greenhouse effect, then its surface temperature could be 72°F (22°C).

LONGEST-RUNNING SETI PROJECT SETI@home, developed by the University of California, U.S.A., is a crowdsourcing project that harnesses the power of PCs to process vast amounts of data. Signals from the Arecibo radio telescope were first made available for download on May 17, 1999 in a screen saver. The most intriguing discovery to date was a signal called SHGb02+14a, found in Mar. 2003, that does not correspond to any known galactic phenomena.

FIRST DIGITAL TIME CAPSULE CHOSEN BY PUBLIC VOTE A radio telescope at Yevpatoria in Ukraine sent a radio message on Oct. 9, 2008 to the planet Gliese 581c, orbiting a star some 20.3 light-years from Earth. Images of landmarks and celebrities (such as singer Cheryl Cole, pictured) were sent, as well as 501 text messages from Bebo users. The message is due to reach Gliese 581c in 2029.

Most Earthlike exoplanet
The Earth Similarity Index (ESI) is a system devised to categorize and rate the increasing number of exoplanetary candidates. It rates how similar each is to Earth, based on size, density, escape velocity, and surface temperature. The ranking ranges from zero to 1, with Earth's value at 1. The exoplanet ranking highest on the ESI is KOI-3284.01, detected by the Kepler telescope in 2012 and given an ESI rating of 0.9. The planet may or may not be rocky, but it does have the potential for liquid water.

Most remote manmade object
Voyager 1, launched on Sep. 5, 1977, is a space probe whose primary mission was to make flybys of Jupiter and Saturn. As of Apr. 9, 2014, it is 11.84 billion mi. (19.06 billion km) from the Sun. *Voyager 1* and *Voyager 2* each contain a tougher version of a vinyl record: a gold-plated copper disk with stylus and instructions to alien life on how to play it (see *Voyager* Golden Record). The disk carries 116 images encoded in audio form and natural sounds of Earth, greetings in 59 languages, and music.

First report of a "flying saucer"
UFOs have been recorded for hundreds of years in various forms, but it was the sighting by pilot Kenneth Arnold on Jun. 24, 1947 that saw newspapers coin the term "flying saucer." Arnold didn't use the exact phrase to describe the nine objects he saw in the sky near Mount Rainier in Washington, U.S.A., though he did say they were like saucers, disks, or pie plates.

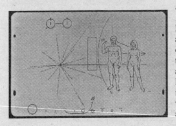

FIRST PHYSICAL MESSAGE SENT INTO DEEP SPACE *Pioneer 10* is a NASA probe launched on Mar. 3, 1972. A gold-strengthened aluminum plaque was attached to the outside showing a man and woman to scale with the probe, along with a map of the Solar System and the location of the Sun relative to pulsars in our galaxy. The probe's mission was to make the **first Jupiter flyby**, achieved on Dec. 3, 1973.

First UFO landing pad St. Paul in Alberta, Canada, is a prairie town with an official UFO landing pad, opened on Jun. 3, 1967 by Canada's Minister of National Defence. The saucer-shape concrete platform sits above a pile of welcoming stones from each province of Canada. A sign declares the pad to be "a symbol of our faith that mankind will maintain the outer universe free from national wars and strife." Inside the pad is a time capsule to be opened on its centenary in 2067.

OLDEST UNEXPLAINED EXTRASOLAR SIGNAL On Aug. 15, 1977, astronomer Jerry Ehman (U.S.A.) detected a radio signal using the *Big Ear* radio telescope at the Ohio State University, U.S.A. The signal was monitored for 72 sec. and closely matched the expected profile of an extraterrestrial signal. Ehman circled the readout and wrote "Wow!" It has never been detected again.

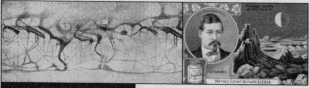

LIFE ON MARS: Examining the Evidence Astronomer Giovanni Schiaparelli (ITA) was the **first person to gather scientific evidence concerning life on Mars**. In 1877, he described telescopic observations of the planet that included *canali*, or channels, a network of lines across the surface. *Canali* was mistranslated as "canals" and later observers mapped them in detail, believing them to be structures built by a civilization instead of natural channels. As telescopes became more powerful, and space probes sent information from the surface, the "canals" were shown to be geological features.

LISA VANDERPERRE-HIRSCH

Gray aliens are alleged extraterrestrial beings of wildly varying description, though they are often shown with oversize heads and black eyes. Lisa Vanderperre-Hirsch (U.S.A.) has the **largest collection of gray alien memorabilia**, with 547 individual items as of Nov. 20, 2011 in Florida, U.S.A. Her collection includes posters, calendars, and even alien-themed toilet paper.

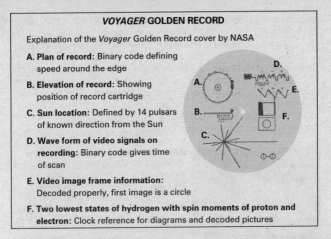

VOYAGER GOLDEN RECORD

Explanation of the *Voyager* Golden Record cover by NASA

A. Plan of record: Binary code defining speed around the edge

B. Elevation of record: Showing position of record cartridge

C. Sun location: Defined by 14 pulsars of known direction from the Sun

D. Wave form of video signals on recording: Binary code gives time of scan

E. Video image frame information: Decoded properly, first image is a circle

F. Two lowest states of hydrogen with spin moments of proton and electron: Clock reference for diagrams and decoded pictures

Largest civilian UFO investigative group The Mutual UFO Network (MUFON) is an American-base organization that investigates UFO sightings. There are branches all over the world and more than 3,000 members. MUFON was started in May 1969.

Largest UFO convention The 23rd International UFO Congress was held in Scottsdale in Arizona, U.S.A., on Feb. 12–16, 2014. An average of 1,500 people attended events throughout the week on topics such as official cover-ups, exopolitics, black projects, crop circles, and visitations.

OBSERVATORIES

Deepest observatory The Sudbury Neutrino Observatory (SNOLAB) is 6,800 ft. (2,075 m) down a mine in Ontario, Canada. There, shielded from cosmic rays that affect experiments into low-energy solar neutrinos, it searches for cosmic dark matter and supernova neutrino.

LARGEST . . .

Primary mirror (nonsegmented) The largest observatory mirrors are those in the dual-tube Large Binocular Telescope (see p. 30), but the largest *single* primary mirror forms part of Japan's Subaru Telescope on Mauna Kea, Hawaii, U.S.A. The 26-ft. 10-in.-wide (8.2-m) mirror is made from 8-in.-thick (20-cm) glass weighing 50,265 lb. (22.8 metric tons). With the help of 261 actuators to constantly keep the mirror focused, warping is limited to less than 0.1 microns (0.00001 millimeters).

Cosmic ray telescope The Pierre Auger Observatory is a vast array of 1,600 particle detectors looking for very high-energy cosmic ray particles, which it is thought may be produced by supermassive black holes. Only one high-energy particle falls per 0.39 sq. mi. (1 km^2) in a century, so the observatory is arranged over a 1,158-sq.-mi. (3,000-km^2) area of Argentina—in an area larger than Luxembourg.

LARGEST MOVABLE MOTOR-DRIVEN STRUCTURE ON LAND The Robert C. Byrd Green Bank Telescope is a radio telescope at the National Radio Astronomy Observatory in West Virginia, U.S.A. The dish measures 328 x 360 ft. (100 x 110 m), and its highest point stands 480 ft. (146 m) above the ground. The structure is fully steerable, and it can observe the whole sky from five degrees above the horizon.

LARGEST BINOCULAR TELESCOPE The Large Binocular Telescope in Arizona, U.S.A., comprises two identical telescopes, each with a 27-ft. 6-in.-wide (8.4-m) primary mirror. Working in tandem, they have an equivalent light-gathering power of a single mirror 38 ft. 8 in. (11.8 m) in diameter and are able to achieve the image sharpness of a 74-ft. 9-in.-wide (22.8-m) aperture.

GLOSSARY

Actuator: Motor that moves the mirror or changes its shape in large reflecting telescopes.

Aperture: The opening in a telescope (or camera) that determines how much light enters and gets focused.

First light: Inaugural use of a telescope to record an astronomical image.

Primary mirror: The main light-gathering surface of a reflecting telescope.

An **11,000-year-old site** in Turkey is thought to have been an early form of observatory.

LARGEST ARRAY OF RADIO TELESCOPES The VLA (Very Large Array) of the U.S. National Science Foundation has 27 mobile antennae on rails in a Y-shape arrangement. Each arm of the Y is 13 mi. (21 km) long, and each antenna has a dish that measures 82 ft. (25 m) in diameter. The VLA, completed in 1980, is located 50 mi. (80 km) west of Socorro in New Mexico, U.S.A.

Dish radio telescope The Arecibo Observatory (see also p. 25) was considered impressive enough to star in the finale to the 1995 James Bond movie *GoldenEye*. The distinctive design consists of a dish with a diameter of 1,000 ft. (305 m), covering 18.5 acres (7.48 ha)—about the same as 14 football fields. The dish surface is covered by 38,778 aluminum panels. A steerable arm measuring 328 ft. (100 m) is above the dish, allowing more of the sky to be seen.

LARGEST CHERENKOV TELESCOPE The H.E.S.S. II telescope, the newest part of the High Energy Stereoscopic System, has a diameter of 91 ft. 10 in. (28 m) and a total collecting surface area of 6,609 sq. ft. (614 m²). It detects faint Cherenkov radiation, which is produced by particles traveling faster than the speed of light. H.E.S.S. II saw its first light in Khomas Highland, Namibia, on Jul. 26, 2012.

FACT: The H.E.S.S. II is larger than many telescopes but, as a Cherenkov detector, it is in a different category to true imaging telescopes.

Gravitational wave detector The Laser Interferometry Gravitational Wave Observatory (LIGO) consists of two similar L-shape structures based in Louisiana and Washington (U.S.A.), ca. 2,000 mi. (3,200 km) apart. The arms of these facilities are each 2.4 mi. (4 km) long, providing LIGO with a high level of sensitivity. The detectors are currently being upgraded to continue the search for gravitational waves predicted in Einstein's general theory of relativity.

Liquid mirror The Large Zenith Telescope (LZT), located east of Vancouver in Canada, uses a mirror made from liquid mercury. By spinning the 6,613-lb. (3-metric-ton), 19-ft. 8-in.-diameter (6-m) mercury mirror, the liquid forms a concave mirror shape. As a zenith telescope it is limited by looking straight up, but it is more economical because mercury is less expensive than glass mirrors.

LARGEST ROBOTIC TELESCOPE The Liverpool Telescope receives requests for data online and autonomously "decides" which observations to make. Located on La Palma in the Canary Islands with a 6-ft. 6-in. (2-m) mirror, the Liverpool reserves 5% of its observing time for use by schools.

LARGEST CONCENTRATION OF HIGH-ALTITUDE TELESCOPES Kitt Peak in Arizona, U.S.A., is a 6,876-ft. (2,096-m) mountain whose atmospheric clarity has attracted 24 major telescopes on its summit since 1958. Two are radio telescopes and the others are optical telescopes. The largest structure is the Nicholas U. Mayall Telescope, a 13-ft. (4-m) mirror housed in a 187-ft.-tall (57-m) building that can be seen from a distance of 50 mi. (80 km).

HIGHEST ASTRONOMICAL OBSERVATORY The University of Tokyo Atacama Observatory (TAO) was established in Chile at an altitude of 18,500 ft. (5,640 m)—double the height at which altitude sickness typically occurs. TAO perches on the summit of Cerro Chajnantor in the Atacama Desert. The observatory has an infrared telescope that was completed in Mar. 2009.

Refracting telescope Refracting telescopes use lenses to gather and focus light, as opposed to reflecting telescopes that use mirrors. The 1897 Yerkes Observatory in Wisconsin, U.S.A., has a primary lens with a diameter of 3 ft. 4 in. (1.02 m).

SCOPE FOR IMPROVEMENT

The **largest reflector telescope** in our 1955 edition was the Hale Telescope of the California Institute of Technology on Palomar Mountain, U.S.A., with its 16-ft. 8-in. unsegmented mirror. The record today—now categorized as the **largest unsegmented primary mirror**—is held by the 26-ft. 10-in.-wide Subaru Telescope on Mauna Kea (see p. 29). The **largest land-base telescope** in *absolute* terms, though, is the segmented Gran Telescopio Canarias (p. 34) at 34 ft. 1 in. wide.

HIGHEST OBSERVATORIES

18,500 ft.
University of Tokyo Atacama Observatory (TAO), Chile

17,155 ft.
Chacaltaya Astrophysical Observatory, Bolivia

17,060 ft.
James Ax Observatory, Chile

17,025 ft.
Atacama Cosmology Telescope, Chile

16,745 ft.
Llano de Chajnantor Observatory (APEX), Chile

16,730 ft.
Shiquanhe Observatory (NAOC Ali Observatory), Tibet

16,665 ft.
Llano de Chajnantor Observatory (QUIET), Chile

16,400 ft.
Llano de Chajnantor Observatory (ALMA), Chile

15,940 ft.
Atacama Submillimeter Telescope Experiment, Chile

15,090 ft.
Large Millimeter Telescope, Mexico

FACT: Three big competitors in the next generation of observatories are the Giant Magellan Telescope (La Serena, Chile), the Thirty Meter Telescope (Mauna Kea, Hawaii), and the European Extremely Large Telescope (Cerro Armazones, Chile). Due for completion in the next decade or so, their budgets will average around $1.18 bn.

MIRROR CALL: Largest Telescope The Gran Telescopio Canarias (GTC) is the **largest land-base optical telescope**, boasting a mirror with an effective aperture of 34 ft. This is also the world's **largest segmented primary mirror**, consisting of 36 hexagonal pieces, each of which can be moved separately to help counter the blurring effect of Earth's atmosphere on stellar light. The GTC, located at an altitude of 7,437 ft. on La Palma in the Canary Islands, has produced images of the Milky Way at a resolution 60 million times greater than human vision.

EARTH

CONTENTS

If all the oceans were combined into a single drop of water, it would be **851 mi**. wide.

TALLEST ILLUMINATED ICEFALLS The waterfalls of Eidfjord in Norway plunge noisily some 1,640 ft. (500 m) in summer. In the winter, when temperatures can drop to -15°F (-26°C), the water is frozen in its tracks. In Jan. 2013, climbers Stephan Siegrist and Dani Arnold (pictured climbing, with Martin Echsner belaying), photographer Thomas Senf, and sports-equipment manufacturer Mammut captured images of these "icefalls" at night. Illuminations were provided by lamps, flashlights, and flares, and involved 2,300 ft. (700 m) of cables.

FACT: The dramatic light show was inspired by stories of the Norse frost giants—a race formed from the drip of an icicle as the fires of creation met the lifeless snows that had come before.

MONITORING EARTH

The history of humanity is defined by our insatiable quest to explore and learn more about our planet. Ever since early explorers crossed the oceans in search of new lands, we have used the latest technology to watch the weather and monitored seas to predict storms. Today, technology is used by scientists to measure the health of the planet.

Our knowledge of the systems governing Earth has increased exponentially over the last 60 years, with increasingly more accurate sensors and comprehensive coverage in telecommunications to monitor the movement of the land and action of the seas. We are constantly seeking to understand the most intimate secrets of the powerful forces that sweep across our world.

Scientists are now able to make measurements of the magnetic properties of the planet. The strength of its gravity field has been mapped at all points to aid in construction projects, and we send robotic vehicles to test environments in which we could not survive.

More recently, advanced systems for data collection have helped us to chart the rate of climate change. Every year we are accumulating a more accurate picture of human processes, such as agricultural irrigation and deforestation. As we do so, we are discovering not only how our planet works but how better to respect and protect it.

1958 Magnetometers are sensitive instruments that measure magnetic fields in orbit. On May 15, 1958, the **first satellite magnetometer** was launched onboard the Soviet Union's *Sputnik 3*—a conical satellite 11 ft. 8 in. (3.57 m) long and 5 ft. 8 in. (1.73 m) wide at its base. It weighed 2,925 lb. (1,327 kg) and possessed 12 scientific instruments (above right). The satellite remained in orbit until Apr. 6, 1960.

1960 The **first successful weather satellite** was the U.S.A.'s *TIROS-1*, which was launched on Apr. 1, 1960. "TIROS"—the "Television Infrared Observation Satellite"—remained operational for 78 days, during which time it employed its high- and low-resolution cameras to record images of cloud formations (above right) that were used by meteorologists worldwide to understand weather systems.

1975 The **first geostationary weather satellite**—*GOES-1* (Geostationary Operational Environmental Satellite)—was launched from Cape Canaveral, Florida, U.S.A., on Oct. 16, 1975. The principal instrument onboard was the Visible Infrared Spin Scan Radiometer (VISSR), which provided day and night imagery of cloud conditions over the full-disk (above right). The satellite had the capability to relay meteorological data from more than 10,000 locations into a central processing center in order to build weather-prediction models.

1984 The **longest-operating Earth-observation satellite** was *Landsat 5*, developed by NASA and launched on Mar. 1, 1984 from Vandenberg Air Force Base, California, U.S.A. Managed by the National Oceanic and Atmospheric Administration (1984–2000) and later the U.S. Geological Survey (2001–13), it was decommissioned in 2013 after capturing more than 2.5 million images of Earth's surface during its 150,000 orbits.

2004 The Argo program uses the **largest fleet of ocean sensors** to monitor global ocean current patterns. The 3,600 free-floating, robotic Argo sensors (mapped above) drift to 6,560 ft. (2,000 m) deep and rise to transmit data via satellites. By Nov. 2012, Argo had collected its millionth profile of temperature and salinity—twice the number obtained by all research vessels during the 20th century.

2005 On Jul. 7, 2005, scientists were able to perform the **first accurate sea-level monitoring by satellite** using a number of different instruments (such as the *Gravity Recovery and Climate Experiment*—or *GRACE*—satellite, left). Satellite data was collected on changes in Earth's gravitational field, the mass of polar ice caps, and ocean topography and circulation (right). Using this data, it was determined that, in the last 50 years, the rate at which the sea level is rising is 0.07 in. (1.8 mm) per year—but in the last 12 years, this rate has increased to 0.118 in. (3 mm) per year.

2006 The **largest-ever unmanned Earth-observation satellite** was *Envisat*, a European Space Agency satellite. It weighed 17,857 lb. (8,100 kg), measured 85 x 32 x 16 ft. (26 x 10 x 5 m), and orbited at an altitude of 487–491 mi. (785–791 km). *Envisat* monitored Earth's land and oceans, ice caps (right), and atmosphere with an array of instruments, before abruptly going silent on Apr. 8, 2012, after 10 years in orbit.

2009 The **fastest-melting Antarctic glacier** is Pine Island Glacier, which is dropping in height by up to 52 ft. (16 m) a year, scientists discovered. Key data came from *Autosub* (left), an autonomous submarine that was sent under the vast glacier, which revealed it has become detached from an undersea ridge, allowing warm water to flow under it and increase the rate of melt.

2009 The **first satellite dedicated to monitoring climate change** was launched on Nov. 2, 2009 by the European Space Agency (ESA). The Soil Moisture and Ocean Salinity (SMOS) mission surveys critical parts of the water cycle between oceans, air, and land by mapping the saltiness of the sea and monitoring water content in the planet's soil. The satellite works by measuring Earth's natural microwave emissions, which alter with the changing moisture levels on land or the salinity of the sea.

2013 From its launch in 2009 until its burn-up in 2013, ESA's *Gravity Field and Steady-State Ocean Circulation Explorer* (*GOCE*, above left) was the **most accurate gravity-mapping satellite**, working to 1 milliGal (a unit used to measure the gravitational field).

The **highest-resolution maps of Earth's gravity field**, however, were created in 2013 by an Australian-German team using data obtained from the U.S. Space Shuttle. The maps (below left) improved the resolution of previous global gravity field maps by a factor of 40, and revealed that the pull of gravity is at its strongest at the North Pole; the lowest is at the top of the Huascarán mountain in the Andes.

2013 The **lowest radiometric Earth temperature recorded by satellite** is -135.76°F (-93.2°C), on a high ridge in Antarctica, as preliminarily announced by NASA in Dec. 2013. Data was collected by satellites including NASA's *Terra* (above right) over 32 years, and it was found that the dry and clear air of the Antarctic allows heat to be efficiently radiated into space.

FACT: The radiometric temperature was measured by the amount of radiation (or lack of it) from the Antarctic Ridge.

60 YEARS OF WEATHER EXTREMES

1959: Greatest snowfall
From Feb. 13 to 19, snow fell to a depth of 188.9 in. on Mount Shasta Ski Bowl in northern California, U.S.A.

1964: Driest place
From 1964 to 2001, the average annual rainfall for the Quillagua meteorological station in the Atacama Desert, Chile, was just 0.019 in.

1966: Highest annual mean temperature
Dallol in Ethiopia recorded a record annual mean temperature of 94°F for the six years between 1960 and 1966.

1970: Most intense rainfall
Basse-Terre, Guadeloupe, in the Caribbean, recorded 1.5 in. of rain in one minute on Nov. 26. This is the accepted highest figure, although scientists agree that it is difficult to assess exact rainfall readings over very short periods.

1983: Lowest temperature recorded on Earth
On Jul. 21, temperatures at the Soviet Union's Vostok research station in Antarctica plunged to -128.6°F. The site was chosen for research with the aim of drilling into ancient ice.

1994: Longest-lasting cyclone
Hurricane/typhoon John formed on Aug. 11 in the eastern Pacific Ocean. It lasted for 31 days, and it also traveled the **farthest distance for a tropical cyclone**: 8,251 mi.

1998: Largest coral reef die-off
In 1998, around 16% of all coral reefs were destroyed or damaged in a once-in-a-millennium event. The 1998 El Niño phenomenon may have triggered the disaster.

2008: Highest ocean temperature
In Aug. 2008, scientists announced that they had recorded water at 867°F spewing from a hydrothermal vent ("black smoker") on the ocean floor 9,842 ft. deep at the Mid-Atlantic Ridge.

2013: Largest measured tornado
A tornado with a diameter of 2.59 mi. was measured using Doppler radar by the U.S. National Weather Service on May 31 in El Reno, Oklahoma, U.S.A.

Greatest temperature range
Verkhoyansk, in the Siberian "Pole of Cold," is in the east of Russia. Temperatures have ranged 189°F: from a record low of -90.4°F to a record high of 98.6°F.

IT CAME FROM OUTER SPACE

Fastest meteor shower The Leonids are a shower of meteors entering Earth's atmosphere at around 44 mi./s (71 km/s) and begin to glow at an altitude of some 96 mi. (155 km). The motion of the parent meteoroid stream, from comet 55P/Tempel–Tuttle, accounts for the speed. It is directly opposite to the orbital motion of Earth around the Sun, resulting in an almost head-on collision between the tiny particles and Earth annually on Nov. 15–20.

Every 33 years, the Leonids look even more impressive as their parent comet swoops near the Sun. On Nov. 16–17, 1966, the Leonid meteors were visible to lucky sky watchers between western North America and eastern Russia (then USSR), passing over Arizona, U.S.A., at a rate of 2,300 per min. for 20 min. from 5 a.m.—the **greatest meteor shower** ever recorded.

Almost **220,400 lb. of meteoroid material** enters Earth's atmosphere every day.

FIRST IDENTIFIED IMPACT CRATER The Barringer Meteorite Crater, aka Meteor Crater, in Arizona, U.S.A., measures around 0.74 mi. (1.2 km) in diameter and 570 ft. (173 m) deep. It was proposed in 1891 to be the result of a meteorite impact, and later determined to be the crater of an iron meteorite. Scientists believe that it landed some 49,000 years ago, with a force 150 times greater than that of the atomic bomb dropped on Hiroshima in 1945.

FIRST PERSON HIT BY SPACE JUNK The first and only person to be hit by a manmade object from orbit is Lottie Williams (U.S.A.). On Jan. 22, 1997, in Tulsa, Oklahoma, U.S.A., she was hit in the shoulder by a piece of blackened metal about 6 in. (15 cm) long that NASA tests showed was probably from a *Delta II* rocket. Williams was unhurt.

First accurately predicted asteroid impact

Analysis of the orbit of asteroid 2008 TC3 indicated that it would hit Earth 21 hr. after being discovered on Oct. 6, 2008. At 2:46 a.m. on Oct. 7, 2008, the asteroid—measuring a few yards across—exploded 23 mi. (37 km) above Sudan with the force of 1 kiloton. Passengers traveling in a plane saw the flash from a distance of 750 nautical mi. (863 mi; 1,389 km).

Greatest impact on Earth The most widely accepted theory of how the Moon came into being is that it was part of Earth until 4.5 billion years ago. A planet the size of Mars is thought to have collided with the young Earth, shearing off much of the mantle and sending huge chunks of it into orbit. Over time, this debris collected under its own gravity to form the Moon.

Greatest recorded impact on Earth (unmeasured) On Jun. 30, 1908, the disintegration of an asteroid 6 mi. (10 km) above the basin of the Podkamennaya Tunguska River in Russia resulted in a huge explosion. An area of 1,500 sq. mi. (3,900 km²) was devastated by the breakup of the meteoroid, which released as much energy as up to five times that of all explosives used in World War II. While there are no exact figures on record from 1908, there are accurate measurements of the recent **greatest measured impact on Earth**. This was the Chelyabinsk impact of Feb. 15, 2013 (see p. 44).

MOST PEOPLE INJURED IN A METEOROID EXPLOSION There have been no confirmed human fatalities found in modern research into meteorite impacts. The worst effects recorded were on Feb. 15, 2013, when a meteoroid exploded over Chelyabinsk Oblast in the Urals in Russia. Around 1,200 people were injured, mostly from flying glass caused by the shock wave following the fireball. Astronomer Alan Harris has calculated that the odds of being killed by an asteroid are 1 in 700,000. Scientists have suggested an asteroid bigger than 6.2 mi. (10 km) across would kill most of humanity; fortunately, these only arrive once every 100 million years.

HEAVIEST MANMADE OBJECT TO REENTER THE ATMOSPHERE The Russian space station *Mir* came out of orbit during a successful controlled reentry of Earth's atmosphere on Mar. 23, 2001. After 15 years in space, the 286,600-lb. (130-metric-ton) laboratory broke into pieces that splashed down in the ocean east of New Zealand. The **largest space station** is now the *International Space Station*.

CRASH TRASH: NASA Litter Fine On Jul. 11, 1979, the defunct U.S. space station *Skylab* (above left) reentered Earth's atmosphere and disintegrated. Large chunks of the station survived to crash in Western Australia, and the Australian Shire of Esperance imposed an AUS$400 (now U.S.$376) fine on NASA for littering, which NASA didn't pay. The bill was finally settled on their behalf in 2009 by U.S. radio host Scott Barley, who raised the money from his audience for the 30th anniversary of *Skylab*'s demise. Pieces of *Skylab* are on display in Esperance's museum, as is a poster declaring the fine paid.

OLDEST IMPACT CRATER ON EARTH On Jun. 29, 2012, scientists at the Geological Survey of Denmark and Greenland announced that they had discovered an impact crater in Greenland that could be 3 billion years old. Known as the Maniitsoq crater, the structure is around 62 mi. (100 km) across. Much of it has eroded and it may once have been much bigger. If such a crater was formed in an impact with Earth today, most life would be wiped out.

A fragment from the Chelyabinsk Oblast meteorite (see p. 44) recovered from Chebarkul Lake, placed in a local museum in 2013. Early analysis by scientists suggests that the meteor is of a common type known as ordinary chondrite.

Big Muley, aka sample 61016, came back with *Apollo 16* on Apr. 27, 1972. At 25 lb. 12 oz., it is the **heaviest rock returned from space**. All rock returned so far is lunar, from the Apollo and Luna programs (see p. 46).

Of the roughly 50 known meteorites on Earth that have originated from the Moon, the **largest lunar meteorite** is Kalahari 009, with a mass of 29 lb. 12 oz. It was discovered in the Kalahari Desert in Botswana in Sep. 1999.

Northwest Africa 7325 (NWA 7325) was discovered in Morocco in 2012 and is thought to be the **first meteorite from Mercury**. Fragments, weighing 12 oz., are chemically consistent with data sent back from a Mercury-orbiting mission.

GLOSSARY

Meteoroid: Metallic or rocky fragments, usually from a comet or asteroid and typically less than 3 ft. 3 in. wide; smaller fragments are known as micrometeoroids.

Meteor: A meteoroid that streaks through the atmosphere emitting heat and light; a "shooting star."

Meteorite: Meteoroid that survives Earth's atmosphere and lands on the ground.

SAMPLE-AND-RETURN

Numerous space missions have sought to return sample material to Earth:

- Apollo (1969–72): 2,415 samples of Moon rock weighing a total of 842 lb.
- Luna (1959–76): Soviet robotic probe missions that collected 11.49 oz. of lunar samples
- Orbital Debris Collector on *Mir* (1996–97) brought back interplanetary dust
- *Genesis* (2001–04): NASA project to collect solar wind molecules (**first material collected beyond the Moon**)

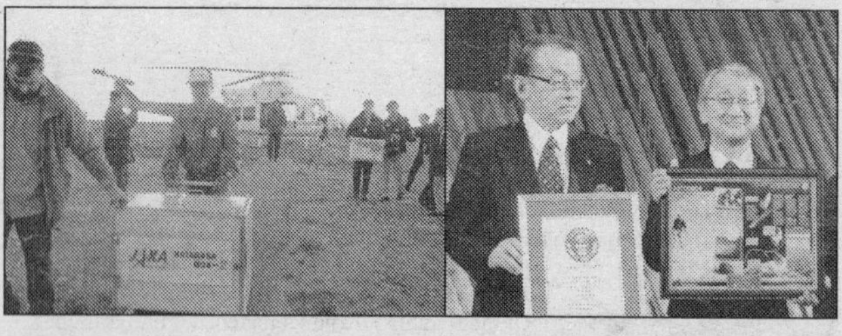

FARTHEST SAMPLE-AND-RETURN MISSION On Jun. 13, 2010, the contents of Japanese space probe *Hayabusa* were retrieved in Australia after a sampling mission to the 25143 Itokawa asteroid some 65.6 million mi. (300 million km) away. The probe had landed on Nov. 25, 2005, and the samples it collected—1,500 tiny grains of dust—are the **first material returned from an asteroid**. The picture above right shows Masaharu Nakagawa (left), science and technology minister for Japan, and *Hayabusa* project leader Junichiro Kawaguchi.

Largest impact crater on Earth The Vredefort crater, near Johannesburg in South Africa, may have lost the title of **oldest impact crater** to Greenland's Maniitsoq crater (see p. 45), but it remains the largest crater, with an estimated diameter of around 186 mi. (300 km). The crater was formed by an impact that occurred about 2 billion years ago.

Largest meteorites

- **Overall:** Hoba meteorite—130,000 lb. (59 metric tons), found in 1920 at Hoba West in Namibia.
- **Exhibited in a museum:** Cape York meteorite—68,085 lb. (30,883 kg), found in 1897 near Cape York in the west of Greenland; now at the Hayden Planetarium in New York City, U.S.A.
- **From Mars:** Zagami meteorite—40 lb. (18 kg), found on Oct. 3, 1962 near Zagami, Nigeria.

Largest tektite Tektites are glassy pieces of rock formed by the melting and cooling of terrestrial rocks after meteor impacts. A tektite weighing 23 lb. 13 oz. (10.8 kg) was discovered in 1971 in Thailand.

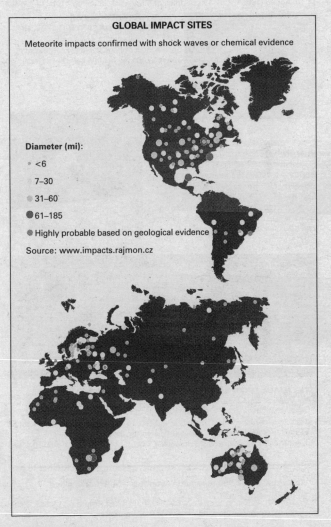

GLOBAL IMPACT SITES

Meteorite impacts confirmed with shock waves or chemical evidence

Diameter (mi):

∘ <6

7–30

31–60

61–185

Highly probable based on geological evidence

Source: www.impacts.rajmon.cz

EARTH FROM SPACE

FIRST FULL-VIEW COLOR PHOTOGRAPH OF EARTH On Nov. 10, 1967, NASA satellite *ATS-3* took a photograph of Earth while in geostationary orbit 23,000 mi. (37,000 km) above Brazil.

FIRST "EARTHRISE" VIEWED BY HUMANS *Apollo 8* was a manned spacecraft that orbited the Moon on Dec. 23–24, 1968. On Christmas Eve, crew members Frank Borman, Bill Anders, and Jim Lovell (all U.S.A.) captured an iconic image of fragile beauty that became known as "Earthrise" and is credited with inspiring increased environmental awareness.

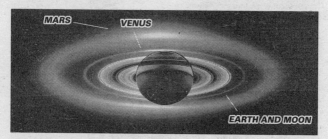

FIRST IMAGE FROM SATURN SHOWING EARTH, THE MOON, MARS, AND VENUS On Jul. 19, 2013, NASA's *Cassini* spacecraft slipped into Saturn's shadow, where it compiled a panoramic mosaic of the planet, seven of its moons, and details of the inner rings. The image was taken 870 million mi. (1.4 billion km) from Earth in a unique viewing geometry that meant the Sun's potentially damaging rays were eclipsed by Saturn itself.

Approximately **2,500 manmade satellites**—both working and defunct—orbit Earth.

FIRST IMAGE OF EARTH FROM LUNAR ORBIT NASA's Apollo precursor *Lunar Orbiter 1* snapped Earth on Aug. 23, 1966 while orbiting the Moon (original shot, above left). Modern technology has allowed for the rendering of higher resolution images from the original sources and the result was unveiled in 2008 (above right).

FIRST IMAGE OF EARTH AND THE MOON IN A SINGLE FRAME FROM SPACE On Sep. 18, 1977, NASA's *Voyager 1* probe was on the way to Jupiter when it captured Earth and the Moon from a distance of 7.25 million mi. (11.66 million km). The image of the Moon was far dimmer than Earth and had to be artificially enhanced by a factor of three to be visible.

MOST DISTANT IMAGE OF EARTH The image called "the pale blue dot" was taken by *Voyager 1* on Feb. 14, 1990 from almost 4 billion mi. (6.5 billion km) away, on the request of astronomer Carl Sagan. "Every 'superstar,' every 'supreme leader,' every saint and sinner in the history of our species lived there," said Sagan, "on a mote of dust suspended in a sunbeam."

LARGEST GEOLOGICAL STRUCTURE DISCOVERED FROM SPACE The "bull's-eye" of the Richat Structure in the Sahara of Mauritania was discovered from orbit by U.S. astronauts Jim McDivitt and Ed White during the *Gemini IV* mission in Jun. 1965. It has a diameter of 30 mi. (50 km).

FIRST HIGH-RESOLUTION IMAGE OF A TOTAL SOLAR ECLIPSE FROM LUNAR ORBIT Earth looks like a diamond ring in this full solar eclipse series taken by Japan's unmanned *Kaguya*, aka the SELENE mission, on Feb. 10, 2009.

FIRST IMAGE OF EARTH FROM SPACE A former Nazi V-2 rocket was launched by the U.S.A. on Oct. 24, 1946 in New Mexico, U.S.A., with a camera taking a frame every 1.5 sec. The rocket soared 65 mi. (104 km) before crashing, with the film preserved in a steel enclosure.

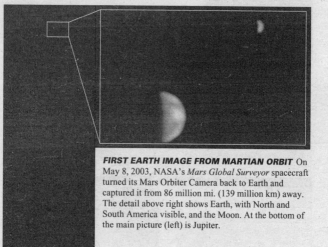

FIRST EARTH IMAGE FROM MARTIAN ORBIT On May 8, 2003, NASA's *Mars Global Surveyor* spacecraft turned its Mars Orbiter Camera back to Earth and captured it from 86 million mi. (139 million km) away. The detail above right shows Earth, with North and South America visible, and the Moon. At the bottom of the main picture (left) is Jupiter.

MOUNTAINS

Highest mountain The summit of Mount Everest, a Himalayan peak on the border between Tibet and Nepal, is at an altitude of 29,029 ft. (8,848 m), higher than any other mountain. For more about the conquests of Everest, see p. 317.

Tallest mountain face The Rupal face of Nanga Parbat, located in the western Himalayas, Pakistan, is a single rise of approximately 16,000 ft. (5,000 m) from the valley floor to the summit. The mountain itself, which reaches an altitude of 26,656 ft. (8,125 m), is the highest mountain in Pakistan and the eighth highest in the world.

Largest vertical extent Both the highest and the lowest points on Earth's exposed surface are in the continent of Asia. Mount Everest, with its peak at 29,029 ft. (8,848 m) above sea level, and the Dead Sea, with its surface at 1,384 ft. (422 m) below sea level, make Asia the continent with the largest difference in vertical extent of 30,413 ft. (9,270 m).

Highest polar ice cap Dome Argus is a vast ice plateau near the center of East Antarctica. Its highest point is some 13,428 ft. (4,093 m) above sea level. It is Antarctica's highest ice feature and overlies the 745-mi.-long (1,200-km) Gamburtsev Mountain Range. For more on the formation of this record breaking range, see p. 54.

HIGHEST ARCTIC MOUNTAIN The summit of Gunnbjørn Fjeld in Greenland's Watkins Range reaches 12,119 ft. (3,694 m) above sea level. It is a type of mountain known as a "nunatak," a rocky peak poking through a glacier or ice field. On the other side of the world, the **highest mountain in Antarctica** is Vinson Massif, one of the Seven Summits, whose peak reaches 16,050 ft. (4,892 m) above sea level.

Every rise of 1,000 ft. in altitude lowers the **boiling point of water** by 1.8°F.

LARGEST PLATEAU The most extensive high plateau is the Tibetan Plateau, which covers 715,000 sq. mi. (1.85 million km²) of Central Asia. Its average altitude is 16,000 ft. (4,900 m). The Himalayan mountain range, to the south of the plateau, is home to 30 of the world's tallest mountains.

HIGHEST FREE-STANDING MOUNTAIN Mount Kilimanjaro in Tanzania, Africa, is 19,341 ft. (5,895 m) above sea level. It is the fourth highest of the world's Seven Summits and the highest mountain in Africa. Standing independent of any range, Kilimanjaro is a dormant or extinct stratovolcano that last erupted around 200,000–150,000 years ago.

MOUNTAIN RANGES

Largest A mountain range is a series of mountains, or hills, that are connected in some way. The Himalayas, in Asia, is the largest mountain range, incorporating 96 of the 109 peaks measuring more than 24,000 ft. (7,300 m).

Longest continental The Andes in South America is 4,700 mi. (7,600 km) long. It spans seven countries, from Venezuela to Argentina, and includes some of Earth's highest mountains. More than 50 of the Andes peaks reach at least 20,000 ft. (6,000 m) high and for most of its extent the range is 200 mi. (300 km) wide.

Highest coastal The Sierra Nevada de Santa Marta is an isolated range of mountains located in Colombia, separated from the Andes. The range rises to an elevation of 18,946 ft. (5,775 m) above sea level. Its considerable biodiversity led UNESCO to designate the mountains as a biosphere reserve in 1979.

Highest tropical Huascarán National Park in Peru's Cordillera Blanca ("White Range") mountain range has its highest point at 22,204 ft. (6,768 m) above sea level. The protected area covers approximately 840,100 acres (340,000 ha) and covers almost the whole of the Cordillera Blanca. The mountain range contains 33 peaks of more than 18,000 ft. (5,500 m) in addition to 80 glaciers and 120 glacial lakes.

Longest submarine The Mid-Ocean Ridge runs 40,000 mi. (65,000 km) from the Arctic Ocean to the Atlantic Ocean, around Africa, Asia, and Australia, and under the Pacific Ocean to the west coast of North America. Its peaks reach 13,800 ft. (4,200 m) above the base ocean depth.

Oldest The Barberton Greenstone Belt in South Africa, also known as the Makhonjwa Mountains, is formed of rocks dating back 3.6 billion years. It was here, in 1875, that the first gold in South Africa was discovered. The mountains rise some 5,900 ft. (1,800 m) above sea level.

Smallest The Sutter Buttes of California, U.S.A., are the eroded remains of a volcano that was active around 1.6–1.4 million years ago. They are isolated within the flat floor of the Sacramento Valley and reach a maximum height of 2,060 ft. (628 m), with a base diameter of around 10 mi. (16 km).

TALLEST MOUNTAIN Measured from its submarine base in the Hawaiian Trough to its peak, Mauna Kea (White Mountain) on the island of Hawaii, U.S.A., has a combined height of 33,480 ft. (10,205 m), of which 13,796 ft. (4,205 m) is above sea level.

HIGHEST MOUNTAIN TABLETOP Monte Roraima, on the border of Brazil, Guyana, and Venezuela, is a sandstone plateau measuring 9,220 ft. (2,810 m) in height. Its harsh environment has deterred human presence and predators; as a result, around one-third of its plant species are unique to the mountain.

FACT: Monte Roraima is thought to have inspired Arthur Conan Doyle's novel *The Lost World*.

MOVING MOUNTAINS Sixty years ago, the height of Mount Everest changed overnight! The Great Trigonometrical Survey of India, a broad study that took place during the 19th century, calculated the height of the summit to be 29,002 ft. in 1856. In 1955, however, this figure was adjusted to the present altitude of 29,029 ft. The mountain was given its present name in 1865, in honor of Sir George Everest (left). As British Surveyor General in India from 1830 to 1843, he had a major role in mapping the Indian subcontinent.

GREATEST VERTICAL DROP
Mount Thor on Baffin Island in Nunavut, Canada, is a granite peak whose west face consists of a vertical drop of 4,101 ft. (1,250 m). It is technically an overhang, with the average angle of repose of the cliff being at 105 degrees—or 15 degrees beyond the vertical.

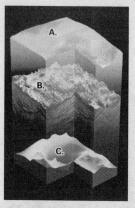

COLD MOUNTAIN: Peaks Under the Ice
The Gamburtsev Mountain Range in eastern Antarctica extends for some 745 mi. across the continent. It reaches 8,858 ft. high but is permanently buried under more than 1,968 ft. of ice, making it the world's **largest subglacial mountain range**.

Studies suggest that the Gamburtsev may date back 1 billion years, the result of mini-continents converging to form a supercontinent and forcing the land between them into a mountain range. In time, this range collapsed under its own weight and was eroded down to a residual root. Tectonic movement tore the land into separate continents and created a rift from present-day eastern Antarctica to India; the root, warmed by the rifting, forced up the land to form eastern Antarctica. As Earth cooled, this land became covered in an ice sheet the size of Canada.

A. Ice sheet
B. Gamburtsev Mountain Range
C. Root

FACT: Chimborazo, an inactive stratovolcano located in the Andes, is 20,564 ft. tall—ca. 6,560 ft. shorter than Mount Everest. Because it is located on the equator, however—which bulges outward more than the rest of the globe—scientists believe that its summit is the **most distant point on Earth from the planet's core**.

FASTEST-RISING MOUNTAIN Nanga Parbat in Pakistan is growing taller at a rate of 0.27 in. (7 mm) per year. The mountain is part of the Himalayan Plateau, which was formed when India began colliding with the Eurasian continental plate between 50 million and 30 million years ago.

PEAK PERFORMANCE: COMPARING THE WORLD'S HIGH POINTS

A. Sea level

B. 16,023 ft.

C. 7,711 ft.

D. 20,000 ft.

E. 27,711 ft.

F. 13,796 ft.

G. 19,684 ft.

H. 33,480 ft.

I. ca. 15,419 ft.

J. ca. 13,615 ft.

K. 29,029 ft.

L. Tibetan Plateau

Highest mountain: Mount Everest, 29,029 ft.; average base elevation of ca. 15,419 ft., giving an average base-to-peak height of ca. 13,615 ft.

Highest island peak: Puncak Jaya, Indonesia, 16,024 ft. above sea level

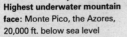

Highest underwater mountain face: Monte Pico, the Azores, 20,000 ft. below sea level

Tallest mountain: Mauna Kea, 33,480 ft. from its submarine base

BLUE PLANET

Lowest river The Jordan River begins in Israel at an elevation of 9,232 ft. (2,814 m) and flows 155 mi. (251 km) south to the Dead Sea. Its lowest elevation here is 1,361 ft. (416 m) below sea level.

This elevation makes the Dead Sea itself the **lowest exposed body of water**. Bordering Israel and Jordan, it is 50 mi. (80 km) long and measures 11 mi. (18 km) at its widest point.

Highest river The Yarlung Zangbo has an average elevation of 13,100 ft. (4,000 m). It rises in Tibet, runs for 6,550 mi. (2,000 km) through China, and becomes the Brahmaputra River in India. It enters the ocean in the Bay of Bengal, where it meets the Ganges to form the **largest delta**, covering 30,000 sq. mi. (75,000 km²).

Biggest rise in sea level since the last ice age Meltwater Pulse 1A was an event occurring around 14,500 years ago, when sea levels rose by ca. 65 ft. (20 m) in less than 500 years. Approximately 3,000 years earlier, as the ice sheets of the last ice age began to retreat, they added fresh water to the oceans. Global sea levels rose at an average of some 0.4 in. (1 cm) per year until Meltwater Pulse 1A speeded things up, probably due to a partial collapse of the Antarctic ice sheets.

LARGEST LAKE WITHIN A LAKE Manitou Lake occupies an area of 41 sq. mi. (106 km²). It is located on the **largest island in a lake**, Manitoulin Island (see above), which covers 1,068 sq. mi. (2,766 km²) of the Canadian section of Lake Huron. Another geographical nesting doll is Vulcan Point, the **largest island in a lake on an island in a lake on an island**. The 130-ft. (40-m) island sits in Crater Lake, the central crater of the Taal volcano in Lake Taal on the island of Luzon in the Philippines.

> **FACT:** Superior is one of the Great Lakes of North America, along with Michigan, Huron, Erie, and Ontario. Spanning more than 745 mi., they contain about a fifth of the world's surface fresh water—only the polar ice caps have more.

LARGEST FRESHWATER LAKE Lake Superior is shared by Canada and the U.S.A., bordered by Ontario and Minnesota to the north and west, and Wisconsin and Michigan to the south. The lake covers 31,700 sq. mi. (82,100 km²). Lake Baikal in Siberia, Russia, has the **greatest volume for a freshwater lake**, estimated at 5,500 cu. mi. (23,000 km³).

LARGEST AREA OF BIOLUMINESCENCE Legends of a "milky sea" date far back in naval history. In 2005, scientists at the U.S. Naval Research Laboratory used satellite imagery to confirm detailed log reports made by the British ship SS *Lima* in 1995. They described an area in the Indian Ocean, near Somalia, measuring around 5,400 sq. mi. (14,000 km²). Vast amounts of bioluminescent bacteria, possibly *Vibrio harveyi*, are believed to be responsible.

LARGEST BAY The Bay of Bengal in the Indian Ocean covers an area of 839,000 sq. mi. (2.17 million km²). One-quarter of the world's population of 7.2 billion live in the countries bordering it: Sri Lanka, India, Bangladesh, Myanmar, and Malaysia.

Chesapeake Bay is the **largest bay by shore length**, stretching 11,684 mi. (18,804 km) along the Atlantic coast of Maryland and Virginia, U.S.A.

Oldest body of seawater The U.S. Geological Survey studied a body of groundwater more than 3,280 ft. (1,000 m) below Chesapeake Bay in the U.S.A. They reported that it dated from the early Cretaceous North Atlantic period, between 145 and 100 million years ago.

Largest desert lake Lake Turkana, in the Great Rift Valley, Kenya, has a surface area of 2,472 sq. mi. (6,405 km²)—the equivalent of 897,058 football pitches.

Oldest lake Lake Baikal in Russia is up to 25 million years old. It formed following a tectonic rift in the Earth's crust.

LARGEST PINK LAKE A combination of microorganisms and minerals gives Lake Retba, or Lac Rose, in Senegal, its distinctive hue. At 2.7 sq. mi. (7.5 km²), it may be the biggest, but it's far from unique. Examples can be found in Canada (Dusty Rose Lake in British Columbia), Spain (two saltwater lakes near Torrevieja), and Australia (Lake Hillier). Lakes become pink through algae, or from organisms that produce carotenoids (as occur in carrots), such as the sea salt field *Dunaliella salina*.

Oceans provide **190 times as much living space** as soil, air, and fresh water combined.

OCEANS

Deepest point Challenger Deep, located in the Mariana Trench in the Pacific Ocean, is 35,797 ft. (10,911 m) at its deepest point. Mount Everest would entirely fit in it, with its peak 6,560 ft. (2,000 m) below the surface.

Largest biome The area in open ocean—away from both seabed and shore—is called the pelagic zone. Globally, its volume is 319 million cu. mi. (1.3 billion km³) and it supports life, making it by far the largest biome. It has many of the planet's larger animals, including whales.

Largest continuous ocean current system The system of ocean circulation that transports cold and salty deep water is called the thermohaline conveyor belt ("thermo" from heat and "haline" from salinity). The water is slowly transported from the north Atlantic down to the Southern Ocean, where it travels east and north to the Indian and Pacific oceans. Here, it rises and becomes warm, traveling back west, where it sinks once again in the north Atlantic. The complete cycle can last for a thousand years.

TIDE OF FILTH: *A Drop in the Ocean* The largest ocean garbage site is in the North Pacific Gyre (above left), a vortex of slowly revolving ocean water that naturally concentrates ever increasing amounts of floating litter in its center. Much of it is made up of plastic, which never degrades but breaks down into tiny fragments that pollute down to 32 ft. below the surface. These tiny, toxic chunks enter the food chain and studies now suggest that waste outweighs nutritious plankton by a factor of six to one. Plastic bags account for more than 50% of all marine litter, the **greatest ocean pollutant** (above right).

IN DEEP WATER

Deepest lake: Lake Baikal, Russia, 5,370 ft. deep

Deepest hypersaline lake: The Dead Sea, Israel/Jordan, 1,240 ft. deep and more than eight times saltier than seawater

Deepest brine pool: Orca Basin, Gulf of Mexico, 7,200 ft. below sea level, filled with water around eight times saltier than the Gulf

---

WATERFALLS

Largest waterfall ever Dry Falls, near Missoula in Montana, U.S.A., is all that remains of a waterfall that stretched over 3.5 mi. (5.6 km) and was 380 ft. (115 m) high. It burst into life when the water from a massive glacial lake—formed 18,000 years ago—broke through the ice, causing a catastrophic flood.

Highest underwater waterfall The Denmark Strait Cataract is underwater in the Denmark Strait, which separates Greenland and Iceland. The 2.17-mi. (3.5-km) waterfall carries around 176.5 million cu. ft. (5 million m^3) of water per sec. The Cataract, the **largest waterfall** of any kind, is formed as cold, denser seawater drops from the Greenland Sea into the slightly warmer Irminger Sea.

Largest plunge pool Plunge pools form at the base of waterfalls as a result of water erosion. Perth Canyon is a plunge pool off the coast of Australia that measures ca. 1,000 ft. (300 m) deep and 4.62 sq. mi. (12 km^2) in area. The prehistoric pool was created when the region was above sea level.

Greatest waterfall flow Boyoma Falls in the Democratic Republic of the Congo flows at a rate of 600,000 cu. ft. (17,000 m^3) per sec. It has seven drops along 60 mi. (100 km) of the Lualaba River.

DEEPEST RIVER In Jul. 2008, scientists from the U.S. Geological Survey and the American Museum of Natural History discovered that the Congo River, which spans 10 countries in Africa, has a maximum depth of at least 722 ft. (220 m). The measurements were performed in the Lower Congo River using echo sounders, advanced GPS, and acoustic doppler current profilers.

LARGEST TIDAL BORES

A tidal bore arises when the Sun, Moon, and Earth align to form dramatic tidal conditions. A solitary wave travels with great speed up a narrow river, forcing the flow upstream.

In 1955, the **largest tidal bore** was the Tsien Tang Kiang, attaining "a height of up to 25 feet and a speed of 13 knots." We later reported the 1993 incident in which one of these waves reached Hangzhou Bay, China. It rose to 30 ft., was 200 mi. long, and pushed 2.3 million gal of water per sec. to the shore, resulting in multiple fatalities.

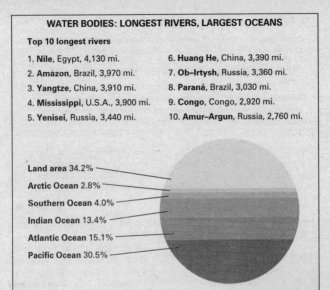

WATER BODIES: LONGEST RIVERS, LARGEST OCEANS

Top 10 longest rivers

1. **Nile**, Egypt, 4,130 mi.
2. **Amazon**, Brazil, 3,970 mi.
3. **Yangtze**, China, 3,910 mi.
4. **Mississippi**, U.S.A., 3,900 mi.
5. **Yenisei**, Russia, 3,440 mi.

6. **Huang He**, China, 3,390 mi.
7. **Ob–Irtysh**, Russia, 3,360 mi.
8. **Paraná**, Brazil, 3,030 mi.
9. **Congo**, Congo, 2,920 mi.
10. **Amur–Argun**, Russia, 2,760 mi.

Land area 34.2%
Arctic Ocean 2.8%
Southern Ocean 4.0%
Indian Ocean 13.4%
Atlantic Ocean 15.1%
Pacific Ocean 30.5%

CAVES

Deepest blue hole Blue holes are found at or just below sea level, and were once dry caves or shafts. They filled with seawater as the ice caps melted and the water levels rose during the last ice age. Dean's Blue Hole is 250 ft. (76 m) wide, a vertical shaft that sinks for 662 ft. (202 m) at Turtle Cove on the Atlantic edge of the Bahamas. It contains 11.8 million cu. ft. (1.1 million m³) of water.

Deepest ice cave descent Janot Lamberton (FRA) descended to 662 ft. (202 m) in a glacial cave in Greenland. The cave, reached by Lamberton in 1998, was formed by a river of meltwater during the Arctic summer.

Deepest lava cave Lava tubes are formed by streaming lava under the hard surface of a lava flow. While a volcano is erupting, the tubes drain lava away, before the rock cools and the process results in a long, cavelike channel. The deepest and longest example is Kazumura Cave in Hawaii, U.S.A. It is 40.7 mi. (65.5 km) long, and descends to a depth of 3,614 ft. (1,101 m).

Longest cave system It has taken some 25 million years for Mammoth Cave to form through the weathering action of the Green River and its tributaries. Situated in Mammoth Cave National Park in Kentucky, U.S.A., the system is a network of limestone caves, of which 400 mi. (644 km) have been explored so far.

Longest gypsum cave Gypsum, a soft mineral, is used to make a type of plaster called plaster of Paris. A cave system called Optymistychna

("Optimistic"), near Korolivka, Ukraine, occurs in a layer of gypsum around 65 ft. 7 in. (20 m) thick. It has been mapped so far at 146 mi. (236 km) in length, under an area covering 0.7 sq. mi. (2 km²).

LARGEST CAVE Vietnamese farmer Ho Khanh found a cave in central Vietnam in 1991—and then forgot where it was. It wasn't until 2009 that he guided a UK team to Hang Son Doong ("Mountain River Cave"), which is 655 ft. (200 m) high, 490 ft. (150 m) wide, and at least 4 mi. (6.5 km) long. Tourists with $3,000 to spare can now visit it—although they must first trek for over a day through jungle and abseil 260 ft. (79 m) to the entrance.

It typically takes **100,000 years** for a cave to grow large enough to accommodate humans.

DEEPEST UNBROKEN VERTICAL SHAFT IN A CAVE

Straight, natural shafts are challenges for cavers—essentially, they are sheer drops without ledges. The Miao Keng Cave, near Tian Xing in China, has a continuous shaft 1,643 ft. (501 m) deep that takes around two hours to abseil. The shaft is about two-thirds of the height of the **tallest building**—the 2,716-ft. (828-m) Burj Khalifa in Dubai, UAE.

LARGEST CAVE CHAMBER

A chamber is the largest order of space in a cave. It is often formed at a junction of passages, where erosion and collapse have exposed more rock, and its maximum size is dictated by the strength of the ceiling. The Sarawak Chamber in the Lubang Nasib Bagus cave of Sarawak, Borneo, is 2,300 ft. (700 m) long. Its average width is 980 ft. (300 m) and it is at least 230 ft. (70 m) high. By way of comparison, that's nearly as long as seven football fields, and taller than Nelson's Column in Trafalgar Square, London.

UNDERGROUND MUSIC

Deepest live radio broadcast: Two-hour CBC Radio Points North (CAN) show, 7,680 ft. down in Creighton Mine in Ontario, Canada, on May 24, 2005

Largest natural underground musical instrument: The Great Stalacpipe Organ—stalactites covering 3.4 acres that produce tones when struck with mallets linked to a keyboard in Luray Caverns, Virginia, U.S.A.

Deepest concert underground: Agonizer (FIN), 4,170 ft. below sea level at Pyhäsalmi Mine in Pyhäjärvi, Finland, Aug. 4, 2007

DEEPEST CAVE

The same year that we published our first edition, we said that six French speleologists discovered the Berger cave near Grenoble in France in Jul. 1955. We called it the **deepest cave**, at 2,959 ft. (902 m).

Today, Gouffre Berger is no longer quite the awesome challenge it once was, and is regularly explored by groups of up to 200. We also now know it is 3,681 ft. deep and that Krubera Cave in Georgia is nearly twice as deep (see below).

GET DOWN: Deepest Cave Gets Deeper It's not often that a geological feature breaks its own record, but that's exactly what happened with the **deepest cave**, Krubera Cave (above left). Or rather, Gennady Samokhin (pictured above right), a Ukrainian caver, extended the known depth of the cave on Aug. 10, 2012 by 20 ft. The cave in the Arabika Massif, Georgia, now has an explored depth of 7,208 ft. The new area is in a sump (submerged section) called Dva Kapitana ("Two Captains") that Samokhin suspects may extend by as much as 6 mi., all the way to the Black Sea. Samokhin was also a member of the previous record attempt team in 2007.

Oldest caves The Sudwala Caves in Mpumalanga, South Africa, are ca. 240 million years old. The series of caves is believed to have formed from Precambrian dolomite rock dating back 3.8 billion years. As well as providing shelter for prehistoric humans, it has been used in modern times for ammunition storage and as a concert venue. The bat guano (droppings) found there are used as fertilizer.

Longest explored cave system underwater Sistema Ox Bel Ha ("Three Paths of Water" in Mayan), in the state of Quintana Roo, Mexico, is a series of underwater passages accessed by surface lakes. As of Mar. 2014, according to cave researcher Bob Gulden at caverbob.com, 151 mi. (243 km) of the system has been mapped.

Greatest vertical extent for a flowstone cascade Flowstone cascades form in sheets when limestone-saturated water runs down cave walls and floors, leaving behind calcite deposits that solidify over time. The largest vertical extent is 492 ft. (150 m), in the Lechuguilla Cave in Carlsbad Caverns National Park, New Mexico, U.S.A.

Longest stalactite Stalactites form to hang from a cave ceiling. The longest free-hanging example is 92 ft. (28 m) and hangs in the Gruta do Janelão in Minas Gerais, Brazil.

Tallest stalagmite A stalagmite is the opposite of a stalactite. It is built up from the floor and the tallest is reported to measure some 230 ft. (70 m). It is located in Zhijin Cave in Guizhou Province, China.

Tallest natural cave column A column measuring 201 ft. 8 in. (61.5 m) in a cave at Tham Sao Hin, Thailand, was created by the merging of a stalactite and stalagmite. Where the two formations met they became one column.

LONGEST UNDERGROUND RIVER In Mar. 2007, cave divers Stephen Bogaerts (UK) and Robbie Schmittner (DEU) announced that they had discovered a 95-mi.-long (153-km) river beneath the Yucatán Peninsula in Mexico. The river, which has many twists and turns, spans around 6 mi. (10 km) of land.

LONGEST SEA CAVE Matainaka Cave on New Zealand's South Island is 5,052 ft. (1,540 m) long and is still forming through wave action from the sea. This length is more than three times that of its nearest rival, Mercer Bay Cave in New Zealand, which extends to 1,542 ft. (470 m). The **largest sea cave** is in the Sea Lion Caves in Oregon, U.S.A. One chamber is 310 ft. (95 m) long, 165 ft. (50 m) wide, and 50 ft. (15 m) high, in a 1,315-ft.-long (400-m) passage.

LARGEST GYPSUM CRYSTAL The Cave of Crystals, below Naica mountain in the Chihuahuan Desert, Mexico, contains translucent single crystals of gypsum measuring up to 36 ft. (11 m) long and weighing up to 121,200 lb. (55 tonnes). They began to form hundreds of thousands of years ago, when the cave was filled with warm, mineral-rich water.

LONGEST CAVES

1. **Mammoth Cave**, U.S.A., 400 mi.

2. **Sistema Sac Actun**, Mexico, 193 mi.

3. **Jewel Cave National Monument**, U.S.A., 166 mi.

4. **Sistema Ox Bel Ha**, Mexico, 151 mi.

5. **Optymistychna Cave**, Ukraine, 146 mi.

6. **Wind Cave**, U.S.A., 141 mi.

7. **Lechuguilla Cave**, U.S.A., 138 mi.

8. **Hölloch**, Switzerland, 124 mi.

9. **Fisher Ridge Cave System**, U.S.A., 122.5 mi.

10. **Gua Air Jernih (Clearwater Cave)**, Malaysia, 122.4 mi.

Source: www.caverbob.com

LIVING PLANET

CONTENTS

There are an estimated **7.77 million animal species** on Earth; to date, only 12% have been described.

LARGEST FISH The largest living fish is the rare, plankton-feeding whale shark (*Rhincodon typus*), which is found in the warmer areas of the Atlantic, Pacific, and Indian oceans. The largest scientifically recorded example was 41 ft. 6 in. (12.65 m) long—about the same length as three-and-a-half Mini Cooper cars—and measured 23 ft. (7 m) around the thickest part of the body. It was captured off Baba Island near Karachi, Pakistan, on Nov. 11, 1949, and weighed an estimated 46,000 lb. (21 metric tons).

FACT: A whale shark egg—the **largest of all fish eggs**—is typically the same size as a football!

NEW DISCOVERIES

It is a tragic but inescapable fact that animal species are becoming extinct all the time—in many cases, as a direct result of human activity. Happily, it is also true that even today a surprising number of previously unknown, entirely new animal species are coming to light: 15,000 each year, on average.

Many of the new species being discovered are small, inconspicuous creatures: mostly insects, worms, and other diminutive invertebrates. But quite a few much more sizable and very spectacular animals are also being uncovered, and on a global scale, not just in a few specific locations.

To demonstrate this heartening and ongoing revelation of previously unknown life forms, our expert Dr. Karl Shuker highlights some of the most notable new animal species that have come to light over the past six decades. All of these creatures have been found, formally described, and classified by scientists since the first edition of the *Guinness Book of Records* was published in 1955, and every one is a GWR record holder.

At the bottom of these pages we present 10 of the most recent, and most remarkable animal finds. Encouragingly, the evidence on these pages suggests that there are still plenty of new species waiting to be discovered!

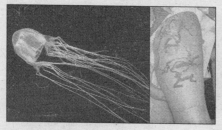

1950s: The year 1955 saw the discovery of the **most venomous jellyfish**, Flecker's sea-wasp (*Chironex fleckeri*), which is found in the waters off Queensland, Australia. Shown near left are sting wounds inflicted on the leg of a swimmer in Jan. 2000.

1960s: During this decade, an extra-large brown spitting cobra was caught by herpetologist James Ashe in Kenya. In 2007, it was found to belong to a previously unknown species—at ca. 9 ft. (3 m) long, the **largest species of spitting cobra**—which was formally named *Naja ashei*, or Ashe's giant spitting cobra.

LARGEST SPECIES OF GERBIL:
Discovered in the 1960s, the great gerbil (*Rhombomys opimus*) can exceed 1 ft. 3 in. (40 cm) in length. It is native to Turkmenistan, Kazakhstan, Mongolia, and several other central and east-central Asian countries.

LARGEST STARFISH: In 1968, a specimen of the very fragile brisingid *Midgardia xandaros* was collected in the Gulf of Mexico. It measured an astonishing 4 ft. 6 in. (1.38 m) from tip to tip. The species was formally classified in 1972.

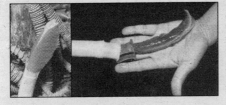

1970s: In 1977, scientists onboard the U.S. research submarine *Alvin* discovered an astonishing new ecosystem thriving around hydrothermal vents on the seafloor off the Galápagos Islands, Ecuador. Among the fauna were new species such as the giant tube worm (*Riftia pachyptila*), with huge, red, plumelike tentacles. It was the **first known ecosystem not to derive its primary energy from sunlight**, which can't penetrate down to it, but from chemical energy instead, released by bacteria.

LARGEST SPECIES OF POISON DART FROG: South America's poison dart frogs have toxic skin secretions used by native Indian tribes to tip their blowgun darts. The largest species, the 1-oz. (30-g) Colombian golden poison dart frog (*Phyllobates terribilis*), remained undiscovered by science until 1974.

1980s: In 1983, scientists created a family of sharks, Megachasmidae, in order to accommodate a large and remarkable new species, the megamouth shark (*Megachasma pelagios*), which was first discovered in 1976 off Hawaii, U.S.A. Megachasmidae remains the **newest shark family**.

1990s: The **newest genus of wild ox**, *Pseudoryx*, was created in 1993 to house a spectacular species first made known to science the previous year in Vu Quang, Vietnam. Now known as the saola or Vu Quang ox (*P. nghetinhensis*), this sizable species differs markedly from other oxen by way of its very long, slender, antelope-like horns and legs.

MOST POISONOUS BIRD: The hooded pitohui (*Pitohui dichrous*) of Papua New Guinea is one of the very few poisonous birds. Discovered in 1990, its feathers and skin contain the potent poison homobatrachotoxin, also secreted by the dart frogs of South America (see above).

SMALLEST SEA HORSE: An adult pygmy sea horse (*Hippocampus denise*) is typically just 0.63 in. (16 mm) long—smaller than an average human fingertip. The species was first discovered in 2003 in the delicate corals of the Flores Sea, off the coast of Indonesia.

2000s: The **newest species of big cat**, the Bornean clouded leopard (*Neofelis diardi*), was thought to be a subspecies until studies confirmed that its DNA and appearance were distinct. It was reclassified in Dec. 2006 as a species in its own right.

2010s: The **newest species of monkey** to have been scientifically recognized is Vieira's titi (*Callicebus vieirai*). Native to the states of Mato Grosso and Pará in central-northern Brazil, it was officially described and named in 2012. It is readily distinguished from all other titis by its unique facial and pelage (hair) coloration.

TEN OF THE MOST RECENT ARRIVALS. NEWEST . . .

Amphibian
2013
Botsford's leaf-litter frog (*Leptolalax botsfordi*) was formally described and classified in late 2013. It was discovered in the high elevations of Vietnam's Mount Fansipan, the tallest mountain in Indochina.

Ape
2010
The northern buff-cheeked gibbon (*Nomascus annamensis*) is native to the tropical rain forests between Vietnam, Laos, and Cambodia. It is distinguished from similar-looking species by its characteristic vocalizations.

Bird of prey
2010
Formally described and named in 2010, the Socotra buzzard (*Buteo socotraensis*) is native exclusively to the Socotra archipelago, a group of tiny islands forming part of Yemen in the Arabian peninsula.

Cat
2013
The selkirk rex is also known as the poodle cat because of its thick, curly fur, composed of three separate layers. The breed was developed from a spontaneous genetic mutation originating in Montana, U.S.A., in 1987.

Freshwater cetacean
2014
Inia araguaiaensis, the Araguaian boto, was officially described and named in Jan. 2014. It is a species of freshwater dolphin native to the Araguaia River basin of Brazil, and is the first such discovery for almost a century.

Lemur
2013
The Marohita mouse lemur (*Microcebus marohita*) and Anosy mouse lemur (*M. tanosi*) are native to Madagascar, as are all lemurs. Each was distinguished from similar species of mouse lemur by sequencing its genes.

Marine cetacean
2012
The latest marine cetacean to have been scientifically recognized is the Burrunan dolphin (*Tursiops australis*), which was officially described and named in 2012. It is endemic to the coastal waters of southeastern Australia.

Owl
2013
The Seram masked owl (*Tyto almae*) was described and named in 2013, but it was first known to science in 1987, when a specimen was photographed (but not collected) in the wild. It is native to the Indonesian island of Seram.

Sea snake
2012
The mosaic sea snake (*Aipysurus mosaicus*) is known from a single specimen in Copenhagen's Natural History Museum. Caught in the 19th century in the seas between New Guinea and Australia, it was only made a new species in 2012.

Tapir
2013
Brazil's kabomani tapir (*Tapirus kabomani*) is one of the largest new mammals to have been discovered for a century, but it is the **smallest living species of tapir**, weighing on average a very modest 242 lb. (110 kg).

MAMMALS

CARNIVORES

Largest bear ever The tyrant polar bear (*Ursus maritimus tyrannus*) evolved from an isolated population of Arctic brown bears during the mid-Pleistocene epoch (250,000–100,000 years ago). With a body length of 12 ft. 2 in. (3.7 m) and a height to the shoulder of 6 ft. (1.83 m), it could weigh more than a ton (2,200 lb.). The tyrant was the first form of polar bear.

Oldest brown bear in captivity On May 24, 2013, a 50-year-old European brown bear (*Ursus arctos*) named Andreas died in a sanctuary built by the World Society for the Protection of Animals (WSPA) in northern Greece. The average lifespan in the wild is 25 years.

Largest euplerid Euplerids were once classed in the civet family and are also known as Madagascan civets. The largest of the 10 species is the fossa (*Cryptoprocta ferox*), which has the size and look of a small puma. It is 2 ft. 3 in.–2 ft. 7 in. (70–80 cm) long with a tail of 2 ft. 1 in.–2 ft. 3 in. (65–70 cm), and weighs 12 lb. 2 oz.–18 lb. 15 oz. (5.5–8.6 kg).

LARGEST CARNIVORE Male (bull) southern elephant seals (*Mirounga leonina*) weigh up to 7,720 lb. (3,500 kg), with an average length of 16 ft. 4 in. (5 m). Also the **largest pinnipeds**, they dwarf even the polar bear (*Ursus maritimus*, p. 75) and are found in the sub-Antarctic islands.

For animals closer to home, try p. 118.

LARGEST FELINE CARNIVORE

The male Siberian tiger (*Panthera tigris altaica*) averages 10 ft. 4 in. (3.15 m) from nose to tail, stands 3 ft. 3 in.–3 ft. 6 in. (99–107 cm) to its shoulder, and weighs around 580 lb. (265 kg). There are about 360 of the tigers in existence, a recovery from a low of 20–30 in the 1930s.

LARGEST TERRESTRIAL CARNIVORE

The polar bear (*Ursus maritimus*) weighs 880–1,320 lb. (400–600 kg) and is 7 ft. 10 in.–8 ft. 6 in. (2.4–2.6 m) long. It feeds on the **largest prey**, killing walruses up to 1,100 lb. (500 kg) and beluga whales of 1,322 lb. (600 kg) to fill a stomach capacity of ca. 150 lb. (68 kg), or 9 lb. (4 kg) more than an adult human male.

Oldest big cat fossil In 2010, fossils from a previously unknown species similar to a snow leopard were unearthed in the Himalayas. The fossils of this species—named *Panthera blytheae*—have been dated to between 4.1 and 5.95 million years old, which supports the theory that big cats evolved in central Asia—not Africa—and spread outward.

Newest species of wild cat Formally named in 2013, the southern Brazilian oncilla (*Leopardus guttulus*) inhabits the Atlantic Forest to the south of the country. They do not interbreed with oncillas elsewhere in Brazil.

Rarest fox The island fox (*Urocyon littoralis*) is native to six of the eight Channel Islands in California, U.S.A., each of which has its own separate subspecies of the species. In 2002, a total of 1,500 specimens was estimated (some of the subspecies numbered fewer than 100). Since then, the species has continued to decline, due in part to predation by golden eagles, disease parasites, and habitat destruction. The International Union for Conservation of Nature (IUCN) categorize it as "Critically Endangered."

Rarest raccoon The Cozumel or pygmy raccoon (*Procyon pygmaeus*) is found on the tiny Cozumel Island, off Mexico's Yucatán Peninsula, which is 184.5 sq. mi. (478 km²) in area. The raccoon is classed as "Critically Endangered": only 250–300 specimens are believed to exist.

Smallest family of land carnivores Two families of land carnivores contain just one single species each. They are Nandiniidae, containing the nandinia (*Nandinia binotata*) of Africa, and Ailuridae, containing as its own living species the lesser or red panda (*Ailurus fulgens*) of Asia.

CETACEANS

Largest cetacean A female blue whale (*Balaenoptera musculus*) killed at Twofold Bay in New South Wales, Australia, in 1910 measured 97 ft. (29.57 m) long.

The **smallest cetaceans** are the Hector's dolphin (*Cephalorhynchus hectori*) and the vaquita (*Phocoena sinus*), both of which grow to a length of just 3 ft. 11 in. (1.2 m).

The **smallest species of baleen whale** (toothless but possessing baleen plates for filtering food from water) is the pygmy right whale (*Caperea marginata*), at 19 ft. 8 in.–21 ft. 3 in. (6–6.5 m) long and weighing around 6,600–7,700 lb. (3–3.5 tonnes).

LARGEST CETACEAN FAMILY The term "cetacean" describes whales, dolphins, and porpoises. Dolphins (*Delphinidae*) have 37 living species, not all of which are called dolphins. This diverse family also includes killer, false killer, and pygmy killer whales and pilot whales. They all breathe through a blowhole situated on top of their heads.

FASTEST MARINE MAMMAL On Oct. 12, 1958, a bull killer whale (*Orcinus orca*) an estimated 20–25 ft. (6.1–7.6 m) in length was timed at 34.5 mph (55.5 km/h) in the northeastern Pacific. Similar speeds have also been reported for Dall's porpoise (*Phocoenoides dalli*) in short bursts.

> The rare **bowhead whale** (*Balaena mysticetus*) can live for longer than a century.

Deepest mammal dive Scientists recorded a 6,500-ft. (2,000-m) dive, lasting 1 hr. 13 min., by a bull sperm whale (*Physeter macrocephalus*) off the coast of Dominica in 1991.

In 1989, a male northern elephant seal (*Mirounga angustirostris*) was recorded diving to 5,017 ft. (1,529 m) off the coast of California, U.S.A., the **deepest dive by a pinniped**.

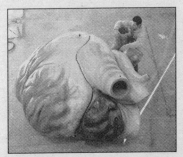

BLUE WHALE: The Biggest Heart on Earth Weighing up to 352,000 lb., the blue whale (*Balaenoptera musculus*) is the **largest mammal**, and the **largest animal** known to have existed. Pictured is a model of a blue whale's heart, made for Museum of New Zealand Te Papa Tongarewa by Human Dynamo Workshop. A blue whale's car-size heart weighs ca. 1,500 lb. and is the **largest heart** of any animal. It beats 4–8 times a minute (**slowest heartbeat**).

MOST EXPENSIVE SPECIES IN CAPTIVITY The giant panda (*Ailuropoda melanoleuca*) indigenous population is owned by China. Four U.S. zoos each pay an annual fee of $1m to China to lease a pair. Cub births, bamboo production, and security all add to the cost, but it can be worth it. Edinburgh Zoo in the UK reported a 51% increase in visitors during the year after giant pandas Sunshine and Sweetie took up residence.

BEAR NECESSITIES

Largest home range for a land-base mammal: Polar bears (*Ursus maritimus*) cover Arctic areas of 11,500 sq. mi.—the size of Italy—in a year.

Most sensitive nose for a land mammal: Typically, polar bears can detect prey, such as seals, from more than 18.6 mi. away and even when the prey is under ice.

Richest bear's milk: Polar bear milk contains up to 48.4% fat, which is as rich as cream and vital in order to build up the fat reserves in cubs, so that they can withstand the extreme conditions.

Fattiest diet: In the spring and summer months, polar bears dine on ringed seal pups, which have up to 50% body fat.

GLOSSARY

Carnivore: Meat-eating animal (order Carnivora)

Cetacean: Aquatic mammal (order Cetacea). Divided into two main groups: toothed whales (dolphins, porpoises, smaller whales) and baleen whales (large filter feeders).

Pinniped: Carnivorous, semiaquatic marine mammal (order Pinnipedia). Comprises seals, sea lions, and the walrus.

CARNIVORE AND CETACEAN SIZES

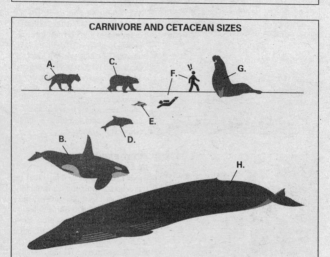

A. Male Siberian tiger: Length 10 ft. 4 in., weight 580 lb.

B. Killer whale: Length 29 ft. 6 in., weight 22,000 lb.

C. Polar bear: Length 8 ft. 6 in., weight 1,300 lb.

D. Common dolphin: Length 8 ft. 6 in., weight 175 lb.

E. Hector's dolphin: Length 3 ft. 11 in., weight 90–130 lb.

F. Adult human male: Height 5 ft. 8 in., weight 141 lb.

G. Elephant seal: Length 16 ft. 4 in., weight 7,720 lb.

H. Blue whale: Length 78 ft. 8 in., weight 352,700 lb.

CHIROPTERANS

Largest bat colony Up to 20 million female Mexican free-tailed bats (*Tadarida brasiliensis*) and offspring live in Bracken Cave in San Antonio, Texas, U.S.A. Up to 500 baby bats occupy 1 sq. ft. (0.09 m²) of space. The colony's nightly flight out for food forms a column that can be picked up on the local airport radar.

Largest bat family As of Nov. 2013, there were 300 species of vesper bat (*Vespertilionidae*), with new ones described every year. Among the members are the common pipistrelles, the European serotine, the noctules, the tube-nosed, the mouse-eared, and the rare barbastelle.

Longest gestation period for a bat The common vampire bat (*Desmodus rotundus*) has a gestation period of seven to eight months, and when the baby bat is born, it suckles its mother for an additional nine months and sometimes even longer. Native to Mexico, Central America, and South America, vampire bats feed solely on blood.

SMALLEST PRIMATE The pygmy mouse lemur (*Microcebus myoxinus*) from Madagascar is about 2.4 in. (62 mm) long with a tail of 5.3 in. (136 mm) and an average weight of 1.1 oz. (30.6 g). A white stripe runs from nose to forehead, and a black stripe runs down its back.

LARGEST BAT Bats are the only mammals capable of true flight (i.e., by flapping wings) instead of gliding. The largest are the flying foxes or fruit bats (*Pteropodidae*), which can have a wingspan of 5 ft. 7 in. (1.7 m).

INSECTIVORES

Largest mammalian brain-to-body mass Shrews have brains that constitute 10% of their total body weight.

Most dangerous insectivore The solenodon is a small, innocuous-looking, ratlike Caribbean mammal. The Haitian solenodon (*Solenodon* *paradoxus*) and the rare Cuban solenodon (*Solenodon cubanus*) have toxic saliva that is potentially dangerous to humans.

Heaviest tree shrew Tree shrews resemble squirrels with pointed snouts and no whiskers. Fully grown male specimens of the Mindanao tree shrew (*Urogale everetti*), native to the Philippines, have been recorded weighing 12 oz. (350 g).

Most sensitive animal organ The star-nosed mole (*Condylura cristata*) takes its name from its 22-probed nose covered with 25,000 sensory receptors—five times the amount of touch-sensitive nerve fibers in a human hand.

SMALLEST MAMMAL ON LAND
Savi's pygmy shrew (*Suncus etruscus*) is no bigger than a human thumb. Its body measures 1.4–2 in. (36–53 mm) and its tail 0.9–1.1 in. (24–29 mm). It weighs just 0.05–0.09 oz. (1.5–2.6 g).

LARGEST INSECTIVORE The moonrat (*Echinosorex gymnurus*) is neither a rat nor from the Moon! Found in southeast Asia, it is actually a giant relative of the hedgehog, but with thick fur instead of spikes. It is 10 in.–1 ft. 6 in. (26–46 cm) long with a tail of 6–9 in. (17–25 cm), and weighs 2 lb. 3 oz.–4 lb. 6 oz. (1–2 kg).

GLOSSARY

Chiropteran: has forelimbs modified as wings; uses echolocation to navigate

Insectivore: insect-eating mammal

Marsupial: characterized by pouch in which mother carries her young

Primate: has large brain and flexible hands and feet; includes humans

---

FACT: Shrews have a big appetite: in just one day, they can eat their own body weight in bugs and worms!

MARSUPIALS

Longest proportionate animal cecum A cecum is a kind of pouch in the large intestine, which in herbivores contains bacteria that help to break down the cellulose present in plant material. The largest in the animal kingdom relative to body size belongs to the koala (*Phascolarctos cinereus*). It is 6 ft. 7 in. (2 m) long and 4 in. (10 cm) in diameter, while the koala's own body length is just 2–2 ft. 9 in. (60–85 cm).

Most nipples The female shrewish short-tailed opossum (*Monodelphis sorex*) has up to 27 nipples (or "mammae"), despite being tiny: 4–5 in. (11–13 cm) with a tail of 2.5–3.3 in. (6.5–8.5 cm).

Most northerly marsupial The Virginia opossum (*Didelphis virginiana*) is the only species of marsupial that lives north of Mexico. It has been recorded as far north as southwestern Ontario in Canada.

LARGEST MARSUPIAL: Red Kangaroo There are nearly 60 species of kangaroo, the biggest being the red (*Macropus rufus*) from the dry center of Australia. The male red measures 5 ft. 10 in. tall and 9 ft. 4 in. long, and can weigh 200 lb. Reds arrive as the **largest newborn marsupial**, but because all marsupials are born very early, the reds weigh just 0.02 oz; it would take 36,000 newborns to equal their mother's weight. The **longest jump by a kangaroo** was in New South Wales, Australia, in 1951, when a female bounded 42 ft.

KOALA BEARS

Sleepiest marsupial: Because of its low-quality diet of eucalyptus leaves, koalas (*Phascolarctos cinereus*) spend up to 18 hr. out of every 24 asleep.

Largest koala litter: Two—a pair of identical twins called Euca and Lyptus, born on Apr. 10–11, 1999 in Queensland, Australia.

Oldest koala: Sarah, who died in 2001 at the age of 23 years, was born in 1978 and lived at the Lone Pine Koala Sanctuary in Queensland, Australia; koalas typically live for 16 years in captivity.

Oldest koala sanctuary: The Lone Pine Koala Sanctuary, where Sarah lived; it was established in 1927 by Claude Reid (AUS) and still operates today.

PRIMATES

Largest primate The male eastern lowland gorilla (*Gorilla beringei graueri*), found in the eastern Congo, weighs up to 360 lb. (163 kg) and has a typical bipedal height of up to 5 ft. 9 in. (1.75 m). The tallest recorded in the wild was a 6-ft. 5-in. (1.95-m) mountain bull shot in the eastern Congo on May 16, 1938.

Largest nocturnal primate The aye-aye (*Daubentonia madagascariensis*) from Madagascar is rodentlike but closely related to lemurs. Under threat for being seen as an omen of death, the aye-aye weighs 5 lb. 15 oz. (2.7 kg) and averages 2 ft. (65 cm) in length for the male, more than half of which is accounted for by its long tail.

Smallest loris Lorises are small, nocturnal primates related to lemurs and bushbabies. The smallest is the pygmy slow loris (*Nycticebus pygmaeus*), which measures 7.6–9 in. (19.5–23 cm) in length, with a tail averaging 0.7 in. (1.8 cm). It weighs 1–2 oz. (36–58 g).

SMALLEST MONKEY Pygmy marmosets (*Callithrix pygmaea*) weigh 0.53 oz. (15 g) at birth and grow to an average of 4.19 oz. (119 g). They are 5.3 in. (136 mm) long, excluding tail. Despite their size, pygmy marmosets can leap 16 ft. 5 in. (5 m) in the air.

SMALLEST MAMMAL Kitti's hog-nosed bat (*Craseonycteris thonglongyai*), aka the bumblebee bat, is 1.14–1.29 in. (29–33 mm) long. Found in caves in Thailand and Myanmar, it was rated as "vulnerable" on the International Union for Conservation of Nature (IUCN) red list of threatened species.

LARGEST MONKEY The male mandrill (*Mandrillus sphinx*) of equatorial West Africa has a head and body length of 2 ft.–2 ft. 6 in. (61–76 cm) and a tail measuring 2–3 in. (5.2–7.6 cm). Males average 55 lb. (25 kg) but can weigh 119 lb. (54 kg). The mandrill's distinctive blue rump, red-stripe face, and yellow beard make it one of the most vividly colored mammals.

The cries of male howler monkeys can be heard from **3 mi. away**.

FACT: The **largest primate of all time** was *Gigantopithecus blacki*—a veritable King Kong, now extinct for 100,000 years—standing 9 ft. 10 in. tall and weighing 3,480 lb.

LARGEST MAMMAL TO BUILD A NEST Male African gorillas (*Gorilla gorilla*) measure 5 ft. 6 in.–6 ft. (1.7–1.8 m) and weigh 300–500 lb. (136–227 kg). They create a new ground nest from the surrounding vegetation every day. The nests are circular and typically measure 3 ft. 3 in. (1 m) in diameter. Some lighter members of the troop build in trees and many make a separate nest during the day for a nap. These constructions are also the **largest nests built by a mammal**.

CHIROPTERAN, INSECTIVORE, AND PRIMATE SIZES

A. Male eastern lowland gorilla: Height 5 ft. 8 in., weight 360 lb.

B. Mandrill: Height 2 ft.–2 ft. 6 in., weight 55 lb.

C. Large and gigantic flying fox (fruit bat): Wingspan 5 ft. 7 in., weight 3 lb. 8 oz.

D. Giant otter shrew: Head-to-tail length 2 ft. 1 in., weight 2 lb. 1 oz.

E. Moonrat: Head-to-tail length 1 ft. 5 in.–2 ft. 4 in., weight 2 lb. 3 oz.–4 lb. 6 oz.

RODENTS

First domesticated rodent The guinea pig or South American cavy (*Cavia porcellus*) was first bred as a food animal in the Andes in around 5000 B.C. It is thought to be a domesticated version of the montane guinea pig (*C. tschudii*) native to the mountains of Peru.

Longest-lived rodent Africa's naked mole rat (*Heterocephalus glaber*) spends its life in underground burrow systems located beneath East Africa's drier tropical grasslands, and can live for 28 years.

Smallest gliding rodent The pygmy scalytail (*Idiurus zenkeri*) is also known as a flying mouse. Native to Central and East Africa, it has a maximum length of 7 in. (18 cm), of which its long, featherlike tail accounts for more than half. It has a gliding membrane between the forelimb and hind limb on each side of its body, which it expands when leaping from a tree, enabling it to glide through the air.

Largest rodent ever *Josephoartigasia monesi* was a 2-million-year-old fossil species that lived in what is today coastal Uruguay. It is currently known only from a single skull measuring 1 ft. 9 in. (53 cm) long, from which scientists estimate that the complete animal probably weighed 2,200 lb. (1 metric ton).

Largest jerboa Jerboas are desert-dwelling rodents that jump and leap on their hind legs like miniature kangaroos. The suitably named great jerboa (*Allactaga major*) has an uppermost head-and-body length of 7 in.

(18 cm), with a tail that can grow to 10.2 in. (26 cm). It primarily inhabits deserts in Russia, Kazakhstan, Turkmenistan, and Uzbekistan.

TALLEST MAMMAL
Giraffes (*Giraffa camelopardalis*) are found in the dry savanna and open woodland areas of sub-Saharan Africa. An adult male giraffe typically measures between 15 ft. and 18 ft. (4.6–5.5 m) in height.

Giraffes give birth standing up, so newborn calves typically fall 5 ft. to the ground.

SMALLEST RODENT Both the northern pygmy mouse (*Baiomys taylori*, left) of Mexico and the U.S.A. and the Baluchistan pygmy jerboa (*Salpingotulus michaelis*) of Pakistan have a 1.4-in. (3.6-cm) head-to-body length and 2.8-in. (7.2-cm) tail.

Largest squirrel

The Indian or Malabar giant squirrel (*Ratufa indica*) is endemic to deciduous and moist evergreen forests in peninsular India. It can grow to 3 ft. 3 in. (1 m) long, of which its long bushy tail constitutes two-thirds.

Fewest teeth for a rodent Also known as the small-toothed moss-mouse, and native to Indonesia and Papua New Guinea, Shaw Mayer's shrew mouse (*Pseudohydromys ellermani*) has eight teeth—four incisors and four molars, with no canines or premolars.

The **most teeth for a rodent** is the silvery mole rat (*Heliophobius argenteocinereus*). Native to Central and East Africa, including Tanzania, Kenya, and the Democratic Republic of the Congo, it has no fewer than 24 grinding teeth (premolars and molars) plus four incisors: 28 teeth in all.

UNGULATES

Smallest rhinoceros Once widespread across southeastern Asia but now confined to Sumatra, the Malay Peninsula, and Borneo, the Sumatran rhinoceros (*Dicerorhinus sumatrensis*) has a maximum head-and-body length of 10 ft. 5 in. (3.18 m), tail length of 2 ft. 3 in. (70 cm), and shoulder height of 4 ft. 9 in. (1.45 m).

SMALLEST UNGULATE
The lesser Malay mouse deer (*Tragulus javanicus*) has a body length of 1 ft. 5 in.–1 ft. 9 in. (42–55 cm), a shoulder height of 8–10 in. (20–25 cm), and weighs 3 lb. 4 oz.–5 lb. 8 oz. (1.5–2.5 kg). Primarily nocturnal, this small ungulate is rarely seen.

FACT: The World Wildlife Fund (WWF) has five ungulates on its critically endangered list: saola (*Pseudoryx nghetinhensis*), Sumatran elephant (*Elephas maximus sumatranus*), Sumatran rhinoceros (*Dicerorhinus sumatrensis*), black rhinoceros (*Diceros bicornis*), and Javan rhinoceros (*Rhinoceros sondaicus*).

LEAST CLASSIFIABLE MAMMAL The African aardvark (*Orycteropus afer*) has cylindrical teeth unlike those of any other mammal and claws instead of the hooves of other ungulates. It has its own order—Tubulidentata ("tube teeth").

LONGEST HAIR FOR A DOMESTIC CATTLE BREED The domestic cattle (*Bos taurus*) with the longest hair is the Highland cattle. Originating in Scotland but subsequently exported worldwide, this famously hirsute breed has an average hair length of 1 ft. 1 in. (35 cm). This is measured from the length of the "dossan" (bangs) and also the length of hair in the ears.

Largest herd of white deer Within the former Seneca Army Depot in Seneca County, New York, U.S.A., is a herd of some 300 white deer. Their species is the North American white-tailed deer (*Odocoileus virginianus*), and their white coat results from a recessive nonalbino mutant gene allele.

The **rarest deer** is the Bawean (*Hyelaphus kuhlii*), limited to the tiny Indonesian island of Bawean. Fewer than 250 mature individuals are believed to exist. It is categorized as "Critically Endangered" by the International Union for Conservation of Nature (IUCN).

LARGEST DEER A male Alaskan moose (*Alces alces gigas*) standing 7 ft. 8 in. (2.34 m) tall and weighing an estimated 1,800 lb. (816 kg) was shot in the Yukon territory of Canada in Sep. 1897. The **smallest deer** is the northern pudu (*Pudu mephistophiles*), which grows to 1 ft. 1 in. (35 cm) tall at the shoulder and weighs up to 13 lb. 3 oz. (6 kg). It is found in Colombia, Ecuador, and Peru.

Largest camel The dromedary or one-humped camel (*Camelus drome-darius*) has a top head-and-body length of 11 ft. 5 in. (3.5 m), with a maximum shoulder height of 7 ft. 10 in. (2.4 m), and it can weigh 1,520 lb. (690 kg). Native to the Middle East, it survives today as a feral animal only in Australia and Spain.

Largest wild pig Central Africa's giant forest hog (*Hylochoerus mein-ertzhageni*) has a head–body length of 6 ft. 10 in. (2.1 m), a shoulder height of 3 ft. 5 in. (1.05 m), and can weigh 600 lb. (275 kg).

LARGEST RHINOCEROS Restricted to southern Africa, the southern white rhinoceros (*Ceratotherium simum simum*) can grow to a length of 13 ft. 9 in. (4.2 m), with an uppermost shoulder height of 6 ft. (1.85 m) and weight of 7,930 lb. (3.6 metric tons).

JUMBO SIZE: African Elephant The adult male African elephant (*Loxodonta africana*) is not only the **largest ungulate** but also the **largest land mammal**. It typically stands 9 ft. 10 in.–12 ft. at the shoulder and, at 8,800–15,400 lb, can weigh more than 100 average-size men. The tallest in Africa are members of the endangered desert race from Damaraland in Namibia. A bull elephant shot near Sesfontein in Damaraland on Apr. 4, 1978 was the tallest recorded example. It measured 14 ft. 6 in. in a line from the shoulder to the bottom of the forefoot—as tall as a London double-decker bus!

NEVER FORGET . . . The **largest land mammal** (African elephant) is nearly 3 million times heavier than the **smallest** (pygmy shrew)!

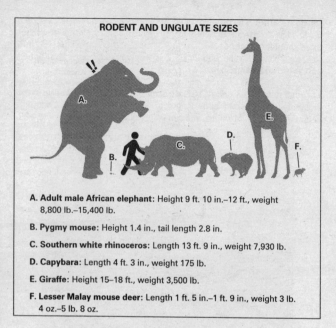

RODENT AND UNGULATE SIZES

A. **Adult male African elephant:** Height 9 ft. 10 in.–12 ft., weight 8,800 lb.–15,400 lb.

B. **Pygmy mouse:** Height 1.4 in., tail length 2.8 in.

C. **Southern white rhinoceros:** Length 13 ft. 9 in., weight 7,930 lb.

D. **Capybara:** Length 4 ft. 3 in., weight 175 lb.

E. **Giraffe:** Height 15–18 ft., weight 3,500 lb.

F. **Lesser Malay mouse deer:** Length 1 ft. 5 in.–1 ft. 9 in., weight 3 lb. 4 oz.–5 lb. 8 oz.

BIRDS

Largest owl The European race of the eagle owl (*Bubo bubo*) has an average length of 2 ft. 2 in.–2 ft. 4 in. (66–71 cm), an average weight of 3 lb. 8 oz.–8 lb. 13 oz. (1.6–4 kg), and a wingspan of more than 5 ft. (1.5 m).

Largest woodpecker The imperial woodpecker (*Campephilus imperialis*) measures up to 1 ft. 11 in. (60 cm) long. It was formerly widespread across Mexico, but due to extensive habitat destruction its numbers rapidly plummeted. The last confirmed sighting was in 1956, but observations by locals continued into the mid-1990s. It is categorized as "Critically Endangered," possibly extinct, by the International Union for Conservation of Nature (IUCN).

Loudest parrot Research conducted at San Diego Zoo in California, U.S.A., recorded shrieks reaching 135 decibels by the Moluccan (salmon-crested) cockatoo (*Cacatua moluccensis*), native to the Moluccas in Indonesia.

LONGEST BILLS The Australian pelican (*Pelecanus conspicillatus*) is the bill to beat, at 1 ft, 1 in.–1 ft. 6.5 in. (34–47 cm). But the **longest beak in relation to body length** is that of the sword-billed hummingbird (*Ensifera ensifera*) of the Andes from Venezuela to Bolivia. The beak measures 4 in. (10.2 cm), making it longer than its body without the tail.

Fastest wingbeat

During its diving courtship displays, the ruby-throated hummingbird (*Archilochus colubris*) has a wingbeat rate of 200 beats per sec., as opposed to the 90 beats per sec. produced by other hummingbirds.

Smallest swan

The smallest swan—but largest species of South American waterfowl—is the black-necked swan (*Cygnus melancoryphus*). It grows up to 4 ft. (1.24 m) long, with a wingspan of 5 ft. 9 in. (1.77 m). The coscoroba swan (*Coscoroba coscoroba*) is slightly smaller, but it is no longer thought to be closely related to true swans and may well be a swan in name only.

Rarest heron The global population of the white-bellied (imperial) heron (*Ardea insignis*) is estimated at no more than 400 birds and is thought to be decreasing. It is categorized as "Critically Endangered" by the IUCN. The species is native to the eastern Himalayan foothills of India, Myanmar, Bhutan, and possibly Bangladesh but is now extinct in Nepal.

LARGEST FAMILY OF BIRDS The Tyrannidae family of tyrant flycatchers has more than 400 species, including the brown-crested flycatcher (*Myiarchus tyrannulus*, center), lesser kiskadee (*Philohydor lictor*, right), and vermilion flycatcher (*Pyrocephalus rubinus*, left). Highly diverse in form, these insectivorous birds live in North, Central, and South America.

FACT: Birds are closely related to dinosaurs. In the U.S.A., there are plans to retro-engineer a dinosaur using chicken DNA.

Rarest kingfisher The Tuamotu kingfisher (*Todiramphus gambieri*) is confined entirely to a very small area on the single island of Niau in the Tuamotu Archipelago of French Polynesia. As of 2013, only 125–135 birds still exist. It is threatened by non-native rats and cats, as well as by cyclone-induced habitat destruction.

Fastest bird in level flight In a report published by French and British researchers working in the sub-Antarctic, the average estimated ground speed for a satellite-tagged grey-headed albatross (*Thalassarche chryso-stoma*) is 78.9 mph (127 km/h), sustained for more than 8 hr. while returning to its nest at Bird Island, South Georgia, in the middle of a storm.

LONGEST-TOED BIRD (RELATIVE TO BODY) The chicken-size northern jacana (*Jacana spinosa*) has four toes, each about 2.8 in. (7 cm) long. When fully extended, they span 26 sq. in. (168 cm²), enabling the bird to walk on lily pads and other floating vegetation.

FASTEST BIRD DIVING The peregrine falcon (*Falco peregrinus*)—found on almost all continents—is thought to reach a terminal velocity of around 186 mph (300 km/h) in a diving stoop. At this point, it is the fastest animal on the planet. Bad news for any prey below.

SMALLEST FLIGHTLESS BIRD Found only on a small area of land in the South Atlantic, the Inaccessible Island rail (*Atlantisia rogersi*) weighs a mere 1.4 oz. (40 g). First discovered in 1870, the birds are around the size of a three-day-old chicken.

SMALLEST BIRD Male bee hummingbirds (*Mellisuga helenae*) of Cuba measure 2.24 in. (57 mm) long, half of which is the bill and tail. They weigh just 0.056 oz. (1.6 g), generally regarded as the lowest limit for warm-blooded animals. Females are slightly larger.

Owls can rotate their heads a full **270 degrees** in either direction.

Most airborne bird After leaving its nesting grounds as a youngster, the sooty tern (*Sterna fuscata*) remains aloft for 3–10 years while maturing, settling on water from time to time before returning to land to breed as an adult.

The **longest bird migration** is that of the Arctic tern (*Sterna paradisaea*). It breeds north of the Arctic Circle, then flies south to the Antarctic for the northern winter and back again—a round trip of approximately 50,000 mi. (80,467 km).

The **longest time for a bird to learn to fly** is exhibited by the wandering albatross (*Diomedea exulans*), whose chicks take 278–280 days on average to make their first flight after hatching. Because it takes so long for the young albatross to get to this stage, the adults breed only once every two years.

LARGEST TOUCAN The largest species of toucan is the toco toucan (*Ramphastos toco*), which weighs up to 1 lb. 14 oz. (876 g) and grows up to 2 ft. 1 in. (65 cm) long—one-third of which is its huge bill. Males are larger than females. It is native to much of eastern and central South America, but particularly Brazil.

BEST OF THE NESTS

- **Highest nest:** Marbled murrelets (*Brachyramphus marmoratus*) nest as high up as 147 ft.

- **Largest ground nest:** Malleefowl (*Leipoa ocellata*) nests contain up to 8,100 cu. ft. of matter and weigh up to 660,000 lb.

- **Longest nest burrow:** Rhinoceros auklet (*Cerorhinca monocerata*) nest burrows typically measure 6–10 ft. long.

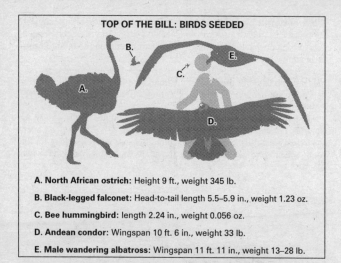

TOP OF THE BILL: BIRDS SEEDED

A. North African ostrich: Height 9 ft., weight 345 lb.

B. Black-legged falconet: Head-to-tail length 5.5–5.9 in., weight 1.23 oz.

C. Bee hummingbird: length 2.24 in., weight 0.056 oz.

D. Andean condor: Wingspan 10 ft. 6 in., weight 33 lb.

E. Male wandering albatross: Wingspan 11 ft. 11 in., weight 13–28 lb.

OSTR-ETCH: Tall Story The North African ostrich (*Struthio camelus camelus*) is the **largest living bird**. Males have been recorded at 9 ft. tall and weighing 345 lb. It cannot fly, but the ostrich makes up for that by being the **fastest flightless bird on land,** reaching 45 mph. Its powerful strides can exceed 23 ft. and are comparable to those of the **fastest land mammal**, the cheetah. It can also attack with a powerful kick. Because of its size, the ostrich is also the bird that lays the **smallest eggs relative to body weight**: only 1.4–1.5% of its total mass.

BRINK OF EXTINCTION

The North American ivory-billed woodpecker (*Campephilus principalis*) remains the **rarest bird**. Sixty years ago, we said that it "may even be extinct. It is believed that less than a dozen still exist in the Florida area." Today, our consultant Karl Shuker says, "I consider there to be good evidence that it survives, albeit very precariously."

Most expensive pigeon On May 18, 2013, pigeon breeder Leo Heremans (BEL) sold his racing pigeon for 310,000 euros ($400,000) on www.pipa.be. The pigeon, Bolt, was named after world-record-holding Jamaican sprinter Usain Bolt and will be used for breeding.

Shortest bills The shortest avian bills in relation to body length belong to the smaller swifts (Apodidae family), and in particular to the glossy swiftlet (*Collocalia esculenta*), whose bill is almost nonexistent.

REPTILES & AMPHIBIANS

Fastest lizard The Costa Rican spiny-tailed iguana (*Ctenosaura similis*) can attain a land speed of 21.7 mph (34.9 km/h).

Highest frequency frog croak The concave-eared torrent frog (*Odorrana tormota*) of eastern China croaks at a frequency of 128 kHz—an ultrasonic emission well beyond the range of human hearing (which cannot detect sound frequencies above 20 kHz). The reason that this frog produces such a high-frequency croak is to overcome the very loud low-frequency sound of the waterfalls near which it lives in order to communicate with others of its species.

Largest caiman Caimans are alligator-related crocodilians and, of their six species, the largest is the black caiman (*Melanosuchus niger*). Old males can sometimes exceed 16 ft. 5 in. (5 m) in length and 880 lb. (400 kg) in weight. The black caiman is native to rivers and swamps in the Amazon basin.

LONGEST LIZARD While the **largest lizard** overall may be the bulky Komodo dragon (*Varanus komodoensis*), Salvadori's monitor (*Varanus salvadorii*) has an impressive tail to tell. Its lengthy appendage brings the total length of the Papua New Guinean lizard up to a maximum of 15 ft. 7 in. (4.75 m).

FACT: A typical Salvadori's monitor might have a body of 3 ft. 11 in. but a tail of more than double that: up to 8 ft. 10 in. By comparison, the average Komodo dragon is 7 ft. 4 in. long.

Largest plant-eating lizard Jim Morrison, singer with The Doors, called himself "The Lizard King." In his honor, an extinct species of iguana was named *Barbaturex morrisoni*. It was almost 6 ft. 6 in. (2 m) in length and inhabited what is now Burma during the Eocene epoch, some 40–36 million years ago. High temperatures may have helped the lizard evolve to its unusual size.

LARGEST TEGU The black-and-white or Argentine giant tegu (*Tupinambis merianae*) is native to east and central South America and can grow to 4 ft. 7 in. (1.4 m) in length and weigh 15 lb. 7 oz. (7 kg). Tegus are predatory, and they are popularly kept as pets by reptile fanciers.

SMALLEST CROCODILIAN Females of the dwarf caiman (*Paleosuchus palpebrosus*) of northern South America rarely exceed a length of 4 ft. (1.2 m) and males often don't grow more than 4 ft. 11 in. (1.5 m). They are generally nocturnal and usually solitary.

HEAVIEST VENOMOUS SNAKE The eastern diamondback rattlesnake (*Crotalus adamanteus*) weighs 12–15 lb. (5.5–6.8 kg), with the biggest on record at 34 lb. (15 kg). Other contenders are the king cobra (*Ophiophagus hannah*), up to 20 lb. (9 kg), and the gaboon viper (*Bitis gabonica*), weighing 18 lb. 12 oz. (8.5 kg).

MOST LEGS FOR A WORM LIZARD As their name suggests, worm lizards resemble earthworms and are generally limbless. But four of the 180-plus species—known as ajolotes (*Bipes spp.*) and confined to Mexico—possess a pair of small forelimbs with large clawed feet positioned behind the head. These limbs are sometimes mistaken for ears.

More than **6,000 species of lizard** are known to exist.

RAREST TREE FROG Rabbs' fringe-limbed tree frog (*Ecnomiohyla rabborum*) was only discovered by science in 2005, and just one living specimen is currently known to exist. The male lives at the Atlanta Botanical Garden in Georgia, U.S.A.

LARGEST FROG The goliath frog (*Conraua goliath*) is 1 ft. (30 cm) long on average, the same size as a rabbit. The largest individual specimen was captured in Apr. 1889 in Cameroon with an overall length of 2 ft. 10.5 in. (87.63 cm). Classified as "endangered" by the International Union for Conservation of Nature (IUCN), the frog is found mainly in Central Africa.

Most poisonous newt The California newt (*Taricha torosa*) is poisonous all over: its skin, muscles, and blood contain tetrodotoxin, a toxic and powerful nerve poison that is a hundred times more deadly than cyanide. It's the same stuff that makes the puffer fish (Tetraodontidae) the **most poisonous edible fish**. The newt itself is immune to the effects of venom.

Smallest lizard family The Lanthanotidae family of lizards has just one member—the earless monitor (*Lanthanotus borneensis*). This is an evolutionary oddity known only in Sarawak, Borneo. It lacks external ears, and the nearest relatives of this small family are the true monitors and the venomous Gila monster and beaded lizards.

SCALED UP: Long Snakes The reticulated python (*Python reticulatus*) of Indonesia, southeast Asia, and the Philippines is the world's **longest snake**. A specimen measured in Indonesia in 1912 was 32 ft. 9.5 in. long—equivalent in length to the outstretched arms of eight adult men.

Pictured is Si Belang, a 19 ft. 10 in.-long python adopted by the Toe family in Borneo. The 132-lb. snake lives, sleeps, eats, and bathes with the family, including three-year-old Karim. Si Belang is not a threat to the Toes; he recognizes them as his own family and their home as his territory.

LONGEST IGUANA SPECIES The green, or common, iguana (*Iguana iguana*) can exceed 6 ft. 6 in. (2 m) in length. Found in an extensive range from Brazil and Paraguay to as far north as Mexico and the Caribbean, they are among the largest lizards in the Americas. Iguanas live near water and are excellent swimmers, feeding largely on leaves, flowers, and fruit.

Most geographically restricted python

Liasis mackloti savuensis is confined to the tiny Indonesian island of Savu, south of Java, from which it gets its common name: the Savu Island python. Savu is the largest of the three Savu Islands, whose total area is only 178 sq. mi. (460.84 km²).

Smelliest species of frog

The skunk frog (*Aromobates nocturnus*) of Venezuela is well named. Measuring 2.44 in. (6.2 cm) long, it is a member of the poison-arrow frog family (Dendrobatidae), yet its defensive skin secretion contains not toxin but the same stink-producing compound present in the anal emissions of mammalian skunks.

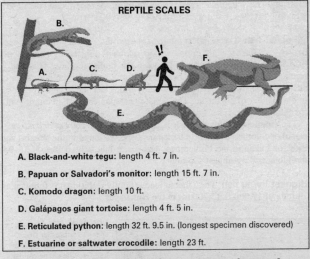

REPTILE SCALES

A. **Black-and-white tegu:** length 4 ft. 7 in.

B. **Papuan or Salvadori's monitor:** length 15 ft. 7 in.

C. **Komodo dragon:** length 10 ft.

D. **Galápagos giant tortoise:** length 4 ft. 5 in.

E. **Reticulated python:** length 32 ft. 9.5 in. (longest specimen discovered)

F. **Estuarine or saltwater crocodile:** length 23 ft.

Most powerful species of vertebrate In terms of watts of power generated per pound of muscle, the giant palm salamander (*Bolitoglossa dofleini*) of Central America is the strongest vertebrate species. Its tongue explodes outward at 818 watts per lb. (18,000 watts per kg) of muscle. It is believed that elastic collagen tissue in the salamander's tongue stores up energy prior to its explosive release, much like a stretched rubber band or a bowstring drawn back.

FISHES

Largest fish ever In 2008, two palaeontology students discovered a specimen of the marine fossil species *Leedsichthys problematicus* in clay pits near Peterborough in Cambridgeshire, UK. Dating back 155 million years, this particular specimen measured 72 ft. (22 m) long, almost twice the length of the whale shark, the **largest fish** alive today (see p. 102).

Largest freshwater fish The largest fish that spends its whole life in fresh or brackish water is the Mekong giant catfish (*Pangasianodon gigas*), principally of the Mekong River basin, and *Pangasius sanitwongsei*, mainly of the Chao Phraya River basin, both native to southeast Asia. Both species are reputed to grow to 9 ft. 10 in. (3 m) and weigh 660 lb.

(300 kg). The *Arapaima gigas* of South America is reported to reach 14 ft. 9 in. (4.5 m) long, but it weighs only 440 lb. (200 kg).

Smallest fish The smallest adult fish—and indeed the **smallest vertebrate**—is a mature male *Photocorynus spiniceps* anglerfish, which is just 0.24 in. (6.2 mm) long and is found in the Philippine Sea. The male's primary purpose is to facilitate reproduction. To do so, he permanently attaches himself to the larger female by biting her back, belly, or sides, in the manner of a parasite. The female is responsible for swimming and for eating.

The **smallest freshwater fish** is the dwarf pygmy goby (*Pandaka pygmaea*), a colorless and nearly transparent species found in the streams and lakes of Luzon in the Philippines. Males are only 0.29–0.38 in. (7.5–9.9 mm) long and weigh just 4–5 mg.

Highest living fish The Tibetan loach (family Cobitidae) is found at an altitude of 17,060 ft. (5,200 m) in the Himalayas.

LONGEST FIN All three species of thresher shark (family Alopiidae) have a huge, scythe-shape caudal (tail) fin that is about as long as the body itself. The largest and most common species, *Alopias vulpinus*, found worldwide in temperate and tropical seas, grows to 19 ft. 8 in. (6 m) in length, of which almost 9 ft. 10 in. (3 m) consists of this greatly elongated upper tail fin.

LARGEST CARP SPECIES The Siamese giant carp (*Catlocarpio siamensis*), aka giant barb, is the largest of the cyprinid (carp) family. The longest specimens currently reported—such as the 225-lb. (102-kg) barb (left)—are around 5 ft. 10 in. (1.8 m) in length, while the longest known specimen measured 9 ft. 10 in. (3 m).

FACT: Thresher sharks are believed to use their tails to herd and then stun schools of milling fish ready for eating.

LONGEST BONY FISH The lengthiest of the bony or "true" fishes (class Pisces, aka Osteichthyes—see Glossary on p. 101) is the oarfish (*Regalecus glesne*), or the "King of the Herrings," which has worldwide distribution. In ca. 1885, a 25-ft.-long (7.6-m) example weighing 600 lb. (272 kg) was caught by fishermen off Pemaquid Point in Maine, U.S.A. The specimen pictured here was found dead in the water off Toyon Bay, California, U.S.A., on Oct. 13, 2013, by staff of the Catalina Island Marine Institute; it measured 18 ft. (5.5 m) long.

FASTEST FISH The cosmopolitan sailfish (*Istiophorus platypterus*) is considered to be the fastest species of fish over short distances, although practical difficulties make measurements extremely hard to secure. Trials at the Long Key Fishing Camp in Florida, U.S.A., suggested a top speed of 68 mph (109 km/h).

Longing for the sea? Turn to p. 327.

FRESHWATER GIANT

In our 1955 edition, the **largest freshwater fish** was the 22-ft.-long giant Russian sturgeon (*Acipenser*), found in the Volga River. "However, we now know that this is not an exclusively freshwater species," says our animal consultant Dr. Karl Shuker. "At 9 ft. 11 in., the largest fish that spends its whole life in fresh water is Asia's Mekong giant catfish." (see p. 97)

FACT: Technically, there is no such thing as a "fish"—the creatures on these pages are from many different animal families.

HEAVIEST BONY FISH The ocean sunfish (*Mola mola*) has been recorded weighing 4,400 lb. (1,995 kg) and measuring 10 ft. (3 m) from fin tip to fin tip. **Mola mola**—named from the Latin for "millstone" in reference to its shape—is found in all oceans in tropical or temperate climates and feeds on zooplankton, small fishes, and algae. Sharks and rays, by contrast, are cartilaginous, not bony as in the case of the ocean sunfish.

Longest fish migration Many fish species undertake long annual migrations between their feeding grounds. The longest straight-line distance known to have been covered by a fish is 5,800 mi. (9,335 km) for a bluefin tuna (*Thunnus thynnus*) that was dart-tagged off Baja California, Mexico, in 1958, and caught 300 mi. (483 km) south of Tokyo, Japan, in Apr. 1963.

The **longest journey by a freshwater fish** is some 3,000–4,000 mi. (4,800–6,400 km), taking about six months, by the European eel (*Anguilla anguilla*). This species spends between 7 and 15 years in fresh water in Europe, before abruptly evolving into breeding conditions, changing color to become silver, and growing a longer snout and larger eyes. The much-altered animal then begins a marathon trek to the species' spawning grounds in the Sargasso Sea, east of North America.

Most venomous fish Poisonous creatures contain poison within their bodies, which they pass on to any creatures that consume, or even touch them, while venomous creatures inject venom into their victims. The stonefish (family Synanceiidae) of the tropical waters of the Indo-Pacific are highly venomous. *Synanceia horrida* has the largest venom glands of any known fish. Direct contact with the spines of its fins, which contain a strong neurotoxic poison, can prove fatal.

The **most poisonous fish** is the puffer fish (*Tetraodon*) of the Red Sea and Indo-Pacific region, which produces a fatally poisonous toxin called tetrodotoxin. Its ovaries, eggs, blood, liver, intestines, and, to a lesser extent, its skin, contain tetrodotoxin. Less than 0.004 oz. (0.1 g) is enough to kill a human adult in as little as 20 min.

SHARK ATTACK: Great White Shark The **largest predatory fish** is the great white shark (*Carcharodon carcharias*, from the Greek for "sharp-toothed"). Adults average 14–15 ft. in length—as long as a typical family sedan car—and generally weigh 1,980 lb. There are many claims of huge specimens up to 33 ft. long, and plenty of circumstantial evidence suggests that some great whites grow to more than 20 ft. in length. Pictured here is a lucky seal escaping the jaws of a great white, snapped in Jul. 2013 off the coast of Seal Island, South Africa, by photographer David Jenkins.

GLOSSARY

Chondrichthyes: cartilaginous fish; have skeletons made of cartilage—a flexible but firm tissue less stiff than bone.

Osteichthyes: bony fish; have skeletons made from bone. There are ca. 28,000 species of Osteichthyes, accounting for 96% of all fish species. They also form the **largest class of vertebrates** (animals with backbones).

FACT: There are more fish in the Amazon River than there are in all of Europe.

SLOWEST FISH The slowest-moving marine fish are the sea horses (family Syngnathidae), of which there are just over 30 species. Some of the smaller species, such as the dwarf sea horse (*Hippocampus zosterae*, left), which reaches a maximum length of only 1.6 in. (4.2 cm), probably never attain speeds of more than 0.001 mph (0.016 km/h).

Most ferocious freshwater fish Piranhas are renowned for their ferocity, particularly those of the genera *Serrasalmus* and *Pygocentrus*, found in the large rivers of South America. Attracted to blood and frantic splashing, a school of piranhas can within minutes strip an animal as large as a horse of its flesh, leaving only its skeleton.

WHAT A WHOPPER! COMPARING FISH SCALES

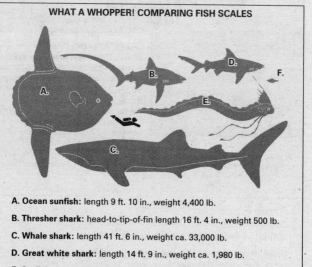

A. **Ocean sunfish:** length 9 ft. 10 in., weight 4,400 lb.

B. **Thresher shark:** head-to-tip-of-fin length 16 ft. 4 in., weight 500 lb.

C. **Whale shark:** length 41 ft. 6 in., weight ca. 33,000 lb.

D. **Great white shark:** length 14 ft. 9 in., weight ca. 1,980 lb.

E. **Oarfish:** length 24 ft. 11 in., weight ca. 600 lb.

F. *Photocorynus spiniceps:* length 0.24 in.

CRUSTACEANS

Deepest-living crustacean In Nov. 1980, live amphipods were found at a depth of 34,450 ft. (10,500 m) in Challenger Deep, the **deepest point on Earth**, in the Mariana Trench of the western Pacific Ocean.

Longest journey by a crab In Dec. 2006, it was reported that an American Columbus crab (*Planes minutus*) had been discovered washed up but still alive on a beach in Bournemouth, UK—5,000 mi. (8,000 km) from its home in the Sargasso Sea, east of Florida, U.S.A. The 6-in. (15-cm) crab is believed to have made its journey by clinging to barnacles on a buoy for three months, surviving storms, predators, and sharp changes in sea temperature.

LARGEST FRESHWATER CRUSTACEAN
The Tasmanian giant freshwater crayfish (*Astacopsis gouldi*) is also the **largest freshwater invertebrate** of any kind. Native to small streams in Tasmania, Australia, it can measure 2 ft. 7 in. (80 cm) and weigh 11 lb. (5 kg). Overfishing and habitat loss have seen the species decline and it is listed as endangered.

LARGEST MARINE CRUSTACEAN The giant spider crab (*Macrocheira kaempferi*), found off the southeastern coast of Japan, has a leg span of up to 12 ft. 1.5 in. (3.69 m). Pictured here is "Big Daddy," whose leg span of 10 ft. 2.5 in. (3.11 m) makes him the **widest crustacean in captivity**. The leggy crab—named after a famous British wrestler—was measured at Sea Life in Blackpool, UK, on Aug. 8, 2013.

A female skeleton shrimp **consumes the male** shortly after mating.

HEAVIEST MARINE CRUSTACEAN The American or North Atlantic lobster (*Homarus americanus*) is the heaviest marine crustacean. On Feb. 11, 1977, a specimen weighing 44 lb. 6 oz. (20.14 kg) and measuring 3 ft. 6 in. (1.06 m) from tail fan to the tip of its largest claw was caught off Nova Scotia, Canada. It was sold to a New York restaurant owner.

Fastest-swimming crustacean Henslow's swimming crab (*Polybius henslowii*), native to the eastern Atlantic Ocean, has been timed at 4 ft. 3 in./s (1.3 m/s) in captivity. It is probable that it would be able to swim even faster under natural conditions in the wild.

First venomous crustacean *Xibalbanus* (previously *Speleonectes*) *tulumensis* feeds upon other crustaceans. Its claws inject a cocktail of chemicals, including a paralyzing neurotoxin similar to rattlesnake venom. The toxin breaks down the victim's body tissues, turning it into liquid to be sucked up from its prey's exoskeleton. The blind crustacean inhabits underwater caves of the Caribbean, Canary Islands, and Western Australia. *Xibalbanus tulumensis* is a member of the remipede class and is the only crustacean that possesses venom.

Largest extent of color vision Stomatopods, such as mantis prawns, have eight different types of color photoreceptor in their eyes (humans have three). These reef-dweller crustaceans can distinguish numerous shades within the electromagnetic spectrum's ultraviolet waveband—

entirely invisible to humans. Their clear-eye vision is used to identify prey (which is often semi-transparent) and dodge predators.

Sharpest night vision for an animal *Gigantocypris* is a marine crustacean living at depths of more than 3,300 ft. (1,000 m) with almost no sunlight. But this genus of ostracod has eyes with an f-number (a measure of light sensitivity) of 0.25. In comparison, humans measure around f-2.55. Each eye possesses a pair of high-power parabolic reflectors that direct the dim light onto the retina.

Largest barnacle The giant acorn barnacle (*Balanus nubilus*) stands up to 5 in. (12.7 cm) high and measures 2.76 in. (7 cm) across. It lives as far down as 300 ft. (91 m) and its side plates withstand strong currents. The barnacle is food for whelk snails, which can drill into the shell.

Largest copepod *Pennella balaenopterae* is a parasite living on the backs of fin whales (*Balaenoptera physalus*). It can attain a length of 1 ft. 0.5 in. (32 cm).

RAREST CRAYFISH The endangered Shasta crayfish *(Pacifastacus fortis)* is native to Shasta County in California, U.S.A., where it is found along portions of the Pit River. It occurs in only 5 sq. mi. (13 km²) of the river, and its fragmented population probably numbers no more than 300 in total.

MOST ABUNDANT ANIMAL Copepods, found almost everywhere with water, comprise 12,000 species and form groups that can reach a trillion individuals. Most are less than 0.04 in. (1 mm) long.

SMALLEST CRAB Parasitic pea crabs (*Pinnotheres pisum*) can measure 0.25 in. (6.3 mm) across. They live in the organ cavity of bivalve mollusks, such as oysters and mussels, where they tuck into food collected by their molluskan host's gills.

PURSE CRAB: _Island Monster_ The **largest (and heaviest) land-living crustacean** is the purse (or robber, coconut, or tree) crab (*Birgus latro*), which lives on tropical islands and atolls in the Indo-Pacific. It can weigh as much as 9 lb. and has a leg span of up to 3 ft. 3 in. This type of hermit crab feeds on rotting coconuts, but it will eat a variety of other food. It has been hunted almost to extinction on many islands in the Indian and Pacific oceans, due to its size and its use as a culinary delicacy. The young are hatched in the sea but return to land and lose the ability to survive in the water.

FASTEST LAND CRUSTACEAN Tropical ghost crabs of the genus *Ocypode* can scuttle up to 6 ft./s. (2 m/s.)—not bad for sideways sprinters. This is equivalent to a human running at 201 mph (324 km/h).

HERMIT CRABS

Hermit crabs (Paguroidea) aren't true crabs (they have three instead of four pairs of walking legs), but they are crustaceans. They don't have shells; instead, they reuse those that have been abandoned by other creatures. The hermit crab is the **animal with the most chromosomes** (the body's hereditary information), with 127 pairs, compared with just 23 pairs in humans.

GLOSSARY

Arthropod: Animal from the phylum Arthropoda (meaning "jointed leg") that includes insects, arachnids, and crustaceans; arthropods account for 80% of all animal species.

Crustacean: A group (or sub-phylum) of arthropod comprising 67,000 described species, from the minuscule 0.003-in.-long *Stygotantulus stocki* up to the giant spider crab (*Macrocheira kaempferi*) with its 12-ft. 1.5-in span from claw to claw (see below). They are distinguished from other groups of arthropods by their two-parted limbs and the form taken by their larvae.

CRUSTACEAN LENGTHS

A. **Tasmanian giant freshwater crayfish:** 2 ft. 7 in.

B. **Parasitic pea crab:** 0.25 in.

C. **Common sea slater:** 1.2 in.

D. **Purse crab:** 3 ft. 3 in.

E. **Water fleas (branchiopods):** 0.009 in.

F. **Giant acorn barnacle:** 2.76 in.

G. **Giant spider crab:** leg span 12 ft. 1.5 in.

Largest wood louse The common sea slater (*Ligia oceanica*) can grow to 1.2 in. (3 cm) long and is twice as long as it is broad. Its speed when startled has earned it the nickname "sea cockroach." It is an aquatic species that breathes air and lives on rocky coasts of temperate waters.

Smallest crustacean *Stygotantulus stocki* measures 0.003 in. (0.094 mm), making it the **smallest arthropod** of any kind. It is an ectoparasite—a parasite on the surface—of crustaceans called harpacticoid copepods. The **smallest nonparasitic crustaceans** are water fleas (branchiopods) of the genus *Alonella*. These freshwater fleas measure less than 0.009 in. (0.25 mm).

INSECTS & ARACHNIDS

Fastest insect on land A speed of 3.36 mph (5.4 km/h), or 50 body lengths per sec., was registered by *Periplaneta americana,* the familiar American cockroach of the order Dictyoptera, in 1991.

The **fastest caterpillar** is the larva of the mother-of-pearl moth (*Pleuroptya ruralis*), which can travel at 0.8 mph (1.37 km/h).

The **fastest flying insect** is the Australian dragonfly (*Austrophlebia costalis*), at 36 mph (58 km/h) in short bursts. In 1917, a ground velocity of 61.3 mph (98.6 km/h) was recorded over 240–270 ft. (73–82 m).

The **fastest insect wing-beat** under natural conditions is 62,760 beats per min. by a tiny midge of the genus *Forcipomyia.*

LOWEST TEMPERATURE ENDURED BY INSECTS The woolly bear caterpillar of the Greenland tiger moth (*Gynaephora groenlandica*) lives in the high Arctic. It can survive being frozen at -58°F (-50°C) for 10 months of the year.

HEAVIEST PRAYING MANTIS Native to India, Myanmar, Nepal, and Sri Lanka, the weightiest species of praying mantis is the giant Asian mantis *Hierodula membranacea*. The heaviest specimen on record was a well-fed female that was reliably weighed and found to tip the scales at 0.3 oz. (9 g)—approximately the same as nine paper clips.

HEAVIEST MOTH Native to Australia, the heaviest species of moth is the giant wood moth (*Endoxyla cinereus*). The weightiest specimen on record is an adult female that measured 1.1 oz. (31.2 g). Females have a wingspan of approximately 9.8 in. (25 cm), while males are only about half that size.

Loudest insect The African cicada (*Brevisana brevis*), discovered in 1850, produces a calling song with a mean sound pressure level of 106.7 decibels at a distance of 1 ft. 7 in. (50 cm). Songs play a vital role in cicada communication and reproduction.

Most times for an insect to molt All insects molt several times during the course of their lifetime. Up to 60 molts have been recorded for the firebrat (*Thermobia domestica*), a primitive, wingless insect that is widely distributed in North America and other temperate regions worldwide. The firebrat molts throughout its life, whereas most insects do so only during their juvenile (nymph, or larval) stage.

HARDIEST BEETLE The most indestructible beetle is a small species known as *Niptus hololeucus*. Researcher Malcolm Burr has revealed that no fewer than 1,547 specimens were discovered alive inside a bottle of casein protein that had been stoppered for 12 years.

FASTEST SPIDER The giant house spider (*Tegenaria gigantea*) is native to North America. An adult female studied during tests in the UK in 1970 attained a running speed of 1.18 mph (1.90 km/h) over short distances. This is equivalent to covering 33 times her own body length in 10 sec.

For every human, there are an estimated **1.4 billion insects** alive right now.

MOST TOXIC INSECT VENOM

Pogonomyrmex maricopa is a stinging species of harvester ant native to Arizona, U.S.A. The LD$_{50}$ value of its venom (the dosage required to kill 50% of mice subjected to it) is 0.0000019 oz./lb. when injected intravenously into mice.

Most aggressive butterfly The powerful flier *Charaxes candiope* of Uganda actively dive-bombs people who invade its territory.

Most dangerous bee The Africanized honeybee (*Apis mellifera scutellata*) will generally attack only when provoked but is persistent in pursuit. It is very aggressive and fiercely protective of territories up to a 0.5-mi. (0.8-km) radius. Its venom is no more potent than that of other bees, but it attacks in swarms so the number of stings inflicted can be fatal.

LEAST CLASSIFIABLE INSECT

A newly discovered nymph (juvenile) form of plant hopper resembles nymphs from at least four taxonomic families but has defied classification. It was found in the rain forest of southeastern Suriname.

MOST VENOMOUS SPIDER The Brazilian wandering spiders of the genus *Phoneutria* are highly venomous, particularly the Brazilian huntsman (*P. fera*), which has the most active neurotoxic venom of any living spider. Just 0.006 mg of its venom is sufficient to kill a mouse.

LONGEST INSECT TONGUE The tongue, or proboscis, of Morgan's sphinx (hawk) moth (*Xanthopan morganii praedicta*) measures up to 1 ft. 1 in. (35 cm)—more than twice the entire length of the moth. It enables the moth to reach the nectar deep inside the star-shape flowers of the comet, or Darwin's, orchid. The insect is native to Madagascar.

Most bee stings removed The greatest number of bee stings sustained by any surviving human subject is 2,443, by Johannes Relleke at the Kamativi tin mine, Gwaii River, in Wankie District, Zimbabwe (then Rhodesia), on Jan. 28, 1962. All the stings were removed and counted.

Most painful insect sting In 1983, entomologist Justin O. Schmidt (U.S.A.) published a detailed pain index of insect stings, based on a four-point scale. The most painful sting, registering 4.0+ on his index, was that of the bullet ant (*Paraponera clavata*), native to Central and South America. Schmidt described its sting as "like walking over flaming charcoal with a 3-in. [8-cm] rusty nail in your heel."

LARGEST . . .

Wasp A female giant tarantula-hawk wasp (*Pepsis heros*) found in Peru had a wingspan of 4.75 in. (12.15 cm) and body length of ca. 2.25 in. (6.2 cm).

Bee Females of the king bee (*Chalicodoma pluto*) from the Moluccas Islands of Indonesia measure 1.5 in. (3.9 cm) long. The **smallest species of bee** is *Perdita minima* of southwestern U.S.A., measuring just under 0.07 in. (2 mm) long and weighing only 0.333 mg (that's 3,330 bees to the gram, or 85,133 to the ounce).

Scorpion A specimen of *Heterometrus swannerdami* found during World War II in the village of Krishnarajapuram, India, measured 11.5 in. (29.2 cm) in length from the tips of the pedipalps (pincers) to the end of the sting.

Cockroach A preserved female *Megaloblatta longipennis* in the collection of Akira Yokokura (JPN) measures 3.8 in. (9.7 cm) long and 1.75 in. (4.5 cm) across.

LARGEST APPETITE RELATIVE TO WEIGHT The caterpillar of the North American silk moth (*Antheraea polyphemus*) eats more food relative to its own body weight than any other animal. Living on the leaves of oak, birch, willow, and maple trees, it eats up to 86,000 times its own weight during the first 56 days of its life.

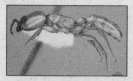

LARGEST ANT The wingless queen of the fulvous driver ant *Dorylus fulvus* is native to South Africa. It grows to a maximum length of 1.9 in. (5 cm), some 0.7 in. (2 cm) longer than the male of the species. The term "fulvous" describes the ant's characteristic tawny brown coloration.

BEE-SUITED: Attracting a Mantle A "mantle" is an enormous cluster of bees that forms a protective layer around the queen bee. By wearing the queen in a locket around the neck, an individual can encourage a mantle of bees to form around their body. This rippling mass of bees can weigh many pounds, with the **heaviest mantle of bees** record currently standing at 134 lb. 14 oz.—about the same weight as an adult man—by Ruan Lianming (CHN) on May 6, 2012. Ruan used 56 queens to attract an estimated 621,000 bees in Fengxin County, Jiangxi Province, China.

APIAN ALERT: BEES AT RISK

Since around 2006, many bee populations have collapsed—a phenomenon known as colony collapse disorder. Possible causes include poisoning from pesticides, destruction of the bees' natural environments, and parasites that feed on bees' blood. The welfare of the bee impacts directly on our own food chain; with no bees to pollinate them, up to half of our fruit and vegetable plants would disappear, along with animal-feed crops.

WHAT'S THE BUZZZZZ?

First use of apitherapy: The Greek physician Galen (A.D. 129–200) is said to have used honey and bee venom to treat baldness.

Largest bee house: A bee house measuring 42 ft. 7 in. x 4 ft. 2 in. x 1 ft. 2 in. was built in Barking, London, UK, on Jun. 18, 2011.

Largest wasp nest: A nest measuring 12 ft. 1 in. x 5 ft. 8 in. and ca. 18 ft. in circumference was found at Waimauku, New Zealand, in Apr. 1963.

OUTSIZE INSECTS, CENTIPEDES, AND ARACHNIDS

A. Chan's megastick: length 13.9 in.

B. Hercules beetle: length including horns 6.6 in.

C. Fulvous driver ant (wingless queen): length 1.9 in.

D. Giant water bug: length 4.5 in.

E. Giant centipede: length 10.2 in.

F. Goliath bird-eating spider: leg span 11 in.

G. Titan beetle: body length 5.9 in.

MOSTLY MOLLUSKS

Deepest octopus The dumbo octopus (*Grimpoteuthis*) lives as far down as 5,000 ft. (1,500 m). Its body, 7.8 in. (20 cm) long, is soft and semigelatinous, enabling the octopus to resist the great pressure found at this depth. It travels by moving its fins, pulsing its webbed arms (octopus limbs are called arms rather than tentacles), or pushing water through a funnel as a form of jet propulsion.

Most bioluminescent octopus Squids include many bioluminescent species, but only *Stauroteuthis syrtensis* lights up the octopus world in a significant way. It uses a row of suckerlike structures that glow blue-green and emit light at 470 nanometers (a wavelength that travels well under water). Researchers believe the flashing entices prey within reach.

Smallest octopus With an average arm span of less than 2 in. (5.1 cm), *Octopus arborescens* is the smallest species. It is found in Sri Lanka.

First complete nervous system In 2013, scientists announced a nervous system had been found in a 1.18-in.-long (3-cm) fossil belonging to a previously unknown species of segmented marine arthropod. This creature is an ancestor of chelicerates (spiders, scorpions, and horseshoe crabs). Belonging to the extinct genus *Alalcomenaeus*, it lived more than 520 million years ago in the Cambrian period in the seas of southwest China.

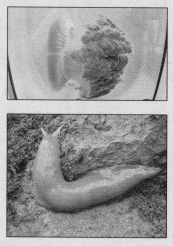

RAREST JELLYFISH The Cookii Monster (*Crambione cookii*) of Australia is pink, 1 ft. 8 in. (50 cm) long, and very venomous. Recorded in 1910 in Cooktown, Queensland, the species disappeared until a specimen was caught in 2013 off Queensland's Sunshine Coast by Puk Scivyer of nearby UnderWater World, where it now resides.

NEWEST SLUG Science was already aware of the giant pink slug (*Triboniophorus aff. graeffei*) of New South Wales, Australia, but it was thought to be an unusual color variety of the red triangle slug (*Triboniophorus graeffei*). In Jun. 2013, genetic results revealed it to be a species in its own right.

For news of life off Earth, turn to p. 24.

OLDEST MOLLUSK In Oct. 2007, at Bangor University in Wales, UK, scientists announced that the annual growth rings in the shell of a quahog clam (*Arctica islandica*) showed it to be 405–410 years old. This was later revised to 507. Alas, the clam was killed in dating.

Heaviest colossal squid Colossal squid are shorter than giant squid, but they make up for it in weight. One specimen of adult male colossal squid (*Mesonychoteuthis hamiltoni*) weighed ca. 990 lb. (450 kg) when caught by fishermen in the Ross Sea of Antarctica in 2007.

Most venomous gastropod Predatory marine shells called cone shells (genus *Conus*) deliver a fast-acting neurotoxic venom. While several species are capable of delivering enough toxin to kill humans, the geographer cone (*C. geographus*) of the Indo-Pacific is particularly dangerous and should never be handled.

Longest bivalve mollusk Bivalves, such as clams and oysters, have a hinged shell. The longest bivalve is the giant shipworm (*Kuphus polythalamia*), a marine species that lives in a tubular shell. The longest specimen measured 5 ft. (1.53 m).

LARGEST . . .

Centipede The giant centipede (*Scolopendra gigantea*) of Central and South America is 10 in. (26 cm) long. It preys on mice, lizards, and frogs—and one group was found in Venezuela hanging upside down from cave roofs to feed on bats. The centipede uses modified jaws to catch its food, delivering venom that feels like an insect sting in humans and can cause swelling and fever.

Millipede A fully grown African giant black millipede (*Archispirostreptus gigas*) owned by Jim Klinger of Coppell, Texas, U.S.A., measures 1 ft. 3.2 in. (38.7 cm) in length and 2.6 in. (6.7 cm) in circumference, and has 256 legs. The average length for this type of millipede is 6–11 in. (16–28 cm).

> **FACT:** Centipedes don't have 100 legs but do have an even number of leg pairs.

Octopuses don't have eight legs—they have **two legs and six arms**.

LARGEST INVERTEBRATE An Atlantic giant squid (*Architeuthis dux*) that washed up in Thimble Tickle Bay, Newfoundland, Canada, on Nov. 2, 1878 had a body measured at 20 ft. (6.1 m) long and one tentacle reaching 35 ft. (10.7 m), giving a total of 55 ft. (16.8 m). Pictured is a giant squid snapped in Feb. 1996 in New Zealand.

Horseshoe crab The Atlantic horseshoe crab (*Limulus polyphemus*) measures up to 1 ft. 11.5 in. (60 cm) in length, yet despite its name it is not a crab. An aquatic relative of arachnids, its appearance has been relatively unchanged for millions of years.

LARGEST SNAIL An individual African giant snail (*Achatina achatina*) was recorded at 1 ft. 3.5 in. (39.3 cm) when fully extended, with a shell length of 10.75 in. (27.3 cm). Weighing 2 lb. (900 g), this specimen was named Gee Geronimo and was kept in Hove in the UK after being collected in Sierra Leone in Jun. 1976.

FACT: Gee Geronimo's owner, Chris Hudson (UK), got divorced after his wife complained that the house was too full of snails—and that he even had a bucket of them under their bed.

LARGEST CLAM The marine giant clam (*Tridacna gigas*) lives on the Indo-Pacific coral reefs. A specimen measuring 3 ft. 9 in. (1.15 m) and weighing 734 lb. (333 kg) was collected off Ishigaki Island, Okinawa, Japan, in 1956. It was examined in 1984 when experts estimated that it weighed over 750 lb. (340 kg) when alive.

Marine snail
The largest marine gastropod is the trumpet or baler conch (*Syrinx aruanus*) of Australia. A specimen collected in 1979 had a shell 2 ft. 6.4 in. (77.2 cm) long, with a maximum girth of 3 ft. 3.75 in. (1.01 m). It weighed nearly 40 lb. (18 kg) when alive.

Eye-to-body ratio
Vampyroteuthis infernalis—the "vampire squid from hell"—has a body measuring 11 in. (28 cm) in length and eyes with a diameter of 0.9 in. (2.5 cm). The ratio is almost 1:11—the human equivalent of eyes the size of table tennis bats! Squid also have the largest eyes in absolute terms (see p. 118).

BIG SUCKERS: Giant Octopus The **largest octopus** is the Pacific giant octopus (*Enteroctopus dofleini*, left), the biggest specimen of which sported an arm span of 31 ft. 6 in.—the same arm span of eight adult men! Despite their size, they are not exempt from predators, but, like most cephalopods, they have a good defense mechanism: center is a Pacific giant squirting a plume of ink in its wake as it evades attack. They are also masters of camouflage and can change color—and even texture—to match their surroundings (right).

FULL OF VENOM

All octopuses, cuttlefish, and some squid are venomous. Fortunately, only the venom of one—the blue-ringed octopus—is powerful enough to kill humans.

SUPERLATIVE SQUID

Smallest: 0.5-in.-long *Parateuthis tunicata*.

Most bioluminescent: Firefly squid (*Watasenia scintillans*) emit flashes of light.

First video of giant squid in natural habitat: Jul. 2012, filmed south of Tokyo in the Pacific Ocean.

First giant squid captured: Seven juveniles caught off the coast of New Zealand in Mar. 2002.

SIZING CEPHALOPODS, MYRIAPODS, AND MOLLUSKS

A. Ash-black slug: length 11.8 in.

B. Giant centipede: length 10 in.

C. Atlantic horseshoe crab: length 1 ft. 11.5 in.

D. African giant black millipede: length 1 ft. 3.2 in.

E. Atlantic giant squid: length up to 55 ft., has the **largest eye of any animal** (p. 117), at 1 ft. 3.7 in. in diameter

F. African giant snail: snout-to-tail length 1 ft. 3.5 in.

PETS

First pet hedgehog A relative of the Algerian hedgehog (*Atelerix algirus*) was domesticated during the 4th century B.C. by the Romans. They were primarily raised for their meat and quills but were also kept as pets, as several different species are today. Modern popular breeds are the Egyptian long-eared hedgehog (*Hemiechinus auritus auritus*), the Indian long-eared hedgehog (*H. collaris*), and the African pygmy hedgehog (*A. albiventris*), which is a hybrid of the Algerian and the four-toed hedgehog.

Most intelligent breed of dog The Border collie is the smartest pooch of all, followed by the poodle and German shepherd, according to Professor Stanley Coren (U.S.A.) of the University of British Columbia, Canada, and 200 professional dog obedience judges. Top dogs understand a vocabulary of 250 words—as many as a two-year-old human child. Bottom of the class are the bulldog, the Basenji, and, last of all, the Afghan hound.

Largest breed of spaniel Named after Clumber Park in Nottingham, UK, the Clumber spaniel has been a favorite of aristocracy and royalty. The breed standard specifies a weight of 86 lb. (39 kg) and a height of 20 in. (51 cm). The Clumber is loyal but a little demanding: its white coat sheds throughout the year, and the breed tends to slobber and snore.

OLDEST BEARDED DRAGON
Guinness (b. Jul. 26, 1997), a bearded dragon owned by Nik Vernon (UK), was 16 years 129 days old when he died on Dec. 2, 2013. Bearded dragons generally live to about eight years in the wild in Australia and typically a maximum of 14 years in captivity.

SMALLEST DOG Vanesa Semler of Dorado, Puerto Rico, owns a female Chihuahua called Milly, who measured 3.8 in. (9.65 cm) tall on Feb. 21, 2013. As a puppy, she was fed using an eyedropper and was small enough to fit on a teaspoon.

MOST EXPENSIVE SHEEPDOG
Shepherd Eddie Thornalley (UK) bought Marchup Midge (both left) from UK breeder and trainer Shaun Richards at an auction in Skipton in North Yorkshire, UK, on Oct. 26, 2012. His winning bid was £10,080 ($16,216).

OLDEST PIG EVER Pig Floyd (b. Feb. 17, 1992)—a potbellied pig owned by Kris and Tricia Fernandez of Baton Rouge, Louisiana, U.S.A.—was 21 years 166 days old when assessed on Aug. 2, 2013.

More amazing animals: pp. 120–125.

NERO THE FRIENDLY LION

George Wombwell (UK, 1777–1850) had a successful traveling menagerie. It included Nero, a lion so docile that he refused to fight dogs when his owner arranged a bout. Wombwell's tomb is still viewable today; he was buried in London's gothic Highgate Cemetery, under a statue of sleepy Nero, lying with his head on his paws.

Smallest breed of poodle Poodles can be found in standard, miniature, and—the smallest—toy categories. To qualify, a toy poodle must have a maximum height to the withers of either 11 in. (28 cm) or 10 in. (25.4 cm), depending on the guidelines of different international bodies.

Smallest breed of horse Originally developed in Argentina in 1868, the smallest recognized breed of horse is the Falabella miniature horse, which has an average height at the withers of 8 hands (32 in.; 81.2 cm). While miniature horses are shorter, they are also smaller—their limbs and body grow in proportion. The use of a "hand" (10.1 cm; 4 in.) as a unit of measurement goes back to ancient Egypt.

Largest breed of horse The English Shire horse is a type of draft horse. Stallions stand 17 hands (5 ft. 8 in.; 1.72 m) or even taller at maturity. It was one of these working animals that was the **tallest** and **heaviest** horse ever to be documented. Sampson (later renamed Mammoth) was a Shire gelding born in 1846. By 1850, he measured 21.2½ hands (7 ft. 2.5 in.; 2.19 m) and later weighed 3,359 lb. (1,524 kg). Mammoth was bred by Thomas Cleaver of Toddington Mills in Bedfordshire, UK.

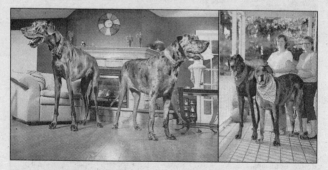

TALLEST DOGS Zeus (U.S.A., above left), a Great Dane, measured 3 ft. 8 in. (111.8 cm) tall on Oct. 4, 2011. Owned by Denise Doorlag and family of Otsego in Michigan, U.S.A., Zeus is both the **tallest male dog** and the **tallest dog ever**. The **tallest female dog** is also a Great Dane: Morgan (above right), owned by Dave and Cathy Payne of Melbourne in Ontario, Canada, measured 3 ft. 2.6 in. (98.15 cm) to the shoulder on Jan. 9, 2013. The two dogs met for the first time in Oct. 2013.

SHORTEST CAT Lilieput, a nine-year-old female Munchkin cat, measured 5.25 in. (13.34 cm) from the floor to the shoulders on Jul. 19, 2013. She is owned by Christel Young of Napa, California, U.S.A.

Gone but not fur-gotten is Colonel Meow (above right), the characterful **cat with the longest fur**, who passed away on Jan. 30, 2014. His fur measured 9 in. (22.87 cm) and his owner was Anne Marie Avey (U.S.A.).

TALLEST DONKEY Romulus is an American Mammoth Jackstock who measured 17 hands (5 ft. 8 in.; 1.72 m) tall on Feb. 8, 2013. He is owned by Cara and Phil Yellott of Red Oak in Texas, U.S.A. His brother, Remus, was measured at over 16 hands (5 ft. 4 in.; 1.62 m). The minimum height for the big breed is 14.2 hands (4 ft. 10 in.; 1.47 m).

Largest breed of pony The Connemara pony of North America ranges in height from 13 to 15 hands (4 ft. 4 in.–5 ft.; 132–152.4 cm).

The **smallest breed of pony** is the Shetland pony. Often used by children learning to ride, its maximum accepted height is 3 ft. 6 in. (107 cm) at the withers, with a minimum of 2 ft. 4 in. (71 cm). Dwarf ponies have a genetic mutation that may make them smaller, but Shetland ponies are the smallest of the pure breeds.

FIRST PETS: *Domestic Bliss* As our ancestors formed settlements, animals became domesticated for practical uses. They were used for food and clothing or would help us work. Dogs became the **first domestic animals**, around 13,000 B.C. in the Middle East. The bones of the **oldest known domestic cat** date back 9,500 years, and were discovered in a neolithic village on Cyprus next to its presumed owner. Records of the **first domestic elephants** tell of their use as beasts of burden at least 4,000 years ago in the present-day area covering Pakistan and India.

COLOSSAL COMPANIONS

A. Tallest horse: 6 ft. 10.5 in., Big Jake, Belgian gelding

B. Tallest donkey: 5 ft. 8 in., Romulus, American mammoth jackstock

C. Largest pony breed: 5 ft., Connemara

D. Largest pet canary: 8.66 in., Parisian frill

E. Tallest male dog: 3 ft. 8 in., Zeus, Great Dane

F. Tallest female dog: 3 ft. 2.6 in., Morgan, Great Dane

G. Tallest domestic cat: 19 in., Trouble, Savannah Islands

H. Largest domestic rabbit: 2 ft. 11.75 in., Flemish giant rabbit

There are **70 million** pet dogs and **74.1 million** pet cats in the U.S.A.

AND FINALLY . . .

- **Longest tail on a dog:** Finnegan, from Calgary, Canada, is an Irish wolfhound with a 2-ft. 4.46-in. tail, as of Aug. 15, 2013.
- **Largest donation of pet food in one week:** Full Stride Media (Pty) Ltd (ZAF) collected 22,066 lb. of pet food for animal charities on Oct. 6–13, 2013, in Johannesburg, South Africa.

ANIMALS IN ACTION

HIGHEST-RANKING PENGUIN Colonel-in-Chief Sir Nils Olav is the male king penguin mascot of Norway's Hans Majestet Kongens Garde (King's Guard) unit. He lives in the UK's Edinburgh Zoo, which received its first king penguin, from Norway, in 1913. In 1972, when the Norwegian King's Guard visited the zoo, a penguin was adopted and was named Nils Olav in honor of King Olav V. The current incumbent became Colonel-in-Chief on Aug. 18, 2005.

MOST TREATS BALANCED ON A DOG'S NOSE Despite his name, Monkey is a dog, and on Jul. 2, 2013 he balanced 26 treats on his nose, appearing with handler Meghan Fraser (U.S.A.) on the set of *Guinness World Records Unleashed* in California, U.S.A.

GWR's human talent always faces fierce **furry or feathered competition** . . .

FACT: Nifty Norman also rides bicycles (with training wheels, of course), skateboards, and surfboards.

FASTEST 30 M ON A SCOOTER BY A DOG Owner Karen Cobb (U.S.A.) didn't need to do much to encourage her enthusiastic four-year-old Briard, Norman, to scoot 30 m (98 ft.) in 20.77 sec., at All-Tournament Players Park in Georgia, U.S.A., on Jul. 12, 2013.

FIRST DOG TO DETECT DIABETIC EPISODES Armstrong the Labrador was trained in 2003 by Mark Ruefenacht (U.S.A.) to detect, via scent, the chemical changes leading to hypoglycemia (low blood sugar)—a condition that can cause a diabetic to slip into a coma. The Dogs for Diabetics charity was founded in 2004, following Armstrong's success.

LARGEST WORKING RODENT The Gambian giant pouched rat (*Cricetomys gambianus*) measures 3 ft. (90 cm) long and is used to sniff out land mines in Mozambique. The rats are trained to associate the scent of explosives with a food reward and identify the presence of explosives by grooming and scratching at the ground.

MOST BEVERAGE CANS OPENED BY A PARROT Zac the macaw opened 35 cans using just his beak in San Jose, California, U.S.A., on Jan. 12, 2012. The talented bird also set the record for the **most slam dunks by a parrot in one minute**, with 22 dunks into a specially designed net on Dec. 30, 2011.

LONGEST JUMP BY A CAT Flying feline Alley cat-apulted himself to a record with a 6-ft. (1.82-m) leap on Oct. 27, 2013. Alley, a rescue cat owned by Samantha Martin (U.S.A.), is part of the Amazing Acro-Cats touring show.

FASTEST DOG TO RETRIEVE A PERSON FROM WATER Search-and-rescue dog Jack, a black vom Mühlrad Newfoundland dog, is handled by Hans-Joachim Brückmann (DEU). On Jun. 11, 2013, Jack retrieved one of his handler's aides from 82 ft. (25 m) in 1 min. 36.81 sec. on the Kaarster See lake in Kaarst, Germany.

FASTEST 10 M ON HIND LEGS BY A DOG Jiff the Pomeranian covered 10 m (32 ft.) in 6.56 sec. at TOPS Kennels in Grayslake, Illinois, U.S.A., on Sep. 9, 2013. The plucky Pom, who performs various tricks, can also walk on his front paws (above right), covering 5 m (16 ft.) in a record 7.76 sec.—the **fastest 5 m on front legs by a dog**.

FACT: Jiff appeared in a Katy Perry video ("Dark Horse," 2013) and in the movie *Adventures of Bailey: A Night in Cowtown* (U.S.A., 2013).

Animals in Action

PLANTS

First use of spices in cooking Garlic mustard plant seeds were used between 6,150 and 5,800 years ago (around 4000 B.C.). In 2013, archaeologists announced that the spice had been found in European pottery shards.

Largest cashew nut tree Natal's cashew tree (*Anacardium occidentale*) in Rio Grande do Norte, Brazil, covers around 80,700 sq. ft. (7,500 m²) with a perimeter of around 1,640 ft. (500 m). That's a lot of nuts—indeed, the yield is up to 80,000 fruit per year. Some estimate the tree to be up to 1,000 years old, although it is also said that it was planted in 1888 by local fisherman Luiz Inácio de Oliveira.

Largest corm A corm is an underground plant stem that is used for storage by some plants to survive adverse surface conditions throughout the seasons. The largest is produced by the titan arum (*Amorphophallus titanum*) and commonly weighs around 110 lb. (50 kg). The heaviest specimen weighed 257 lb. 15 oz. (117 kg) and was recorded in 2006 in the Botanical Garden of Bonn University in Germany.

The titan arum is also the **smelliest plant** when it blooms—which is fortunately relatively rarely. It releases an odor, comparable to that of rotten flesh, that can be smelled at a great distance to attract the carrion beetles and flesh flies that pollinate it. Like the **largest living flower** (below), its stench gives it the nickname "corpse flower."

SHINIEST LIVING OBJECTS Marble berry (*Pollia condensata*) is a 3-ft. 3-in.-tall (1-m) herb native to Ghana. Resembling Christmas ball decorations, its vivid fruit is approximately 30% as reflective as a silver mirror. This is the highest reported light reflectivity of any biological material.

LARGEST LIVING FLOWER *Rafflesia arnoldii* gets its nickname "corpse flower" owing to its smell of rotting flesh (see also **smelliest plant**, above). And there is a lot of flower to sniff—it measures up to 3 ft. (91 cm) across and weighs up to 24 lb. (11 kg), with petals that are 0.75 in. (1.9 cm) thick. The rare flower is native to southeast Asia and grows as a parasite inside and upon jungle vines.

LARGEST PREY OF CARNIVOROUS PLANTS Of all the carnivorous plants, the ones that digest the largest prey belong to the Nepenthaceae family (genus *Nepenthes*). Both *N. rajah* and *N. rafflesiana* have been known to eat large frogs, birds, and even rats. These species are commonly found in the rain forests of Asia, in particular Borneo, Indonesia, and Malaysia. By using their color, smell, and nectar to attract prey, the plants then trap, kill, and digest enzymes, before absorbing what is needed for nutrition.

Largest horsetail One of the oldest plant genera to survive, horsetail is a living fossil. It is the only surviving member of the Equisetopsida class that once featured strongly in late Mesozoic period forests for up to 100 million years. Today, the Mexican giant horsetail (*Equisetum myriochaetum*) is the largest species, a primeval-looking plant reaching 24 ft. (7.3 m) in height.

Largest poppy flowers Coulter's Matilija poppy (*Romneya coulteri*) has silky white flowers around an eye-catching ball of golden stamens and grows to 5.12 in. (13 cm) across. It grows in southern California, U.S.A., and northern Mexico and its bold display of flowers makes it a popular ornamental plant.

Most massive plant by area A network of quaking aspen trees (*Populus tremuloides*) grows in the Wasatch mountains, Utah, U.S.A., covering 106 acres (43 ha) and weighing an estimated 13,227,700 lb. (6,000 metric tons), making it also the **heaviest organism**. The clonal system is genetically uniform and acts as a single organism, with all the component trees changing color or shedding leaves in unison. The network looks like a forest, but it is made up of plants that have grown from the root system of a single tree dating back at least 80,000 years.

A notch or limb on a tree stays the **same distance** from the ground.

Smallest bromeliad While the best-known member of the bromeliad clan is the pineapple, its unlikely relation is Spanish moss (*Tillandsia usneoides*). Neither a moss nor Spanish, the beardlike growth is made up of the smallest bromeliads, with slender stems bearing tiny flowers and a series of leaves that cling together. It produces hanging threadlike chains that stretch up to 19 ft. 8 in. (6 m) long.

Tallest banksia Banksias are Australian wildflowers of the genus Banksia, some of which are so large that they grow as tall as trees. The tallest species are the coast banksia (*Banksia integrifolia*) and the river banksia (*B. seminuda*), both of which can grow to 100 ft. (30 m) in height.

Tallest cycad Cycads can look like palm trees and are sometimes grouped with them, but they are coning plants (like pine trees). Hope's cycad (*Lepidozamia hopei*) from Queensland, Australia, is the largest, growing to heights of 49 ft. (15 m).

Tallest moss Dawson's giant moss (*Dawsonia superba*), a New Zealand native, can grow to 23.6 in. (60 cm) tall, but its spores are no more than 0.00039 in. (0.01 mm) in size.

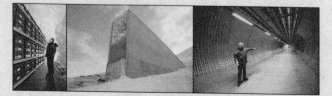

VAULTING AMBITION: Seed Storage The Svalbard Global Seed Vault is an underground facility on the Norwegian island of Spitsbergen designed to store samples of the world's seeds as insurance against threats to biodiversity. Opened on Feb. 26, 2006, it is the **largest seed vault**. The goal is to store a total of 4.5 million samples (about 2 billion seeds) from 100 countries and, as of 2013, more than 770,000 samples had been deposited. The vault cost $8.3m and the location—426 ft. into the permafrost of a mountain—was chosen for being the best suited to keeping the temperature of samples at a stable 64.4°F.

MARINE PLANTS

Deepest: Algae at 882 ft., found by Mark and Diane Littler (both U.S.A.), the Bahamas, Oct. 1984

Fastest growing: Giant kelp (*Macrocystis pyrifera*), growing 1 ft. 1.3 in. per day

Largest clonal colony: DNA-sharing colony of Neptune grass, aka Mediterranean tapeweed (*Posidonia oceanica*), 4.9 mi. across, Mediterranean Sea, discovered 2006

> **FACT:** If evenly distributed, a mature giant water lily leaf can support up to 100 lb. of weight.

LARGEST WATER LILY Native to freshwater lakes and bayous in the Amazon basin, the giant water lily (*Victoria amazonica*) has floating leaves measuring up to 10 ft. (3 m) across and is held in place on an underwater stem 23–26 ft. (7–8 m) long. The leaves are supported by riblike cross ridges that are said to have inspired the metal girders of Crystal Palace in London, UK, built in 1851.

LARGEST BRANCHED INFLORESCENCE A branched inflorescence is a cluster of flowers on a multibranched stem instead of on a single stem. The largest is that of the talipot palm (*Corypha umbraculifera*), which consists of up to several million creamy white flowers. The palm is native to parts of India and Sri Lanka. Its inflorescence grows at the apex of the tree's trunk and is 19–26 ft. (6–8 m) long.

TREES OF THE AMAZON

The Amazon basin and Guiana Shield area of South America has an estimated 16,000 tree species, of which just 227 species (1.4%) account for half of all Amazon trees. The rarest 11,000 species account for just 0.12% of the total number of trees in the region. The study from which this data is extracted, published in *Nature* in 2013, suggests that there are a total of 400 billion trees alive today in the Amazon rain forest.

Plants

LARGEST PLANT SIZES

A. Redwood: height 379 ft. 1 in.

B. Raffia palm: leaf length 65 ft. 7 in.,
stem length 13 ft.

C. Talipot palm: length 19–26 ft.

D. *Puya raimondii*: height 35 ft.

E. Giant water lily: width up to 10 ft.

F. *Rafflesia arnoldii*: width 3 ft.,
weight 24 lb.

PALMED OFF

Before the leaf of the raffia palm took the record, it was the giant water
lily that was considered the **largest leaf**, in 1955 reported as 21 ft. Back
then, it was called *Victoria regina* before the name *Victoria amazonica*
became widely used. Its common name is the royal water lily.

HUMANS

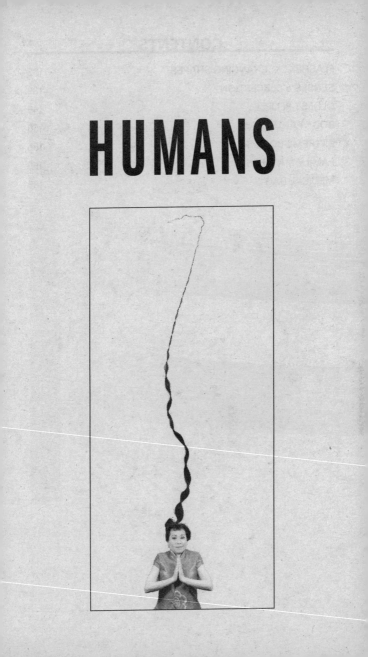

CONTENTS

> The surface area of a human lung is equivalent to the **size of a tennis court.**

LONGEST FINGERNAILS ON A PAIR OF HANDS She's nailed it: Chris "The Dutchess" Walton (U.S.A.) has a set of fingernails measuring 11 ft. 10 in. (3.62 m) for her left hand and 12 ft. 1 in. (3.68 m) for her right hand—a total of 23 ft. 11 in. (7.3 m). Chris's twisting talons were measured in London, UK, on Sep. 16, 2013.

> **FACT:** Fingernails grow at around 0.1 in. per month. And men's nails usually grow faster than women's.

CHANGING SHAPES

One constant in Guinness World Records's 60-year history has been the popularity of the Human Body chapter. It's the part of the book that most people flip to first, and many of the colorful characters who've filled the pages over the years have attained iconic status. Here, we look back at how some of these records have changed since our first edition in 1955.

Ask anyone to name a favorite record holder from the *Guinness World Records* book and the chances are they'll recall someone from the Human Body chapter. With visually striking record holders such as Robert Wadlow (**tallest man ever**), Lee Redmond (**longest fingernails**), and Robert Earl Hughes (**largest chest measurement** and former **heaviest man**), it comes as no surprise. It helps that their stories are so memorable. Who could forget that Wadlow died as a result of a blister from ill-fitting footwear? Or that Hughes was buried in a coffin the size of a piano case?

In this Flashback, we examine a selection of iconic Human Body superlatives that appeared in our first edition and identify who now holds the record. In some cases, such as the **tallest man ever**, the record hasn't changed in 60 years; in others, such as the **longest hair**, the current claimant has surpassed the original holder by a long way . . .

MOST CHILDREN

MOST CHILDREN DELIVERED AT A SINGLE BIRTH TO SURVIVE (2015) Nadya Suleman (U.S.A.) claimed headlines across the world on Jan. 26, 2009, when she gave birth to six boys and two girls in Bellflower, California, U.S.A. Dubbed "Octomom" by the U.S. press, Suleman conceived with the aid of *in vitro* fertilization (IVF), swelling her family from 6 children to 14.

"MULTIPLE BIRTHS" (1955) Our first edition mentions fanciful accounts of women having as many as 36 children in a single birth (illustrated right is "Dorothea," who reportedly had 11 babies in 1755). Turning to "medically more acceptable cases," however, we go on to discuss the five Dionne babies—then, one of only three examples of quintuplets to survive—born on May 28, 1934.

OLDEST WOMAN

OLDEST LIVING WOMAN (2015) As we go to press, 115-year-old Misao Okawa of Japan is the oldest woman—and **oldest person**—alive on Earth (see p. 148). She's not the **oldest woman ever**, of course: the all-time holder, also a woman, is Jeanne Louise Calment (FRA), who died on Aug. 4, 1997 at the remarkable age of 122 years 164 days.

"OLDEST CENTENARIANS" (1955) Longevity is a subject that has clearly always been controversial. "Few subjects have been so obscured by deceit and falsehood," we wrote in 1955. The oldest woman then on record "for whom there exists acceptable evidence" was vicar's daughter Katherine Plunkett of County Louth, Ireland, who lived for 111 years 328 days from 1820 to 1932.

LONGEST MUSTACHE

LONGEST MUSTACHE (2015) Measured at 14 ft. (4.29 m) on Mar. 4, 2010, the face furniture of Ram Singh Chauhan (IND) earned him a place in the record books for the longest 'stache of all time. Ram started growing his facial hair in 1970 and, with his wife's help, grooms his whiskers daily with coconut and mustard oils.

"LONGEST MUSTACHE" (1955) Our earliest edition makes reference to Mr. John Roy of Glasgow, UK, whose 16.5-in.-long (41.91-cm) mustache is the "longest mustache owned by a member of Britain's 'Handlebar Club.'" Roy, a smoker, once tried to have his mustache insured because of the fire risk, but he couldn't afford the premiums.

HEAVIEST MAN

HEAVIEST LIVING MALE (2015)
Although his peak weight of 1,235 lb. (560 kg) secured Manuel Uribe (MEX, pictured right) the extant world record in 2006, he's not the **heaviest man ever**. That accolade goes to Jon Brower Minnoch (U.S.A., 1941–83, see p. 157), whose weight was estimated by doctors at an unparalleled 1,400 lb. (635 kg) in 1978.

"HEAVIEST HEAVYWEIGHT" (1955)
Now known as the man with the **widest chest measurement** (10 ft. 4 in; 315 cm), Robert Earl Hughes's (U.S.A.) first appearance in GWR was as the **heaviest living man**, at 946 lb. (429 kg). We also named the "heaviest man recorded in medical history" as Miles Darden (U.S.A., 1799–1857), who peaked "slightly in excess of 1,000 lb." (453 kg).

LONGEST HAIR

LONGEST HAIR (FEMALE) (2015)
The world's lengthiest locks (female) belong to Xie Qiuping of China at 18 ft. 5.5 in. (5.62 m). She has been growing her hair since 1973, from the age of 13. "It's no trouble at all. I'm used to it," she said. "But you need patience and you need to hold yourself straight when you have hair like this."

"LONGEST TRESSES" (1955)
The "longest recorded feminine tresses," we said in 1955, "appear to be those of the 19th-century exhibitionist named Miss Owens, which were measured at 8 ft. 3 in. [251.4 cm]." Millie Owens was the "Queen of Long Hair" and enjoyed a career showing off her tresses and selling picture postcards.

FACT: Xie travels with an assistant to hold her hair and help her manage her plentiful tresses.

GREATEST VOCAL RANGE

GREATEST VOCAL RANGE (2015) Brazil's Georgia Brown has a vocal range that spans an incredible eight octaves (from G2 to G10), as verified at Aqui Jazz Atelier Music School in São Paulo on Aug. 18, 2004—a record that has remained unchallenged for more than a decade!

"GREATEST RANGE" (1955)
The singer with the greatest range in 1955 was named as Miss Yma Sumac (born Zoila Augusta Emperatriz Chávarri del Castillo, 1922–2008), an acclaimed soprano from Peru: "She is reputed to have a range of five octaves from A# to B."

TALLEST MAN

TALLEST LIVING MAN (2015) Towering 2 ft. 8 in. (81.2 cm) over GWR Editor-in-Chief Craig Glenday is Sultan Kösen of Turkey, who took the title of tallest living man—and human—in Feb. 2009. Currently standing at 8 ft. 3 in. (251 cm), Sultan is one of just eight people over 8 ft. (243 cm) to be ratified in the past 60 years.

FACT: As a teenager, Sultan was signed to play basketball for Galatasaray in Turkey but proved too tall to compete!

"TALLEST GIANTS" (1955) "The only admissible evidence upon the true height of giants is that of recent date made under impartial medical supervision." So said Norris and Ross McWhirter in 1955 before going on to dismiss the likes of Og, King of Bashan at 9 Assyrian cubits (16 ft. 2.5 in.; 494.03 cm) due to "confusion of units" from the Bible. They then named Robert Wadlow as the tallest man "of whom there is irrefutable evidence." Find out more on p. 158.

SHORTEST MAN AND WOMAN

SHORTEST LIVING MAN AND WOMAN (2015) Pictured here is GWR's Head of Records, Marco Frigatti, with the current shortest living humans. Jyoti Amge (IND, near left) measured 24.7 in. (62.8 cm) in Nagpur, India, on Dec. 16, 2011, while two months later, at a clinic in Kathmandu, Nepal, on Feb. 26, 2012, Chandra Bahadur Dangi (NPL, far left) reached just 21.5 in. (54.6 cm). Mr. Dangi is also officially ratified as the **shortest man ever measured** using modern medical equipment.

"SHORTEST DWARFS" (1955) Sixty years ago, we named Miss Edith Barlow (above left) as the UK's "shortest living dwarf," at 22 in. (55.8 cm), making her the world's **shortest living woman** by default. Only Walter Boehning, aka Böning (DEU, d. 1955, above right) was shorter in absolute terms, claiming to be the "smallest dwarf in the world" at an unconfirmed height of just 20.5 in. (52 cm). By 1964, Boehning was removed from the book due to a lack of supporting evidence for his claimed stature.

SENSES & PERCEPTION

HEARING

Highest detectable pitch The upper limit of human hearing is accepted to be 20,000 Hz (hertz, or cycles per second), although this figure decreases with age. By way of comparison, bats emit pulses at up to 90,000 Hz.

The average accepted **lowest detectable pitch** by the human ear is 20 Hz, although in ideal conditions a young person can hear frequencies down to 12 Hz. Inaudible infrasound waves in the range of 4–16 Hz can be felt by the human body as physical vibrations.

> The eyes can process around **36,000 pieces of information** every hour.

QUIETEST PLACE Tests performed on Oct. 18, 2012 in the Anechoic Test Chamber at Orfield Laboratories in Minneapolis, Minnesota, U.S.A., gave a background noise reading of just -3 dBA (decibels A-weighted). The term "dBA" denotes sound levels audible to the human ear—i.e., excluding extreme highs and lows.

Smallest bone The stapes, or stirrup bone, measures 0.1–0.13 in. (2.6–3.4 mm) in length and weighs 2–4.3 mg. One of the three auditory ossicles in the middle ear, the stapes plays a vital role in hearing.

NOISIEST WORKPLACE The cockpit of a Formula One car is the loudest place on Earth in which any human works for a sustained period. The noise level directly in front of the engine where a driver sits has been measured at 140 dB. All drivers wear tailor-made earplugs.

FACT: Quieter V6 engines were introduced in the 2014 season—to the disappointment of many F1 fans!

SIGHT

Farthest object visible to the naked eye Gamma-ray bursts are the birth cries of black holes. At 2:12 EDT on Mar. 19, 2008, NASA's *Swift* satellite detected a gamma-ray burst from a galaxy some 7.5 billion light-years away. Some 30–40 sec. later, the optical counterpart of the burst was seen on Earth and captured by a robotic telescope. The explosion, known as GRB 080319B, was visible to the naked eye for around 30 sec.

Most active muscle Scientists have estimated that human eye muscles move more than 100,000 times a day. Many of these rapid eye movements take place during the dreaming phase of sleep.

Most sensitive color vision The average human eye can perceive approximately a million colors. Our powers of color vision derive from three types of cone cells in the eye, each responsive to different wavelengths of light. Our brains combine the signals to produce the perception of color. Work completed by neuroscientist Gabriele Jordan at the University of Newcastle, UK, proved that some people have four cones, enabling them to see more colors—about 99 million more, in fact. Jordan and her team created a test in which three subtle color circles flashed on a screen. Only one person was able to distinguish them every time—an English female doctor known as "cDa29"—who has the most sensitive color vision measured.

HOW MANY SENSES DO WE HAVE?

Conventionally, we think of ourselves as having five senses: sight, hearing, taste, touch, and smell. But if to "sense" something simply means to be aware of it, then we have many more than just these five "primary" senses. Here are a few others to consider:

 Temperature: We can tell hot from cold and adjust accordingly

 Pain: A mechanism for the body to sense damage

 Balance: We are sensitive to body movement, direction, and acceleration

 Time: We sense time passing

Interoception: Our internal senses alert us when we are feeling hungry or tired

Kinesthetics: The brain's parietal cortex enables us to tell where every part of our body is in relation to its other parts. (Test this by trying to touch your nose with your eyes closed!)

The loudness, or intensity, of a sound is usually measured in decibels (dB). Decibels are calculated according to a logarithmic scale, which increases by a set ratio.

Total silence would measure 0 dB; a sound 10 times greater would be 10 dB, but a sound 100 times louder than 0 dB would measure only 20 dB, and sounds 1,000 times louder than 0 dB would register just 30 dB.

Listed here are typical decibel readings, recorded from a distance of 32 ft. away from the source.

DECIBEL (DB) READINGS

All readings from 32-ft. distance

dB	Sound
150	Jet engine
114	Train whistle
110	Subway train
107	Pneumatic riveter
89	Power saw
64	City traffic from inside car
46	Normal piano practice

SMELL

Smelliest substance The manmade foul-smelling substances "Who-Me?" and "U.S. Government Standard Bathroom Malodor" have five and eight chemical ingredients respectively. Bathroom Malodor smells primarily of human feces and becomes incredibly repellant to people at a ratio of just two parts per million. It was originally developed to test the power of deodorizing products.

Smelliest molecule The chemicals ethyl mercaptan (C_2H_5SH) and butyl seleno-mercaptan (C_4H_9SeH) have a distinctive smell reminiscent of a combination of rotting cabbage, garlic, onions, burned toast, and sewer gas.

MOST VALUABLE NOSE On Mar. 19, 2008, Lloyd's reported that Ilja Gort (NLD) had his nose insured for 5 m euro ($7.8 m). Gort, the owner of the vineyard Château la Tulipe de la Garde in Bordeaux, France, insured his nose in an attempt to protect his livelihood.

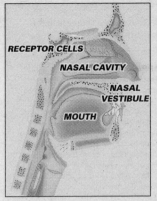

TALKING SCENTS: *Our Sense of Smell* Smell accounts for around 80% of our sense of taste. The first sense to develop, it is functional before we are born and is generally most sensitive in childhood. We can detect some 10,000 odors, but prolonged exposure to a smell causes our awareness of it to reduce quickly. We are more sensitive to smells in spring and summer, because the air is more moist then; exercise also increases the moisture in our nostrils, improving our sense of smell. Women have a stronger sense of smell than men—it is particularly acute during pregnancy.

Smells enter the nasal vestibule (nostril), where small hairs filter out dust and other fine particles. At the top of the nasal cavity are ca. 40 million olfactory receptor cells, which detect the odorant molecules and send a message to the brain. When you eat, you "taste" the food using these same cells, which detect food odors in the mouth.

TASTE

Bitterest substance The bitterest-tasting substances are based on the denatonium cation and have been produced commercially as benzoate and saccharide. Taste detection levels are as low as just one part in 500 million, while a dilution of just one part in 100 million will leave a lingering taste.

MOST VALUABLE TONGUE On Mar. 9, 2009, Lloyd's reported that the tongue of Gennaro Pelliccia (UK) was insured for £10 m ($14 m). Pelliccia tastes every single batch of coffee beans made for Costa Coffee (UK) stores and has now learned to distinguish between thousands of different flavors.

SWEETEST SUBSTANCE Thaumatin, aka talin, from arils (appendages found on certain seeds) of the katemfe plant (*Thaumatococcus daniellii*) found in West Africa, is 3,250 times sweeter than sugar when compared with a 7.5% sucrose solution.

MAPPING THE SENSES This oddly shaped figure is a "sensory homunculus." This is what you'd look like if your body parts were in proportion to the areas of the brain concerned with sensory perception. Based on a model at the UK's Natural History Museum, it shows which areas of our bodies are the most sensitive to touch.

Lips have many sense receptors—which is one of the reasons why babies put objects into their mouths to learn about them.

When it comes to detecting our world, the tongue is highly sensitive, with a very dense concentration of neural connections.

Our fingers feel the world in sensory high definition by containing the highest density of touch receptors in the body. Sense receptors are more concentrated in smaller fingers. As a result, women tend to have a more developed tactile sensitivity than men.

The calves are among the least sensitive body parts—the brain can only distinguish two points of contact around 1.77 in. apart, compared with 0.07 in. for the fingers.

The 100,000–200,000 sense receptors on the sole of each foot help stabilize the whole body. They are at their most effective when we walk barefoot.

TOUCH

Most touch-sensitive part of the body Our fingers have the highest density of touch receptors in the body. The fingers are so sensitive that we can feel two points of contact just 0.07 in. (2 mm) apart. They can also detect a movement of just 0.02 microns—that's 31-millionths of an inch (or 200-thousandths of a millimeter).

AND FINALLY . . .

• **Longest echo:** 1 min. 15 sec. by Trevor Cox and Allan Kilpatrick (both UK) inside a disused oil tank at Inchindown in Highland, UK, on Jun. 3, 2012.

• **Fastest time to boil water by passing electricity through body:** 1 min. 22.503 sec., to heat 5.28 fl. oz. of water from 77°F to 206°F by Slavisa "Biba" Pajkic (SRB) in Istanbul, Turkey, on Jul. 13, 2013.

OLDEST PEOPLE

Longest separated twins Twins Ann and Elizabeth were born to unmarried mother Alice Lamb in Aldershot, Hampshire, UK, on Feb. 28, 1936. A decision was made to separate the twins for adoption, and Ann grew up unaware of her sister Lizzie, who now lives in Portland, Oregon, U.S.A. The pair were finally reunited on May 1, 2014 after a record 77 years 289 days apart.

OLDEST . . .

Person (ever) The greatest fully authenticated age to which any human has ever lived is 122 years 164 days by Jeanne Louise Calment (FRA, Feb. 21, 1875–Aug. 4, 1997). She lived through two World Wars and the development of television, the modern automobile, and airplanes. When asked on her 120th birthday what she expected of the future, she replied: "A very short one."

LARGEST GATHERING OF CENTENARIANS On May 19, 2013, the Regency Jewish Heritage Nursing & Rehabilitation Center in Somerset, New Jersey, U.S.A., hosted a gathering of 31 people at the age of 100 years or over—only two of whom were men. Their combined ages stretched back to about 1100 B.C., when the ancient Phoenicians were inventing the alphabet.

OLDEST SOLO PARACHUTE JUMP (FEMALE) Dilys Margaret Price (UK, b. Jun. 3, 1932) made a parachute jump at Langar Airfield in Nottingham, UK, on Apr. 13, 2013 at the age of 80 years 315 days. The **oldest solo parachute jump (male)** was made by Milburn Hart (U.S.A., 1908–2010) in Washington, U.S.A., on Feb. 18, 2005. He was 96 years 63 days old.

The number of people over 65 is expected to **double to 800 million** by 2025.

Parent-child (aggregate) The highest combined age for a parent and child alive at the same time is 215 years in the case of 119-year-old Sarah Knauss (U.S.A., 1880–1999) and her 96-year-old daughter Kathryn Knauss Sullivan (U.S.A., 1903–2005). Knauss was the second-oldest human ever, reaching 119 years 97 days.

Adoptive parent Frances Ensor Benedict (U.S.A., 1918–2012) was 83 years 324 days old when she adopted her foster daughter Jo Anne Benedict Walker (U.S.A.) on Apr. 5, 2002 in Putnam County, Tennessee, U.S.A. At 65 years 224 days, Jo Anne (b. Aug. 24, 1936) is also the **oldest adoptee**.

Fashion model Aged 85 years 295 days as of Apr. 22, 2014, Daphne Selfe (UK, b. Jul. 1, 1928) is the oldest professional fashion model. Her 60-year career includes appearances for Dolce & Gabbana and Gap, modeling in *Vogue* and *Marie Claire*, and posing for photographers David Bailey and Mario Testino.

LYING ABOUT AGE IS NOTHING NEW

In our first edition, we cautioned against "deceit and falsehood" encountered in claimed ages. Using information investigated by the Canadian government, we listed the greatest age reached by a male as 113, by Pierre Joubert, a French Canadian bootmaker (b. Jul. 15, 1701, buried Nov. 18, 1814). An investigation in 1990, however, established that Joubert was actually 82 at the time of his death, and that the person buried in 1814 was Joubert's homonymous ("same name") son, born in 1732.

FACT: Life expectancy has risen worldwide on average by four months each year since 1970.

MY LIFE WILL GO ON

The greatest age reached by a survivor of the *Titanic* was 104 years 72 days. Mary Wilburn, née Davis (UK, 1883–1987), was 28 when the ship sank in 1912.

Actor to win an Oscar Christopher Plummer (UK, b. Dec. 13, 1929) was 82 years 65 days old when he won the 2012 Best Supporting Actor Oscar for *Beginners* (2010). The **oldest actress to win an Oscar** is Jessica Tandy (UK, 1909–1994), who won the 1990 Best Actress award at 80 years 295 days for the title role in *Driving Miss Daisy* (1989).

Newspaper delivery person Ted Ingram (UK, b. Feb. 14, 1920) delivered the *Dorset Echo* from the 1940s until Nov. 9, 2013, when he was 93 years 268 days old.

OLDEST COMPETITIVE SPRINTER Hidekichi Miyazaki (JPN, b. Sep. 22, 1910) was 103 years 15 days old when he competed at the International Gold Masters in Kyoto, Japan, on Oct. 6, 2013. He took part in the 100 m race, which he finished in 34.10 sec., shaving 2.67 sec. off his previous best.

OLDEST BASE JUMPER Donald Cripps (U.S.A., b. Sep. 12, 1929) was 84 years 37 days old when he parachuted off the 876-ft.-high (267-m) New River Gorge Bridge near Fayetteville in West Virginia, U.S.A., on Oct. 19, 2013. BASE jumping—from Buildings, Antennas, Spans (bridges), and Earth (cliffs)—is the most dangerous form of parachuting, due to the short falls involved.

OLDEST SUPERCENTENARIANS

As of Apr. 14, 2014, there were 74 people whose age had been verified as passing the 111-year mark. The estimated worldwide total of living supercentenarians is 300–450 persons.

Who	Born	How old?
Misao Okawa (JPN)	Mar. 5, 1898	116 years 40 days
Jeralean Talley (U.S.A.)	May 23, 1899	114 years 326 days
Susannah Mushatt Jones (U.S.A.)	Jul. 6, 1899	114 years 282 days
Bernice Madigan (U.S.A.)	Jul. 24, 1899	114 years 264 days
Emma Morano-Martinuzzi (ITA)	Nov. 29, 1899	114 years 136 days
Anna Henderson (U.S.A.)	Mar. 5, 1900	114 years 40 days
Antonia Gerena Rivera (U.S.A.)	May 19, 1900	113 years 330 days
Ethel Lang (UK)	May 27, 1900	113 years 322 days
Nabi Tajima (JPN)	Aug. 4, 1900	113 years 253 days
Blanche Cobb (U.S.A.)	Sep. 8, 1900	113 years 218 days

Source: Gerontology Research Group

OLDEST LIVING PERSON Misao Okawa (JPN, b. Mar. 5, 1898) turned 116 in 2014. Misao, who lives in a nursing home in Osaka, Japan, became the **oldest living woman** on Jan. 12, 2013 and **oldest living person** on Jun. 12, 2013. She is also the ninth oldest verified person ever.

Soccer referee As of Apr. 14, 2013, Peter Pak-Ngo Pang (U.S.A., b. IDN, Nov. 4, 1932) was still refereeing in the adult men's league in San Jose, California, U.S.A., aged 80 years 161 days.

Convicted bank robber On Jan. 23, 2004, 92-year-old J. L. Hunter Rountree (U.S.A., b. 1911) received 12 years 7 months for robbing a bank (unarmed) in Texas, U.S.A.

OLDEST NEWSPAPER DELIVERY PERSON (FEMALE) At 88 years 346 days old as of Mar. 27, 2014, Beryl Walker (UK, b. Apr. 15, 1925) was still delivering newspapers six mornings a week in Gloucester, Gloucestershire, UK. She has now given up her evening round.

OLDEST LIVING MAN Shortly before going to press, we heard of the passing of Arturo Licata (ITA, May 2, 1902–Apr. 24, 2014), who had briefly been the oldest living man, aged 111 years 357 days at his death. His successor, Dr. Alexander Imich (POL/RUS, now U.S.A., b. Feb. 4, 1903), took the title at the age of 111 years 79 days. He is pictured here in his Upper West Side home in New York.

OLDEST DANCE TROUPE The Hip Op-eration Crew (NZ) are hip-hop dancers whose ages range from 67 to 95, giving an average of 79 years 197 days (as of May 10, 2014). The 23 core members, from the small island of Waiheke, New Zealand, include 12 in their eighties and nineties. Their performances include a guest slot at 2013's World Hip Hop Dance Championship final in Las Vegas, Nevada, U.S.A. Respect.

Theater actor On Nov. 29, 2013, Radu Beligan (ROM, b. Dec. 14, 1918) was still performing at the National Theatre in Bucharest, Romania, at 94 years 350 days old.

ELDER STATESMEN: Current National Leaders Combining political power with staying power, Shimon Peres (right), the ninth President of Israel, is the **oldest living head of state**. Born Szymon Perski in Wiszniew, Poland (now Vishnyeva, Belarus), on Aug. 2, 1923, he celebrated his 90th birthday in 2013.

Only six months younger is the President of Zimbabwe, Robert Mugabe (left), born on Feb. 21, 1924. Almost exactly a year younger than Peres is Saudi Arabia's King Abdullah bin Abdulaziz al-Saud (center). Born on Aug. 1, 1924, he has already outlived two of his crown prince heirs.

LONGEST CAREERS

Professional hairdresser: Dorothy McKnight (U.S.A., b. Feb. 27, 1922) of Lake Worth, Florida, U.S.A., since Jun. 13, 1939

Church pianist/organist: Martha Godwin (U.S.A., b. Jan. 17, 1927) in Southmont, North Carolina, U.S.A., since Apr. 1940

Stuntman: Rocky Taylor (UK, b. Feb. 28, 1945), since Mar. 1961. He appeared in *World War Z* (released Jun. 2013)

Painter Alphaeus Philemon Cole (U.S.A., 1876–1988), whose work is in the permanent collections of the National Portrait Gallery (UK) and the Brooklyn Museum (U.S.A.), painted and exhibited his work up to the age of 103. A portraitist, Cole began his art career in the 1890s with Seurat and Signac as contemporaries.

Chess master Zoltan Sarosy (HUN, b. Aug. 23, 1906) was the Canadian Correspondence Chess Champion three times (1967, 1972, 1981) and, according to ChessGames.com, continues to play at 107 years of age.

BODY PARTS

Stretchiest skin Garry Turner (UK) is able to stretch the skin of his abdomen to a distended length of 6.25 in. (15.8 cm) due to a rare medical condition called Ehlers-Danlos Syndrome. With this condition, the collagen that strengthens the skin and determines its elasticity becomes defective, resulting in, among other things, a loosening of the skin and "hypermobility" of the joints.

Largest hairy family Victor "Larry" Gomez, Gabriel "Danny" Ramos Gomez, Luisa Lilia De Lira Aceves, and Jesus Manuel Fajardo Aceves (all MEX) are four of a family of 19 that span five generations with a rare condition called congenital generalized hypertrichosis—excessive facial and torso hair. The women are covered with a light-to-medium coat of hair while the men have thick hair on approximately 98% of their body apart from their hands and feet.

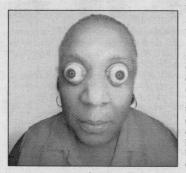

FARTHEST EYEBALL POP Kim Goodman (U.S.A.) popped her eyeballs to a protrusion of 0.47 in. (12 mm) beyond her eye sockets in Istanbul, Turkey, on Nov. 2, 2007, beating her previous record of 0.43 in. (11 mm) in 1998. Kim discovered her talent when she was hit on the head by a hockey mask, but can now pop her eyes out on cue.

Adults are made up of around
7,000,000,000,000,000,000,000,000,000 atoms.

TALLEST AND SHORTEST

A. **Robert Wadlow** 8 ft. 11.1 in.
B. **John William Rogan** 8 ft. 8.0 in.
C. **John F. Carroll** 8 ft. 7.7 in.
D. **Väinö Myllyrinne** 8 ft. 3.0 in.
E. **Sultan Kösen** 8 ft. 3.0 in.
F. **Don Koehler** 8 ft. 2.0 in.
G. **Bernard Coyne** 8 ft. 2.0 in.
H. **Zeng Jinlian** 8 ft. 1.7 in.
I. **Patrick Cotter (O'Brien)** 8 ft. 1.0 in.
J. **Brahim Takioullah** 8 ft. 0.9 in.

K. **Lin Yih-Chih** 2 ft. 3 in.
L. **Khagendra Thapa Magar** 2 ft. 2.4 in.
M. **Calvin Phillips** 2 ft. 2.4 in.
N. **Younis Edwan** 2 ft. 1.5 in.
O. **Madge Bester** 2 ft. 1.5 in.
P. **Jyoti Amge** 2 ft. 0.7 in.
Q. **Pauline Musters** 2 ft.
R. **Junrey Balawing** 1 ft. 11.5 in.
S. **Gul Mohammed** 1 ft. 10.5 in.
T. **Chandra Bahadur Dangi** 1 ft. 9.5 in.

Hairiest teenager In 2010, trichologists (medical experts specializing in hair) used the Ferriman-Gallwey method to evaluate the hirsutism (hairiness) of Supatra "Nat" Sasuphan (THA, b. Aug. 5, 2000). Ten areas of her body were scored from 1 to 4 according to the density of the hair. Nat received a score of 4 on four areas: face, neck, chest, and upper back.

Tallest Mohawk spike Kazuhiro Watanabe (JPN) has a spike measuring 48 in. (1.23 m), dwarfing even Eric Hahn's full Mohawk (see box on p. 154). The length was verified at Dwango Hanzomon Studio in Chiyoda, Tokyo, Japan, on Apr. 23, 2014.

SIMMONDS' DISEASE

The lightest recorded adults of average height are those who have Simmonds' disease (hypophyseal cachexia)—brought about by a failure of the pituitary gland. Losses of up to 65% of the original bodyweight have been recorded in females, with a low of 45 lb. documented in the case of Emma Schaller (U.S.A., 1868–90), who stood 5 ft. 1 in. tall.

LARGEST...

Human skull The largest documented skull was that of an adult male with a 120-cu.-in. (1,980-cm³) cranial capacity. The average skull has a capacity of 57.9–109 cu. in. (950–1,800 cm³), depending on age and size.

Hands Robert Wadlow's (U.S.A.) hands measured 1 ft. 0.75 in. (32.3 cm) from wrist to tip of middle finger—not surprising given his status as **tallest man ever** (see pp. 151 and 158). The current **tallest man**, Sultan Kösen (TUR, see p. 156), has the **largest hands on a living person**: 11.22 in. (28.5 cm) long.

Feet If cases of elephantiasis are excluded, the largest feet ever measured belonged to Robert Wadlow, who wore U.S. size 37AA shoes—the equivalent of 1 ft. 6.5 in. (47 cm).

The **largest feet on a living person** are those of Brahim Takioullah (MAR)—at 8 ft. 0.9 in. (246.3 cm), the world's second tallest living human—whose left foot measured 1 ft. 3 in. (38.1 cm) and his right 1 ft. 2.76 in. (37.5 cm) on May 24, 2011.

LONGEST FINGERNAILS ON ONE HAND The aggregate measurement of the five nails on Shridhar Chillal's (IND) left hand was 23 ft. 1.5 in. (7.05 m) on Feb. 4, 2004. His thumbnail was the longest, at 5 ft. 2.2 in. (1.58 m), and his index finger was the shortest, at 4 ft. 3.5 in. (1.31 m). Chillal stopped cutting his fingernails in 1952.

THE SKINNY ON WEIGHT LOSS

In 1955, we reported on a 31-in.-tall dwarf as the "thinnest human": "The lowest recorded human bodyweight was the 12 lb. [5.44 kg] of the Welshman, Hopkin Hopkins, at his death in Glamorganshire in March 1754. At no time in his 17 years of life did he attain a weight of more than the 17 lb. [7.7 kg] he was at 14 years."

The record, since retitled **lightest person** and now open only to adults aged 18 or older, is held by 26.37-in.-tall Lucia Xarate (aka Lucia Zarate, MEX, 1863–89), whose adult weight peaked (at 20 years old) at 13 lb.

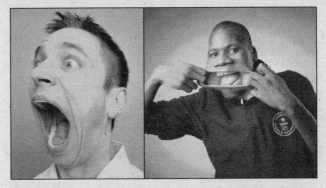

LARGEST GAPE A mouth gape stretches from the incisal edge of the maxillary central incisors to the incisal edge of the mandibular central incisors. J. J. Bittner (U.S.A., left) is able to open his mouth to a gape of 3.30 in. (8.4 cm). Meanwhile, Francisco Domingo Joaquim "Chiquinho" (AGO, right) has the **widest mouth**, measuring 6.69 in. (17 cm) on Mar. 18, 2010 in Rome, Italy.

LONGEST TONGUE Nick "The Lick" Stoeberl's (U.S.A.) lengthy licker measured 3.97 in. (10.10 cm) from tip to closed lip when examined in Salinas, California, U.S.A., on Nov. 27, 2012. The bank teller and stand-up comedian has been known to use his tongue, wrapped in plastic wrap, to paint artworks!

Fellow American Chanel Tapper has the record for the **longest tongue (female)**, measuring 3.80 in. (9.75 cm) when examined in California, U.S.A., on Sep. 29, 2010.

Tonsils The palantine tonsils (the lymphatic tissue at the back of the mouth) of Justin Werner (U.S.A.) measured 2.1 x 1.1 x 0.7 in. (5.1 x 2.8 x 2 cm) and 1.9 x 1 x 0.7 in. (4.7 x 2.6 x 2 cm). They were removed at the ExcellENT Surgery Center in Topeka, Kansas, U.S.A., on Jan. 18, 2011.

MOST . . .

Tattoos Lucky Diamond Rich (AUS, b. NZ) has spent more than 1,000 hr. having his body modified. Lucky had a 100% covering of black inked over his existing tattoos and is now adding white designs on top of the black, and colored designs on top of the white.

Maria Jose Cristerna (MEX) is the **most tattooed woman**: she had a total body coverage of 96% on Feb. 8, 2011.

HAIR-RAISING: *Incredible Coiffures* Joining the GWR family in 2013 was Alan Edward Labbe (above left) of Waltham, Massachusetts, U.S.A., whose hairdo—measured at 5-ft. in circumference on Jul. 26—earned him a certificate for the **largest male afro**. Alan joins the likes of Eric Hahn (U.S.A., above right), whose 27-in. fan of hair was verified as the **tallest Mohawk** on Nov. 14, 2008, and Xie Qiuping (CHN, right), who has grown the **longest hair (female)**—her terrific tresses, last measured on May 8, 2004, stretch for 18 ft. 5 in.

HOLE AGAIN

Most piercings . . .

- **On a senior citizen (single count):** "Prince Albert," aka John Lynch (UK), 241, as of Oct. 17, 2008

- **In the tongue:** Francesco Vacca (U.S.A.), 16, as of Feb. 17, 2012

- **On the face:** Axel Rosales (ARG), 280, as of Feb. 17, 2012

Piercings (lifetime) Elaine Davidson (BRA/UK) had been pierced 4,225 times as of Jun. 8, 2006. She also received the **most piercings in a single count** with 462 in one sitting on May 4, 2000.

Rolf Buchholz (DEU) had the **most piercings in a single count (male)**, with 453 on Aug. 5, 2010. As of Dec. 16, 2012, Rolf had 516 modifications, including a split tongue, two subdermal horn implants, four ear expanders, and five magnetic fingertips in his right hand, making him the **most modified person**.

WIDEST TONGUE At its widest point, Byron Schlenker's (U.S.A.) tongue measures 3.26 in. (8.3 cm). Three separate measurements were made in New Hartford, New York, U.S.A., on Oct. 30, 2013—3.22 in. (8.2 cm), 3.30 in. (8.4 cm), and 3.26 in. (8.3 cm)—with the average taken as the final record value.

EXTREME BODIES

HEAVIEST TWINS Billy Leon (1946–79) and Benny Loyd (1946–2001) McCrary, alias McGuire (both U.S.A.), were average in size until the age of six. But by Nov. 1978, Billy and Benny weighed 743 lb. (337 kg) and 723 lb. (328 kg) respectively. Each brother had a waist measuring 6 ft. 11.8 in. (2.13 m) in circumference.

Kuwaiti citizens have the **highest body mass index**: 27.5 for men, 31.4 for women.

TALLEST LIVING PERSON At 8 ft. 3 in. (251 cm), Sultan Kösen (TUR) had feared that he might be too tall to find true love. But on Oct. 26, 2013, his dream of finding a soul mate came true when he married 5-ft. 9-in.-tall (175-cm) Merve Dibo in Mardin, Turkey.

LARGEST WAIST At his peak weight of approximately 1,200 lb. (544 kg), Walter Hudson (U.S.A., 1944–91) had a waist measurement of 9 ft. 11 in. (302 cm).

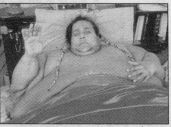

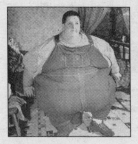

LARGEST CHEST MEASUREMENT Robert Earl Hughes (U.S.A., 1926–58) had a chest circumference of 10 ft. 4 in. (315 cm). In our first edition of 1955, he was listed as the **heaviest human**, with a weight of 946 lb. (429.6 kg), although when he was weighed shortly before his death he had reached 1,067 lb. (484 kg).

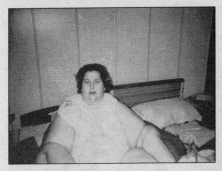

HEAVIEST WOMAN EVER Rosalie Bradford (U.S.A.) was claimed to have registered a peak weight of around 1,200 lb. (544 kg) in Jan. 1987. Although she had some success in controlling her size, it continued to be a problem throughout her life and she died from weight-related complications in Nov. 2006.

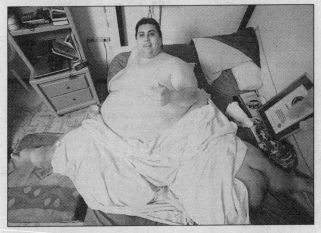

HEAVIEST LIVING MAN In 2006, Manuel Uribe (MEX) peaked in weight at 1,235 lb. (560 kg), but by Mar. 2012 he had slimmed down to 980 lb. (444.6 kg). He remains the heaviest living man weighed by GWR.

FACT: GWR discovered Manuel after he asked for help to lose weight on Mexican television.

FACT: The **heaviest man ever** was Jon Brower Minnoch (U.S.A., 1941–83), whose weight peaked at an estimated 1,400 lb. (635 kg).

SHORTEST LIVING WOMAN Jyoti Amge (IND) was measured at 2 ft. 0.7 in. (62.8 cm) on Dec. 16, 2011—her 18th birthday. She towers over the **shortest living man** (and **shortest man ever**), Chandra Bahadur Dangi (NPL), who was measured at 1 ft. 9.5 in. (54.6 cm) tall on Feb. 26, 2012.

SHORTEST WOMAN EVER Pauline Musters (NLD) was born in Ossendrecht, Netherlands, on Feb. 26, 1876, measuring 12 in. (30.5 cm). By the time she died of pneumonia with meningitis on Mar. 1, 1895 in New York City, U.S.A., at the age of 19, she had grown to only 2 ft. (61 cm).

TALLEST MAN EVER Robert Pershing Wadlow of Alton, Illinois, U.S.A., was listed as the tallest man in our first edition and his record has never been beaten. When last measured, on Jun. 27, 1940, he was 8 ft. 11.1 in. (2.72 m). He died less than a month later, on Jul. 15.

FAMILY MATTERS

Highest combined age for nine living siblings As of Jun. 24, 2013, the nine Melis siblings born to Francesco Melis and his wife Eleonora Mameli of Perdasdefogu, Italy, had an aggregate age of 828 years 45 days.

Largest family reunion On Aug. 12, 2012 at Saint-Paul-Mont-Penit in Vendée, France, 4,514 members of the Porteau-Boileve family came together for a truly great reunion.

Largest proportion of children Niger has the highest proportion of children, with 50% of the total population 0–14 years old in 2012.

The **smallest proportion of children** is that of the two Special Administrative Regions of China: Hong Kong and Macau. Just 12% of their respective populations were 0–14 years old in 2012.

MOST TWINS IN ONE ACADEMIC YEAR AT A SCHOOL A total of 24 pairs of twins were enrolled in fifth grade at Highcrest Middle School in Wilmette, Illinois, U.S.A., for the academic year 2012–13. That's eight more pairs than the previous record holders!

In Senegal, the average household has **8.9 family members**; in Germany, it's just 2.0.

> **FACT:** In Tudor and medieval England, the term "family" also included servants.

LONGEST MARRIAGE Herbert Fisher (U.S.A., 1905–2011) and Zelmyra Fisher (U.S.A., 1907–2013) were married on May 13, 1924 in North Carolina, U.S.A. They had been married 86 years 290 days at the time of Herbert's death.

Lowest birth rate In 2011, Germany had the lowest crude birth rate—the number of babies born per 1,000 people—with 8.1 births. In the same year, Germany had the 16th-largest population in the world, at 82.2 million.

As of 2011, Niger remained the country with the **highest birth rate** with 48.2 births for every 1,000 people.

Greatest number of descendants In polygamous countries, the number of descendants can become incalculable. In terms of documented cases, at the time of his death on Oct. 15, 1992, at 96 years old, Samuel S. Mast of Fryburg, Pennsylvania, U.S.A., was known to have 824 living descendants. The roll call comprised 11 children, 97 grandchildren, 634 great-grandchildren, and 82 great-great-grandchildren.

The last Sharifian Emperor of Morocco, Moulay Ismail (1672–1727), was reputed to have fathered a total of 525 sons and 342 daughters by 1703 and produced a 700th son in 1721. However, it is impossible for these figures to be fully verified.

Most prolific mother A total of 69 children were born to the wife of Feodor Vassilyev (1707–ca. 1782), a peasant from Shuya, Russia. In 27 confinements, she gave birth to 16 pairs of twins, seven sets of triplets, and four sets of quadruplets.

Most children delivered in a single birth Nine children were born to Geraldine Brodrick (AUS) at the Royal Hospital for Women in Sydney, Australia, on Jun. 13, 1971. All the children (five boys and four girls) died within six days.

On Jan. 26, 2009, Nadya Suleman (U.S.A.) gave birth to six boys and two girls at the Kaiser Permanente Medical Center in Bellflower, California, U.S.A.—the **most children delivered in a single birth to survive**. The babies were conceived with the aid of in vitro fertilization (IVF) treatment and were nine weeks premature when they were delivered by Cesarean section.

MOST EXPENSIVE WEDDINGS

A. Diana Spencer to Prince Charles, 1981, $110 m

B. Vanisha Mittal to Amit Bhatia, 2004, $66 m

C. Kate Middleton to Prince William, 2011, $34 m (estimated)

D. Coleen McLoughlin to Wayne Rooney, 2008, $8 m

E. Chelsea Clinton to Marc Mezvinsky, 2010, $5 m

F. Liza Minnelli to David Gest, 2002, $4.2 m

G. Elizabeth Taylor to Larry Fortensky, 1991, $4 m

H. Heather Mills to Paul McCartney, 2002, $3.6 m

I. Elizabeth Hurley to Arun Nayar, 2007, $2.6 m

J. Christina Aguilera to Jordan Bratman, 2005, $2.2 m

Source: Business Insider. *Figures adjusted for inflation.*

Heaviest birth Giantess Anna Bates (née Swan, CAN), who measured 7 ft. 11 in. (241.3 cm), gave birth to a boy weighing 22 lb. (9.98 kg) and measuring 2 ft. 4 in. (71.12 cm) at her home in Seville, Ohio, U.S.A., on Jan. 19, 1879. The baby died 11 hr. later.

Donna Simpson (U.S.A.) weighed 532 lb. (241 kg) when she delivered daughter Jacqueline in Feb. 2007, making her the **heaviest woman to give birth**.

Lightest birth The lightest birth for a surviving infant of which there is evidence is 9.17 oz. (260 g) for Rumaisa Rahman (U.S.A.), born at Loyola University Medical Center in Maywood, Illinois, U.S.A., on Sep. 19, 2004, after a gestation period of just 25 weeks 6 days.

Rumaisa was born with her twin sister Hiba, who weighed 1 lb. 4.4 oz. (580 g). Together, they hold the record for the **lightest birth for twins**, with a total weight of 1 lb. 13.57 oz. (840 g).

OLDEST FIRST-TIME GRANDMOTHER
Marianne Wallenberg (DEU, b. Feb. 7, 1913) was 95 years 81 days old when her first grandson, Joshua Fritz Wallenberg (CAN), was born at Sinai Hospital in Toronto, Ontario, Canada, on Apr. 29, 2008. Joshua's twin, Karina Diana, was delivered at the same birth.

RUNNING IN THE FAMILY The **most family members from multiple generations to complete a marathon** is eight, by the Shoji family (JPN, left) at the 40th Honolulu Marathon in Hawaii, U.S.A., on Dec. 9, 2012. The **most siblings to complete a marathon** is 16, by the Kapral family (U.S.A., right) in Appleton, Wisconsin, U.S.A., on Sep. 20, 2009.

HIGH DO: Tallest Married Couple On Aug. 4, 2013, Sun Mingming—the world's **tallest active basketball player**—and handball player Xu Yan (both CHN) were married in Beijing, China, generating speculation that they had become the world's **tallest married couple**.

On Nov. 14, 2013, Guinness World Records was able to confirm this as a record when the towering twosome were measured by doctors at the Oasis Healthcare Centre in Beijing in the presence of official adjudicators. Mingming and Yan reached 7 ft. 9 in. and 6 ft. 1.7 in. respectively, giving a record combined height of 13 ft. 10.7 in. and beating the previous record by 1.7 in.

FACT: The **tallest married couple ever recorded** in history was Anna Haining Swan (CAN) and Martin van Buren Bates (U.S.A.), whose combined height was 15 ft. 8 in. when they married in St Martin-in-the-Fields church in Trafalgar Square, London, UK, on Jun. 17, 1871. Anna later gave birth to the **heaviest baby** (see main text p. 162).

For more group records, see below.

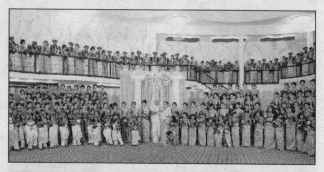

MOST BRIDESMAIDS TO A BRIDE Nisansala Kumari Ariyasiri (LKA) was attended to by a record retinue of 126 bridesmaids at her wedding to Nalin Pathirana at the Avenra Garden Hotel in Negombo, Colombo, Sri Lanka, on Nov. 8, 2013. Around 700 guests were also present.

Longest interval between birth of triplets
The greatest gap between the birth of a first and third triplet was 66 hr. 50 min. for the arrival of Christine, Catherine, and Calvin, children of Louise and Robert Jamison (all U.S.A.) in 1956. Christine was born at 3:05 A.M. on Jan. 2, Catherine was born at 10 a.m. on Jan. 3, and Calvin was born at 9:55 P.M. on Jan. 4.

Peggy Lynn (U.S.A.) gave birth to a girl, Hanna, on Nov. 11, 1995. Hanna's twin, Eric, was not delivered until Feb. 2, 1996—84 days later—at the Geisinger Medical Center in Pennsylvania, U.S.A.—a delay that represents the **longest interval between the birth of twins**.

Largest gathering of . . .
- **Multiple births:** 4,002 sets (3,961 pairs of twins, 37 sets of triplets, four sets of quads) amassed outside Taipei City Hall in Chinese Taipei on Nov. 12, 1999.
- **People born via IVF:** 1,232, by The Infertility Fund R.O.C. in Taichung, Chinese Taipei, on Oct. 16, 2011.
- **People born prematurely:** 386, by UNICEF in Buenos Aires, Argentina, on Sep. 30, 2012.
- **People with the same birthday:** 228 people, all born on Jul. 4, by Stichting Apenheul (NLD) in Apeldoorn, Netherlands, on Jul. 4, 2012.

MEDICAL BAG

First recorded lithopedion The 1582 autopsy on 68-year-old Madame Colombe Chatri (FRA) revealed an ossified child (lithopedion or "stone-child"). The fetus had died in pregnancy and was calcified by her body to prevent infection from the tissue.

First proven case of superfetation Superfetation is the conception of twins from two different menstrual cycles—and potentially different fathers. A 1980 case of disputed paternity of twins in Germany used genetic testing to establish the putative father of Twin Two with 99.995% probability, while excluding him as the father of Twin One.

Largest waiting mortuary German physician Christoph Wilhelm Hufeland (1762–1836) designed "waiting hospitals" to avoid burying the living. The largest of these was in Munich around 1880, and had room for 120 corpses. "Patients" were tied to an alarm system triggered by movement.

First safety coffin Duke Ferdinand of Brunswick-Wolfenbüttel (DEU) suffered from taphophobia (see p. 167). Ahead of his death in 1792, he ordered a coffin with a window, an air hole, and a lid that was unlockable instead of nailed down.

Faroppo Lorenzo (ITA) underwent the **longest voluntary burial** in a safety coffin, from Dec. 17, to Dec. 26, 1898. He was an assistant to the coffin's inventor, Count Michel de Karnice-Karnicki (RUS). It had a periscope-like tube reaching aboveground to let in air for the prematurely buried. Lorenzo said of his Christmas break that it had been "damned smelly down there."

Fig. 181

LONGEST HUMAN HORN There are many historical instances of humans growing large horns, usually from the head. Madame Dimanche (FRA), who lived in Paris, France, in the early 19th century, had a horn measuring 10 in. (25 cm) in length and 2 in. (5 cm) in diameter at the base.

The 14th-century outbreak of the Black Death killed up to **200 million** people.

First three-headed baby

In 1834, Dr. Raina and Dr. Galvagni (both ITA) described a stillborn, three-headed infant. This was the first reported instance of extreme conjoined twinning; one of the necks had two heads.

Longest human tail

Indian plantation worker Chandre Oram showed a tail measuring 1 ft. 1 in. (33 cm) in length to the world's media in 2008. Other notable cases include a 12-year-old boy in French Indochina who was said to have sported a 9-in. (22.8-cm) tail. In 1901, anatomist Dr. Ross Granville Harrison described a baby boy with a 3-in.-long (7.6-cm) tail that was examined by Harrison after amputation.

Most ascarides expelled

Ascarides are roundworm parasites that live in the small intestine. They sometimes appear by the hundreds, but in 1880, Dr. Fauconneau-Dufresne reported on the case of a Frenchman who had managed to expel around 5,000 ascarides in less than three years, largely through vomiting.

Most tapeworms expelled

It is possible for more than one tapeworm to exist in the body. In 1883, Dr. Aguiel described an unnamed patient who

expelled a 2-lb. 3-oz. (1-kg) lump containing 113 ft. 2 in. (34.5 m) of tapeworm. Three years later, Dr. Garfinkel saw a peasant with 238 ft. (72.5 m) of tapeworm with 12 heads.

LIGHTEST PERSON

Lucia Zarate (aka Xarate, MEX) weighed 2 lb. 6 oz. (1.1 kg) at birth and 4 lb. 11 oz. (2.1 kg) at the age of 17. By 1884, when she was 20, she weighed 13 lb. (5.9 kg). Born with a variant of dwarfism, she reached a height of 2 ft. 2 in. (67 cm).

TOP 10 CAUSES OF DEATH WORLDWIDE IN 2011

	Low-income countries	Lower-middle-income countries	Upper-middle-income countries	High-income countries	Number of deaths
Heart disease	7	43	55	24	129
Stroke	8	34	58	14	114
Respiratory infection	15	28	10	6	59
COPD*	4	23	21	6	54
Diarrheal diseases	10	22	2	1	35
HIV/AIDS	10	11	7		28
Trachea bronchus**	1	3	13	10	27
Diabetes	3	9	9	4	25
Road injury	3	9	10	2	24
Premature birth	6	12	2		20

*COPD is chronic obstructive pulmonary disease
**also includes lung cancers
Source: World Health Organization, 2013

These are the leading causes of death in 2011 in a representative sample of 1,000 people worldwide from the following groups:

- 141 from low-income countries
- 368 from lower-middle-income countries
- 322 from upper-middle-income countries
- 169 from high-income countries
- **Total deaths from these causes: 515**

FIRST DOCUMENTED ACCOUNT OF A PIG-FACED LADY Papers published by G. J. Boekenoogen (NLD) trace the legend of girls born with the face of a pig back to the 1630s. A Dutch print goes farther back, recounting the tale of a girl from 1621 who grew up to eat from a trough and talk in grunts. Such fanciful accounts were spread in pamphlets and ballads that were in general circulation during the 17th and 18th centuries.

SMALLEST WAIST Ethel Granger (UK, 1905–82) reduced her natural waist from 24 in. (56 cm) to 13 in. (33 cm) from 1929 to 1939 by wearing increasingly tighter corsets. The same measurement was matched by actress Mlle Polaire, aka Émilie Marie Bouchaud (FRA, 1874–1939).

FIRST RECORDED ASYMMETRICAL CONJOINED TWINS Lazarus Colloredo (ITA, b. 1617) had a parasitic twin complete with head and three deformed extremities growing from his chest. The twin was apparently considered to be a separate individual and was given the name Joannes Baptista. Lazarus toured to exhibit his twin, who displayed some reaction to stimulus, implying limited autonomous functionality.

LONGEST NOSE EVER Thomas Wedders (UK) was a traveling circus sideshow act in the 1770s, with a nose that was reputed to measure 7.5 in. (19 cm) long.

Most deadly outbreak of listeriosis

Sources differ, but somewhere between 47 and 84 people were killed in California, U.S.A., in the 1985 outbreak of listeriosis. It was caused by the bacteria listeria in cheese and, even at the lowest figure, it remains the instance with the highest number of fatalities. It is also the deadliest outbreak of bacterial food-borne disease in the U.S.A.

Oldest dwarf Hungarian-born Susanna Bokoyni of New Jersey, U.S.A., was 105 when she died on Aug. 24, 1984. Born in Apr. 1879, she was 3 ft. 4 in. (101.5 cm) tall and is one of two centenarian dwarfs on record. The other was Anne Clowes (UK), who died on Aug. 5, 1784 at the age of 103 and was 3 ft. 9 in. (114 cm) tall.

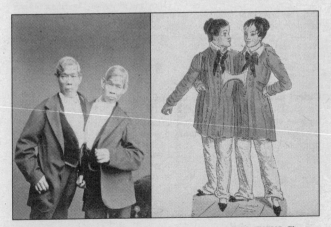

MOST CHILDREN BORN TO UNSEPARATED CONJOINED TWINS Chang and Eng Bunker (1811–74) were born in Thailand, then called Siam—the origin of the now-defunct term "Siamese twins." The two men fathered 21 children, the descendants of whom held their 24th annual reunion in Mount Airy, North Carolina, U.S.A., in 2013.

FACT: The decision to separate conjoined twins is not taken lightly, and many twins—such as Lori and George (below right) and Chang and Eng Bunker (p. 169)—opt to stay together. Complications arise when twins share vital organs. In the case of the Bunkers, their livers were fused; the procedure to separate them would be relatively simple today, but not so back in the 1800s, hence their decision to stay together.

TOGETHER: *Conjoined Twins* Masha and Dasha Krivoshlyapova (both USSR, left) suffered from *dicephalus tetrabra-chius dipus* (two heads, four arms, and two legs), a very rare form of conjoined twinning. They were born on Jan. 3, 1950 and, until their death on Apr. 17, 2003, were the **oldest living conjoined female twins**. The title then went to the craniopagus (joined at the head) twins born on Sep. 18, 1961 as Lori and Dori Schappell (both U.S.A., right). As of May 8, 2014 they were 52 years 232 days old. In 2007, Dori announced that he was transgender, identifying himself as a male called George.

Oldest ever male conjoined twins Giacomo and Giovanni Battista Tocci (ITA) were born on Oct. 4, 1877 and lived to be 63. They were separate above the waist, but shared an abdomen, pelvis, and two legs. Having made money from touring Europe and the U.S.A., they retired from public life.

RECORDMANIA

CONTENTS

LARGEST COLLECTION OF SOFT-DRINK CANS Davide Andreani's (ITA) mania for Coca-Cola cans began at the age of five, when he started collecting unfamiliar cans brought home by his father from European business trips. At the last count, confirmed on Aug. 14, 2013, Coke addict Davide owned a record 10,558 unique single-brand cans from 87 countries.

FACT: Most of Davide's cans are unopened. He empties them by piercing a hole in the bottom so the cans don't explode!

MR. VERSATILITY

No sooner had work started on the first edition of *The Guinness Book of Records* in London than a boy was born in New York City, U.S.A., who would go on to become the undisputed king of breaking records. His name was Keith Furman, but today he's better known by his spiritual name: Ashrita.

Mania: noun, from the Greek, *be mad*; an excessive enthusiasm or passion

That the man who holds the Guinness World Records title for **most Guinness World Records titles held** was born within a month of the company is a coincidence, but it's a joyous one. Keith Furman was born on Sep. 16, 1954. It would be 25 years before he set the first of many Guinness World Records, but he has achieved more in 36 years than most people could do in 10 lifetimes.

The manager of a health food store, Furman was given the name Ashrita—Sanskrit for "Protected by God"—by his spiritual teacher Sri Chinmoy (IND, 1931–2007), who taught him self-transcendence and meditation. Using these lessons, Ashrita set his first record in 1979—achieving 27,000 jumping jacks—and he hasn't looked back. As of May 1, 2014, he had set 521 records, of which 182 are still current.

Come with us on a journey through just some of the records set by Mr. Versatility . . .

ASHRITA . . . IN HIS OWN WORDS "My teacher's philosophy of self-transcendence—of overcoming your limits and making progress spiritually, creatively, and physically using the power of meditation—really thrills me. If you can connect with your inner source and be receptive to a higher Grace, you can accomplish anything.

"Attempting records has become an inherent part of my spiritual journey. I scour the *Guinness World Records* book looking for categories I think will be challenging and fun. Many of the records involve childlike activities, such as juggling, hopscotch, unicycling, pogo-sticking, and balancing objects on my head and chin. I get joy not only in practicing the activity itself, but also in seeing my progress toward achieving a goal. The particular event is unimportant as long as it gives you the opportunity to dance on the edge of your capacity."

1986 Most consecutive forward rolls: 8,341

1997 Farthest distance jumped on a pogo stick: 23.11 mi. (37.18 km)

FOR THE RECORD Ashrita set his 100th record on Sep. 24, 2005, **spinning the largest hula hoop**—16 ft. (4.8 m) in diameter—three times around his waist on the set of *Richard & Judy* in London, UK.

FURMAN'S FAVORITES

Ashrita has broken records on all seven continents, including the **fastest mile on a pogo stick** in Antarctica and the **fastest mile on a kangaroo ball (spacehopper)** along the Great Wall of China. Here, he picks his most memorable records.

Most consecutive forward rolls	8,341
Farthest distance with milk bottle on head	80.96 mi.
Pogo-stick jumping (in Mount Fuji foothills)	11.5 mi.
Underwater pogo-stick jumping (in the Amazon River)	3,647 jumps 3 hr. 40 min.
Fastest sack race mile (against a yak)	16 min. 41 sec.
Most jumping jacks—Ashrita's first record!	27,000
Pool cue balancing (at the pyramids, Egypt)	7 mi.
Fastest mile pushing an orange with nose	22 min. 41 sec.
Fastest 8 km on stilts	39 min. 56 sec.
Fastest 5 km skipped without a rope	30 min.

1998 **Farthest distance walked with a milk bottle on the head**: 80.96 mi. (130.3 km)

1999 **Farthest distance carrying a 9-lb. (4.08-kg) brick nonstop (male)**: 85.05 mi. (136.87 km)

2003 **Fastest marathon skipping (no rope)**: 5 hr. 55 min. 13 sec.

2004 **Fastest mile while hula-hooping**: 14 min. 25 sec.

2004 **Fastest time to walk 8 km on stilts**: 39 min. 56 sec.

2006 Fastest mile spinning a whip top: 25 min. 13 sec.

2007 Farthest distance jumped underwater on a pogo stick: 1,680 ft. (512.06 m)

2007 Most skips on spring-loaded stilts in one minute: 106

	Record set then later lost	Still holds record			Record set then later lost	Still holds record
1979	1	0		1997	3	0
1980	1	0		1998	3	2
1981	2	0		1999	1	2
1982	1	0		2000	1	1
1983	2	0		2001	4	3
1984	0	0		2002	8	0
1985	0	0		2003	4	1
1986	3	1		2004	6	3
1987	6	1		2005	12	0
1988	3	0		2006	30	7
1989	6	0		2007	30	11
1990	2	0		2008	36	8
1991	4	0		2009	45	9
1992	3	0		2010	26	27
1993	4	0		2011	40	24
1994	4	0		2012	23	38
1995	3	0		2013	18	37
1996	3	0		2014	0	7

Current as of May 1, 2014

2007 Fastest mile on a pogo stick while juggling three balls: 23 min. 28 sec.

2008 Fastest mile on stilts: 12 min. 23 sec.

2009 Fastest mile balancing a book on the head: 8 min. 27 sec.

2009 Fastest 10 m balancing a pool cue on the chin: 3.02 sec.

2010 Longest duration juggling three objects underwater: 1 hr. 19 min. 58 sec.

2010 Fastest one-mile piggy-back race: 12 min. 47 sec.

2010 Longest control of a golf ball with one club: 1 hr. 20 min. 42 sec.

2010 Fastest 100 m frog jumping: 7 min. 18 sec.

2011 **Most baseballs held in a glove:** 24

2011 **Most apples snapped in one minute:** 40

2012 **Longest duration balancing a chain saw on the chin:** 1 min. 25.01 sec.

2012 **Fastest mile bounce-juggling three objects:** 7 min. 27 sec.

2012 **Fastest 5 km joggling in swim fins:** 32 min. 3 sec.

COLLECTIONS

These are the latest collections to be added to the GWR database:

Airline boarding passes Having flown with 90 airlines in 28 years, João Gilberto Vaz of Brasilia, Brazil, had saved 2,558 boarding passes as of Jan. 23, 2014. He flies an average of 91.35 flights per year.

Bagpipes Daniel Fleming of Cleethorpes in Lincolnshire, UK, owned 105 sets of playable bagpipes as of Oct. 24, 2013.

DOCTOR WHO *MEMORABILIA*

Ian O'Brien (UK) had acquired 1,573 unique items relating to everyone's favorite Timelord, as of Sep. 6, 2013, in his home in Manchester, UK. He started his collection in 1974 with a yellow Dalek (a Louis Marx toy) and received *The Dr. Who Annual* every Christmas. His personal favorites are a TARDIS console released by Dapol and a very rare nursery toy Dalek by Selcol.

JAMES BOND MEMORABILIA

Nick Bennett (UK) began his bond with Bond in 1995 and his collection of 12,463 items, as verified on Nov. 21, 2013, is now housed in a warehouse in Warrington, UK. The collection includes Roger Moore's shoes from *The Man with the Golden Gun* (UK, 1974), a unique 007 doll worth in the region of £10,000 ($16,000), and a speedboat from *Live and Let Die* (UK, 1973).

Coins from the same year Rahul G. Keshwani (IND) has 11,111 coins from the year 1989. The collection, made up of the defunct 25-paise coin, was verified on Jul. 28, 2013 in Mumbai, India.

Cookbooks Sue Jimenez (U.S.A./CAN) had 2,970 cookbooks as of Jul. 14, 2013 in Albuquerque, New Mexico, U.S.A.

Electronic calculators Gerhard Wenzel (DEU) has no fear of wrongly counting his collection of calculators—not with 4,113 examples to help add them up, as of Sep. 7, 2013, in Solingen, Germany.

There are an estimated **five million stamp collectors** in the U.S.A.

Ganesha-related items Ram and Lalita Kogata (IND) own 10,631 items relating to Ganesha, the Hindu god with the head of an elephant. Their collection was counted on Sep. 14, 2013 in Udaipur, Rajasthan, India. The couple also have the **largest collection of Ganesha statues**, with 2,930.

Gift cards (gift tokens) In 2007, teenage brothers Aaron and David Miller (U.S.A./CAN) wanted to make shopping with their mother more interesting, so they started to collect gift tokens. As of Aug. 30, 2013, they had amassed 3,215 different cards.

Horse-related items Equine enthusiast Edgar Rugeles (COL) had collected 2,762 models of horses, among other items of horse memorabilia, as of Aug. 26, 2013, in Bogotá, Colombia.

PIZZA BOXES When Scott Wiener (U.S.A.) orders a pizza, he's usually more interested in the box than the food. As of Oct. 23, 2013, the pizza buff—who has even written a book about his passion, *Viva La Pizza!: The Art of the Pizza Box*—had amassed a collection of 595 boxes from 42 different countries.

FAKE FOOD Plastic food replicas are a common sight in Japanese restaurants . . . and in the home of Akiko Obata in Sanbu-gun, Chiba, Japan. Obata's collection of 8,083 fake dishes—plus food-related keyrings, toys, and magnets—was verified on Jan. 24, 2014.

CHARACTER COLLECTIONS

Collection	Amount	Record holder	Date counted
X-Men	15,400	Eric Jaskolka (U.S.A.)	Jun. 28, 2012
James Bond (see p. 179)	12,463	Nick Bennett (UK)	Nov. 21, 2013
Winnie the Pooh	10,002	Deb Hoffmann (U.S.A.)	Sep. 14, 2013
Mickey Mouse	6,726	Janet Esteves (U.S.A.)	Nov. 11, 2013
Conan the Barbarian	4,670	Robert and Patricia Leffler (both U.S.A.)	Apr. 2, 2003
Hello Kitty	4,519	Asako Kanda (JPN)	Aug. 14, 2011
Trolls	2,990	Sherry Groom (U.S.A.)	Oct. 26, 2012
Donald Duck	2,775	Steffen Gerdes (DNK)	Jun. 27, 2012
The Simpsons (A.)	2,580	Cameron Gibbs (AUS)	Mar. 20, 2008
Batman (B.)	2,501	Kevin Silva (U.S.A.)	Oct. 25, 2013
Doctor Who (see p. 179)	1,573	Ian O'Brien (UK)	Sep. 6, 2013
Charlie's Angels (C.)	1,460	Jack Condon (U.S.A.)	Feb. 6, 2007
Superman	1,253	Herbert Chavez (PHL)	Feb. 22, 2012
Daleks	1,202	Rob Hull (UK)	May 14, 2013
Harry Potter	807	Jayne Gradel (U.S.A.)	Jun. 13, 2013

Keys Lisa J. Large of Kansas City, Missouri, U.S.A., owned 3,604 different keys as of Nov. 20, 2013.

Ozzy Osbourne memorabilia As of Oct. 18, 2013, Claus Solvig of Rødovre, Denmark, had acquired 1,811 items relating to heavy-metal legend Ozzy Osbourne.

COLLECT CALL: Anything Goes Guinness World Records has at least 169 collection categories for which a record has yet to be awarded. Now's the time to check behind the couch—perhaps you have the **largest collection of** . . . *Alice in Wonderland* memorabilia; Aloha (Hawaiian) shirts; autographed golf balls; autographed soccer memorabilia; baby bibs; baseball jerseys; basketball memorabilia; beauty pageant sashes; bedpans; boxed PC games; branded cans; Buddhist statues; camel-related items; candy canes; cleaning brushes; collie-related items; crotcheted items . . . Find out how to register your claim on p. xxix.

TOP 10 LARGEST CATEGORIES OF COLLECTIONS

1: Tobacco
4.65 million items

2: Human body
2.17 million items

3: Publishing
1.65 million items

4: Food and drink
1.45 million items

5: Clothing and accessories 806,698 items

6: Leisure, games, and hobbies 551,046 items

7: Travel
459,249 items

8: Stationery
381,101 items

9: Household
237,006 items

10: Animal
184,946 items

Total: **12,558,180** as of Apr. 22, 2014

MODEL MAKING

Largest toothpick sculpture Michael Smith (U.S.A.) used more than 3 million toothpicks to create "Alley," a 15-ft.-long (4.5-m) alligator that weighed 292 lb. (132.4 kg) when measured in Prairieville, Louisiana, U.S.A., on Mar. 22, 2005.

Largest display of toothpick sculptures A full miniature orchestra—comprising 62 musicians with their instruments, plus a conductor—was modeled by Go Sato (CAN) using 12,500 toothpicks and displayed in Ottawa, Ontario, Canada, on Jun. 18, 2013.

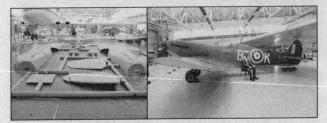

LARGEST MODEL AIRCRAFT KIT In the TV series *Toy Stories* (BBC, 2009), presenter James May (UK) took part in the construction of a model aircraft from a fully scaled-up Airfix kit, resulting in a 1:1 replica of a Supermarine Spitfire Mk1 with a wingspan of 36 ft. 9 in. (11.2 m) and a length of 29 ft. 11 in. (9.12 m). It was built at the Royal Air Force Museum Cosford in Shropshire, UK.

Airfix originally sold **inflatable rubber toys**; it didn't sell model-making kits until 1952.

LARGEST DALEK SCULPTURE Snugburys Ice Cream (UK) has made straw sculptures for over 10 years and, in 2013, built a 35-ft.-tall (10.6-m) Dalek. The sculpture, made in celebration of *Doctor Who*'s 50th anniversary, took 700 hr. to complete and used 13,440 lb. (6 metric tons) of straw and 11,200 lb. (5 metric tons) of steel.

TALLEST TOOTHPICK SCULPTURE Stan Munro (U.S.A.) created a model of the Burj Khalifa tower in Dubai, UAE, the world's **tallest building**. The 16-ft. 8-in.-tall (5.09-m) sculpture was measured at the Phelps Art Center in Phelps, New York, U.S.A., on Jun. 22, 2013. It took Munro around six months to make and includes approximately 250,000 toothpicks.

TALLEST MATCHSTICK MODEL A scale replica of the Eiffel Tower, built from matchsticks by Toufic Daher (LBN), stands at 21 ft. 5 in. (6.53 m) tall. It was unveiled at City Mall, Beirut, Lebanon, on Nov. 11, 2009, in celebration of GWR Day.

Also known as "baby houses," these dolls' houses date back at least to the 16th century. The early versions were usually replicas of grand houses of rich families instead of toys. By the 18th century, "doll cabinets"—miniature houses set in fine cabinets—were common. The Victorian era saw the birth of the dolls' house as we know it today: a beautifully crafted child's plaything.

MINI-MARVEL: *Queen Mary's Dolls' House* Built in 1921–24 by architect Sir Edwin Landseer Lutyens (UK) at a scale of 1:12, Queen Mary's Dolls' House includes plumbing, electricity, and a cellar stocked with drinkable wine. It is the **most visited dolls' house**, having been on display for many years at Windsor Castle in Windsor, UK, which attracted more than 9 million visitors between 2004 and 2013 alone. Its miniature library contains the **most works of literature made for a dolls' house**; the 206 unique literary works include a handwritten book of poetry by Rudyard Kipling and *How Watson Learned the Trick*, a story specially written by Arthur Conan Doyle.

Largest Plasticine model Martin and Nigel Langdon (UK) have spent thousands of hours since the early 1960s painstakingly modeling their ideal city with more than 500 lb. (226 kg) of Plasticine. The model, complete with Roman-style colosseum and American-inspired skyscrapers, now covers an area 15 ft. (4.5 m) long by 4 ft. (1.2 m) wide. The only things not made of Plasticine are the tree trunks, which are made of dyed matchsticks.

Largest matchstick model "Cathedrals of the Sea" is a North Sea oil production platform modeled from 4,075,000 matchsticks. It was made by David Reynolds (UK) and completed in Jul. 2009.

PIETRO D'ANGELO Since 2008, Italian artist Pietro D'Angelo has been creating a series of sculptures made from paper clips—all handmade in his own home. Created in 2008, Pietro's *Pole Dance* is the **tallest paper clip sculpture** in the world, stretching 7 ft. 5 in. Each sculpture takes Pietro two to three months to produce and includes 10–20,000 paper clips. The dextrous D'Angelo used iron paper clips at first, but now has stainless steel versions specially made for him by a paper clip factory.

Largest collection of military models Francisco Sánchez Abril (ESP) started collecting miniature military vehicles in 1958 and, as of Feb. 2012, had amassed 2,815 unique items representing the military might of 25 countries.

Largest model airport Knuffingen Airport, located at Miniatur Wunderland in Hamburg, Germany, is built to a scale of 1:87. The 494-sq.-ft. (45.9-m²) model is based on the international airport serving Hamburg, and took seven years to complete.

Fastest rocket-powered model car The Heathland School Rocket Car Club in Hounslow, UK, built "Möbius," a jet-propelled model car that reached an incredible speed of 204.95 mph (329.84 km/h) on Jun. 14, 2013.

Longest model train A model train measuring 925 ft. 6 in. (282.11 m) and comprising 31 locomotives and 1,563 carriages was constructed by the Wilmington Railroad Museum Model Railroad Committee. It was presented in Wilmington, North Carolina, U.S.A., on Apr. 23, 2011.

The **longest model train track** is the Great American Railway, which boasts a total of more than 9.5 mi. (15.2 km) of HO (1:87 scale) track. Built by Bruce Williams Zaccagnino (U.S.A.), it is the star exhibit at the Northlandz attraction in Flemington, New Jersey, U.S.A.

LARGEST SHIP IN A BOTTLE "Nelson's Ship in a Bottle" is a scale replica of HMS *Victory* contained within a giant bottle. The artwork was made by Yinka Shonibare MBE (UK) and measures 15 ft. 5 in. (4.7 m) in length and 9 ft. 2 in. (2.8 m) in diameter. It was originally displayed on the Fourth Plinth in Trafalgar Square, London, UK, in 2010.

LARGEST COLLECTION OF DIORAMAS A diorama is a 3D model of a landscape or scene containing numerous elements, and the largest collection on record is owned by Nabil Karam (LBN). Among his 333 dioramas— which were counted in Zouk, Lebanon, on Nov. 17, 2011— are famous battles, a train station, an airport, and scenes from classic movies.

Most model rocket kits launched simultaneously Boy Scout Jacob Smith (U.S.A.) launched 3,130 model rockets at the same time to commemorate the 100th anniversary of the Boy Scouts of America. The launch took place in College Station, Texas, U.S.A., on Oct. 9, 2010.

Smallest ship in a bottle In 1956, Arthur V. Pedlar (UK) constructed a ship inside a 1-cc glass phial measuring 0.9 in. (2.38 cm) long and 0.3 in. (0.9 cm) wide, with a neck of just 0.07 in. (0.2 cm). The galleon had three masts, five sails, and three flags.

Largest display of ships in a bottle Kjell Birkeland (NOR) owned a fleet of 655 model ships, as of Feb. 15, 2013. The bottled boats are displayed at the Arendal Bymuseum in Arendal, Norway.

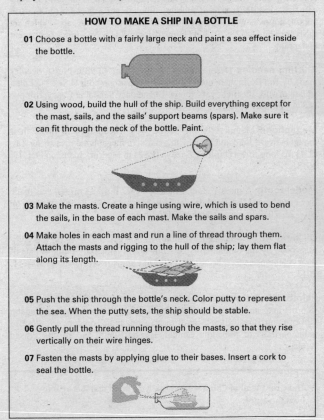

HOW TO MAKE A SHIP IN A BOTTLE

01 Choose a bottle with a fairly large neck and paint a sea effect inside the bottle.

02 Using wood, build the hull of the ship. Build everything except for the mast, sails, and the sails' support beams (spars). Make sure it can fit through the neck of the bottle. Paint.

03 Make the masts. Create a hinge using wire, which is used to bend the sails, in the base of each mast. Make the sails and spars.

04 Make holes in each mast and run a line of thread through them. Attach the masts and rigging to the hull of the ship; lay them flat along its length.

05 Push the ship through the bottle's neck. Color putty to represent the sea. When the putty sets, the ship should be stable.

06 Gently pull the thread running through the masts, so that they rise vertically on their wire hinges.

07 Fasten the masts by applying glue to their bases. Insert a cork to seal the bottle.

BIG STUFF

LARGEST . . .

Envelope Ajmal Khan Tibbiya College (IND) made an envelope measuring 58 ft. 7 in. (17.86 m) in length and 42 ft. 11.7 in. (13.10 m) in width in Aligarh, Uttar Pradesh, India, on Apr. 3, 2013.

Hot dog cart Marcus Daily (U.S.A.) built a 12-ft. 3-in.-tall (3.72-m) cart that, despite its size, is mobile, although at 23 ft. 2 in. (7.06 m) in length, it moves with difficulty. Marcus plans to turn the cart—which set the record on Oct. 28, 2013 in Union, Missouri, U.S.A.—into a permanent restaurant.

Knitting needles Despite being 13 ft. 0.75 in. (3.98 m) long, needles made by Jim Bolin were used by Jeanette Huisinga (both U.S.A.) to knit a square of 10 x 10 stitches at Monroe Elementary School in Casey, Illinois, U.S.A., on May 20, 2013.

Megaphone Members of the public were encouraged to make their thoughts heard loud and clear with a massive megaphone measuring 8 ft. (2.43 m) long. It was built by Bezoya (ESP) in Madrid, Spain, on Oct. 10, 2013.

Model tooth A massive molar measuring 27 ft. (8.23 m) tall was made by Sensodyne (MEX) and displayed in Mexico City's Parque México on Nov. 25, 2013 to raise awareness of tooth decay.

Oil lamp An oil lamp with a volume of 172.4 gal. (652.8 liters) was commissioned by the municipality of Almócita in Almeria, Spain, as part of their celebrations for The Night of the Oil Lamps festival held on May 11, 2013.

Paintbrush Indian artist Sujit Das made a paintbrush measuring 28 ft. (8.5 m) long and weighing 48 lb. 8 oz. (22 kg). It was used at Nagaon Government Boys' High School in Nagaon, India, on Jun. 19, 2012 to paint portraits of Mahatma Gandhi, Bhagat Singh, and Bishnu Prasad Rabha.

> The **Great Wall of China** is big—but it's a myth that it is visible from the Moon.

LARGEST FLOOR LAMP Fredrik and Martin Raddum (NOR) were the bright sparks behind a lamp measuring 30 ft. (9.16 m) high in Oslo, Norway, in Feb. 2013. The lamp shade is made of polyester and fiberglass and is 13 ft. (3.98 m) in diameter. The supporting pole is made of steel.

LARGEST SOCCER SHIRT The Nigerian national squad—the Super Eagles—had a shirt made by Guinness Nigeria plc. It measured 241 ft. (73.55 m) wide and 294 ft. (89.67 m) long in Lagos, Nigeria, on Jan. 25, 2013.

Paper aircraft It's one thing to make a paper plane with a wingspan of 59 ft. 9 in. (18.21 m); it's another to make it fly. Yet Braunschweig Institute of Technology (DEU) did just that in Braunschweig, Germany, on Sep. 28, 2013. Launched from an 8-ft.-high (2.47-m) platform, the aircraft flew 59 ft. (18 m).

Playing cards A pack of playing cards measuring 4 ft. 3 in. x 3 ft. 1 in. (1.295 m x 0.939 m) was unveiled by Viejas Casino & Resort in Alpine, California, U.S.A., on Sep. 12, 2013. The cards were played in a hand of

blackjack on the world's **largest blackjack table**—a fully functioning gaming table covering an area of 2,226.51 sq. ft. (206.85 m²)—made to celebrate the venue's 21st anniversary.

Mailbox A 2,418.49-cu.-ft. (68.484-m³) mailbox was erected by Yamaguchi University's Choshu Enjoying Science Innovation Project in Ube, Yamaguchi, Japan, on Dec. 27, 2012. A first-class effort all round!

LONGEST BOARD CUT FROM ONE TREE Daniel Czapiewski (POL) cut a board measuring 152 ft. 7 in. (46.53 m) in Szymbark, Poland, on Jun. 9, 2012. For more from Daniel, see Big Orchestra on p. 194.

BIG NEWS

In 1955, we reported on the "most massive single issue of a newspaper yet published": a 490-page edition of *The New York Times* from Sep. 12, 1954. This has since been beaten by the Sep. 14, 1987 Sunday edition of *The New York Times*—a single issue that contained 1,612 pages. At a back-breaking 11 lb. 14 oz., it's also the **heaviest newspaper ever**.

LARGEST POSTER The boss of all posters is a poster to promote *Boss*, a 2013 Bollywood movie. It took 30 hr. to print and had an area of 34,814 sq. ft. (3,234 m²), longer than 12 tennis courts. It was made by Team Akshay (IND) and Macro Art Ltd (UK) and unveiled on Oct. 3, 2013.

LONGEST GOLF CLUB Karsten Maas (DNK) made a 14-ft. 5-in.-long (4.37-m) golf club and drove a ball 542 ft. 10 in. (165.46 m) at the Golf in Wall course in Wall, Germany, on Apr. 30, 2013. Karsten, who performs in his own trick golf shows, last set the record in 2009. Normal golf drivers are usually around 3 ft. 9 in.–4 ft. (1.14–1.22 m).

Sand castle Ed Jarrett (U.S.A.) became king of the (sand) castle with his 38-ft. 2-in.-tall (11.63-m) effort at Point Pleasant Beach in New Jersey, U.S.A., on Oct. 29, 2013.

Silver ring A 201-lb. 5-oz. (91.32-kg) ring made from 99.99% pure silver was made by Valentine Diamond (TUR). The ring, which has an inner diameter of 3 ft. (92 cm), was measured in Istanbul, Turkey, on Sep. 27, 2013.

> **FACT:** In Brazil, Santa Claus is known as Papai Noel. He comes through the window and hides presents in shoes left out for him.

LARGEST SANTA CLAUS Shopping Center Norte unveiled a Santa towering 65 ft. 7 in. (20 m) tall, 23 ft. (7 m) wide, and 13 ft. (4 m) deep in São Paulo, Brazil, on Nov. 7, 2013. It was estimated that up to 5 million shoppers would pass through the mall over Christmas to admire the styrofoam and fiberglass giant. Next to Santa was a wrapped present that itself stood 13 ft. (4 m) high.

LARGEST CLOTHESPIN Karl Josef Biller (DEU, pictured near left) devised a fully functioning wooden clothespin—just don't get your finger caught in it! It measured 11 ft. 5 in. (3.5 m) long and 2 ft. (65 cm) high, and was unveiled on Sep. 9, 2012 in Regensburg, Germany.

MAKING IT SUPERSIZE

"Big stuff" records typically require claimants to recreate a scaled-up version of a regular-size object, maintaining proportions where possible and using the same construction materials. Although guidelines may vary, we expect the supersize version to be functional—a giant pencil should still be able to write, for example, no matter how big!

Wooden spoon A traditional folk art spoon made by Centrul Cultural Mioveni of Romania measured 58 ft. 4 in. (17.79 m) long in Mioveni, Romania, on Jun. 7, 2013.

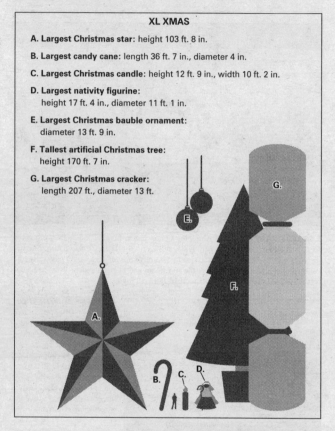

XL XMAS

A. Largest Christmas star: height 103 ft. 8 in.

B. Largest candy cane: length 36 ft. 7 in., diameter 4 in.

C. Largest Christmas candle: height 12 ft. 9 in., width 10 ft. 2 in.

D. Largest nativity figurine:
height 17 ft. 4 in., diameter 11 ft. 1 in.

E. Largest Christmas bauble ornament:
diameter 13 ft. 9 in.

F. Tallest artificial Christmas tree:
height 170 ft. 7 in.

G. Largest Christmas cracker:
length 207 ft., diameter 13 ft.

AND FINALLY . . .

- **Largest marquee:** 435,655 sq. ft., erected by Barrett-Jackson Auction Company in Scottsdale, Arizona, U.S.A., in Jan. 2014.

- **Largest spade:** 14 ft. 9 in. tall with a 3-ft. 1-in.-wide blade, by Rollins Bulldog Tools in Harlow, UK, on Sep. 27, 2013.

- **Largest flag (draped):** 1,097,682 sq. ft., by Moquim Al Hajiri in Doha, Qatar, on Dec. 16, 2013.

KNITTY GRITTY: Longest Scarf Helge Johansen (NOR) is no knit-wit: he's the proud creator of the world's **longest knitted scarf**. It's taken the nimble-finger Norwegian 30 years to knit his neck warmer to an incredible 14,978 ft.—long enough to stretch the entire length of Central Park in Manhattan, New York, U.S.A., or as long as 550 London double-decker buses. In order to measure his knitwear for Guinness World Records Day 2013, Helge unraveled his scarf—which he usually keeps in a ball (left)—in a sport center in Oslo, Norway, snaking the scarf in dozens of tight loops (center and right).

BIG ORCHESTRA

LARGEST ELECTRIC GUITAR Modeled on a 1967 Gibson Flying V, this 12:1-scale replica is 43 ft. 7 in. (13.29 m) tall, 16 ft. 5 in. (5.01 m) wide, and weighs 2,000 lb. (900 kg). It was made by Scott Rippetoe (U.S.A., above) and students from Conroe Independent School District Academy of Science & Technology in Texas, U.S.A. It was first played on Jun. 6, 2000, some seven months after work began.

> The word "orchestra" comes from the ancient Greek *orcheisthai*, meaning **"to dance."**

FACT: Pianos usually have 88 keys. This record-breaking behemoth has 156 of them!

LARGEST PIANO Constructed by Daniel Czapiewski (POL, above), this very grand piano is 8 ft. 2 in. (2.49 m) wide, 19 ft. 10 in. (6.07 m) long, and 6 ft. 3 in. (1.9 m) high. It was played at a concert in the village of Szymbark, Poland, on Dec. 30, 2010. Sadly, Daniel—a gifted woodworker and friend of GWR—died on Dec. 3, 2013.

LARGEST ACCORDION This 8-ft. 3-in.-tall (2.53-m), 6-ft. 2-in.-wide (1.9-m), and 2-ft. 9-in.-deep (85-cm) squeeze-box weighs about 440 lb. (200 kg). Built by Giancarlo Francenella (ITA, left, with his daughter Laura), the instrument is named "Fisarmonica Gigante" and was completed in 2001.

LONGEST ALPHORN Seven months in the making, "Corno vivo Oli" is 86 ft. 9 in. (26.46 m) long and weighs 203 lb. 14 oz. (92.5 kg). It was made by the Rottumtaler Alphornbläser (DEU) out of a single Douglas fir and was presented and measured in Bellamont, Germany, on Sep. 16, 2012.

LARGEST DRUM KIT The Drumartic (AUT) percussion group's kit list includes a bass drum at 9 ft. 6 in. (2.9 m), a floor tom at 6 ft. 11 in. (2.11 m), and a rack tom at 5 ft. 2 in. (1.57 m). The hi-hat cymbals are 5 ft. 8 in. (1.73 m) wide. Their huge creation is called Big Boom.

LARGEST SAXOPHONE With a tube length of 22 ft. 1 in. (6.74 m) and a bell diameter of 1 ft. 3 in. (39.1 cm), this supersize sax was created by J'Élle Stainer (BRA) for the company Below65-4hz.com (ITA) to mark the 200th anniversary of Adolphe Sax. It stands 8 ft. 11 in. (2.74 m) tall, weighs 63 lb. 0.8 oz. (28.6 kg), and was measured in Cerveteri, Italy, on Aug. 3, 2013. Right, project coordinator Gilberto Lopes tries it out.

LARGEST VIOLIN Created by the Vogtland masters of making violins and bows (DEU), this giant violin is 14 ft. (4.27 m) long, has a maximum width of 4 ft. 7 in. (1.4 m), and is played with a 17-ft.-long (5.2-m) bow.

MOST PIECES IN A DRUM KIT In terms of individual elements, the largest drum set belongs to Dr. Mark Temperato (U.S.A., left) and comprises 813 pieces. They were counted in Lakeville, New York, U.S.A., on Mar. 21, 2013. It takes a team of four people more than 20 hr. to set up this colossal kit, and around 45 minutes to hit every piece of percussion in it. Beat that!

FUN WITH FOOD

Fastest field-to-oven-cooked loaf Australian farmer Neil Unger had long wanted to take the "paddock-to-plate" challenge. The record had stood unbroken since 1999, but with a team of assistants he took wheat from a field to produce 13 loaves of bread (a "baker's dozen") in 16 min. 30.83 sec. The feat took place in Cawdor, New South Wales, Australia, on Jan. 11, 2013.

Fastest time to eat a bowl of pasta Furious Pete, aka Peter Czerwinski (CAN, pictured below), ate a bowl of pasta in 41 sec. on the set of *Abenteuer Leben* (Kabel eins) in Sankt Peter-Ording, Germany, on Jul. 13, 2013.

FASTEST TIME TO EAT THREE ÉCLAIRS Furious Pete demolished three chocolate éclairs in 18.02 sec. at MEATMarket in Covent Garden, London, UK, on Jul. 10, 2013. That day he also set a gastronomic record for the **most hamburgers eaten in one minute**, with four. Fans follow his antics on YouTube, with his videos having notched up more than 115 million views by Feb. 1, 2014.

Americans eat **68 quarts of popcorn** a year—enough to fill a bathtub!

Fastest time to crush 10 eggs: 12.64 sec., Mauro Vagnini (ITA), Milan, Italy, Apr. 28, 2011

Most standing jumps onto raw eggs without breaking them: nine, Lan Guangping (CHN), Beijing, China, Sep. 9, 2013

Most eggs held in one hand: 27, Silvio Sabba (ITA), Milan, Italy, May 19, 2013

FASTEST TIME TO DRINK ONE LITER OF LEMON JUICE Michael Jenkins (U.S.A.) won a three-way, head-to-head challenge by drinking a liter of lemon juice through a straw in a record time of 54.1 sec. in Los Angeles, California, U.S.A., on Jun. 20, 2013, beating the next fastest time by 10 sec.

Fastest time to eat a jam doughnut with no hands Oli White (UK) used no hands and didn't lick his lips as he hoovered up a jam doughnut in 28.75 sec. at Alexandra Palace in London, UK, on Aug. 17, 2013. It was the third time in the space of a year that the GWR YouTube presenter managed to break the record.

MOST . . .

Bananas sliced with a sword on a slackline in one minute A slackline is similar in looks to a tightrope, but it is slung much closer to the ground. Veteran record breaker Ashrita Furman (U.S.A.) balanced on a slackline as he was thrown 36 bananas, each of which he cut in two in New York, U.S.A., on Aug. 3, 2013.

Chile	Scoville rating
Peperoncini	100–500
Jalapeño	2,500–5,000
Cayenne	30,000–50,000
Tabasco	
Scotch bonnet	80,000–300,000
Bhut Jolokia	800,000–1.04 million
Naga viper	1.38 million
Carolina reaper (pictured left)	1.56 million (the **hottest chile**)

SPICE UP YOUR LIFE: The Scoville Scale We have American chemist Wilbur Scoville to thank for the scale that rates the chiles we chomp. In 1912, long before high-pressure liquid chromatography tests in labs, he relied on taste alone. A grain of chile was dissolved in an alcoholic solution added to sweetened water until it could barely be noted by a panel of testers. The more dilution required, the higher the rating. See above for some ratings from the scale still used—although technology has replaced tasters.

MOST BHUT JOLOKIA CHILE PEPPERS EATEN IN TWO MINUTES The Bhut Jolokia, or ghost chile, rates at approximately 1,000,000 on the Scoville scale (see above). On Jun. 19, 2013, Jason McNabb (U.S.A.) ate 2.33 oz. (66 g) of these chiles—more than 13 whole peppers—in Los Angeles, California, U.S.A.

FACT: Ghost peppers can burn bare skin, so always wear latex gloves if handling.

> **FACT:** Sabering a bottle of champagne was popular during the Napoleonic Wars. The bottle is held at about 20 degrees and the saber used to crack the collar; the pressure in the bottle then sends the top flying off.

Champagne bottles sabered in one minute

"Sabrage" is a technique used to open champagne by holding the bottle at an angle and sliding a saber (sword) up the neck deftly enough to slice off the collar and cork. On Sep. 8, 2013, Mitchell Ancona (U.S.A.) sabered open 34 bottles in a minute in Ridgefield, Connecticut, U.S.A.

The **most champagne bottles sabered at once** is 277, by Centro Empresarial e Cultural de Garibaldi in Rio Grande do Sul, Brazil, on Oct. 5, 2013.

Using the conventional method of opening, UK TV chef Gino D'Acampo (ITA) recorded the **most champagne corks popped in one minute**, with seven on Jul. 29, 2013.

Cream-filled sponge cakes eaten in one minute

Competitive eater Patrick Bertoletti (U.S.A.) put away 16 creamy sponge delights in Los Angeles, U.S.A., on Jun. 26, 2013.

Eggs held unbroken on a roller coaster

Özgür Tuna held 110 eggs in a basket while Udo Baron (both DEU) gave him advance warning of the roller coaster turns. The pair were at Europa-Park in Rust, Germany, on Jun. 21, 2013.

MOST BITES IN ONE MINUTE WHILE JUGGLING APPLES Entertainer and juggler Michael Goudeau (U.S.A.) took 151 bites from three apples while juggling for 1 min. on the set of *Guinness World Records Unleashed* in Los Angeles, California, U.S.A., on Jun. 20, 2013.

MOST PANCAKES MADE IN ONE HOUR Ross McCurdy (U.S.A.) singlehandedly made 1,092 pancakes in Kingston, Washington, U.S.A., on Aug. 13, 2013.

The **most pancakes made in eight hours by a team** is 76,382, by Batter Blaster (U.S.A.) on May 9, 2009.

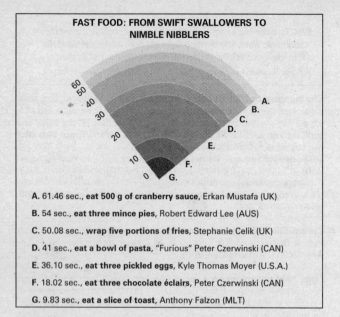

FAST FOOD: FROM SWIFT SWALLOWERS TO NIMBLE NIBBLERS

A. 61.46 sec., **eat 500 g of cranberry sauce**, Erkan Mustafa (UK)

B. 54 sec., **eat three mince pies**, Robert Edward Lee (AUS)

C. 50.08 sec., **wrap five portions of fries**, Stephanie Celik (UK)

D. 41 sec., **eat a bowl of pasta**, "Furious" Peter Czerwinski (CAN)

E. 36.10 sec., **eat three pickled eggs**, Kyle Thomas Moyer (U.S.A.)

F. 18.02 sec., **eat three chocolate éclairs**, Peter Czerwinski (CAN)

G. 9.83 sec., **eat a slice of toast**, Anthony Falzon (MLT)

Hamburgers eaten in three minutes Takeru Kobayashi (JPN) ate 11 hamburgers in Istanbul, Turkey, on Jun. 5, 2013.

Ice cream scoops balanced on one cone Dimitri Panciera (ITA) balanced 85 scoops at a festival of ice cream in Zoppè di Cadore, Italy, on Jul. 21, 2013.

Most nuts crushed by sitting down in 30 seconds Cherry Yoshitake (JPN) crushed 48 walnuts using his buttocks at the Wakamiya Hachimangu shrine in Kawasaki, Kanagawa, Japan, on Jan. 15, 2013.

TRENCHERMEN: EATING TO EXCESS

A "trencher" was a medieval bowl carved out of a loaf of stale bread and, as the first edition of *The Guinness Book of Records* explained in 1955, "trencherman" was the name given to a glutton who enjoys food to excess, often setting records in the process. However, we went on to say that trenchermen records did not match "those suffering from the rare disease of bulimia (morbid desire to eat) and polydipsia (pathological thirst). Some bulimia patients have to spend 15 hr. a day eating, with an extreme consumption of 384 lb. of food in six days by Matthew Daking, age of 12, in 1743 . . . Some polydipsomaniacs are unsatisfied by less than 96 pints of liquid a day."

Mustard drunk in 30 seconds Denis Klefenz (DEU) consumed 10.37 oz. (294 g) from a tube of Kühne Senf Mittelscharf German mustard on Jun. 20, 2013.

Walnuts crushed by hand in one minute Not content with crushing 131 walnuts in his hand in 60 sec. on Dec. 10, 2012, Ashrita Furman went on to set another nutty record, for the **most walnuts cracked against the head in one minute**: 44, on Jan. 8, 2013. Both were set in New York, U.S.A.

BIG FOOD

LARGEST . . .

Bowl of apple sauce Musselman's Apple Sauce (U.S.A.) produced a bowl of apple sauce weighing 716 lb. (324.8 kg) at the Baltimore Running Festival in Maryland, U.S.A., on Oct. 12, 2013.

Cheesecake Philadelphia Cream Cheese (U.S.A.) created a cheesecake weighing in at 6,900 lb. (3,129 kg) in Lowville, New York, U.S.A., on Sep. 21, 2013. It measured 7 ft. 6.2 in. (2.29 m) in diameter, and 2 ft. 7 in. (78.7 cm) tall.

Chewing gum stick Japanese firm Lotte produced the biggest stick of chewing gum, in Sapporo, Hokkaido, Japan, on Oct. 5, 2013. It measured 3 ft. 6.7 in. (1.85 m) long, 11.57 in. (29.4 cm) wide, and 1.14 in. (2.9 cm) deep.

Chocolate mousse A mousse weighing 496 lb. 12 oz. (225.3 kg)—as heavy as three average men—was whipped up for charity at the Aventura Mall in Florida, U.S.A., on Oct. 6, 2012.

There are **more Indian restaurants** in London than in Mumbai and New Delhi combined.

LARGEST MACARON TOWER (left) Sebastien Laurent (FRA) created a 12-tier, 21-ft. 11-in. (6.7-m) display that comprised 8,540 macarons at Château de Montjoux in Thonon-les-Bains, France, on Jun. 8, 2013.

Cinnamon roll Weighing the equivalent of five adult women, the largest cinnamon roll tipped the scales at 609 lb. (276 kg) and was baked by the Second Floor Bakery in Holland, Michigan, U.S.A., on May 4, 2013. The roll measured 6 ft. (1.83 m) in diameter and was 7 in. (17.8 cm) deep.

Crab cake Made from fresh Maryland blue crab meat, the largest crab cake weighed 300 lb. (136 kg). It was made by Handy International Incorporated (U.S.A.) in Timonium, Maryland, U.S.A., on Sep. 1, 2012.

LARGEST PIZZA COMMERCIALLY AVAILABLE Big Mama's & Papa's Pizzeria's Giant Sicilian pizza measures 4 ft. 6 in. x 4 ft. 6 in. (1.37 x 1.37 m). Sold at six locations in Los Angeles, U.S.A., it's large enough to feed between 50 and 100 people. The outsize snack will set you back $199.99 plus tax.

> **FACT:** First made in Naples, Italy, pizzas originally used dough and tomatoes but no cheese.

HUMONGOUS HELPINGS

Most of the records on these pages are for one huge item of food. But in the table below, you'll find records for the largest overall servings—ordinary food served in extraordinary amounts.

What	Quantity	Who	Date
Baked potatoes	3,784 lb. 7 oz. (1,716.6 kg)	Comité Organizador de Fegasur (PER)	Jun. 9, 2012
Chili con carne (A.)	2,420 lb. (1,097.7 kg)	Chris' Dream Chili Team (U.S.A.)	Jun. 15, 2013
Dumplings	1,510 lb. 2 oz. (685 kg)	A Chang Meat Dumpling Restaurant (TPE)	Nov. 18, 2012
Fish and chips (B.)	105 lb. 4 oz. (47.75 kg)	Fish and Chips@ LTD (UK)	Jul. 30, 2012
Fries	987 lb. 10 oz. (448 kg)	Adventure Island (UK)	Jun. 29, 2011
Fruit salad	15,291 lb. (6,935.88 kg)	University of Massachusetts Dining Services (U.S.A.)	Sep. 2, 2013
Lobster (C.)	1,126 lb. 8 oz. (510.99 kg)	International Lobster Festivals, Inc. and San Pedro Fish Markets (U.S.A.)	Sep. 14, 2013
Mussels	10,798 lb. 3 oz. (4,898 kg)	Havfruen Fiskerestaurant (NOR)	Aug. 3, 2012
Papas rellenas	1,867 lb. 1 oz. (846.9 kg)	Municipality of Ventanilla, Sociedad Peruana Cebiche Más Grande del Mundo, and APRIEG (all PER)	Sep. 29, 2013
Pastries	39,550 pastries	2023 Metre Barış ve Kardeşlik Böregi (TUR)	Jun. 3, 2012

LARGEST SERVING OF DOUGHNUTS MEGA Alma-Ata shopping and entertainment mall in Almaty, Kazakhstan, fried up 1,470 lb. (667 kg) of *baursaks* (sweetened fluffy dough) on Nov. 2, 2013. A specially constructed wooden barrel was needed to hold the doughnuts.

LARGEST SAMOSA On Jun. 22, 2012, chefs and students at Bradford College in West Yorkshire, UK, cooked up a supersize Indian pastry weighing 244 lb. 4 oz. (110.8 kg) and measuring 4 ft. 5 in. (1.35 m) long, 2 ft. 9 in. (85 cm) wide, and 11 in. (29 cm) high. The team dubbed their world beater "Big Bertha."

LARGEST CHRISTMAS DINNER This 21-lb. 2-oz. (9.6-kg) festive feast for one comprises a turkey, carrots, parsnips, broccoli, cauliflower, roast potatoes, "pigs in blankets," and 25 Brussels sprouts. It was on the menu of The Duck Inn in Oakenshaw, UK, on Dec. 24, 2013.

FACT: This titanic turkey meal is free for anyone who can eat it—solo—within 45 min.!

Rocky road On Jan. 25, 2013, Australian confectionery company Darrell Lea created a "rocky road"—a chocolate, nut, marshmallow, and cookie candy bar—that weighed 575 lb. 13.5 oz. (261.2 kg).

Smoothie More than 3,200 bananas were liquidized by the Cabot Creamery Cooperative in New York City, U.S.A., on May 3, 2013 to make a 339.9-gal. (1,514-liter) smoothie—enough to fill at least 16 average bathtubs!

LONGEST . . .

Blood sausage Created in Burgos, Spain, during the city's year as the Spanish Capital of Gastronomy 2013, a blood sausage was measured at 576 ft. 5 in. (175.7 m). Weighing in at 465 lb. (211 kg), the *morcilla* was made by more than 450 volunteers, following the local recipe: pork, pork fat, horcal onion, bahia rice, lard, pork blood, spices, and salt, in a casing of tripe.

Cake roll Starting on Apr. 16, 2013, it took 66 pastry chefs from Japan's Kai Corporation two days to create a strawberry-topped cream sponge roll measuring 428 ft. 8 in. (130.68 m) in Tokyo, Japan.

Fruitcake A fruitcake measuring 1,651 ft. 4 in. (503.34 m)—as long as nine jumbo jets parked wing to wing—was made by Panaderia Schick at the Centro Comercial Managua in Nicaragua on Nov. 17, 2013.

BIG BURGER RECIPE

The Black Bear Casino Resort (U.S.A.) shares their recipe for the **largest hamburger**. You will need:

2,014 lb. beef (about 3.5 cows)	19 lb. pickles
52 lb. 8 oz. tomatoes	40 lb. American cheese
50 lb. lettuce	16 lb. 8 oz. bacon
60 lb. onions	

Cook the beef for 4 hr. on a 14-ft. 9-in. skillet, using a crane to flip the patty. Once it's done, add toppings and serve in a giant bun!

HAM-MADE: *Grow Your Own Burger* Professor Mark Post (center), a Dutch vascular biologist at Maastricht University in the Netherlands, demonstrated the **first laboratory-grown hamburger** during a launch event in London, UK, on Aug. 5, 2013. The *in vitro* meat—the first example of what its creator says could provide an answer to global food shortages and help combat climate change—was fried in a pan and tasted by two volunteers.

The result of years of research by Professor Post, the meat in the burger was made by knitting together around 20,000 strands of protein cultured from cattle stem cells in his lab. Post and his team are working to show that meat grown in petri dishes might one day be a true alternative to meat from livestock.

Garlic bread Etienne Thériault (CAN) created a stick of garlic bread 54 ft. 10 in. (16.71 m) long at École Ola-Léger in Bertrand, New Brunswick, Canada, on Jul. 6, 2013.

Hot dog A hot dog measuring 668 ft. 7 in. (203.8 m) was created by Novex SA in the city of Mariano Roque Alonso, Paraguay, on Jul. 15, 2011—long enough to fill 1,132 regular hot dog buns!

Ice cream dessert On Aug. 18, 2013, a 1,249-ft. 11-in. (380.97-m) line of ice cream scoops decorated with chocolate syrup, nuts, and sprinkles was served—in an array of (clean!) gutter pipes—by PGA National Resort & Spa and Luke's Ice Cream in Palm Beach Gardens, Florida, U.S.A.

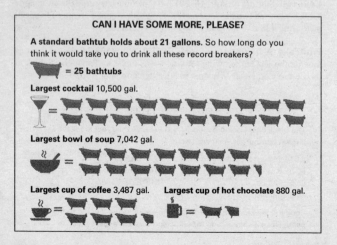

CAN I HAVE SOME MORE, PLEASE?

A standard bathtub holds about 21 gallons. So how long do you think it would take you to drink all these record breakers?

= 25 bathtubs

Largest cocktail 10,500 gal.

Largest bowl of soup 7,042 gal.

Largest cup of coffee 3,487 gal.   **Largest cup of hot chocolate** 880 gal.

CURIOUS CLAIMANTS

SIMON ELMORE Here's a record that really sucks! Britain's Simon Elmore managed to stuff 400 regular drinking straws into his mouth at once on Aug. 6, 2009. And, as per Guinness World Records guidelines, he held them in place for a full 10 sec. Unfortunately for Simon, he was two straws short of his personal goal, but he still did enough to earn himself the world record.

NATHAN DICKENS There was plenty of bizarre behavior on American TV when *Guinness World Records Unleashed* aired in 2013. Among the records established was the **most targets hit by blindfolded tennis serves in two minutes** (15), by the U.S.A.'s Nathan Dickens.

STEPHEN KISH A regular in the first series of the BBC's *Officially Amazing* TV show, "Sizzlin'" Stephen Kish (UK) bounced his way to a record for the **most table tennis balls bounced into a beer glass in one minute** (six).

You don't need to be **Usain Bolt or Edmund Hillary** to be a record breaker . . . luckily for this heroic lot!

28 Number of dice that Silvio stacked into a tower—using just his mouth—in a minute on Jul. 3, 2013.

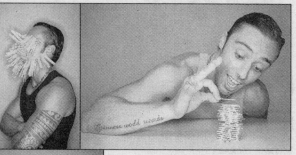

SILVIO SABBA With 48 current Guinness World Records to his name—all achieved in less than three years—Italy's Silvio Sabba is one of our most prolific claimants and king of the one-minute records. He's pictured here attempting the **most matchsticks stacked into a tower** (74), **most dice stacked using chopsticks** (44), and **most clothespins clipped to the face** (51).

MICHAEL PERICOLOSO Putting the "breaking" into record breaking is Michael Pericoloso (U.S.A.), who earned his certificate for the **most yardsticks broken over the head in one minute** (37) on *Guinness World Records Unleashed* in Jun. 2013. Ouch!

BRANDON KEE Ever heard the phrase "Don't shoot 'til you see the whites of his eyes"? It could've been coined for Brandon "Youngblood" Kee (U.S.A.), holder of the record for the **fastest time to hit five targets by squirting milk from the eye** (34.9 sec.). How does he get it there? He snorts it up his nose, then forces it out of his tear ducts. Eye caramba!

GARY DUSCHL The latest surveyor's report on Gary Duschl's (U.S.A.) epic **longest chewing gum wrapper chain** gives a total of 14.8 mi. (23.9 km)—that's almost 230 soccer pitches long! Gary has been linking gum wrappers since Mar 11, 1965, and as of Mar. 2014 has made 3,743,076 links to 1,871,538 wrappers.

JOHN CASSIDY When it comes to balloon-shaping, John Cassidy (U.S.A.) leaves the competition feeling deflated. John's records include the **fastest time to create a balloon dog sculpture** (6.5 sec.), the **most balloon sculptures made in one minute** (13), and the **most made in one hour** (747).

SHOW OF STRENGTH

Fastest time to pull a train over 20 meters using rice-bowl suction By pressing a bowl on his abdominal muscles, Zhang Xingquan (CHN) created enough suction to pull a train weighing 291,000 lb. (132 metric tons), with two drivers weighing 330 lb. (150 kg). It took him 1 min. 18.92 sec. to cover 20 m (65 ft. 6 in.) in Erlianhaote, Inner Mongolia, China, on Jul. 24, 2013.

Greatest weight lifted in one hour by kettlebell snatch On Dec. 23, 2013, Sergey Trifanov (BLR) lifted 66,165 lb. (30,012 kg) by snatching kettlebells at the State Technological University in Vitebsk, Belarus.

Most baseball bats broken with the back in one minute Matt Dopson (U.S.A.) was on the set of *Guinness World Records Unleashed* to snap 19 baseball bats over his back in Los Angeles, California, U.S.A., on Jun. 24, 2013.

Most wins of the Lumberjack World Championships Jason Wynyard (NZ) won the Tony Wise All-Around Champion title 15 times between 1999 and 2013. The nine events include standing chop, hot saw, springboard chop, and 60-ft. (18-m) speed climb. The World Championships are held annually in Hayward, Wisconsin, U.S.A.

The **most Lumberjack World Championships won by a woman** is nine, by Nancy Zalewski (U.S.A.). She won the title of Lady Jill (men are lumberjacks, women are lumberjills) in 2003–04 and 2007–13. The All-Around Lady Jill title is given to the woman who scores highest over the entire competition.

MOST SKILLETS ROLLED IN ONE MINUTE
Steve Weiner (U.S.A.) rolled 12 skillets, or frying pans, in Los Angeles, California, U.S.A., on Jun. 25, 2013. The **most skillets rolled by a female** is five, by Polish powerlifter Aneta Florczyk in Beijing, China, on Nov. 14, 2008.

Danish strong man John Holtum could **catch cannonballs** fired straight at him.

> **FACT:** Daniella's death-defying act includes a bed of nails, lying on broken glass, and charming snakes.

FASTEST TIME TO BREAK 16 CONCRETE BLOCKS ON THE BODY (FEMALE) Daniella D'Ville, aka Danielle Martin (UK), had 16 concrete blocks smashed on her body—one at a time—in 30.40 sec. with a sledgehammer wielded by fellow performer Johnny Strange (UK) at the Tattoo Jam in Doncaster, South Yorkshire, UK, on Oct. 12, 2013. Each of the slabs had a minimum density of 41 lb. per cu. ft. (650 kg/m³).

MOST APPLES CRUSHED WITH THE BICEP IN ONE MINUTE Mama Lou, aka Linsey Lindberg (U.S.A.), used muscle power to squash eight apples in Los Angeles, California, U.S.A., on Jun. 26, 2013. Once an accountant, she quit to be a performer and now blows up and pops hot water bottles and rips telephone directories in half.

HEAVIEST . . .

Boat pulled by a team of swimmers A team of 73 people organized by lifeguard association SLRG Luzern (CHE) pulled a boat weighing 712,534 lb. (323.2 metric tons) on Sep. 14, 2013 in Lucerne, Switzerland. They took 4 min. 34.72 sec. to pull the boat 328 ft. (100 m).

George Olesen (DNK) recorded the **heaviest boat pulled by an individual**. The boat was a ferry weighing 22.7 million lb. (10,300 metric tons) and he heaved it 16 ft. 8.8 in. (5.1 m) in Gothenburg, Sweden, in Jun. 2000.

For more physical feats, turn to p. 246.

Tire spun around the body As well as breaking records with ordinary hula hoops, Paul Blair (U.S.A.) has shaken his stuff with a tire weighing 116 lb. 10 oz. (52.9 kg). Paul, who performs as Dizzy Hips, set his latest record on Sep. 8, 2013.

Vehicle pulled with an arm-wrestling move Kevin Fast (CAN) challenged a truck to an arm-wrestling contest—and won! With his elbow on a table in an arm-wrestling position, the multiple record holder pulled a truck weighing 24,380 lb. (11,060 kg) in Cobourg, Ontario, Canada, on Apr. 26, 2013. Kevin also holds records for the **heaviest aircraft pulled by a man** (a Boeing C-17 Globemaster III weighing 416,299 lb.; 188.83 metric tons), and the **heaviest house pulled by a man** (79,145 lb.; 35.9 metric tons). You can also see him setting a new caber-tossing record on p. 231.

HEAVIEST WEIGHT LIFTED BY BEARD Antanas Kontrimas (LTU) used his beard to lift 141 lb. (63.8 kg)—in the shape of *Rekorlar Dünyası* presenter Gupse Özay'ın—in Istanbul, Turkey, on Jun. 26, 2013. It was his 10th consecutive successful attempt at a record he first set in 2000, when he lifted 122 lb. 11 oz. (55.7 kg).

GREATEST WEIGHT LIFTED

"The greatest weight ever raised by a human being," according to our 1955 book, "is 4,333 lb. (1.84 tons) by the 25-stone [350-lb.] French-Canadian Louis Cyr (1863–1912) in Chicago in 1896 in a back-lift (weight raised off trestles). Cyr had a 60½-in. chest and 22-in. biceps." Today, the fully notarized record stands at 5,340 lb. for two cars (plus drivers) on a platform backlifted by Gregg Ernst (CAN) in Jul. 1993.

PULLING VEHICLES

Heaviest road vehicle pulled by teeth: Igor Zaripov (RUS), double-decker bus weighing 27,249 lb. in London, UK, on Oct. 15, 2012

Heaviest train pulled by teeth: Velu Rathakrishnan (MYS), two trains weighing 287.4 tons in Kuala Lumpur, Malaysia, on Oct. 18, 2003

Heaviest vehicle pulled by nipples: "The Great Nippulini," aka Sage Werbock (U.S.A.), a wagon loaded with people weighing a total of 2,179 lb. 4 oz. in Milan, Italy, on Mar. 25, 2011

HEAVIEST VEHICLE PULLED OVER 100 FEET (FEMALE)

Lia Grimanis (CAN) dragged a 2014 International 8600 tandem axle cab weighing 17,820 lb. (8,083 kg) across a distance of 100 ft. at the Toronto Convention Centre in Toronto, Ontario, Canada, on Dec. 12, 2013.

HEAVIEST WEIGHT LIFTED BY PIERCED EARS Johnny Strange (UK) lifted a 32-lb. 13.5-oz. (14.9-kg) keg attached to a hook through his pierced ears in Doncaster, South Yorkshire, UK, on Oct. 12, 2013. Along with Daniella D'Ville (p. 211), Johnny performs as part of the Institution of Human Marvels.

Yoke walk over 10 meters The yoke is a metal bar carried over the shoulders with weights on either side. Patrik Baboumian (DEU, b. IRN) carried a weight of 1,224 lb. (555 kg) in Toronto, Ontario, Canada, on Sep. 8, 2013.

Weight lifted with one ear using a clamp Rakesh Kumar (IND) used an ear clamp to lift 182 lb. 1 oz. (82.6 kg) in Istanbul, Turkey, on Jul. 25, 2013.

Vehicle pulled with ears (female) On Jun. 20, 2013, Asha Rani (IND) used both ears to pull a 3,745-lb. (1,700-kg) van in Leicestershire, UK. Back in Aug. 2012, she had pulled a double-decker bus—at 26,678 lb. (12,101 kg), the **heaviest vehicle pulled by a woman using her hair**—a distance of 56 ft. 5 in. (17.2 m).

GYM KING: *Endurance Weightlifter* Eamonn Keane (IRL) holds 22 records, as of Mar. 2014, for endurance weightlifting. The champion lifter's most recent feat was the **most weight lifted by incline dumbbell flies in one minute** (in which dumbbells are held in each hand on an incline bench before bringing them together over the chest), with 4,761 lb. in Louisburgh, Ireland, on Oct. 16, 2013. His oldest record still standing dates back to 2003: the **heaviest weight lifted in one hour by bench press**, an astonishing 305,300 lb. He did 1,280 repetitions with 200 lb. and 493 reps with 100 lb.

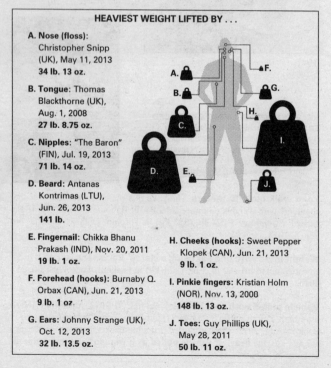

HEAVIEST WEIGHT LIFTED BY . . .

A. Nose (floss): Christopher Snipp (UK), May 11, 2013 **34 lb. 13 oz.**

B. Tongue: Thomas Blackthorne (UK), Aug. 1, 2008 **27 lb. 8.75 oz.**

C. Nipples: "The Baron" (FIN), Jul. 19, 2013 **71 lb. 14 oz.**

D. Beard: Antanas Kontrimas (LTU), Jun. 26, 2013 **141 lb.**

E. Fingernail: Chikka Bhanu Prakash (IND), Nov. 20, 2011 **19 lb. 1 oz.**

F. Forehead (hooks): Burnaby Q. Orbax (CAN), Jun. 21, 2013 **9 lb. 1 oz.**

G. Ears: Johnny Strange (UK), Oct. 12, 2013 **32 lb. 13.5 oz.**

H. Cheeks (hooks): Sweet Pepper Klopek (CAN), Jun. 21, 2013 **9 lb. 1 oz.**

I. Pinkie fingers: Kristian Holm (NOR), Nov. 13, 2000 **148 lb. 13 oz.**

J. Toes: Guy Phillips (UK), May 28, 2011 **50 lb. 11 oz.**

FLEXIBLE FRIENDS

Fastest escape from a straitjacket Sofia Romero (UK) freed herself from a regulated Posey straitjacket in 4.69 sec. at the Aylestone Leisure Centre in Leicester, UK, on Jun. 9, 2011.

The **fastest escape from a straitjacket and chains while suspended** is 10.6 sec. and was achieved by Lucas Wilson (CAN) at Holy Trinity Catholic High School in Simcoe, Ontario, Canada, on Jun. 8, 2012.

Wilson also recorded the **fastest escape from a straitjacket underwater**—23.16 sec.—at École St. Patrick high school in Yellowknife, Northwest Territories, Canada, on Oct. 5, 2013.

Most people belly dancing simultaneously
Danone Canarias (ESP) organized a mass belly dance that involved 842 performers at Playa de Las Canteras in Las Palmas, Gran Canaria, Spain, on May 29, 2011.

LONGEST TIME TO HOLD THE MARINELLI BEND POSITION
This extraordinarily demanding position requires the performer to sustain his or her entire body weight via a mouth grip on a short pole. Tsatsral Erdenebileg (MNG) maintained a Marinelli bend for 4 min. 17 sec. on the set of *Rekorlar Dünyası* in Istanbul, Turkey, on Jul. 17, 2013.

Overall, **women are more flexible** than men of the same age.

FASTEST TIME TO CRAM INTO A BOX (MALE) Mr. Yogi Laser, aka Kenneth Greenaway (U.S.A.), took 5.35 sec. to squeeze into a box measuring 20 x 20 x 17.5 in. (50.8 x 50.8 x 44.4 cm) in California, U.S.A., on Jun. 27, 2013. The **fastest time to cram into a box (female)**—a space of just 20.4 x 17.7 x 17.7 in. (52 x 45 x 45 cm)—is 4.78 sec., by Skye Broberg (NZ) on Sep. 15, 2011.

YOGA

Longest yoga chain A chain of 696 students from the CK School of Practical Knowledge (IND) formed a yoga chain in Cuddalore, India, on Jan. 30, 2013. They performed five different yoga poses, including: Cow's Face (Gomukhasana), Child's (Balasana), Half Lotus (Padmasana), and Easy Seated (Sukhasana).

Longest yoga marathon (female) During a 32-hr. marathon, Yasmin Fudakowska-Gow (CAN) completed 1,008 yoga positions at Om West Centre Holistique in Quebec, Canada, on Aug. 2–3, 2010.

The **longest yoga marathon (male)** lasted 29 hr. 4 min. and was achieved by Michael Schwab (AUT) in Vienna, Austria, on Sep. 26–27, 2009.

SUPPLE DIFFERENCE

Babies have a greater amount of soft cartilage than bone. In time, however, much of it hardens into bone—which is why adults are so much less flexible than babies.

ACROBATICS

Longest backflip Lukas Steiner (AUT) carried out a 13-ft. 11.7-in. (4.26-m) backflip in Milan, Italy, on Apr. 28, 2011.

Steiner also recorded the **longest jump from feet to handstand (male)**. From a standing start, he leaped 8 ft. 4.39 in. (2.55 m), landed on his hands, and pressed himself into a handstand, held for 5 sec. The attempt was undertaken in Mittweida, Germany, on Nov. 10, 2011.

On May 24, 2010, Chase Armitage (UK) performed the **longest backflip off a wall**, measuring 11 ft. 5 in. (3.48 m), for *Zheng Da Zong Yi – Guinness World Records Special* in Beijing, China.

The **most backflips against a wall in one minute** is 29, by Miguel Marquez (ESP) for the same TV series in Beijing, China, on Jun. 19, 2009.

MOST HULA HOOPS SPUN SIMULTANEOUSLY AROUND THE WAIST (TEAM) Marawa the Amazing (AUS) and her Majorettes whirled into the record books by spinning 264 hula hoops at once at the Shaftesbury Theatre in London, UK, on Nov. 14, 2013, in celebration of Guinness World Records Day. For more Marawa, spin over to p. 234.

MOST JACKHAMMER HOPS IN ONE MINUTE Bryan Nguyen (U.S.A.) performed 49 jackhammer hops—a staple break-dancing move—in a minute on the set of *Guinness World Records Unleashed* in Los Angeles, California, U.S.A., on Jun. 19, 2013. The guidelines require that the hand leaves the ground on each hop.

FARTHEST ARROW SHOT USING FEET Nancy Siefker (U.S.A.) shot an arrow into a target 20 ft. (6.09 m) away using only her feet on the set of *Guinness World Records Unleashed* in Los Angeles, California, U.S.A., on Jun. 20, 2013. The guidelines require that the target should be no more than 12 in. (30 cm) in diameter. However, Nancy, a circus performer, hit a target measuring just 5.5 in. (13.9 cm).

Most circular jumps on a wall in one minute

To make a circular jump, performers use only their hands to spin the body 360 degrees against a wall. On Mar. 24, 2010, Aung Zaw Oo (U.S.A.) carried out 11 circular jumps on a wall in Rome, Italy.

Longest forward-jump flip/somersault

Hasit Savani (UK) achieved a 19-ft. 7-in. (6-m) forward-jump flip at Talacre Community Sports Centre in London, UK, on Feb. 15, 2012.

Most forward-roll front flips in one minute

Mathew Kaye (UK) managed 17 forward-roll front flips in a minute at Parkour Park in Chineham, Hampshire, UK, on Sep. 8, 2010. On the same day, he also recorded the **most pistol squats on a scaffold pole in one minute**, with 29. A pistol squat is a bodyweight squat done on one leg to full depth. Mathew can be seen performing parkour in Coldplay's video for "Charlie Brown" (2011).

Oldest person to perform a backflip

Walter Liesner (DEU, b. Jan. 14, 1913) was 94 years 268 days old when he backflipped into a swimming pool in Wetzlar, Germany, on Oct. 9, 2007. Walter, a part-time gymnastics teacher for most of his life, shot to local fame at the age of 17 when he performed a handstand on the handrail at the top of the Wetzlar church tower, 137 ft. (42 m) above the ground.

GLOSSARY

Parkour: The discipline of moving rapidly through a typically urban environment by means of performing acrobatic feats such as jumping, climbing, and flipping to negotiate obstacles. It began in France and was popularized by David Belle and Sébastien Foucan. Parkour practitioners are known as "traceurs"; they "trace" their way through their environment.

LARGEST ACTIVITY EVENTS

Largest aerobics display:
50,420 participants,
Aug. 15, 2011

Largest yoga class:
29,973 students,
Nov. 19, 2005

Largest dance class:
9,223 participants, Apr. 30, 2010

Largest Zumba class:
6,671 participants, Sep. 15, 2012

Largest pilates class:
3,486 participants, Jun. 2, 2013

Largest limbo dance:
1,208 children, Oct. 1, 2011

☝ = **1,000 participants**

JOINT SESSION: Pros and Cons of Hypermobility People with extreme flexibility are often said to be double-jointed or even triple-jointed. There is disagreement about the accuracy of these terms, however, and some scientists prefer the term "hypermobility" to describe unusually unrestricted joint movements. For dancers or gymnasts, such flexibility can improve performance, but it can also give rise to problems, including dislocation of the joints, back pain, and damage to soft tissue. Superflexibility, however, can be helpful to contortionists such as Zlata, aka Julia Gunthel (DEU, above left, **fastest time to burst three balloons with the back**: 12 sec.), and Daniel Browning Smith (U.S.A., above right), who achieved the **fastest time to enter a locked straitjacket** (2 min. 8 sec.) on Aug. 16, 1999.

FACT: U.S. gymnast George Eyser won six medals at the 1904 Olympics—despite his wooden leg.

PERFORMERS

Farthest distance walked balancing a lawn mower on the chin
Multiple record holder The Space Cowboy, aka Chayne Hultgren (AUS),
walked 93 ft. 2 in. (28.4 m) with an unpowered lawn mower on his chin in
Sydney, Australia, on Nov. 14, 2013. His other records include the **most
hat flicks from foot to head on a unicycle in one minute**, with 10 in
London, UK, on Sep. 28, 2012.

Greatest distance traveled on a slackline by unicycle Slack-
lines are less rigid to cross than tightropes and German "extreme uni-
cyclist" Lutz Eichholz went 51 ft. 4 in. (15.66 m) in Beijing, China, on
Sep. 9, 2013.

Greatest height by a human cannonball The Bullet, aka David
Smith, Jr. (U.S.A.), was fired 85 ft. (26 m) vertically on Jul. 8, 2013 in
California City, California, U.S.A. He also holds the record for the **farthest distance for a human cannonball**, with 193 ft. 8.8 in. (59.05 m)
in Milan, Italy, on Mar. 10, 2011. Cannonballing began on Apr. 2, 1877,
when 14-year-old Zazel, aka Rosa Richter (UK), became the **first human cannonball**. She was shot a distance of 20 ft. (6 m) at Westminster
Aquarium in London, UK.

*LONGEST CAREER AS
A RINGMASTER* Norman
Barrett (UK) had been a
ringmaster for 56 years, as
of Mar. 20, 2014. But he
didn't need to run away to
join the circus—his father
owned one and he was born
into the life on Dec. 20, 1935.
Norman was 12 when he first
performed.

JEFF DUNHAM

American ventriloquist and stand-up comedian Jeff Dunham holds
the record for the **most tickets sold for a stand-up comedy tour**—
his "Spark of Insanity" tour, which was performed in 386 venues
worldwide from Sep. 13, 2007 to Aug. 21, 2010, sold an incredible
1,981,720 tickets, presumably leaving Dunham laughing all the way to
the bank.

"Circus" is from the Latin for "**ring**"—rounded arena for entertainment.

MOST MELONS CHOPPED ON THE STOMACH ON A NAIL BED Daniella D'Ville had 10 watermelons sliced on her stomach while lying on a bed of nails at Doncaster's Tattoo Jam on Oct. 12, 2013.

The **most watermelons chopped on the stomach in one minute** (no bed of nails) is 48, sliced by Bipin Larkin on Ashrita Furman (both U.S.A.) in Jamaica, New York, U.S.A., on Nov. 30, 2012.

Largest free-floating soap bubble SamSam BubbleMan, aka Sam Heath (UK), made a bubble indoors with a volume of 117 cu. ft. (3.3 m³) on Jan. 11, 2013 in London, UK, for *Officially Amazing* (Lion TV).

Most poi weaves in one minute Poi is the art of swinging weights on lengths of material in different rhythmic patterns. Joe Dickinson (UK) achieved 74 three-beat poi weaves in one minute at the Secret Garden Party in Cambridgeshire, UK, on Jul. 22, 2012.

Youngest person to do a quadruple somersault Michael Martini (ITA, b. Nov. 17, 1999) performed a quadruple somersault when 13 years 196 days old at Circo Orfei in Massafra, Italy, on Jun. 1, 2013. Michael is a professional performer; GWR does not otherwise monitor this category for under-16s.

MOST SOAP BUBBLES BLOWN INSIDE ONE LARGE BUBBLE Andy Lin, aka Kuo-Sheng Lin (TWN), blew 152 soap bubbles inside a larger bubble at the World Trade Center in Taipei City, Chinese Taipei, on Dec. 23, 2011. On Apr. 17, 2012, Kuo-Sheng also set a record for the **most bounces of a soap bubble**, with 195 consecutive bounces.

More performance feats on p. 210.

MOST ROTATIONS OF A SWORD BALANCED ON A DAGGER
Specialist circus sideshow performer Daniella D'Ville, aka Danielle Martin (UK), set a new record when she rotated a sword balanced on a dagger nine times in a minute at Doncaster's Tattoo Jam on Oct. 12, 2013.

MOST SWORDS SWALLOWED UNDERWATER
The Space Cowboy, aka Chayne Hultgren (AUS), swallowed three swords underwater at the Olympic Park Aquatic Centre in Sydney, Australia, on Nov. 14, 2013.

MOST APPLES HELD IN OWN MOUTH AND CHAIN SAWED IN ONE MINUTE
Johnny Strange (UK) chain sawed eight apples in his mouth in a minute at Doncaster's Tattoo Jam in South Yorkshire, UK, on Oct. 12, 2013. Teaming up with Daniella D'Ville (see p. 211), Johnny also set a record for the **most apples held in the mouth and cut in half by chain saw in one minute**, with 12.

JUGGLING

Fastest time for a pair to exchange costumes while juggling
Matt Baker and Joe Ricci (both U.S.A.) swapped outfits in 2 min. 52 sec. in Jiangsu, China, on Jan. 8, 2014. The two men also recorded 13 changeovers—passing while leaping over each other—the **most complete changeovers juggling three objects in one minute**, on Jan. 1, 2012.

Greatest distance on a slackline while juggling three objects
Carson Firth (U.S.A.) combined slacklining with juggling to walk a record 28 ft. 4 in. (8.65 m) in Florida, U.S.A., on Aug. 9, 2013.

Most consecutive ax juggling catches Having demonstrated the potency of his axes by chopping wood, Max Winfrey (U.S.A.) juggled three of them, making 163 catches, in Winter Garden, Florida, U.S.A., on Jun. 7, 2013.

Most objects juggled while sword swallowing The Space Cowboy juggled five balls after swallowing a sword in London, UK, on Sep. 14, 2012. Luther Bangert (U.S.A.) matched this feat in Iowa City, U.S.A., on Jul. 7, 2013. Luther kept the balls aloft for 11.72 sec; The Space Cowboy kept them airborne for 6.5 sec.

Most juggling catches on a circus pole in one minute Isabelle Noël (DEU), a performer and circus teacher, perched on a 160-ft. (49-m) pole to make 179 catches at Europa-Park in Rust, Germany, on Jun. 21, 2013.

GREATEST WEIGHT JUGGLED Ukrainian strong man Hercules, aka Denys Ilchenko, juggled three tires weighing a total of 59 lb. 7 oz. (26.98 kg) in Nairn in the Scottish Highlands, UK, on Jul. 17, 2013. The tires stayed aloft for 32.43 sec. on Denys's third attempt.

CIRQUE DU SOLEIL PRESENTS . . .

Most people simultaneously stilt walking in multiple venues: 1,908 on Jun. 16, 2009

Largest underwater stage hydraulic lift system: Handling Specialty Manufacturing (CAN) built a 3,650-ft. stage in a pool of 1.47 million gallons of water in 1999 for Cirque du Soleil

Fastest 50 m hand walking on stilts: Carlos Rodriguez Diaz (CUB), 1 min. 30 sec. in Florida, U.S.A., on Jun. 16, 2009

LARGEST ANIMAL CIRCUS ACTS

Lions: 40, Alfred Schneider (UK), Bertram Mills Circus, London, UK, 1925

Mixed lions and tigers: 43, Clyde Beatty (U.S.A.), 1938

Polar bears: 60–70, Willy Hagenbeck (DEU), Circus Paul Busch, Berlin, Germany, 1904

CIRCUS ANIMALS

As the graphic above suggests, Guinness World Records has had a long and varied history of documenting records involving circus animals. Today, circuses are much more sensitive to the welfare of animals, and many have banned animal acts outright. Similarly, we no longer monitor records involving circus animals where we cannot be 100% sure of the animals' treatment and welfare.

CIRQUE DU SOLEIL: Circus Maximus Montreal-based Cirque du Soleil, cofounded and run by Guy Laliberté (CAN), is the **largest circus organization**, with 19 touring and resident global productions. The record-breaking company (see p. 223) turns over more than U.S.$1 bn annually and has 5,000 employees. Cirque du Soleil faces increased competition and tougher markets, but Laliberté still found the time and money to enjoy a $35-m break on the *International Space Station* in 2009—one of seven visitors since 2001 to experience the **most expensive tourist trip**.

INDOOR PURSUITS

Largest plastic-cup pyramid in 30 minutes Uri, Jonathan, Daniel, and Oded Ish-Shalom (all U.S.A.) built a pyramid using 652 plastic cups in 30 min. in Jerusalem, Israel, on Feb. 22, 2012.

Fastest sport stacking (individual cycle stack) William Polly (U.S.A.) set an individual cycle stack time of 5.59 sec. at the WSSA U.S. National Sport Stacking Championships in Maryland, U.S.A., on Mar. 24, 2013.

Most people playing a board game simultaneously The Dokter Toy company (IDN) assembled 1,239 people to play the Crazy Birds board game in Tribeca Central Park, Jakarta, Indonesia, on Jun. 16, 2013.

MOST SCRABBLE OPPONENTS PLAYED AT ONCE Chris May (AUS) won 25 of the 28 games of Scrabble he played simultaneously at Oxford University Press in Oxford, UK, on Jun. 11, 2013. Then ranked No. 9 in the world at Scrabble, May took more than four hours to finish all the games.

MOST PEOPLE PLAYING PINBALL SIMULTANEOUSLY On May 16, 2013, 100 paddle flippers amassed at First Canadian Place in Toronto, Canada, to play pinball. The free-to-play event was organized by the Stratford Festival to promote the Avon Theatre's production of *Tommy,* the musical that features the song "Pinball Wizard."

A 3 x 3 Rubik's Cube has **43,252,003,274,489,856,000 permutations.**

LARGEST BALL BATH On Oct. 30, 2013, the swimming pool at the Kerry Hotel in Pudong, Shanghai, China, was drained and filled with one million green and pink balls as part of Breast Cancer Awareness Month. The balls, which covered a surface area of 3,397 sq. ft. (315.6 m²), were later sold to raise funds for charity.

TALLEST DOMINO STRUCTURE A domino tower 19 ft. 9.2 in. (6.02 m) high and consisting of 11,465 dominoes was erected and toppled by Yspertal Domino Team (AUT) in Yspertal, Austria, on Nov. 3, 2013. Pictured is Marcel Pürrer, one of the team of four who built the tower.

FACT: The tower formed the final part of a 100,101-domino array built by 44 people over four days.

MOST SOLVES OF RUBIK'S CUBES IN ONE YEAR

Name	Solves	Attempts	Year
Sébastien Auroux (DEU)	2,033	2,122	2012
François Courtès (FRA)	1,651	1,780	2013
Zoé de Moffarts (BEL)	1,518	1,575	2012
Arnaud van Galen (NLD)	1,481	1,568	2012
Erik Akkersdijk (NLD)	1,477	1,609	2010
Jan Bentlage (DEU)	1,452	1,517	2012
Bence Barát (HUN)	1,349	1,392	2010
Clément Gallet (FRA)	1,213	1,249	2011
Tim Reynolds (U.S.A.)	1,205	1,281	2012
Laura Ohrndorf (DEU)	1,193	1,295	2013

Source: World Cube Association, as of Dec. 31, 2013

MOST SOLVES IN RUBIK'S CUBE COMPETITIONS IN A SINGLE YEAR In 2012, Sébastien Auroux (DEU) solved 2,033 Rubik's Cubes in official World Cube Association competitions. This equates to 5.5 competitive solves every day and doesn't include any cubes solved outside of formal events.

PRICEY PASTIMES

Most expensive . . .

Toy model car: 1930s W. E. Boyce delivery van, £19,975 ($35,728)

Mickey Mouse toy: clockwork Mickey Mouse motorcycle, £51,000 ($83,466)

Toy soldier: 1963 prototype G.I. Joe, $200,000 (£124,309)

Doll: 1914 French doll by Albert Marque, $263,000 (£162,181)

CAPTAINS OF CUP: Sport Stacking The eighth annual STACK UP! was organized by the World Sport Stacking Association (U.S.A.) on Nov. 14, 2013. They assembled more than half a million people to record the **most people sport stacking in multiple venues**. Speed stackers use special cups, which they arrange in specific sequences as fast as possible and then take them down again, often too quickly for a casual observer to follow. The 555,932 stackers represented 2,631 schools and organizations from 29 countries. Stacking fans claim that it improves hand and eye coordination with its emphasis on dexterity.

Longest board game marathon Brett Carow and Sam Hennemann (both U.S.A.) played 116 back-to-back games of Strat-O-Matic Baseball for 61 hr. 2 min. in New York City, U.S.A., on Jun. 7–9, 2012.

CHESS

Fastest time to arrange a chess set Ray Butler (U.S.A.) set up a chess board in 41.87 sec. in Las Vegas, Nevada, U.S.A., on Sep. 18, 2013. The **fastest time to arrange a set by a team of two** is 41.24 sec., by Tyler Eichman and John Walker (both U.S.A.) in Oconto, Wisconsin, U.S.A., on Nov. 27, 2013.

Longest chess marathon On Dec. 17–19, 2010, Daniel Häußler and Philipp Bergner (both DEU) played chess for 40 hr. 20 min. in Ostfildern, Germany. Häußler won 191 to Bergner's 114 games, with 50 draws.

Most chess games played in one location The Sports Authority of Gujarat (IND) ran 20,480 games simultaneously at the University of Gujarat Sports Grounds in Ahmedabad, India, on Dec. 24, 2010.

Largest chess set On May 27, 2009, the Medicine Hat Chess Club of Alberta, Canada, unveiled a set measuring 19 ft. 4 in. (5.89 m) on each side. The king was 3 ft. 10 in. (1.19 m) tall and 1 ft. 2 in. (37.4 cm) wide at its base.

DOMINOES

Most dominoes toppled by an individual Liu Yang (CHN) single-handedly arranged and then toppled 321,197 dominoes at CITIC Guoan Grand Epoch City in Beijing, China, on Dec. 31, 2011.

WORLD CUBE ASSOCIATION FASTEST SINGLE SOLVES

 2 x 2: Christian Kaserer (ITA), 0.69 sec.

 3 x 3: Mats Valk (NLD), 5.55 sec.

 4 x 4: Feliks Zemdegs (AUS), 24.66 sec.

 5 x 5: Feliks Zemdegs (AUS), 50.50 sec.

 6 x 6: Kevin Hays (U.S.A.), 1 min. 40.86 sec.

 7 x 7: Bence Barát (HUN), 2 min. 40.11 sec.

 Megaminx: Simon Westlund (SWE), 42.28 sec.

 Square-1: Andrea Santambrogio (ITA), 7.41 sec.

 Pyraminx: Oscar Roth Andersen (DEN), 1.36 sec.

 Skewb: Brandon Harnish (U.S.A.), 2.19 sec.

 Rubik's Clock: Sam Zhixiao Wang (CHN), 5.27 sec.

Correct as of Feb. 26, 2014

HOW THE MIGHTY HAVE FALLEN: MOST DOMINOES TOPPLED BY A GROUP

A. 1,605,757
Netherlands
1998

B. 2,472,480
Netherlands
1999

C. 2,751,518
China
1999

D. 3,407,535
China
2000

E. 3,847,295
Netherlands
2002

F. 3,992,397
Netherlands
2004

G. 4,002,136
Netherlands
2005

H. 4,079,381
Netherlands
2006

I. 4,345,027
Netherlands
2008

J. 4,491,863
Netherlands
2009

▮ = 15,000 dominoes

Longest domino wall Germany's Sinners Domino Entertainment holds multiple records for setting up and toppling dominoes. On Jul. 6, 2012, at the Wolfgang Ernst Gymnasium School in Büdingen, Germany, Sinners erected—and then toppled—a 98-ft. 5-in.-long (30-m) wall built from 31,405 dominoes. On the same day, Sinners also set a record for the **most dominoes toppled in a pyramid**, with 13,486.

They were back in action on Oct. 23, 2012, this time in Kefenrod, Germany, with the **most dominoes toppled in 30 seconds**, setting up and toppling 60 pieces.

Six months later, Sinners set another record for the **most toppled in a spiral**, with 55,555 on Jul. 12, 2013.

Most toppled in one minute Gemma Hansen (UK) set up and toppled 75 dominoes at Butlin's in Minehead, UK, on Aug. 7, 2010. At the 2011 event, also on Aug. 7, Andy James (UK) stacked 39 dominoes in a single pile: the **most dominoes stacked in one minute**. Paul Lusher (UK) equaled his record on Sep. 4, 2011.

OUTDOOR PURSUITS

BUNGEE

Highest dunk of a doughnut Ron Jones (U.S.A.) dunked a doughnut by bungee from 198 ft. 8 in. (60.55 m) into a coffee cup measuring 3.5 in. (8.89 cm) in diameter in California City, California, U.S.A., on Jul. 7, 2013.

LONGEST CUMULATIVE ABSEIL IN ONE HOUR— TEAM OF 10 In a stunt organized by ECCO Shoes (DEU), ten abseilers—all wearing high heels—descended the 339-ft. 2-in.-tall (103.4-m) Park Inn hotel in Berlin, Germany, in one hour on Jul. 6, 2013. A total of 32 descents were logged: a cumulative distance of 2.05 mi. (3.3 km).

Highest bungee jump dive into water Raymond Woodcock (UK) was 72 years old when he bungee-jumped 380 ft. (115.9 m) from a crane into water in Chepstow, UK, on Aug. 18, 2013.

Most jumps in one hour Mike Heard (NZ) jumped 80 times under Auckland Harbour Bridge on Sep. 16, 2011, using a cord measuring 31 ft. 2 in. (9.5 m).

The **most bungee jumps in 24 hours** stands at 105, by Kevin Scott Huntly (ZAF) at Bloukrans Bridge, Garden Route, South Africa, on May 8, 2011. His time was 7 hr. 42 min.—an average of one jump every 4.5 min., with a cord measuring 131 ft. 3 in. (40 m).

MOST CABER TOSSES IN THREE MINUTES Kevin Fast (CAN) tossed 14 cabers in Quinte West, Ontario, Canada, on Sep. 7, 2013. Kevin has been setting records for many years and currently holds eight records for feats of strength.

HIGHEST FORWARD FLIP JUMP ON A POGO STICK Biff Hutchison (U.S.A.) jumped 8 ft. 2 in. (2.49 m) in Tompkins Square Park, New York, U.S.A., on Jul. 27, 2013. The next day he set the **highest jump on a pogo stick** at 9 ft. 7.5 in. (2.93 m).

Skateboarding was **banned in Norway** from 1978 to 1989 because of the high accident rate.

FLYING DISK (FRISBEE)

Fastest relay over 20 m On May 6, 2012, a team of five threw a disk in 8.74 sec. Tim, Daniel, Lindsey, and Elyse Habenicht and Cliff West (all U.S.A.) were in College Station, Texas, U.S.A.

Longest throw caught by a dog Robert McLeod (CAN) threw a flying disk 402 ft. (122.5 m) to Davy Whippet in Thorhild, Alberta, Canada, on Oct. 14, 2012.

Another canine disk master is Beibei the border collie. His owner Liu Haiwang (CHN) helped him set the **most catches by a dog over 10 m in three minutes**, with 18 in Beijing, China, on Sep. 7, 2013.

Longest throw to hit a target Brodie Smith (U.S.A.) dunked a disk into a basketball hoop from 150 ft. (45.7 m) in Patterson Park in Austin, Texas, U.S.A., on Dec. 3, 2013. Brodie was not allowed to hit the backboard in the attempt.

Most beverage cans hit in one minute Robert McLeod (CAN) hit 28 cans at Edgemont World Health club in Calgary, Canada, on Jan. 28, 2012. His other achievements include setting the **longest throw, run, and catch on ice skates**, with 240 ft. (73.2 m) on Feb. 24, 2013, and the **longest time for a disk to stay aloft thrown from ice skates**, with 12.03 sec. in Edmonton, Canada, on Feb. 23, 2013.

LONGEST JOURNEY BY WATER JET PACK On Nov. 8, 2013, TV presenter Pollyanna Woodward (UK) jetted off from Gozo Marina in Malta using a jet pack that draws in water and forces it out under pressure, providing lift. She covered a record 22.64 mi. (36.45 km) in 4 hr. 45 min.

MOST WATERSKIERS TOWED BY ONE BOAT On Jan. 27, 2012, a total of 145 skiers were towed behind a boat at the Horsehead Water Ski Club in Strahan, Tasmania, Australia.

DID YOU KNOW?

In the late 1990s, the U.S. Marine Corps experimented with skateboards in urban-military exercises, using them to detect trip wires in buildings and draw out sniper fire.

FACT: Mountain biking was adopted as an Olympic sport in 1996. BMX followed in 2008.

POGO STICK

Fastest mile dribbling a basketball On Aug. 9, 2013, Ashrita Furman (U.S.A.) pogo-sticked a mile—while controlling a bouncing basketball—in 23 min. 2.91 sec. in New York City, U.S.A. Ashrita's eight pogo records include the **fastest mile**, set on Jul. 24, 2001 at 12 min. 16 sec.

Most consecutive jumps James Roumeliotis (U.S.A.) recorded 70,271 consecutive pogo jumps, i.e., without a break and without falling off, at Pogopalooza 10 in New York, U.S.A., on Jul. 26, 2013.

James had previously set the record for the **most bounces in a pogo marathon,** with an ankle-crushing 206,864 jumps. His attempt took 20 hr. 13 min. at Pogopalooza 8 in California, U.S.A., on Jul. 29, 2011. James commented afterward, "My calves are killing me. My ankles are swollen. I can't actually feel my hands, my right thumb especially."

POGO POWER: BOUNCING INTO THE RECORD BOOKS

A. **Fastest one mile:** 12 min. 16 sec., Ashrita Furman (U.S.A.), Jul. 24, 2001

B. **Most balloons popped in one minute:** 57, Mark Aldridge (UK), Apr. 1, 2010

C. **Most consecutive front flips:** 5, Jake Gartland (U.S.A.), Jul. 28, 2011

D. **Most consecutive backflips:** 17, Fred Grzybowski (U.S.A.), Dec. 19, 2013

E. **Farthest distance underwater:** 1,680 ft., Ashrita Furman (U.S.A.), Aug. 1, 2007

A.   B.   C.   D.   E.

FASTEST 100 M IN HIGH-HEEL ROLLER SKATES Marawa Ibrahim (AUS) glided 100 m (328 ft.) in 26.10 sec. in Regent's Park, London, UK, on Aug. 21, 2013 while wearing her custom-made 5.1-in.-high (13-cm) high-heel roller skates. "Marawa the Amazing," as she is known, manages a troupe of majorettes who perform in the UK.

ROLLER SKATING

Longest forward jump Jeff Dupont (U.S.A.) jumped 20 ft. 3 in. (6.18 m) without using a ramp at the Willamalane Center for Sports and Recreation in Springfield, Oregon, U.S.A., on Feb. 12, 2012.

Most spins while carrying two people On Dec. 10, 2012, Liu Jiangshan made 17 consecutive 360-degree spins on roller skates while hanging onto Wang Chenyu and Yang Liangliang (all CHN) in Beijing, China.

GET YOUR SKATES ON

Fastest time to roller-skate across the U.S.A.: Russell "Rusty" Moncrief (U.S.A.), 69 days 8 hr. 45 min., Mar 15, 2002.

Fastest time to roller-skate the length of the UK: Damian Magee (UK), 9 days 5 hr. 23 min., Jun. 19–28, 1992.

Tallest moving human pyramid on roller skates: NSA Roller Gymnastics Team (U.S.A.), four stories high, Pennsylvania, U.S.A., 1985.

LONGEST CHAIN OF ROLLER SKATERS The Clyde 1 radio station and ScotRail (both UK) set in motion 254 participants in a roller-skating line in Glasgow, UK, on Sep. 8, 2013. They were led by Clyde 1 DJ Diane Knox-Campbell.

PIE'S THE LIMIT: *Flying Disk History* As long ago as ancient Greece, the discus was in use (above left), and a clay disk found in Utah, U.S.A., suggests that Native Americans used something similar. In the 1870s in Connecticut, U.S.A., a baker called Russell Frisbie started stamping "Frisbie's pies" on the bottom of his light, circular pans. Students at nearby Yale played throw and catch with the pans, shouting "Frisbie!" as an alert. In California, Wham-O adopted the name for its plastic disk, changed the spelling, and patented the Frisbee. More than 100 million Frisbees have now been produced, but the bakery itself closed in 1958.

SLINGSHOT

Longest slingshot The greatest distance for launching an object from a sling is 1,565 ft. 4 in. (477.10 m), using a 4-ft. 2-in.-long (1.27-m) sling and a 2.25-oz. (62-g) dart, by David Engvall (U.S.A.) at Baldwin Lake, California, U.S.A., on Sep. 13, 1992.

Most cans hit in one minute Michael McClure (U.S.A.) used metal balls to strike 13 beverage cans with a slingshot—from 33 ft. (10 m)—at the East Coast Slingshot Tournament in Alverton, Pennsylvania, U.S.A., on Jun. 8, 2013.

WHEELIE GOOD

First double loop by a car Gary Hoptrough (UK) conquered the "Deadly 720" by completing two 360-degree loops—each 26 ft. (8 m) in diameter—in a Rage R180 buggy on *Top Gear Live* at Moses Mabhida Stadium in Durban, South Africa, on Jun. 16, 2012.

Longest individual ATV side wheelie On Oct. 30, 2012, Daniel Adams (U.S.A.) executed a 16.89-mi. (27.17-km) wheelie on the side wheels of an all-terrain vehicle (ATV) near Grantsville in Utah, U.S.A.

Longest UTV ramp jump Tanner Godfrey (U.S.A.) made a 105-ft. 3-in. (32.08-m) ramp jump in a utility terrain vehicle (UTV) at Eureka Casino Resort in Mesquite, Nevada, U.S.A., on Feb. 22, 2013.

LONGEST VEHICLE DRIFT In a drift, a driver controls a vehicle through a sustained rear-wheel skid. Johan Schwartz (U.S.A.) maintained a 51.27-mi. (84.13-km) drift at the BMW Performance Center in Spartanburg, South Carolina, U.S.A., on May 11, 2013.

LONGEST WHEELIE BY A SKID LOADER On Jul. 28, 2012, Jake R. Hatch (U.S.A.) carried out a 71-ft. 9-in.-long (21.88-m) wheelie in a Bobcat skid steer at Taylor Rodeo Grounds in Taylor, Arizona, U.S.A.

SHORTEST BRAKING DISTANCE BY A VEHICLE ON ICE On Jan. 8, 2013, Fulda Reifen—a tire brand of Goodyear Dunlop Tires Germany—set a braking distance of 157 ft. 11 in. (48.132 m) for a car driven at 30.1 mph (48.5 km/h) on the frozen Schwatka Lake near Whitehorse, Yukon, Canada.

FACT: The 2011 film *Drive* (U.S.A.), starring Ryan Gosling, was directed by Nicolas Winding Refn, who has never owned a driver's license.

BICYCLE

Most 180-degree jumps in one minute The most 180-degree jumps on a bicycle in a minute is 43, by Daniel Rall (DEU) at Comtech Arena in Aspach, Germany, on Jul. 13, 2013.

Highest vertical drop Wayne Mahomet (UK) made a vertical drop of 13 ft. 5 in. (4.1 m) on his bicycle at the Dounby Show in Dounby, Orkney Islands, UK, on Aug. 8, 2013.

Fastest 10-obstacle slalom (blindfolded) On Jul. 23, 2013, Juan Ruiz (MEX) negotiated his bicycle around 10 obstacles set randomly on a 66-ft. (20-m) slalom course in 25.43 sec. on the set of *Guinness World Records—Rekorlar Dünyası* in Istanbul, Turkey. Juan has been blind since birth and used echolocation to achieve the feat.

Fastest 100 miles Ian Cammish (UK) took 3 hr. 11 min. 11 sec. to cycle 100 mi. (161 km) on Aug. 10, 1993.

The **fastest 100 miles by a woman** is 3 hr. 49 min. 42 sec., by Pauline Strong (UK) on Oct. 18, 1991.

Farthest wheelie on front wheel with feet off the pedals Andreas Lindqvist (SWE) carried out a 1,036-ft. 8-in. (316-m) front-wheel wheelie without his feet touching the pedals of his bike on the set of *Guinness Rekord TV* at Liljeholmshallen, Stockholm, Sweden, on Oct. 6, 2001.

On the same show, Lindqvist also performed the **longest duration bicycle wheelie on the front wheel with feet off the pedals**, staying aloft for 2 min. 20 sec.

FASTEST 400-M HURDLES ON A BICYCLE On Aug. 26, 2013, Austrian cyclist Thomas Öhler negotiated a 400-m hurdles course by bicycle in 44.62 sec. in Linz, Austria.

MOST STEPS CLIMBED BY BICYCLE Krystian Herba (POL) climbed all 2,754 steps of the World Financial Center in Shanghai, China, by bike on Mar 17, 2013. He did so, without touching the walls or putting his feet on the floor, in a time of 1 hr. 21 min. 53 sec.

Most BMX megaspins in 30 seconds A BMX megaspin involves standing on a rear peg, holding onto the handlebars, and, with the front wheel raised, kicking the rear tire so that the bike spins. On Jul. 19, 2013, Takahiro Ikeda (JPN) performed 45 spins in 30 sec. in Kōtō, Tokyo, Japan.

MOTORCYCLE

Longest jump with backflip on a minimoto On Oct. 9, 2012, Ricardo Piedras (ESP) carried out a 48-ft. 4-in.-long (14.74-m) jump with backflip on a minimoto (minibike) in Barcelona, Spain.

FASTEST MOTORCYCLE WHEELIE ON ICE On Jan. 27, 2013, Ryan Suchanek (U.S.A.) carried out a wheelie at a speed of 108.5 mph (174.6 km/h) across the frozen Lake Koshkonong in Wisconsin, U.S.A. In doing so, he broke his own existing world record by 13.5 mph (21.7 km/h). The speed was measured over a distance of 328 ft. (100 m).

FACT: Ryan Suchanek (above) rode a 2005 Kawasaki ZX10R. Its tires were studded to provide better traction on ice.

LONGEST DIRT-TO-DIRT MOTORCYCLE RAMP JUMP
The greatest distance covered in a dirt-to-dirt motorcycle ramp jump is 297 ft. 6 in. (90.69 m), by Alex Harvill (U.S.A.) at the Horn Rapids Motorsports Complex in West Richland, Washington, U.S.A., on Jul. 6, 2013. He reached a speed of 96 mph (154 km/h) on the approach to the takeoff ramp.

Longest stoppie The greatest distance for a stoppie (aka endo or front-wheel wheelie) on a motorcycle is 1,320 ft. 4 in. (402.42 m). It was achieved by Jesse Toler (U.S.A.) at the Charlotte Diesel Super Show staged at the ZMAX Dragway in North Carolina, U.S.A., on Oct. 5, 2012.

Most switchback zero rotations in one minute For this record, a rider must be seated back-to-front on a motorcycle ("switchback zero"), without touching it with his or her hands, and rotate the machine through 360 degrees. On Aug. 22, 2013, British rider Mark Van Driel completed a total of 13 motorcycle switchback zero rotations in one minute on the set of *Officially Amazing* in Mildenhall, Suffolk, UK.

SKATEBOARD

Fastest 110-m hurdles by hippy jumps A hippy jump involves jumping off a moving board and over an obstacle while the skateboard passes beneath. Steffen Köster (DEU) hippy-jumped along a 110-m (360-ft.) hurdle course in 29.98 sec. in Rust, Germany, on Jun. 19, 2013.

Fastest time to slalom 100 cones On Aug. 16, 2013, Jānis Kuzmins (LVA) slalomed his board through 100 cones in 19.41 sec. on the set of *CCTV Guinness World Records Special* at the Asia-Pacific Experimental School of Beijing Normal University in Beijing, China.

> The **skateboard ollie** is named after its inventor, Alan "Ollie" Gelfand.

GREATEST STUNT DISTANCES: LONGEST RAMP JUMP BY . . .

Car in reverse: 61 ft. 2 in., *Top Gear* stuntman (UK)

Skateboard: 79 ft., Danny Way (U.S.A.)

Rollerblades: 98 ft. 5 in., Chris Haffey (U.S.A.)

Bicycle (assisted): 116 ft. 11 in., Colin Winkelmann (U.S.A.)

Monster truck: 214 ft. 8 in., Dan Runte (U.S.A.)

Car: 269 ft., Travis Pastrana (U.S.A.)

Motorcycle: 351 ft., Robbie Maddison (U.S.A.)

***MONSTER FEATS:** Bigfoot* It may have recorded the **longest monster truck ramp jump** with a leap of 214 ft. 8 in, but *Bigfoot 18* isn't the biggest in the *Bigfoot* family. *Bigfoot 5*, built in 1986, has the accolade of being the **largest monster truck**, standing 15 ft. 6 in. tall with 10-ft.-high tires and weighing in at 38,000 lb. The man behind the monsters is Bob Chandler (U.S.A.), who began building them in 1975 as a way of publicizing his four-wheel-drive center in Missouri, U.S.A.

Farthest distance in 24 hours Andrew Andras (U.S.A.) traveled 261.8 mi. (431.33 km) on his skateboard in 24 hr. at the Homestead-Miami Speedway in Homestead, Florida, U.S.A., on Jan. 7–8, 2013.

On the same date and at the same venue, Colleen Pelech (U.S.A.) achieved the **farthest distance traveled on a skateboard in 24 hours (female)**: 167.2 mi. (269.08 km).

Most ollie 180s in a minute Eric Carlin (U.S.A.) performed 25 skateboard ollie 180s in 60 sec. in Mount Laurel, New Jersey, U.S.A., on Jul. 2, 2013.

Longest stationary manual Brendon Davis (U.S.A.) remained stationary on one set of wheels for 19 min. 39.56 sec. at the Society skate shop in San Carlos, California, U.S.A., on May 11, 2013.

Most shove-its On Sep. 5, 2013, Gabriel Pena (U.S.A.) executed 33 shove-its (a 180-degree-or-more board spin) in 30 sec. in Houston, Texas, U.S.A.

MASS PARTICIPATION

LARGEST . . .

AED training session Automated External Defibrillators (AED) diagnose and treat heart conditions. A training session for 2,109 participants on the machines was held by AED4all.com, Anne-Marie Willems and René Verlaak (all NLD) in Nijmegen, Netherlands, on May 29, 2013.

Baking lesson Much dough was kneaded by 426 students of Green Grin Club Limited, Grin Kitchen Limited, and Ma On Shan Tsung Tsin secondary school (all HKG) in Hong Kong, China, on Sep. 7, 2013.

Barbecue Try to guess how much food you need for a barbecue for 45,252 people. Ingredients used by Estado de Nuevo León (MEX) included 34,000 lb. (15.5 tonnes) of beef with 39,500 lb. (18 tonnes) of onions, and 33,000 lb. (15 tonnes) of corn tortillas, topped with 35,000 lb. (16 tonnes) of salsa. It took place in Parque Fundidora in Monterrey, Mexico, on Aug. 18, 2013.

LARGEST GATHERING OF PEOPLE DRESSED AS PENGUINS Children's hospice Richard House got 325 oversize penguins to waddle together in Wood Wharf, London, UK, on Guinness World Records Day on Nov. 13, 2013.

A gathering of 9,768 firefighters in Oct. 2011 is almost **four times the population** of the Falkland Islands.

LARGEST GATHERING OF PEOPLE DRESSED . . .

Category	People	Organizer/Event	Location	Date
as Mohandas Gandhi (A.)	2,955	Sowdambikaa Group of Schools	Tiruchirappalli, India	Oct. 11, 2013
with false moustaches	2,268	City of Fairfield & Fairfield RAGBRAI Committee	Fairfield, Iowa, U.S.A.	Jul. 26, 2013
as witches (B.)	1,607	La Bruixa d'Or	Sort, Lleida, Spain	Nov. 16, 2013
as *Star Trek* characters (C.)	1,063	Media 10 Ltd.	ExCeL, London, UK	Oct. 20, 2012
as Saint Patrick (D.)	882	Saint Brigid's National School	Castleknock, Dublin, Ireland	Mar. 14, 2013
as fairies	871	St. Giles Hospice	Lichfield, Staffordshire, UK	Jun. 22, 2013
as Superman	867	Escapade, Kendal Calling	Lowther Deer Park, Cumbria, UK	Jul. 27, 2013
in one-piece pajamas (onesies)	752	Henry Allen Onesie Angels	StadiumMK, Milton Keynes, UK	Nov. 2, 2013
as nurses	691	Dubai Health Authority	Dubai, UAE	Jan. 24, 2014
as trees	516	Ośrodek Kultury Leśnej w Gołuchówie	Gołuchów, Poland	Sep. 30, 2013
as cows	470	Chick-fil-A	George Mason University, Virginia, U.S.A.	Jul. 2, 2013
as monks	463	Ardfert Central National School	Ardfert, County Kerry, Ireland	May 11, 2013
in Disney costumes	361	Walsgrave Church of England Primary School	Coventry, UK	Jul. 12, 2013

LARGEST HORSE RACE The Federation of Mongolian Horse Racing Sport and Trainers registered 4,249 runners in an 11.18-mi. (18-km) race in Khui Doloon Khudag, Ulan Bator, Mongolia, on Aug. 10, 2013. The youngest rider was seven years of age and the oldest was 79.

Barefoot walk The National Service Scheme Cell of Acharya Nagarjuna University (IND) took 7,050 people for a shoe-free stroll in Guntur, Andhra Pradesh, India, on Dec. 12, 2012.

Gathering of professional clown doctors Clown doctors can ease difficult and frightening procedures in hospitals for sick young people. On Jan. 30, 2013, a group of 153 clowns marked the 20th anniversary of the clown doctoring work done by the Theodora Foundation, headquartered in Bern, Switzerland.

LARGEST GATHERING OF ZOMBIES A brain-munching 9,592 members of the walking dead did the New Jersey Zombie Walk in Asbury Park, New Jersey, U.S.A., on Oct. 5, 2013. They shuffled their way to regaining the record from the Zombie Pub Crawl of Minneapolis, U.S.A.

BIG BANQUETS

In our 1962 edition, one of the earliest examples of a mass participation record was reported. "Lyons catered for the world's largest banquet at Olympia, London, on August 8, 1925. A total of 6,600 guests were seated at 5 miles of tables served by 1,360 waitresses supported by 700 cooks and porters. The occasion was a War Memorial fund raising effort by Freemasons."

MOST PEOPLE . . .

On the same drum Queen's "We Will Rock You" was an anthemic choice for 263 people playing a drum measuring 32 ft. 9 in. (10 m) in diameter and 5 ft. 2 in. (1.6 m) high. Organized by PLAY (POL), the event took place at Przystanek Woodstock in Kostrzyn nad Odra, Poland, on Aug. 2, 2013.

Singing a national anthem simultaneously A total of 121,653 employees from the Sahara India Pariwar company sang India's national anthem in Lucknow, India, on May 6, 2013.

Caroling The Waukesha Downtown Business Association (U.S.A.) cajoled 1,822 carol singers in Waukesha, Wisconsin, U.S.A., on Nov. 22, 2013.

On a single bed Leaving no room to roll over, 54 people were crammed on a single bed by Xilinmen Furniture in Beijing, China, on Sep. 7, 2013.

Blowing bubble gum bubbles Lester B. Pearson Public School in Aurora, Canada, organized 544 people to simultaneously blow gum bubbles on Jun. 6, 2013.

Blowing up balloons A different kind of blowing saw Bayer Yakuhin (JPN) organize 2,639 simultaneous balloon inflations on Jan. 14, 2014, in Osaka, Japan.

LOUDEST STADIUM CROWD ROAR Fans of the Seattle Seahawks (U.S.A.) achieved a 137.6-dB(A) roar at CenturyLink Stadium in Seattle, Washington, U.S.A., on Dec. 2, 2013, in a match against the New Orleans Saints. The term "dB(A)" denotes decibel levels audible to the human ear—i.e., excluding extreme highs and lows.

MOST PEOPLE TWERKING On Sep. 25, 2013, GWR adjudicator Charlie Weisman witnessed 358 people twerking simultaneously in New York City, U.S.A. The event was organized by hip-hop artist Big Freedia (U.S.A.).

GREATEST GATHERINGS

A. Largest religious crowd: 30 million, India, 2013

B. Largest funeral: 15 million, India, 1969

C. Largest papal crowd: 4 million, Philippines, 1995

D. Largest gathering of Sikhs: 3.5 million, India, 1999

E. Largest antiwar rally: 3 million, Italy, 2003

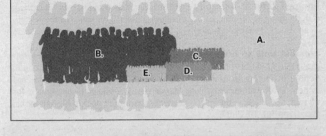

HINDU PILGRIMAGE: Kumbh Mela Festival Between 80 and 100 million people attended the 55-day Kumbh Mela festival, which began in Allahabad, India, in Jan. 2013. A Hindu pilgrimage to bathe in a sacred river is usually held every three years in one of four cities, but 2013 was a special version, the Maha Kumbh Mela, which occurs every 144 years. The city prepared for the onslaught—more than the entire population of the UK—with 14 temporary hospitals, 243 doctors on call, around 30,000 police and security staff on duty, and 40,000 restroom facilities. The cost was approximately 11.5 bn rupees ($182 m), but it was hoped that the festival would earn as much as 120 bn rupees ($1.9 bn).

AND FINALLY . . .

- **Most people shaking cocktails simultaneously:** 1,710, Diageo (UK), Sep. 18, 2013

- **Most people popping party poppers:** 743, Grey Court School (UK), Jul. 17, 2013

- **Longest high-five chain:** 695 people, St. Francis of Assisi Primary School and Calwell High School (both AUS), Sep. 27, 2013

Painting buildings at once On May 18, 2013, Slovenian paint manufacturer Helios put 1,272 painters to work across nine venues.

NO PAIN, NO GAIN

Longest time in full-body contact with snow Oleksiy Gutsulyak (UKR) endured 60 min. 8 sec. of close contact with snow in the Kyrylo Tryliovski City Park in Kolomyia, Ukraine, on Jan. 25, 2013.

Longest time to hold the breath voluntarily (male) Stig Severinsen (DNK) held his breath underwater for exactly 22 min. at the London School of Diving in London, UK, on May 3, 2012. The female record is held by Karoline Mariechen Meyer (BRA), who held her breath for 18 min. 32.59 sec. in the Racer Academy swimming pool in Florianópolis, Brazil, on Jul. 10, 2009.

Longest full-body burn (without oxygen) The greatest duration for a full-body burn without oxygen is 5 min. 25 sec. The fiery feat was accomplished by Jayson Dumenigo (U.S.A.) in Santa Clarita, California, U.S.A., on Mar. 27, 2011.

The **most people to perform simultaneous full-body burns** is 21, achieved during an event organized by Ted Batchelor and Hotcards.com (both U.S.A.) at the Hotcards Burn in Cleveland, Ohio, U.S.A., on Oct. 19, 2013.

The **fastest time to run through 10 locked and burning doors** is 12.84 sec., performed by Chris Roseboro (U.S.A.) on the set of *Guinness World Records Unleashed* in California City, California, U.S.A., on Jul. 7, 2013.

LONGEST TIME SPENT IN FULL-BODY CONTACT WITH ICE Wim Hof (NLD) spent 1 hr. 53 min. 2 sec. immersed in ice in Naarden, Netherlands, on Oct. 18, 2013. When it comes to withstanding sub-zero temperatures, Wim has consistently proved himself to be one cool customer: he has held this record 16 times in the past.

Due to a genetic anomaly, **redheads** are more susceptible to pain.

MOST ANIMAL TRAPS RELEASED ON THE BODY IN ONE MINUTE On Oct. 12, 2013, Johnny Strange (UK) set off six vintage animal traps on his body in a minute at Doncaster's Tattoo Jam, held at Doncaster Racecourse in South Yorkshire, UK. All of the traps were once used to catch rabbits. It's one of six GWR records that this sideshow entertainer extraordinaire currently holds.

MOST NAILS REMOVED FROM WOOD WITH TEETH IN ONE MINUTE Tommy Heslep (U.S.A.) yanked 16 nails from a length of wood using just his teeth in a nail-biting 60 sec. on the set of *Guinness World Records Unleashed* in Los Angeles, California, U.S.A., on Jun. 19, 2013. Around 300 lb. (135 kg) of pressure was needed to remove each nail.

Most nails inserted into the nose in 30 seconds Burnaby Q. Orbax (CAN) inserted 12 nails, into—then out of—his nose, one at a time, in 30 sec. in London, UK, on Jun. 22, 2013. Each nail was 4 in. (10 cm) long.

Heaviest vehicle pulled using a hook through the nasal cavity and mouth On Jun. 5, 2013, Ryan Stock (CAN) pulled a 2,167-lb. (983-kg) Volkswagen Beetle—with two women inside it—using a hook fed through his nasal cavity and out of his mouth for *Rekorlar Dünyası* in Istanbul, Turkey.

MOST . . .

Arrows broken by the neck in one minute Fitness enthusiast Michael Gillette (U.S.A.) snapped 12 arrows by placing the sharp end of each one against his throat, in the jugular notch, and forcing the other end against a wall in Los Angeles, California, U.S.A., on Jun. 27, 2013.

FACT: William Staub created the home treadmill in the 1960s. It was initially sold under the name PaceMaster.

FACT: Tommy is also known for his remarkably strong grip—so much so that a technique for bending metal is named after him!

MOST COCONUTS SMASHED WITH THE ELBOWS IN ONE MINUTE On Jun. 24, 2013, actor and martial arts expert Jeffrey James Lippold (U.S.A.) used his elbows to smash through 21 coconuts in one minute on the set of *Guinness World Records Unleashed* in Los Angeles, California, U.S.A.

LASTING ACHIEVEMENTS

You might think that the human capacity for athletic endurance was fairly well set by now, but committed individuals have a way of confounding expectations. Back in 1998, Rory Coleman (UK) held the record for the **fastest time to run 100 miles on a treadmill (male)**, with a time of 23 hr. 43 min. By 2003, Andrew Rivett (UK) was more than 7 hr. faster (16 hr. 23 min. 16 sec.). The current record, held by Suresh Joachim (AUS), is 13 hr. 42 min. 33 sec.—around 10 hr. faster than the 1998 record holder!

PADDY DOYLE TAKES THE STRAIN

Most jumping jacks in one minute carrying a 100-lb. pack: 33, on Nov. 10, 2013

Most step-ups in one minute carrying a 100-lb. pack: 31, on Aug. 17, 2013

Fastest cross-country half marathon carrying a 100-lb. pack: 4 hr. 18 min., on Jun. 22, 2013

Most squat thrusts in one minute with a 40-lb. pack: 21, on Mar. 28, 2011

HARD TO BEAT: *Paddy Doyle* If one man knows all about pushing the body to the limits of its physical capacity, it's Paddy Doyle (UK). This tough and tenacious character has been setting and breaking GWR endurance records for years—his oldest current record goes all the way back to 1989 (**most push-ups in 12 hours:** 19,325)! Along the way, he's also survived the **most competitive full-contact rounds** (6,324) and performed the **most push-ups using the back of the hands in one hour carrying a 40-lb. pack** (663). See box at top for more examples of Doyle's derring-do

---

GREATEST DISTANCES RUN ON A TREADMILL IN . . .

1 week (female): 517.6 mi., Sharon Gayter (UK) Dec. 14–21, 2011

1 week (male): 510.9 mi., Pierre-Michael Micaletti (FRA), May 13–19, 2012

48 hr. (male): 271.79 mi. Tony Mangan (IRL), Aug. 22–24, 2008

48 hr. (female): 192.5 mi. Martina Schmit (AUT), Mar. 10–12, 2006

24 hr. (male): 160.2 mi., Suresh Joachim (AUS), Nov. 28–29, 2004

24 hr. (female): 153.6 mi., Edit Bérces (HUN), Mar. 8–9, 2004

12 hr. (male): 76.67 mi., Eusébio Bochons (CHE/ESP), Dec. 7, 2013

12 hr. (female): 60.14 mi., Theresa Dugwell (CAN), Mar. 2, 2013

FACT: There were 3,000 nails in the board on Jon's chest and the board weighed 125 lb.

MOST ROPE JUMPS ON A BED OF NAILS OVER A PERSON As if lying on a bed of nails isn't testing enough, Amy Bruney jumped 117 times on top of a bed of nails balanced over her husband Jon Bruney (both U.S.A.) on the set of *Guinness World Records Unleashed* in Los Angeles, California, U.S.A., on Jun. 25, 2013.

Ceramic slabs broken by the head by forward flips in one minute In just 60 sec., Michael Gonzalez (U.S.A.) smashed 43 ceramic slabs with his head, following a forward flip, on the set of *Guinness World Records Unleashed* in Los Angeles, California, U.S.A., on Jul. 2, 2013.

Concrete blocks broken in one minute (male) Ali Bahçetepe (TUR) smashed 1,175 concrete blocks by hand in Datça Cumhuriyet Meydanı, Turkey, on Nov. 17, 2012.

Ali is something of a past master when it comes to concrete deconstruction. Over the years, he has also recorded the **most concrete blocks broken in 30 seconds** (683) and the **most concrete blocks broken in one stack** (36).

Ice blocks broken by a human battering ram Uğur Öztürk (TUR) rammed through 14 ice blocks for *Rekorlar Dünyası* in Istanbul, Turkey, on Jun. 26, 2013.

Pine boards broken with the elbow in one minute Mohammad Rashid (PAK) broke 68 pine boards with his elbow in one minute at the Punjab Youth Festival in Lahore, Pakistan, on Mar. 13, 2013. At the same event on the same day, 1,450 attendees also set the record for the **most people arm wrestling**.

The following year, perhaps looking for less painful records to attempt, the festival organizers formed the **largest human flag**, involving 28,957 participants at the National Hockey Stadium in Lahore on Feb. 15.

MODERN
WORLD

CONTENTS

There are **250 births** every minute . . . and 105 deaths.

LARGEST COLLECTION OF U.S. PRESIDENTIAL MEMORABILIA Ronald
Wade (U.S.A.) owned 6,960 items of memorabilia with a U.S. presidential theme
as of Oct. 14, 2013. Ronald started his collection with a badge at the age of 10
and, after graduation, he became a White House page during Richard Nixon's
presidency (1969–74). He has also donated many items to the Bush Library outside
Dallas and has had a replica of the Oval Office built in his house in Longview,
Texas.

FACT: The site for the White House was chosen by the first U.S.
president, George Washington, in 1791. John Adams, the second
president, was the first one to actually live there, in 1800.

RICHE$T PEOPLE

**Meet the oil barons, retail magnates, and tech tycoons who are all
members of the exclusive Guinness World Records Super-Rich Club—
the 16 men (and yes, they're all men, and all but four of them American) who've held the record for the wealthiest living person over the
past 60 years.**

Even if he spent $1 m a day, it would still take the **richest man** nearly 200 years to spend all of his cash!

FACT: The business card of gangster Alphonse Gabriel "Al" Capone read: "Secondhand furniture dealer."

AL CAPONE Our 1960 edition records the belief that Chicago gangster Al Capone (U.S.A., 1899–1947) held the record for the **highest gross income ever achieved in a single year by a private citizen**. Adjusted for inflation, in 1927 he earned $1.41 bn from a trade we said included "illegal liquor trading and alky-cookers (illicit stills)" as well as "dog tracks, dance halls . . . and vice."

KING BHUMIBOL ADULYADEJ
One surefire way to riches is to be born to them. Thailand's King Bhumibol Adulyadej, with assets of $30 bn, is the **richest monarch**. Here, he is with Brunei's Sultan Haji Hassanal Bolkiah (near right), the second richest monarch with a mere $20 bn—but what's a few billion between royal friends?

WHO WANTS TO BE A QUADRILLIONAIRE?

In Jun. 2013, it was reported that Christopher Reynolds (U.S.A.) became the **first trillionaire** and **first quadrillionaire** when a (brief) bank error in his favor resulted in a balance of $92,233,720,368,547,800 in his PayPal account. Reportedly, when asked what he would have spent the money on, Reynolds said, "I probably would have paid down the national debt." He would have been able to do that and then some, given that his balance was 1,200 times greater than the GDP of every country in the world combined!

FACT: If Bill Gates were still worth $120 bn today, his wealth would be greater than the GDP of 134 of the world's 192 countries.

THE GWR RICH LIST: HIGHEST ROLLERS, 1955–2015

John Thoburn Williamson (CAN, 1907–58)
Record: 1955–56
Industry: Minerals, founded Williamson diamond mine
Peak: $60 m
Adjusted: $514 m

Jean Paul Getty (U.S.A., 1892–1976)
Record: 1958, 1960–61, 1964–67
Industry: Oil, building on empire of father George Franklin Getty
Peak: $3 bn
Adjusted: $22.2 bn

Haroldson Lafayette Hunt (U.S.A., 1889–1974)
Record: 1962
Industry: Oil empire based in Texas, after running cotton plantation
Peak: $2 bn
Adjusted: $15.2 bn

Howard Hughes (U.S.A., 1905–76)
Record: 1968–71
Industry: Inherited father's tool business, moved into aviation, also movie production
Peak: $1.37 bn
Adjusted: $9 bn

Daniel K. Ludwig (U.S.A., 1897–1992)
Record: 1972–77, 1979–81
Industry: Shipping, oil, banking, cattle, insurance, property, hotels
Peak: $3 bn
Adjusted: $16.5 bn

John D. MacArthur (U.S.A., 1897–1978)
Record: 1978
Industry: Insurance (with wife Catherine), property, mainly in Florida, U.S.A.
Peak: $1.72 bn
Adjusted: $6 bn

Forrest Mars, Sr. (U.S.A., 1904–99)
Record: 1982–83
Industry: Food, building on father's Mars candy business, leaving company in 1969
Peak: $1 bn
Adjusted: $12.3 bn

David Packard (U.S.A., 1912–96)
Record: 1984–85
Industry: IT and computing, cofounding Hewlett-Packard with Bill Hewlett in 1939
Peak: $1.8 bn
Adjusted: $3.98 bn

Gordon Getty (U.S.A., b. 1933)
Record: 1986
Industry: Father's oil empire, selling to Texaco in contentious deal for $10 bn in 1984
Peak: $4.1 bn
Adjusted: $9.06 bn

Sam Walton (U.S.A., 1918–92)
Record: 1987–88
Industry: Retailing empire based around Walmart chain stores, founded 1962
Peak: $21 bn
Adjusted: $42.4 bn

Yoshiaki Tsutsumi (JPN, b. 1934)
Record: 1989–1992
Industry: Developing and expanding father's property-base business empire
Peak: $21 bn
Adjusted: $38.9 bn

S. Robson Walton (U.S.A., b. 1944)
Record: 1993
Industry: Oldest son of Sam Walton, chairman of Walmart (biggest retailer in 2013)
Peak: $10 bn
Adjusted: $15.9 bn

John Werner Kluge (DEU, 1914–2010)
Record: 1994
Industry: Mainly media, including TV, radio, and advertising
Peak: $8.1 bn
Adjusted: $12.5 bn

Warren Buffett (U.S.A., b. 1930)
Record: 1995–96, 2009
Industry: Investing in a diverse range of companies all over the world
Peak: $62 bn
Adjusted: $66.1 bn

THE GWR RICH LIST (continued)

Bill Gates (U.S.A., b. 1955)
Record: 1997–2008, 2010, 2014
Industry: Software engineering, founder of Microsoft
Peak: $90 bn
Adjusted: $120 bn

Carlos Slim Helú (MEX, b. 1940)
Record: 2011–13
Industry: Telecoms, after stockbroking, investment, and general business
Peak: $74 bn
Adjusted: $74 bn

Adjusted wealth estimated in 2014 using the consumer price list

TOP 10 RICHEST PEOPLE IN 2014

Of the **richest person** record holders over the last 60 years, only three feature in the current top 10.

Name	Amount	Industry	Age
Bill Gates (U.S.A.)	$75.9 bn	Software	58
Carlos Slim Helú (MEX)	$71 bn	Telecoms	73
Amancio Ortega (ESP)	$62.7 bn	Textiles	77
Warren Buffett (U.S.A.)	$58.6 bn	Investment	83
Ingvar Kamprad (SWE)	$51.9 bn	Retail	87
Charles Koch (U.S.A.)	$46.9 bn	Engineering	78
David Koch (U.S.A.)			73
Larry Ellison (U.S.A.)	$43 bn	Software	69
Christy Walton (U.S.A.)	$36.9 bn	Retail	59
Sheldon Adelson (U.S.A.)	$35.4 bn	Casinos	80

Wealth average taken from: bloomberg.com, celebritynetworth.com, citywire.co.uk, forbes.com, londonlovesbusiness.com, and nationaljournal.com

"The meek shall inherit the Earth, but not its mineral rights." So said Jean Paul Getty (U.S.A.), the oil baron who was the world's **richest person** for seven of the last 60 years. He was not alone in oil—one in four of our featured billionaires owed their megabucks to a vicelike grip on our natural resources.

Oil is no longer such a king. More recent entrants to the Billionaires' Club found their fortunes by trading in less tangible goods such as software and media rights, or have a near magical ability to read the stock markets.

In real terms, the richest man to emerge since we started publishing in 1955 is Bill Gates (U.S.A.). Adjusted for inflation, his software-base fortune via Microsoft reached an almost inconceivable $120 bn in 2000. It was built on the back of the dot-com boom, which, in the U.S.A., saw the value of shares on the NASDAQ stock exchange more than double in the year up to Mar. 10, 2000. Alas, all good things come to an end, and the wheel of fortune crushed many of those same companies: just 12 months later, most NASDAQ dot-coms had ceased trading.

Bill Gates survived, although, by the end of 2001, even he was down to his last $77.8 bn.

WORLD AT WAR

Most peaceful country As of 2013, Iceland was No. 1 on the Global Peace Index (see p. 265) with a score of 1.162. Denmark was second and New Zealand was ranked third.

Highest defense budget The U.S.A. had a defense budget totaling $645.7 bn in 2012.

Least secure nation in relation to nuclear weapons In 2012, the Economist Intelligence Unit and the Nuclear Threat Initiative (a nongovernmental organization) reported that of the 32 nations with more than 2.2 lb. (1 kg) of weapons-grade nuclear material, North Korea is the least secure. The state's leader, Kim Jong-un—at the age of 31, according to official reports—is the **youngest state leader to control nuclear weapons**.

As of 2012, these sources rank Australia as the **most secure nation in relation to nuclear weapons**.

There has not been a 25-year period without war since **1495**.

LEAST PEACEFUL COUNTRY Created by the Institute for Economics and Peace, the Global Peace Index ranks countries by the safety of their citizens, the extent of conflict, and the degree of militarization. The index runs from 1 to 5, where 1 represents peace. As of 2013, Afghanistan was rated least at peace (3.440), with Somalia second-least peaceful, and Syria third.

Most civilian deaths in an undeclared civil war Accurately recording deaths in any conflict is difficult and subject to variation of numbers. However, the United Nations estimated on Jul. 24, 2013 that 100,000 people had died in Syria since the start of hostilities in Mar. 2011. On Sep. 24, 2013, France is reported to have told the UN General Assembly that 120,000 people had been killed in Syria. In Oct. 2013, the Syrian Observatory for Human Rights, based in the UK, also reported 120,000 fatalities.

Deadliest conflict for children (current) In the Nov. 2013 report "Stolen Futures" (spanning Mar. 2011 to Aug. 2013) by the Oxford Research Group, 11,420 victims 17 years old and under are believed to have been killed in the Syrian civil war. Of these, more than 112 were tortured, 389 were killed by sniper fire, and some 764 were summarily executed.

The number of Syrian child refugees is now 1 million (the **most refugee children**), most of whom are under the age of 11.

LARGEST REFUGEE CAMP According to the humanitarian aid charity Cooperative for Assistance and Relief Everywhere (CARE), the Dadaab refugee camp in Kenya, Africa, is the largest in the world. On Apr. 29, 2013, its registered refugee population stood at 423,496—nearly five times the size the camp was originally built to accommodate. Most of the refugees are from neighboring Somalia.

FACT: During World War I, the average life expectancy of soldiers in the trenches was around six weeks.

HIGHEST DEATH TOLLS IN CONFLICTS SINCE 1955

✝✝
Second Congo War 2.5–5.4 million, 1998–2003

✝✝✝✝✝✝✝✝✝✝✝✝✝✝✝✝✝✝✝✝✝✝✝✝✝✝✝✝✝✝✝✝✝✝✝✝✝✝
Vietnam War 800,000–3.8 million, 1955–75

✝✝✝✝✝✝✝✝✝✝✝✝✝✝✝✝✝✝✝✝✝✝✝✝✝✝✝✝✝
Nigerian Civil War 1–3 million, 1967–70

✝✝✝✝✝✝✝✝✝✝✝✝✝✝✝✝
Soviet War in Afghanistan
ca. 960,000–1.6 million, 1979–89

✝✝✝✝✝✝✝✝✝✝✝✝
Iran-Iraq War ca. 1 million, 1980–88

✝✝✝✝✝✝✝✝✝✝✝
Second Sudanese Civil War ca. 1 million, 1983–2005

✝✝✝✝✝✝✝✝✝✝
Mozambican Civil War 900,000–1 million, 1975–94

✝✝✝✝✝✝✝✝✝
Rwandan Civil War 800,000–1 million, 1990–93

✝✝✝✝✝✝✝✝
First Congo War 800,000, 1996–97

✝✝✝✝✝✝
Eritrean War of Independence 570,000, 1961–91

KEY:
✝ x1 = 100,000 deaths
✝✝✝✝✝✝✝✝✝✝
= lowest estimate
✝✝✝✝✝✝✝✝✝✝
= highest estimate

NOTHING CIVIL ABOUT WAR

Civil wars have brought about the death of around 25 million people since the conclusion of the last global conflict in 1945.

LONGEST CIVIL WAR OF MODERN TIMES The civil war in Myanmar started shortly after the country—formerly known as Burma—achieved independence from the UK on Jan. 4, 1948, and it continues to the present day. Small armed groups are active in the west and, according to Amnesty International, clashes in Rakhine State started in Jun. 2012 and have continued since.

CASUALTIES OF WAR

The first *Guinness Book of Records* was published only 10 years after the end of World War II. That conflict featured in our debut edition as the **bloodiest war,** with overall casualties of around 56.4 million. Poland suffered most in proportion to its population, with 6,028,000 (or 17.2%) of its 35,100,000 citizens killed. It is a measure of the magnitude of this loss of life that it still represents history's **highest wartime death toll.**

MOST TERRORIST ATTACKS PER COUNTRY The survey "Country Reports on Terrorism 2012," published in May 2013 by the U.S. National Consortium for the Study of Terrorism and Responses to Terrorism, identified Pakistan as the country with the most terrorist attacks during 2012. It saw 1,404 attacks during that 12-month period, in which 1,848 people were killed and 3,643 injured. Iraq was placed second in the survey and Afghanistan third.

Most refugees by country of origin According to UNHCR, the UN refugee agency, a combined total of 2,585,605 refugees had escaped from Afghanistan as of Jan. 2013, the greatest number from any country.

The **country with the largest population of refugees** is Pakistan. In Jan. 2013, it housed 1,638,456 refugees, nearly all of whom have fled from Afghanistan.

LARGEST SPECIAL FORCES
Special forces are trained military units with nonconventional tasks. North Korea has the largest such force, with around 60,000 operatives and some 130,000 personnel with special forces–like characteristics, according to U.S. military officials.

WAGING WARFARE

Shortest war: Between Britain and Zanzibar (now part of Tanzania); lasted from 9:00 a.m. to 9:45 a.m. on Aug. 27, 1896

Longest continuous international war: Thirty Years War (1618–48), between various European countries; ended with Peace of Westphalia

Highest death toll from a civil war: Russian Civil War (1917–22), with the death of ca. 1.5 million soldiers and more than 8 million civilians

Military hardware? Turn to p. 427.

Largest peace-keeping force (one operation) A United Nations Protection Force (UNPROFOR) peace-keeping mission was deployed in the former Yugoslavia from Feb. 1992 to Mar. 1995. In Sep. 1994, the mission reached a strength of 39,922 military personnel, including a "Rapid Reaction Force."

At present, the UN is undertaking 15 peace-keeping operations worldwide, with one special political mission in Afghanistan. The **largest peace-keeping force deployed on one operation (present day)** is the stabilization mission in the Democratic Republic of the Congo. Of the 26,024 UN personnel deployed there, 19,557 are military troops.

Lowest score on the Press Freedom Index Based on data for deaths, violence, censorship, media independence, and other factors, the African dictatorship of Eritrea is rated as the country with the least press freedom, according to the 2013 Press Freedom Index.

According to the Committee to Protect Journalists, as of Dec. 19, 2013, the **most dangerous country for the media (current year)** was Syria: 21 journalists were killed there in 2013. In all, 52 journalists were killed in 2013 worldwide with a "confirmed" motive—i.e., where a murder is in direct reprisal for their work, or in crossfire, combat, or during dangerous assignments, such as coverage of a street protest.

First post–World War II head of state convicted by an international war crimes court The international Special Court for Sierra Leone based in the Hague, Netherlands, found Charles Taylor, the ex–President of Liberia, Africa, guilty of 11 crimes. These included rape, murder, and the use of child soldiers during the civil war in Sierra Leone between 1991 and 2002, in which around 50,000 people died. He was sentenced to 50 years' imprisonment in May 2012 for aiding the rebels who committed atrocities.

LARGEST EMERGENCY AID APPEAL On Jun. 7, 2013, the United Nations launched an appeal for $5 bn in humanitarian aid for Syria to help more than 10 million people by the end of that year. The UN estimates that 4 million children are in need of humanitarian assistance as a result of the three-year conflict. The war has forced more than 6 million people out of their homes and caused 2 million to flee the country.

REMOTE-CONTROLLED DEATH: Striking Drones Drones are remotely controlled, armed, and unmanned aerial vehicles. According to nongovernmental organizations and Pakistan government sources cited by Amnesty International in its "Will I Be Next?" report on U.S. drone strikes in Pakistan, the U.S.A. launched some 330–374 drone strikes in that country between 2004 and Sep. 2013. Another estimate, from the New America Foundation public policy institute, puts the figure at 364 U.S. drone strikes in Pakistan as of Jul. 2013. Either estimate represents the **most drone strikes**.

HOT SPOTS

Most murders per capita While Brazil has the most murders in an absolute sense (see p. 264), per capita the record is held by Honduras. The Central American country has 82.1 murders per 100,000 people, according to research by *The Economist*.

Most prisoners per capita According to the International Center for Prison Studies, in 2011 the U.S.A. had a record prison population of 2,239,751, and a rate of 716 prisoners for every 100,000 residents—the most prisoners per capita. By comparison, the micro-state of San Marino had just two prisoners—or 6 prisoners per 100,000.

Most dangerous place to fly The 2012 Annual Review of the International Air Transport Association (IATA) reported that the most dangerous place to fly is Africa—nine times more dangerous than the global average. In 2011, Africa suffered 3.27 aircraft destroyed or written off for every million flights taken. Reasons included an aging fleet of turboprop aircraft, and inadequate air-traffic control.

The **average life expectancy in 1955** was 48 years; today, it is 67.2.

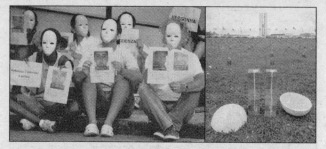

MOST MURDERS PER COUNTRY There were 47,106 murders in Brazil during 2012, corresponding to 24.5 homicides per 100,000 of the population. In Nov. 2012, protesters concerned by these figures amassed outside the Brasilia National Congress, where more than 900 blood-red bricks were laid out: one for each victim in a typical week.

Country with the highest percentage of the poor
Despite India's growing economy, its borders contain 41.01% of the world's poor. China comes second with 22.12%. The UN Department of Economic and Social Affairs defines poverty as "equating to those who earn $1.25 a day or less."

Lowest GDP per head
Gross Domestic Product (GDP) reflects all the goods and services produced by a nation in a year, stated as a value per head of population. The citizens of Malawi, an East African country with an undeveloped economy, have a GDP per head of $223. Luxembourg has the **highest GDP** (excluding the tiny principalities of Monaco and Liechtenstein) at $110,424.

Largest global toxic threat
According to a report from 2010 by the Blacksmith Institute (U.S.A.), 10 million people are at risk from lead poisoning. The next most toxic global pollutants, in order, are: mercury, chromium, arsenic, pesticides, and radionuclides. These can cause mental and physical disabilities, cancers, and even death.

DEADLIEST PLACE TO TRAVEL BY ROAD The World Health Organization (WHO) in 2013 reported that the Dominican Republic recorded 41.7 road deaths per 100,000 population during the year 2010, the highest rate of nations with a population of more than 1 million. Globally, 1.24 million people died on the road in 2010.

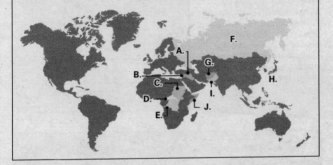

GLOBAL PEACE INDEX: THE LEAST PEACEFUL COUNTRIES

The Global Peace Index 2013 ranks 162 nations on a scale of 1 to 5 (1=most peaceful), using 22 indicators ranging from military expenditure to relations with neighboring countries and the percentage of prison population.

A. Iraq **3.245**

B. Syria **3.393**

C. Sudan **3.242**

D. Central African Republic **3.03**

E. Dem. Rep. of the Congo **3.085**

F. Russia **3.060**

G. Afghanistan **3.440**

H. North Korea **3.044**

I. Pakistan **3.106**

J. Somalia **3.394**

Source: Institute for Economics and Peace

Worst air pollution In 2011, the World Health Organization (WHO) reported that the air in Mongolia had an annual average of 279 micrograms of PM_{10} per cubic meter (see Glossary p. 267). Many of the country's factories burn coal and many people live in *gers*: yurtlike felt-lined tents with central stoves. See page 266 for the **most polluted major city**.

On a lighter note, the WHO report also stated that Whitehorse in Yukon, Canada, has an annual average of only 3 micrograms of PM_{10}, making it the **least polluted city**.

COUNTRY COMPARISONS

Highest death rate: Ukraine, with 16.2 deaths per 1,000 population projected for 2010–15.

Highest cancer death rate: Hungary, with 316 deaths per 100,000 population in 2009.

Highest heart disease death rate: Ukraine, with 1,070.5 deaths per 100,000 population in 2011.

Highest obesity rate: The island state of Nauru in the South Pacific, with 71.1% of people in 2008.

MOST FATAL SNAKEBITES PER COUNTRY India reports a greater number of fatalities from snakebites than any country, recording 81,000 "envenomings" annually. Of these, 11,000 eventually prove to be fatal, according to conservative estimates published in *The Global Burden of Snakebite* (2008).

MOST POLLUTED MAJOR CITY A 2011 report by the WHO measured air pollution by the mass of particles smaller than 10 microns in diameter per cubic meter of air (known as PM_{10}). Ahwaz in Iran was the main offender, with a PM_{10} of 372 micrograms per cubic meter.

MOST DEATHS FROM NATURAL DISASTERS In 2013, the Centre for Research on the Epidemiology of Disasters, Belgium, provided a report of fatalities from disasters such as earthquakes, floods, and hurricanes during 2012. The most deaths—2,385—occurred in the Philippines, with China in second place with 802. In Dec. 2012, almost 2,000 people in the Philippines were killed by Typhoon Bopha alone.

MOST ROBBERIES PER CAPITA In 2013, *The Economist* reported that Belgium has 1,714 robberies for every 100,000 people in a population of 10.8 million. The figures include an audacious heist on Feb. 18, 2013, when cars with police markings were used to steal $50 m of diamonds from a plane at Brussels Airport—without a shot being fired.

HARD NEWS: *Journalists in Danger* The **most dangerous country for journalists** is Iraq, with 153 killed since 1992. A total of 1,014 journalists have been killed worldwide since 1992, according to the Committee to Protect Journalists (CPJ). The problem is compounded by impunity—when governments deliberately don't investigate murders because they don't want to have abuses of power and human rights violations reported. The second most dangerous country is the Philippines, with 73 journalists killed since 1992.

STATE OF DANGER

From our first edition: "Taking figures for the decade (1940–1950) that part of the world with the highest annual average murder rate is the state of Georgia, U.S.A., with 167.3 per million." By 2012, the figure had dropped to 59 per million, according to the FBI. The record holder per capita is now Honduras (see p. 263).

MOST DANGEROUS RESORT FOR SHARK ATTACKS New Smyrna Beach in Florida, U.S.A., has recorded 238 attacks, and the beach has become known as the shark attack capital of the world, although most of the bites have been nibbles from hungry juveniles. Pictured here are surfers with a blacktip shark not far behind them—a photo snapped in 2008 by Kem McNair, who had finished surfing for the day.

Worst land pollution In Nov. 1994, thousands of tons of crude oil flowed across the pristine Arctic tundra of the Komi Republic near Usinsk, Russia. Estimates of the amount of oil lost vary from about 15,400 to 220,000 tons, and the total contaminated area measured 227.11 million sq. ft. (21.1 million m²), almost the same area occupied by El Salvador. The cost of the accident was estimated at more than 311 billion roubles ($11 bn).

Unhappiest country According to a survey of 156 nations conducted in 2013 by the UN Sustainable Development Solutions Network, the citizens of the West African nation of Togo are the unhappiest, with a score of 2.936 out of 10. The survey looked at factors such as quality and quantity of life, mental health, and personal liberty. At the other end of the scale was Denmark with a score of 7.693—making it the **happiest country**.

Most tornadoes by area The Netherlands has one twister for every 769 sq. mi. (1,991 km²) of land. The U.S.A. has one per 3,161 sq. mi. (8,187 km²).

TRAVEL & TOURISM

Highest tourist receipts In 2011, global receipts (earnings) from tourism topped $1 tr for the first time in history, according to the United Nations World Tourism Organization (UNWTO). In 2012, however, total exports from international tourism rose once again, to reach an unprecedented level of $1.3 tr.

Mexico City is sinking by 3 ft. 3 in. per year—**10 times faster** than Venice.

MOST NORTHERLY SKI RESORT
The Tromsø Alpinsenter ski resort is located in Kroken, Norway, more than 186 mi. (300 km) inside the Arctic Circle. The resort has two drag lifts, a 1,640-ft. (500-m) children's tow, and four slopes with varying levels of difficulty. The longest run extends for some 1.2 mi. (2 km).

FASTEST-GROWING TOURIST REGION
Tourist arrivals in Asia and the Pacific rose 7% in 2012, the equivalent of 15 million more international tourist visitors than in 2011. Among Asian subregions, southeast Asia posted the highest growth, with 9% more arrivals than the previous year, and Thailand saw a growth of 16% in absolute terms over 2011. This was the second year in a row that this region posted a record increase, according to the UNWTO.

Greatest spending on tourism (country) The Chinese spent $102 bn on tourism in 2012—an increase of 37% on the country's 2011 spending and an eightfold increase from the $13 bn spent in 2000. Germany's tourists spent the next largest amount internationally—$83.8 bn—with the U.S.A. third, spending $83.5 bn.

Highest earnings from tourism According to the UNWTO, tourism in the U.S.A. was worth $126.2 bn in 2012 and single-handedly accounted for 8.5% of international tourism takings. Spain was second, with $56 bn, and France third, with $54 bn.

Most international tourist arrivals in one year In 2012, according to a UNWTO report, the number of international tourist arrivals was 1.035 billion.

The same source reports that the **most popular country for tourism** is France, with 83 million international arrivals. The country accounts for just over 8% of the global tourism market. Its nearest rivals are the U.S.A. (with 67 million visitors) and China (with 57.7 million).

Europe remains the **most-visited tourism region**, with 534.2 million arrivals in 2012, according to the UNWTO. Asia and the Pacific are its nearest rivals, with 233.6 million arrivals. In third place are the Americas, with 163.1 million.

Travel & Tourism

LARGEST APARTMENT SHIP Launched in 2002, MS *The World* incorporates 165 residential units comprising 106 apartments, 19 studio apartments, and 40 studios. While it continuously circumnavigates the world, its residents are able to conduct their professional lives while living and relaxing onboard. The average stay lasts for around three to four months of the year and average occupancy is 150 residents (with an average age of 65).

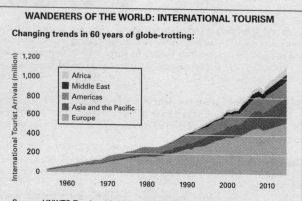

WANDERERS OF THE WORLD: INTERNATIONAL TOURISM

Changing trends in 60 years of globe-trotting:

International Tourist Arrivals (million)

- Africa
- Middle East
- Americas
- Asia and the Pacific
- Europe

Source: UNWTO Tourism Highlights 2013 Edition

Transportation mode
Road 40%
Rail 2%
Water 6%
Air 52%

Purpose of visit
Health; religion; friends/family;
    other 27%
Leisure 52%
Business 14%
Not specified 7%

For truly epic journeys, see p. 337.

PLUS ÇA CHANGE . . .

China has overtaken the U.S.A. in terms of tourist spending, and over the years London and Paris have vied for the honor of being the most-visited city. But for years now, one country has consistently proved to be the most popular for tourists: France. Back in 1999, it welcomed 73 million visitors. As of 2012, 83 million of us chose France for its rich cultural heritage, beautiful countryside, beaches, ski resorts, culinary delights, historic castles, and cathedrals . . . and, of course, to see the "city of light," Paris.

FACT: Only an estimated 1,000th of 1% of the world's population has visited Antarctica.

TOWERING ACHIEVEMENT

Every seven years, the Eiffel Tower receives a fresh coat of paint. In all, 132,275 lb. of paint are required to cover its 2.69 million-sq.-ft. surface area.

Most continents visited in one calendar day Gunnar Garfors (NOR) and Adrian Butterworth (UK) visited five continents in one calendar day, taking scheduled transport between the east side of Istanbul in Turkey (Asia), Casablanca in Morocco (Africa), Paris in France (Europe), Punta Cana in the Dominican Republic (North America), and Caracas in Venezuela (South America) on May 18, 2012. The entire trip took 28 hr. 25 min., but the changing time zones ensured that Garfors and documentary filmmaker Butterworth cleared customs in each country on the same day.

LARGEST MARINA In terms of inhabitants, Marina del Rey in Los Angeles County, California, U.S.A., is the largest marina, with a population of 8,866 according to a 2010 census. It is home to 6,500 boats. The Dubai Marina, however—a 2-mi.-long (3-km) canal city in Dubai, UAE, inaugurated in 2003—will accommodate approximately 120,000 people. It has a provisional completion date of 2015.

MOST POPULAR CITY FOR TOURISM According to the MasterCard Global Destination Cities index, the city that attracted the greatest number of tourists in 2012 was London, UK, with an estimated 16.9 million international visitors. The same report noted that tourists to London spent $21.1 bn, a 10.3% increase on 2011. No doubt the city's role as host of the 2012 Olympics played a part in this achievement.

MOST-VISITED ART GALLERY
The Louvre Museum in Paris, France, attracted 9,720,260 visitors in 2012. Housed in the Palais du Louvre on the Right Bank of the Seine, the museum first opened in 1793. In 1989, a glass pyramid designed by architect I. M. Pei was controversially added to its main courtyard (above).

According to *The Economist*, the Tate Modern in London, UK, remains the **most-visited modern art gallery**. In 2012, it drew 5,300,000 art lovers.

Most national capitals visited in 24 hours by scheduled transport
Sarah Warwick and Lucy Warwick (both UK) visited London, Brussels, Prague, Paris, Bratislava, and Vienna from Sep. 24 to 25, 2013.

THE FINAL FRONTIER

First space tourist: Businessman Dennis Tito (U.S.A.), trip to *International Space Station* (*ISS*), Apr. 28 to May 6, 2001

First space tourist (female): Anousheh Ansari (IRN), trip to *ISS*, Sep. 18 to 29, 2006

Most trips into space by a tourist: Charles Simonyi (U.S.A., b. HUN) embarked on first trip to *ISS* on Apr. 7, 2007; made second trip, at the age of 60, on Mar. 26, 2009

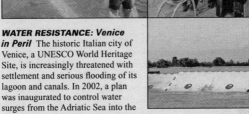

WATER RESISTANCE: Venice in Peril The historic Italian city of Venice, a UNESCO World Heritage Site, is increasingly threatened with settlement and serious flooding of its lagoon and canals. In 2002, a plan was inaugurated to control water surges from the Adriatic Sea into the lagoon. Named the Moses Project, it envisages building 78 giant steel gates across three inlets to the lagoon, and sinking 660,000-lb. hinged gates (see bottom right)—each around 88 ft. wide—into huge concrete bases dug into the seabed. This represents the **largest project to save a tourist resort**.

Most international visits by a U.S. president Two U.S. presidents have each visited 74 unique nations in office. The first was Bill Clinton, whose trips began on Apr. 3–4, 1993 in Vancouver, Canada, where he had a summit meeting with President Yeltsin (RUS) and a meeting with Canadian Prime Minister Brian Mulroney. His final trip was to the UK on Dec. 12–14, 2000, and included meetings with Prime Minister Tony Blair and Queen Elizabeth II. In all, Clinton made 133 trips.

George W. Bush, the 43rd president, visited 74 unique nations during 140 trips in his two terms. The first, on Feb. 16, 2001, was to San Cristóbal in Mexico, where he met with President Fox. The final visit was to Kabul in Afghanistan, from Dec. 14 to 15, 2008, to meet President Karzai and visit U.S. military personnel.

Largest national park The Northeast Greenland National Park covers 375,290 sq. mi. (972,000 km²), from Liverpool Land in the south to the northernmost island, Oodaaq, off Peary Land. Established in 1974 and enlarged in 1988, much of the park is covered by ice and is home to a variety of protected flora and fauna, including polar bears, musk ox, and birds of prey.

The **oldest national park** is Yellowstone National Park, U.S.A. It was given its status in 1872 by U.S. president Ulysses S. Grant, who declared that it would always be "dedicated and set apart as a public park or pleasuring ground for the benefit and enjoyment of the people." It covers 3,470 sq. mi. (8,980 km²), mostly in the state of Wyoming.

SHIPPING

Busiest shipping lane The Dover Strait marks the narrowest part of the English Channel between the UK and continental Europe. Through its shipping lane pass 500–600 ships a day.

First container ships Shipborne containers were employed—usually on short sea routes—from the early 20th century. Modern containerization started in the 1950s, one of the first vessels being the former tanker *Ideal X*, modified by Sea-Land Service (U.S.A.) in 1955. Standard container sizes were adopted in the 1960s alongside the introduction of purpose-built ships. A unit of cargo capacity can be measured by TEU—Twenty-foot Equivalent Unit—based on the volume of one standard, 20-ft.-long (6.1-m) container.

Largest container shipping line Maersk (DNK) runs more than 600 vessels that make a total of 3.4 million container moves annually. The company reported that they call at 35,000 ports annually and, in 2012, their work included shipping 8.4 billion bananas.

Fastest shipbuilding The World War II shipbuilding program at Kaiser's yard in Portland, Oregon, U.S.A., built 22-million-lb. (10,000-metric-ton) ships in as little as 4 days 15 hr. 30 min. In 1942, the SS *Robert E. Peary* had her keel laid on Nov. 8, launched on Nov. 12, and was operational on Nov. 15. Prefabrication speeded up production.

GREATEST LIFTING CAPACITY FOR A SHIP
The MV *Fairplayer* and MV *Javelin*, operated by Jumbo Shipping of Rotterdam (NLD), are J-class mega ships. Equipped with two Huisman mast cranes, each can carry a load of 2 million lb. (900 metric tons), giving a maximum lifting capacity of 4 million lb. (1,800 metric tons).

In a year, the average container ship will cover the distance of a trip to the **Moon and halfway back**.

LARGEST SHIPS

A. *For comparison: Eiffel Tower, 1,062 ft. tall*

B. Largest privately owned yacht: *Azzam*, owned by Sheikh Khalifa bin Zayed Al Nahyan (UAE), 590 ft. (cost: approx. $654 m)

C. Largest passenger liner: Royal Caribbean International Oasis class, 1,187 ft., DWT (deadweight tonnage) 33 million lb.

D. Largest oil tanker: Daewoo Shipbuilding & Marine Engineering T1 class, 1,243 ft., DWT 973.5 million lb.

E. Longest container ship: Maersk Triple E class, 1,312 ft., DWT 432 million lb.

F. Largest ship ever: *Mont*, 1,504 ft., DWT 1.24 billion lb.

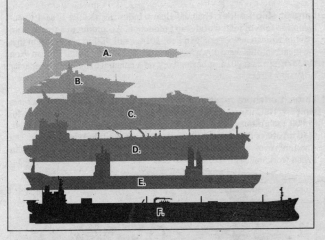

DEADWEIGHT TONNAGE (DWT)

Largest oil tanker—current: *Hellespont Alhambra*, Daewoo Shipbuilding & Marine Engineering (KOR), Jun. 11, 2001, 973 million lb.

Largest bulk carrier ship: *Vale Beijing* (Dec. 2011) and *Vale Qingdao* (Jun. 2012), STX Offshore & Shipbuilding (KOR), 891 million lb.

Largest dry bulk carrier ship: *Berge Stahl*, Bergesen (NOR), 1986, 804 million lb.

Largest pipe-laying ship: *Solitaire*, Allseas Group (NDL), 1998, 280 million lb.

BUSIEST OCEAN TRADE ROUTE A
total of 7.52 million cargo containers were
transported from North America to Asia
in 2012, and 14.42 million containers
shipped in the opposite direction. In all,
the route saw 21.94 million units.

Largest ship builder Hyundai Heavy Industries (KOR) is said to account for 15% of total world ship production. According to a report from
a South Korean news agency in Feb. 2014, a fall in ship prices meant that
the giant's profits were down 86% in 2013, at 146.3 bn South Korean Won
($136 m). In Jan. 2014, it began work on a container ship with a capacity
of 19,000 TEU.

Largest offshore mast crane Onboard the *Seven Borealis* is a crane,
built by Huisman (NLD), that lifts payloads of up to 11 million lb.
(5,000 metric tons). The *Seven Borealis* crane extends a record 492 ft.
(150 m) above deck level, although other cranes lift heavier weights. The
structure revolves on a bearing that is 36 ft. (11 m) in diameter. The ship
began work in 2012.

LONGEST CONTAINER SHIP The Maersk (DNK) Triple E-class ships are each
1,312 ft. (400 m) long and 20 have been ordered. The lead, *Maersk Mc-Kinney
Møller*, was launched in Geoje, South Korea, on Feb. 24, 2013. Each of the ships
will contain as much steel as eight Eiffel Towers and, placed in Times Square, New
York City, U.S.A., would tower above the billboards and most of the buildings.
Each ship has enough space to accommodate 36,000 cars or 863 million cans of
beans.

LARGEST SHIP EVER The oil tanker *Mont* (formerly *Jahre Viking*, *Happy Giant*, and *Seawise Giant*) had a deadweight tonnage of 622,544 tons (564,763 tonnes). She was 1,504 ft. (458.45 m) long, 226 ft. (68.8 m) wide, and had a draft of 80 ft. 9 in. (24.61 m). In 2010, she became the **largest ship to be scrapped**.

BUSIEST PORT FOR CARGO VOLUME The Port of Shanghai turned over 811 million tons (736 million metric tons) of cargo in 2012, handling more than 32 million containers. It has a total quay length of around 12.43 mi. (20 km), with 125 berths for container ships.

Largest open-deck transport ship The semi-submersible *Dockwise Vanguard* is 902 ft. (275 m) long and has a flat deck measuring 230 x 902 ft. (70 x 275 m). It can carry oversize cargo weighing 242.5 million lb. (110,000 metric tons). The carrier, operated by Dockwise (NLD), submerges its deck to a depth of 52 ft. (16 m) to allow it to load cargoes, such as oil and gas platforms, by floating underneath them.

MOST POWERFUL NUCLEAR-POWERED CARGO SHIP The Russian *Sevmorput* is not only the most powerful but is now the only nuclear-powered cargo ship left of the four that were originally produced. Nuclear power has not been widely adopted in shipping, and *Sevmorput* itself was to be scrapped until it was announced in Dec. 2013 that it is to be restored by 2016.

FACT: In 1992, 29,000 plastic yellow ducks and other toys were released into the wild when they were spilled from a container ship in the Pacific.

SPINNING AROUND: A Propeller with a Twist The *Emma Maersk* was launched in 2006 and featured the world's **largest propeller**. Made by Mecklenburger Metallguss GmbH (DEU), the single-piece, 286,600-lb. propeller has six blades and measures 31 ft. 6 in. in diameter. Because of its size, the metal alloy from which it's made required two weeks to cool after casting. The blades are turned by a 14-cylinder Wärtsilä-Sulzer RTA96C two-stroke engine, the world's **largest diesel engine**. In Feb. 2013, however, as the ship entered the Suez Canal, an engine-room flood put it out of service for some months.

LONGEST BIG SHIP CANAL The Suez Canal has allowed ships to navigate from the Red Sea to the Mediterranean Sea, without sailing around Africa, since opening on Nov. 17, 1869. Ten years in the making, it is 100.8 mi. (162.2 km) in length and varies in width between 984 ft. (300 m) and 1,198 ft. (365 m).

SHIPWRECKS

Deepest The *Rio Grande* was a German World War II blockade runner, evading enemies to deliver cargo. In Jan. 1944, she was sunk by American ships and was discovered in 1996 by Blue Water Recoveries (UK) at a depth of 18,904 ft. (5,762 m).

Another World War II casualty was UK merchant ship SS *Gairsoppa*, from which was retrieved the **deepest salvage of cargo from a shipwreck**. She was sunk by a German U-boat submarine and lay at a depth of 15,420 ft. (4,700 m). In 2011, the ship was discovered by Odyssey Marine Exploration (U.S.A.), who had retrieved 105,821 lb. (48 metric tons) of silver by Jul. 2013.

Largest The 708-million-lb. (321,186-metric-ton) deadweight crude oil carrier *Energy Determination* broke in two in the Strait of Hormuz, Persian Gulf, on Dec. 12, 1979. She was not carrying any cargo but had a hull value of $58 m.

Oldest A single-mast sailing ship, discovered in 1912, was wrecked off Uluburun, near Kaş in southern Turkey, in the 14th century B.C.

WORLD OF CHANCE

Greatest winning streak In Dec. 1992, Greek-American Archie Karas arrived in Las Vegas, U.S.A., with $50 in his pocket. By early 1995, he had turned this sum into $40 m by playing pool, poker, and dice. It's the largest winning streak in history, and even has its own name in gambling lore: "The Run." Karas's love of dice and (later) baccarat were his downfall: by mid-1995, he had lost all of the money.

MOST MONEY LOST BY A NATION TO GAMBLING PER CAPITA According to international gambling organization H2 Gambling Capital, during 2010 the average Australian 17 years old or over lost U.S.$1,199. Around 70% of Australians are believed to participate in some form of gambling.

In 2013, **$9.4 bn** was gambled by the 39.7 million people who visited Las Vegas.

LARGEST WIN IN A TELEVISED POKER GAME Tom Dwan (U.S.A.) picked up £0.6 m ($1.1 m) from one hand of televised poker against fellow American Phil Ivey during Full Tilt Poker's Million Dollar Cash Game, filmed in London, UK, in Sep. 2009. Both players had drawn a "straight" (five cards of any suit ranked in order), but Dwan's 3-4-5-6-7 beat Ivey's ace-2-3-4-5.

First bookmaker The first person to turn a profit as a bookmaker is thought to have been Harry Ogden (UK), who operated on Newmarket Heath, Suffolk, UK, during the mid-1790s. Prior to this, people who wanted to bet on horse racing would simply make bets against one another. Ogden was the first to look at the entire field and offer different odds on every horse, calculating its chance of winning so that he would make a profit.

First offshore bookmaker Victor Chandler International, now trading as BetVictor, decided to move its entire operation offshore in 1997 to evade the UK gambling tax, a move that was completed in 1999. The company relocated to Gibraltar—where the betting tax is zero. Many other bookmakers now also have a presence on the "Rock."

LARGEST CLAW MACHINE "Santa Claw" is a claw machine measuring 17 x 8 x 12 ft. (5.1 x 2.4 x 3.6 m) that was operated via the Internet on thesantaclaw.com website between Jan. 3 and May 2011. Around 100,000 players tried their luck during this period, and more than 4,000 prizes were grabbed; winners received their prizes by mail.

LARGEST LOTTERY WIN DONATED TO CHARITY In Jul. 2010, Canadians Allen and Violet Large won CAN$11.2 m ($10.8 m) on the Lotto 6/49 draw. They gave away some 98%—CAN$10.9 m ($10.5 m)—to local groups, including the Red Cross and hospitals where Violet had cancer treatment.

TOP 10 BIGGEST GAMBLING LOSSES PER ADULT (PER ANNUM)

In absolute terms, populations of larger countries, such as the U.S.A. and China, naturally lose more money to gambling than smaller countries. (Macau in China is the **largest gambling city by revenue**—more than $38 bn was generated by its casinos and other gaming services in 2012.) But measured in proportion to their overall population, gambling's biggest losers tend to be the smaller nations:

A. Spain: $389
B. Greece: $391
C. Norway: $416
D. Hong Kong: $468
E. Italy: $481

F. Finland: $514
G. Canada: $528
H. Ireland: $547
I. Singapore: $1,093
J. Australia: $1,199

Source: H2 Gambling Capital, 2011; all figures quoted in U.S.$

FACT: The chances of winning the jackpot in a 6/49 lottery (i.e., selecting six numbers correctly out of a choice of 49) are 1 in 13,983,816.

FIRST FACEBOOK GAME TO OFFER CASH PRIZES

On Aug. 7, 2012, British online gaming company Gamesys launched the first Facebook game to offer real cash prizes. Titled *Bingo Friendzy*, it featured 90 mini games. Only Facebook users over the age of 18 are legally allowed to play the game.

Largest horse-racing win Scottish racehorse owner Harry Findlay scooped £1.85 m ($3 m) over the British May Bank Holiday weekend in 2007. Findlay had placed bets of £140,000 ($276,000) with online pool betting firm RaceO. He ended up with 16 winners, comprising two eight-horse accumulators (a multiple, high-risk bet that only pays out if every horse wins).

GREATEST NATIONAL LOTTERY JACKPOT

By Mar. 30, 2012, the American Mega Millions lottery jackpot reached an annuity value of $656 m, or $474 m in cash. The three unidentified winners (all U.S.A.) split the cash sum between them.

LONGEST CRAPS ROLL

On May 23, 2009, at the Borgata Hotel Casino in Atlantic City, New Jersey, U.S.A., craps player Patricia Demauro (U.S.A.) threw a pair of dice 154 times before a 7 ended her winning streak. It took her 4 hr. 18 min., beating odds of 1,560 billion to 1.

Most successful horse-racing gambler William Benter (U.S.A.) makes some $10 m per year betting on horses at the two tracks in Hong Kong, China. Benter trained as a physicist, and he used his scientific skills to build a computer model that takes into account more than 100 statistics—quantifying horses, jockeys, trainers, tracks, and race conditions—to calculate each runner's exact chance of winning.

Largest win in a poker competition Antonio Esfandiari (U.S.A., b. Iran) won $18,346,673 at the World Series of Poker tournament (WSOP2012) in Las Vegas, Nevada, U.S.A., on Jul. 3, 2012.

Largest online poker tournament PokerStars (UK) organized an online poker tournament with 225,000 participants on Jun. 16, 2013. Each player paid 60p ($1), with a £15,000 ($25,000) top prize.

LOTTERY WINNERS: What do they spend it on? As of Mar. 2012, the **largest national lottery** (see Lottery legends, above) had created 3,000 millionaires, each winning an average of $4.68 m. So how did they choose to spend their windfalls?

A. Property: $5.5 bn

B. Investments: $3.5 bn

C. Future needs (inc. provisions for children): $2.67 bn

D. Cars: $774 m

E. Dream vacations: $35 m

Source: Camelot Group

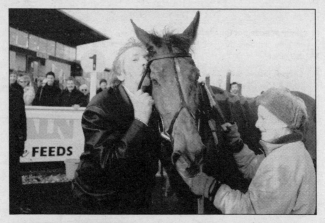

LARGEST TOTE BETTING WIN Sixty-one-year-old Steve Whiteley (UK) won an incredible £1,445,671.71 ($2,356,444.89) on a £2 ($3.25) Tote Jackpot accumulator bet in which he successfully predicted the winner of all six races from the meeting at Exeter, UK, on Mar. 8, 2011. Afterward, he was quoted as saying: "I'm a heating engineer—well, I was."

Largest slot machine tournament A total of 3,001 players attended a slot machine event organized by Bally Technologies (U.S.A.) at Mohegan Sun in Uncasville, Connecticut, U.S.A., on Apr. 27, 2013.

Most lottery prizes given in a year Pronósticos para la Asistencia Pública (MEX) awarded 97,909,447 lottery prizes during 2008, distributed across eight different games.

Most members of a family to win a national lottery In Sep. 2012, teenager Tord Oksnes became the third member of his family to hit the jackpot in the Norwegian National Lottery when he won 12.2 m kroner ($2.1 m). Three years previously, Tord's sister Hege Jeanette claimed 8.2 m kroner ($1.27 m). Three years before that, Tord and Hege's father Leif scooped a win of 8.4 m kroner ($1.5 m).

FAKES, FRAUDS, & FORGERIES

Most prolific art forger At his trial in 1979, Thomas Keating (UK, 1917–84) put his output of fake pictures at more than 2,000 works, representing 121 different artists across a 25-year period.

In 1496, the young **Michelangelo** faked an "ancient" statue of Cupid.

MOST EXPENSIVE FAKE DIARIES In 1983, *Stern* magazine paid some 9 million German marks ($5 m) for 62 diaries allegedly written by Adolf Hitler, Germany's leader during World War II. U.S. expert Kenneth W. Rendell later proved that they were forged. The forger, Konrad Kujau (DEU), was jailed for 3 years 6 months, as was the man who had "uncovered" the diaries, Gerd Heidemann (DEU, above).

Highest career earnings for a forger

Han van Meegeren (NLD, 1889–1947) is often cited as the most successful and influential art forger of all time. Estimates of his earnings vary, but by 1943 he had made the equivalent today of $25–30 m, and also had property investments in the region of $500 m. He focused on forgeries of work by the artists Johannes Vermeer and Pieter de Hooch.

Most lucrative art fraud by a woman

On Sep. 16, 2013, Glafira Rosales (MEX) pleaded guilty in New York City, U.S.A., to nine counts of fraud. She had taken part in a scheme to sell more than 60 fakes of abstract and Impressionist art, allegedly by 73-year-old American-Chinese artist Pei-Shen Qian, for more than $80 m. The forgeries included copies of works by Mark Rothko and Jackson Pollock.

LARGEST COLLECTION OF FAKE MASTERPIECES French artist Christophe Petyt owns just over 2,500 fake paintings of some of the world's most famous artworks. His company, L'Art du Faux, employs a selection of highly talented artists to copy masterpieces, which are then officially registered as a reproduction and sold.

MOST LUCRATIVE WINE FRAUD On Oct. 16, 2013, two Italian wine merchants suspected of faking at least 400 bottles of the exclusive Romanée-Conti burgundy wine were arrested. The fraudsters may have made some $2.75 m from the scheme.

Most prolific forger of Shakespearean work

In 1794–95, manuscripts appeared in London, UK, supposedly written by William Shakespeare (1564–1616), among them a love poem to his wife, a letter from Queen Elizabeth I, revisions to his work, and two new plays. They were, in fact, forgeries by William Henry Ireland (UK). One of the new dramas, *Vortigern and Rowena*, was performed in 1796.

CONFOUNDING THE COUNTERFEITERS

The Swiss have the most secure banknotes (see p. 287). Security features include:

A. Color-shifting ink—changes color when viewed from different angles
B. Holographic strip
C. Watermark, visible when held up to the light
D. Hidden numbers, visible when held up to the light
E. Very fine lines—difficult to replicate
F. Security thread, embedded in the note
G. Raised printing
H. Microprint text—difficult to replicate
I. Made from multilayer polymer plastic; changes color when tilted

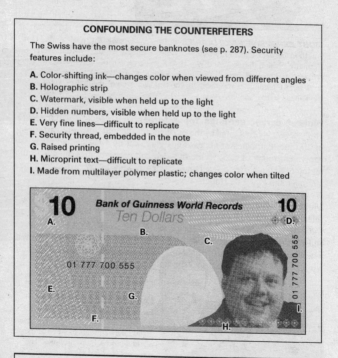

FACT: In all, 830 million UK banknotes—worth £11.4 bn ($19.1 bn)—were destroyed in 2013 due to poor condition.

SPLASHING THE PLASTIC

In 2006, we declared Swiss franc notes to be the **most secure banknote**. The 1,000-franc note incorporated 14 security features, including micro lettering, fluorescent ink, and braille. Several nations—including Australia, Canada, and Brunei—have now abandoned paper notes in favor of plastic film. They are also four times more durable than paper banknotes; on average, the U.S. dollar bill lasts for only around 18 months before it wears out.

FINANCE AGENTS

The U.S. Secret Service, a law-enforcement agency, was originally created at the end of the American Civil War (1861–65) to tackle counterfeit currency.

MOST SUCCESSFUL DEFENSE EQUIPMENT FAKER On May 2, 2013, James McCormick (UK) received a 10-year sentence for selling devices that he claimed could detect explosives and drugs, but which were actually modified novelty golf-ball finders. He sold them for around £27,000 ($40,000) each, making an estimated £50 m ($77 m) overall.

Largest ATM fraud In May 2013, it was reported that cyber criminals had stolen $45 m by hacking into a database of prepaid credit cards in a scheme dubbed "PIN cashing" or "carding." Seven U.S. citizens were arrested and accused of removing withdrawal limits, creating access codes, and using associates to spread the data online to leaders of "cashing crews," who drained cash machines.

LARGEST BITCOIN FRAUD Bitcoin—a virtual monetary system based on digital tokens—was conceived in 2008, and by Nov. 2013, its value had soared to $1,000 per bitcoin. The currency has already suffered from fraud losses, the worst being that of the Bitcoin Savings and Trust. By the time it was shut down in 2012, the savings scheme had reportedly lost the equivalent of $5.6 m.

Fakes, Frauds, & Forgeries

GREATEST GOLDSMITH FRAUD

In 1896, the Louvre Museum in Paris, France, exhibited a large gold helmet weighing more than 1 lb. 12 oz. (800 g). The "Tiara of Saitaphernes" allegedly dated from either the late third or second century B.C. The Louvre bought the object for 200,000 gold French francs, but it was later shown to be a fake that had been crafted by Russian goldsmith Israel Rouchomovsky.

LARGEST FAKE ARMY Before Allied forces invaded Europe, via Normandy in France, on "D-Day" (Jun. 6, 1944), a ruse was invented. Operation Bodyguard gave the illusion of two field armies, one set to menace Pas-de-Calais, comprising 1 million men. As a result, many German troops stayed in Pas-de-Calais instead of Normandy—preserving many Allied lives on the day of the invasion.

Largest fine for mortgage fraud

On Nov. 19, 2013, the largest U.S. bank—JPMorgan Chase—concluded a settlement with officials from the U.S. Justice Department. This included a fine that amounted to $13 bn—the largest civil settlement with any one company resulting from the sale and misrepresentation of residential mortgage-backed securities (RMBS).

Largest fine for pharmaceutical fraud

In Jul. 2012, British company GlaxoSmithKline received a £1.9-bn ($3-bn) penalty after admitting to history's biggest healthcare fraud. From 1997 to 2004, the company was alleged to have bribed doctors to prescribe drugs linked with safety concerns and promoted drugs that were not approved for their intended purpose.

For genuine works of art, view p. 372.

FINANCIAL FINAGLING

Longest prison sentence for fraud: 141,078 years, for Chamoy Thipyaso (THA) and seven associates in 1989, for swindling some 16,000 Thai citizens out of their life savings.

Greatest banknote forgery: the Third Reich's Operation Bernhard, during World War II, produced approximately 9 million counterfeit British notes valued at around £130 m ($520 m).

HIGHEST ANNUAL COST OF CYBERCRIME Stolen identities, raided bank accounts, and hacked e-mails are all forms of cybercrime. The 2013 Norton Report puts the annual cost of consumer cybercrime at $113 bn, or $298 per victim, of which there are more than 1 million every day or one every 3 sec.

Largest fraud by a rogue trader On Jan. 24, 2008, French bank Société Générale declared that it had uncovered 4.9 bn euros ($7.16 bn) of losses following rogue trading by a member of its staff. Bank trader Jérôme Kerviel (FRA) was taken into police custody and was said to have admitted hiding his activities from his superiors. He was sentenced to five years in prison, with two years suspended. In 2010, however, he published a memoir entitled *Downward Spiral: Memoirs of a Trader* in which he claims that his employers were aware of his trading activity.

WORRYING SIGNS: The Rogue Interpreter Nelson Mandela's memorial service took place on Dec. 10, 2013 in the 95,000-capacity FNB Stadium in Soweto, South Africa. It was attended by leaders and dignitaries from more than 100 countries and some 60,000 South Africans. As U.S. President Barack Obama and South African President Jacob Zuma spoke, the official interpreter for the deaf stood beside them and made signs. These were later described by experts as childish hand gestures relating neither to the signs associated with the country's 11 official languages, nor to any of the related facial gestures. According to one international expert, the man—identified as Thamsanqa Jantjie—had also falsely interpreted at a military event in 2012.

Fakes, Frauds, & Forgeries

Longest time under an assumed identity In 1914, newspaper editor Anton Ekström (SWE) had a breakdown after the death of his wife and the loss of his wealth. He became a hermit in the countryside under the name Magnusson. In 1955, after 41 years, he was exposed and reunited with his bewildered children.

MONEY & ECONOMICS

Fastest rising brand Facebook's brand value increased by 43% to take it to No. 52 in the Interbrand list of 2013, the only social media brand to claim a place on the Top 100 Best Global Brands. Its global user base increased by 26% to an incredible 1.19 billion MAU (monthly active users), and its mobile user base went up by 51% to 751 million in the year to Sep. 2013.

Largest advertising agency In Jul. 2013, Publicis (FRA) and Omnicom (U.S.A.) announced that they would merge to create the Publicis Omnicom Group, which would have had $23 bn in revenue had it been in existence during 2012. As it stands, WPP reported record revenues of $16.8 bn in the same period.

LARGEST GENDER GAP According to the World Economic Forum's 2013 Global Gender Gap Index, Yemen has the largest gender gap of any country. The measurement is made by scoring four indicators: economic participation and opportunity, educational attainment, health and survival, and political empowerment. Yemen scored 0.5128 (with 1 as the highest possible score). The country with the **smallest gender gap** was Iceland, scoring 0.8731. The U.S.A. scored 0.7392 and the UK 0.7440.

MOST UNEQUAL SOCIETY According to World Bank data from 2009 (the most recent figures available), South Africa is the economy in which disparities of income between richest and poorest are at their worst. The country with the **most equal distribution of income** is Slovakia.

1,781 tons of gold was recycled in 2012, generating **$23.5 bn**.

HIGHEST ANNUAL EARNINGS BY A CEO
John H. Hammergren (U.S.A.), chief executive of the pharmaceutical firm McKesson, received $131.19 m in 2012. Of this, "just" $1.66 m was earned as salary; $4.65 m was a bonus, $112.12 m was given as stock options, and the remaining $12.76 m came under the heading of "other."

RICHEST MEDIA TYCOON
Former mayor of New York City Michael Bloomberg (U.S.A.) is the richest media mogul. His Bloomberg LP empire, which includes the Bloomberg financial news firm, is worth $27 bn according to Forbes' list of billionaires from Mar. 2013.

Greatest economic freedom
With a score of 89.3 (out of 100), Hong Kong, China, enjoys the greatest economic freedom according to the Heritage Foundation's Index of Freedom. Economic freedom is a measurement of the right of workers to control their own labor, consumption, investments, and property.

Highest economic growth Sierra Leone ended a decade of often barbaric civil war in 2002, and growth has been relatively speedy given how poor its citizens are in absolute terms. The country saw a 15.2% increase in GDP (Gross Domestic Product) in 2011–12. However, citizens also have the lowest **average life expectancy**, at 45 years.

In 2011, South Sudan gained independence from Sudan after another long civil war. The fledgling country went on to experience the **lowest economic growth**, with an enormous drop of 55.8% in 2011–12. Next door, Sudan recorded the second lowest growth with -10.1%.

PROSPEROUS PEOPLE

Richest person (ever): John D. Rockefeller (U.S.A., 1839–1937), $189 bn—if adjusted to 2013 figures.

Richest person (current): Bill Gates (U.S.A.), $75.9 bn, Feb. 2014.

Richest investor: Warren Buffett (U.S.A.), $58.6 bn, Feb. 2014.

Richest woman: Christy Walton (U.S.A.), $36.9 bn, Feb. 2014.

ECONOMY SIZES: LARGEST GDP

A. U.S.A. $16.24 tr
B. China $8.22 tr
C. Japan $5.95 tr
D. Germany $3.42 tr
E. France $2.61 tr

F. UK $2.47 tr
G. Brazil $2.25 tr
H. Russia $2.01 tr
I. Italy $2.01 tr
J. India $1.84 tr

Source: worldbank.org

A.   B.   C.   D. E. F. G. H. I. J.

MOST VALUABLE BRAND According to the 2013 Interbrand Top 100 Best Global Brands rankings, Apple is worth $98.31 bn—which is a 28% rise over the previous year. The record ends 13 years of domination by Coca-Cola, which dropped to third behind Google. There are 72 million Mac computers in use, and 9 million iPhone 5s and 5c models were sold in launch weekend alone. In 2013, the App Store reached the 50-billion download mark after just five years.

Most innovative economy As of Jul. 2013, Switzerland had a score of 66.59 in the annual Global Innovation Index, published by Cornell University, the business school INSEAD, and the World Intellectual Property Organization. Measurements are taken in such areas as institutions, infrastructure, research, the sophistication of the market, and in business, creativity, and technology.

FACT: The GDP of the U.S.A. is $16.24 tr. But how long would it take you to count this out in $1 bills? Fast (human) money counters can count 200 notes in a minute; at 12,000 per hr., that's more than 154,000 years—nonstop—to count all 16.24 trillion bills!

WORST MODERN RECESSION The ongoing downturn in Greece has been more severe than in any other country in the developed world since World War II. In 2013, the economy shrank by 23–25%, compared with 20% in 2012. The jobless rate increased from 25% to 27% and youth unemployment leaped from 50% to 60%.

LARGEST MUNICIPAL BANKRUPTCY On Jul. 18, 2013, Detroit in Michigan, U.S.A., filed for the largest bankruptcy in modern times, with debts estimated at $18–20 bn. Up to 40% of streetlights are broken in the city that is home to more than 150,000 deserted buildings. Among them is the former Packard car factory (pictured), a 3.5-million-sq.-ft. (325,160-m²) property that is the **largest abandoned factory**. Closed since 1956, Packard once produced 75% of the world's cars in Detroit—known as "Motor City."

COSTLY QUAFFS

As an indicator of how our spending habits have changed since 1955, the **most expensive bottle of wine** then was a 1949 Feinste Trockenbeerenauslese priced at $22; adjusting for inflation means that it would cost $294 today. But the most expensive wines commercially available now sell for ca. $52,900—that's 180 times more than the adjusted figure!

STARSHIP ENTER-PRISE: High Transactions Russian cosmonaut Pavel Vinogradov was in the *International Space Station* orbiting at 260 mi. (419 km) above Earth when he made the **highest-altitude financial transaction**, a land tax payment of 616 roubles ($18.51) on Apr. 22, 2013. The money was transferred to the Federal Tax Service of Russia in an event organized by Mikhail Mishustin and Vladimir Bezrukov. This transaction represents the first time that anyone has paid their tax bill—or, indeed, any kind of bill—from space!

Highest budget for . . .

• **Defense:** According to *The Economist*, Iraq spent 11.3% of its GDP on defense in 2012.

• **Health:** World Bank figures from 2011 put Liberia top of spending on health with 19.5% of its GDP.

• **Education:** In 2012, Lesotho put 13% of its GDP toward education, according to figures from *The Economist*.

Highest budgetary expenditure The U.S.A. spent $3.53 tr in 2012, a figure that excludes social benefits of approximately $2.3 tr. The U.S.A. accounts for more than 15% of worldwide budgetary expenditure and also brings in the **highest revenue**, with an estimated $2.44 tr in 2012. This excludes social contributions revenue of approximately $1 tr.

Highest cost of living According to a Dec. 2012 survey by the Economist Intelligence Unit, Japan is the most expensive nation to live in for expatriate executives and their families. Prices for products of international comparable quality in stores in New York City, U.S.A., are used as a base, with the U.S.A. scoring 100. Japan is the priciest, with a score of 152, followed by Australia (137). The country with the **lowest cost of living** is Pakistan, with a rating of 44.

GROSS WORLD PRODUCT

Totaling the gross domestic product (GDP) of every country gives you the "gross world product"—i.e., the value of all goods and services in the world. Sixty years ago, this figure stood at $5.43 tr (or $1,966 per person); in 2014, this is an estimated $72.21 tr (or $10,316 per person). This means our economy today is more than 13 times bigger than it was back in 1955.

INTERNET

First Google hoax On Apr. 1, 2000, Google perpetrated the "Mental-Plex" hoax to mark April Fool's Day. It invited users of its search engine to stare at an animated gif on its home page and think of what they wanted to find on the net.

First Webcam In 1991, computer scientists at Cambridge University, UK, set up a camera and a computer to monitor the status of their coffeepot without having to leave their room. The system was upgraded in Nov. 1993, when it was linked to the net, and live images of the famous coffeepot were broadcast until the feed was turned off in 2000.

MOST VIEWED ONLINE VIDEO ADVERTISEMENT

"Dove Real Beauty Sketches" was watched 134,265,061 times—in 25 languages in more than 110 countries—as of May 1, 2014, by which date it had been shared 4,517,422 times. The video was posted on Apr. 14, 2013, and data was collected by Unruly for their Viral Video Chart.

MOST FACEBOOK "LIKES" ON AN ITEM On Nov. 30, 2013, *Fast & Furious* star Paul Walker (U.S.A., left on car) died in a car crash in California, U.S.A. Friend Vin Diesel, aka Mark Vincent (U.S.A., right on car), posted a photo of them together on Facebook (above right), where it had received 6,817,898 "likes" as of May 7, 2014. The previous record holder was a 2012 photo on Barack Obama's Facebook page showing his embrace with wife Michelle after being elected U.S. president for a second term. As of May 7, 2014, it had 4,433,487 "likes."

By 2015, **44%** of the world will have Internet access at home.

> **FACT:** Google's Trekker helped collect images for the **southernmost Street View** (below). Trekker is a backpack with a battery-powered camera on a mast. Its 15 lenses are differently angled and their images were later joined into a 360-degree panorama.

SOUTHERNMOST LOCATION ON GOOGLE STREET VIEW

On Jul. 17, 2012, Google released images on its ground-level perspective Street View service showing the South Pole. Other areas of Antarctica available on Street View include penguin colonies, Ernest Shackleton's hut, and Robert Falcon Scott's supply hut. Users can guide their cursors inside the buildings and take a virtual tour of these shrines of exploration.

MOST MENTIONS OF A BRAND NAME ON TWITTER IN 24 HOURS

A chocolate-coated cookie stick called Pocky was mentioned 3,710,044 times on Twitter on Nov. 11, 2013. That works out at slightly over 4,294 mentions per sec. for the Ezaki Glico Co., Ltd. (JPN) snack. Everything from emojis (Japanese smileys) to straight retweets were counted in the attempt.

Highest Earth–Moon bandwidth

In Oct. 2013, NASA and the Massachusetts Institute of Technology successfully demonstrated the first two-way communications laser link to the Moon. They sent signals to a spacecraft orbiting the Moon, and achieved a download data rate of 622 megabits per second. Mission engineers were able to download the spacecraft's entire 1-gigabyte science data in less than five min.—an operation that would have taken three days if conventional radio waves were used.

WHAT HAPPENS IN AN INTERNET MINUTE

e-mail 204 million e-mails sent
flickr 20 million photo views
Google 2 million searches
facebook 1.8 million "likes"
skype 1.4 million connection minutes
twitter 278,000 tweets
YouTube 3 days of video uploaded
tumblr 20,000 new photos
iTunes 15,000 tracks downloaded
Pinterest 11,000 active users

Source: Intel and qmee.com, 2013

E-MAIL SPAMMING

Anyone who has ever used e-mail has received spam—unsolicited messages. Billions of the nuisances are sent daily but, before the phenomenon had a name, Gary Thuerk (U.S.A.) sent the **first spam**, on May 3, 1978. His memo was quite innocent—a message to 397 e-mail accounts on the ARPANet of the U.S. Department of Defense, with an invitation to attend a product demonstration.

FACT: Tim Berners-Lee had the idea for the **first hypertext browser**—what became the World Wide Web—in Mar. 1989. Marking its 25th anniversary, in 2014 Berners-Lee called for a bill of rights to keep the Web free and open. "Our rights are being infringed . . . on every side and the danger is that we get used to it . . . the key thing is getting people to fight for the Web."

FIRST INSTAGRAM FROM SPACE

"Back on *ISS*, life is good" wrote Steve Swanson (U.S.A.) from the *International Space Station* on Apr. 7, 2014, posing in a T-shirt from cult TV sci-fi show *Firefly* (U.S.A., 2002).

The **most "liked" image on Instagram** (above right) shows actor Will Smith (U.S.A.) and Justin Bieber (CAN), posted in Aug. 2013. "Me and uncle Will," noted the pop star, who posted the image. It has been "liked" more than 1.5 million times.

MOST RETWEETED MESSAGE ON TWITTER The selfie organized by 2014 Oscars host Ellen DeGeneres (U.S.A.) exceeded 1 million retweets within about an hour of being tweeted on Oscars night, Mar. 3, 2014. Smiling alongside stars such as Bradley Cooper, Jennifer Lawrence, Brad Pitt, Kevin Spacey, and Meryl Streep, DeGeneres tweeted, "If only Bradley's arm was longer. Best photo ever. #oscars." As of May 5, 2014, the message had been retweeted 3,428,897 times.

For more top tech, turn to pp. 459–64.

FACT: Robert Downey Jr. also operates a Facebook account that had been "liked" by 16,373,295 fans as of May 7, 2014.

FASTEST TIME TO REACH 1 MILLION FOLLOWERS ON TWITTER

On Apr. 11, 2014, Twitter was a-flutter to learn that Robert Downey Jr. (U.S.A.) had joined the site with a "Talk to me, Twitter" (@robertdowneyjr). Within a day, the star had attracted 1,017,322 fans, but he still lags behind the **most followers on Twitter for an actor**. Ashton Kutcher (U.S.A.; @aplusk) had 16,022,147 followers as of May 6, 2014.

Largest Internet census by a botnet A botnet ("robot network") consists of many computers linked together to run services. In 2012, an anonymous hacker hijacked 420,000 devices that had only default passwords and used them to conduct an illegal mapping of the Internet, particularly insecure devices. His control program was called the Carna Botnet.

Largest seizure of virtual currency On Oct. 25, 2013, the U.S. Federal Bureau of Investigation (FBI) revealed that it had seized a total of 144,000 bitcoins worth around $28.5 m. The FBI allege that the tranche of bitcoins—a currency that exists only online—belonged to Ross Ulbricht (U.S.A.), who is accused of running the Silk Road, an online marketplace for drugs.

TURN IT OFF AND ON AGAIN: *Rebooting the Net* Seven experts—including Moussa Guebre (BFA), middle left—form the **first international group capable of rebooting the World Wide Web**, or at least certain aspects of it, in the event of a major catastrophe such as a cyber attack. They are the backup for a security system called DNSSEC that adds a digital signature to website names, helping in the battle to stop hackers redirecting surfers to fake sites. Should a disaster take out DNSSEC, five of the seven global keyholders would be summoned to a secure U.S. location to save the day. Each of the team has a swipe card that provides one-fifth of the reboot key.

Northernmost underwater communications cable Longyearbyen in Norway, at a latitude of 78.22°N, is the landing point of the Svalbard Undersea Cable System, which provides a fiber-optic Internet connection with the Norwegian mainland. The two-cable system is 1,686 mi. (2,714 km) long and provides fast access to data from Svalbard's SvalSat. This is one of only two ground stations optimally located to download data from all 14 polar-orbiting satellites.

Most consecutive daily personal video blogs on YouTube As of May 6, 2014, Charles Trippy (U.S.A.) had posted 1,831 vlogs consecutively, without missing a day, on his YouTube channel Internet Killed Television. In Apr. 2014, he documented his split from wife and fellow vlogger Alli.

Most expensive property sold at online auction A plot of land in the same area of Dubai as the Burj Khalifa sold for 94,176,000 United Arab Emirates dirham ($25,634,707) on Feb. 19, 2013, through Emirates Auction (UAE).

Most subscribers on YouTube As of May 6, 2014, "PewDiePie," aka Felix Arvid Ulf Kjellberg (SWE), had 26,540,250 YouTube subscribers for his comedic video-gaming highlights.

CROWDSOURCING

First use of the term "crowdsourcing" In 2005, U.S. journalist Jeff Howe coined the term "crowdsourcing" while pitching an article about how the Internet was being used to outsource work to the general public, or "crowd." The article appeared in the Jun. 2006 edition of *Wired* under the title "The Rise of Crowdsourcing."

A **bank robber used crowdsourcing** to hire a team of identically dressed workmen, aiding his escape.

MOST MONEY PLEDGED FOR A KICKSTARTER COMIC PROJECT Graphic designer Rich Burlew (U.S.A.) couldn't afford to reprint *The Order of the Stick* himself, so turned to his fans. Almost 15,000 people had pledged $1,254,120 by the time the project closed on Feb. 21, 2012.

MOST MONEY PLEDGED FOR A KICKSTARTER PROJECT The Pebble (U.S.A.) is a customizable watch with Internet connectivity, message and e-mail alerts, and access to sports and fitness apps. The watch received pledges of $10,266,845 by May 19, 2012, surpassing its goal 10-fold.

Largest platform for crowdfunding From Kickstarter's launch on Apr. 28, 2009 until Mar. 4, 2014, 5.7 million people pledged a total of $1,001,567,335. This support has aided 57,171 projects to meet their funding goals.

First crowdsourced military vehicle design The XC2V Flypmode, made by Local Motors and the U.S. Defense Advanced Research Projects Agency (DARPA), used design ideas from more than 150 people. Built to replace the Humvee, the prototype was presented to President Obama in 2011.

Highest chart placing by a crowdfunded album *Theatre Is Evil*, an album by Amanda Palmer and The Grand Theft Orchestra (U.S.A., see p. 303), achieved a top 10 placing on the *Billboard* 200 on its release in Sep. 2012—the highest position achieved by a crowdfunded music release.

WHAT IS KICKSTARTER?

Kickstarter was founded by Perry Chen, Yancey Strickler, and Charles Adler (all U.S.A.) in New York, U.S.A., and launched on Apr. 28, 2009. The concept allows investors to pledge money toward creative projects in return for rewards and experiences. However, the funds are only handed over if the project's entire funding goal is met.

For more on cars, turn to p. 409.

FIRST CROWDSOURCED CAR DESIGN The Rally Fighter, an off-road racer produced by Local Motors (U.S.A.), represents the culmination of 35,000 designs by 2,900 people from more than 100 countries. The car made its debut at the Specialty Equipment Market Association Show in Las Vegas, Nevada, U.S.A., on Nov. 3, 2009.

Fastest Kickstarter project to reach $1 m On Oct. 27, 2013, "Reaper Miniatures Bones II" (U.S.A.)—a project created to fund an expansion of the miniatures range—sped to a pledge total of $1 m in just 2 hr. 41 min. 51 sec.

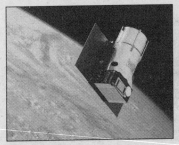

MOST MONEY PLEDGED ON KICKSTARTER FOR PHOTOGRAPHY On Jul. 1, 2013, U.S.-based Planetary Resources raised more than $1.5 m for "A Space Telescope for Everyone." The project aims to launch a publicly accessible telescope that can take photos of space or allow people to have their photo displayed above Earth (artist's impression left).

Crowdsourcing

GROUP EFFORTS: The History of Crowdsourcing Crowdsourcing is nothing new. In the UK, the Oxford English Dictionary (bottom left) received six million suggestions from the public when it first solicited entries in the 1850s, while Nelson's Column (near right, erected 1843) was paid for in part from public subscriptions (crowdfunding). In 1567, England's Queen Elizabeth I effectively crowdfunded the enlarging of the Navy by initiating the first national lottery. Competitions can also be considered a form of crowdsourcing; the Longitude Prize in the 1700s, for example, sought to find a solution to determining a ship's longitude at sea—a problem finally solved in 1756 by John Harrison (top left).

MOST MONEY PLEDGED FOR A KICKSTARTER . . .

Art project The Marina Abramović Institute, a performance and education center in New York City, U.S.A., aimed to raise $600,000. The goal was surpassed on Aug. 25, 2013 with pledges of $661,452.

Dance project STREB Extreme Action (U.S.A.) beat their $45,000 goal on Nov. 25, 2013 with pledges of $45,512. *FORCES* is described as a theatrical show centered on "action."

Fashion project Jake Bronstein (U.S.A.) is so sure of his lifetime-lasting hoodie that he provides a 10-year free mending service. He passed his funding goal on Apr. 21, 2013 with pledges of $1,053,830.

MOST CROWDFUNDED STAGE PROJECT The story of serial killer Patrick Bateman may seem an unlikely source for a musical, but *American Psycho* opened in London, UK, in Dec. 2013 with ex-*Doctor Who* star Matt Smith as the lead. Producer Jesse Singer of Act 4 Entertainment (U.S.A.) had raised pledges of $154,929 in May 2013 to help fund the production.

MOST CROWDFUNDED PROJECT (OVERALL) Efforts to fund *Star Citizen*, a space-base trading and combat adventure video game, resulted in the largest single amount ever raised via crowdsourcing. As of Mar. 4, 2014, publisher Cloud Imperium Games (U.S.A.) had raised $39,680,576 via its own website appeal alone. Chris Roberts designed the game, scheduled for release in 2015.

MOST CROWDFUNDED MUSIC PROJECT
Amanda Palmer (U.S.A.) initiated a Kickstarter appeal to fund her album with the aim of raising $100,000. By the time the appeal closed on Jun. 1, 2012, she had received pledges of $1,192,793, making hers the most successful crowdfunded music project of any kind.

Food project Scott Heimendinger's (U.S.A.) "Sansaire Circulator" uses *sous vide*—a method of cooking using exact temperature control—in a product designed for the home cook. Final pledges reached $823,003 on Sep. 6, 2013.

KICKSTARTER CATEGORIES WITH THE MOST SUCCESSFUL PROJECTS

Category	Total	Funded	Unfunded
Music	$94.20 m	15,011	12,208
Movie/Video	$163.95 m	13,096	19,594
Art	$30.24 m	5,613	6,101
Publishing	$40.42 m	5,125	10,756
Theater	$19.69 m	3,556	1,974
Games	$189.97 m	2,948	5,435
Design	$125.13 m	2,537	4,040
Food	$30.69 m	2,089	3,121
Comics	$22.96 m	1,762	1,814

Source: kickstarter.com, Mar. 4, 2014

MOST CROWDFUNDED VIDEO-GAME CONSOLE The Kickstarter appeal to back the OUYA (U.S.A.) raised $8,596,474 by Aug. 9, 2012. The $99 eighth-generation console is an Android-based device that connects to a standard modern TV set and allows users to play free-to-try games.

Publishing project Planet Money's (U.S.A.) project leads the consumer on an innovative journey through a T-shirt's creation. Each T-shirt has a bar code linking to a Web page featuring photos of the people who made it, from cotton growers to factory workers. Pledges of $590,807 were received by May 14, 2013.

Theater project Tim O'Connor (U.S.A.) raised $175,395 by Sep. 24, 2012 to upgrade Catlow Theater in Barrington, Illinois, U.S.A., with modern audio and visual equipment.

GREAT
JOURNEYS

CONTENTS

Each continent has a **Pole of Inaccessibility**—its farthest point from an ocean.

FIRST 360-DEGREE PANORAMA FILMED ON THE SUMMIT OF MOUNT EVEREST The first fully spherical 360-degree video from the summit of Mount Everest was recorded in May 2013. The footage was captured with 360Heros' 360-degree video gear for a documentary by Everest Media Productions about Nepalese climber Apa Sherpa, who was a consultant for the shoot. The veteran sherpa summited the mountain 21 times between 1990 and 2011, the **most conquests of Mount Everest**.

SLIPPING INTO PLACE The 3D-printed H3PRO6 holder was invented by Michael Kintner (U.S.A.), CEO of 360Heros. On Everest, six GoPro cameras were slipped into the holder and software was later used to create the final footage.

"LITTLE PLANET" MODE As well as being available as a fully interactive 3D video, the panorama can also be viewed in "little planet" or "miniplanet" mode, which creates a spherical or "stereographic" projection.

FACT: In Nepal, the name of Everest is *Sagarmatha* ("forehead of the sky"), and in Tibet it is *Chomolungma* ("mother goddess of the world").

NORTH POLE

Most polar expeditions completed by an individual Richard Weber (CAN) has successfully completed eight polar expeditions. He reached the geographic North Pole from the coast six times between May 2, 1986 and Apr. 14, 2010, and the geographic South Pole twice from the coast on Jan. 7, 2009 and Dec. 29, 2011.

First solo expedition to the North Pole At 4:45 A.M. GMT on May 1, 1978, Japanese explorer and mountaineer Naomi Uemura became the first person to reach the North Pole in a solo expedition across the Arctic sea ice. He had traveled 478 mi. (770 km), setting out on Mar. 7, 1978 from Ellesmere Island in Canada. The expedition was supported by dogs, and Uemura had access to resupplies.

THREE POLES CHALLENGE The first person to complete the Three Poles Challenge was Erling Kagge (NOR), who reached the North on May 8, 1990, the South on Jan. 7, 1993, and Everest on May 8, 1994. The latest challenger was Johan Ernst Nilson (SWE, above), who topped Everest in May 2007. He began the polar stages by being dropped at the North Pole on Jun. 22, 2011 and walking to land, and completed a South Pole trek on Jan. 19, 2012. Having left from 90°N, Nilson achieved the **first Three Poles Challenge—North Pole to land**.

The ocean at the North Pole is more than **13,100 ft. deep.**

FIRST TRAVERSE OF THE NORTH POLE BY WHEELED VEHICLE The Russian Marine Live-Ice Automobile Expedition MLAE 2013 (Sergey Isayev, Nikolay Kozlov, Afanasy Makovnev, Vladimir Obikhod, Alexey Shkrabkin, and Andrey Vankov, led by Vasily Elagin) left Golomyanny Island, Russia, on Mar. 1, 2013. Driving two 6 x 6 low-pressure-tire ATVs, the team arrived at the North Pole on Apr. 6, then continued to the Canadian coast, which they reached on Apr. 30. The 60-day journey covered approximately 2,480 mi. (4,000 km) in all.

YOUNGEST FEMALE TO SKI TO THE NORTH POLE (UNSUPPORTED, UNASSISTED) Amelia Darley (née Russell, UK, b. Aug. 29, 1982) was 27 years 239 days old when she reached the geographic North Pole on Apr. 25, 2010. Her journey of 484 mi. (780 km) began at Cape Discovery, McClintock Inlet, on Ward Hunt Island, Canada. Amelia traveled in a two-person expedition accompanied by her boyfriend, Dan Darley (UK).

First person to ski to both poles (unassisted and unsupported)

Polish-born Marek Kamiński (U.S.A.) reached the North Pole from Cape Columbia on May 23, 1995 and the South Pole from Berkner Island on Dec. 27, 1995. He completed both trips under his own power and without any external assistance.

FASTEST . . .

Surface journey to the North Pole

On Mar. 21, 2005, Tom Avery and George Wells (both UK), Matty McNair and Hugh Dale-Harris (both CAN), Andrew Gerber (ZAF), and a team of 16 husky dogs left Cape Columbia on Ellesmere Island in Canada. They reached the North Pole 36 days 22 hr. 11 min. later on Apr. 26, 2005. Their journey was an attempt to re-create as closely as possible the disputed 1909 expedition of explorer Robert Peary.

THE "THREE POLES"

Adventurers consider Earth to have three poles: the North and South poles and Mount Everest. The latter is regarded as a "pole" in this context, due to its relative inaccessibility.

A. Magnetic North Pole: Unlike the geographic North Pole, this is not a fixed point; it moves by some 37 mi. each year, driven by fluctuations in Earth's magnetic field. This is the "north" to which magnetic compasses align themselves.

B. Geographic North Pole: Also known as "True North," this is located at 90°N. All the lines of longitude on Earth converge at this point.

C. Norway

D. Svalbard archipelago

E. Greenland

F. Canada

Ski journey to the North Pole by a women's team
Catharine Hartley and Fiona Thornewill (both UK) skied to the North Pole (with support in the form of resupplies en route) in 55 days between Mar. 11 and May 5, 2001. They began their expedition from Ward Hunt Island in Nunavut, Canada.

Trek to the North Pole
David J. P. Pierce Jones (UK), Richard Weber and Tessum Weber (both CAN), and Howard Fairbanks (ZAF) took 41 days 18 hr. 52 min. to trek to the North Pole, from Mar. 3 to Apr. 14, 2010. The team set out from 82°58'02"N and 77°23'3"W and were picked up after reaching the North Pole, at 90°N, on Apr. 14, 2010.

Solo trek to the North Pole (unsupported)
Børge Ousland (NOR) skied his way to the North Pole from Cape Arkticheskiy on the archipelago of Severnaya Zemlya in the Russian Federation. He undertook the trip without external assistance in 52 days, from Mar. 2 to Apr. 23, 1994. This also makes him the **first person to make a solo journey to the North Pole from land (unassisted and unsupported)**.

The fastest trek to the North Pole by a woman (unsupported)
was achieved by Cecilie Skog (NOR). She left Ward Hunt Island with Rolf Bae and Per Henry Borch (both NOR) on Mar. 6, 2006, reaching the Pole 48 days 22 hr. later.

FASTEST JOURNEY FROM THE NORTH POLE TO LAND (UNSUPPORTED, UNASSISTED)

In 1895, Fridtjof Nansen and Hjalmar Johansen (both NOR) almost became the first people to reach the North Pole, but were forced to retreat at 86°14'N. In 2012, Audun Tholfsen (NOR) and Timo Palo (EST), pictured right, set out on what would have been Nansen and Johansen's return route. The duo left the North Pole on Apr. 23, 2012. Using skis and kayaks, but no external support or resupplies, they negotiated about 715 mi. (1,150 km) of drifting ice and curious polar bears to reach Phippsøya island, in Norway's Svalbard archipelago, 55 days later. They arrived at Longyearbyen, Svalbard, on Jul. 3, having covered 1,060 mi. (1,620 km) in all.

A. "Our carbon paddles were lightweight, but durable. The sharp blade helped us to cut through thin ice layers and make a channel."

B. "This small outdoor weather station allowed us to measure wind speed, temperature, air pressure, and humidity. It was also of some help to us in predicting the weather."

C. "A very simple and ordinary GPS. It's lightweight and consumes less energy than those with color maps. In the Arctic Ocean, there is no need for GPS maps: there is nothing to be mapped."

D. "Ski goggles protect the eyes and part of the face in harsh weather conditions. The yellow and red lenses also enhance contrast and give a better definition in overcast and white-out conditions."

E. "A waterproof 'spray skirt' covers the cockpit and prevents water from getting in when we paddle in high winds and heavy waves."

F. "To protect our hands from the wind and cold, weatherproof mittens are a must."

G. "Waterproof Gore-Tex dry suits made paddling through the freezing cold Arctic waters both comfortable and safe."

H. "This type of camping stove is simple and sturdy—exactly what you need in the Arctic Ocean. It is such a crucial part of our gear that we had a spare."

I. "For some reason, we managed to break all our plastic spoons. So we had to improvise and combine new ones from the leftovers."

J. "A sled, rather than this kayak, would have been more appropriate to pull across the sea ice of the Arctic Ocean. But we needed it to cross the large open areas of water at the later stages of the expedition in order to get on land and continue along the fjords."

Marathon on each continent and the North Pole (male) From Feb. 26 to Apr. 9, 2013, Ziyad Tariq Rahim (PAK) ran a marathon on each continent and one at the North Pole, taking 41 days 20 hr. 38 min. 58 sec. in all.

THREE POLES CHALLENGE

First woman to complete the Three Poles Challenge Sweden's Tina Sjögren reached the North Pole on May 29, 2002 with her husband Thomas. She had summited Everest on May 26, 1999, and reached the South Pole on Feb. 1, 2002. The couple's two polar journeys also mark the **fastest time to reach both poles unsupported**.

First person to complete the Three Poles Challenge without the use of oxygen on Everest As of Mar. 2014, the only person to complete the Three Poles Challenge unsupported and without the use of supplementary oxygen on Everest is Antoine de Choudens (FRA), who achieved this breathtaking feat from Apr. 25, 1996 to Jan. 10, 1999.

Fastest time to complete the Three Poles Challenge The shortest time taken to reach the three extreme points on Earth is 1 year 217 days by Adrian Hayes (UK). He summited Everest on May 25, 2006, reached the North Pole on Apr. 25, 2007 (from Ward Hunt Island, Canada), and claimed the South Pole, journeying from the Hercules Inlet in western Antarctica, on Dec. 28, 2007.

The **fastest time to complete the Three Poles challenge by a woman** is 1 year 336 days, and was accomplished by Cecilie Skog (NOR). She summited Mount Everest on May 23, 2004, reached the South Pole on Dec. 27, 2005, and got to the North Pole on Apr. 24, 2006.

SOUTH POLE

First expedition to reach the South Pole The South Pole was conquered on Dec. 14, 1911 by a Norwegian party of five men led by Captain Roald Amundsen, after a 53-day march with dog sleds from the Bay of Whales, then part of Antarctica's Ross Ice Shelf.

A total of 19 expeditions in Antarctica were undertaken in 2011, the **most expeditions to the South Pole in a single year**. Most of the expeditions were launched with the aim of marking the centenary of Captain Robert Scott (UK) and Roald Amundsen's race to the South Pole. Around 500 people were involved in the various attempts, either as participants or working as support staff.

The **first person to walk to both poles** was Robert Swan OBE (UK).

He led the three-man "In the Footsteps of Scott" expedition, which reached the South Pole on Jan. 11, 1986, and three years later headed the eight-man "Icewalk" expedition, which arrived at the North Pole on May 14, 1989.

First solo expedition to the South Pole Erling Kagge (NOR) became the first person to reach the South Pole after a solo and unsupported surface trek on Jan. 7, 1993. His 870-mi. (1,400-km) journey from Berkner Island took 50 days.

The **first woman to complete a journey to the South Pole solo (unsupported)** was Liv Arnesen (NOR), who trekked solo from the Hercules Inlet on Nov. 4, 1994, arriving at the pole 50 days later on Dec. 24.

YOUNGEST PERSON TO TREK TO THE SOUTH POLE Lewis Clarke (UK, b. Nov. 18, 1997) was 16 years 61 days old when he reached the geographic South Pole on Jan. 18, 2014. He had skied 698.18 mi. (1,123.61 km) from Hercules Inlet on the Ronne Ice Shelf with guide Carl Alvey (30 years old). The duo were unsupported but were assisted with three resupplies by air.

Approximately **90% of the ice on Earth** is located in Antarctica.

FASTEST TREK TO THE SOUTH POLE BY A TEAM (UNSUPPORTED) Norwegians Mads Agerup (left), Christian Eide (photographer, reflected), Morten Andvig, and Rune Midtgaard skied from the Messner Start on the Filchner Ice Shelf to the geographic South Pole in 24 days 8 hr. 57 min. between Dec. 2 and Dec. 26, 2008.

FARTHEST DISTANCE SKIED BY A TEAM (UNSUPPORTED) James Castrission and Justin Jones (both AUS, left and right) skied 1,410 mi. (2,270 km) from the Hercules Inlet to the South Pole and back, finishing on Jan. 27, 2012 after an 89-day trek. They crossed the finish line with Aleksander Gamme (NOR, center), who had completed the trip solo (see p. 317).

FIRST PERSON TO CYCLE TO THE SOUTH POLE British cyclist Maria Leijerstam (above) departed from the edge of the Ross Ice Shelf in Antarctica on Dec. 17, 2013, on her recumbent tricycle. She reached the South Pole 10 days 14 hr. 56 min. later on Dec. 27, 2013, having covered 396.43 mi. (638 km).

Records for the **first** and **fastest person to reach the South Pole by bicycle**— that is, a two-wheel cycle—are currently in research. Two expeditions were attempted during the winter of 2013/14 but evidence has yet to be collated.

Fastest journey to the South Pole overland

Two-man team Jason De Carteret and Kieron Bradley (both UK) set off from Patriot Hills in western Antarctica on Dec. 18, 2011 in their Thomson Reuters polar vehicle. They arrived at their destination 1 day 15 hr. 54 min. later. Having covered 692 mi. (1,114 km) at an average speed of 17.34 mph (27.9 km/h), they also recorded the **fastest average speed to the South Pole overland**.

Fastest walk to the South Pole (unsupported, unassisted)

Ray Zahab, Kevin Vallely, and Richard Weber (all CAN) reached the South Pole from the Hercules Inlet, on the southwestern edge of the Ronne Ice Shelf, on Jan. 7, 2009 after just 33 days 23 hr. 30 min.

MOST EXPEDITIONS TO THE SOUTH POLE Hannah McKeand (UK) made six expeditions to the South Pole from Nov. 4, 2004 to Jan. 9, 2013. By skiing to the pole in 39 days 9 hr. 33 min. from Nov. 19 to Dec. 28, 2006, she also made the **fastest solo journey to the South Pole by a woman (unsupported, unassisted)**.

A. Ronne-Filchner Ice Shelf: second-largest ice shelf in Antarctica, covering 11,580 sq. mi.

B. South Pole: Located at 90°S. Ice is about 9,180 ft. thick here. As with the North Pole, there is also a magnetic South Pole, which fluctuates with Earth's magnetic field. It is presently in the Southern Ocean, some 1,755 mi. from the geographic South Pole.

C. Hercules Inlet: Located on the southwest edge of the Ronne Ice Shelf, this ice-packed inlet is frequently chosen as a starting point for Antarctic treks.

D. Ross Ice Shelf: Earth's most southerly navigable point. It is some 182,240 sq. mi. in size.

FACT: Antarctica is larger than the U.S.A. (and bigger than the entire continent of Europe), and is nearly twice the size of Australia.

FIRST SOLO ANTARCTIC TRAVERSE BY A WOMAN

In Nov. 2011, Felicity Aston (UK) skied solo from the Ross Ice Shelf to the South Pole, then carried on across Antarctica to the Hercules Inlet on the Ronne Ice Shelf, arriving 59 days later on Jan. 23, 2012. Aston made the 1,084-mile (1,744-km) journey—with resupplies—on Nordic cross-country skis, dragging 187 lb. (85 kg) of provisions on two sleds in temperatures as low as -40°F (-40°C).

A. "Antarctica is right beneath the ozone hole, so there is little or no natural protection from the Sun's harmful UV rays. Without these ski goggles for eye protection, I would quickly have gone snow-blind."

B. "In the extreme cold, my face had to be covered at all times. This face mask has a clever system that allows me to breathe freely without losing too much heat."

C. "These meals were made especially for me, with added carbohydrate and fat for energy. Once cooked, the meals are dehydrated to make them light to carry. To eat them, I simply had to pour hot water into the bag and wait a few minutes."

D. "These mittens have both a fleece inner glove and down outer glove for extra warmth and are completely windproof."

E. "This jacket is lightweight but it is a very effective wind barrier and so keeps me warm when I am skiing. It has deep, well-placed pockets so that I had easy access to the equipment I needed while skiing."

F. "The sleds were made of strengthened plastic that was lightweight and resilient. I dragged two sleds, one behind the other, together containing all my equipment."

G. "These boots are handmade in Norway, based on a traditional design. Inside the canvas and leather outer boot is an inner liner made of pressed wool surrounded by a fleece sock."

H. "The highlight of my day was crawling into the tent when I had finished skiing, taking off my ski boots, and slipping my feet into my treasured down booties. Warm and comfortable, I often slept in them too!"

I. "One of the major hazards in Antarctica are crevasses that are hidden from the surface by a thin layer of snow. Skis, especially long ones, spread out the skier's weight and reduce the likelihood of falling through the snow into an unseen crevasse."

J. "This shovel was a vital piece of kit. At the end of each day, the tent has to be dug into the snow for protection against high winds. And in the morning, all the snow that has accumulated overnight has to be dug away."

Farthest distance skied solo (unsupported) Aleksander Gamme (NOR) skied solo for 1,410 mi. (2,270 km) across Antarctica, completing his epic journey on Jan. 25, 2012 (local time). He set off from the Hercules Inlet and traveled to the South Pole, then returned to 0.6 mi. (1 km) from his start. There, he waited two days to cross the finish line with two other skiers—James Castrission and Justin Jones (both AUS)—who had traveled a similar route.

On Jan. 27, 2012, the three men returned to their starting point at the Hercules Inlet. They had traveled without food drops, snowmobiles, kites, or other means of assistance, thereby setting the record for the **first ski trip to the South Pole and back (unassisted)**.

Youngest person to traverse Antarctica (wind-supported, assisted) Teodor Johansen (NOR, b. Aug. 14, 1991) traversed Antarctica at the age of 20 years 151 days. Johansen started out on his journey from the Axel Heiberg Glacier on Nov. 26, 2011, reaching the South Pole on Dec. 18, 2011, and completing the trip at the Hercules Inlet on Jan. 12, 2012. In all, Johansen covered 1,034 mi. (1,665 km).

First circumnavigation via both poles (surface) Sir Ranulph Fiennes (UK)—named in 1984 by GWR's Founding Editor Norris McWhirter as the greatest living explorer—traveled south with Charles Burton (UK) from Greenwich in London, UK, on Sep. 2, 1979. They reached the South Pole on Dec. 15, 1980, the North on Apr. 10, 1982, and returned to Greenwich on Aug. 29, 1982, after a 35,000-mi. (56,000-km) journey.

MOUNT EVEREST

Most ascents of Everest (female) Lakpa Sherpa (NPL) reached the 29,029-ft.-high (8,848-m) summit of Mount Everest for the sixth time on May 11, 2006. She made the climb accompanied by her husband, Gheorghe "George" Dijmarescu (ROM/U.S.A.), who was completing his eighth ascent of Everest. For the **most conquests of Everest** overall, see p. 307.

Most ascents of Everest in one day On May 19, 2012, a total of 243 climbers summitted Everest—the most on a single day. The **most ascents of Everest in one year** came in 2013, with 658 ascents, up from 623 in 2007.

It took **16 attempts** before the highest peak was finally conquered.

Tragically, an avalanche near Everest's base camp on Apr. 18, 2014 killed 16 Nepalese climbers, the **most deaths on Mount Everest in one day**.

Longest stay on the summit of Everest Babu Chhiri Sherpa (NPL) completed a stay of 21 hr. at the summit of Mount Everest, without the use of bottled oxygen, in May 1999.

Oldest man to climb Everest Yuichiro Miura (JPN, b. Oct. 12, 1932) reached the top of Everest on May 23, 2013 at the age of 80 years 223 days. This is the third time that he has held this record: he previously climbed to the highest point on Earth as the world's oldest summiteer in 2003 and again during 2008. The achievement also makes Miura the **oldest man to climb any mountain over 8,000 m (26,246 ft.)**.

Tamae Watanabe (JPN, b. Nov. 21, 1938) climbed Everest for the second time on May 19, 2012 at the age of 73 years 180 days, making her the **oldest woman to climb Everest**.

FIRST ASTRONAUT TO SUMMIT EVEREST On May 20, 2009, former NASA astronaut Scott Parazynski (U.S.A.) successfully topped Everest, becoming the first person to travel in space and climb Earth's highest peak. According to NASA, Parazynski participated in five space flights and spent more than 1,380 hr. in space. Once at the top of Everest, he left a small Moon rock that had been collected by the crew of Apollo 11.

FIRST TWINS TO SUMMIT EVEREST On May 23, 2010, Damián and Willie Benegas (b. ARG, now U.S.A.) became the first twins to climb Mount Everest. They set out from the South Col—a pass located between Everest and Lhotse (the world's fourth-highest mountain, at 27,940 ft.; 8,516 m)—situated on Nepalese territory.

YOUNGEST WOMAN TO CLIMB EVEREST (SOUTH SIDE) Ngim Chhamji Sherpa (NPL, b. Nov. 14, 1995) reached the summit from the Nepali side on May 19, 2012 aged 16 years 187 days. She and her father, Dendi Sherpa (NPL), are the **first father and daughter to climb Everest together**. The **youngest woman to climb from the north side** (Tibet) was 15-year-old Mingkipa Sherpa (NPL, b. 1987) on May 22, 2003.

Fastest time to ski down Everest Slovenian ski instructor Davo Karničar skied from the summit of Everest to Base Camp (located at an altitude of 17,550 ft., or 5,350 m) in just 5 hr. on Oct. 7, 2000. By contrast, it took him a whole month to get to the mountaintop, as he was obliged to stop at several camps to acclimatize to the extreme altitude.

Fastest ascent of Everest (south side) Pemba Dorje Sherpa (NPL) climbed from Base Camp to the peak of Mount Everest in a time of 8 hr. 10 min. on May 21, 2004.

FIRST . . .

Ascent of Everest At 11:30 A.M. on May 29, 1953, Edmund Percival Hillary (NZ) and Tenzing Norgay (IND/Tibet) became the first people to conquer Mount Everest. The successful expedition was led by Colonel (later Honorary Brigadier) Henry Cecil John Hunt. Hillary was knighted by Queen Elizabeth II and Norgay awarded the George Medal.

Junko Tabei (JPN) achieved the **first ascent of Everest by a woman**, reaching the summit on May 16, 1975.

Ascent of Everest without oxygen Reinhold Messner (ITA) and Peter Habeler (AUT) made the first successful ascent of Mount Everest without supplemental oxygen on May 8, 1978. This feat is regarded by some purist mountaineers as the first "true" ascent of Everest, because overcoming the effects of altitude (i.e., the low oxygen content of the air) is the greatest challenge facing high-altitude climbers.

On Aug. 20, 1980, Messner also became the **first person to ascend Everest solo**. It took him three days to make the ascent from his base camp at 21,325 ft. (6,500 m), again without bottled oxygen.

FIRST FEMALE TWINS TO SUMMIT EVEREST Tashi and Nungshi Malik (both IND) are the first twin sisters to have climbed Everest, doing so on May 19, 2013. They reached the peak alongside Samina Baig, the first Pakistani woman to complete the climb. All three successful climbers raised the flags of both countries in a symbolic gesture of peace.

Blind person to climb Everest

Erik Weihenmayer (U.S.A.) was born with retinoschisis, an eye condition that left him blind by the age of 13. Despite this, on May 25, 2001, he topped Everest, the first—and so far only—blind person to have done so.

Erik's other notable feats include his 2008 completion of the Seven Summits—climbing the highest mountain on each of the seven continents of the world. This makes him the **first blind person to climb the Seven Summits including Carstensz**.

Married couple to climb Everest

Andrej and Marija Štremfelj (both SVN) became the first married couple to conquer Mount Everest, on Oct. 7, 1990.

On the same day, Jean-Noël and his son Bertrand "Zébulon" Roche (both FRA) became the **first father and son team to summit Everest**.

FASTEST TIME TO CLIMB HEIGHT OF EVEREST BY . . .

Machine (such as a Versaclimber stepping machine). Requires climbing the equivalent of 29,029 ft.

Individual	2 hr. 53 min. 47 sec.	Richard Pemberton (AUS)
Male (team)	1 hr. 56 min. 8 sec.	Richard Saville, Edward Kerry, Steve Wilson, Chris Grimshaw, Charlie Boyes, Dan Levy, Dave Rome, and Kevin Williams (all UK)
Female (team)	2 hr. 45 min. 53 sec.	Bridget Funnell, Victoria Brown, Natasha Jones, Sarah Ruscombe-King, Sandra Heard, Margaret Reeve, Sandra Cann, and Nicola Hammond (all UK)

Indoor climbing wall

Individual	13 hr. 25 min	Tom Lancaster (UK)
Team	4 hr. 24 min. 33 sec.	The Climbing Society at Texas A&M University-Commerce (U.S.A.)

FIRST PERSON TO CLIMB EVEREST FROM BOTH SIDES IN ONE SEASON

David Liaño González (MEX) reached the peak of Mount Everest from Nepal on the south side on May 11, 2013, and returned to the peak on May 19, 2013, climbing from Tibet on the north side. This is the first time that any climber has scaled the mountain from both sides in one climbing season.

A. "Oxygen levels at the summit of Everest are approximately one-third of those available at sea level. This mask mixes pure oxygen from a tank with ambient air."

B. "These goggles protect my eyes from hurricane-speed winds and the Sun reflected on the snow, which can cause blindness. The LED head lamp illuminates my way when I'm climbing at night."

C. "For nourishment at high altitudes, I rehydrate freeze-dried food by adding water to it from melting ice."

D. "The outermost layer of this suit is filled with goose down, which is still one of the best materials for insulation while climbing."

E. "I use this ice axe for self-arrest in case I have a fall and for additional support while climbing."

F. "This is an ascender: a safety device that allows climbers to clip into ropes and anchors already set up on the route. It's attached to the mountaineering harness by a length of climbing cord."

G. "Fingers are one of the first body parts to get injured because of extreme cold. These mittens are filled with goose down to protect my hands against frostbite."

H. "The double-layer boots protect the toes against frostbite and are comfortable enough to be worn for hours and hours. The crampons are easily attached to the boots, and allow climbers to ascend steep ice sections where boots alone would slip."

I. "This solar panel provides clean energy to power electronics, such as radios, satellite phones, and cameras on the mountain."

J. "The backpack is expandable, to accommodate big loads—such as those carried to the lower camps—and small loads—such as those carried on summit day."

MOUNTAINEERING

FIRST . . .

Person to climb the Seven Summits The highest mountains on each of the continents are collectively known as the "Seven Summits" (see table on p. 323). Two lists have been compiled: the "Bass list," which includes Mount Kosciuszko in New South Wales, Australia, and the more difficult "Messner list," which recognizes Oceania's highest point as Puncak Jaya in Indonesia. Patrick Morrow (CAN) completed the Messner list on Aug. 5, 1986 with a summit of Puncak Jaya.

Woman to climb the Seven Summits On Jun. 28, 1992, Junko Tabei (JPN) topped Puncak Jaya, completing Messner's list. Tabei also recorded the **first ascent of Everest by a woman**, when she climbed it on May 16, 1975.

It took Vanessa O'Brien (U.S.A.) 295 days to climb both Messner's and Bass's list—the **fastest Seven Summits ascent (female)**. She began with Everest on May 19, 2012 and finished on Kilimanjaro on Mar. 10, 2013.

FASTEST TIME TO CLIMB THE SEVEN SUMMITS (BOTH LISTS) Vernon Tejas (U.S.A.) climbed the combined Kosciuszko and Carstensz lists of summits, beginning with Vinson Massif on Jan. 18, 2010 and ending with McKinley, aka Denali, on May 31, 2010. This musically minded climber has also played guitar on top of each of the summits and at the North and South poles.

> The Seven Summits' combined height is the equivalent of 113 Eiffel Towers.

FIRST ASCENT OF NANGA PARBAT VIA THE MAZENO RIDGE In 1953, Hermann Buhl (AUT) became the **first person to climb Nanga Parbat**—the ninth-highest mountain, situated in the Himalayas at 26,656 ft. (8,125 m). It was not until Jul. 15, 2012 that it was ascended via the technically difficult Mazeno Ridge or west-southwest route—one of the most demanding challenges in alpinism—by Sandy Allan and Rick Allen (both UK).

FIRST ASCENT OF PUNCAK JAYA The 16,024-ft.-high (4,884-m) peak of Puncak Jaya, aka Carstensz Pyramid, in Indonesia was first ascended by Heinrich Harrer (AUT), Philip Temple, Russell Kippax (both NZ), and Albertus Huizenga (NLD). The team reached the summit on Feb. 13, 1962. It is considered the most difficult of the Seven Summits to climb.

THE SEVEN SUMMITS

As with many mountaineering distinctions, the definition of the "Seven Summits" is disputed. Some climbers include Kosciuszko in Australia instead of Carstensz. Others place Elbrus within the borders of Asia, and thus regard Mount Blanc as Europe's highest mountain.

Continent	Mountain	Location	Height	First Climbed
Africa	Kilimanjaro	Tanzania	19,350 ft.	Oct. 6, 1889
Antarctica	Vinson Massif	Antarctica	16,049 ft.	Dec. 18, 1966
Asia	Everest	Nepal/China	29,029 ft.	May 29, 1953
Australasia	Puncak Jaya, aka Carstensz	Indonesia	16,024 ft.	Feb. 13, 1962
Europe	Elbrus	Russia	18,510 ft.	Jul. 27, 1874
North America	McKinley, aka Denali	U.S.A.	20,321 ft.	Jun. 7, 1913
South America	Aconcagua	Argentina	22,841 ft.	Jan. 14, 1897

Source: www.8000ers.com

FIRST TO SUMMIT ANNAPURNA VIA THE SOUTH FACE (FEMALE)
Wanda Rutkiewicz (POL) (left) reached the peak of Annapurna (26,545 ft.; 8,091 m) from the south face in the Himalayas, Nepal, on Oct. 22, 1991. Rutkiewicz was also the **first woman to ascend K2**, doing so on Jun. 23, 1986.

Person to climb all 8,000er mountains

Reinhold Messner (ITA) began his quest to climb each of the 14 mountains higher than 8,000 m—or 26,246 ft.—in Jun. 1970. He ended the feat with a summit of Lhotse, on the Nepal-Tibet border, on Oct. 16, 1986. The feat is so difficult that as of Apr. 25, 2014—nearly 30 years later—only 32 people had climbed all 14 mountains.

Woman to climb all 8,000er mountains On May 17, 2010, Edurne Pasaban Lizarribar (ESP) completed her climb of the 14 mountains over 8,000 m (undisputed) by summiting Shisha Pangma in Tibet. A month earlier, Korea's Oh Eun-Sun had claimed this title, but doubt was cast on her summit of Kangchenjunga and her record remains disputed.

The **first woman to summit all 8,000ers without bottled oxygen** was Gerlinde Kaltenbrunner (AUT) on Aug. 23, 2011.

Person to complete the Explorers' Grand Slam

The Explorers' Grand Slam comprises climbing the Seven Summits, the 14 mountains over 8,000 m, and trekking to the North and South poles on foot. Park Young-Seok (KOR) began by climbing Everest on May 16, 1993, and finished the slam when he reached the North Pole on Apr. 30, 2005. Sadly, Park died in Oct. 2011 on Annapurna, the **deadliest mountain**.

Ascent of K2

On Jul. 31, 1954, Italy's Achille Compagnoni and Lino Lacedelli completed the first ascent of K2, which at 28,251 ft. (8,611 m) is the world's second-highest mountain. K2 is situated in the Karakoram range, on the border between Pakistan and China.

Wanda Rutkiewicz (POL) became the **first woman to climb K2**, on Jun. 23, 1986.

Russia's Andrew Mariev and Vadim Popovich completed the **first ascent of K2's west face**, on Aug. 21, 2007, after a grueling 10-week climb. The pair—led by Viktor Kozlov (RUS)—conquered this notoriously vicious face and reached the peak without the use of bottled oxygen.

Ascent of Kangchenjunga The third-highest mountain (28,169 ft.; 8,586 m) was first climbed on May 25, 1955 by George Band and Joe Brown (both UK).

The **first female to climb Kangchenjunga** was Ginette Harrison (UK), who summited via the northwest face on May 18, 1998.

OLDEST . . .

Person to climb the Seven Summits (Messner list) **Male:** Takao Arayama (JPN, b. Oct. 4, 1935) completed his final Seven Summits climb on Kilimanjaro in Tanzania on Feb. 18, 2010, at the age of 74 years 138 days.

Female: Carol Masheter (U.S.A., b. Oct. 10, 1946) completed her last Seven Summits climb by ascending Carstensz Pyramid on Jul. 12, 2012, aged 65 years 276 days.

Masheter also climbed Kosciuszko on Mar. 17, 2012, thus becoming the **oldest female to climb the Bass list of the Seven Summits**.

Person to climb the Seven Summits (Bass list) Ramón Blanco (ESP, b. Apr. 30, 1933) completed the last mountain on the Bass list on Dec. 29, 2003, at 70 years 244 days old.

Person to climb an 8,000er without bottled oxygen Only five people older than 65 have summited an 8,000er without the use of supplementary oxygen. The oldest of these was Boris Korshunov (RUS, b. Aug. 31, 1935), who climbed Cho Oyu on Oct. 2, 2007 aged 72 years 32 days. However, as some alpinists dispute Korshunov's claim, the undisputed record goes to Carlos Soria (ESP, b. Feb. 5, 1939), who summited Manaslu on Oct. 1, 2010, aged 71 years 238 days.

FASTEST TIME TO CLIMB ALL 8,000ERS Kim Chang-Ho (KOR) climbed the 14 mountains over 26,246 ft. (8,000 m) in 7 years 310 days, starting with his successful summit of Nanga Parbat on Jul. 14, 2005 and ending with Everest on May 20, 2013. Significantly, he completed all climbs without supplemental oxygen.

FACT: Kim Chang-Ho made a sea-to-summit ascent of Everest, starting from sea level at the Bay of Bengal.

FIRST PERSON TO CLIMB THE TRIPLE SEVEN SUMMITS Building on the idea of the Seven Summits, the Triple Seven Summits refers to climbing the three highest mountains on each continent. Christian Stangl (AUT) was the first to achieve the feat when he finished with Europe's third-highest mountain, Shkhara, on Aug. 23, 2013.

While achieving this hat trick, Stangl also became the **first person to climb the Seven Second Summits** and the **Seven Third Summits**, having conquered the second-highest mountain on each continent by Jan. 15, 2013.

A. "Helmet: To protect the head from falling rocks and chunks of ice."

B. "Glasses: To protect the eyes from the Sun's UV radiation and wind."

C. "Gloves: To protect against the cold."

D. "Rope: For protection in case of a fall and to rappel [abseil]."

E. "Ice ax: To climb on icy terrain."

F. "Harness: Provides the link between your body and the rope."

G. "Pants and jacket: Waterproofed and with insulation."

H. "Carabiners and quickdraws: For safety and to provide quick connection to the rope while climbing."

I. "Crampons: Steel frame with spikes, essential to get a grip on icy ground."

J. "Boots: Waterproofed and with good insulation."

Continent	Second Summits	Third Summits
Africa	Batian (17,057 ft.)	Mawenzi (16,889 ft.)
Antarctica	Tyree (15,918 ft.)	Shinn (15,288 ft.)
Asia	K2 (28,251 ft.)	Kangchenjunga (28,169 ft.)
Australasia	Sumantri (15,977 ft.)	Puncak Mandala (15,610 ft.)
Europe	Dykh-tau (17,076 ft.)	Shkhara (17,037 ft.)
North America	Logan (19,550 ft.)	Orizaba (18,490 ft.)
South America	Ojos del Salado (22,614 ft.)	Pissis (22,293 ft.)

CROSSING THE SEAS

Fastest single-handed sail from Cádiz to San Salvador Following a similar route to that of Christopher Columbus (leading to its name "The Discovery Route"), Armel Le Cléac'h (FRA) sailed from Cádiz in Spain to San Salvador in the Bahamas in 6 days 23 hr. 42 min. Le Cléac'h sailed in his 103-ft. (31.4-m) trimaran *Banque Populaire 7* and completed the 3,884-nautical-mi. (4,469.62-mi.; 7,193.17-km) route on Jan. 23–30, 2014, at an average speed of 23.16 knots (26.65 mph; 42.89 km/h).

On Jan. 26–27, during the voyage, veteran sailor Le Cléac'h also achieved the **greatest distance sailed in 24 hours single-handedly**, covering 682.85 nautical mi. (785.81 mi.; 1,264.64 km).

YOUNGEST PERSON TO ROW ACROSS ANY OCEAN (NONSOLO) Eoin Hartwright (UK, b. Jan. 17, 1997) was 16 years 340 days old when he left La Gomera in the Canary Islands, Spain, to row the Atlantic Ocean east to west. The team, also consisting of Simon Hartwright (Eoin's uncle), Matthew Collier, and Tom Alden, reached Antigua in the *Trilogy Extra* on Feb. 4, 2013, in just under 44 days.

As of Sep. 2013, a total of **340 ocean rows** had been successfully completed.

FIRST PERSON TO ROW ACROSS TWO DIFFERENT OCEANS IN A YEAR
Livar Nysted (DNK) rowed the Atlantic east to west in a team of eight from Gran Canaria to Barbados from Jan. 17 to Feb. 22, 2013. After a few months' rest, on Jun. 9, he rowed a second ocean, crossing the Indian Ocean east to west in a team of three from Australia to Mauritius (see below), arriving on Aug. 5, 2013. He spent a total of 93 days 4 hr. at sea during the two voyages.

Fastest single-handed transatlantic sailing Francis Joyon (FRA) sailed from New York City, U.S.A., to Cornwall, UK, in 5 days 2 hr. 56 min. He arrived on Jun. 16, 2013, after a trip of 2,880 nautical mi. (3,314 mi.; 5,333 km). Joyon still holds the **fastest global solo circumnavigation sailing** record, set back in 2008 at 57 days 13 hr. 34 min. He sailed 21,600 nautical mi. (24,170 mi.; 38,900 km).

Fastest row across the Indian Ocean, east to west Maxime Chaya (LBN), Livar Nysted (DNK), and Stuart Kershaw (UK) rowed from Geraldton, Australia, to Mauritius onboard *tRIO*. Their trip—which took 57 days 15 hr. 49 min., from Jun. 9 to Aug. 5, 2013—also represents the **first team of three to row an ocean**.

LONGEST UNSUPPORTED OPEN OCEAN JOURNEY BY JET SKI
Frederico Rezende (PRT) jet-skied 598.4 mi. (963 km) in the Atlantic Ocean between the Portuguese cities of Lisbon and Funchal on Sep. 11–13, 2013. The voyage took him 48 hr. 55 min., during which time he was the sole pilot and had no sleep.

LONGEST DISTANCE ROWED SOLO NONSTOP IN THE ATLANTIC (FEMALE)

Janice Jakait (DEU) (left) rowed 3,545 mi. (5,705 km) as the crow flies, east to west from Portugal to Barbados, from Nov. 23, 2011 to Feb. 21, 2012. This also makes her the **first woman to row across the Atlantic east to west from mainland Europe to the West Indies solo**, a feat unmatched as of Apr. 2014.

First person to row mid-Pacific west to east solo

Sarah Outen (UK) rowed onboard *Happy Socks* from Chōshi in Japan to Adak in Alaska, U.S.A., taking 149 days 13 hr. between Apr. 27 and Sep. 23, 2013.

Prior to this, at the age of 23 years 310 days, Outen (b. May 26, 1985) had become the **youngest female to row the Indian Ocean solo**. She made her epic east-to-west crossing between Apr. 1 and Aug. 3, 2009.

Youngest person to row solo across an ocean

On Mar. 14, 2010, Katie Spotz (U.S.A., b. Apr. 18, 1987) completed her 70-day row across the Atlantic, east to west from Senegal to Guyana. When she set off on Jan. 3, 2010, she was at the age of 22 years 260 days.

Tommy Tippetts (UK, b. Mar. 26, 1989) was 22 years 301 days old at the start of his trip east to west across the Atlantic, making him the **youngest male to row solo across an ocean**. His trip took place from Jan. 21 to Apr. 12, 2012.

YOUNGEST TANDEM ROW ACROSS AN OCEAN

UK rowers Jamie Sparks (b. Jan. 11, 1992) and Luke Birch (b. Jul. 4, 1992) set off on Dec. 4, 2013 in the *Maple Leaf* from La Gomera, Spain, on the Talisker Whisky Atlantic Challenge. At, respectively, 21 years 327 days and 21 years 153 days old on departure, they reached English Harbour in Antigua 54 days 5 hr. 56 min. later, on Jan. 27, 2014, having covered 2,934.48 mi. (4,722.6 km).

FASTEST MONOHULL SOLO CIRCUMNAVIGATION (40-FT. CLASS) Guo Chuan (CHN, left) sailed the world in 137 days 20 hr. 1 min., finishing on Apr. 4, 2013. In 2005–06, he was the first Chinese sailor to take part in the Clipper Round the World Yacht Race, founded by Sir Robin Knox-Johnston (UK, right, with GWR's Frank Chambers). Sir Robin became the **first person to sail solo around the world (nonstop)** on Apr. 22, 1969, as the only finisher of the Golden Globe Race.

TASMAN SEA

First solo row From Feb. 6 to Apr. 10, 1977, Colin Quincey (NZ) rowed solo in the *Tasman Trespasser* across the Tasman Sea—a stretch of water approximately 1,200 mi. (2,000 km) wide and known locally as "The Ditch." Quincey rowed from Hokianga in New Zealand to Marcus Beach in Queensland, Australia, taking 63 days 7 hr.

The **first person to row across the Tasman Sea west to east** (from the mainland) is Shaun Quincey (NZ)—Colin's son. He rowed in *Tasman Trespasser 2* from New South Wales in Australia to Ninety Mile Beach in New Zealand. The trip took him 53 days, between Jan. 20 and Mar. 14, 2010.

First team to row east to west Steven Gates, Andrew Johnson, Kerry Tozer, and Sally Macready (all AUS) rowed from Hokianga in New Zealand to Sydney Harbour, Australia, between Nov. 29 and Dec. 30, 2007.

The **first team to row west to east** was Nigel Cherrie, Martin Berka, James Blake, and Andrew McCowan (all NZ), from Sydney to the Bay of Islands, between Nov. 26, 2011 and Jan. 16, 2012.

FIRST CROSSING OF THE TASMAN SEA BY KAYAK James Castrission and Justin Jones (both AUS) traveled from Australia to New Zealand across the Tasman Sea in *Lot 41*. They left Foster in Victoria on Nov. 13, 2007 and rowed 2,061.7 mi. (3,318 km) over 62 days, reaching New Plymouth in New Zealand on Jan. 13, 2008.

MOST OCEAN ROWS BY ONE PERSON Simon Chalk (UK, b. Sep. 12, 1972) has made a total of eight ocean rows. He rowed east to west across the Atlantic Ocean in teams of two (1997), five (2007/08), six (2013), eight (2012 and 2014), and 14 (2011). He rowed the Indian Ocean east to west, solo, in 2003—making him the **youngest male rower to cross the Indian Ocean**—and in a team of eight in 2009.

A. "A tracking beacon charts the boat's progress every step of the way and relays data to team members on dry land."

B. "White flares are set off to avoid collision and red flares are to ask for help."

C. "The sun hat provides neck protection, which is vital in temperatures exceeding 104°F on the mid-Atlantic route."

D. "An offshore life jacket with spray hood, whistle, and reflective tape; this is designed to keep a rower's head above water in case of becoming unconscious."

E. "Specifically designed for ocean rowing, the oars provide the only means of propelling the boat."

F. "A safety harness keeps the rower attached to the rowing boat at all times."

G. "The satellite phone is for safety first and foremost but it's good to hear news from back at home and tell loved ones how the rowers are getting on."

H. "Fenders are only used in port and not taken on the trip. They prevent damage to the boat when moored."

I. "Desalinated water is heated in the Jetboil cooker to rehydrate the freeze-dried food rations—and is good for making the odd cup of tea, too!"

J. "The throwing line is used as a first rescue attempt in the event of man overboard."

Crossing the Seas

ENDURANCE

Fastest speed in a human-powered vehicle (multiple riders)
On Sep. 14, 2013, Tom Amick and Phil Plath (both U.S.A.) reached
73.08 mph (117.61 km/h) in their streamlined recumbent bicycle *Glow-
worm* on a flat road surface at the World Human Powered Speed Challenge near Battle Mountain in Nevada, U.S.A.

Fastest circumnavigation by bicycle (female) In just 152 days 1 hr.,
Juliana Buhring (DEU) cycled a total distance of 18,063 mi. (29,069 km).
The journey started and finished at Piazza Plebiscito in Naples, Italy, and
lasted from Jul. 23 until Dec. 22, 2012.

Fastest human-powered propeller submarine In Jun. 2007, the
two-person, propeller-driven submarine *OMER 5* reached 8.035 knots
(9.2 mph; 14.9 km/h) at the 9th International Submarine Races held at the
David Taylor Model Basin in Bethesda, Maryland, U.S.A. It was piloted
by Sebastien Brisebois and Joel Brunet (both CAN) of the École de Tech-
nologie Supérieure at the University of Quebec, Canada.

FASTEST SPEED IN A HUMAN-POWERED VEHICLE (SINGLE RIDER)
Sebastiaan Bowier (NLD) notched up a speed of 83.13 mph (133.78 km/h) in
his streamlined recumbent bicycle *VeloX3* at the World Human Powered Speed
Challenge near Battle Mountain in Nevada, U.S.A., on Sep. 14, 2013. Sebastiaan is
pictured above, with teammate Wil Baselmans.

We can survive for about two months without food, but only around
five days **without water**.

FARTHEST DISTANCE TO SWIM UNDER ICE WITH BREATH HELD
Wearing fins and a diving suit, Stig Åvall Severinsen (DNK) swam 500 ft. (152 m) under ice, with his breath held, at Qorlortoq Lake on Ammassalik Island, Greenland, on Apr. 16, 2013. He returned the next day to make the **farthest swim under ice with breath held (no fins, no diving suit)**: 250 ft. (76 m).

FASTEST CROSSING OF THE U.S.A. BY BICYCLE During the Race Across America in 2013, Christoph Strasser (AUT) cycled across the U.S.A. in 7 days 22 hr. 11 min., completing the trip on Jun. 19. In doing so, the indefatigable cyclist also became the first person to cross the U.S.A. coast to coast in under 8 days.

Most countries visited by bicycle in seven days Between Apr. 29 and May 5, 2013, Glen Burmeister (UK) cycled through 11 countries, from Břeclav in the Czech Republic to Shkodër in Albania. Burmeister passed through Austria, Slovakia, Hungary, Slovenia, Croatia, Romania, Serbia, Bosnia and Herzegovina, and Montenegro.

Longest time flying in a human-powered vehicle Kanellos Kanellopoulos (GRC) kept his *Daedalus 88* aircraft aloft for 3 hr. 54 min. 59 sec. on Apr. 23, 1988, while pedaling the 71.93 mi. (115.11 km) between Heraklion, Crete, and the Greek island of Santorini. Unfortunately, a gust of wind broke off the plane's tail and it crashed just before reaching shore.

LONGEST JOURNEY . . .

By bicycle (individual) The greatest mileage amassed in a cycle tour was more than 402,000 mi. (646,960 km), by the itinerant lecturer Walter Stolle (CZE) from Jan. 24, 1959 to Dec. 12, 1976. He visited 159 countries, starting out from Romford in Essex, UK.

On crutches From Mar. 21 to Jul. 27, 2011, Guy Amalfitano (FRA) journeyed 2,488 mi. (4,004 km) through France on crutches. His journey took him from Salies-de-Béarn to the Centre Hospitalier in Orthez.

LONGEST WALK ON FLOWER PETALS Between Jan. 2 and 27, 2013, a group of 1,128 Buddhist monks walked 278.6 mi. (448.4 km) between temples, across eight provinces in Thailand, stepping on marigold petals. The walk was part of the Second Dhammachai Dhutanga pilgrimage to welcome in the year 2013.

FARTHEST DISTANCE BAREFOOT (24 HOURS) Peter Wayne Botha (NZ, b. ZAF) ran 131.43 mi. (211.51 km) barefoot on Oct. 5–6, 2013, in the 16th annual Sri Chinmoy 24-hour race in Auckland, New Zealand. En route, he clocked the **fastest 100 km barefoot**, in 8 hr. 49 min. 42 sec.

FASTEST TIME TO CLIMB EL CAPITAN (FEMALE) Mayan Smith-Gobat (NZ, above) and Libby Sauter (U.S.A.) successfully climbed the "Nose" route of El Capitan in Yosemite National Park in California, U.S.A., on Sep. 29, 2013. The duo took 5 hr. 39 min. to complete the ascent, beating the previous record by almost two hours.

FASTEST SPEED IN A HUMAN-POWERED VEHICLE (FEMALE) On Sep. 15, 2010, Barbara Buatois (FRA) (left) reached a speed of 75.69 mph (121.81 km/h) pedaling her streamlined recumbent bicycle *Varna Tempest*. She achieved the feat on a flat road surface at the World Human Powered Speed Challenge near Battle Mountain in Nevada, U.S.A.

On roller skis Between May 11 and Jul. 5, 2012, César Baena (VEN) traveled 1,395.73 mi. (2,246.21 km) on roller skis from Stockholm in Sweden to Oslo in Norway.

On inline skates Khoo Swee Chiow (SGP) covered a distance of 3,782 mi. (6,088 km) on inline skates. Khoo departed from Hanoi in Vietnam on Oct. 20, 2007 and arrived in Singapore on Jan. 21, 2008.

Swimming in open water Martin Strel (SVN) swam 3,273 mi. (5,268 km) down the length of the Amazon River in Peru and Brazil from Feb. 1 to Apr. 8, 2007.

Walking backward To date, the greatest exponent of reverse pedestrianism is Plennie L. Wingo (U.S.A.). From Apr. 15, 1931 to Oct. 24, 1932, he walked 8,000 mi. (12,875 km) from Santa Monica in California, U.S.A., to Istanbul in Turkey at a rate of 15.47 mi. (24.89 km) per day.

LONGEST ONGOING PILGRIMAGE

As of Apr. 24, 2013, the greatest distance claimed for an "around the world" pilgrimage is 40,235 mi. (64,752 km) by Arthur Blessitt (U.S.A.), who has been walking on a mission since Dec. 25, 1969. He has visited all seven continents, including Antarctica, having traversed 321 nations, island groups, and territories carrying a 12-ft.-tall (3.7-m) wooden cross and preaching from the Bible throughout.

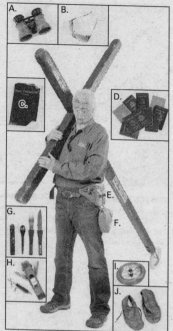

A. "I used these beat-up binoculars for 20–30 years. They were small but clear for finding a way over difficult mountains or ravines. Also, to see in wars, where the shooting and bombing was."

B. "I wore these sunglasses out in two years across Africa. The dust on dirt roads from passing trucks rose up in huge clouds. I also wore contact lenses. These were almost priceless."

C. "My greatest treasure and necessity. When faced with dangers, death, and struggles I pull it out and hold it in my hand."

D. "Keep the passport dry, out of sight, and away from sticky fingers—some border police of remote areas would hold the passport for a bribe. Interestingly, it's the smallest countries that have a full-page stamp!"

E. "I've used this hipster for 20 years. It carries my small Bible and sometimes my passport. Sometimes I have food snacks in it, too. It's like a small backpack. I still use it."

F. "My water canteen, last used in the Darién Gap in Panama/Colombia in 1978. I've never gotten sick from the water sources I used on the roads of the world. Jesus did it. It is very emotional to see this . . ."

G. "A true pleasure, these utensils fit inside a plastic holder with a salt and pepper shaker. So even with dirty hands on the road and awful food at least I have something clean to eat with."

H. "My army knife is one thing that always goes with me. It fits right on my belt with its bottle and can opener, sewing kit, paper, writing pen, magnifying glass, saw, wrench, scissors, screwdriver, and stone for sharpening."

I. "The wheel for my cross, this one used on my trip across southern Africa in 1985–86 and China in 1987. The cross wood wears away as it drags on the rocks and pavement, and I'd have to replace the cross every few weeks without the wheel."

J. "In 1969, there were only working boots—it was years before specialty walking shoes became developed. I learned the hard way to get walking shoes that were larger than my typical shoe size; I would have to cut holes on the side for my toes. I tighten my shoelaces in the morning and loosen them as my feet expand."

EPIC JOURNEYS

BY AIR

Fastest circumnavigation by microlight Colin Bodill (UK) circled the globe in his Mainair Blade 912 Flexwing microlight aircraft in 99 days from May 31 to Sep. 6, 2000, starting and landing at Brooklands airfield in Weybridge, Surrey, UK. Accompanying him was Jennifer Murray (UK), who made the **fastest circumnavigation by helicopter (female)** on the trip, flying in a Robinson R44. The pair covered some 21,750 mi. (35,000 km).

YOUNGEST PERSON TO CIRCUMNAVIGATE BY AIRCRAFT Between May 2 and Jun. 29, 2013, Jack Wiegand (U.S.A., b. Jun. 22, 1992) flew around the world in a Mooney M20R Ovation aircraft, covering approximately 24,000 mi. (38,600 km) in all, and making 22 stops en route. Jack was 21 years 7 days old when he touched down in Fresno, California, U.S.A., at the end of his trip.

> We walk the equivalent of about **four times** around Earth in a lifetime.

Longest journey . . .

• **By ultralight aircraft:** Roberto Bisa and Antonio Forato (both ITA) of ASD Riding the Skies flew an ultralight aircraft 12,505 mi. (20,126 km) from Cassola in Italy to Southport in Queensland, Australia, from Oct. 8 to 31, 2013.

• **Kitesurfing in 24 hours:** On Feb. 26, 2012, Rimas Kinka (LTU) covered 401.2 mi. (645.6 km) off the coast of Islamorada in Florida, U.S.A.

• **Kitesurfing (female):** No woman has kitesurfed for longer than Germany's Anke Brandt, who covered 135.16 nautical mi. (155.54 mi.; 250.32 km) between Amwaj Marina and Al Dar Island, Bahrain, on Mar. 1, 2014.

LONGEST JOURNEY BY 50-CC SCOOTER Theodore Rezvoy and Evgeniy Stoyanov (both UKR) rode 8,968 mi. (14,434 km) from Odessa in Ukraine to Ulan-Ude in Russia on two 50-cc Honda Zoomer scooters between Jul. 11 and Sep. 11, 2013. In doing so, they surpassed the previous record, set in 2010, by approximately 1,240 mi. (2,000 km).

LONGEST JOURNEY BY ELECTRIC MOTORCYCLE As part of the Meneghina Express event—a project to investigate global food nutrition and sustainability— Nicola Colombo and Valerio Fumagalli (both ITA) covered 7,691 mi. (12,379 km) on electric motorcycles. The duo rode from Shanghai, China, to Milan, Italy, between Jun. 10 and Jul. 23, 2013.

BY LAND

Fastest circumnavigation by car The record for the first and fastest man and woman to have circumnavigated the Earth by car covering six continents under the rules applicable in 1989 and 1991 embracing more than an equator's length of driving (24,901 road miles; 40,075 km), is held by Saloo Choudhury and his wife Neena Choudhury (both India). The journey took 69 days 19 hr. 5 min. from Sep. 9 to Nov. 17, 1989. The couple drove a 1989 Hindustan "Contessa Classic" starting and finishing in Delhi, India.

Longest journey . . .

- **Barefoot:** Michael Essing (DEU) walked 924.65 mi. (1,488.09 km) on his bare feet between the German towns of Flensburg and Efringen-Kirchen from May 30 to Sep. 5, 2013.
- **By car:** As of Apr. 3, 2013, Emil and Liliana Schmid (both CHE) had covered 420,842 mi. (677,281 km) in a Toyota Land Cruiser. Their trip began on Oct. 16, 1984.
- **By nonsolar electric vehicle:** Duane Leffel (U.S.A.) drove 3,534.77 mi. (5,688.68 km) from Charleston in South Carolina to Laguna Hills in California, U.S.A., from Jul. 4 to Aug. 24, 2013.
- **By motorcycle in one country:** Buck Perley (U.S.A.) and Amy Mathieson (UK) rode 20,727.13 mi. (33,357.15 km) across China from Jul. 19 to Dec. 11, 2013.
- **By motorized bicycle:** From Jul. 14 to Sep. 4, 2012, Danny Halmo (CAN) rode 4,176 mi. (6,721 km) within Canada, from English Bay in Vancouver, British Columbia, to Halifax Harbour, Nova Scotia.
- **By rickshaw:** Tim Moss (UK) rode a rickshaw 856.22 mi. (1,377.96 km) from Aviemore to West Molesey, UK, between Apr. 26 and May 19, 2010.

LONGEST JOURNEY BY SOLAR-POWERED CAR A team from SolarCar Projekt Hochschule Bochum (DEU) carried out an 18,487-mi. (29,753-km) trip by electric vehicle, leaving Adelaide in Australia on Oct. 26, 2011 and arriving in Mount Barker, Australia, on Dec. 15, 2012. They spent a total of 168 days driving. Eight days were devoted to recharging the vehicle; the remaining days were spent exhibiting the SolarCar at various locations, events, and universities and being transported between continents.

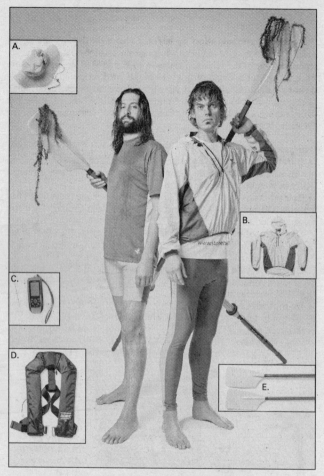

FIRST ROW OF THE NAVIGABLE LENGTH OF THE AMAZON Embarking from Nauta in Peru on Sep. 13, 2013, Anton Wright (UK, left) and Dr. Mark de Rond (NLD, right) rowed down the Amazon River to Macapá in Brazil, arriving on Oct. 14, 2013. Altogether, they covered more than 2,000 mi. (3,200 km) in their Woodvale Pairs-class ocean rowing boat, made out of plywood and reinforced with glass fiber and resins.

A. "Wearing a sun hat is a must when rowing the Amazon to prevent sunstroke and provide protection from the blistering Sun."

B. "Tropical storms can whip up quickly in the Amazon basin. These JL splash jackets provided ideal protection from the torrential rain."

C. "One of our most important pieces of equipment by far was this GPS device. It would indicate where we were on the river, how much progress we'd made, and what we could expect ahead."

D. "A life vest is a non-optional accessory, and for good reason: tropical storms and strong currents have claimed the lives of plenty of strong swimmers in the past."

E. "Oars made of reinforced carbon fiber are ideal for their durability and strength. They are also surprisingly lightweight."

LONGEST JOURNEY BY . . .

Vehicle	Distance	Record holders	Dates
Bus	54,287 mi.	Hughie Thompson, John Weston, and Richard Steel (all UK)	Nov. 6, 1988–Dec. 3, 1989
Fire engine	31,663 mi.	Stephen Moore (UK)	Jul. 18, 2010–Apr. 10, 2011
Hovercraft	4,970 mi.	British Trans-African Hovercraft Expedition, led by David Smithers (UK)	Oct. 15, 1969–Jan. 3, 1970
Motorcycle	456,707 mi.	Emilio Scotto (ARG)	Jan. 17, 1985–Apr. 2, 1995
Quad bike	34,945 mi.	Valerio De Simoni, Kristopher "Ted" Davant, and James Kenyon (all AUS)	Aug. 10, 2010–Oct. 22, 2011
Skateboard	7,555 mi.	Rob Thomson (NZ)	Jun. 24, 2007–Sep. 28, 2008
Tandem	23,700 mi.	Phil and Louise Shambrook (UK)	Dec. 17, 1994–Oct. 1, 1997
Tractor	13,172 mi.	Vasilii Hazkevich (RUS)	Apr. 25–Aug. 6, 2005
Wheelchair	24,901 mi.	Rick Hansen (CAN)	Mar. 21, 1985–May 22, 1987

BY WATER

First person to swim from Cuba to Florida without a shark cage
Diana Nyad (U.S.A., b. Aug. 22, 1949) swam from Havana, Cuba, to Key West, Florida, U.S.A., in 52 hr. 54 min. 18.6 sec. on Aug. 31–Sep. 2, 2013, aged 64 years 11 days.

Longest journey . . .
• **Swimming nonstop in open water (male):** Martin Strel (SVN) swam 313.1 mi. (504.5 km) down the Danube, from Melk in Austria to Paks in Hungary, in 84 hr. 10 min. on July 3–6, 2001. He was escorted by four kayakers, a safety escort boat, and six road vehicles.
• **Rowed in 24 hours by a team (men):** On Jun. 14–15, 2013, Dutch rowers Ansgar John Brenninkmeijer, Gert Jan Keizer, Oscar Dinkelaar, Jacques Klok, Jeroen van Renesse, and Hans-Jan Rijbering covered 183.4 mi. (295.2 km) up- and downstream on the Amstel River in the Netherlands.

ARTS & MEDIA

CONTENTS

The top 10 most visited museums had a total of **52.9 million visits** in 2012.

HIGHEST-GROSSING ACTION-MOVIE HEROINE The phenomenal success of the first two *Hunger Games* movies (U.S.A., 2012 and 2013) means that the character of Katniss Everdeen—portrayed by Jennifer Lawrence (U.S.A.)—is the movie industry's most successful action heroine at the box office, with both movies grossing a total of $1.55 bn internationally. *The Hunger Games: Catching Fire* was the **highest-grossing post-apocalypse movie**, taking $424,668,047 in the U.S.A. and grossing $864,565,663 worldwide.

FACT: According to Forbes' 2013 list of the most powerful celebrities, Jennifer Lawrence was the second-highest-scoring actress. Only Angelina Jolie (U.S.A.) ranked higher.

60 YEARS ON SCREEN

The movie industry has seen a huge increase in technological sophistication over the past six decades, but how has this affected our appetite for movies? Are we going to the movies more than ever? Are we releasing as many movies? And are new releases just as successful if you account for inflation?

All figures in U.S.$

In the past 60 years on screen, everything has changed, and yet nothing has changed. In 1955, the highest-grossing movie of all time was *Gone with the Wind* (U.S.A., 1939). Adjusting for current inflation, it seems probable it will still be the highest-grossing movie of all time at the end of 2015.

American movie houses made today's equivalent $10.68 billion in 1954, and $10.90 billion in 2012. Does this mean that movies are as popular as they've ever been? Well, it's estimated that U.S. movie houses sold about 2.5 billion tickets in 1955, compared with 1.3 billion in 2012. While most people go to the movies less regularly than they did in 1955, the rise of blockbusters—with their ever-spiraling budgets and technical breakthroughs—means that the public is prepared to pay more when they do.

The rise of affordable video technology has also helped the total number of movies made around the world each year to spiral, creating grassroots industries such as Nigeria's Nollywood, which now produces over 1,000 movies each year, beating the U.S.A. into third place on the list of the most prolific moviemaking countries.

NUMBER OF FEATURE MOVIES RELEASED PER YEAR (WORLDWIDE)

There has been a steady increase in the number of movies released annually, from 1,904 in 1955 to 10,048 in 2013. The affordability of high-end filmmaking technology has led to a rapid rise in the past 10 years.
• Peak of 3,248 releases in 1968; not surpassed until 1990
• Peak of 3,482 releases in 1990; not surpassed until 1999
• Releases exceed 4,000 for first time; 1,041 of them originate in India

CLEOPATRA *(U.S.A., 1963)*
Most expensive movie produced (adjusted): $306.86 m in today's money

E.T.: THE EXTRA-TERRESTRIAL *(U.S.A., 1982)* Most weekends at No. 1: Enjoys 16 (nonconsecutive) weekends as the highest-ranking movie; seen by an estimated 161 million people in the U.S.A. alone

**THE RESCUERS DOWN UNDER
(U.S.A., 1990) First fully digital
feature movie:** Made using a digital
ink system developed by Disney and
Pixar (both U.S.A.)

**AVATAR (U.S.A., 2009) First
movie to gross $2 bn:** Surpasses
$2 bn globally by the weekend of
Jan. 29–31, 2010

AVERAGE PRICE OF A U.S. MOVIE TICKET

Prices have crept up over the last six decades, as you would expect, but
when adjusted for inflation, there is plenty of variation over the years, peak-
ing in 1971. Of course, this is just the cost of the seat, not the parking, the
popcorn, the drinks, the 3D glasses . . .

• Average ticket price peaks in 1971 at $9.35 (in today's money)

**DOCTOR ZHIVAGO (U.S.A.,
1965) First movie to win five
Golden Globe awards:** Best Film,
Director, Actor, Screenplay, and
Score; five Globes is also a record,
shared with four other movies

**TRUE LIES (U.S.A., 1994) First
movie to have a $100-m budget:**
James Cameron ups the ante on the
spectacle of moviemaking; it ends up
making back $378 m

FACT: The average amount spent in a U.S. movie house in 2013
was $20 per person, of which only $8.12 was for the seat.

FACT: The Japanese pay the most for their movie tickets, as of
2013—the equivalent of $22 per seat.

THE TWILIGHT SAGA: ECLIPSE (U.S.A., 2010)
Widest movie release: Opens in 4,468 movie houses in U.S.A. on Jun. 30, 2010.

U.S. MOVIE HOUSE ADMISSIONS

It's been a bumpy ride when it comes to movie house admissions. As ticket prices grew, so the number of visits to the movies dropped drastically, reaching a low at the start of the 1970s. The advent of the blockbuster and multiplexes has seen this trend reverse, but not back to the glory days of the 1940s and 50s.

• The Golden Age of Hollywood peaked at 4.7 billion admissions in 1947; by 1964, with the rise of TV, the figure had dropped below 1 billion

• Record low of 709 million admissions in 1971

• Attendances peak at 1.6 billion in 2002, with *The Lord of the Rings*, *Harry Potter*, *Men in Black*, and *Star Wars* all enjoying chart-topping sequels

JAWS (U.S.A., 1975) First blockbuster movie: The first movie to earn $100 m at the box office

TRON (U.S.A., 1982) First major motion picture to use CGI: Producers desperate to keep movie audiences growing discover the benefits of computer-generated imagery

TITANIC (U.S.A., 1997) Most consecutive weekends at No. 1: 15 weekends as the highest-ranking movie

THE AVENGERS (U.S.A., 2012) Fastest time to gross $100 m at the domestic box office: Two days (May 4–5)

TOTAL U.S. BOX-OFFICE GROSS

The money earned by the theaters has fluctuated annually between a high of ca. $12 bn and a low of $6 bn.

- Adjusted peak of $11.98 bn in 1956; remains unbeaten until 2002
- *Star Wars* helps annual grosses to peak at $9.5 bn in 1978—a figure not surpassed for another 20 years
- *Titanic* (see p. 351) becomes the **first movie to gross $1 bn**
- U.S. box-office takings peak in 2003, with combined adjusted earnings of $12.06 bn
- The 12 biggest movies of 2009's Christmas weekend (Dec. 25–27) earn a combined $259.9 m in three days at the domestic (U.S.) box office—the **biggest weekend at the movies**

2001: A SPACE ODYSSEY (U.S.A./UK, 1968) Largest movie budget for special effects: Stanley Kubrick's mind-altering sci-fi classic spends more than 60% of its budget on special effects

STAR WARS (U.S.A., 1977) Highest-grossing sci-fi series: George Lucas's blockbuster and its sequels (and prequels) go on to gross an adjusted $2.65 bn

SUPER MARIO BROS. (U.S.A., 1993) First live-action movie based on a video game: Movie producers, looking for inspiration from popular licenses, turn to video-gaming for the first time

HARRY POTTER AND THE DEATHLY HALLOWS PART 2 (UK/U.S.A., 2011) Highest-grossing movie—single day: Earns $91 m on Jul. 15 in the U.S.A. alone

BLOCKBUSTERS PRE-1955 Below is a list of the highest-grossing movies since 1955. Only two movies in the all-time top 10 list of **most successful movies** predate 1955: *Gone with the Wind* (1939) and *Snow White and the Seven Dwarfs* (1937). When adjusted to today's ticket prices, the former remains at the No. 1 slot, with a gross of $3.44 bn.

TOP 10 MOVIES OF THE PAST 60 YEARS . . .

Ranking based on number of tickets sold, seat prices, and box-office gross

1956
The Ten Commandments
Chart position: 6
Ticket sales: 262.0 m
Adjusted gross: $2.187 bn
Biblical epic starring Charlton Heston as Moses, tasked with freeing the Hebrew slaves

1961
101 Dalmatians
Chart position: 10
Ticket sales: 199.8 m
Adjusted: $1.003 bn
A litter of Dalmatian dogs must be rescued before they become the fashion victims of Cruella de Vil

1965
Doctor Zhivago
Chart position: 7
Ticket sales: 248.2 m
Adjusted: $2.073 bn
A doctor/poet experiences illicit love and hardship during the Bolshevik Revolution

1965
The Sound of Music
Chart position: 4
Ticket sales: 283.3 m
Adjusted: $2.366 bn
The hills are alive with the sound of children and their nanny fleeing Nazi-occupied Austria

1973
The Exorcist
Chart position: 9
Ticket sales: 214.9 m
Adjusted: $1.794 bn
The Church is called in after a demonic entity takes possession of a young girl

1975
Jaws
Chart position: 8
Ticket sales: 242.8 m
Adjusted: $2.027 bn
A man-eating great white shark terrorizes a U.S. tourist hotspot at the height of the summer season

1977
Star Wars
Chart position: 2
Ticket sales: 338.4 m
Adjusted: $2.825 bn
Swashbuckling adventure set a long time ago in a galaxy far, far away . . .

1982
E.T.: The Extra-Terrestrial
Chart position: 5
Ticket sales: 276.7 m
Adjusted: $2.310 bn
An alien visitor to Earth is left stranded and befriends a young boy, who helps him "phone home"

1997
Titanic
Chart position: 3
Ticket sales: 301.3 m
Adjusted: $2.516 bn
James Cameron's epic tale of the sinking of the "unsinkable" ocean liner

2009
Avatar
Chart position: 1
Ticket sales: 238.6 m
Adjusted: $3.02 bn
Cameron again, this time setting the sci-fi action on the distant planet Pandora

MOST PROLIFIC MOVIE INDUSTRY
India continues to be the source of more movies than any other country: 1,255 releases in 2011, compared with 819 in the U.S.A. In May 2013—during Bollywood's 100th anniversary year—Vijay Krishna Acharya (IND) released *Dhoom 3*, the **highest-grossing Bollywood movie**, which raked in $88 m internationally.

MOVIES

Most expensive year in Hollywood The 50 biggest blockbusters released by major Hollywood studios in 2010 cost a combined total of $5.2 bn—the highest total in one year in U.S. cinematic history.

In 2013, the U.S.A. experienced the **highest box-office summer gross**, with movie theaters taking a total of $4.76 bn between May 1 and Aug. 31.

Most extensive digital object For the final battle sequence in *Ender's Game* (U.S.A., 2013), U.S. effects studio Digital Domain created 333,443 individual spaceships, all of which appeared simultaneously in shots comprising more than 27 billion polygons.

HIGHEST BOX OFFICE FILM GROSS FOR AN ANIMATION
Frozen (U.S.A., 2013) surpassed *Toy Story 3* (U.S.A., 2010) as the most successful animated movie at the global box office, earning $1.112 bn (£664.7 m)—and counting—as of Apr. 14, 2014. The Disney musical, inspired by Hans Christian Andersen's fairy tale *The Snow Queen*, broke the record while still on general release.

Movie theater visits in Senegal cost the **equivalent of 63¢**.

Largest total movie theater attendance (current) There were some 3.17 billion trips made to movie theaters in India in 2011. The **largest annual movie theater attendance** in a given year occurred in 1929, when 4.49 billion admissions were made to U.S. movie theaters.

Largest international movie market North America represents the largest market for movies, with box-office receipts in the U.S.A. and Canada totaling $10.8 bn in 2012.

HIGHEST BOX-OFFICE GROSS FOR A ZOMBIE MOVIE The 2013 blockbuster *World War Z* (UK/U.S.A.) took a worldwide box-office gross of more than $540 m by the time it closed in movie theaters on Oct. 10, 2013. The movie is based on a book of the same name by Max Brooks and stars Brad Pitt. In Jun. 2013, it was announced that there would be a *World War Z* sequel.

FACT: Max Brooks, author of *World War Z*, is the son of comedy director Mel Brooks, whose movies include horror spoofs *Young Frankenstein* (U.S.A., 1974) and *Dracula: Dead and Loving It* (U.S.A., 1995).

BUDGET vs. BOX OFFICE: BIGGEST RETURNS ON INVESTMENT

Charted here are the top 10 most profitable movies, as identified by the-numbers.com as of May 14, 2014. Profit is estimated from global box-office figures and domestic video/DVD sales. At the top is *Paranormal Activity* (U.S.A., 2009), which cost $450,000 to make but netted $89.7 m.

	Return on investment (%)
A. *Paranormal Activity* (2009)	19,850%
B. *The Devil Inside* (2012)	3,644%
C. *Peter Pan* (1953)	3,443%
D. *Grease* (1978)	3,056%
E. *Paranormal Activity 2* (2010)	2,474%
F. *Insidious* (2011)	2,079%
G. *Jaws* (1975)	1,730%
H. *Reservoir Dogs* (1992)	1,632%
I. *The King's Speech* (2010)	1,154%
J. *Beauty and the Beast* (1991)	1,148%

■ Budget
■ Gross
■ Return

Budget   Profit (estimated)   Return on investment (%)

A.
B.
C.
D.
E.
F.
G.
H.
I.
J.

Source: www.the-numbers.com/Nash Information Services; budget and profit scales are not proportional

Largest annual movie output According to UNESCO, India is the most prolific movie-making nation. The Bollywood industry produces up to 1,000 feature movies a year, and in 2011 1,255 movies were made, in 24 languages, compared with 819 movies made in the U.S.A.

MOST TIMES AN ACTOR HAS PLAYED THEMSELVES Legendary *lucha libre* wrestler El Santo (MEX) starred as himself in 50 action-adventure movies made over 24 years, beginning with *Santo contra el cerebro del mal* in 1958 and concluding with *Santo en la furia de los karatekas* in 1982.

HIGHEST-GROSSING SUPERHERO MOVIE Marvel's *The Avengers* (U.S.A., 2012) took $1.51 bn at the international box office in its 22 weeks on general release between May 4 and Oct. 4, 2012. The movie, directed by Joss Whedon (U.S.A.), accounted for 52% of all domestic box-office takings in the U.S.A. for the month of May.

Most movies made in one language

The most recent UNESCO cinematic survey found that in 2011, 1,302 movies were made exclusively in English. French came second with 293 movies and Spanish was third with 263. Although India makes the most movies, a range of languages were featured including Hindi, Tamil, and Telugu.

MOST EXTENSIVE LIGHTING ON A MOVIE SET "Zero-gravity" footage for the movie *Gravity* (U.S.A., 2013) was filmed within a custom-built light box containing 1.8 million high-powered LEDs. The LEDs were individually controlled by the movie's effects team to help re-create the natural light and shade of outer-space photography. The light box took the form of a hollow cube, within which the actors were suspended.

For more movies, turn the page.

CROWDFUNDED: *Veronica Mars* *Veronica Mars* (right) is the **most crowdfunded movie**, having received $5,702,153 via the Kickstarter crowdfunding site as of Apr. 13, 2013. The appeal, which began in response to the cancellation of the *Veronica Mars* TV show, funded the movie, which premiered on Mar. 14, 2014, a year and a day after the appeal launch.

The **first crowdfunded Oscar winner**, *Inocente* (left), won the Best Documentary (short feature) award on Feb. 24, 2013. The movie, about a homeless Californian girl's efforts to become an artist, was directed by Sean Fine and Andrea Nix.

Most expensive movie *Pirates of the Caribbean: At World's End* (U.S.A.) had a production budget of $300 m in 2007. Even if movie budgets are adjusted for inflation to 2014 prices, *At World's End* remains the most expensive production of all time. Its $339-m budget narrowly beats *Cleopatra* (1963, U.S.A.), starring Elizabeth Taylor and Richard Burton (both UK), which cost $44 m in 1963—the equivalent of $337 m today.

Most expensive movie series The eight *Harry Potter* movies (U.S.A./UK, 2001–09) had a combined production budget of $1.15 bn. However, it is *James Bond* that takes the record of **most expensive movie series adjusted for inflation**, with costs of around $2.07 bn across 23 movies and 50 years.

STANDOUT STUDIOS

Most billion-dollar movies by a studio: Buena Vista International (U.S.A.), seven (*Pirates of the Caribbean: Dead Man's Chest, Alice in Wonderland, Toy Story 3, Pirates of the Caribbean: On Stranger Tides, The Avengers, Iron Man 3,* and *Frozen*)

Highest average gross for a studio: Pixar (U.S.A.) has earned an average of $252.6 m across 14 movies

HIGHEST GROSSING . . .

- **Movie:** *Avatar* (U.S.A., 2009), $2.78 bn
- **Bollywood movie:** *Dhoom: 3* (IND, 2013), $88 m
- ***James Bond* movie:** *Skyfall* (UK/U.S.A., 2012), $1.10 bn
- **Post-apocalypse movie:** *The Hunger Games: Catching Fire* (U.S.A., 2013), $864 m

MOVIEMAKERS

Highest box-office movie gross for a director The 27 theatrically released movies thus far directed by Steven Spielberg (U.S.A.)—from *The Sugarland Express* (U.S.A., 1974) to *Lincoln* (U.S.A., 2012)—have grossed a total of $9.01 bn worldwide.

BOLLYWOOD BIG-HITTERS Topping the *Forbes* list as the **highest-earning Bollywood actor** is Shah Rukh Khan (IND), with estimated earnings in 2013 of 220.5 crore (2.2 bn rupees; $37.06 m). Khan is pictured here in the 2012 romantic drama *Jab Tak Hai Jaan* (*As Long as I Live*) with Katrina Kaif (HKG/UK), the **highest-earning Bollywood actress**, with earnings of 63.75 crore (637 m rupees; $10.7 m) during the same period.

MOST POWERFUL ACTOR Best known for his role as Wolverine, Hugh Jackman (AUS) topped Forbes' 2013 list of most powerful actors and is 11th overall in the list of most powerful celebrities. The list measures fame in terms of factors such as earnings, media exposure, and Internet presence.

Johnny Depp once worked for a **telemarketing** firm, selling pens.

HIGHEST BOX-OFFICE GROSS FOR A FEMALE DIRECTOR With a total worldwide box-office gross of $1,152,567,728 for her six movies as director, including *What Women Want* (U.S.A., 2000) and *It's Complicated* (U.S.A., 2009), U.S. moviemaker Nancy Meyers remains the highest-grossing female movie director of all time.

HIGHEST AVERAGE BOX-OFFICE GROSS FOR A LEADING ROLE *Harry Potter* star Emma Watson (UK) has an average box-office gross of $775,303,380. Her *Harry Potter* costar Daniel Radcliffe (UK) took top billing in one more non–*Harry Potter* movie than Watson, which has reduced his per-movie lead role average slightly to $712,856,021.

Most billion-dollar movies at the box office for a director

Three directors have each made two movies that have grossed at least $1 bn at the box office. They are: Canada's James Cameron, for *Titanic* (U.S.A., 1997) and *Avatar* (U.S.A./UK, 2009); New Zealand's Sir Peter Jackson, for *The Lord of the Rings: The Return of the King* (U.S.A./NZL, 2003) and *The Hobbit: An Unexpected Journey* (U.S.A./NL, 2012); and the UK's Christopher Nolan, for *The Dark Knight* (U.S.A./UK, 2008) and *The Dark Knight Rises* (U.S.A./UK, 2012).

HOLLYWOOD ROYALTY: THE MOST INDIVIDUAL OSCAR WINS

Most Oscars won in a lifetime: Walt Disney (U.S.A.), 26

Most Oscars won in a lifetime (female): Edith Head (U.S.A.), eight

Most Best Director Oscars won: John Ford (U.S.A.), four

Most Best Actress Oscars won: Katharine Hepburn (U.S.A.), four

Most Best Actor Oscars won: Daniel Day-Lewis (UK), three

Most overpaid actor According to business magazine *Forbes*, Adam Sandler (U.S.A.) returned an average of $3.40 for every $1 he was paid, based on the last three movies he starred in to Jun. 1, 2013. For the same period, *Forbes* ranked Katherine Heigl (U.S.A.) as the **most overpaid actress**, with an average return of $3.50 for every $1 earned. (See also: "Payback with interest," above.)

MOST BILLION-DOLLAR MOVIES AT THE BOX OFFICE FOR AN ACTOR
Johnny Depp achieved three billion-dollar box-office smashes with *Pirates of the Caribbean* movies *On Stranger Tides* and *Dead Man's Chest*, and *Alice in Wonderland*. Hugo Weaving (AUS, top left) matches him with *The Hobbit: An Unexpected Journey*, *Transformers: Dark of the Moon*, and *The Lord of the Rings: The Return of the King*. Gary Oldman (UK, bottom left) scores for *Harry Potter and the Deathly Hallows: Part 2*, *The Dark Knight*, and *The Dark Knight Rises*.

MOST BANKABLE HOLLYWOOD FIGURE Steven Spielberg (U.S.A.) contributed the equivalent of $26,344,040 annually to the movie industry as of Feb. 2014, according to the-numbers.com. His annual earnings (see **highest earnings for a producer**, below) also make Spielberg the **highest-earning director**.

Oldest actress in a leading role Lillian Gish (U.S.A., b. Oct. 14, 1893) was 93 years old when she starred in *The Whales of August* (U.S.A.), released on Oct. 16, 1987.

The **oldest actress to debut in a leading role** is Harue Akagi (JPN, b. Mar. 14, 1924), who was 88 years 175 days old when she starred in *Pekorosu no Haha ni Ai ni Iku* (JPN), released on Nov. 9, 2013.

HIGHEST . . .

Annual earnings for a producer Steven Spielberg (U.S.A.) earned $100 m from Jun. 2012 to Jun. 2013 according to Forbes' Celebrity 100 list. The total gross of Spielberg-produced movies stands at more than $6.4 bn.

HIGHEST ANNUAL EARNINGS FOR AN ACTOR According to Forbes, two actors share the record for the highest earnings over a 12-month period. Robert Downey Jr. (U.S.A., top left) earned around $75 m from Jun. 2012 to Jun. 2013, benefiting from the success of *The Avengers* and *Iron Man 3*. Tom Cruise (U.S.A., top right) earned a similar figure from May 2011 to May 2012, during which *Mission: Impossible: Ghost Protocol* (U.S.A./UAE/CZE, 2011) grossed some $700 m.

CRUISING TO SUCCESS

In the past eight years, Tom Cruise, seen above as Jack Reacher, has been the highest-earning movie actor three times. His big-screen debut came back in 1981.

SUPERCAMEO-MAN: Stan Lee With movies based on his creations breaking box-office records around the world, it's perhaps unsurprising that Marvel Comics mastermind Stan Lee (U.S.A.), at 91 years 68 days old as of Mar. 5, 2014, would want to play his part in the action. The 19 movies in which he has made cameo appearances since his cinematic debut in *Mallrats* (U.S.A., 1995)—including *X-Men 3: The Last Stand* (U.S.A., 2006; top right), *Spider-Man 3* (U.S.A., 2007; center right), and *Fantastic Four* (U.S.A., 2005; bottom right)—have grossed $10,077,831,163 at the global box office, making Stan Lee the **highest-grossing actor from cameo appearances**.

Box-office gross for an actor Samuel L. Jackson (U.S.A.) has a career worldwide gross of $12,126,213,694 from the 94 movies in which he has appeared. These include supporting roles in box-office record breakers *The Avengers* and *Iron Man 2* (U.S.A., 2010).

Average box-office gross for a director (male) Lee Unkrich (U.S.A.) has an average U.S. gross of $332.9 m as a director, with a worldwide overall gross of $2.97 bn as of Nov. 8, 2013. His highest-grossing movie is *Toy Story 3* (U.S.A., 2010).

Average earnings for a movie composer John Williams (U.S.A.) has written scores for 76 movies, each grossing an average of $289.6 m at the box office. They include the six *Star Wars* movies and several of the *Harry Potter* movies. The **highest career box-office movie gross for a composer** is $22.48 bn by Hans Zimmer (DEU), nearly $4 bn more than John Williams, his nearest rival. His credits include *The Dark Knight Rises* and three *Pirates of the Caribbean* movies.

AND FINALLY . . .

- **Most appearances in $100-m-grossing movies:** Bruce Willis (U.S.A.), with 25 such movies as of Jan. 21, 2014.

- **Most powerful actress:** Angelina Jolie (U.S.A.), ranked 41 in Forbes' 2012–13 Celebrity 100 list.

- **Most screenwriters credited:** 51, for *50 Kisses* (UK, 2014), produced by the London Screenwriters' Festival (UK).

POP MUSIC

Most Facebook "likes" for a musician As of Apr. 25, 2014, Shakira (COL) had the most "likes" with 90,938,442. Not far behind was Rihanna (BRB) with 87,042,153, and at No. 3 was Eminem (U.S.A.) with 86,136,651.

Over on Twitter, the **musician with the most followers** is Katy Perry (U.S.A.) with 52,463,838. Next up are Justin Bieber (CAN) with 51,140,907 and Lady Gaga (U.S.A.) with 41,297,293.

FIRST ACT TO DEBUT AT NO. 1 IN U.S.A. WITH FIRST THREE ALBUMS One Direction (UK) completed a hat-trick of No. 1 debuts on the *Billboard* 200 albums chart when *Midnight Memories* entered in pole position with first-week sales of 546,000 on Dec. 14, 2013. It followed the chart-topping success of *Up All Night* and *Take Me Home* in 2012.

MOST TRAVELED MUSICIAN IN ONE YEAR According to research carried out by the live music events website Songkick, electro-house musician, DJ, and producer Steve Aoki (U.S.A.) traveled 241,850 mi. (389,221 km) performing a total of 168 shows in 41 countries in 2012.

There are more than **26 million songs** in the iTunes catalog.

FASTEST-SELLING iTUNES ALBUM On Dec. 13, 2013, Beyoncé (U.S.A.) unexpectedly released self-titled studio album *BEYONCÉ*—with 14 new tracks and 17 videos—exclusively on iTunes. In its first three days of availability as a download, it sold 828,773 copies worldwide.

Highest-earning dead celebrity
American singer Michael Jackson earned $160 m from Oct. 2012 to Oct. 2013. If Forbes included the dead, he would top the 2013 list of highest-earning celebs.

LONGEST-RUNNING ALBUM SERIES There have been 87 albums in the *NOW That's What I Call Music!* series (Virgin/EMI). The first was released in 1983 and the most recent on 7 Apr. 2014.
- ***FIRST:*** *NOW That's What I Call Music!*, Nov. 28, 1983
- ***EDITIONS:*** 87
- ***SONGS:*** 3,440
- ***UNITS SOLD:*** more than 100 million
- ***MOST APPEARANCES:*** Robbie Williams (33)
- ***MOST APPEARANCES ON ONE ALBUM:*** Calvin Harris (3)

STILL A "WHITE CHRISTMAS"

The **best-selling single** (or "gramophone record" as it was then known) in 1955 was "White Christmas" (1942), written by Irving Berlin. Including Bing Crosby's famous version, it had sold 18 million copies. Today, the record is held by . . . "White Christmas," the festive favorite having sold an estimated 50 million copies (this figure can be doubled if you include sales of albums on which it has appeared).

BIGGEST MUSIC FESTIVALS BY ATTENDANCE

Source: mtviggy.com

Exit (SRB) 200,000 in 2013

Paléo (CHE) 230,000 in 2013

Ultra (U.S.A.) 330,000 in 2013

Sziget (HUN) 385,000 in 2011

Przystanek (POL) 550,000 in 2012

Coachella (U.S.A.) 675,000 in 2013

Rock in Rio (BRA) 700,000 in 2011

Summerfest (U.S.A.) 840,000 in 2013

Mawazine (MAR) 2.5 million in 2013

Donauinselfest (AUT) 3.2 million in 2013

SILVER STARS

Oldest U.S. Hot 100 entrant: Fred Stobaugh (U.S.A.), 96 years 23 days ("Oh Sweet Lorraine," No. 42, Sep. 14, 2013).

Oldest UK albums chart-topper: Dame Vera Lynn (UK), 92 years 183 days (*The Very Best of Vera Lynn—We'll Meet Again*, Sep. 19, 2009).

Oldest UK singles chart-topper: Robert "Bobby" Elliott (UK, Hollies drummer), 71 years 21 days ("He Ain't Heavy, He's My Brother" by The Justice Collective, Dec. 29, 2012).

Most consecutive years with a UK No. 1 single Three acts in the 62-year history of the UK's Official Singles Chart have achieved No. 1 singles in seven consecutive years: Elvis Presley (U.S.A.) in 1957–63, The Beatles (UK) in 1963–69, and in 2007–13 Rihanna, whose latest chart-topper, "The Monster," debuted at No. 1 on Nov. 9, 2013.

MOST WORDS IN A HIT SINGLE "Rap God" by Eminem (U.S.A.) packs 1,560 words into a fast and furious 6 min. 4 sec.—that's a tongue-twisting average of 4.28 words every second! In one 15-second segment alone, "Slim Shady" spits out 97 words (6.46 words per sec.) at supersonic speed.

BEST-SELLING FEMALE ARTIST Madonna has sold more than 300 million albums in her career. Her earnings of $125 m for Jun. 2012–Jun. 2013 were also the **highest annual earnings ever for a female pop star**, dwarfing those of record holder Celine Dion for 1998—$56 m ($80 m today).

First act to play a concert on every continent Metallica (U.S.A.) became the first music act to play on all seven continents when they entertained 120 scientists and competition winners at Antarctica's Carlini Station on Dec. 8, 2013. The show was dubbed "Freeze 'Em All."

Longest officially released song "Zwei Jahre" ("Two Years"), performed by German band Phrasenmäher, lasts 1 hr. 30 min. 10 sec. It was released via iTunes, Amazon, and Spotify on Jan. 10, 2014.

Longest time between UK No. 1 albums On Jun. 22, 2013, British rock band Black Sabbath returned to the top of the UK albums chart with their 19th studio set, *13*, some 42 years 255 days after first topping the chart with their second album, *Paranoid*, on Oct. 10, 1970.

GWR'S POP MUSIC POWER INDEX

	Name	Power rating
1	Lady Gaga (U.S.A.)	100
2	Justin Bieber (CAN)	75.5
3	Taylor Swift (U.S.A.)	66.8
4	Katy Perry (U.S.A.)	66.2
5	Rihanna (BRB)	64.2
6	Shakira (COL)	62.9
7	One Direction (UK/IRL)	56.2
8	Madonna (U.S.A.)	49.0
9	Britney Spears (U.S.A.)	47.0
10	Miley Cyrus (U.S.A.)	46.3

Index accounts for earnings, social media presence, video views, and search hits, as of Mar. 6, 2014; benchmarked to Lady Gaga = 100.

MOST WEEKLY RADIO IMPRESSIONS Robin Thicke's (U.S.A./CAN) controversial single "Blurred Lines" had 228.9 million audience impressions on *Billboard*'s Radio Songs chart on Aug. 24, 2013. Impressions are calculated according to the number of times a song is played and the radio station's audience size.

Most cover versions of a single charted before the original

Seven cover versions of "I Love It," by Swedish duo Icona Pop and singer-songwriter Charli XCX, aka Charlotte Aitchison (UK), made the Top 200 of the UK's Official Singles Chart before the original debuted at No. 1 on Jul. 6, 2013.

Largest TV audience for a Super Bowl half-time performance

The half-time show by Bruno Mars and the Red Hot Chili Peppers (both U.S.A.) at Super Bowl XLVIII attracted 115.3 million U.S. viewers, according to data supplied by Nielsen. The 2014 Super Bowl was contested by the Denver Broncos and the Seattle Seahawks at MetLife Stadium in East Rutherford, New Jersey, U.S.A., on Feb. 2. The game itself was watched by an average of 111.5 million—the **largest TV audience for a Super Bowl**.

CALVIN CLIMBS: Superstar DJ The **highest-paid DJ in one year** is Calvin Harris (UK), with earnings of $46 m in the 12 months to Jun. 2013, according to Forbes, including up to $300,000 for one night's work in Las Vegas, U.S.A. Electronic dance music has become very popular in the U.S.A. in the last decade and is worth more than $4 bn a year. Harris proved his worth on May 16, 2013 when he was named Songwriter of the Year at the 58th Ivor Novello Awards. Harris has collaborated with artists such as Rihanna, Dizzee Rascal, Kylie Minogue, and Tinchy Stryder.

Most searched-for pop star According to Google, Miley Cyrus (U.S.A.) was the most searched-for pop star in 2013. No. 5 on the overall list, her Internet popularity peaked after she "twerked" with Robin Thicke at the 2013 MTV Video Music Awards.

Best-selling album ever *Thriller* by Michael Jackson (U.S.A.), released in Nov. 1982, has sold more than 65 million copies worldwide. *Thriller* and the Eagles' (U.S.A.) *Their Greatest Hits (1971–1975)* have been certified 29x platinum by the Recording Industry Association of America (RIAA) and are joint holders of the **best-selling album in the U.S.A.**

According to the Official Charts Company, the **best-selling album in the UK** is Queen's *Greatest Hits* (1981). In 2014, it became the first album to sell 6 million copies in the UK.

Most weeks on U.S. singles chart (one single) "Radioactive," by U.S. rock band Imagine Dragons, spent a total of 86 nonconsecutive weeks on the U.S. Hot 100 singles chart between Aug. 18, 2012 and May 3, 2014. It reached a peak chart position of No. 3.

POP VIDEOS

1958: FIRST MUSIC VIDEOS The Big Bopper, aka Jiles Perry Richardson (U.S.A.), booms "Hello, baby!" in his "Chantilly Lace" video of 1958, miming into a prop phone. He was the first to use the term "music video," only weeks before he died in the plane crash that also claimed Buddy Holly. The Bopper filmed clips for three songs on the same day.

After Robin Thicke performed "Give it 2 U" at 2013's MTV MVAs, the single's sales **leaped by 251%**.

1981: FIRST MUSIC VIDEO SHOWN ON MTV On Aug. 1, 1981, MTV used "Video Killed the Radio Star" by The Buggles (UK duo Geoff Downes and Trevor Horn) as its opening track. On Feb. 27, 2000, the same video was the millionth to be broadcast by the channel.

1982: FIRST MUSIC VIDEO BANNED BY MTV Tame by today's standards, Queen's "Body Language" was full of sweaty, writhing, Lycra-clad bodies in a dimly lit steam room. While the band was fully clothed, the flesh and alleged "homoerotic undertones" worried MTV.

1982: FIRST GRAMMY FOR VIDEO OF THE YEAR *Elephant Parts* (Pacific Arts, 1981) was an hour-long mix of five songs with comedy by former Monkee Michael Nesmith (U.S.A.) that won at the 1982 Grammys. Short- and long-form video awards were separated in 1984.

1986–99: MOST WINS AT THE MTV MUSIC VIDEO AWARDS Madonna (U.S.A.) has won a total of 20 MTV Music Video Awards (MVAs): Video Vanguard Award (1986); one for "Papa Don't Preach" (1987); three for "Express Yourself" (1989); one for "Like a Prayer" (1989); three for "Vogue" (1990, pictured); one for *The Immaculate Collection* (1991); two for "Rain" (1993); one for "Take a Bow" (1995); five for "Ray of Light" (1998); one for "Frozen" (1998); and one for "Beautiful Stranger" (1999).

1987: MOST MTV MVAS FOR A SINGLE VIDEO In 1987, Peter Gabriel's (UK) "Sledgehammer" (1986) won nine awards, including Best Special Effects and Video of the Year. Lady Gaga, aka Stefani Germanotta (U.S.A.), is second with seven awards for "Bad Romance" (2009).

TOP OF THE POPS: MOST VIEWED AND TOP TRENDING MUSIC VIDEOS OF 2013

Listed here are the top five most viewed music videos of 2013 alongside the year's top five trending music videos. Both sets of figures represent the total viewing figures for each video as of Dec. 2013.

	Most viewed music videos of 2013	Top trending music videos of 2013
1	PSY—"Gentleman M/V" **598 million**	Ylvis—"The Fox (What Does The Fox Say?)" **265 million**
2	Miley Cyrus—"Wrecking Ball" **393 million**	Kenneth Håkonsen—"Harlem Shake (Original Army Edition)" **95 million**
3	Miley Cyrus—"We Can't Stop" **304 million**	Steve Kardynal—"Wrecking Ball (Chatroulette Version)" **67 million**
4	Katy Perry—"Roar (Official)" **251 million**	thelonelyisland—"YOLO (feat. Adam Levine & Kendrick Lamar)" **53 million**
5	P!nk—"Just Give Me A Reason" (feat. Nate Ruess) **236 million**	ERB—"Mozart vs Skrillex: Epic Rap Battles of History Season 2" **41 million**

1991: LARGEST TV AUDIENCE FOR A MUSIC VIDEO PREMIERE
An estimated 500 million people in 27 countries watched "Black or White" by Michael Jackson (U.S.A.) on Nov. 14, 1991. The 11-min. clip was filmed by "Thriller" director and moviemaker John Landis.

2004: FIRST OFFICIAL FAN-MADE MUSIC VIDEO
Placebo (BEL/SWE/UK) were so impressed by fan Grégoire Pinard's (ZAF) claymation clip for "English Summer Rain" that they adopted it as the official promo video for the song.

VIDEO FIRSTS

First video featuring unauthorized use of an act's music: "Up All Night" (2011), Blink-182, compiled from clips taken from fan-made videos

First video in Simlish: "Smile" (2007), Lily Allen in *The Sims 2: Seasons* (2007)

First video to receive one billion views on YouTube: "Gangnam Style", PSY, Dec. 2012

2010: MOST PRODUCT PLACEMENT IN A VIDEO Lady Gaga has approximately a dozen brands on show in "Telephone" (featuring Beyoncé), including Virgin Mobile, Beats Electronics, Polaroid, Chanel sunglasses, Wonder bread, Kraft salad dressing, and Diet Coke cans imaginatively utilized as her hair rollers.

2013: FIRST VIDEO IN SPACE On May 12, 2013, Commander Chris Hadfield (CAN) posted a video of himself singing David Bowie's "Space Oddity" onboard the *International Space Station.* Read an interview with Chris on p. 5.

2013: LONGEST VIDEO Pharrell Williams (U.S.A.) released the "world's first 24-hour music video." *Happy* features fans dancing to the four-min. track of the same name, which is looped 360 times. Pharrell appears in the video on the hour every hour.

DISTINCTIVE DYLAN

Described by one website as "a Dylan cable network with 16 channels of mindless entertainment," the star-studded interactive video (see below) features a host of celebrities and musicians including vintage footage of Dylan himself performing "Like a Rolling Stone." According to the video's creator, Interlude, no viewer will see the same video twice.

2013: LONGEST WAIT FOR AN OFFICIAL VIDEO An interactive video for Bob Dylan's (U.S.A.) "Like a Rolling Stone" appeared on his website on Nov. 19, 2013, more than 48 years after the song was a hit. Viewers could flick through different "channels" to watch artists lip sync the song.

TAKE YOUR PARTNERS: Biggest Dances Record attempts can be inspired by music videos. Pictured bottom left is the **largest "Thriller" dance**, in which 13,597 "zombies" pulled Michael Jackson moves in Mexico City, Mexico, on Aug. 29, 2009. "Harlem Shake" by Baauer inspired the **highest Harlem Shake** (top left), danced at an altitude of 62,300 ft. on a British Airways plane on Mar. 10, 2013. "Cha Cha Slide" (DJ Casper, 2000) prompted 3,231 dancers to achieve the **largest Cha Cha Slide** (right) at the Pleasure Beach in Blackpool, UK, on Oct. 8, 2011.

WORKS OF ART

MOST FREQUENTLY STOLEN PAINTING
The Ghent Altarpiece—also known as *The Adoration of the Mystic Lamb*—is a large, early-15th-century Flemish panel painting by Hubert and Jan van Eyck. It has been stolen seven times since it was first unveiled. Police are still searching for one missing panel.

MOST EXPENSIVE SCULPTURE (LIVING ARTIST) On Nov. 12, 2013, the 12-ft.-tall (3.6-m) stainless steel sculpture entitled *Balloon Dog (Orange)* by Jeff Koons (U.S.A.) sold for $58.4 m at Christie's in New York City, U.S.A.

On Aug. 21, 1911, the ***Mona Lisa*** was stolen from Paris's Louvre.

MOST EXPENSIVE SCULPTURE

A 6-ft.-tall (1.8-m) bronze sculpture entitled *L'Homme qui marche I (The Walking Man I)* (1960), created by Alberto Giacometti (CHE), sold to an anonymous bidder at Sotheby's in London, UK, for £65 m ($104 m) on Feb. 3, 2010.

OLDEST SCULPTURE

In Sep. 2008, excavations at Hohle Fels Cave in southwest Germany uncovered a 35,000–40,000-year-old female figurine carved from a mammoth's tusk.

MOST EXPENSIVE PAINTING

The Card Players, painted by Paul Cézanne (FRA), was sold to the royal family of Qatar for $250 m in 2011. The painting, which was created in the early 1890s, is one of five in a series by the renowned post-Impressionist artist.

MOST EXPENSIVE PAINTING SOLD AT AUCTION

On Nov. 12, 2013, *Three Studies of Lucian Freud* (1969), a triptych by Francis Bacon (UK), was sold to an unnamed client for $142.4 m at Christie's in New York City, U.S.A.

LARGEST HORSE-HEAD SCULPTURES

In Nov. 2013, two 100-ft.-tall (30-m) equine sculptures were unveiled in Falkirk, UK. *The Kelpies* were designed by artist Andy Scott (UK) as a tribute to the local tradition of working horses.

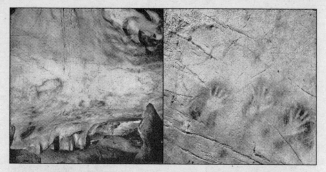

OLDEST PAINTING Discovered in the 1870s, paintings of animals and handprints from a cave called El Castillo in Puente Viesgo in the province of Cantabria, Spain, have now been proved to be at least 40,800 years old.

LARGEST RUBIK'S CUBE MOSAIC Created by Josh Chalom (U.S.A.), the largest mosaic made out of Rubik's Cubes measured 225 ft. 7 in. (68.78 m) long by 13 ft. 2 in. (4.03 m) high and was unveiled at One Central Macau, China, on Dec. 7, 2012. The mosaic depicted famous views in Macau and comprised 85,626 cubes.

ANAMORPHIC ART: SEEING IS BELIEVING Anamorphic art is two-dimensional but appears to have three dimensions when viewed from one point. The **largest anamorphic sidewalk art** (right) covers 16,899 sq. ft. (1,570 m²) and was created to promote tourism in Wilhelmshaven, Germany, on Aug. 4, 2012. Above left is the **largest anamorphic print**: a 45,504-sq.-ft. (4,227.5-m²) image commissioned by Renault Trucks (FRA) and realized by François Abélanet (FRA) in Lyon, France, on Jul. 6, 2013.

SMALLEST HANDMADE SCULPTURE

Golden Journey is a gold sculpture measuring just 0.006 in. (0.1603 mm) long. It was crafted by hand by artist Willard Wigan (UK) and sits in a hollowed-out section of a single hair. The measurement was verified in Birmingham, UK, on Jun. 19, 2013.

LONGEST WOOD SCULPTURE Designed by Zheng Chunhui (CHN), the lengthiest wooden carving measures 40 ft. 3 in. (12.28 m) and was unveiled in Putian, Fujian, China, on Nov. 14, 2013. It took the record holder and his 20 coworkers four years to complete the highly intricate work from camphor wood.

PUBLISHING

BEST-SELLING . . .

Fiction book Due to a lack of audited figures, it is impossible to state categorically which single work of fiction has the highest sales. However, Charles Dickens' (UK) *A Tale of Two Cities* (1859) is believed to have sold in excess of 200 million copies.

Harry Potter creator J. K. Rowling **does not have a middle name**.

Children's book series J. K. Rowling's (UK) seven-part *Harry Potter* saga began in 1997 and ended in 2007, with *Harry Potter and the Deathly Hallows*. By 2008, the series had sold a combined total of ca. 400 million copies.

The **best-selling children's trilogy** is Suzanne Collins' (U.S.A.) *Hunger Games*; during 2012 alone, the three books—*Hunger Games* (2008), *Catching Fire* (2009), and *Mockingjay* (2010)—sold a total of 27.7 million copies across both printed and digital formats.

Nonfiction book Even without exact sales numbers, there is little doubt that the Bible is the world's best-selling and most widely distributed book. A survey by the Bible Society concluded that around 2.5 billion copies were printed between 1815 and 1975, but more recent estimates put the number at more than 5 billion.

Regularly updated book The *Xinhua Zidian* (New China Character Dictionary) is the world's most popular reference work. Originally published in 1953, the dictionary has been revised 11 times, had more than 200 print runs, and sold well in excess of 400 million copies.

LARGEST COMIC BOOK COLLECTION Bob Bretall (U.S.A.) has amassed a collection of 94,268 comic books. The tally was made at his home in Mission Viejo, California, U.S.A., on May 1, 2014 and includes only unique comic books. Bretall began collecting comics when he was eight years old, when he purchased *The Amazing Spider-Man* #88.

FACT: Bob's collection weighs an estimated 16,800 lb.—about the same as 118 adult men!

HIGHEST-GROSSING LITERARY CREATIONS AT THE MOVIES

Based on total movie gross of each creation, measured in billions of dollars

A. *Harry Potter* (J. K. Rowling)		7.72
B. *James Bond* (Ian Fleming)		6.11
C. *The Lord of the Rings* (J. R. R. Tolkien)		4.72
D. *Shrek* (William Steig)		3.51
E. *The Twilight Saga* (Stephenie Meyer)		3.34
F. *Jurassic Park* (Michael Crichton)		2.01
G. *The Chronicles of Narnia* (C. S. Lewis)		1.58
H. *The Hunger Games* (Suzanne Collins)		1.52
I. John McClane/*Die Hard* (based on Detective Joe Leland in *Nothing Lasts Forever* (Roderick Thorp)		1.43
J. Robert Langdon/*The Da Vinci Code* (Dan Brown)		1.24

LUCRATIVE LITERATURE

Highest annual earnings for an author: $95 m, E. L. James (UK), *Fifty Shades . . .* trilogy.

Highest annual earnings for a children's author: $55 m, Suzanne Collins (U.S.A.), *Hunger Games* trilogy.

Largest advance for a nonfiction book: $15 m, U.S. President Bill Clinton for his memoir, *My Life*.

FACT: Self-published author John Locke (U.S.A.) has sold more than 2 million Kindle-formatted eBooks on Amazon using the Kindle Direct Publishing service. He passed the 1-million milestone in Jun. 2011, and to date has published 21 novels plus one nonfiction book, entitled—appropriately enough—*How I Sold 1 Million eBooks in 5 Months*.

HIGHEST NEW YORK TIMES RANKING FOR A "MASH-UP" A "mash-up" is a work of fiction that combines preexisting text—often a literary classic—and new text written by a contemporary author. *Pride and Prejudice and Zombies*—a hybrid of Jane Austen's 19th-century period romance and Seth Grahame-Smith's (above) alternative-universe zombie horror—reached No. 3 on the *New York Times* best-seller list in 2009.

FIRST . . .

Encyclopedia Speusippus compiled the earliest known encyclopedia in Athens, Greece, in ca. 370 B.C. As of 2014, it would have been compiled 2,384 years ago.

Detective novel According to the British Library, *The Notting Hill Mystery* (1863) by Charles Felix (UK) was the first detective novel. Starting with a murder, the plot reveals the twists and turns leading up to the crime, establishing many features of the now-ubiquitous detective genre.

Digital library Currently offering around 133,000 free eBooks, Project Gutenberg was established in 1971 with the aim of making 10,000 of the most consulted books available to the public at little or no cost.

Graphic novel The term "graphic novel" first appeared in 1976 on the dust jacket of *Bloodstar* by Richard Corben and Robert E. Howard (both U.S.A.).

Author to earn $1 bn In 2004, J. K. Rowling (UK)—one of only five self-made female billionaires—became the first author to earn $1 bn. Her *Harry Potter* books have been published in at least 55 languages.

Author to sell one million eBooks By Jul. 6, 2010, James Patterson (U.S.A.), creator of *Alex Cross* and *Women's Murder Club*, had exceeded sales of one million eBooks.

YOUNGEST BOOKER PRIZE WINNER

Eleanor Catton (NZ, b. Sep. 24, 1985) was 28 years 22 days old when she won the Booker Prize on Oct. 15, 2013 for her novel *The Luminaries*.

LARGEST BOOK A photo book measuring 16 ft. 5 in. x 26 ft. 6 in. (5.01 x 8.08 m) was created by Samsung Electronics in Berlin, Germany, on Sep. 7, 2013. The 16-page book consists of 28,000 photos sent via Facebook to Samsung. It was unveiled in the Museum für Kommunikation Berlin.

SMALLEST PRINTED BOOK The illustrated reference book *Flowers of the Four Seasons* measures 0.02 x 0.02 in. (0.74 x 0.75 mm) and was printed by Toppan Printing Co. Printing Museum in Bunkyo, Tokyo, Japan.

FACT: Only 250 copies of the 22-page book were printed between Apr. and Dec. 2012.

MOST . . .

Prolific computer-assisted author With a little help from computers, a team of programmers, and a clever software algorithm that he designed, Philip M. Parker (U.S.A.) has "written" in excess of 200,000 books. His algorithm gathers information freely available in the public domain and compiles it into book form. Digital files are produced in around 13 min. and printed on demand. Given the specialized nature of the content, cover prices are often high—for example, $1,300 in the case of *The 2007–2012 World Outlook for Floor Lamps*.

Booker Prize wins Awarded since 1969, the Booker Prize has been won twice by four authors as of 2013: J. G. Farrell (UK), J. M. Coetzee (ZAF), Peter Carey (AUS), and Hilary Mantel (UK).

DIAMOND SELLER: The Record-Breaking Record Book The 100-millionth copy of *Guinness World Records* was sold in 2004, although the book by then had already earned its own entry in the records archive. In the edition published in 1975 (left), our founding editors Norris and Ross McWhirter announced that, in Nov. 1974, the *Guinness Book of Records* "first sold in October 1955 and [with] total sales in 14 languages now running at 60,000 a week, surpassed the 23,916,000 of *The Common Sense Book of Baby and Child Care* by Dr. Benjamin Spock." We continue to be the **biggest-selling annual book**.

NOBEL PRIZE IN LITERATURE

The Nobel Prize in Literature has been awarded to 110 authors since 1901. According to Alfred Nobel's will, the winner should have produced ". . . the most outstanding work in an ideal direction . . ." Doris Lessing (UK, 1919–2013) was the **oldest recipient of the Literature Prize**, winning it in 2007 at the age of 87 years 355 days.

AND FINALLY . . .

• **Fastest-selling nonfiction book (UK):** *My Autobiography*, by retired soccer manager Sir Alex Ferguson (UK), published on Oct. 24, 2013—first week sales of 115,547 copies.

• **Fastest-selling video game guide (UK):** *Grand Theft Auto V Signature Series Strategy Guide*, published on Sep. 17, 2013—first week sales of 21,530 copies.

Pseudonyms A total of 325 pen names were listed for humorist Konstantin Arsenievich Mikhailov (RUS) in the 1960 *Dictionary of Pseudonyms*. Most were abbreviations of his real name.

Translated author According to the Index Translationum—UNESCO's book translation inventory—Agatha Christie (UK) has had an astonishing 6,598 translations of her novels, short stories, and plays.

Blank pages in a published book Sheridan Simove's (UK) book *What Every Man Thinks About Apart from Sex . . .* (2011) contains 196 blank pages.

TV

First 3D television We often think of 3D TV as a modern invention, but stereoscopic 3D television was first demonstrated by Scottish inventor John Logie Baird at his company's premises at 133 Long Acre in London, UK, on Aug. 10, 1928. Baird pioneered a variety of 3D TV systems using electro-mechanical and cathode-ray tube techniques, including simultaneous left- and right-eye images for true stereoscope viewing. It took until Apr. 12, 2008, however, for the **first commercially available 3D TV set** to go on sale, made by Hyundai in Japan.

MOST PIRATED TV PROGRAM *Game of Thrones* retains the No. 1 spot in Torrent Freak's top 10 list of most pirated TV shows, with 5,900,000 downloads per episode in 2013. One reason is HBO's refusal to license the series to Netflix; HBO and Warner Bros. executives also stated, controversially, that "receiving the title of 'most-pirated' was better than an Emmy," creating a "much-needed cultural buzz."

Bermuda has **more TV sets per capita** than any other country (1,024 per 1,000).

LONGEST CAREER AS A TV NEWS ANCHOR (SAME PROGRAM) Guillermo José Torres (U.S.A.) worked on WAPA-TV's *Noticentro* in Guaynabo, Puerto Rico, for 43 years 303 days until Aug. 5, 2013. He was awarded his GWR certificate as a surprise during his final telecast.

HIGHEST-RATED TV SERIES (CURRENT) As of the 2013–14 season, the first series of Canal+'s *The Returned* (aka *Les Revenants*, FRA) had a rating of 92 out of 100 on Metacritic. Based on the French 2004 movie *Les Revenants*, the creepy story revolves around a French village where the dead start to return from the grave.

LARGEST TV DRAMA SIMULCAST At 7:50 p.m. (GMT) on Nov. 23, 2013, the 50th-anniversary episode of *Doctor Who* (BBC, UK) was broadcast in 98 countries across six continents. Themed around a Time War between Timelords and Daleks, the episode featured three Doctors, played by Matt Smith, David Tennant, and John Hurt (above right). The above left picture shows (left to right) Executive Producer Steven Moffat, Matt Smith, and Jenna-Louise Coleman, who plays the Doctor's companion Clara.

Most powerful person in television According to Forbes, Oprah
Winfrey (U.S.A.) tops the list of most powerful celebrities. The list as-
sesses fame by taking into account income, exposure in print and on TV,
Internet presence, public opinion, and marketability. Her estimated earnings from Jun. 2012 to Jun. 2013 were $77 m, the **highest annual earn-
ings for a TV personality (female)**.

Ashton Kutcher (U.S.A.), who joined sitcom *Two and a Half Men* (CBS,
2003–present) in 2011, earned an estimated $24 m from Jun. 2012 to
Jun. 2013, the **highest annual earnings for a TV actor (current)**.

Highest annual earnings for a TV chef Gordon Ramsay (UK) earned
$38 m between Jun. 2012 and Jun. 2013, according to Forbes. He is
known for TV shows such as *Hell's Kitchen* and *The F Word*.

Highest box-office gross for a TV simulcast The *Doctor Who:
The Day of the Doctor* simulcast on Nov. 23, 2013 (see p. 382) grossed
$10.2 m at the global movie-theater box office. In the U.S.A. alone,
320,000 tickets were sold, earning $4.7 m at more than 650 sites. That
made it the second biggest attraction of the day after *The Hunger Games:
Catching Fire* (U.S.A., 2013), but the per-screen average for *Doctor Who*
was higher at $13,607, compared with $12,300.

**A DOSE OF REAL-
ITY: Got Talent** The
most successful reality
television format is
Got Talent (Fremantle
Media/Syco), sold to
58 countries—including
India, below right—
since debuting as
Britain's Got Talent in
the UK in Jun. 2007.
Simon Cowell (UK,
far left) and Howard
Stern (U.S.A., top
right)—judges on the
UK and U.S. editions
respectively—enjoy
the **highest annual earnings by a TV celebrity**. Each earned $95 m for the year
ending Jun. 2013. In Forbes' annual list of the most powerful celebrities, however,
Cowell (No. 17) outranks Stern (No. 45), factoring in areas such as marketability
and social media ranking.

Most Primetime Emmy Awards for a TV series *Saturday Night Live* (NBC, U.S.A., 1975–present) won four trophies at the 2013 Primetime Emmy Awards, bringing its overall haul to 40 awards. The late-night comedy sketch show, which was created by Lorne Michaels and developed by Dick Ebersol, is in its 39th season as of 2014.

As of the 2013 ceremony, *Saturday Night Live* had also received the **most Primetime Emmy Award nominations** (171).

LONGEST-RUNNING TV SERIES BY CATEGORY

Documentary series: *Meet the Press* (NBC, U.S.A.), Nov. 6, 1947–present	66 years 119 days
Sports program: *Hockey Night in Canada* (CBC, CAN), Oct. 11, 1952–present	61 years 145 days
Children's magazine program: *Blue Peter* (BBC, UK), Oct. 16, 1958–present	55 years 140 days
Cooking show: *Hasta La Cocina* (Canal 4, MEX), Dec. 1, 1960–present	53 years 94 days
Soap opera: *Coronation Street* (ITV, UK), Dec. 9, 1960–present	53 years 86 days
Quiz show: *It's Academic* (NBC4, U.S.A.), Oct. 7, 1961–present	52 years 149 days
Variety show: *Sábado Gigante* (Univision Television Network, CHL/U.S.A.), Aug. 8, 1962–present	51 years 209 days
Educational show: *Teleclub* (Canal 13, CRI), Feb. 8, 1963–present	51 years 25 days
Animated series: *Sazae-san* (Fuji Television Network, JPN), Oct. 5, 1969–present	44 years 151 days
Medical drama: *Casualty* (BBC, UK), Sep. 6, 1986–present	27 years 180 days

SMALL-SCREEN MILLIONAIRES

In 1954, U.S. comedian Jackie Gleason signed the most lucrative TV contract up to that date: $65,000 per episode for CBS's *The Honeymooners*, a half-hour, once-weekly TV show. Even though this is worth a cool $555,000 in today's money, it still doesn't beat Ashton Kutcher (U.S.A.), currently the **highest-paid TV actor per episode**, who picks up $750,000 for each installment of *Two and a Half Men*.

Most Emmy Awards won by an individual Producer Sheila Nevins (U.S.A.), President of Documentary and Family Programming for HBO and Cinemax, has won 25 Primetime Emmy Awards. Most recently, she took home two statuettes in 2013: Outstanding Documentary or Nonfiction Special for *Manhunt* (2013) and Exceptional Merit in Documentary Filmmaking for *Mea Maxima Culpa: Silence in the House of God* (2012).

Camera operator Hector Ramirez (U.S.A.) has been nominated for an Emmy Award 71 times in his 40-year career, the **most Emmy Award nominations received by an individual**. His first nod came in 1978 for *CBS: On the Air*. As of the 2013 ceremony, he had won 17 awards.

The **most nominations for a game-show producer** is 37 for Harry Friedman (U.S.A.), Executive Producer of *Wheel of Fortune* and *Jeopardy!*

HIGHEST ANNUAL EARNINGS FOR A TV ACTRESS (CURRENT)

Modern Family star Sofia Vergara (COL) celebrates her second year as the best-paid actress on TV, with earnings estimated at $30 m by Forbes. This makes her the **highest paid actor in absolute terms**—earning more than her male counterpart, Ashton Kutcher (see p. 383).

HIGHEST-RATED REALITY-COMPETITION SERIES As of Feb. 2014, *Project Runway: Season 2* (Lifetime/Bravo, U.S.A., 2005–06) boasted a Metacritic rating of 86. The 14-week show, fronted by model Heidi Klum, saw designers compete to have their work selected for the catwalk in New York Fashion Week.

MOST BAFTA CHILDREN'S AWARDS WON BY A TV SERIES The BBC's educational sketch series *Horrible Histories* (UK) is the first program to win four successive BAFTAs at the Children's Awards (2010–13). Commissioned by CBBC and produced by Richard Bradley of Lion TV, it is based on Terry Deary's award-winning books.

VIDEO GAMERS

LARGEST COMPETITIVE POKÉMON GAMING FAMILY *Pokémon*'s family-friendly charm is amply affirmed by the five-strong Arnold family from Frankfort, Illinois, U.S.A., who take part in official *Pokémon* video game world championships. Pictured from left to right are Ryan, mom Linda, Ryan's twin David, dad Glenn, and youngest child Grace.

According to the ESA, **58% of Americans** play video games.

LONGEST NHL VIDEO GAME MARATHON Hockey-mad Canadians James Evans (left) and Bruce Ashton (right) racked up a thumb-numbing 24-hr. 2-min. game of *NHL 10* (EA, 2009) in Orillia, Ontario, Canada, from Jul. 30 to 31, 2011. Bruce's Winnipeg Jets fantasy team won the 45-game series against James and his Detroit Red Wings by a score of 32–13.

LONGEST MARATHON ON A DANCE VIDEO GAME Carrie Swidecki (U.S.A.) danced herself into the record books with a body-pumping 49-hr. 3-min. 22-sec. session on *Just Dance 4* (Ubisoft, 2012) at Otto's Video Games & More! in Bakersfield, California, U.S.A., between Jun. 15 and 17, 2013.

YOUNGEST PRO GAMER Born on May 6, 1998, "Lil Poison," aka Victor De Leon III (U.S.A.), picked up a Dreamcast Controller at the age of just two to play *NBA 2K* (Sega). In 2005, at seven, he signed an exclusive deal with the organizers of Major League Gaming.

FASTEST COMPLETION OF SUPER MARIO KART *CIRCUIT 1*

Speedy Sami Çetin (UK) took the checkered flag for the fastest completion of the iconic Circuit 1 on the first game in the series, *Super Mario Kart* (Nintendo, 1992). Sami holds the record on both the PAL and NTSC versions of the game, with times of 58.34 sec. and 56.45 sec. respectively.

FASTEST COMPLETION OF BATMAN: ARKHAM CITY On May 27, 2012, Sean "DarthKnight" Grayson (U.S.A.) flew through *Batman: Arkham City* in just 2 hr. 3 min. 19 sec. The game settings were single-segment (played without stopping) and "normal" difficulty (including Catwoman DLC story-driven episodes).

HIGHEST SCORE AT LEVEL 1-1 OF "POACHED EGGS" ON ANGRY BIRDS *FOR CHROME*

Stephen Kish (UK) notched up 37,510 points at this level on *Angry Birds* for Chrome (Rovio, 2011) in East Sussex, UK, on Aug. 23, 2011.

On the same day, he also ran up the **highest score on *World's Biggest PAC-Man*** (Soap Creative, 2011), with 5,555,552 points.

MOST INTERNATIONAL STREET FIGHTER COMPETITION WINS

Ryan Hart (UK) won more than 450 *Street Fighter* events from 1998 to 2011. On Mar. 27, 2010, he also set the record for the **longest winning streak on *Street Fighter IV*** with 169 unbeaten matches at GAME in Hull, UK. Hart is pictured here with "Kayane," aka Marie-Laure Norindr (FRA)—the **first woman to win a pro-*Street Fighter* event**.

HIGHEST SCORE ON GUITAR HERO III (FEMALE)

On Sep. 30, 2010, at her home in San Francisco, California, U.S.A., Annie Leung achieved a record score of 789,349—the highest by a female gamer—playing the DragonForce track "Through the Fire and Flames" on *Guitar Hero III: Legends of Rock* (Neversoft, 2007).

LARGEST JOY PAD Officially verified in Aug. 2011 as the largest console game pad, this fully functional NES pad measures 12 ft. x 5 ft. 3 in. x 1 ft. 8 in. (3.66 x 1.59 x 0.51 m). Its main creator is engineering student Ben Allen (above), who was helped by Stephen van't Hof and Michel Verhulst, all students at Delft University of Technology in the Netherlands at the time.

GUINNESS WORLD RECORDS GAMER'S EDITION All these gamers were photographed for our record book dedicated to video gaming. Look out for *Gamer's Edition 2015*—packed with new gaming achievements and available now!

TECHNOLOGY & ENGINEERING

CONTENTS

There are **766 cars** for every 1,000 people in Liechtenstein.

FACT: Frederick's titanic cart has a capacity of 965 cu. ft., making it 227 times bigger than a typical 4.2-cu.-ft. shopping cart.

LARGEST MOTORIZED SHOPPING CART Powered by a 7,439-cc engine, this mammoth cart measures 27 ft. (8.23 m) long, 15 ft. (4.57 m) tall, and 8 ft. (2.43 m) wide and incorporates 7,200 lb. (3,265 kg) of stainless steel. Built by Frederick Reifsteck (U.S.A.), it was displayed in South Wales, New York, U.S.A., on Apr. 20, 2012.

However, it's not the **largest shopping cart** overall. That honor goes to a 31-ft. 5-in.-long (9.6-m), 44-ft. 7-in.-tall (13.6-m), 27-ft.-wide (8.23-m) behemoth created by Migros Ticaret A.Ş. (TUR) in Istanbul, Turkey, and unveiled on Jun. 14, 2012.

TELECOMS REVOLUTION

In just one lifetime, we've undergone an unprecedented transformation in how we communicate with each other. Here, we chart the development in technology that has underpinned this telecoms revolution over the past 60 years.

The entirety of the data on the Internet **weighs about the same as a strawberry**.

When Guinness World Records launched in 1955, it wasn't even possible to make a transatlantic telephone call; today, we can send all of the data in this book down a phone line between our London and New York offices in seconds. We are living through a truly epoch-defining digital revolution.

The time line below highlights the major record-breaking milestones that have dictated style, fashion, and communication trends over the past 60 years and reveals the extent of this spectacular change. The technology we have today can transmit audio and video at a blistering pace that would have been inconceivable to our colleagues in the 1950s. Just imagine what we've got to look forward to in the next 60 years.

1955/56 First transatlantic telephone call becomes possible after TAT-1 cable is laid between Gallanach Bay in Scotland, UK, and Clarenville, Canada, in 1955; public phone service starts on Sep. 25, 1956

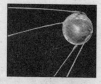

1957 First artificial satellite, *Sputnik 1*, put in orbit from Kazakhstan on Oct. 4; transmits signals for three weeks to Soviet scientists and radio enthusiasts

1958 First monolithic integrated circuit (microchip) patented by Jack Kilby (U.S.A., left); he and Robert Noyce (U.S.A.) etch transistors and connections onto silicon, key to modern telecoms.

1962 First active direct relay communications satellite is *Telstar 1*, launched on Jul. 10; transmits intercontinental TV, phone, and telegram signals

1963 First touch-tone telephone used at Bell Labs (U.S.A.) on Nov. 18, replacing "pulse" dialing

1964 First fax machine or Long Distance Xerography (LDX) is launched by Xerox

1969 First remote computer connection made from the University of California, U.S.A., to Stanford Research Institute

1971 **First e-mail** sent is the somewhat unimaginative "QWERTYUIOP" by Ray Tomlinson (U.S.A.), who programs a system to exchange messages between computers in the same office (left) linked through the U.S. Department of Defense's ARPANET

1972 **First all-in-one desktop computer** is the HP 9830, launched by Hewlett-Packard

1973 **First cellular phone** invented by Motorola's Martin Cooper (U.S.A.), who first uses it to call his rival at Bell Labs, Joel Engel

1974 **First Voice over Internet Protocol (VoIP)** carried out in Aug. 1974, using Network Voice Protocol (NVP) over the ARPANET; enables multiple computers to "talk" to each other over a single wire connection

1976 **First public fiber-optic cable network** installed in Hastings, UK, by Rediffusion (UK), leading to faster and farther telecommunications

1977 **Voyager 1 launches**; in 2014, it is still sending back data, from 11.8 billion mi. away—the **longest communications distance**

1979 **First true laptop** is the GRiD Compass, designed by William Moggridge (UK) for GRiD Systems (U.S.A.); boasts 512 K of RAM

1981 **First IBM Personal Computer** (model 5150) launches, operating with Microsoft's MS-DOS; becomes the first "true" home PC

1981 Oldest archived Usenet post, written by Mark Horton (U.S.A.), describes how the bulletin board forerunner should be run; unlike forums, Usenet content is sent between servers as news feeds

1982 First digital emoticons entered by Scott Fahlman (U.S.A.) on a bulletin board to signify emotion and avoid misunderstandings in e-mails: :-) and :-(

1984 First successful PC using a graphical user interface (GUI) is the Apple Macintosh; Microsoft's DOS interface is text-only

1987 First MMORPG (multiplayer online video game) with graphics, *Air Warrior*, is released by Kesmai on the GEnie (U.S.A.) service

1988 First ISDN (Integrated Services Digital Network) standard defined by the International Telecommunication Union to allow digital transmission over copper telephone wires

1990 First hypertext browser launched by Tim Berners-Lee (UK, right) and released on the Internet as the World Wide Web in 1991

1991 First e-mail sent from space by Shannon Lucid (left) and James C. Adamson (both U.S.A.) on an Apple Macintosh Portable on the Space Shuttle

1993 First Internet radio show, "Geek of the Week," produced by Internet Talk Radio (U.S.A.)

1996 First public GPS network introduced, although already used by the U.S. government since the 1980s

2000 Longest submarine fiber-optic cable, the Sea-Me-We 3. It is 24,233 mi. long and connects users in Europe, Australia, and Japan

2002 Scientists at Essex University, UK, transmit data at a rate of 1.02 terabits per sec. (equivalent to 15.9 million phone calls), becoming the **first fiber transmission system to exceed 1 terabit per sec.**

2005 Facebook—originally known as thefacebook—launches worldwide to become the **largest social network**, with 1.19 billion monthly active users by late 2013

2006 **First tweet** sent by Twitter founder Jack Dorsey (U.S.A., right) at 9:50 P.M. PST on Mar. 21, 2006: "just setting up my twittr"

2007 **First land-base cell phone call from the summit of Mount Everest** is made, at 29,028 ft., by Rod Baber (UK) on a Motorola MOTO Z8 satellite phone

2007 **Best-selling smartphone** is the original Apple iPhone; in its first month on sale, 2.31 million units were sold

2008 **First online legal summons** served by lawyers Mark MacCormack and Jason Oliver (both AUS) on Facebook

2009 **First 3D broadcast on the Internet** is a 20-min. set by rock band Keane (UK) from Abbey Road Studios in London, UK

2009 **First video phone watch** is LG's GD910 Watch Phone, with color screen, voice recognition, and video-call capability

2010 **Fastest-selling consumer electronics device** is the iPad (pictured with Apple's Steve Jobs), 3 million of which are sold in the first 80 days of its launch; the iPad 2, launched in Mar. 2011, sells at a rate of 311,666 per day

2011 **Highest-capacity communications satellite**, with a throughput of 134 gigabits per sec., is *ViaSat-1* in geostationary orbit above North America

2012 **Largest e-mail service provider** becomes Google's Gmail, with 425 million users, surpassing previous record holders Yahoo! Mail and Microsoft Hotmail

2012 First Google+ Hangout in space conducted with Akihiko Hoshide (JPN) of the Japan Aerospace Exploration Agency (JAXA) onboard the *International Space Station*

2012 Fastest Internet connection reaches 200 Gbit per sec. at The Gathering IT event in Norway, meaning users can download a BluRay movie in 2 sec.

2012 FIRST NEUTRINO MESSAGE On Mar. 13, 2012, it was announced that scientists working at Fermilab in Batavia, Illinois, U.S.A., had used a beam of neutrinos to send a message to a detector for the very first time. The word "neutrino" was sent across 1.6 mi.—262 yd. of which was solid rock—at a data rate of 0.1 bits per sec. Subatomic neutrinos pass through matter easily, because they rarely interact with it, but they require huge equipment to be detected so are unlikely to replace e-mail any time soon.

2014 Facebook buys the instant messaging service WhatsApp for $19 bn—**the largest acquisition of a venture-backed company**

ROLLER COASTERS

Most roller coasters in one country The nation with the greatest number of coasters of any kind is China, which has 824. Next up is the U.S.A. with 653 and then Japan with 212.

Most roller coasters in one theme park As of Jan. 20, 2014, Six Flags Magic Mountain in Valencia, California, U.S.A., has 18 operating roller coasters. The theme park opened on May 29, 1971.

There are **3,360 roller coasters** in the world: 3,186 steel and 174 wood.

Most roller coasters ridden in 24 hours

The greatest number of different roller coasters ridden in one 24-hour period is 74. On Aug. 9, 2001, Philip A. Guarno, Adam Spivak, John R. Kirkwood, and Aaron Monroe Rye (all U.S.A.) rode cars in 10 parks in four U.S. states, using helicopters to travel between them.

Most naked people on a theme park ride

On Aug. 8, 2010, 102 coaster fans bared all on the *Green Scream* roller coaster at Adventure Island in Southend-on-Sea, UK.

Most costumed riders on a theme park ride

Dorney Park & Wildwater Kingdom in Allentown, Pennsylvania, U.S.A., saw 330 costumed riders—all dressed as zombies—enjoy the *Steel Force* roller coaster on Aug. 18, 2011.

LARGEST ROLLER COASTER LOOP

Full Throttle at Six Flags Magic Mountain in Valencia, California, U.S.A., has the largest loop, at 127 ft. 1 in. (38.75 m). Its name doesn't lie. Riders accelerate into the record-breaking loop at a fearsome 70 mph (110 km/h) and are turned upside down twice in less than a minute.

HIGHEST THRILL RIDE The aptly named *Sky Drop* sits at the top of the 1,591-ft. (485-m) mast of the Canton Tower in Guangzhou, Guangdong, China. Visitors are dropped 101 ft. 8 in. (31 m) back to the top deck at 48 ft./s (16 m/s).

FACT: When looping the loop, acceleration is stronger than gravity at the top, keeping you in your seat.

MOST TRACK INVERSIONS ON A ROLLER COASTER *The Smiler* at Alton Towers Resort in Staffordshire, UK, inverts its riders 14 times. The (possibly misleadingly named) ride also includes optical illusions, blinding lights, and near misses as it reaches speeds of 52.82 mph (85 km/h) through drops of up to 98 ft. (30 m).

Longest marathon on a roller coaster Richard Rodriguez (U.S.A.) rode the *Pepsi Max Big One* and *Big Dipper* roller coasters at the Pleasure Beach in Blackpool, UK, for 405 hr. 40 min. from Jul. 27 to Aug. 13, 2007.

Fastest accelerating roller coaster *Dodonpa*, the 170-ft. 7-in.-tall (52-m) steel roller coaster at Fuji-Q Highland in Fujiyoshida, Yamanashi Prefecture, Japan, accelerates its eight riders from 0 to 106.9 mph (172.03 km/h) in 1.8 sec.

Oldest roller coaster operating continuously *The Scenic Railway*, a traditional wooden coaster at Luna Park in St. Kilda, Victoria, Australia, opened on Dec. 13, 1912 and has been running ever since.

Oldest roller coaster fully restored *Leap-the-Dips*, another old wooden ride, was built at Lakemont Park in Altoona, Pennsylvania, U.S.A., in 1902. It closed, seemingly for good, in 1985, but funds were raised for its restoration and it reopened in 1999.

LARGEST PLEASURE BEACH

Stretching 27 mi. along the Atlantic Ocean is Virginia Beach in Virginia, U.S.A., which offers 147 hotels and 2,323 campsites. Back in 1955, the record was held by Coney Island in New York, U.S.A. "As well as its five-mile beach, it features more than 350 business and amusement places . . . An estimated 50 million visit Coney Island and each spends about $1.25."

STEEL VERSUS WOOD

The first roller coasters were made out of wood, with tubular-steel coasters appearing in the 1950s. Steel coasters are stronger and more flexible than wooden ones, so can include more complex twists and turns, require fewer supports, and give a smoother ride. Wooden roller coasters sway more than steel versions and generally give a bumpier ride—although for many people this simply adds to the thrill of the experience.

STEEPEST WOODEN ROLLER COASTER

Outlaw Run at Silver Dollar City in Branson, Missouri, U.S.A., has a drop at an 81-degree angle. The coaster—which can achieve a reported speed of 68 mph (109 km/h)—has been open since Mar. 15, 2013 and is estimated to have cost more than $10 m to build.

BIGGEST DROP ON A WOODEN ROLLER COASTER

El Toro at Six Flags Great Adventure near Jackson, New Jersey, U.S.A., is 188 ft. (57.3 m) tall and features a drop of 176 ft. (54 m). As if that weren't enough, this heart-stopping plunge is tilted at a 76-degree angle and is taken at 70 mph (110 km/h).

FASTEST ROLLER COASTER

After going from 0–62 mph (100 km/h) in 2 sec., the steel *Formula Rossa* at Ferrari World Abu Dhabi, in the UAE, can accelerate to 149 mph (240 km/h) and move 170 ft. (52 m) upward—higher than the Statue of Liberty—in as little as 4.9 sec.

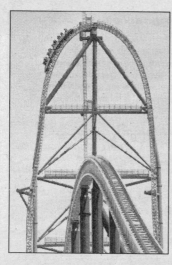

BIGGEST ROLLER COASTER
DROP *Kingda Ka* at Six Flags Great Adventure near Jackson, New Jersey, U.S.A., includes a drop of 418 ft. (127.4 m) and sees riders reach 128 mph (206 km/h) just seconds after launch. *Kingda Ka* is no ordinary ride—at 456 ft. (139 m), it's the world's **tallest roller coaster**.

Most expensive roller coaster

Expedition Everest at Walt Disney World Resort in Florida, U.S.A., opened in 2006 at a cost of $100 m. The concept is a train journey through the Himalayas via Forbidden Mountain, wherein lies a huge Yeti: a 22-ft.-tall (6.7-m) audio-animatronic beast covered in around 1,000 sq. ft. (93 m²) of fur.

LONGEST . . .

Roller coaster Don't hold your breath on *Steel Dragon 2000* at Nagashima Spa Land in Kuwana, Mie, Japan—it's 1.54 mi. (2.48 km) long.

Flying roller coaster Six Flags Magic Mountain in Valencia, California, U.S.A., has the longest flying coaster, *Tatsu*, measuring 0.68 mi. (1.09 km), as well as the **longest stand-up coaster**, *The Riddler's Revenge*, which is 0.82 mi. (1.33 km) long.

Floorless roller coaster *The Dominator* at Kings Dominion in Doswell, Virginia, U.S.A., continues for 0.79 mi. (1.28 km).

Wooden roller coaster The 1.40-mi. (2.28-km) *Beast*, at Kings Island in Ohio, U.S.A., lasts for 3 min. 40 sec.

STEEPEST STEEL ROLLER COASTER The
Takabisha ride at Fujikyu (aka Fuji-Q) Highland amusement park, Fujiyoshida City, Japan, stands 141 ft. (43 m) at its highest. Its steepest drop—at a 121-degree angle down an 11-ft. 2-in. (3.4-m) stretch—takes a mere 0.38 sec.

Technology & Engineering

THE FORCE IS WITH YOU:
WHAT A ROLLER COASTER DOES TO YOUR BODY

In 2013, the *Washington Post* provided a fascinating step-by-step guide to what happens to your body during a roller coaster ride.

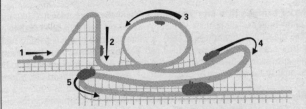

1: A linear G-force (G for gravity) launch of 0–120 mph in under 5 sec. pushes riders back, and fear and adrenaline kick in.

2: The drop makes riders feel extra-heavy—positive G-force, anything up to 5G, briefly.

3: Upside-down riders stay in their seats through centripetal force exerted over the course of the loop. Riders may feel queasy, though, as gravity isn't keeping their lunch where it should be.

4: Just the right amount of negative G-force makes your insides float momentarily (too much would make your eyeballs explode).

5: Bumpy corners make you feel the lateral G-force that—when uncontrolled, such as in car crashes—can result in whiplash injuries.

Source: "Roller coasters: feeling loopy," washingtonpost.com, Jul. 1, 2013

TRACK RECORDS: Coasters Identified In addition to the typical "sit down" coaster (which you ride above the track in a seated position), look out for:
Flying: riders are strapped parallel to the track, as if flying (above left: *Tatsu*, Six Flags, Valencia, California, U.S.A.).
Fourth dimension: riders sit either side of the track, allowing seats to rotate (above middle left: *Eejanaika*, Fuji-Q, Yamanashi, Japan).
Floorless: riders are seated above the track but with their legs dangling (above middle right: *Griffon*, Busch Gardens, Williamsburg, Virginia, U.S.A.).
Inverted: seats are suspended under the track (above right: *Wicked Twister*, Cedar Point, Ohio, U.S.A.).

BRIDGES & TUNNELS

Most bridges in a city Hamburg in Germany has between 2,300 and 2,500 bridges—more than Venice, Amsterdam, and London combined. The oldest is Zollenbrücke (1663). A more accurate figure is hard to find, partly because bridges are added and destroyed all the time and partly because sources disagree on how big a river, stream, or channel has to be to qualify for needing a bridge.

First Leonardo da Vinci bridge to be built Italy's master artist and inventor Leonardo da Vinci designed the Golden Horn bridge in 1502 to cross the Bosphorus in Istanbul, Turkey. It would have been the longest bridge in the world, but Ottoman Empire ruler Sultan Bayezid II believed the bridge wouldn't work and it was not until 2001 that the design was realized. It was finally built as a footbridge, measuring 328 ft. (100 m) long and 26 ft. 3 in. (8 m) wide, over the E18 highway in Ås, Norway. It was created by artist Vebjørn Sand (NOR) with Norway's National Roads Authority.

Highest sky bridge A double-decker bridge connects the Petronas Twin Towers in Kuala Lumpur, Malaysia, at the 41st and 42nd floors. (The buildings are distinct, instead of one structure as with other contenders.) The bridge is 558 ft. (170 m) above the ground, 190 ft. (58 m) long, and weighs 1.65 million lb. (750 metric tons).

FIRST TILTING BRIDGE The Millennium or "Winking" Bridge was opened on Jun. 28, 2001 over the River Tyne in Newcastle upon Tyne, UK. The bridge rotates instead of lifting up, turning on pivots on both sides of the river. Its nickname comes from the way it mimics a (very slow) blink of an eye when opening to allow for boats to pass underneath.

The bridge that inspired Winnie the Pooh's **Pooh sticks** cost $47,280 to renovate.

Largest spiral bridge access Traffic approaches the Nanpu Bridge over the Huangpu River in Shanghai, China, via a sweeping swirl of an elevated road section that minimizes the steepness of the gradient. The final section is 590 ft. (180 m) in diameter and 4.66 mi. (7.5 km) long, and cars complete two full rotations on the way up. The road, opened in 1991, was designed by the Shanghai Municipal Engineering Design Institute and Tongji Architectural Design and Research Institute.

Longest canal bridge The Mittellandkanal and Elbe-Havel canals in Germany are joined by the Magdeburg Water Bridge over the Elbe River. The bridge is 3,012 ft. (918 m) long and was opened on Oct. 10, 2003. The 142-ft.-wide (43-m) structure contains 52.9 million lb. (24,000 metric tons) of steel and carries ships of up to 2.9 million lb. (1,350 metric tons).

Longest self-anchored suspension span bridge While a suspension bridge is anchored in the ground, a self-anchored bridge is secured to the road deck ends. The latter form was chosen to replace the eastern span of the San Francisco–Oakland Bay Bridge, U.S.A., which centers on Yerba

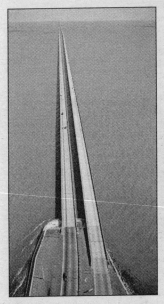

Buena Island. The span is 2,047 ft. (624 m) long, supported from a 525-ft.-high (160-m) tower.

Largest system of military infiltration tunnels The tunnels of Cu Chi in Ho Chi Minh City, Vietnam, became a key part of the Viet Cong insurgency fight against a South Vietnamese government backed by the U.S.A. in the 1960s. At their peak, the claustrophobic, snake-and-spider-infested tunnels stretched for 150 mi. (250 km), an extent of which has been preserved to be explored by tourists.

LONGEST BRIDGE OVER WATER (CONTINUOUS) The Lake Pontchartrain Causeway joins Mandeville and Metairie in Louisiana, U.S.A. It is 23.87 mi. (38.42 km) long and was completed in 1969. It runs alongside a slightly shorter bridge that was opened in 1956—each has two lanes for traffic.

FACT: The Causeway withstood the effects of Hurricane Katrina in 2005, when nearby bridges were destroyed.

LONGEST MULTICOLOR LIGHT TUNNEL The Bund Sightseeing Tunnel connects East Nanjing Road and Pudong in Shanghai, China: a distance of 2,121 ft. (646 m). Tourists ride on driverless trains through the tunnel, illuminated with different colored lights and accompanied by sound effects.

LARGEST FERRIS WHEEL BRIDGE
The Tianjin Eye on the Yongle Bridge is 394 ft. (120 m) high. Opened on Apr. 5, 2009 in Tianjin, China, the wheel bisects the bridge and road itself. The bridge has two layers: the upper for six lanes of traffic and the lower for pedestrians and the entrance to the Eye.

LARGEST DOUBLE HELIX BRIDGE
Taking inspiration from the structure of DNA, the Helix Bridge in Singapore was designed by Cox Architecture and Architects 61. If the steel that created its complex tubular truss was to be stretched out, it would measure 1.4 mi. (2.25 km)—but the bridge still uses five times less steel than its regular box girder equivalent.

First tunnel under a navigable waterway The Thames Tunnel was 1,300 ft. (365 m) long and completed in 1843 by engineer Sir Marc Brunel (FRA) to connect Rotherhithe and Wapping in London, UK. On the opening day, 50,000 people paid a penny each to wander through the attraction and within 10 weeks one million had visited it, although it was never used for traffic. It is today part of the London rail network. The tunnel used the

first tunneling shield, also developed by Brunel, to act as a temporary support structure. The basic idea is still used to allow workers to install permanent support systems in unstable conditions.

Most expensive rail tunnel The rail link underneath the English Channel between the UK and France was opened in 1994 at a total cost of around £12 bn ($20 bn), including train stock. The link consists of two 31-mi. (50-km) rail tunnels, each 25 ft. (7.6 m) in diameter, and one 16-ft.-diameter (4.8-m) service tunnel that runs between them.

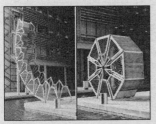

FIRST CURLING BRIDGE Instead of opening up rigidly, the Rolling Bridge curls up its eight segments, like a scorpion's tail, to let boats pass. Thomas Heatherwick (UK) designed the pedestrian bridge and it was built in 2004 in London's Paddington Basin, UK.

LONGEST BRIDGE-SUPPORTED AIRPORT RUNWAY A runway extension to accommodate larger aircraft at Madeira Airport was built partly over the sea. A bridge supporting this section is 3,346 ft. (1,020 m) long and 591 ft. (180 m) wide, and it sits on 180 pillars. It cost 520 m euros ($707.76 m) to build and was opened in Dec. 2011.

TUNNEL VISION

- **Deepest road tunnel:** Eiksund road tunnel, Norway, 941 ft. below sea level

- **Most expensive road tunnel:** Central Artery/Tunnel Project, Boston, U.S.A., $14.6 bn

- **Longest sewage tunnel:** Chicago TARP (Tunnels and Reservoir Plan), currently 109 mi. (extending to 131 mi. when completed in 2029)

> **FACT:** The Channel Tunnel between England and France was first proposed in 1802 by French engineer Albert Mathieu-Favier. It was finally completed in 1994.

CHANGING CHANNELS: Bridge Tunnels The **longest bridge tunnel** is the Chesapeake Bay Bridge Tunnel, which was opened to traffic on Apr. 15, 1964, extending 17.6 mi. from the Eastern Shore region of the Virginia Peninsula to Virginia Beach, Virginia, U.S.A. Bridges on each side give way to a tunnel, allowing ships access from the Atlantic along the Thimble Shoals and Chesapeake shipping channels. The longest bridge section is Trestle C at 4.56 mi. and the longest tunnel is the Thimble Shoal Channel Tunnel at 1.08 mi.

RECORD BREAKING BRIDGES AND TUNNELS

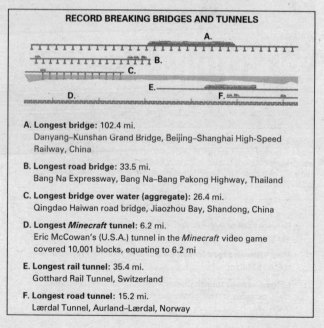

A.

B.

C.

E.

D.

F.

A. Longest bridge: 102.4 mi.
Danyang–Kunshan Grand Bridge, Beijing–Shanghai High-Speed Railway, China

B. Longest road bridge: 33.5 mi.
Bang Na Expressway, Bang Na–Bang Pakong Highway, Thailand

C. Longest bridge over water (aggregate): 26.4 mi.
Qingdao Haiwan road bridge, Jiaozhou Bay, Shandong, China

D. Longest *Minecraft* tunnel: 6.2 mi.
Eric McCowan's (U.S.A.) tunnel in the *Minecraft* video game covered 10,001 blocks, equating to 6.2 mi

E. Longest rail tunnel: 35.4 mi.
Gotthard Rail Tunnel, Switzerland

F. Longest road tunnel: 15.2 mi.
Lærdal Tunnel, Aurland–Lærdal, Norway

CARS

Largest producer of vehicles Toyota (JPN) ended General Motors' 77-year winning streak as the biggest maker of cars in 2008, and the two companies have traded places twice since. In 2013, Toyota sold 9.98 million vehicles across all its divisions, again ahead of General Motors (9.71 million) and just short of 10 million units—a figure as yet never reached by a manufacturer in a single year.

Best-selling two-seater sports car The Mazda MX-5 (known as the Miata in North America) has held the record for best-selling two-seater since 1999. By the first half of 2014, it had sold over 940,000 units.

First folding car An electric car with a chassis that folds itself up, the Hiriko Fold shrinks from a length of 8 ft. 7 in. (2.63 m) to 6 ft. 9 in. (2.07 m). Three Hirikos can park in the same space as one four-door sedan. The two-seater car was invented by the Massachusetts Institute of Technology (U.S.A.) and developed by Denokinn (ESP), but as of Apr. 2014 this model is yet to be launched commercially.

LARGEST PRODUCTION CAR ENGINE (EVER) Three cars had engines of 823.8-cu.-in.-capacity (13.5-liter): the Pierce-Arrow 6-66 Raceabout (1912–18, right), the Peerless 6-60 of 1912–14, and a 1918 Fageol (all U.S.A.). But big is not always better. Their power output was 65.7 hp (49 kW), roughly the same as a typical modern family car with a capacity of 79.3–122 cu. in. (1.3–2 liters).

MOST EXPENSIVE CAR AT AUCTION A 1963 Ferrari 250 GTO racer was sold to a private buyer in Oct. 2013 for $52 m. The competition car was formerly owned by U.S. collector and racer Paul Pappalardo. Only 39 of the GTO cars were made, with an original retail price of around $18,000 (today's equivalent would be $135,000).

Every year, commuters in the U.S.A. spend an average of **38 hr. stuck in traffic.**

First hydrogen-powered production car Hydrogen-powered cars are good for the environment in that they create no carbon emissions once they are on the move. The Honda FCX, introduced in 2002, was the first hydrogen-powered production car. Although only a handful are currently on the road, manufacturers such as Toyota and Honda are planning to have more affordable versions available by 2016.

Highest vehicle mileage On Sep. 18, 2013, Irvin Gordon (U.S.A.) clocked up his three-millionth mile (4.28 million km) in the 1966 Volvo P1800S that he had driven continuously for 48 years. By May 1, 2014, the retired science teacher had driven 3,039,122 mi. (4.89 million km). Irv now has a brand-new XC60R AWD, and plans to "give my 1800 a bit of a break."

MOST EXPENSIVE CAR COMMERCIALLY AVAILABLE Prices for cars in Bugatti's six-part "Legends" series range from 2.09 m euros ($2.84 m) for the "Meo Costantini" to 2.35 m euros ($3.2 m) for the "Ettore Bugatti," the final edition to be unveiled. The Legends series—based on the Veyron 16.4 Grand Sport Vitesse—is limited to just three cars per edition. Prices exclude tax and transportation.

FACT: The $3-m "Rembrandt," above, is named after founder Ettore Bugatti's younger brother.

FACT: Drifting was the subject of Justin Lin's hit action movie *The Fast and the Furious: Tokyo Drift* (2006).

FASTEST VEHICLE DRIFT
Regular drivers might react with panic when taking a turn so fast that their back wheels swing out and their car slides into an uncontrolled drift. For others, it's a skill and a sport. Jakub Przygoński (POL) drifted at a speed of 135.44 mph (217.97 km/h) at Biała Podlaska Airport near Warsaw, Poland, on Sep. 3, 2013.

LARGEST PRODUCTION CAR ENGINE (CURRENT) Chrysler's (U.S.A.) 2014 SRT Viper has a 512-cu.-in. (8.39-liter) V10 engine. Even Bugatti's mighty Veyron has only a 488-cu.-in. (8-liter) engine. The Viper can produce 640 hp (477 kW) of power, 600 lb./ft. (814 Nm) of torque, and accelerates from 0 to 60 mph (96.5 km/h) in 3.3 sec.

MOST PEOPLE CRAMMED IN . . .

an original Fiat 500: 14 students from ESSCA business school in Paris, France, on Apr. 2, 2011.

a classic model Mini Cooper: 25 people organized by Virgin Mobile in Johannesburg, South Africa, on Oct. 2, 2013.

a new model Mini: 28 people organized by Dani Maynard and the David Lloyd Divas (UK) in London, UK, on Nov. 15, 2012.

a Smart car: 20 people organized by Glendale College Cheerleading Team (U.S.A.) in Los Angeles, U.S.A., on Sep. 28, 2011.

OLDEST "HORSELESS CARRIAGE"

The Grenville Steam Carriage was a three-wheeled vehicle built in 1875. More than 45 years after featuring in our first edition as the oldest "horseless carriage" still in working order, it completed the 54-mi. London to Brighton Veteran Car Run of 2000 in under 9 hr. In 2009, it was moved from Bristol to the Beaulieu National Motor Museum—and, as of Apr. 2014, is still in working order. Robert Neville Grenville of Somerset, UK, designed the self-propelled vehicle, which holds four passengers and boasts a top speed of 14.9 mph.

FIRST 10-MILLION-SELLING CAR On Jun. 4, 1924, the 10-millionth Model T rolled off the assembly line at Ford (U.S.A.). Henry Ford (U.S.A.) had done much to innovate—his Model T production line lowered costs, enabling him to sell 15 million units in total.

FIRST 20-MILLION-SELLING CAR On May 15, 1981, Volkswagen's iconic Beetle—originally designed in 1938 for the Nazis as a cheap option for the German masses—hit the 20-million milestone. By the time that production ceased in 2003, around 22 million Beetles had been made.

FIRST 30-MILLION-SELLING CAR In 2005, the Toyota Corolla sold its 30-millionth car, and in 2013, as reported by the manufacturer, was the **first car to sell 40 million units**, making the Corolla overall the **best-selling car**.

Longest fuel range (standard tank) Marko Tomac and Ivan Cvetković (both HRV) drove a Volkswagen Passat 1.6 TDI BlueMotion for 1,581.88 mi. (2,545.8 km) on one tank of fuel between Jun. 27 and 30, 2011 in Croatia.

Longest journey by car in a single country Durga Charan Mishra and Jotshna Mishra (both IND) toured continuously throughout India between Feb. 23 and Apr. 1, 2014, driving 11,469 mi. (18,458 km). They started and finished their epic 38-day road trip in Puri in the state of Odisha, averaging 301.7 mi. (485.7 km) per day.

Most expensive veteran car Only cars built before 1905 are classed as "veteran"—qualifying for entry in the UK's annual London to Brighton Veteran Car Run. A Rolls-Royce built in 1904 was sold for £3.52 m ($7.24 m) in the UK on Dec. 3, 2007. It has the serial number 20154 and is the oldest existing Rolls-Royce.

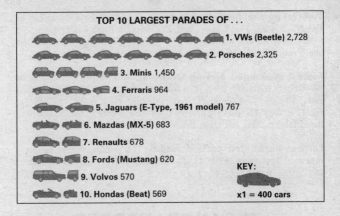

TOP 10 LARGEST PARADES OF . . .

1. VWs (Beetle) 2,728
2. Porsches 2,325
3. Minis 1,450
4. Ferraris 964
5. Jaguars (E-Type, 1961 model) 767
6. Mazdas (MX-5) 683
7. Renaults 678
8. Fords (Mustang) 620
9. Volvos 570
10. Hondas (Beat) 569

KEY:
x1 = 400 cars

DRIVING SEAT: Big Producers China was the **largest producer of cars** in 2013, making 18,085,213 of a total of 65,386,596 automobiles (excluding commercial vehicles). This contributes to 2013 being the **biggest year on record for car sales**, according to data from the International Organization of Motor Vehicle Manufacturers. Japan was in second place, with 8,189,323 sales, and Germany came in third with 5,439,904. According to industry experts WardsAuto, the number of vehicles on the road (including commercial traffic) hit 1 billion in 2010, rising from 250 million in 1970.

FACT: In 2010, there were an estimated 1 billion vehicles in operation (see above). According to predictions made by the International Monetary Fund, by 2050 the number of cars on the road will have risen to 3 billion worldwide. CO_2 emissions from cars could contribute 8.1% to the overall figure of emissions.

Tightest parallel parking of two cars On Jan. 9, 2014, in the city of Jiangyin, China, Tian Linwen and Xia Hongjun (both CHN) drove into a parking space that was just 16.5 in. (42 cm) longer than their two cars combined. This was less than the length of a sheet of tabloid paper.

Fastest automated parking facility At Volkswagen's Autostadt in Wolfsburg, Germany, cars fresh from the production line are retrieved and delivered by an automated system that travels at up to 3 ft. 3 in. per sec. (2 m/sec). The parking process from the entrance of the Autostadt to the farthest parking box takes 1 min. 44 sec.

Largest automated parking facility The parking lot at Emirates Financial Towers in Dubai, UAE, stores up to 1,191 cars in an area of 297,150 sq. ft. (27,606.14 m²).

URBAN TRANSPORT

First congestion program In 1975, Singapore implemented the Area Licensing Scheme (ALS). Owners of vehicles entering the Central Business District or the "Restricted Zone" had to buy a special paper license. In 1998, the system was upgraded to the Electronic Road Pricing (ERP) program.

LARGEST SHIPS BY CAPACITY Although other ships can potentially carry more passengers, the vessels with the largest "standard" passenger loads are the Staten Island Ferry sister ships *Andrew J. Barberi* and *Samuel I. Newhouse* in New York City, U.S.A., each of which can carry 6,000 passengers. They are 310 ft. (95 m) long and 69 ft. 10 in. (21 m) wide, with a service speed of 16 knots (19 mph; 30 km/h).

Japan is home to **45 of the 51 busiest train stations** in the world; almost half are in Tokyo alone.

MOST CYCLE RICKSHAWS IN ONE CITY There are some 500,000 cycle rickshaws in Dhaka, Bangladesh (left). In this city of 15 million people, they account for nearly 40% of all trips.

As of 2012, an estimated 120,000–160,000 autorickshaws were active in Mumbai, India (right), the **most autorickshaws in one city**. They are used by up to 85% of residents.

Busiest underground network (current)

The Tokyo Metro served a ridership of 3.102 billion passengers in 2012. The underground system runs for 190 mi. (310 km) altogether and serves a metropolitan area of 35 million residents. It incorporates 13 lines and 290 stations in total.

The Moscow Metro is the **busiest underground network ever**, with 3.3 billion passenger journeys in a year at its peak, although by 1998 the figure had declined to 2.55 billion. The system has been serving the Russian capital since 1935, and incorporates 3,135 coaches covering 159 stations and 132 mi. (212 km) of track.

The **longest metro system by total length** is the Seoul Metropolitan Subway in South Korea, with 580 mi. (940 km) of routes across 17 lines as of 2013.

Largest underground train depot (metro)

Singapore's Kim Chuan Depot, which opened in 2009, measures 2,624 ft. (800 m) long, 524 ft. (160 m) wide, and 75 ft. (23 m) high, and has a volume of 1,057 million cu. ft. (2.9 million m³).

The depot took five years and 295 million Singapore dollars (U.S. $209 m) to construct. It houses equipment and stabling, and provides maintenance facilities for up to 70 three-car driverless trains.

PREMIER SERVICE

First regular passenger railroad service: The Oystermouth Railway, later the Swansea and Mumbles Railway, in Swansea, UK, began on Mar. 25, 1807.

First motorized taxicab service: Operated by the Daimler Motorized Cab Company in Stuttgart, Germany, in 1897. The taxi was able to travel 43 mi. a day. The fleet was increased to seven vehicles just two years later.

Most expensive public transit commute According to the UBS Price and Earnings Report 2012, which assessed 72 cities in 58 countries, Oslo in Norway has the most expensive transit ticket fare (based on a 10-stop bus, streetcar, or subway trip): $5.12.

The same report also noted that Zurich in Switzerland offers the **most expensive taxi ride**, at $28.93. This calculation is based on a taxi journey over a distance of 3 mi. (5 km), taken during the day within the city limits.

Farthest distance by a battery-powered streetcar (one charge) in 24 hours Stadler Pankow GmbH (DEU) ran the battery-powered Variobahn streetcar 11.79 mi. (18.98 km) on a single charge at Velten/Hennigsdorf rail-test track near Berlin, Germany, on May 25, 2011.

The **most southerly streetcar terminus** is at Brighton East in Melbourne, Victoria, Australia, on route number 64 at the junction of Hawthorn Road and Nepean Highway.

The **longest streetcar route** is the Kusttram service; it runs along the Belgian coast from Knokke in the north to Adinkerke in the south—a distance of 42 mi. (68 km).

LONGEST BUSES Currently trialing in Germany is the AutoTram Extra Grand (pictured above), a bi-articulated (three-section) bus 100 ft. 9 in. (30.7 m) long that is designed to carry 256 passengers. In China, meanwhile, the Youngman JNP6250G bus is being piloted: an 82-ft.-long (25-m) vehicle that will transport 300 passengers.

Neither will beat the **longest buses ever**, though: the 105-ft. 7-in.-long (32.2-m) articulated DAF Super CityTrain buses in the Democratic Republic of the Congo.

LONGEST INTRACITY STREETCAR ROUTE The 501 Queen route in Toronto, Canada, is 15.2 mi. (24.5 km) long, and averages 52,000 passengers daily, 24 hr. a day, seven days a week. It runs from Long Branch in the west to Neville Park in the east.

LARGEST BICYCLE-SHARE PROGRAM The Hangzhou Public Bicycle program in Hangzhou, China, is the largest bicycle-sharing system. In 2013, its fleet included 69,750 bicycles, with 2,965 stations spread across the city. Users can easily access the system as stations are placed less than 0.6 mi. (1 km) apart.

LONGEST DRIVERLESS METRO NETWORK The two lines of the driverless Dubai Metro have a combined length of 46.41 mi. (74.69 km). They were constructed by the Roads & Transport Authority in Dubai, UAE, and officially inaugurated on Sep. 9, 2011.

At 32.3 mi. (52.1 km) in length, the Dubai Metro Red Line is the **longest driverless metro line**. The second line, Green Line, is 13.9 mi. (22.5 km) long.

TRAM-PACKED

The **largest urban streetcar network ever** was in Argentina's capital Buenos Aires. Inaugurated in 1897, by the 1960s it had 532 mi. of streetcar lines, including some underground. The lines were discontinued to save money and make way for buses. Today's **most extensive streetcar system** is more than three times smaller. Located in Melbourne, Victoria, Australia, it runs "just" 155 mi., with 487 streetcars, 1,763 stops, and 30 routes.

> **FACT:** In Japan, some metro cars are set aside for women to provide greater personal safety.

Largest bus rapid transit (BRT) system The TransJakarta bus rapid transit system in Jakarta, Indonesia, boasts some 120 mi. (194 km) of dedicated busways. It carries more than 300,000 passengers daily on 12 "corridors."

Oldest railroad tunnel British engineer Benjamin Outram (UK) built an 88-ft.-long (27-m) railroad tunnel at Fritchley near Crich in Derbyshire, UK, in 1793. It remained in use until 1933. Both ends were sealed in the 1960s.

As of Jan. 2014, the **oldest railroad workshop in continuous operation** is the Boston Lodge Works of the Ffestiniog Railway near Minffordd, UK. Wagon maintenance began there in 1838 with a blacksmith's shop, from which the current complex has grown.

Liverpool Road station in Manchester, UK, is the **oldest railroad station**. It opened on Sep. 15, 1830 and closed on Sep. 30, 1975.

Largest rail freight yard Bailey Yard in North Platte, Nebraska, U.S.A., is 8 mi. (12.8 km) long and covers an area of 4.4 sq. mi. (11.5 km²). It is operated by the Union Pacific Railroad.

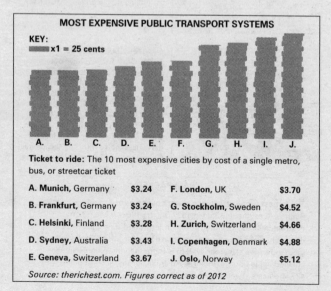

MOST EXPENSIVE PUBLIC TRANSPORT SYSTEMS

KEY:
x1 = 25 cents

A. B. C. D. E. F. G. H. I. J.

Ticket to ride: The 10 most expensive cities by cost of a single metro, bus, or streetcar ticket

A. **Munich,** Germany	$3.24	F. **London,** UK	$3.70
B. **Frankfurt,** Germany	$3.24	G. **Stockholm,** Sweden	$4.52
C. **Helsinki,** Finland	$3.28	H. **Zurich,** Switzerland	$4.66
D. **Sydney,** Australia	$3.43	I. **Copenhagen,** Denmark	$4.88
E. **Geneva,** Switzerland	$3.67	J. **Oslo,** Norway	$5.12

Source: therichest.com. Figures correct as of 2012

METRO MANIA: Station Masters For some, going underground provides a direct route to breaking records. Chris Solarz and Matthew Ferrisi (both U.S.A., left) achieved the **fastest time to travel to all New York City Subway stations** (22 hr. 52 min. 36 sec.) from Jan. 22 to 23, 2010. Tim Littlechild and Chantel Shafie (both UK; Chantel seen center) recorded the **fastest time to travel to all Hong Kong metro stations** (8 hr. 18 min. 8 sec.) on Dec. 30, 2013. Geoff Marshall and Anthony Smith (both UK, right) set the **fastest time to travel to all London Underground stations** (16 hr. 20 min. 27 sec.) on Aug. 16, 2013.

ALTERNATIVE TRANSPORT

Longest cable car beneath sea level A 4,359-ft.-long (1,328-m), 12-cabin cable car connects Elisha's Spring with the Mount of Temptation in Jericho, Palestine. The lower station is 721 ft. 3 in. (219.86 m) below sea level; the upper station is 164 ft. 11 in. (50.29 m) below sea level.

Longest cable car ever A cable car of approximately 60 mi. (96 km) in length was first opened in 1943 to transport ore from Kristenberg to Boliden in Sweden. Constructed in lieu of a road, due to the shortage of rubber and gasoline during World War II, the system was only decommissioned for ore transport as late as 1987. Still in operation today, it is now used as an 8.2-mi.-long (13.2-km) tourist ride.

Longest nonstop aerial tram Wings of Tatev, constructed in collaboration with the National Competitiveness Foundation of Armenia, is a nonstop cable-car line measuring 18,871 ft. (5,752 m) long. It links the Tatev monastery and Halidzor, Armenia.

Highest ascent by a nonstop cable car The Bà Nà Hills single-track cable car in Da Nang, Vietnam, opened on Mar. 29, 2013, takes 15 min. to rise 4,488 ft. (1,368 m) between its start and end stations.

As of 2013, around 95.4% of the U.S.A.'s energy needs are still met by **fossil fuels**.

AERIAL SURVEY

All cable-car records on this spread refer to aerial carriages propelled by a steel cable. The term "cable car" is also sometimes used to refer to cable-drawn cars at street level.

Longest monorail The most extensive monorail system is 46.2 mi. (74.4 km) long and forms part of the Chongqing Rail Transit. The most recent stretch of line was completed in Dec. 2012.

The **longest monorail line** is line 3 of the Chongqing Rail Transit system. It is 34 mi. (55 km) in length.

First maglev train to enter public service A 1,970-ft. (600-m) maglev line operated between Birmingham International Airport and the nearby Birmingham International Interchange in West Midlands, UK, from 1984 to 1995. It was taken out of service due to the high cost of replacing worn parts and succeeded by a conventional cable-drawn shuttle system.

Fastest maglev train A MLX01 maglev train operated by the Central Japan Railway Company and Railway Technical Research Institute attained a speed of 361 mph (581 km/h) on the Yamanashi Maglev Test Line in Yamanashi Prefecture, Japan, on Dec. 2, 2003.

The **fastest maglev train in public service** links China's Shanghai International Airport and the city's financial district and reaches a speed of 267 mph (431 km/h) on each 18-mi. (30-km) trip. Built by Germany's Transrapid International, the train had its official maiden run on Dec. 31, 2002.

LONGEST FUNICULAR The Sierre to Crans-Montana funicular is 2.604 mi. (4.192 km) long. It connects passengers to the ski resort of Crans-Montana from the Swiss city of Sierre and was built in 1911 as two separate funiculars. The two lines were merged and rebuilt as one system in 1997. The funicular travels at speeds of 26 ft. per sec. (8 m/sec) and completes the journey in 12 min.

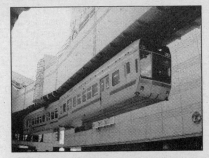

LONGEST SUSPENDED MONORAIL

Measuring 9.45 mi. (15.2 km), the Chiba Urban Monorail near Tokyo, Japan, is the longest suspended monorail train system. The first 1.98-mi. (3.2-km) stretch opened on Mar. 20, 1979, but the line has been expanded three times since then. The monorail has 18 stations, and an average of 120 trains run on the system per day.

FIRST "DUCK" TOUR "Ducks" are amphibious vehicles widely used in sight-seeing tours. The first-ever duck tour company was established in 1946 by Mel Flath and Bob Unger (both U.S.A.) in Wisconsin Dells, Wisconsin, U.S.A. The original company has changed ownership since then, and today operates under the name Original Wisconsin Ducks. Flath's family also owns another duck tour company, bearing the name Dells Army Ducks.

HIGHEST CABLE CAR ABOVEGROUND

The Peak 2 Peak Gondola in Whistler, British Columbia, Canada, rises to 1,430 ft. (436 m). The three-cable gondola lift runs for around 2.7 mi. (4.4 km) and connects the peaks of the Whistler and Blackcomb mountains. The vertiginous ride also incorporates the **longest unsupported span between two cable-car towers**—a length of 9,921 ft. (3,024 m).

GLOSSARY

Funicular: A cable railroad, enabling travel on gradients too steep for conventional trains. The word is derived from the Latin *funiculus*, meaning "rope" or "cord."

Maglev: Abbreviation of "magnetic levitation." Maglev vehicles are propelled by magnets—supported by a magnetic field that runs around the train tracks—instead of fuel-powered wheels.

STEEPEST RAILROAD GRADIENT The
Katoomba Scenic Railway in the Blue Mountains of
New South Wales, Australia, has a 52-degree-angle
slope. The 1,017-ft.-long (310-m) funicular was built
in 1878, originally for mining purposes, but was
converted into a tourist ride in 1945.

Highest-capacity funicular The Funicular
de Montjuïc in Barcelona, Spain, can transport
16,000 people per hr. (8,000 people each way).
It can hold 400 people at a time and reach a
speed of 32 ft. per sec. (10 m/sec) or 22 mph
(36 km/h).

First public electric railroad The earliest
public electric railroad opened on May 12,
1881 in Lichterfelde near Berlin, Germany. It
was 1.5 mi. (2.5 km) long, ran on 100-V current, and carried 26 passengers at 30 mph (48 km/h).

The Volk's Electric Railway, which runs along the seafront at Brighton, UK, between the pier and the marina, is the **oldest electric railroad in
operation**. Designed by Magnus Volk (UK), the railroad first opened for
business on Aug. 4, 1883.

Largest fleet of electric taxis Shenzhen in China is home to a fleet
of 800 "e6" model electric taxis built by the Chinese automobile manufacturer BYD. Each taxi can travel 185 mi. (300 km) on one charge. The
fleet's total mileage is estimated to have
now exceeded 62 million mi. (100 million km).

SHORTEST FUNICULAR The Fisherman's
Walk Cliff Railway in Bournemouth, UK, is
128 ft. (39 m) long. Built in 1935 by borough
engineer F. P. Dolamore, the system travels on
a 5-ft. 10-in.-gauge (1.77-m) railway track with
a 45-degree incline. It has transported more
than 4 million passengers.

BUSIEST PUBLIC-TRANSIT CABLE CAR
Line K of the Metrocable system in Medellín,
Colombia, is the busiest cable-car line built
for public transportation, with a ridership of
6,330,713 passengers in 2012. The 1.2-mi.
(2-km) line, opened in 2004, was designed to
connect the impoverished hillside communities
to the city's metro network.

For cutting-edge science, see p. 449.

WHO'S DRIVING THIS? *Driverless Cars* For several years now, Google has been testing driverless cars (left), controlled by onboard computers that also keep track of the cars' locations. A qualified driver would still be required to sit at the wheel—but only to take over in emergencies. To date, Google's autonomous automobiles have racked up more than 186,000 mi. on the road without any major incidents, and the company claims that they could be safer than human drivers. Center: Children peer inside a self-driving car at Google's HQ in California, U.S.A. Right: A street as interpreted by a driverless car.

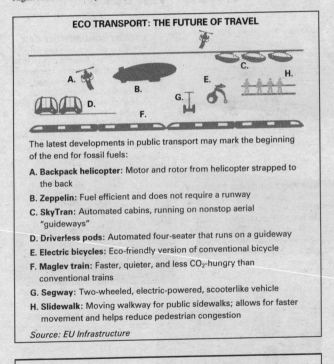

ECO TRANSPORT: THE FUTURE OF TRAVEL

The latest developments in public transport may mark the beginning of the end for fossil fuels:

A. Backpack helicopter: Motor and rotor from helicopter strapped to the back

B. Zeppelin: Fuel efficient and does not require a runway

C. SkyTran: Automated cabins, running on nonstop aerial "guideways"

D. Driverless pods: Automated four-seater that runs on a guideway

E. Electric bicycles: Eco-friendly version of conventional bicycle

F. Maglev train: Faster, quieter, and less CO_2-hungry than conventional trains

G. Segway: Two-wheeled, electric-powered, scooterlike vehicle

H. Slidewalk: Moving walkway for public sidewalks; allows for faster movement and helps reduce pedestrian congestion

Source: EU Infrastructure

FACT: The first flight of a zeppelin took place on Jul. 2, 1900 over Lake Constance in Germany.

WACKY WHEELS

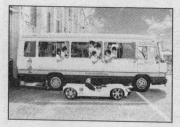

LOWEST ROADWORTHY CAR
The *Mirai* car measures just 1 ft. 5 in. (45.2 cm) from the ground to its highest part. Students and teachers of the Automobile Engineering Course of Okayama Sanyo High School in Asakuchi, Japan, unveiled it on Nov. 15, 2010. *Mirai* means "future" in Japanese.

HEAVIEST RIDEABLE TRICYCLE
Wouter van den Bosch (NLD) has constructed a tricycle that's truly off the scale, weighing in at a colossal 1,650 lb. (750 kg). Wouter took his heavyweight creation for a ride in Arnhem, Netherlands, in May 2010.

SMALLEST ROADWORTHY CAR
The ideal complement for the smallest caravan, this diminutive car measures 2 ft. 1 in. (63.5 cm) high, 2 ft. 1.75 in. (65.4 cm) wide, and 4 ft. 1.75 in. (1.26 m) long. It was made by Austin Coulson (U.S.A.) and measured in Carrollton, Texas, U.S.A., on Sep. 7, 2012.

Wheels were first used for transport more than **5,500 years** ago, but not like this!

LONGEST GOLF CART From bumper to bumper, the longest golf cart stretches an impressive 31 ft. 6 in. (9.62 m) and was created by Mike's Golf Carts (U.S.A.). The cart was measured in Perry, Georgia, U.S.A., on May 30, 2013.

FASTEST MOTORIZED SHOPPING CART Bringing a whole new meaning to the words "fast food," Matt McKeown (UK) reached 70.4 mph (113.2 km/h) in a shopping cart at Elvington Airfield in North Yorkshire, UK, on Aug. 18, 2013.

FACT: Matt smashed his own record for this feat—a mere 45 mph—which he had set during the previous month.

LOUDEST BICYCLE HORN Not content simply with creating the **smallest caravan** (bottom), the Environmental Transport Association has developed a bicycle horn capable of emitting a honk measuring 136.2 dB(A) (decibels) from a distance of 8 ft. 2 in. (2.5 m). *The Hornster* uses a modified freight train horn powered by a scuba-diving tank and was demonstrated by Yannick Read on Feb. 13, 2013 in Weybridge, Surrey, UK.

FASTEST BATHROOM The *Bog Standard* consists of a motorcycle and sidecar hidden under a bathroom set comprising a Victorian-style throne toilet, bathtub, sink, and laundry bin. Created by Edd China (UK), this mobile restroom can reach a speed of 42.25 mph (68 km/h).

A past master in mobile furniture, Edd has also made the **fastest garden shed** (58 mph; 94 km/h), **bed** (69 mph; 111 km/h), and **office** (87 mph; 140 km/h).

SMALLEST CARAVAN The QTvan is just 7 ft. 10 in. (2.39 m) long, 5 ft. (1.53 m) high, and 2 ft. 7 in. (79 cm) wide. It was manufactured by the Environmental Transport Association (UK) and measured in Aylesbury, UK, on Jun. 5, 2013. Left, designer Yannick Read (UK) shows off his compact creation.

For wild wheel skills, flip to p. 236.

LARGEST MONSTER TRUCK
Bigfoot 5 is 15 ft. 6 in. (4.7 m) tall with 10-ft.-high (3-m) tires and weighs in at more than 38,000 lb. (17 tonnes). It is one of a fleet of 17 Bigfoot trucks created by Bob Chandler (U.S.A.) and was built in 1986. Permanently parked in St. Louis, Missouri, U.S.A., *Bigfoot 5* makes occasional exhibition appearances at local shows.

TALLEST LIMOUSINE CAR
Gary and Shirley Duval (both AUS) have made a lofty limo that measures 10 ft. 11 in. (3.33 m) tall. The record-breaking car has an eight-wheel independent suspension system and sits on eight monster truck tires. It has eight-wheel steering, two engines, and took a little more than 4,000 hours (166 days) to complete.

MILITARY HARDWARE

ON LAND

First javelin A study published by the journal *PLOS ONE* on Nov. 13, 2013 dated the use of projectile weapons akin to javelins to more than 279,000 years ago. An examination of fossils indicated that pointed stone artifacts were used on throwing weapons. The stone-tipped weapons were found at Gademotta in Ethiopia, suggesting that eastern Africa was a source of more modern culture and biology than previously thought. The weapons ultimately allowed humans to leave Africa and out-compete Neanderthals.

First hand grenades Grenades appeared in the Eastern Roman (Byzantine) Empire in ca. A.D. 741, when soldiers realized that Greek fire—a buoyant incendiary weapon—could be thrown at the enemy in stone, ceramic, or glass containers. The use of grenades spread, with evidence found in a Chinese military writing from 1044, *Wujing Zongyao* (*Compilation of Military Classics*).

IN THE AIR

First air-to-air refueling by hose On Jun. 27, 1923, at Rockwell Field in San Diego, California, U.S.A., a successful refueling of one aircraft from another took place. An Airco DH.4B passed 75 gal. (284 L) of gasoline through a hose to a craft of the same type.

First manned missile In 1944, during World War II, German V1 missiles were found to lack accuracy. This led the German Research Institute for Sailplane Flight to design a manned missile. The Fieseler Fi 103R-4 Reichenberg could be guided to its target by a pilot, who would bail out. The plan was abandoned, because getting out of a 400-mph (650-km/h) speeding missile was impossible without death or serious injury.

MOST EXPENSIVE MILITARY AIRCRAFT PROGRAM By 2012, the Lockheed Martin F-35 Lightning Joint Strike Fighter had costs of $336 bn—a 52.8% increase from 2001—with some reports putting it as high as $392 bn, for the U.S.A. This 50-year, multinational program has an estimated sustainment cost for the U.S.A. of $0.85–1.5 tr over its lifetime.

LONGEST-SERVING BOMBER The Boeing B-52 jet bomber, which entered service with the U.S. Air Force in 1954, is the longest-serving currently operational bomber aircraft. With 60 years of service already, it is scheduled to remain in use until 2044 and will receive a further $24.6 m of upgrades to increase its ability to carry smart weapons.

Largest non-nuclear submarine: 396.9-ft.-long World War II I-400 Japanese submarines of the Sen-Toku class (1946)

Longest-range stealth mini-submarine: Torpedo SEAL, 2013, capable of transporting two divers and equipment at 4 knots (4.5 mph) over a range of 10 nautical mi. (11.5 mi.)

Newest class of submarine: Iran's Fateh class, 2013, a diesel-electric submarine

First pilotless aircraft to cross the Pacific Ocean

On Apr. 23, 2001, the Northrop Grumman RQ-4A began its flight at the Edwards Air Force Base in California, U.S.A. The unmanned aerial vehicle (UAV) flew for 22 hr. nonstop across the Pacific Ocean before landing at the Royal Australian Air Force Base in Edinburgh, Adelaide, Australia.

Most expensive UAV

A U.S. General Accountability Office Report in Mar. 2013 gave the Northrop Grumman Global Hawk a unit cost of $222 m, making it the most expensive UAV yet.

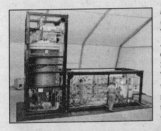

NEWEST DEPLOYABLE CHEMICAL WEAPON DESTROYER

The U.S. Defense Threat Reduction Agency commissioned a mobile unit that can destroy chemical weapons, following Syria's agreement to surrender them. The Field Deployable Hydrolysis System works by splitting chemical weapon molecules into small fragments that can then be disposed of like normal hazardous waste.

FIRST 3D-PRINTED PISTOL In 2013, Solid Concepts, based in Austin, Texas, U.S.A., produced a 3D-printed gun using "laser-sintering"—a process that creates objects from powders, in this case metal powders. The gun is a replica of the 1911 Browning pistol and has fired 50 rounds successfully. The purpose of the project was to demonstrate that 3D metal printing provides strong, reliable, and accurate products.

IN THE SEA

First sea mine A reference to sea mines can be found in *Huolongjing,* a Chinese military manual from the early Ming dynasty (1368–1644). It describes the "Submarine Dragon King"—a wrought-iron mine weighted by stones with an explosive contained in an ox bladder, ignited via a joss stick enclosed in a goat's intestine.

First successful combat submarine On Feb. 17, 1864, during the American Civil War, the *H. L. Hunley* became the first combat submarine to sink an enemy warship when it sunk the U.S.S. *Housatonic* off Charleston in South Carolina. The 40-ft.-long (12-m) *H. L. Hunley*—which sank minutes after engagement—was recovered in 2000 and, after restoration work, displayed in Jan. 2013.

First self-propelled torpedo In 1866, Robert Whitehead (UK) developed a new weapon in the shape of a self-propelled underwater torpedo, which was fired via compressed air. Whitehead's weapon could hit a target as far away as 2,100 ft. (640 m) with an 18-lb. (8-kg) charge of explosive, at a speed of 7 knots (8 mph; 13 km/h).

The **first ship sunk by a self-propelled torpedo** was *Intibah* in Jan. 1878. Whitehead torpedoes launched from Russian torpedo boats sank the Turkish ship during the 1877–78 Russo-Turkish War.

LARGEST ANTI-MINE NAVAL EXERCISE
On May 13, 2013, a fleet of 34 ships, 100 divers, and 18 unmanned submarines began an anti-mine exercise in the Persian Gulf. The aim was to show how the strategically important Strait of Hormuz—a critical route for the world's oil supplies—could be kept open in the event that a hostile nation would seek to block it.

FIRST DRONE LAUNCH FROM A SUBMERGED COMBAT SUBMARINE
On Dec. 5, 2013, the XFC (eXperimental Fuel Cell) unmanned aerial system was launched from a submerged submarine. It can undertake video reconnaissance and intelligence missions, and relay its output to its command center.

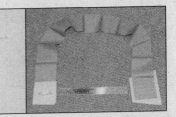

MOUSE DROPPINGS: Aerial Assault The snake population on the island of Guam in the Pacific grew to some 2–3 million following their arrival in freight from Australia and Papua New Guinea. The snakes threatened native fauna and cost the Guam Power Authority up to $4 m annually in repairs. The solution? The **largest aerial assault by paramice.** On Dec. 1, 2013, 2,000 dead mice tied to miniature parachutes (above) were air-dropped onto Guam by U.S. authorities. Each mouse contained 80 mg of the over-the-counter painkiller acetaminophen: a fatal dose for snakes.

MILITARY MIGHT—GLOBAL FIREPOWER 2014

		Manpower	Land Vehicles	Aircraft	Seacraft
1.	U.S.A.	145,212,012	39,162	13,683	473
2.	Russia	69,117,271	57,503	3,082	352
3.	China	749,610,775	23,664	2,788	520
4.	India	615,201,057	15,681	1,785	184
5.	UK	29,164,233	6,935	908	66
6.	France	28,802,096	8,672	1,203	120
7.	Germany	36,417,842	5,124	710	82
8.	Turkey	41,637,773	15,948	989	115
9.	South Korea	25,609,290	13,158	1,393	166
10.	Japan	53,608,446	4,611	1,595	131

Source: globalfirepower.com

MOST EXPENSIVE SUPERCARRIER The U.S.S. *Gerald R. Ford*, a 1,092-ft.-long (332-m) carrier, is scheduled for service in 2016. It has capacity for 75 fighter and strike aircraft, and comes equipped with a new type of catapult—the Electromagnetic Aircraft Launch System—which can launch up to 220 air strikes a day. It cost $13 bn to build, but will save $4 bn over its lifetime compared with the current Nimitz-class carriers.

AND FINALLY . . .

- **Most common fighter aircraft (current):** U.S. F-16 Fighting Falcon, made by U.S. General Dynamics and Lockheed Martin: 2,281 combat aircraft (15% of global total)

- **Largest air force by number of fighter aircraft (current):** U.S.A.: 2,271 active fighters/interceptors, according to globalfirepower.com (see full table, p. 431)

ARCHITECTURE

Largest architectural practice (employees) According to the "2013 World Architecture 100" survey by the UK's *Building Design* magazine, the largest firm of architects in terms of the number of employees is Gensler, with a 1,468-strong workforce on its books. Gensler's headquarters are in San Francisco, U.S.A., but it also has 43 offices in 14 countries worldwide.

Logically enough, according to the "Top 300 Architecture Firms" list compiled by U.S. magazine *Architectural Record*, the **largest firm of architects by revenue** is also Gensler, with earnings of $807 m in 2012.

"Skyscraper" originally referred to a triangular sail at the top of a ship's mast.

OLDEST . . .

Continuously inhabited city Archaeologists have discovered settlements in Jericho, part of the Palestinian territories, that date back to 9000 B.C. The city, located near the Jordan River in the West Bank, is today home to approximately 20,000 people. Its population in 8000 B.C. is thought to have numbered 2,000 to 3,000.

Minaret The Great Mosque of Kairouan in Tunisia houses a minaret that was largely built in the ninth century and completed by A.D. 836. It is 103 ft. 4 in. (31.5 m) high and rests on a square base measuring 35 ft. 1 in. x 35 ft. 1 in. (10.7 x 10.7 m).

Surviving skatepark The Albany Skate Track in Albany, Western Australia, was completed in Mar. 1976. It consists of a 459-ft.-long (140-m) concrete "snake run" with steeply banked sides, varying from 19 ft. 8 in. to 26 ft. 2 in. (6–8 m) wide. The facility cost AUS$15,000 ($18,600).

LARGEST GLASS GREENHOUSE The Flower Dome greenhouse at Gardens by the Bay in Singapore covers 3.16 acres (1.28 ha) under its glass roof. Designed by architects Wilkinson Eyre, the column-free grid shell and arch shape allow for maximum sunlight and climate control. Along with the smaller Cloud Forest conservatory, it was completed in Jun. 2012.

SCRAPING THE SKY

In 1955, the **tallest building** was the Empire State Building in New York City, U.S.A., measuring "1,472 feet [488.6 m] high to the top of the television tower." A succession of buildings have held that coveted title since, the latest being the Burj Khalifa, which is nearly twice as tall as that 1955 record holder. The Sky City skyscraper in Changsha, China, was to top out at 32 ft. 9 in. taller but, by 2013, work stalled on the challenging prefabricated design.

Architecture

LARGEST . . .

Airport passenger terminal roof The roof of the Hajj terminal at King Abdulaziz International Airport near Jeddah, Saudi Arabia, covers 2.8 million sq. ft. (260,129 m²). Designed by Skidmore, Owings & Merrill, the Teflon-coated roof modules are supported by 147-ft.-high (45-m) pylons.

Basket-shape building Completed in 1997, the seven-story headquarters of the Longaberger basket company in Ohio, U.S.A., resembles a giant basket and has 180,000 sq. ft. (16,722 m²) of floor space. With a maximum length of 208 ft. (63.4 m) and a width of 142 ft. (43.3 m), it is 160 times larger than Longaberger's "Medium Market Basket."

TALLEST BUILDING Developed by Emaar Properties, the 2,716-ft.-tall (828-m) Burj Khalifa opened in Dubai, UAE, on Jan. 4, 2010. Almost 26,000 hand-cut glass panels were used in the exterior cladding of the building, which has residential, office, and hotel use.

TALLEST SUMMIT CROSS Built in 1926–28 to honor the dead of World War I, Heroes' Cross (aka the Caraiman Cross) is 129 ft. 7 in. (39.5 m) tall with its concrete base. It sits 7,516 ft. (2,291 m) up Mount Caraiman in Romania's Bucegi Mountains.

LARGEST BUILDING SHAPED LIKE A MUSICAL INSTRUMENT The Piano House in Huainan, China, is around 52 ft. (16 m) tall. It was designed by students of Hefei University of Technology in 2007. Visitors enter through a "violin," then proceed via an escalator that takes them into the main, piano-shape section of the building.

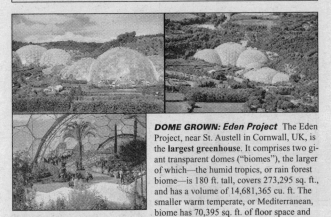

DOME GROWN: *Eden Project*

The Eden Project, near St. Austell in Cornwall, UK, is the **largest greenhouse**. It comprises two giant transparent domes ("biomes"), the larger of which—the humid tropics, or rain forest biome—is 180 ft. tall, covers 273,295 sq. ft., and has a volume of 14,681,365 cu. ft. The smaller warm temperate, or Mediterranean, biome has 70,395 sq. ft. of floor space and a volume of 3,023,640 cu. ft. Both are made of steel frames carrying hexagons and pentagons of flourine-base plastic. The site also features an unroofed outdoor biome.

LARGEST PLANETARIUM

The planetarium of Nagoya City Science Museum in Japan has a hemispherical dome with an internal diameter of 114 ft. 10 in. (35 m). The almost perfectly spherical section that houses the planetarium measures 129 ft. (39.2 m) tall and is suspended 37 ft. (11.4 m) above the ground.

TALLEST ART NOUVEAU CHURCH

La Sagrada Família in Barcelona, Spain, was begun in 1882 under architect Francisco de Paula del Villar y Lozano and taken over in 1883 by Antoni Gaudí (both ESP). It is not expected to be completed until at least 2026. Currently 351 ft. (107 m) high, the tallest of the 18 towers will reach 560 ft. (170 m) when finished.

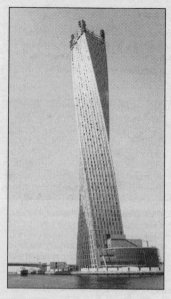

TALLEST TWISTED TOWER The Cayan Tower in Dubai, UAE, stands 1,008 ft. (307.3 m) tall and features a 90-degree twist. Each floor has a 1.2-degree rotation, which creates a helix shape. It was developed by Cayan Real Estate Investment & Development and opened on Jun. 10, 2013.

The **first twisted skyscraper** was the HSB Turning Torso in Malmö, Sweden (2005).

Opera house Designed by architect Wallace K. Harrison, the Metropolitan Opera House at the Lincoln Center in New York City, U.S.A., can accommodate an audience of 3,975, based on it having 3,800 seats and 175 standing-room places. It cost $45.7 m and was opened on Sep. 16, 1966.

Television building The China Central Television building in Beijing is 768 ft. (234 m) tall, contains 54 floors, and cost 850 million euros ($1.17 bn) to construct. It was designed by architects Office for Metropolitan Architecture (NDL) with engineers Arup (UK), and officially completed on May 16, 2012. The total floor space measures 5,091,300 sq. ft. (473,000 m²)—equivalent to more than 85 football fields—and includes areas for news and program production, TV broadcasting, and parking. Beijing residents have nicknamed the building the "giant shorts" due to its unique shape.

Vertical garden Keppel Land Limited completed a 22,879.33-sq.-ft. (2,125.56-m²) green wall in Singapore's Ocean Financial Centre on Sep. 13, 2013. It took three years to create the garden, which features 25 plant species.

HIGHEST BUILDING JACK-UP The Main Yuzhen Palace Gate, East Palace Gate, and West Palace Gate of the Ancient Building Complex in Hubei Province, China, were lifted 50 ft. (15 m)—from an elevation of 524 ft. (160 m) to 574 ft. (175 m)—between Aug. 15, 2012 and Jan. 16, 2013 to avoid the risk of flooding from a water-diversion project.

TALLEST BUILDINGS AROUND THE WORLD

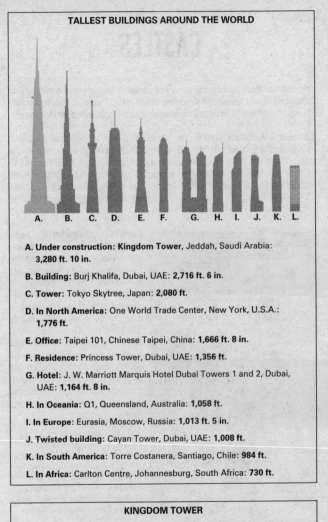

A. Under construction: Kingdom Tower, Jeddah, Saudi Arabia: **3,280 ft. 10 in.**

B. Building: Burj Khalifa, Dubai, UAE: **2,716 ft. 6 in.**

C. Tower: Tokyo Skytree, Japan: **2,080 ft.**

D. In North America: One World Trade Center, New York, U.S.A.: **1,776 ft.**

E. Office: Taipei 101, Chinese Taipei, China: **1,666 ft. 8 in.**

F. Residence: Princess Tower, Dubai, UAE: **1,356 ft.**

G. Hotel: J. W. Marriott Marquis Hotel Dubai Towers 1 and 2, Dubai, UAE: **1,164 ft. 8 in.**

H. In Oceania: Q1, Queensland, Australia: **1,058 ft.**

I. In Europe: Eurasia, Moscow, Russia: **1,013 ft. 5 in.**

J. Twisted building: Cayan Tower, Dubai, UAE: **1,008 ft.**

K. In South America: Torre Costanera, Santiago, Chile: **984 ft.**

L. In Africa: Carlton Centre, Johannesburg, South Africa: **730 ft.**

KINGDOM TOWER

So far, work has only begun on its foundations, but when completed—possibly by 2019, and at a cost of around $1.2 bn—the Kingdom Tower will become the first building ever to break the 1-km (0.6-mi.) barrier. Its sloping exterior and triangle-shape footprint are designed to help reduce the impact of wind on the supertall building.

CASTLES

Oldest castle The earliest recorded castle is located in the old city of Sana'a, Yemen. Known as Gomdan or Gumdan Castle, it dates from before A.D. 200 and is believed to have originally comprised 20 stories.

Largest inhabited castle The royal residence of Windsor Castle at Windsor, Berkshire, UK, is originally of 12th-century construction and takes the form of a waisted parallelogram measuring 1,890 x 540 ft. (576 x 164 m). The entire site covers 570,000 sq. ft. (53,000 m²)—the area of nearly 10 football fields—in the center of which stands the iconic 214-ft.-tall (65.5-m) Round Tower topped off with gothic-style battlements.

Largest nonpalatial residence St. Emmeram Castle (or Abbey) in Regensburg, Germany, has 517 rooms and a floor area of 231,000 sq. ft. (21,460 m²). Originally a Benedictine monastery (founded in A.D. 739), it was acquired in 1812 by the Thurn und Taxis family, who built up a fortune from their exclusive control of the mail service in Bavaria over the course of 200 years. Princess Gloria von Thurn und Taxis still uses the castle as her primary residence.

TALLEST SELF-BUILT CASTLE

The 160-ft.-tall (48.75-m) stone-and-steel Bishop Castle in Colorado, U.S.A., has been a work in progress by American welder Jim Bishop since Jun. 1969. It features stained-glass windows, three towers, a grand ballroom, and a sculpture of a fire-breathing dragon.

Castle stairwells usually turn **clockwise**, giving right-handed swordsmen an advantage in attacks.

LARGEST CAVE CASTLE More than 115 ft. (35 m) in height, Predjama Castle near Postojna, Slovenia, is built in the entrance to a cave system (above right). Set halfway up a 403-ft.-high (123-m) cliff face, the castle dates back to at least the 13th century, and was rebuilt in a Renaissance style in 1570.

Longest castle siege The cathedral fort of Ishiyama Hongan-ji, in what is today Osaka, Japan, first came under attack from the renowned warrior Oda Nobunaga in Aug. 1570, but the defending Ikkō-ikki warrior monks under Abbot Kōsa held out for a decade until Aug. 1580, when the complex was finally burned to the ground. Osaka Castle was constructed on the site and continues to be a popular tourist destination.

Northernmost castle The small Kajaani Castle in Finland, at a latitude of 64.2295 degrees, is the most northerly castle. It was built on a small river island between 1604 and 1619 and first used as a prison. It survives only as stone ruins today.

LARGEST ANCIENT CASTLE
Prague Castle in the Czech Republic was constructed in the ninth century. It is an oblong irregular polygon with an axis of 1,870 ft. (570 m) and an average transverse diameter of 420 ft. (128 m), resulting in a total surface area of 18 acres (7.28 ha).

LARGEST BRICK CASTLE
Poland's Malbork Castle was built largely in the 13th and 14th centuries by Teutonic Order crusader knights. It encompasses a 52-acre (21-ha) site and is built almost entirely from locally made bricks of a distinctive red hue. Its grandiose Knights' Hall refectory could house up to 400 visiting knights and guests.

Oldest museum The Royal Armouries museum in the Tower of London (UK)—the city's most famous castle—is the oldest museum. It first opened its doors to the public in 1660, although it was possible to view the collection by appointment for up to eight years prior to this date.

Tallest theme-park castle The Cinderella Castle at Disney's Magic Kingdom in Florida, U.S.A., is 189 ft. (57.3 m) high. Partly based on picturesque real-life castles, such as those at Neuschwanstein (Germany), Segovia (Spain), and Moszna (Poland), the "forced-perspective" design of the steel, concrete, and fiber-glass structure makes it seem even taller than it is. It opened in 1971.

LONGEST CASTLE Constructed mainly between ca. 1255 and 1490, the Burg zu Burghausen measures 3,448 ft. (1,051 m) long and is built on a ridge that runs above the town of Burghausen in Germany. It was once a residence of the dukes of Bavaria, and it is composed of a main inner courtyard—where the family lived—and five large outer courtyards, all of which would have been protected by portcullises, moats, and drawbridges.

LARGEST TRIANGULAR CASTLE

Wewelsburg Castle in Büren, Germany, was constructed between 1603 and 1609. The Renaissance-style structure has a total perimeter of 787 ft. (240 m). Originally used by the Prince-Bishopric of Paderborn, it later became notorious as one of the centers for the Nazi SS under Heinrich Himmler.

Largest inflatable (bouncy) castle Designed by Dana Caspersen and William Forsythe (both U.S.A.) and produced in three weeks by Southern Inflatables, UK, the largest inflatable castle stands 39 ft. (12 m) tall and is 62 sq. ft. (19 m²) at the base. Made from 29,330 sq. ft. (2,725 m²) of white-PVC-coated polyester, it takes 6 hr. to fully construct and 15 min. to fill with 13,500 cu. ft. (385 m³) of air. Between Mar. 24 and May 11, 1997, it served as an architectural installation in Camden, London, UK. Since then, it has been used at a range of events worldwide.

A more modest inflatable, measuring 12 x 15 ft. (3.6 x 4.5 m) at the base, was used for the **longest marathon on a bouncy castle by a team.** Eight bouncers from the logistics company Wincanton and the Tesco supermarket in Rugby, Warwickshire, UK, clocked a time of 37 hr. 14 sec. on Aug. 30–31, 2013.

NARROW ADVANTAGE

The term "loophole" originally referred to the narrow slit in a castle wall through which arrows could be fired.

Largest suit of armor made for an animal: Adult Asian elephant suit, weighing 260 lb., in Royal Armouries museum, Leeds, UK

Most expensive suit of armor sold at auction: Suit of armor made for Henri II in 1545 by Giovanni Negroli, sold for £1,925,000 ($3,032,800) on May 5, 1983, from Hever Castle collection, Kent, UK

Tallest suit of armor: 6.7 ft. high, dated to ca. 1535, in the White Tower at HM Tower of London, UK

SPELLBINDING SCHOOL: Hogwarts One of the most instantly recognizable castles is Hogwarts School of Witchcraft and Wizardry from J. K. Rowling's Harry Potter series. The **largest model of Hogwarts castle** was made by the art department of Warner Bros. (UK) in 2011. The 1:24-scale model (pictured top left, with model supervisor José Granell) is 50 ft. wide and can be visited at the Warner Bros. studio tour in London.

The **largest model of Hogwarts made from LEGO®** was created by Alice Finch (U.S.A., bottom left) in 2012; 13 ft. long, it used around 400,000 bricks.

Largest can sculpture An 18-ft.-tall (5.5-m) reproduction of Yoshida Castle in Toyohashi, Japan, was built from 104,840 aluminum drink cans by Junior Chamber International in Toyohashi Park, Aichi, Japan, on Sep. 21, 2013.

GLOSSARY

Castle: Specifically, a defensively constructed residence for rulers, often with state-of-the-art military hardware. Sometimes a generic term for fortified structures.

Citadel: A fort or fortress used to defend a town or city.

Fort: A heavily defended military outpost but not always designed as a residence for royalty or aristocracy.

Palace: The nonfortified residence of a leader.

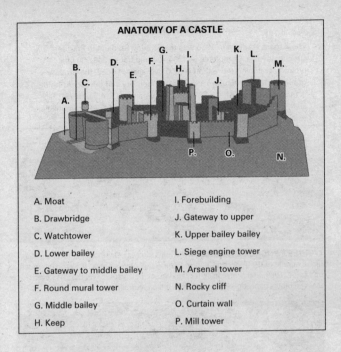

ANATOMY OF A CASTLE

A. Moat

B. Drawbridge

C. Watchtower

D. Lower bailey

E. Gateway to middle bailey

F. Round mural tower

G. Middle bailey

H. Keep

I. Forebuilding

J. Gateway to upper

K. Upper bailey bailey

L. Siege engine tower

M. Arsenal tower

N. Rocky cliff

O. Curtain wall

P. Mill tower

SPORTS ARCHITECTURE

Largest ancient stadium The Circus Maximus in Rome, Italy, could accommodate 255,000 spectators in a triple-bank structure measuring some 2,000 ft. (610 m) long and 650 ft. (200 m) wide. Writer Pliny the Younger said it rivaled the beauty of Rome's temples. First begun in the 6th century B.C., the Circus Maximus reached its largest form under Trajan in A.D. 103. It remains most famous for the chariot races that were re-created in *Ben-Hur* (U.S.A., 1959), as well as for track and field events and gladiator combat. The last race in the Circus Maximus was recorded in A.D. 550.

A UK home valued at $117.39 m in 2005 boasted a **squash court, bowling alley, and five pools**.

LARGEST STADIUM

The **largest stadium** in 1955 was the Strahov Stadium in Prague, Czechoslovakia. Completed in 1934, it could house 240,000 fans, typically watching more than 40,000 gymnasts. Today, the Strahov's grand gymnastic displays are a distant memory and the record-holder is the Indianapolis Motor Speedway in Indiana, U.S.A., with 257,325 seated. The future for Prague's striking monolith of the Communist era remains uncertain.

LARGEST SOCCER STADIUM The Rungnado May Day Stadium is on an island in the middle of the Taedong River in Pyongyang, North Korea. It was inaugurated on May 1, 1989, and is also used for the Arirang Festival (above, the 2013 event) that celebrates the country's late leaders. It has a current capacity of 150,000.

LARGEST SOLAR-POWERED STADIUM

The National Stadium in Kaohsiung, Chinese Taipei, is topped with 8,844 solar panels covering 152,362 sq. ft. (14,155 m²). They can generate 1.14 million kWh of electricity every year: 80% of the venue's needs. If it were powered by traditional power stations, 1.45 million lb. (660 metric tons) of carbon dioxide would be released annually. Designed by Toyo Ito (JPN), the stadium's shape is said to be based on that of a curled dragon.

LARGEST TENSILE STADIUM ROOF Tensile structures are held in place using tension, anchored by cables instead of bent or compressed with poles. The King Fahd International Stadium in Riyadh, Saudi Arabia, covers 505,900 sq. ft. (47,000 m²) and was completed in 1987 from a design by Ian Fraser Associates. Its 24 masts support an 807-ft.-wide (246-m) roof shaped like Bedouin tents. The roof protects more than 67,000 spectators from the desert climate.

Largest marble stadium The Panathenaic Stadium is unique in being constructed almost entirely out of white marble. It was first built in the 6th century B.C. in Athens, Greece, rebuilt in marble in 329 B.C. by Lycurgus, and has been enlarged and renovated many times since. It hosted the first modern Olympic Games in 1896.

Highest-capacity Olympic stadium Stadium Australia was constructed to hold approximately 110,000 people for the Sydney Olympics of 2000, but more than 114,000 spectators crammed into the stadium for the closing ceremony. Also known as the ANZ Stadium, the venue is still used, although with a reduced capacity of 83,500. Four other Olympic cities have had stadia with capacities of more than 100,000: Los Angeles, U.S.A. (101,574 in 1932); Berlin, Germany (110,000 in 1936); Melbourne, Australia (100,000 in 1956); and Moscow, Soviet Union (103,000 in 1980).

LONGEST MOTOR-RACING CIRCUIT The longest purpose-designed circuit in use is Nürburgring in Nürburg, Germany. Built in 1927, the "Nordschleife" ("north loop") measures 12.93 mi. (20.81 km) and the "Südschleife" ("south loop"), which was rebuilt in 1984, is 3.199 mi. (5.148 km) long. When combined for the annual 24-hr. endurance event, the track is 16.129 mi. (25.958 km) long, with more than 180 corners.

FACT: The tree-lined track claims between three and 12 lives each year. Formula One legend Jackie Stewart calls it "The Green Hell."

TOP 10 LARGEST STADIA BY CAPACITY

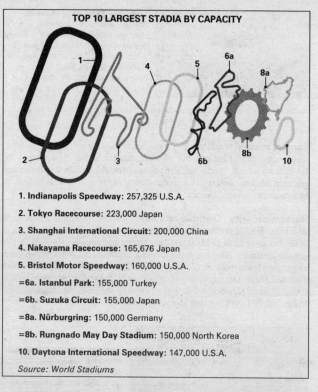

1. **Indianapolis Speedway:** 257,325 U.S.A.

2. **Tokyo Racecourse:** 223,000 Japan

3. **Shanghai International Circuit:** 200,000 China

4. **Nakayama Racecourse:** 165,676 Japan

5. **Bristol Motor Speedway:** 160,000 U.S.A.

=6a. **Istanbul Park:** 155,000 Turkey

=6b. **Suzuka Circuit:** 155,000 Japan

=8a. **Nürburgring:** 150,000 Germany

=8b. **Rungnado May Day Stadium:** 150,000 North Korea

10. **Daytona International Speedway:** 147,000 U.S.A.

Source: World Stadiums

SKY-HIGH SPORTS: Top Courts You'd need serious danger money to be a ball boy on the **highest tennis court**, 692 ft. above the ground. The court was temporarily installed on the helipad of the Burj Al Arab hotel in Dubai, UAE, on Feb. 22, 2005 as Roger Federer (CHE) and Andre Agassi (U.S.A.) played a friendly game to promote the ATP's Dubai Duty Free Men's Open. "Do you think I can knock this guy off his boat?", joked Agassi as they paused to peer over the side of the sheer drop to the shallows far below. If you were ever on the beach in Dubai and wondered where that tennis ball came from—it was from former world No. 1 Andre Agassi!

LARGEST FLOATING SPORTS PLATFORM The Float at Marina Bay, Singapore, was completed in 2007 and has 214,847 sq. ft. (19,960 m²) of usable space plus a grandstand for 27,000 fans on the shore. The platform is secured by six pylons and can support the weight of 9,000 people.

LARGEST FLOATING GOLF GREEN To play the 14th hole of the Coeur d'Alene golf course in Idaho, U.S.A., you have to take a boat trip. Measuring some 15,000 sq. ft. (1,390 m²), the green is on a computer-controlled island that can be moved between 246 ft. (75 m) and 574 ft. (175 m) from the shore. Golfers reach the island by an electrically powered water taxi in a course that was completed in 1991.

Largest sumo stadium The Ryōgoku Kokugikan in Tokyo, Japan, has a capacity of 11,908. Spectators in the *suna-aburi-seki* ringside seats are so close to the action in the *dohyō* central ring that they are often sprayed with sand during bouts. The venue opened in Jan. 1985 and holds three of the country's six official sumo tournaments.

Longest bobsled track The 2014 Winter Olympics track at the Sliding Center Sanki in Sochi, Russia, is the most fiendish yet. It has a competition length of 0.93 mi. (1.5 km) and drops 432 ft. 8 in. (131.9 m) at an average grade of 9.3% over its 18 curves. Riders can reach speeds as high as 83.9 mph (135 km/h).

Tallest ski-flying hill Ski flying is a more extreme version of ski jumping. The ski-jump facility at Vikersundbakken in Vikersund, Norway, is partly manmade and partly modified natural hill. It reaches a dizzying height of 738 ft. (225 m)—almost two-and-a-half times the height of the Statue of Liberty. Begun in 1935, Vikersundbakken had been modified into its current form by 2011. On Feb. 11 of that year, Johan Remen Evensen (NOR) set the **longest competitive ski jump** on the hill, with a distance of 809 ft. (246.5 m).

Newest real tennis court The court may be new, but the game is old. Real tennis is a precursor of modern tennis, played on a hard court surrounded by four walls. Fewer than 50 courts exist today; their numbers were swelled in 2012 by the Racquet Club of Chicago, Illinois, U.S.A.

The **oldest surviving real tennis court** is at Falkland Palace in Fife, UK. It was constructed for James V of Scotland between Apr. 1539 and late 1541 and is home to the Falkland Palace Royal Tennis Club, which was founded in 1975.

FIRST RETRACTABLE GRASS PITCH The GelreDome in Arnhem, Netherlands, opened on Mar. 25, 1998. Home to soccer club Vitesse Arnhem, its playing surface sits in a concrete tray that takes 5 hr. to slide outside the stadium (above) to prepare for concerts.

The **largest retractable roof** covers the Toronto Blue Jays' Rogers Center (formerly SkyDome) in Toronto, Canada. It spans 685 ft. (209 m) and covers 8 acres (3.2 ha).

SUPERSIZE STADIA

Building for top sports comes at a cost. Portugal spent 536.5 m euros ($745.4 m) to host soccer's Euro 2004, with seven new stadia in a country about the size of Indiana, U.S.A. For the 2002 soccer World Cup, Japan spent ¥526 bn ($5.1 bn) on new venues and renovations. For the Olympics, Greece's 2004 Games cost 9.4 bn euros ($13 bn) and China spent ¥293 bn ($47.8 bn) in 2008.

CUTTING-EDGE SCIENCE

First country to mine gas hydrates Gas hydrates, aka "flammable ice," are a solid resembling water ice. They contain methane gas trapped in a crystalline structure and occur beneath sediments on the ocean floor. In Mar. 2013, Japan announced that it had successfully extracted methane gas from hydrate deposits in the Nankai Trough, 30 mi. (50 km) offshore from Japan. Scientists estimate that there could be enough hydrate deposits in the Nankai Trough to meet Japan's energy needs for a decade.

First photon interaction In Sep. 2013, researchers from Harvard University and the Massachusetts Institute of Technology (both U.S.A.) completed an experiment that compared the interaction of protons to the behavior of light sabers, the fictional weapons used in *Star Wars*. Researchers observed an attractive force between two photons—the basic particles that form light—which interacted to form a joined, two-photon molecule. This indicated that photons could be manipulated to create a solid "blade" of light, like a light saber.

Highest manmade RPM Scientists at the University of St. Andrews in the UK created a tiny sphere of calcium just 4 micrometers (0.00015 in; 0.004 mm) across, around 10 times narrower than a human hair. They suspended the sphere using laser light inside a vacuum and made it spin by altering the polarity of the light. On Aug. 28, 2013, the team published the results of their research, which observed the calcium sphere reaching 600 million revolutions per min. (RPM) before disintegrating.

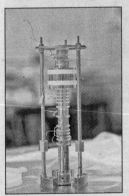

MOST ACCURATE ELECTRON MASS MEASUREMENT On Feb. 19, 2014, the Max Planck Institute for Nuclear Physics (DEU) announced the mass of an electron measured at 0.000548579909067 of an atomic mass unit. It was measured by binding a single electron to a bare carbon nucleus in a Penning trap (left) and manipulating it with electric and magnetic fields. The result is ca. 13 times more accurate than previous efforts.

As helium was first **discovered on the Sun**, it was named after Helios, the Greek sun god.

FIRST EARTHQUAKE DETECTED FROM ORBIT On Mar. 17, 2009, the European Space Agency launched *GOCE*, a satellite that can map Earth's gravitational field from an orbit of 158.3 mi. (254.9 km). On Mar. 11, 2011, as it passed through the weak sound waves of Earth's thermosphere, the spacecraft detected the devastating earthquake that struck Japan.

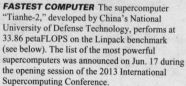

FASTEST COMPUTER The supercomputer "Tianhe-2," developed by China's National University of Defense Technology, performs at 33.86 petaFLOPS on the Linpack benchmark (see below). The list of the most powerful supercomputers was announced on Jun. 17 during the opening session of the 2013 International Supercomputing Conference.

FACT: A supercomputer's performance is measured in FLOPS—FLoating-point Operations Per Second. A floating-point operation is the calculation of a mathematical equation, so a petaFLOP, as used to measure the fastest supercomputer (above), means 1,000,000,000,000,000 calculations per sec.

LARGEST NEUTRINO DETECTOR IceCube is a U.S.-led international telescope designed to detect neutrinos, subatomic particles with almost no mass. Located at the Amundsen-Scott South Pole Station in Antarctica, it consists of 5,160 detectors in 86 vertical cables buried 4,750–8,050 ft. (1,450–2,450 m) below sea level, where the ice is optically clear.

Thinnest manmade material In Oct. 2004, British and Russian scientists announced the discovery of the nanofabric graphene. With a thickness of just one single atom of carbon, graphene can exist as a single sheet of a theoretically infinite size.

In Jan. 2012, researchers from the University of California in Riverside (U.S.A.) showed that when just 10% graphene was added to other materials, a 23-fold increase in thermal conductivity was seen—the **highest increase in thermal conductivity by a material**. These composite materials have potential for use as thermal interface materials; for example, they are used in electronic devices to avoid overheating, by absorbing the heat generated.

Thinnest transistor A transistor is a device that opens or closes an electrical circuit, or amplifies a signal. On Feb. 19, 2012, scientists from the Centre for Quantum Computation & Communication Technology (AUS) unveiled a transistor less than 1 nanometer (0.000001 mm) high—the same height as one atom. The active element in this transistor is a single phosphorus (P) atom set within a silicon (Si) crystal. All elements of the device are fabricated on a single atomic plane, so the entire transistor is only one atomic layer in height. It is termed a "single atom transistor."

Highest projectile velocity Scientists at the Naval Research Laboratory in Washington, D.C., U.S.A., have used the Nike krypton fluoride laser to propel a sphere less than 12-thousandths of an inch (300 micrometers) in size to velocities in excess of 621 mi./s. (1,000 km/s). This figure is some 186 mi./s. (300 km/s) faster than previous attempts.

AIRY AEROGEL: Least Dense Solid Professor Gao Chao and his team from the Department of Polymer Science and Engineering at Zhejiang University in China have created graphene aerogel with a density of just 0.00009 oz./cu. in. The team freeze-dried solutions of carbon nanotubes and large sheets of graphene oxide, then chemically removed oxygen to leave a conductive, elastic, solid foam. Aerogel is lighter than air and has numerous applications, from mopping up oil spills to capturing dust from comet tails. The breakthrough was announced in *Nature* magazine on Feb. 27, 2013.

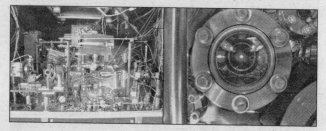

MOST ACCURATE CLOCK Researchers at the Joint Institute for Laboratory Astrophysics (JILA)—a project initiated by the University of Colorado and the U.S. National Institute of Standards and Technology—have used the element strontium to create an atomic clock that will neither gain nor lose a second in 4.5 billion years. The research was announced on Jan. 22, 2014. Because the SI definition of the second is based on the caesium atom, caesium clocks were previously regarded as the most accurate.

GLOSSARY

Caesium: An alkali metal element ($_{55}$Cs) that provides the basis of the SI unit of measurement for the second; one second equals 9,192,631,770 oscillations of a caesium atom with an atomic weight of 133 atomic units ($^{133}_{55}$Cs).

Carbon nanotube: An allotrope of carbon ($_8$C) in which the molecules are in the shape of a cylinder 50,000 times smaller than a human hair.

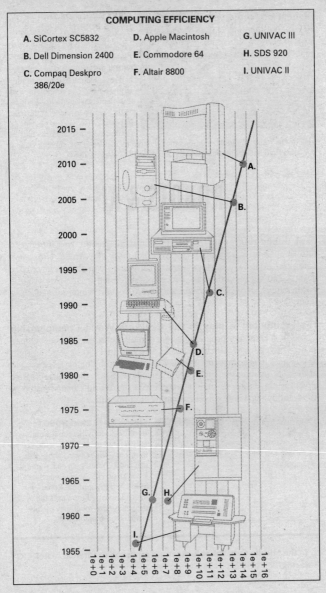

COMPUTING EFFICIENCY

A. SiCortex SC5832

B. Dell Dimension 2400

C. Compaq Deskpro 386/20e

D. Apple Macintosh

E. Commodore 64

F. Altair 8800

G. UNIVAC III

H. SDS 920

I. UNIVAC II

FIRST PROOF OF THE HIGGS BOSON On Mar. 14, 2013, it was confirmed that an experiment performed at the Large Hadron Collider (left) at CERN in Geneva, Switzerland, had revealed the existence of the Higgs boson. The confirmation of this elementary particle—known as the "God particle"—is the most important discovery in physics for decades. It strengthens the idea of the Standard Model, a unified theory about the nature of the universe that connects fundamental particles and the forces acting between them.

ROBOTS & AI

First public reference to robots The word "robot" was introduced into English by Karel Čapek (CZE) in his 1921 play *R.U.R.* (*Rossum's Universal Robots*). The story features "artificial people" who have been designed to enjoy hard work. The word, suggested by the playwright's brother Josef, derives from the Czech word *robota*, which means "slave labor."

First computer to play in the Checkers World Championship Chinook, a computer program designed to play checkers, was developed at the University of Alberta, Canada, in 1989. In 1990, it won the right to compete in the Checkers World Championship by being rated second in the U.S. nationals behind Marion Tinsley (U.S.A.), one of the greatest checkers players of all time. Chinook won the World Championship in 1994, following Tinsley's retirement due to ill health.

LIGHTEST FLYING ROBOT RoboBee is a flylike robot weighing only 0.0028 oz. (80 mg), with wafer-thin, 1-in.-wide (3-cm) wings that can flap 120 times per sec. Harvard University, U.S.A., published details of the first flight of the RoboBee in 2013, saying future uses for the penny-size robot may include artificial crop pollination.

In the Middle East, **robot jockeys** are replacing children in camel racing.

FIRST ROBOT TRUMPETER A bipedal robot made by Toyota (JPN) in 2004 mastered the embouchure (complex coordination of mouth, lips, and tongue) to play the trumpet. Fellow robots were constructed to play tuba and drums.

Most dexterous robot band Z-Machines
is a band created by engineers at the University of Tokyo, Japan, in 2013. As well as keyboardist Cosmo, the group consists of guitarist Mach (who boasts 78 "fingers") and drummer Ashura (who can play with 22 drumsticks). The group released their debut album, composed by the UK electronic music artist Squarepusher, in Apr. 2013.

Longest journey by an unmanned autonomous surface vehicle On Feb. 14, 2013,
"Benjamin Franklin" the Wave Glider®—developed by Liquid Robotics (U.S.A.)—finished a 7,939-nautical mile (14,703-km) journey across the Pacific Ocean from San Francisco in California, U.S.A., to Lady Musgrave Island in Queensland, Australia. It is one of four Wave Gliders; they convert wave energy into thrust and use solar energy to generate electricity for sensors, communications, and navigation.

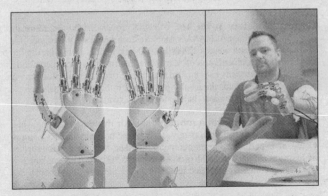

FIRST BIONIC HAND WITH REAL-TIME SENSORY FEEDBACK Dennis Aabo Sørensen (DNK) was the test subject for a prosthetic hand that was wired into his nerves. According to a report issued on Feb. 5, 2014 by École Polytechnique Fédérale de Lausanne in Switzerland, he was able to tell how hard he was grasping and to distinguish between objects, including their shape and softness.

NO ROBOT JOB TOO SMALL

Smallest robotic lunar rover: *Jade Rabbit* (CHN), 4 ft. 11 in. long, landed on Dec. 14, 2013.

Smallest robotic minesweeper: *RoboClam*, designed by Massachusetts Institute of Technology, U.S.A., based on Atlantic razor clam, burrows 0.39 in. per sec. and can dig to a mine to detonate it.

Smallest robotic tweezers: University of Toronto, Canada, developed tweezers that can sense how to move a 10-micrometer heart cell with the correct force.

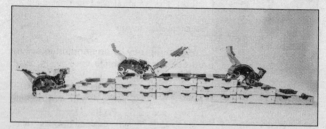

FIRST SELF-ORGANIZING ROBOT CONSTRUCTION SWARM TERMES robots are the size of a shoe and their design, by Harvard University, U.S.A., was inspired by termites. As reported on Feb. 14, 2014, TERMES robots are able to use blocks to construct towers, pyramids, and other structures. They require no centralized command, operating as a swarm to complete the task collectively.

Largest planetary rover The *Curiosity* rover landed on Mars on Aug. 6, 2012 as part of NASA's Mars Science Laboratory mission. It is 9 ft. (3 m) long and weighs 1,900 lb. (900 kg), including 176 lb. (80 kg) of scientific instruments. As of Mar. 2014, the rover had traveled almost 3 mi. (5 km). *Curiosity* uses an arm and "hand" to collect samples; having analyzed them, it sends the resulting data back to Earth. Scientists believe that its current location may have once been a riverbed.

First person to control a robot hand with the mind Matthew Nagle (U.S.A.), who had been paralyzed from the neck down, had a BrainGate—an experimental brain-computer interface—attached to the surface of his motor cortex in 2004 in Massachusetts, U.S.A. The implant was linked to a computer and used his brain waves to allow him to open and close a robotic hand.

Farthest distance by a quadruped robot BigDog, developed by Boston Dynamics (p. 457), is a four-legged robot designed to be a "pack mule" for soldiers. In Feb. 2009 it was announced that BigDog had walked 12.8 mi. (20.5 km) autonomously by following a GPS tracking system.

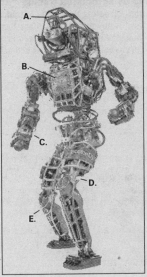

BOSTON DYNAMICS: RISE OF THE ROBOTS

Boston Dynamics (U.S.A.) is one of the world's most advanced robotics companies and was bought by Google in Dec. 2013. Their *Atlas* robot (left) is the **most agile humanoid robot**, able to run over rocky terrain and stay balanced when hit with a 20-lb. (9-kg) medicine ball (above left). Boston Dynamics' *WildCat* is the **fastest-running untethered, quadruped robot** (above right), running up to 16 mph (25 km/h) on flat terrain.

Materials are mostly aluminum, steel, and titanium—which helps in crash protection.

Atlas is 6 ft. 2 in. tall and has been designed to resemble a full-size adult with joints that facilitate near-human movement.

A. Head-mounted stereo cameras, sensors, and perception algorithms.

B. A computer on its chest checks sensors, controls actuators (devices that activate a mechanism or system), collects data, and can communicate with a remote user.

C. Wrist accessories can be swapped for different units by third-party manufacturers.

D. *Atlas* stays upright with the help of 28 hydraulically actuated joints, which allow it to crouch, kneel, and jump down.

E. Crumple-zone cages around limbs protect the sensors in case of collision.

GLOSSARY

Artificial narrow intelligence: Typically focused on a narrow task, such as playing chess or fulfilling requests, as Apple's Siri does in iOS.

Artificial general intelligence: Theory of humanlike intelligence, including the ability to display reason, strategy, planning, and make complex judgments.

Largest automated factory In 2011, Grupo Modelo (MEX) opened a fully automated bottling factory that uses robots and laser-guided trolleys to achieve production capabilities of 6,000 or 144,000 bottles per hr.

Deadliest anti-personnel robot South Korea deploys Super aEgis 2 robot sentries that can lock on to targets up to 1.8 mi. (3 km) away. They are deployed in the demilitarized zone between North and South Korea, picking off intruders on sight using heavy-duty machine guns and grenade launchers.

Largest stock market crash caused by automated trading "Algorithmic trading" refers to AI computers executing thousands of trades per sec. On May 6, 2010, the U.S. Dow Jones plunged by more than 600 points, with algorithmic trading thought to be to blame. The index recovered 20 min. later, leading to the event being nicknamed the "flash crash."

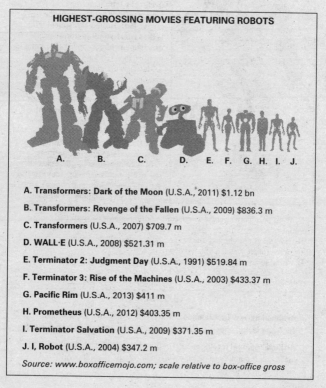

HIGHEST-GROSSING MOVIES FEATURING ROBOTS

A. **Transformers: Dark of the Moon** (U.S.A., 2011) $1.12 bn

B. **Transformers: Revenge of the Fallen** (U.S.A., 2009) $836.3 m

C. **Transformers** (U.S.A., 2007) $709.7 m

D. **WALL·E** (U.S.A., 2008) $521.31 m

E. **Terminator 2: Judgment Day** (U.S.A., 1991) $519.84 m

F. **Terminator 3: Rise of the Machines** (U.S.A., 2003) $433.37 m

G. **Pacific Rim** (U.S.A., 2013) $411 m

H. **Prometheus** (U.S.A., 2012) $403.35 m

I. **Terminator Salvation** (U.S.A., 2009) $371.35 m

J. **I, Robot** (U.S.A., 2004) $347.2 m

Source: www.boxofficemojo.com; scale relative to box-office gross

HELLO, WORLD: Machines Answer Back In 2011, IBM's *Watson* (top right) responded in real time to questions to record the **highest score by a computer on Jeopardy!** (U.S.A., 1964–present). Its $77,147 total beat the show's two human contestants. IBM also built *Deep Blue*, the **first computer to beat a world chess champion under regular time controls**, defeating Garry Kasparov (RUS) on May 11, 1997 (bottom right). Mike Dobson and David Gilday (both UK) built *CUBESTORMER 3* (above left), which achieved the **fastest time to solve a Rubik's Cube by a robot**, taking just 3.253 sec. on Mar. 15, 2014.

TOP TECH

First bluetooth gloves commercially available In Oct. 2012, Italian company hi-Fun released a range of knitted and leather gloves with built-in bluetooth communication for cell phones. Users can make calls by speaking into the glove's pinkie finger and listening via the thumb.

FASTEST TIME TO TYPE A TEXT MESSAGE BLINDFOLDED Mark Encarnación (U.S.A.) used a smartphone to type a specified text message in 25.9 sec. in Redmond, Washington, U.S.A., on Apr. 24, 2013. Without a blindfold, the **fastest time to type a text message on a smartphone** is 18.44 sec., achieved by Gaurav Sharma (U.S.A.), who was also in Redmond, on Jan. 16, 2014.

> **"Gadget":** may originate from French, *gâchette* ("lock tumbler") or *gagée* ("tool").

LARGEST LOOP-THE-LOOP BY A REMOTE-CONTROLLED VEHICLE

On Jun. 15, 2013, Jason Bradbury—host of *The Gadget Show* (Channel 5, UK) and pictured above with cohost Rachel Riley—guided a remote-controlled car in a 10-ft. 5-in.-wide (3.18-m) loop-the-loop. Other records from the show include the **heaviest machines moved using a brain-control interface** (in which cranes weighing 123,899 lb. (56.2 metric tons) were used to move a car with an electromagnet in 2011, bottom left) and the **largest architectural projection-mapped game** (a game of *PAC-Man* covering 23,881 sq. ft. (2,218.65 m²) played in London, UK, in 2013, bottom right).

REMOTE-CONTROL MODEL VEHICLES

Fastest speed by a jet-powered aircraft: 439.29 mph on Sep. 14, 2013, by a turbine-powered 4-ft. 3-in.-long plane built by Niels Herbrich (DEU).

Fastest speed by a battery-powered car: 171.95 mph on Dec. 19, 2012, by the R/C Bullet, designed, built, and driven by Nic Case (U.S.A.).

Longest ramp jump by a remote-control car: 121 ft. by a Carson Specter 6S, controlled by Thomas Strobel (DEU) on Jul. 30, 2011.

For cutting-edge science, turn to p. 449.

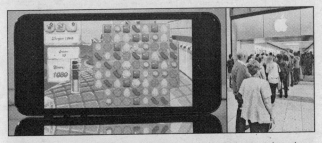

FASTEST-SELLING PORTABLE GAMING SYSTEM Apple reported opening-weekend sales of the iPhone 5c and 5s in Sep. 2013 of 9 million units, breaking its own record of 5 million for the iPhone 5 in 2012 and becoming the fastest-selling device capable of playing video games. Apple's sales were boosted by releasing two models instead of one, and for the first time debuting in China on the same day as the U.S.A.

MOST USED SMARTPHONE APP A global study of smartphone owners 16–64 years old (left) asked them to complete an online questionnaire that found 54% use Google Maps. The GlobalWebIndex data was published in Aug. 2013, showing users opened the app at least once in the previous month. In second place (44%) was the Facebook mobile app.

Highest power drawn from a fruit battery

Da Vinci Media (DEU), an educational TV channel, generated 1.21 watts by connecting 1,500 lemons together in Budapest, Hungary, on Apr. 27, 2013.

Largest animated cell-phone mosaic

At the inaugural China Smart Device Games—held at the National Olympic Sports Centre in Beijing on Jul. 13, 2013—China Unicom, Sohu IT, and HTC created an animated cell-phone mosaic using 400 smartphones. The devices were linked via China Unicom's WCDMA HSPA+ network; each screen showed a different video that, in combination with the others, formed a video ad.

Most consumer electronics recycled in 24 hours

Sims Recycling Solutions (U.S.A.) recycled electronics weighing a total of 126,344 lb. (57,308 kg) at seven locations in the U.S.A. and Canada on Apr. 20, 2013. The event, staged as part of Earth Day 2013, saw the company collecting unwanted electronics from locations in California, Hawaii, Illinois, Nevada, New Jersey, and Ontario.

FIRST SELFIE In Oct. 1839, Robert Cornelius (U.S.A.) took a self-portrait using the daguerreotype technique: a photographic process employing a polished silver plate that is afterward exposed to mercury vapor. He sat for the shot—which typically would need 3–15 min. to expose—in the backyard of his family's store in Philadelphia.

FIRST SELFIE IN SPACE On Jul. 18, 1966, *Gemini 10* launched with astronauts John Young and Michael Collins (both U.S.A.). A day later, while in orbit, Collins took this picture of himself sitting in the capsule.

FIRST SELFIE IN OPEN SPACE On Nov. 13, 1966, Edwin "Buzz" Aldrin, Jr. (U.S.A.) started the second of three spacewalks during the *Gemini 12* mission. During the 2-hr. 6-min. tethered walk in open space, he took photos of the visible star fields and of himself.

3D PRINTING

Fastest ultrahigh-resolution 3D printer Researchers have developed a printer that can make models the size of a grain of sand. The superfast nano printer at the Vienna University of Technology in Austria uses a liquid resin, which is hardened by a laser beam. The applications for the printer's nano models in the future include biomedical technology and nanotechnology.

Largest 3D object from a desktop 3D printer Skylar Tibbits, Marcelo Coelho (both U.S.A.), Natan Linder, and Yoav Reches (both ISL) used a desktop 3D printer to create "folded" items within a print chamber measuring 4.9 x 4.9 x 6.5 in. (12.4 x 12.4 x 16.5 cm). The 2013 project linked each part of the larger structure in a chain and the team created a chandelier approximately five times larger in volume than the printer's chamber.

Most 3D printers operating simultaneously Students of Dr. Jesse French (U.S.A.) in 2013 were required to make a 3D printer as part of their engineering course at LeTourneau University in Longview, Texas, U.S.A. A total of 102 undergraduates assembled with their printers on Apr. 4, 2014 and printed a special coin designed for the event.

First 3D-printed complete lower-jaw implant In Jun. 2011, an 83-year-old woman underwent surgery at the Orbis medical center in the Netherlands, during which she was implanted with a lower jaw "printed" from titanium powder fused together using a laser. It was created by Layer-Wise in collaboration with scientists at Hasselt University (both BEL).

FIRST 3D-PRINTED TITANIUM ALLOY BICYCLE FRAME
Empire Cycles (UK) designed a bike frame that was constructed by UK manufacturing firm Renishaw from titanium. The 3D laser melting process ensured that there was less waste, and made it easier to create a more organic form. The MX-6 Evo prototype frame of 2014 weighs 3 lb. (1.4 kg), making it 33% lighter than conventional frames.

NEED FOR 3D: Real Printing The **first 3D-printed football cleat shoes** (left) were tailored by Nike in 2013 for NFL footballers. Nike's Vapor Laser Talon boots have soles made by "selective laser sintering," in which lasers fuse small particles of plastic. The **first 3D-printed record** (above center) was made in 2013 by researcher Amanda Ghassaei (U.S.A.), who wrote code to transform audio files into 3D files. And Blizzident (ESP) produced the **first 3D-printed toothbrush** (right) in 2013, in which 400 bristles are mounted in a plastic mold made from scans of your mouth; you brush using a chewing motion.

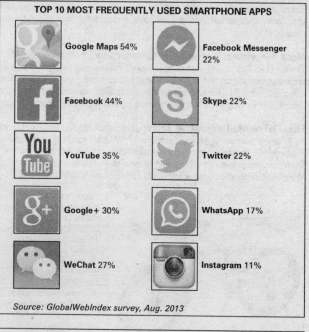

TOP 10 MOST FREQUENTLY USED SMARTPHONE APPS

Google Maps 54%

Facebook Messenger 22%

Facebook 44%

Skype 22%

YouTube 35%

Twitter 22%

Google+ 30%

WhatsApp 17%

WeChat 27%

Instagram 11%

Source: GlobalWebIndex survey, Aug. 2013

MOST MONEY PLEDGED FOR A KICKSTARTER 3D-PRINTER PROJECT
As of May 1, 2014, the Micro printer by M3D had attracted pledges of $3.15 m—toward an initial goal of $50,000—on the crowdsourcing website kickstarter.com. As 3D printing is becoming increasingly popular, it is used to create everything from plastic ornaments to whole houses, and the price of printers has been coming down. The Micro is aimed at the consumer market, with a cube-shape printer chamber measuring 7.3 in. (18.5 cm) on each side. It costs $299.

SPORTS

CONTENTS

On average, a tennis game lasts for two-and-a-half hours—of which the ball is in action for just **20 min**.

FACT: Serena's sister Venus shares a world record with Brenda Schultz-McCarthy (NLD) for the **fastest tennis serve (female)**—an incredible 129 mph.

MOST "POWERFUL" SPORTS STAR (FEMALE) The highest-ranked female athlete in Forbes' "most powerful" list is tennis player Serena Williams (U.S.A.). The list measures fame by taking into account celebrity earnings, exposure in print and on television, the strength of a star's Internet presence, public opinion, and marketability.

Serena also became the **first female athlete to win $50 million in prize money** when she won the U.S. Open at Flushing Meadows in New York, U.S.A., on Sep. 8, 2013. And on Oct. 27, 2013, at the age of 32 years 31 days, she became the **oldest female tennis player to be ranked world No. 1**.

What's more, she has enjoyed the **longest span of Grand Slam titles in the open era**, male or female. Her win over Victoria Azarenka at the U.S. Open on Sep. 8, 2013 came 13 years 362 days after her maiden Slam against Martina Hingis, in the same tournament, on Sep. 11, 1999.

FOOTBALL

NFL

Most seasons played George Blanda played for four different teams across 26 NFL seasons. He first played in 1949 and ended his career with the Oakland Raiders in 1967–75.

Most seasons played for the same team Jason Hanson spent 21 seasons (1992 to 2012) with the Detroit Lions.

Most games played Between 1982 and 2007, place kicker Morten Andersen (DNK) played in 382 games with the New Orleans Saints, Atlanta Falcons, New York Giants, Kansas City Chiefs, and Minnesota Vikings.

Andersen also scored records for the **most points** (2,544), **most successful field goals** (565), and **most attempted field goals** (709) in an NFL career.

Most consecutive games played Jeff Feagles appeared in 352 consecutive games between 1988 and 2009 while playing for the New England Patriots, Philadelphia Eagles, Arizona Cardinals, Seattle Seahawks, and New York Giants.

LONGEST NFL FIELD GOAL Denver Broncos' Matt Prater set the NFL field goal record by kicking a 64-yard goal in a game against the Tennessee Titans on Dec. 8, 2013. The previous mark of 63 yards was set by New Orleans Saints' Tom Dempsey in 1970 and had later been tied three times.

The 2013 Super Bowl was watched on TV by **164.1 million people**.

For soccer, see pp. 537–47.

MOST NFL CAREER INTERCEPTION RETURNS FOR TOUCHDOWN Rod Woodson scored 12 touchdowns after intercepting a pass during an NFL career played with the Pittsburgh Steelers, Baltimore Ravens, and Oakland Raiders from 1987 to 2003.

FIRST PLAYER TO RECORD 200 RECEIVING YARDS IN CONSECUTIVE NFL GAMES Josh Gordon of the Cleveland Browns recorded 237 receiving yards on Nov. 24, 2013, and then 267 receiving yards on Dec. 1, 2013. It marked the first time in NFL history that a player had logged consecutive 200-yard receiving games.

Most points by a player in a season San Diego Chargers' LaDainian Tomlinson scored 186 points in 2006. In the same year, the running back secured the **most touchdowns in a season**, with 31.

Most points by a team in a season Colorado's Denver Broncos scored 606 points during the 2013 season.

Most points in a game Ernie Nevers scored 40 points for the Chicago (now Arizona) Cardinals on Nov. 28, 1929. Also in 1929, Nevers racked up the **most touchdowns in an NFL game** (six), a feat matched by William "Dub" Jones in 1951 and Gale Sayers in 1965.

Most consecutive games scoring a touchdown Two footballers managed at least one touchdown in 18 consecutive games: Lenny Moore from 1963 to 1965 and LaDainian Tomlinson in 2004–05.

Most field goals in a season David Akers kicked 44 field goals in the 2011 season for the San Francisco 49ers. In the same year, he recorded the **most field goals attempted in a season** (52).

All players and teams U.S.A. unless otherwise stated.

LONGEST NFL TOUCHDOWN RUN BY A QUARTERBACK Terrelle Pryor of the Oakland Raiders ran for 93 yards before scoring a touchdown. The record run was set during an NFL (National Football League) game against the Pittsburgh Steelers on Oct. 27, 2013.

MOST TACKLES IN AN NFL GAME Luke Kuechly of the Carolina Panthers made 24 tackles in a game against the New Orleans Saints on Dec. 22, 2013, tying the single-game NFL record set by David Harris of the New York Jets, playing against the Washington Redskins, on Nov. 4, 2007.

Most yards rushing in a game On Nov. 4, 2007, Minnesota Vikings running back Adrian Peterson gained 296 yards rushing in a game. The 2007 season saw Peterson named NFL Offensive Rookie of the Year.

Most pass completions in a playoff game Drew Brees completed 40 passes for the New Orleans Saints in a playoff game against the San Francisco 49ers on Jan. 12, 2014.

Most career return touchdowns Devin Hester and Deion Sanders have achieved 19 return touchdowns each.

Most career receiving yards by a tight end Tony Gonzalez gained 15,127 receiving yards for the Kansas City Chiefs and the Atlanta Falcons from 1997 to 2013.

SUPER BOWL

Most games played Mike Lodish has played in six Super Bowl games: four for the Buffalo Bills in 1991–94 and two for the Denver Broncos in 1998–99.

Most points in a game Four players have scored 18 points in a Super Bowl game: Roger Craig in 1985; Jerry Rice twice, in 1990 and 1995; Ricky Watters in 1995; and Terrell Davis in 1998.

Most career touchdowns Jerry Rice racked up eight touchdowns in Super Bowl games, as well as the **most career NFL touchdowns** (208) in 1985–2004.

SUPER BOWL GAME RECORDS

Most yards gained passing	407	St. Louis Rams (2000)
Most yards gained rushing	280	Washington Redskins (1988)
Most yards gained by interceptions	172	Tampa Bay Buccaneers (2003)
Most rushing attempts	57	Pittsburgh Steelers (1975)
Most points	55	San Francisco 49ers (1990)
Largest margin of victory	45	San Francisco 49ers vs. Denver Broncos, 55–10 (1990)
Most passes completed	34	Denver Broncos (2014)
Most first downs	31	San Francisco 49ers (1985)
Most penalties	12	Dallas Cowboys (1978)
		Carolina Panthers (2004)
Most punts	11	New York Giants (2001)
Most kickoff returns	9	Denver Broncos (1990)
		Oakland Raiders (2003)
Most turnovers	9	Buffalo Bills (1993)
Most fumbles	8	Buffalo Bills (1993)
Most touchdowns	8	San Francisco 49ers (1990)
Most punt returns	6	Washington Redskins (1983)
		Green Bay Packers (1997)
Most interceptions	5	Tampa Bay Buccaneers (2003)
Most field goals	4	Green Bay Packers (1968)
		San Francisco 49ers (1982)

Correct as of Feb. 3, 2014

Most career field goals Adam Vinatieri scored seven field goals in Super Bowl games in 2001–06.

Most yards rushing in a game During Super Bowl XXII (1988), the Washington Redskins' Timmy Smith gained 204 yards rushing.

CFL

Most touchdown passes in a career Anthony Calvillo has thrown 455 touchdown passes in his CFL (Canadian Football League) career. He played for the Las Vegas Posse and Canada's Hamilton Tiger-Cats and Montreal Alouettes from 1994 to 2013.

Highest pass completion percentage in a season Ricky Ray completed 77.23% of his passes (234 of 303) for the Toronto Argonauts (CAN) in 2013.

Most career pass completions From 1994 to 2013, Anthony Calvillo set many CFL records, including 5,892 pass completions and the **most pass attempts in a career** (9,437).

Most yards rushing in a Grey Cup game The 101st CFL Grey Cup on Nov. 24, 2013 saw Kory Sheets run for 197 yards while leading the Saskatchewan Roughriders (CAN).

MOST NFL CAREER YARDS GAINED BY INTERCEPTION RETURN
Baltimore Ravens, Houston Texans, and New York Jets star Ed Reed accumulated 1,590 interception return yards from 2002 to 2013. He also recorded the **longest interception return for a touchdown**, with 107 yards while playing for the Ravens against the Philadelphia Eagles on Nov. 23, 2008. He broke his own record of 106 yards, set against the Cleveland Browns on Nov. 7, 2004.

PIG IN A BLANKET

American footballs were originally made from natural materials, most commonly a pig's bladder wrapped in leather.

TRACK & FIELD

Most IAAF Athlete of the Year trophies won Male: Usain Bolt (JAM) has won the International Association of Athletics Federations' (IAAF) Athlete of the Year trophy five times, in 2008–09 and 2011–13.

Female: The women's record belongs to Yelena Isinbayeva (RUS) with three wins, in 2004–05 and 2008.

DIAMOND LEAGUE

Youngest meeting winner Male: Conseslus Kipruto (KEN, b. Dec. 8, 1994) won the 3,000-m steeplechase Diamond League title in 2012 aged 17 years 225 days old.

Female: Francine Niyonsaba (BDI, b. May 5, 1993) is the youngest female winner, taking the 800-m crown on Sep. 7, 2012 at the age of 19 years 126 days.

***MOST MEDALS WON AT THE IAAF WORLD CHAMPIONSHIPS* Male:** The most medals accumulated by a man at the World Championships is 10, by Carl Lewis (left), who won eight gold, one silver, and one bronze between 1983 and 1993. His feat was equaled by Usain Bolt (right), who won eight gold and two silver medals between 2007 and 2013.

Female: Merlene Ottey (JAM) won 14 medals—three gold, four silver, and seven bronze—from 1983 to 1997.

LEAGUE OF THEIR OWN

The Diamond League was established in 2010, replacing the Golden League as the premier annual track & field competition.

If he could sustain his peak speed, it would take Usain Bolt **44 days** to sprint around the globe.

OUTDOOR TRACK EVENTS (MALE)

Event	Time	Name (Nationality)	Date
100 m	9.58	Usain Bolt (JAM)	Aug. 16, 2009
200 m	19.19	Usain Bolt (JAM)	Aug. 20, 2009
400 m	43.18	Michael Johnson (U.S.A.)	Aug. 26, 1999
800 m	1:40.91	David Lekuta Rudisha (KEN)	Aug. 9, 2012
1,000 m	2:11.96	Noah Ngeny (KEN)	Sep. 5, 1999
1,500 m	3:26.00	Hicham El Guerrouj (MAR)	Jul. 14, 1998
1 mile	3:43.13	Hicham El Guerrouj (MAR)	Jul. 7, 1999
2,000 m	4:44.79	Hicham El Guerrouj (MAR)	Sep. 7, 1999
3,000 m	7:20.67	Daniel Komen (KEN)	Sep. 1, 1996
5,000 m	12:37.35	Kenenisa Bekele (ETH)	May 31, 2004
10,000 m	26:17.53	Kenenisa Bekele (ETH)	Aug. 26, 2005
20,000 m	56:26.00	Haile Gebrselassie (ETH)	Jun. 27, 2007
25,000 m	1:12:25.4	Moses Cheruiyot Mosop (KEN)	Jun. 3, 2011
30,000 m	1:26:47.4	Moses Cheruiyot Mosop (KEN)	Jun. 3, 2011
3,000 m steeple-chase	7:53.63	Saif Saaeed Shaheen (QAT)	Sep. 3, 2004
110 m hurdles	12.80	Aries Merritt (U.S.A.)	Sep. 7, 2012
400 m hurdles	46.78	Kevin Young (U.S.A.)	Aug. 6, 1992
4 x 100 m relay	36.84	Jamaica	Aug. 11, 2012
4 x 200 m relay	1:18.68	Santa Monica Track Club (U.S.A.)	Apr. 17, 1994
4 x 400 m relay	2:54.29	U.S.A.	Aug. 22, 1993
4 x 800 m relay	7:02.43	Kenya	Aug. 25, 2006
4 x 1,500 m relay	14:36.23	Kenya	Sep. 4, 2009

MOST POINTS IN DIAMOND LEAGUE TRACK & FIELD MEETINGS
Female: The most points scored in a Diamond League career is 94, by Valerie Adams (NZ, left) in the shot put in 2010–13. An athlete scores points by finishing in the top three at a meeting.

Male: Renaud Lavillenie (see p. 476) has scored the most points for a man. By the end of the 2013 Diamond League season, he had 86 points.

Oldest meeting winner Male: Discus thrower Virgilijus Alekna (LTU, b. Feb. 13, 1972) was 39 years 175 days old when he won the London meet in 2011.

Female: Brigitte Foster-Hylton (JAM, b. Nov. 7, 1974) took the 100-m hurdles crown in Doha, Qatar, at the age of 37 years 187 days in 2012.

Most titles won A man and a woman have each won four Diamond Race titles. Renaud Lavillenie (FRA, p. 476) won the pole vault from 2010 to 2013 and Milcah Chemos Cheywa (KEN) won four 3,000-m steeplechase events between 2010 and 2013.

OLYMPICS

Most northerly Summer Games The XV Olympiad (1952) in Helsinki, Finland, was located at 60.1-degree latitude and 24.6-degree longitude. By contrast, the 1956 Summer Games in Melbourne, Australia, were the **most southerly**, at a 37.5-degree latitude and 144.6-degree longitude.

The **highest altitude Summer Games** were the 1968 Games in Mexico City, Mexico, at 7,380 ft. (2,250 m) above sea level.

Most track & field golds Male: Paavo Nurmi (FIN) won nine track & field golds in 1920–28. Carl Lewis (U.S.A.) matched his feat between 1984 and 1996.

Female: Six women have four golds to their name, the most recent being Sanya Richards-Ross (U.S.A.) and Allyson Felix, who added to their tallies in 2012.

OUTDOOR FIELD EVENTS (MALE)

Event	Meters	Name (Nationality)	Date
High jump	2.45	Javier Sotomayor (CUB)	Jul. 27, 1993
Pole vault	6.14	Sergey Bubka (UKR)	Jul. 31, 1994
Long jump	8.95	Mike Powell (U.S.A.)	Aug. 30, 1991
Triple jump	18.29	Jonathan Edwards (UK)	Aug. 7, 1995
Shot put	23.12	Randy Barnes (U.S.A.)	May 20, 1990
Discus	74.08	Jürgen Schult (GDR)	Jun. 6, 1986
Hammer	86.74	Yuriy Sedykh (USSR)	Aug. 30, 1986
Javelin	98.48	Jan Železný (CZE)	May 25, 1996
Event	**Points**	**Name (Nationality)**	**Date**
Decathlon	9,039	Ashton Eaton (U.S.A.)	Jun. 23, 2012

Statistics correct as of Mar. 12, 2014

HIGHEST INDOORS POLE VAULT (MALE) Renaud Lavillenie (FRA) achieved 20 ft. 2.5 in. (6.16 m) in the indoors pole vault at Pole Vault Stars in Donetsk, Ukraine, on Feb. 15, 2014. The previous record of 20 ft. 2.12 in. (6.15 m), set by pole vault legend Sergey Bubka, had stood for almost 21 years.

PARALYMPICS

Most track & field medals Male: Heinz Frei (CHE) competed in 14 Paralympic competitions between 1984 and 2012—both Winter and Summer Games. He won 22 track & field medals in total.

Female: Chantal Petitclerc (CAN) won 21 Paralympic track & field medals between 1992 and 2008 in distances between 100 m and 1,500 m.

Chantal also holds the record for the **most Paralympic track & field gold medals** (14), a record she shares with male athlete Franz Nietlispach (CHE).

SPRINTING HAT-TRICK Shelly-Ann Fraser-Pryce (JAM) became the **first woman to win three sprint golds at one World Championships** when she won the 100 m, 200 m, and 4 x 100 m relay at the 2013 IAAF event on Aug. 12–18. Maurice Greene (U.S.A.) was the **first athlete** to achieve the feat, doing so at the 1999 World Championships in the same three events.

OUTDOOR TRACK EVENTS (FEMALE)

Event	Time	Name (Nationality)	Date
100 m	10.49	Florence Griffith-Joyner (U.S.A.)	Jul. 16, 1988
200 m	21.34	Florence Griffith-Joyner (U.S.A.)	Sep. 29, 1988
400 m	47.60	Marita Koch (GDR)	Oct. 6, 1985
800 m	1:53.28	Jarmila Kratochvílová (TCH)	Jul. 26, 1983
1,000 m	2:28.98	Svetlana Masterkova (RUS)	Aug. 23, 1996
1,500 m	3:50.46	Yunxia Qu (CHN)	Sep. 11, 1993
1 mile	4:12.56	Svetlana Masterkova (RUS)	Aug. 14, 1996
2,000 m	5:25.36	Sonia O'Sullivan (IRL)	Jul. 8, 1994
3,000 m	8:06.11	Junxia Wang (CHN)	Sep. 13, 1993
5,000 m	14:11.15	Tirunesh Dibaba (ETH)	Jun. 6, 2008
10,000 m	29:31.78	Junxia Wang (CHN)	Sep. 8, 1993
20,000 m	1:05:26.6	Tegla Loroupe (KEN)	Sep. 3, 2000
25,000 m	1:27:05.9	Tegla Loroupe (KEN)	Sep. 21, 2002
30,000 m	1:45:50.0	Tegla Loroupe (KEN)	Jun. 6, 2003
3,000 m steeple-chase	8:58.81	Gulnara Samitova-Galkina (RUS)	Aug. 17, 2008
100 m hurdles	12.21	Yordanka Donkova (BGR)	Aug. 20, 1988
400 m hurdles	52.34	Yuliya Pechenkina (RUS)	Aug. 8, 2003
4 x 100 m relay	40.82	U.S.A.	Aug. 10, 2012
4 x 200 m relay	1:27.46	U.S.A. "Blue"	Apr. 29, 2000
4 x 400 m relay	3:15.17	USSR	Oct. 1, 1988
4 x 800 m relay	7:50.17	USSR	Aug. 5, 1984
4 x 1,500 m relay	17:09.75	Australia	Jun. 25, 2000

OUTDOOR FIELD EVENTS (FEMALE)

Event	Meters	Name (Nationality)	Date
High jump	2.09	Stefka Kostadinova (BGR)	Aug. 30, 1987
Pole vault	5.06	Yelena Isinbayeva (RUS)	Aug. 28, 2009
Long jump	7.52	Galina Chistyakova (USSR)	Jun. 11, 1988
Triple jump	15.50	Inessa Kravets (UKR)	Aug. 10, 1995
Shot put	22.63	Natalya Lisovskaya (USSR)	Jun. 7, 1987
Discus	76.80	Gabriele Reinsch (GDR)	Jul. 9, 1988
Hammer	79.42	Betty Heidler (DEU)	May 21, 2011
Javelin	72.28	Barbora Špotáková (CZE)	Sep. 13, 2008
Event	Points	Name (Nationality)	Date
Heptathlon	7,291	Jackie Joyner-Kersee (U.S.A.)	Sep. 24, 1988
Decathlon	8,358	Austra Skujytė (LTU)	Apr. 15, 2005

Statistics correct as of Mar. 12, 2014

IAAF WORLD CHAMPIONSHIPS

Most appearances Male: Spanish 50-km walker Jesús Ángel García competed in 11 IAAF World Championships between 1993 and 2013.

Female: Susana Feitór (POR) also appeared 11 times, contesting three different events between 1991 and 2011: the 10,000-m walk, 10-km walk, and 20-km walk.

Most gold medals Four athletes—three men and one woman—have won eight gold medals at the World Championships. Carl Lewis was the first in 1983–91, a feat matched by Michael Johnson (1991–99), Allyson Felix (all U.S.A., 2005–11), and Usain Bolt (JAM, 2009–13).

YOUNGEST WORLD CHAMPIONSHIPS RELAY MEDALIST
Female: Dina Asher-Smith (UK, b. Dec. 4, 1995) (left) won 4 x 100-m bronze at 17 years 247 days old in 2013.

Male: Darrel Brown (TTO, b. Oct. 11, 1984) was 16 years 305 days old when he won 4 x 100-m silver in 2001.

Most 200-m wins **Female:** Allyson Felix won three consecutive 200-m golds, in 2005–09.
Male: Usain Bolt matched her record in 2009–13.

Most consecutive 4 x 400-m relay wins LaShawn Merritt (U.S.A.) won gold in four World Championships in a row in 2007–13.

BALL SPORTS

Largest attendance for a netball match The Allphones Arena in Sydney, Australia, recorded an official attendance of 14,339 for the Australia vs. New Zealand international game on Nov. 13, 2004. Australia won 54–49.

Highest total score in a women's World Handball Championship final On Dec. 14, 2003, France and Hungary met in the World Championship final in Croatia. France won by 32 points to 29 for an aggregate score of 61.

Most World Polo Championships Argentina has won the World Championships four times since its inauguration in 1987, taking the crown in 1987, 1992, 1998, and 2011.

HIGHEST TEAM SCORE IN A NETBALL WORLD SERIES FINAL
New Zealand scored the most points in a final of netball's top competition, aka Netball Fast5, when they beat Australia on Nov. 10, 2013. The Ferns won by 29, with a final score of 56–27.

A brutal Mayan ball game played 3,000 years ago may have used **severed human heads**.

Career games	426	Michael Tuck (1972–91)
Consecutive games	244	Jim Stynes (1987–98)
Career goals	1,360	Tony Lockett (1983–2002)
Goals in a season	150	Bob Pratt (1934)
		Peter Hudson (1971)
Goals in a game	18	Fred Fanning (1947)

FIELD HOCKEY

Most World Cups Female: The Dutch women's team won the field hockey World Cup six times between 1974 and 2006.

Male: Pakistan holds the record for the most men's World Cup wins with four between 1971 and 1994.

Most international goals scored Defender Sohail Abbas (PAK) scored 348 goals between Mar 1, 1998 and Aug. 5, 2012.

Most wins of the men's African Cup for Nations The field hockey African Cup for Nations is a qualifier for the World Cup and in some years the Olympic Games. The greatest number of wins is seven, by South Africa between 1993 and 2013.

Largest margin of victory in an Olympic match Male: The third men's field hockey match at the 1932 Olympics in Los Angeles, California, U.S.A., saw India beat the home team 24–1.

Female: South Africa beat the U.S.A. 7–0 at London 2012 on Aug. 6.

MOST GOALS BY AN INDIVIDUAL IN THE EURO HOCKEY LEAGUE The top scorer in the Euro Hockey League (field hockey's top competition) is Jeroen Hertzberger (NLD). The striker notched up 32 goals for HC Rotterdam between Oct. 27, 2007 and Oct. 25, 2013.

FACT: In 1363, hockey was banned in England by King Edward III, along with soccer and other "idle games."

Career games	408	Lui Passaglia (1976–2000)
Consecutive games	353	Bob Cameron (1980–2000)
Career touchdowns	147	Milt Stegall (1992–2008)
Touchdowns (season)	23	Milt Stegall (2002)
Touchdowns (game)	6	.Eddie James (1932)
		Bob McNamara (1956)

GAA

Most All-Ireland Hurling championships won The GAA (Gaelic Athletic Association) sport of hurling is a fast-moving Irish stick-and-ball sport (not unlike a free-form version of hockey). Kilkenny won its top competition—contested by intercounty teams—34 times between 1904 and 2012.

LARGEST WINNING MARGIN IN A MEN'S WORLD HANDBALL CHAMPIONSHIP FINAL The biggest score difference in an International Handball Federation men's World Championship final is 16 goals. It was achieved by Spain, who beat Denmark 35–19 in the 2013 final at the Palau Sant Jordi stadium in Barcelona, Spain, on Jan. 27. Pictured is pivot Julen Aguinagalde (ESP, left) vying with Denmark's left back Mikkel Hansen.

> **FACT:** A type of handball was played by the ancient Greeks in Homer's _Odyssey_, using a ball made of purple wool.

Most All-Ireland Senior Camogie championships Camogie is hurling, but played by women. Dublin has the greatest number of All-Ireland titles with 26.

Most All-Ireland Gaelic Football championships Gaelic football is roughly a cross between rugby and soccer. Kerry has won 36 championships—more than any other side.

KORFBALL

Highest score in a mixed World Championship final Korfball is a mixed-gender sport similar to netball and basketball. The final on Nov. 5, 2011 saw the Netherlands score 32 points against Belgium in Shaoxing, China.

Most Europa Cup titles Dutch team PKC won the Europa Cup seven times, in 1985, 1990, 1999–2000, 2002, 2006, and 2014.

The Dutch national team have the **most World Games titles** (8) having won every korfball tournament at the World Games between 1985 and 2013.

MOST ALL-IRELAND HURLING CHAMPIONSHIPS WON (INDIVIDUAL) Henry Shefflin (IRL) secured nine medals—and countless battle scars—while playing for Kilkenny in 2000, 2002–03, 2006–09, 2011, and 2012. One of the game's greats, Waterford-born Shefflin (nicknamed "King Henry") is a center forward—and works as a bank official when not winning trophies.

MOST POINTS SCORED IN A LACROSSE SEASON The highest points tally accumulated in a single Major League Lacrosse season is 72, by Paul Rabil (U.S.A.) while playing for the Boston Cannons in the 2012 season.

LACROSSE

Most men's World Championship titles Between 1967 and 2010, the men's U.S.A. team won nine World Lacrosse Championship titles. The U.S.A. also holds the record for **most women's Lacrosse World Cup titles**, with seven golds between 1982 and 2013.

Fastest shot Mike Sawyer (U.S.A.) recorded 114 mph (183 km/h) in Charlotte, North Carolina, U.S.A., on Jul. 13, 2013.

VOLLEYBALL

Most men's FIVB Volleyball World League titles The Fédération Internationale de Volleyball World League is an annual event in which teams compete in pools before the best sides progress to the final round. The most men's World League wins is nine, by Brazil in 1993, 2001, 2003–07, and 2009–10.

MOST TOURNAMENT TITLES IN WOMEN'S BEACH VOLLEYBALL Kerri Walsh Jennings (U.S.A.) has the most tournament wins with 113. This total comprises 67 domestic and 46 international wins from May 2001 to Oct. 28, 2013. Walsh Jennings has won 113 (60%) of the 189 tournaments she has entered, mostly alongside Misty May-Treanor (U.S.A.), whose record she broke on Oct. 28, 2013.

MOST WOMEN'S VOLLEYBALL WORLD GRAND CHAMPIONS CUPS Brazil became the first women's team to win the FIVB World Grand Champions Cup twice when they triumphed in Tokyo, Japan, on Nov. 17, 2013. The first five editions were won by different countries; Brazil had previously won it in 2005.

Most FIVB Volleyball World League participants (men) In 2013, 18 countries from four continents took part in the FIVB Volleyball World League. Russia was the eventual winner, seeing off Brazil 3-0 in the final.

Most appearances by a pair in men's FIVB beach volleyball events Norwegian duo Vegard Høidalen and Jørre Kjemperud recorded 135 appearances in FIVB beach volleyball events between 1987 and 2010.

BASEBALL

Most combined wins and saves Andy Pettitte (U.S.A.) and Mariano Rivera (PAN) combined for a win and a save 72 times while pitching for the New York Yankees from 1996 to 2013.

Oldest player to hit a walk-off home run A walk-off home run is a game-ending homer on the final pitch of the game that results in a victory for the home team. At 42 years 202 days old, Jason Giambi (U.S.A., b. Jan. 8, 1971) is the oldest player in MLB history to perform such a feat. Giambi accomplished the record with a pinch-hit homer in the ninth inning to defeat the Chicago White Sox on Jul. 29, 2013.

Most doubles hit in a season Earl Webb (U.S.A.) hit 67 doubles playing for the Boston Red Sox in 1931. The **most triples hit in a season by an individual player** is 36, by "Chief" Wilson (U.S.A.) for the Pittsburgh Pirates in 1912.

To improve grip for pitchers, every MLB baseball is rubbed in **mud from a secret site** in New Jersey.

Most grand slam home runs in a MLB career A grand slam home run is a homer hit with batters on all the bases. Since 1994, Alex Rodriguez has hit 24 of them for the Seattle Mariners, Texas Rangers, and New York Yankees.

MOST SAVES IN A CAREER The MLB record for most career saves is 652, achieved by Mariano "Sandman" Rivera (PAN) playing for 19 seasons with the New York Yankees from 1995—when he made his MLB debut—to his retirement in 2013. New York mayor Michael Bloomberg declared Sep. 22, 2013 "Mariano Rivera Day" in his honor.

THE LAST 42 IN HISTORY

Rivera was the last baseball player to wear a number 42 shirt in baseball history. The shirt was retired across the major leagues on Apr. 15, 1997 in memory of baseball legend Jackie Robinson of MLB's Brooklyn Dodgers.

MOST GAMES . . .

Finished in a career Playing for the New York Yankees between 1995 and 2013, Mariano Rivera (PAN) was the last pitcher for his team in 952 games. With the Yankees, he also recorded the **most games pitched with one team**: 1,115.

Won consecutively by a pitcher Masahiro Tanaka (JPN) won 30 successive games pitching for Japan's Tohoku Rakuten Golden Eagles from Aug. 26, 2012 to Oct. 27, 2013.

Tanaka also recorded the **most consecutive baseball games won by a pitcher during regular-season play** (28), again for the Tohoku Rakuten Golden Eagles, from Aug. 26, 2012 to Oct. 8, 2013. For the same team, Tanaka registered the **most consecutive baseball games won by a pitcher in a season** (24), from Apr. 2 to Oct. 8, 2013.

Won consecutively by a pitcher in the MLB Roger Clemens (U.S.A.) won 20 consecutive games for the Toronto Blue Jays and New York Yankees from Jun. 3, 1998 to Jun. 1, 1999.

MAJOR LEAGUE BASEBALL (MLB) WORLD SERIES RECORDS

Team		
Most titles (first awarded in 1903)	27	New York Yankees
Most consecutive titles	5	New York Yankees, 1949–53
Largest cumulative attendance	420,784	Six games between Los Angeles Dodgers and Chicago White Sox, Oct. 1–8, 1959; Dodgers won 4–2
Individual		
Most home runs, one series	5	Chase Utley (U.S.A.) of Philadelphia Phillies, 2009 World Series against New York Yankees
		"Reggie" Jackson (U.S.A.) of New York Yankees, 1977 World Series against Los Angeles Dodgers
Most games pitched	24	Mariano Rivera (PAN) of New York Yankees, 1996, 1998–2001, 2003, 2009
Most MVP (Most Valuable Player) awards	2	Sanford "Sandy" Koufax (U.S.A.), 1963, 1965
		Robert "Bob" Gibson (U.S.A.), 1964, 1967
		"Reggie" Jackson (U.S.A.), 1973, 1977

Statistics correct as of the end of the 2013 season

MOST CONSECUTIVE BASEBALL CROWD SELLOUTS The longest home sellout streak in major pro sports history (i.e., Major League Baseball, the National Basketball Association, the National Football League, and the National Hockey League) lasted 820 games. The Boston Red Sox set it with every home game at Fenway Park in Boston, U.S.A., from May 15, 2003 to Apr. 10, 2013.

MOST HOME RUNS . . .

By a catcher Mike Piazza (U.S.A.) hit 396 home runs (with an overall total of 427) while playing for the Los Angeles Dodgers, Florida Marlins, New York Mets, San Diego Padres, and Oakland Athletics from 1992 to 2007.

By a switch hitter Playing for the New York Yankees from 1951 to 1968, Mickey Mantle (U.S.A.) hit 536 home runs.

MOST HOME RUNS IN A CAREER BY A DESIGNATED HITTER David Ortiz (DOM) has hit 381 career home runs—a Major League Baseball (MLB) record for a designated hitter—from an overall total of 431 home runs, playing for the Minnesota Twins and the Boston Red Sox since 1997. His 47 home runs for the Red Sox in 2006 represent the **most home runs by a designated hitter in a season**. His overall home run total was 54.

FIRST FATHER-AND-SON HOME RUNS IN SEQUENTIAL AT BATS Ken Griffey and his son Ken, Jr. (U.S.A.) hit back-to-back home runs for the Seattle Mariners on Sep. 14, 1990. They also became the **first father-son duo to play on the same team at the same time**, on Aug. 31, 1990.

By a second baseman Jeff Kent (U.S.A.) scored 351 home runs as a second baseman (with an overall total of 377) with the Toronto Blue Jays, New York Mets, Cleveland Indians, San Francisco Giants, Houston Astros, and LA Dodgers from 1992 to 2008.

The **most home runs in one season hit by a third baseman** stands at 52 (with an overall total that season of 54), scored by Alex Rodriguez (U.S.A.) for the New York Yankees in 2007.

YOUNGEST PLAYER TO HIT 30 HOME RUNS AND STEAL 30 BASES IN A SEASON At the age of 21 years 53 days, Mike Trout (U.S.A., b. Aug. 7, 1991, above left) became the youngest MLB player ever to hit 30 or more home runs and steal 30 or more bases within just one season. He accomplished this feat while playing for the Los Angeles Angels of Anaheim in 2013. Before Trout, the youngest person to do this had been 22-year-old Alex Rodriguez, while playing for the Seattle Mariners in 1998.

FIRST SIBLINGS TO HIT HOME RUNS IN SUCCESSIVE AT BATS On Apr. 23, 2013, B. J. Upton and his brother Justin (U.S.A., left) struck back-to-back home runs for the Atlanta Braves against the Colorado Rockies, becoming only the second pair of siblings to do so. The first were Lloyd and Paul Waner (U.S.A.) of the Pittsburgh Pirates, who hit successive homers on Sep. 15, 1938. The Uptons' feat marked the 27th time in MLB history that brothers had homered in the same game.

MOST STRIKEOUTS . . .

By a batter in a postseason Alfonso Soriano (DOM) struck out 26 times in 17 games while playing for the New York Yankees in the 2003 postseason.

By a pitching staff in a postseason series Detroit Tigers pitchers struck out 73 Boston Red Sox batters over the course of the six-game American League Championship Series in 2013.

By a batter in a season The MLB record for most strikeouts by a batter in a season is 223, by Mark Reynolds (U.S.A.) for the Arizona Diamondbacks in 2009. In doing so, he surpassed his own mark of 204, established in 2008.

By a pitcher in a career Nolan Ryan (U.S.A.) recorded 5,714 strikeouts while playing for the New York Mets, California Angels, Houston Astros, and Texas Rangers from 1966 to 1993.

By a team in a season Houston Astros (U.S.A.) batters struck out 1,535 times during the 2013 season, surpassing the previous mark of 1,529 by the Arizona Diamondbacks in 2010.

By batters in a postseason (team) Boston Red Sox (U.S.A.) batters struck out 165 times in 16 playoff games during the 2013 postseason.

Across all teams in a season Major league batters struck out 36,710 times in the 2013 regular season.

MOST STRIKEOUTS BY A PITCHING STAFF IN A SEASON Detroit Tigers pitchers struck out 1,428 batters during the 2013 season. Their achievement surpasses the previous record of 1,404 by the Chicago Cubs' pitching staff in 2003.

BASKETBALL

NBA

Most career minutes During Kareem Abdul-Jabbar's 20-year NBA pro career, he spent 57,446 min. on court for the Milwaukee Bucks and the Los Angeles Lakers (1969–89)—that's almost 40 days!

First players to win an NBA and Olympic title in one year In 1992, Michael Jordan and Scottie Pippen won the NBA finals playing with the Chicago Bulls, then won an Olympic basketball gold as part of the U.S.A. team.

Most consecutive games played A. C. Green played in 1,192 consecutive games for the Los Angeles Lakers, Phoenix Suns, Dallas Mavericks, and Miami Heat from Nov. 19, 1986 to Apr. 18, 2001.

Youngest player to reach 9,000 rebounds Dwight Howard (b. Dec. 8, 1985) had recorded 9,000 rebounds at just 27 years 130 days old. He took the record while playing for the Los Angeles Lakers in a game against the Houston Rockets on Apr. 17, 2013.

Oldest player to record 20 rebounds in a game On Mar. 2, 2007, at the age of 40 years 251 days, Dikembe Mutombo (COD, b. Jun. 25, 1966)

of the Houston Rockets became the oldest player in NBA history to get more than 20 rebounds in a game, with 22.

MOST POINTS SCORED IN AN NBA CAREER Kareem Abdul-Jabbar scored 38,387 points (at an average of 24.6 points per game) in his regular-season career from 1969 to 1989. He also scored 5,762 points in playoff games, which ranks second to 5,987 by Michael Jordan from 1984 to 1998.

The late "Chick" Hearn is credited with coining the phrase **"slam dunk."**

FEWEST TURNOVERS IN AN NBA GAME The Oklahoma City Thunder committed just two turnovers against the Los Angeles Lakers on Mar. 5, 2013, equaling the mark set by the Milwaukee Bucks in 2006 and Cleveland Cavaliers in 2009.

The **fewest turnovers in an NBA Finals game** is four, by the Detroit Pistons on Jun. 16, 2005 and San Antonio Spurs on Jun. 6, 2013.

Most free throws attempted in a game Dwight Howard equaled his own record of 39 while playing for the Los Angeles Lakers on Mar. 12, 2013.

Most three-pointers in a season Stephen Curry accumulated 272 three-point field goals while playing for the Golden State Warriors during the 2012–13 season, surpassing the 269 recorded by Ray Allen in 2005–06.

As of Apr. 16, 2014, Allen still holds the record for the **most three-point field goals in a career**, with 2,973 sunk since 1996. Allen joined Miami Heat in 2012.

All players and teams U.S.A. unless otherwise stated.

NBA & WNBA—CAREER RECORDS

Individual	NBA		WNBA	
Most points	Kareem Abdul-Jabbar (1969–89)	38,387	Tina Thompson (1997–present)	7,488
Most rebounds	Wilt Chamberlain (1959–73)	23,924	Lisa Leslie (1997–2009)	3,307
Most field goals made	Kareem Abdul-Jabbar (1969–89)	15,837	Tina Thompson (1997–present)	2,630
Most assists	John Stockton (1984–2003)	15,806	Ticha Penicheiro (PRT, 1998–2012)	2,599
Most free throws made	Karl Malone (1985–2004)	9,787	Tamika Catchings (2002–present)	1,709
Most blocks	Hakeem Olajuwon (NGA, 1984–2002)	3,830	Margo Dydek (POL, 1998–2008)	877
Most steals	John Stockton (1984–2003)	3,265	Tamika Catchings (2002–present)	930
Team	NBA		WNBA	
Most Championship titles	Boston Celtics (1957, 1959–66, 1968–69, 1974, 1976, 1981, 1984, 1986, and 2008)	17	Houston Comets (1997–2000)	4
Most Finals appearances	Los Angeles Lakers (1949–50, 1952–54, 1959, 1962–63, 1965–66, 1968–70, 1972–73, 1980, 1982–85, 1987–89, 1991, 2000–02, 2004, and 2008–10)	31	Houston Comets (1997–2000)	4
			Detroit Shock (2003, and 2006–08)	
			New York Liberty (1997, 1999, 2000, and 2002)	

Correct as of Feb. 12, 2014

Most consecutive games scoring a three-pointer Kyle Korver's run of scoring a three-pointer per game hit 127, ending on Mar. 5, 2014. It began on Nov. 4, 2012, and beat Dana Barros' 89-game record on Dec. 6, 2013.

Most three-pointers in a game Kobe Bryant (Los Angeles Lakers) and Donyell Marshall (Toronto Raptors) each scored 12 three-pointers, on Jan. 7, 2003 and Mar. 13, 2005 respectively.

The **most three-pointers in a game by a team** is 23, a record shared by the Orlando Magic (Jan. 13, 2009) and the Houston Rockets (Feb. 5, 2013).

MOST THREE-POINTERS IN AN NBA FINALS
Danny Green scored 27 three-point field goals in the 2013 NBA Finals. Green was playing for the San Antonio Spurs against Miami Heat in the Finals, which lasted seven games. He beat Ray Allen's 22 with the Boston Celtics in 2008.

LONGEST BASKETBALL SHOT On Nov. 11, 2013, Corey "Thunder" Law of the Harlem Globetrotters threw a basketball 109 ft. 9 in. (33.45 m) into the net. His record-breaking basket occurred at the U.S. Airways Center in Phoenix, Arizona, U.S.A., in celebration of GWR Day 2013. Three fellow Globetrotters gave it their best shot, but they fell short of Law's length.

Most three-pointers in a quarter Joe Johnson scored eight three-pointers for the Brooklyn Nets on Dec. 16, 2013, equaling Michael Redd's 2002 record.

WNBA

Most games in a career As of Dec. 20, 2013, Tina Thompson had played in 496 Women's National Basketball Association (WNBA) games. Her career began in 1997 with the Houston Comets; she has since played with the Los Angeles Sparks and is currently with Seattle Storm.

Thompson has also clocked up the **most minutes played in a WNBA career**, with 16,088—the equivalent of more than 11 days on court.

Most free throws attempted in a game Two women have attempted 24 free throws in a game: Cynthia Cooper did so on Jul. 3, 1998, and Tina Charles followed suit on Jun. 29, 2013.

Highest rebounds per game average Tina Charles—playing for the Connecticut Sun since 2010—also holds the record for rebounds per game: an unrivaled average of 10.8.

Most three-pointers in a career Katie Smith had scored 906 three-pointers as of Feb. 12, 2014, since her career began in 1999. Smith has played for five teams: Minnesota Lynx, Detroit Shock, Washington Mystics, Seattle Storm, and New York Liberty.

On Sep. 8, 2013, Riquna Williams scored the **most three-pointers in a game**, with eight for the Tulsa Shock. Williams equaled the mark set twice by Diana Taurasi for Phoenix Mercury, on Aug. 10, 2006 and May 25, 2010.

Largest half-time lead Connecticut Sun led New York Liberty by a massive 34 points (61–27) at half-time on Jun. 15, 2012. The Suns went on to win the match with a comfortable 97–55 victory. Their half-time lead bested Seattle Storm's 33-point margin against Tulsa Shock on Aug. 7, 2010.

MOST GAMES IN AN NBA CAREER Robert Parish played 1,611 NBA (National Basketball Association) regular-season games from 1976 to 1997. His 21-season career saw him play for the Golden State Warriors (1976–80), Boston Celtics (1980–94), Charlotte Hornets (1994–96), and Chicago Bulls (1996–97).

MOST FREE THROWS IN A WNBA CAREER
As of Feb. 12, 2014, Tamika Catchings had made 1,709 free throws in Women's National Basketball Association (WNBA) games. Catchings—who has played for the Indiana Fever since 2002—also holds the record for **most steals in a WNBA career,** with 930.

MOST THREE-POINTERS ATTEMPTED BY A TEAM IN AN NBA SEASON The New York Knicks attempted 2,371 three-point field goals during the 2012/13 season, 891 of which were successful—the **most three-pointers scored in a season.** The Knicks also hold the record for the **longest postseason losing streak,** with 13 consecutive playoff games lost from 2001 to 2012.

FACT: The NBA three-point line is 23 ft. 9 in. from the middle of the basket, while the WNBA line is 22 ft. 1.75 in. from the top of the key.

MOST WINS OF DEFENSIVE PLAYER OF THE YEAR Two players have been named NBA Defensive Player of the Year four times, as of the end of the 2014 season. Dikembe Mutombo (COD) won for the Denver Nuggets, Atlanta Hawks, and Philadelphia 76ers between 1994 and 2001, and Ben Wallace (above center) was awarded the title for the Detroit Pistons between 2001 and 2006.

COMBAT SPORTS

BOXING

Most world title fights Julio César Chávez (MEX) won 31 of his 37 fights contested between 1984 and 2000 in the super featherweight, lightweight, and light welterweight divisions.

Most flash KOs in a pro career Mike Tyson (U.S.A.) managed nine under-60-sec. knockouts during his career.

Shortest world title fight Just 17 sec. was all it took for Daniel Jiménez (PRI) to knock out Harold Geier. Jiménez was defending his WBO super bantamweight title at Wiener Neustadt in Austria on Sep. 3, 1994.

HIGHEST-SELLING PAY-PER-VIEW BOXING MATCH The junior middleweight fight between Saúl "El Canelo" Álvarez (MEX, left) and Floyd Mayweather Jr. (U.S.A., right) on Sep. 14, 2013 grossed $150 m from 2.2 million TV viewers. In addition, the venue in Las Vegas, Nevada, U.S.A., sold out and another $20 m was taken in gate receipts.

Size matters: There are **no weight divisions** in pro sumo wrestling.

BOXING WINS—OLDEST AND YOUNGEST

Record	Age	Boxer	Title (date)
Oldest . . .			
World champion (male)	48 years 53 days	Bernard Hopkins (U.S.A., b. Jan. 15, 1965)	IBF light heavyweight (Mar. 9, 2013)
World champion (female)	46 years 61 days	Alicia Ashley (U.S.A./JAM, b. Aug. 23, 1967)	WBC super bantamweight (Oct. 23, 2013)
Youngest . . .			
World champion (male)	17 years 176 days	Wilfred Benítez (U.S.A., b. Sep. 12, 1958)	WBA light welterweight (Mar. 6, 1976)
World champion (female)	18 years 342 days	Ju Hee Kim (KOR, b. Jan. 13, 1986)	IFBA light flyweight (Dec. 19, 2004)

Correct as of Jan. 23, 2014

MOST SIBLINGS TO WIN WORLD BOXING TITLES As of Aug. 1, 2013, brothers Kōki, Daiki, and Tomoki Kameda (JPN) had each won a world boxing title. Tomoki won the WBO bantamweight title, Kōki secured the WBA bantamweight crown, and Daiki started the brothers' success by winning the WBA flyweight title.

WRESTLING

Most freestyle wrestling world titles (male) Two men have won seven freestyle wrestling world titles: Aleksandr Medved (BLR) in the over-100-kg class between 1962 and 1971, and Valentin Jordanov (BGR) in the 55-kg class between 1983 and 1995.

Heaviest living athlete Sumo wrestler Emmanuel "Manny" Yarborough of Rahway, New Jersey, U.S.A., stands 6 ft. 8 in. (203 cm) tall and weighs 704 lb. (319.3 kg).

Most arm wrestling matches in 24 hours On Feb. 12, 2012, world champion Ion Oncescu (ROM) contested 1,024 arm wrestles in Bucharest, Romania. He won every match.

FENCING

Most individual world fencing titles **Male:** Christian d'Oriola (FRA) won six foil titles in World Championships and Olympics between 1947 and 1956. Russian Stanislav Pozdnyakov matched this feat with six saber wins from 1996 to 2007.

Female: Valentina Vezzali (ITA) won nine individual foil titles: three Olympic golds and six at the World Fencing Championships. She won the titles in 1999–2011.

Most golds at the World Championships (country) In 2013, Italy became the first nation to win more than 100 golds at the Fencing World Championships. As of the end of 2013, their tally stood at 101 gold, 97 silver, and 114 bronze medals.

MOST CAREER MATCHES WON BY A SUMO WRESTLER Kaiō Hiroyuki (JPN) won 1,047 (of 1,731) bouts between Mar. 1988 and Jul. 2011. Remarkably, Kaiō initially doubted if he was good enough to make it as a sumo wrestler.

MARTIAL ARTS

Most World Taekwondo Championships wins Male: Steven López (U.S.A.) won five Championships: lightweight in 2001 and four welterweights in 2003–09.

Female: Jung Myung-suk's (KOR) three heavyweight wins came in 1993–97, a feat equaled by Brigitte Yagüe (ESP), who won finweight in 2003 and flyweight in 2007 and 2009.

Most single-leg martial arts kicks in one minute Raul Meza (U.S.A.) performed 335 single-leg kicks at Meza's Karate America in Sioux Falls, South Dakota, U.S.A., on Nov. 17, 2011.

Most men's team kumite World Karate Championships wins The first World Karate Championships were held in 1970. Since then, the French men's team have won the kumite title seven times, in 1972, 1994, 1996, 1998, 2000, 2004, and 2012.

MOST SIBLINGS TO WIN GOLD AT A TAEKWONDO CHAMPIONSHIPS The López family (U.S.A.) won three gold medals at the World Taekwondo Championships in Madrid, Spain, in Apr. 2005. Steven won the welterweight title, younger brother Mark the featherweight crown, and sister Diana took featherweight gold. Their coach was dad Jean.

MOST WORLD JUDO CHAMPIONSHIPS WINS Male: Teddy Riner (FRA) has won six titles—five at heavyweight (over-100 kg) in 2007, 2009–11, and 2013, and one with the French men's team in 2011.

Female: Ryoko Tani (JPN) won seven titles in the under-48-kg category in 1993–2007.

For more strength, turn to p. 210.

UFC

Most fights won by decision Georges St-Pierre (CAN) won 12 Ultimate Fighting Championship (UFC) fights by decision from Apr. 16, 2005 to Nov. 16, 2013. St-Pierre also holds the record for the **most UFC wins—19**—from Jan. 31, 2004 to Nov. 16, 2013.

Most fights won by KO Anderson "The Spider" Silva (BRA) secured 20 knockout wins between 2000 and 2012. Silva also has the **most consecutive UFC wins—17**—in 2006–12.

Shortest average contest time The shortest average UFC contest time is 2 min. 20 sec., achieved by Drew McFedries (U.S.A.) in 17 fights from Sep. 8, 2001 to Jan. 25, 2013.

Tallest UFC fighter Stefan "Skyscraper" Struve (NLD), who competes as a heavyweight in the UFC, measures 6 ft. 11 in. (211 cm); he also reportedly has a phenomenal 7-ft. (2.13-m) reach.

LONGEST TOTAL FIGHT TIME IN A UFC CAREER The longest overall time spent in the octagon (the eight-side enclosure where Ultimate Fighting Championship bouts take place) is 5 hr. 28 min. 21 sec., achieved by Georges St-Pierre (CAN) between Jan. 25, 2002 and Nov. 16, 2013. Pictured is St-Pierre (left)—fighting Jake Shields—on his way to successfully defending the welterweight title on Apr. 30, 2011.

> **FACT:** The only rules for the freestyle combat sport of pankration (recorded in the Olympic Games of 648 B.C.) were no biting and no eye gouging.

CRICKET

Most Champions League Twenty20 wins The annual Champions League Twenty20 (T20) is contested by leading domestic teams from seven countries. Mumbai Indians (IND) are the only team to have won the title twice. Their first win came on Oct. 9, 2011, and most recently they claimed a 33-run win against Rajasthan Royals (IND) in Delhi, India, on Oct. 6, 2013.

Highest single-day Test match attendance A crowd of 91,092 people packed out the Melbourne Cricket Ground in Australia on day one of the fourth Ashes Test between Australia and England on Dec. 26, 2013.

Longest cricket ban In Sep. 2013, Indian bowler Shanthakumaran Sreesanth was handed a lifetime ban from cricket. He was found guilty of "spot-fixing," or fixing the game, in the Indian Premier League match between Rajasthan Royals and Kings XI Punjab on May 9, 2013.

Fastest delivery of a cricket ball Shoaib Akhtar (PAK) bowled a ball at 100.23 mph (161.3 km/h) on Feb. 22, 2003, during a World Cup match against England in Cape Town, South Africa.

Most wins of a domestic first-class cricket competition New South Wales won Australia's Sheffield Shield 45 times between 1895–96 and 2007–08.

With ca. 3 billion fans, cricket is the world's **second most popular sport**.

FIRST MULTI-FORMAT SERIES IN INTERNATIONAL CRICKET A Test match, three Twenty20 Internationals, and three One-Day Internationals determined the winner of the multi-format women's Ashes series between England and Australia in Aug. 2013. Captained by Charlotte Edwards, hosts England clinched the series by 12 points to 4 and regained the Ashes crown that they had lost on Australian soil in 2011.

RUNS, WICKETS, AND CATCHES

Test matches (men)

Most runs	15,921	Sachin Tendulkar (IND), 1989–2013
Most wickets	800	Muttiah Muralitharan (LKA), 1992–2010
Most catches	210	Rahul Dravid (IND), 1996–2012

Test matches (women)

Most runs	1,935	Janette Brittin (ENG), 1979–98
Most wickets	77	Mary Duggan (ENG), 1949–63
Most catches	25	Carole Hodges (ENG), 1984–92

One-Day Internationals (men)

Most runs	18,426	Sachin Tendulkar (IND), 1989–2012
Most wickets	534	Muttiah Muralitharan (LKA), 1993–2011
Most catches	201	Mahela Jayawardene (LKA), 1998–2013

One-Day Internationals (women)

Most runs	5,432	Charlotte Edwards (ENG), 1997–2014
Most wickets	180	Cathryn Fitzpatrick (AUS), 1993–2007
Most catches	50	Jhulan Goswami (IND), 2002–14

Source: www.espncricinfo.com, as of Feb. 4, 2014
(catches excluding wicket keepers)

MOST WICKETS IN A T20 INTERNATIONAL CAREER (FEMALE) Spin bowler Anisa Mohammed (TTO) is the leading wicket taker in women's Twenty20 Internationals. As of Mar. 9, 2014, she had claimed 74 wickets in 59 matches playing for the West Indies, at an average of 13.68 runs conceded per wicket.

WICKETS

Most wickets without conceding a run in a women's ODI Two women have taken three wickets without conceding a run in an ODI (One-Day International). Olivia Magno (AUS) snapped up three tail-end wickets in 1.4 overs on Dec. 14, 1997, a feat matched by England's Arran Brindle in two maiden overs in Mumbai, India, on Feb. 5, 2013.

RUNS

Highest Test match 10th-wicket partnership Australians Ashton Agar (98) and Phillip Hughes (81 not out), batting at 11 and 6 respectively, made 163 runs in 31.1 overs in the 2013 Ashes at Trent Bridge in the UK on Jul. 11.

Most runs in a T20 match Chris Gayle (JAM) finished on 175 not out—the highest score by a player in any professional T20 innings—for Royal Challengers Bangalore in the Indian Premier League on Apr. 23, 2013. Gayle hit 100 runs in 30 balls—the **fastest T20 century**—and 13 fours and 17 sixes, the **most T20 runs scored in boundaries** (154).

MOST RUNS BY A NO. 11 BATSMAN IN A TEST MATCH INNINGS Test match debutant Ashton Agar (AUS) rewrote the record books when he scored 98 runs in the opening Test of the 2013 Ashes series against England at Trent Bridge in Nottingham, UK, on Jul. 11. Agar's astonishing 101-ball knock featured 12 fours and two sixes and rescued Australia from a perilous 117 for 9.

FACT: Cricketers batting in positions 8 to 11 are known as the lower order or "tail."

For sports architecture, see pp. 443–48.

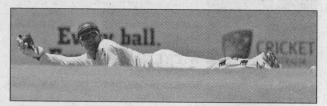

MOST CATCHES BY A WICKET KEEPER IN A TEST SERIES Australia gloveman Brad Haddin broke a 30-year-old Test record when he claimed 29 catches in the 2013 Ashes series between hosts England and Australia—despite his team losing the five-match series 3–0. Haddin pouched the record on Aug. 25, 2013—day five of the fifth Test—from another Australian wicket keeper, Rod Marsh, who took 28 catches in five Test matches in 1982–83.

MOST RUNS SCORED BY A PLAYER IN A T20 INTERNATIONAL The highest individual score in a Twenty20 International is 156 runs, by Australian Aaron Finch against England at the Ageas Bowl in Southampton, UK, on Aug. 29, 2013. Opening batsman Finch hit 14 sixes in his 63-ball innings to guide Australia to a formidable 248 for 6.

Fastest international century Corey Anderson (NZ) hit a century from just 36 balls in an ODI against the West Indies on Jan. 1, 2014. Anderson struck 14 sixes and six fours in an unbeaten 131 from 47 balls.

Highest match aggregate in a T20 International England made 209 for 6 in reply to Australia's 248 for 6 at the Ageas Bowl in Hampshire, UK, on Aug. 29, 2013, for a match aggregate of 457 runs.

THE CENTURION OF CRICKET

Sachin Tendulkar's career totals (1989–2013)	
Most centuries in internationals	100
Most centuries in Test matches	51
Most centuries in One-Day Internationals	49
Most international centuries scored in a partnership (career)—with Sourav Ganguly (IND)	38

Source: www.espncricinfo.com

SIXES

Highest aggregate in a Test match series In the five-match 2013–14 Ashes series between Australia and England, 65 sixes were recorded. Australia, who won the series 5–0, contributed 40 maximums—the **most sixes by one team in a Test match series**. Chief contributions came from Aussies Brad Haddin (nine) and George Bailey (eight), with six each from Shane Watson (AUS), Ian Bell, and Stuart Broad (both ENG).

Bailey hit three of his sixes in one over during the third Test in Perth on Dec. 16, 2013, when he equaled the 28-run record for the **most runs scored off an over in a Test match**. West Indies batsman Brian Lara had achieved the feat on Dec. 14, 2003.

Most in an ODI Rohit Sharma (IND) hit 16 sixes in Bangalore, India, on Nov. 2, 2013. Opening batsman Sharma made 209—the second highest score in ODI history—off 158 balls.

Most in a Test match innings Wasim Akram (PAK) scored 12 sixes in an innings of 257 not out against Zimbabwe in Sheikhupura, Pakistan, on Oct. 19–20, 1996.

Most in an IPL career At the conclusion of the 2013 Indian Premier League tournament on May 26, 2013, Chris Gayle (JAM) had scored a total of 180 maximums in his five-season career (2009–13).

Most by a team in a T20 International The Netherlands struck 19 sixes in a World T20 group match against Ireland at Sylhet Stadium, Bangladesh, on Mar. 21, 2014, reaching their target of 190 with 37 balls to spare to progress to the Super 10 stage of the tournament.

MOST SIXES BY A PLAYER IN A T20 INNINGS Jamaican cricketer Chris Gayle cleared the boundary 17 times on his way to a Twenty20 record of 175 not out. His set of sixes came in the record breaking Indian Premier League match on Apr. 23, 2013 (see p. 503).

MOST TEST MATCHES PLAYED Batsman Sachin Tendulkar (IND)—known by his fans as the "God of Cricket"—retired on Nov. 16, 2013 after a 24-year career, but not before playing a record 200th Test, against the West Indies at Mumbai's Wankhede Stadium. Tendulkar has 20 Guinness World Records titles to his credit, the highlights of which are listed in the tables on p. 504.

CYCLING

Greatest distance cycled in 12 hours Marko Baloh (SVN) cycled 295.31 mi. (475.26 km) solo and unpaced in 12 hr. at the Montichiari Velodrome in Brescia, Italy, on Oct. 8, 2010. He completed 1,901 full laps of the 820-ft. (250-m) course in the allotted time.

Baloh continued his solo, unpaced cycling for another 12 hr. and went on to achieve the **greatest distance cycled in 24 hours** with 561.57 mi. (903.76 km), or 3,615 full laps.

Largest cycling race The 2004 Cape Argus Pick n Pay Cycle Tour held in Cape Town, South Africa, on Mar. 14, 2004 began with 42,614 entrants, 31,219 of whom finished the race.

Most riders to finish a Grand Tour The greatest number of cyclists to complete an edition of a Grand Tour is 175, during the 2012 Vuelta a España (Tour of Spain) from Aug. 18 to Sep. 9, 2012.

Fastest 4-km pursuit (women) The Great Britain team consisting of Katie Archibald, Elinor Barker, Danielle King, and Joanna Rowsell completed the 4-km team pursuit in 4 min. 16.552 sec. to win gold at the Union Cycliste Internationale (UCI) Track Cycling World Cup in Aguascalientes, Mexico, on Dec. 5, 2013.

OLDEST OLYMPIC ROAD CYCLING GOLD MEDALIST
When Kristin Armstrong (U.S.A., b. Aug. 11, 1973) successfully defended her time trial title at the 2012 Games in London, UK, on Aug. 1, she became the oldest road cycling winner. At the age of 38 years 356 days, Kristin rode the 18-mi. (29-km) course in 37 min. 34.82 sec.

MOST OLYMPIC CYCLING MEDALS WON (FEMALE)
Leontien Zijlaard-van Moorsel (NLD) won six Olympic cycling medals including four golds. Her medals were won at Sydney 2000 and Athens 2004.

Most **bicycles are "right-handed"**: the chain is typically located on the right of the frame.

TRACK CYCLING–ABSOLUTE

Men	Start	Time/Distance	Name & Nationality	Place	Date
200 m	flying	9.347	François Pervis (FRA)	Aguascalientes, Mexico	Dec. 6, 2013
500 m	flying	24.758	Chris Hoy (UK)	La Paz, Bolivia	May 13, 2007
1 km	standing	56.303	François Pervis (FRA)	Aguascalientes, Mexico	Dec. 7, 2013
4 km	standing	4:10.534	Jack Bobridge (AUS)	Sydney, Australia	Feb. 2, 2011
Team 4 km	standing	3:51.659	Great Britain (Steven Burke, Ed Clancy, Peter Kennaugh, and Geraint Thomas)	London, UK	Aug. 3, 2012
1 hour	standing	49.7 km	Ondřej Sosenka (CZE)	Moscow, Russia	Jul. 19, 2005
Women	**Start**	**Time/Distance**	**Name & Nationality**	**Place**	**Date**
200 m	flying	10.384	Kristina Vogel (DEU)	Aguascalientes, Mexico	Dec. 7, 2013
500 m	flying	29.481	Olga Streltsova (RUS)	Moscow, Russia	May 29, 2011
3 km	standing	3:22.269	Sarah Hammer (U.S.A.)	Aguascalientes, Mexico	May 11, 2010
1 hour	standing	46.065 km	Leontien Zijlaard-van Moorsel (NLD)	Mexico City, Mexico	Oct. 1, 2003

Statistics correct as of Dec. 7, 2013

MOST UCI TRIALS WORLD CHAMPIONSHIPS WON Male: Benito Ros Charral (ESP) won nine elite men's UCI Trials World Championships, in 2003–05 and 2007–12.

Female: Karin Moor (CHE) won the women's title nine times between 2001 and 2011.

OLYMPICS

Most cycling medals The greatest number of Olympic cycling medals won by an individual is seven, by Bradley Wiggins and Chris Hoy (both UK). Wiggins won four gold, one silver, and two bronze medals in 2000–12. Hoy's seven came from six golds and one silver, also between 2000 and 2012.

Chris Hoy's six golds give him the record for the **most Olympic track cycling gold medals**. He picked up gold in the 1-km time trial at Athens 2004, the individual sprint, team sprint, and Keirin at Beijing 2008, and the team sprint and Keirin at London 2012.

Most cycling gold medals won at one Olympic Games On Aug. 5, 1904, at the Olympic Games in St. Louis, U.S.A., Marcus Hurley (U.S.A.) won four gold medals, in the quarter mile, third mile, half mile, and 1 mile events.

Most medals won at both Summer and Winter Olympics (female) Canadian athlete Clara Hughes won a total of six medals across both Summer and Winter Games. She won two bronze medals in cycling events at the 1996 Summer Games in Atlanta, U.S.A., before switching to speed skating. In this new discipline, Hughes won a bronze medal at the 2002 Winter Olympics in Salt Lake City, U.S.A., a gold and silver medal at the 2006 Games in Turin, Italy, and another bronze medal at the 2010 Winter Olympics in Vancouver, Canada.

First to win the Tour de France and Olympic gold in the same year Bradley Wiggins capped a memorable summer for British cycling when he eased to victory in the men's time trial in 50 min. 39 sec. at the London Olympics on Aug. 1, 2012—just 10 days after becoming the first Brit to win the Tour de France.

TOUR DE FRANCE

Longest In 1926, the Tour de France totaled 3,569 mi. (5,745 km) and was won by Lucien Buysse (BEL).

MOST PODIUM FINISHES IN THE TOUR DE FRANCE Raymond Poulidor (FRA) finished in the top three of the Tour de France eight times. He came second on three occasions (1964, 1965, and 1974) and third five times (1962, 1966, 1969, 1972, and 1976).

FACT: Prior to Horner's victory, the oldest Grand Tour winner was Firmin Lambot (BEL), who won the Tour de France in 1922 at 36 years old.

OLDEST PERSON TO WIN A CYCLING GRAND TOUR Chris Horner (U.S.A., b. Oct. 23, 1971) won the 2013 Vuelta a España at the age of 41 years 327 days in Madrid, Spain, on Sep. 15, 2013. He also became the **oldest winner of a stage in a Grand Tour** when he took stage 10 of the race at the age of 41 years 314 days in Alto de Hazallanas, Spain, on Sep. 2, 2013.

FIRST PERSON TO WIN THE CYCLING TRIPLE CROWN The inaugural winner of cycling's Triple Crown was Eddy Merckx (BEL), who won the Tour de France, Giro d'Italia, and UCI Road World Cycling Championships in 1974. The only other person to achieve this feat was Stephen Roche (IRL) in 1987.

MOST WORLD CHAMPIONSHIPS IN CYCLO-CROSS (FEMALE) Marianne Vos (NLD) has won six cyclo-cross World Championships, in 2006 and consecutively in 2009–13. The championships began in 2000. She also won Olympic gold in different cycling events at the Beijing and London games.

Most wins Four riders have won the Tour five times: Jacques Anquetil (FRA) in 1957 and 1961–64; Eddy Merckx (BEL) in 1969–72 and 1974; Bernard Hinault (FRA) in 1978–79, 1981–82, and 1985; and Miguel Indurain (ESP) in 1991–95. With 34 victories, Merckx also enjoyed the **most Tour de France stage wins**, between 1969 and 1978.

Closest In the 1989 Tour de France, after 2,030 mi. (3,267 km) ridden over a period of 23 days (July 1–23), Greg LeMond (U.S.A.) finished the race in 87 hr. 38 min. 35 sec., beating Laurent Fignon (FRA) by only 8 sec.

Largest attendance at a sporting event The most spectators at any sporting event is an estimated 12 million people over a three-week period for the 2012 Tour de France. The Tour took place in Belgium, Switzerland, and France from Jun. 30 to Jul. 22. The organizers estimate that 80% of spectators were French and that 70% were men.

BMX

Most World Championships won
Male: The most UCI BMX World Championships won by an individual is three, by Kyle Bennett (U.S.A.) in 2002–03 and 2007.

Female: Two women have won three titles: Gabriela Diaz (ARG) in 2001–02 and 2004, and Shanaze Reade (UK) in 2007–08 and 2010.

MOST UCI MOUNTAIN BIKE MARATHON WORLD CHAMPIONSHIPS
Christoph Sauser (CHE) has won the UCI Mountain Bike Marathon World Championships a total of three times, in 2007, 2011, and 2013.

A bit too slow? Try Motor Sports, p. 528.

Most Olympic medals BMX was first incorporated into the Olympics in 2008. Since then, only one rider has won two medals. Māris Štrombergs (LVA) won the individual men's event in 2008 and 2012.

GOLF

Longest golf hole The seventh hole (par 7) of the Satsuki gold course in Sano, Japan, measures 964 yd. (881 m) long.

Longest hole in one in a PGA Tour event On Jan. 25, 2001, Andrew Magee (U.S.A.) shot a 332-yd. (303-m) hole in one on the 17th hole (par 4) in the first round of the Phoenix Open at TPC of Scottsdale in Arizona, U.S.A.

The **longest hole in one in the U.S. Masters** is 213 yd. (194 m), by Jeff Sluman (U.S.A.) at the par-3 fourth hole at Augusta National Golf Club in Georgia, U.S.A., on Apr. 9, 1992.

Most consecutive PGA Tour titles won Byron Nelson (U.S.A.) won 11 PGA Tour titles in a row in 1945. The run, commonly referred to as "The Streak," was part of the 18 Tour titles that Nelson won in the same year. He turned professional in 1932 and retired from full-time golf in the 1946 season, by which time he had amassed a career total of 52 PGA titles.

LONGEST HOLE IN ONE IN THE RYDER CUP
Paul Casey (UK, left) holed a 213-yd. (194-m) drive at the 14th hole (par 3) at the K Club in Straffan, County Kildare, Ireland, on Sep. 23, 2006. Incredibly, the feat was repeated by Scott Verplank (U.S.A.) the next day at the same hole on the final day of the tournament. The Ryder Cup is contested every two years between the U.S.A. and Europe.

The word **"caddy"** comes from the French *cadet*, meaning junior or student.

Most PGA Player of the Year awards The greatest number of PGA Player of the Year awards won by an individual golfer is 11, by Tiger Woods (U.S.A.) in 1997, 1999–2003, 2005–07, 2009, and 2013. Inaugurated in 1948, this award is based on a points system, including variables such as wins, top 10 finishes, performances in major tournaments, and scoring average. Woods has almost twice as many awards as his nearest rival, Tom Watson (U.S.A.), who won the award on six occasions.

LOWEST ROUNDS

Lowest single-round score (18 holes) in the U.S. Masters Two players have each recorded a single-round score of 63 at the U.S. Masters, which is played at the Augusta National Golf Club. They are Nick Price (ZWE) in 1986 and Greg Norman (AUS) in 1996.

Lowest score at the British Open Eight players have played a round of 63 at the British Open golf championships: Mark Hayes (U.S.A.) at Turnberry, South Ayrshire, in 1977; Isao Aoki (JPN) at Muirfield, East Lothian, in 1980; Greg Norman (AUS) at Turnberry in 1986; Paul Broadhurst (UK) at St. Andrews, Fife, in 1990; Jodie Mudd (U.S.A.) at Royal Birkdale, Southport, in 1991; Nick Faldo (UK) and Payne Stewart (U.S.A.), both at Royal St. George's, Sandwich, in 1993; and Rory McIlroy (UK) at St. Andrews in 2010.

LOWEST SCORE BELOW PAR AFTER 54 HOLES IN A PGA TOUR EVENT
Patrick Reed (U.S.A.) scored 27 under par after 54 holes during the 2014 Humana Challenge on the PGA West course in La Quinta, California, U.S.A., on Jan. 16–18. Reed received a congratulatory call afterward from former U.S. President Bill Clinton. The tournament is held in partnership with the Clinton Foundation.

> **FACT:** The 2014 Humana Challenge had a total prize purse of $5.7 m, with $1.026 m going to Patrick Reed for winning the event.

Lowest score under par in a pro golf tournament (single round)
Richard Wallis (UK) shot 59 at the PGA Southern Open Championship
OOM Pro-Am on the par-73 course at The Drift Golf Club, East Horsley,
Surrey, UK, on Jun. 2, 2013. This represents a score of 14 under par.

Lowest below-age score Two golfers have had a score of 17 below
their ages. James D. Morton (U.S.A.) hit a 72 at Valleybrook Golf and
Country Club, Hixson, Tennessee, U.S.A., on Apr. 21, 2001, at 89 years
old, and Keith Plowman (NZ) hit 72 at Maungakiekie Golf Club, Auck-

land, New Zealand, also at 89
years old, on Nov. 20, 2007.

***HIGHEST ANNUAL EARNINGS
FROM GOLF*** Released in 2013,
Forbes' Celebrity 100 list ranked
Tiger Woods (U.S.A.) as both
the highest-earning golfer and
the **highest-earning athlete**. His
earnings for 2012–13 came to an
estimated $78 m.

MOST WINS AND LOWEST SCORES (72 HOLES)

British Open		
Most wins	6	Harry Vardon (UK)
Lowest total score	267	Greg Norman (AUS), 1993
U.S. Open		
Most wins	4	Willie Anderson (U.S.A.)
		Bobby Jones Jr. (U.S.A.)
		Ben Hogan (U.S.A.)
		Jack Nicklaus (U.S.A.)
Lowest total score	268	Rory McIlroy (UK), 2011
U.S. PGA		
Most wins	5	Walter Hagen (U.S.A.)
		Jack Nicklaus (U.S.A.)
Lowest total score	265	David Toms (U.S.A.), 2001
U.S. Masters		
Most wins	6	Jack Nicklaus (U.S.A.)
Lowest total score	270	Tiger Woods (U.S.A.), 2007

Statistics correct as of Feb. 24, 2014

YOUNGEST AND OLDEST

Youngest golfer to make the cut at the U.S. Masters At the age of 14 years 171 days, Guan Tianlang (CHN, b. Oct. 25, 1998) made the cut with 4 over par after 18 holes at the 77th U.S. Masters on Apr. 13, 2013. The tournament was staged at Augusta National Golf Club in Georgia, U.S.A.

Guan had already become the **youngest golfer to play at the U.S. Masters** when he teed off at the same tournament two days beforehand, at 14 years 169 days old. His final score was 300 (73, 75, 77, 75).

Youngest golfer to score their age Tsugio Uemoto (JPN, b. Jul. 3, 1928) scored 68 at the Higashi Hiroshima Country Club, Hiroshima, Japan, on Oct. 22, 1996.

The **oldest player to score their age** is C. Arthur Thompson (CAN, 1869–1975), who scored 103 on the 6,215-yd. (5,682-m) Uplands Golf Club course in Victoria, British Columbia, Canada, in 1973.

MOST APPEARANCES BY A PAIR IN THE RYDER CUP The most frequent pairing in Ryder Cup history is that of Spaniards Severiano "Seve" Ballesteros (far right) and José María Olazábal (near right), who played together 15 times for Europe in foursomes and four-ball from 1987 to 1993. The duo ended with an overall record of 11 wins, 2 draws, and 2 losses.

MOST LPGA PLAYER OF THE YEAR AWARDS Sweden's Annika Sörenstam has won a total of eight Ladies Professional Golfers' Association (LPGA) Player of the Year awards. Her victories came in 1995, 1997–98, and 2001–05.

SOLHEIM CUP

The female equivalent of the Ryder Cup is the Solheim Cup, held every two years since 1990. The U.S.A. has won eight times to Europe's five.

FIRST WINNER OF THE FEDEX CUP AND RACE TO DUBAI IN ONE YEAR
Henrik Stenson (SWE) won the U.S. Professional Golfers' Association (PGA) Tour's FedEx Cup (right) on Sep. 22, 2013, and the PGA European Tour's Race to Dubai (left) on Nov. 17, 2013. The scale of his achievement is indicated by the fact that no player has even won both tours in *different* years before.

MOST CONSECUTIVE GOLF MAJORS WON IN A SINGLE YEAR (FEMALE)
Mildred Ella "Babe" Didrikson Zaharias (U.S.A., left) won three successive majors in 1950, a feat matched by Inbee Park (KOR, right) in 2013. Their three wins also represent the **most majors won in a year (female)**, a record shared with Mary "Mickey" Wright (U.S.A., 1961) and Pat Bradley (U.S.A., 1986).

Youngest Ryder Cup captain Arnold Palmer (U.S.A.) was 34 years 31 days old when he captained the U.S. Ryder Cup team at East Lake Golf Club in Atlanta, Georgia, U.S.A., in 1963.

The **oldest Ryder Cup captain** is Tom Watson (U.S.A., b. Sep. 4, 1949), who was selected on Dec. 13, 2012, at the age of 63 years 100 days, to lead the U.S. team. The 2014 Ryder Cup at Gleneagles in Scotland, UK, begins on Sep. 26, 2014, at which point Watson will be 65 years 22 days old.

Youngest golfer to play in the Ryder Cup Sergio García (ESP, b. Jan. 9, 1980) competed for Europe in the Ryder Cup in 1999, at 19 years 229 days old.

The **oldest golfer to play in the Ryder Cup** is Raymond Floyd (U.S.A., b. Sep. 4, 1942), who competed in the 1993 tournament at 51 years 20 days old. Floyd retired from professional golf in 2010, but Tom Watson recruited him as a vice-captain for his 2014 Ryder Cup team.

Oldest golfer to score a hole in one Switzerland's Otto Bucher (b. May 12, 1885) hit a hole in one on the 130-yd. (119-m) 12th hole at La Manga in Spain on Jan. 13, 1985, at the age of 99 years 244 days.

Oldest golf club president Jack Miles (UK, b. Mar. 10, 1913), the president of Wimbledon Common Golf Club, celebrated his 101st birthday in 2014. Jack has been an active playing member of the club since 1947.

ICE HOCKEY

Most wins in an NHL season The Detroit Red Wings (U.S.A.) won 62 times in the 1995/96 NHL season.

Most assists in an NHL season Wayne Gretzky (CAN) carried out 163 assists playing for the Edmonton Oilers during the 1985/86 NHL season.

Gretzky also recorded the **most assists in an NHL career**, with 1,963 for the Edmonton Oilers, Los Angeles Kings, St. Louis Blues, and New York Rangers from 1979 to 1999.

Most penalty minutes in an NHL game Playing for the Los Angeles Kings in a game against the Philadelphia Flyers on Mar. 11, 1979, Canadian Randy Holt racked up 67 penalty minutes.

The player with the **most penalty minutes in NHL history**, however, is Dave "Tiger" Williams (CAN), with 3,966 in 17 seasons between 1974 and 1988, playing for the Toronto Maple Leafs, Vancouver Canucks, Detroit Red Wings, Los Angeles Kings, and Hartford Whalers.

HIGHEST SAVE PERCENTAGE BY A GOALKEEPER IN AN NHL SEASON Craig Anderson (U.S.A.) recorded a .941 save percentage while playing for the Ottawa Senators during the 2012/13 season, surpassing the previous mark of .940 set by Brian Elliott (CAN) of the St. Louis Blues in 2011–12.

Pucks used to be made from **frozen cow dung**.

MOST NHL CAREER POINTS Wayne Gretzky (CAN) scored a remarkable 2,857 points for the Edmonton Oilers, Los Angeles Kings, St. Louis Blues, and New York Rangers between 1979 and 1999. This total comprises 894 goals and 1,963 assists in 1,487 games. In addition to these regular-season goals and 122 Stanley Cup goals, Gretzky scored 56 goals in the World Hockey Association (WHA) in 1978–79.

MOST INDIVIDUAL WINS OF THE STANLEY CUP Henri Richard (CAN) won the Stanley Cup 11 times with the Montreal Canadiens from 1956 to 1975. The shorter sibling of legendary right winger Maurice "The Rocket" Richard, Henri was nicknamed "The Pocket Rocket."

Fastest coach to reach 200 NHL wins Pittsburgh Penguins' 3–1 win over the Ottawa Senators on Apr. 22, 2013 gave Dan Bylsma (U.S.A.) his 200th win from 316 games coached.

Longest undefeated run by an NHL team From Oct. 14, 1979 to Jan. 6, 1980, the U.S.A.'s Philadelphia Flyers had an unbeaten run of 35 games, with 25 wins and 10 ties. (For the **longest NHL winning streak**, see the table on p. 520.)

Most career games in professional ice hockey Canadian right winger Gordon "Gordie" Howe (b. Mar 31, 1928) featured in 2,421 professional games over 26 seasons from 1946 to 1980, including NHL and WHA (World Hockey Association) games.

When Howe retired in 1980, he was 52 years old, an age that made him the **oldest player in NHL history**.

Most consecutive NHL games played Doug Jarvis (CAN) played 964 games for the Montreal Canadiens, Washington Capitals, and Hartford Whalers from Oct. 1975 to Oct. 1987.

Most consecutive games played by an NHL defenseman Jay Bouwmeester (CAN) had featured in 635 consecutive NHL regular-season games as of the end of the 2012/13 season. Chris Chelios (U.S.A.) played the **most career regular-season games by an NHL defenseman**, with 1,651 for various teams from 1983 to 2010.

Most shootout wins by an NHL goalkeeper Henrik Lundqvist (SWE) achieved 44 shootout wins while playing for the New York Rangers—more than any other NHL goalie.

Most overtime goals in an NHL season The NHL record for overtime goals in a season is five, by Steven Stamkos (CAN) in the 2011/12 season for Tampa Bay Lightning.

Most shootout goals in an NHL career Zach Parise (U.S.A.) has scored 34 shootout goals in the service of the New Jersey Devils and Minnesota Wild since 2005.

Most goals by a rookie in an NHL season In the 1992/93 NHL season, Finland's Teemu Selänne racked up 76 goals for the Winnipeg Jets.

FASTEST NHL HAT-TRICK On Mar. 23, 1952, Canadian right winger Bill Mosienko scored a hat-trick in 21 sec. for the Chicago Blackhawks vs. the New York Rangers at Madison Square Garden, New York City, U.S.A. The Blackhawks went on to triumph 7–6.

MOST GAME-WINNING GOALS IN AN NHL CAREER As of Dec. 30, 2013, the Czech Republic's Jaromír Jágr had scored 122 game-winning goals in his National Hockey League (NHL) career. He has also scored the **most regular-season NHL career goals in overtime**, with 18 for the Pittsburgh Penguins, Washington Capitals, New York Rangers, Philadelphia Flyers, and New Jersey Devils from 1990 to 2013.

FACT: Jágr started playing ice hockey at the age of three.

NATIONAL HOCKEY LEAGUE

Most Stanley Cup Final appearances	34	Montreal Canadiens (CAN), 1916–93
Most Stanley Cup wins	24	Montreal Canadiens (CAN), 1916–93
Most games played in a career	1,767	Gordie Howe (CAN), for the Detroit Red Wings and Hartford Whalers, 1946–80
Longest winning streak	17	Pittsburgh Penguins (U.S.A.), from Mar. 9 to Apr. 10, 1993
Most goals scored	894	Wayne Gretzky (CAN), for the Edmonton Oilers, Los Angeles Kings, St. Louis Blues, and New York Rangers
Most goals in a game by a player	7	Joe Malone (CAN), for the Quebec Bulldogs vs. Toronto St. Patricks on Jan. 31, 1920
Most goals in a game by a team	16	Montreal Canadiens, in a 16–3 victory over the Quebec Bulldogs (both CAN) on Mar. 3, 1920
Most goals in a season by a player	92	Wayne Gretzky (CAN), for the Edmonton Oilers in 1981–82
Most goals in a season by a team	446	Edmonton Oilers (CAN), 1983–84
Most saves by a goalkeeper	27,312	Martin Brodeur (CAN), for the New Jersey Devils, 1993–present

All statistics correct as of Jan. 29, 2014

Most goals on an NHL debut On Oct. 9, 2010, Derek Stepan (U.S.A.) became only the fourth player to score a hat-trick on his NHL debut, playing for the New York Rangers in a 6–3 victory over the Buffalo Sabres. The others are: Alex Smart (CAN) on Jan. 14, 1943, Réal Cloutier (CAN) on Oct. 10, 1979, and Fabian Brunnström (SWE) on Oct. 15, 2008.

Most men's ice hockey World Championships The men's IIHF (International Ice Hockey Federation) World Championships were first held in 1920. The Soviet Union/Russia have won more times than any other nation, with 22 victories as the Soviet Union (in 1954, 1956, 1963–71, 1973–75, 1978–79, 1981–83, 1986, and 1989–90) and four wins as Russia (in 1993, 2008–09, and 2012).

Most women's ice hockey World Championships The women's IIHF World Championships was first held in 1990 and has been staged annually since then, apart from Olympic years and in 2003, during the SARS outbreak. The Canadian team have won 10 titles in total: in 1990,

1992, 1994, 1997, 1999–2001, 2004, 2007, and 2012. The U.S.A. has won five times, most recently in 2013.

Youngest captain of a Stanley Cup–winning team At 21 years 309 days, Sidney Crosby (CAN, b. Aug. 7, 1987) became the youngest captain of any team to win the Stanley Cup when the Pittsburgh Penguins beat the Detroit Red Wings in the 2009 finals.

Fewest goals conceded in a Stanley Cup finals series The fewest goals conceded by a goalkeeper in a Stanley Cup finals series is eight, by Tim Thomas (U.S.A.) for the Boston Bruins vs. the Vancouver Canucks in 2011.

OLDEST GOALSCORER IN OLYMPIC ICE HOCKEY

At the age of 43 years 234 days, Teemu Selänne (FIN, b. Jul. 3, 1970) scored twice in the Olympic bronze medal match against the U.S.A. in Sochi, Russia, on Feb. 22, 2014. Selänne's goals helped Finland to a 5–0 victory over the Americans, and also made him the **oldest medalist in Olympic ice hockey**.

MOST TICKETS SOLD FOR AN NHL MATCH A total of 105,491 tickets were sold for the 2014 Bridgestone NHL Winter Classic game between the Detroit Red Wings (U.S.A.) and the Toronto Maple Leafs (CAN). The match was held at the University of Michigan Football Stadium in Ann Arbor, Michigan, U.S.A., on Jan. 1, 2014.

MARATHONS

Deepest marathon The Crystal Mine Underground Marathon is run in an old salt mine located 1,640 ft. (500 m) below sea level. It has taken place in Sondershausen, Thuringia, Germany, annually since 2002.

Coldest marathon In 2001, the Siberian Ice Marathon in Omsk, Russia, registered a temperature of -38°F (-39°C), making it the coldest regular marathon.

Some 169°F (94°C) warmer, the **hottest marathon** is the Badwater Ultramarathon held between Death Valley and Mount Whitney in California, U.S.A., which registers temperatures of 131°F (55°C).

Most northerly marathon The North Pole Marathon held at the geographic North Pole has been run annually since 2002. In 2007, Thomas Maguire (IRL) ran the **fastest men's North Pole marathon** in 3 hr. 36 min. 10 sec. A year later, Cathrine Due (DNK) recorded the **fastest women's** in 5 hr. 37 min. 14 sec.

The **most southerly marathon** is the Antarctic Ice Marathon, held on the Antarctic mainland at a latitude of 80 degrees south.

Fastest aggregate World Marathon Majors time The "World Marathon Majors" comprise the Olympic and World Championship marathons as well as those held in Berlin, Boston, Chicago, London, and New York City. Kjell-Erik Ståhl (SWE) completed the seven Majors in an aggregate time of 15 hr. 36 min. 47 sec. His record-breaking sequence began at the Moscow 1980 Olympic Games and ended in Berlin in 1991.

FASTEST MARATHON (FEMALE)
Paula Radcliffe (UK) finished the London Marathon on Apr. 13, 2003 in 2 hr. 15 min. 25 sec., making her the fastest female marathon runner of all time. She also ran the **fastest Chicago Marathon (female)**, on Oct. 13, 2002, finishing in 2 hr. 17 min. 18 sec.

London Marathon runners have raised some **$1.1 bn** for charity.

FASTEST MARATHON

The Berlin Marathon in Germany was the setting for the fastest marathon ever. It took Wilson Kipsang (KEN) just 2 hr. 3 min. 23 sec. to complete the course on Sep. 29, 2013. Kipsang has also won the Frankfurt Marathon twice (2010–11) and the London Marathon twice (2012 and 2014).

BIGGEST MARATHONS

Marathon	Most finishers	Fastest (male)	Fastest (female)
Berlin, Germany (A.)	36,544 Sep. 29, 2013	Wilson Kipsang (KEN), 2:03:23, Sep. 29, 2013	Mizuki Noguchi (JPN), 2:19:12, Sep. 25, 2005
Boston, Massachusetts, U.S.A. (B.)	35,868 Apr. 15, 1996	Geoffrey Mutai (KEN), 2:03:02, Apr. 18, 2011	Rita Jeptoo (KEN), 2:18:57, Apr. 21, 2014
Chicago, Illinois, U.S.A. (C.)	39,122 Oct. 13, 2013	Dennis Kimetto (KEN), 2:03:45, Oct. 13, 2013	Paula Radcliffe (UK), 2:17:18, Oct. 13, 2002
London, UK	36,672 Apr. 22, 2012	Wilson Kipsang (KEN), 2:04:29, Apr. 13, 2014	Paula Radcliffe (UK), 2:15:25, Apr. 13, 2003
New York City, New York, U.S.A.	50,062 Nov. 3, 2013	Geoffrey Mutai (KEN), 2:05:06, Nov. 6, 2011	Margaret Okayo (KEN), 2:22:31, Nov. 2, 2003
Osaka, Japan	27,674 Oct. 27, 2013	Ser-Od Bat-Ochir (MNG), 2:11:52, Nov. 25, 2012	Lidia Simon (ROM), 2:32:48, Oct. 30, 2011
Paris, France	38,690 Apr. 7, 2013	Kenenisa Bekele (ETH), 2:05:04, Apr. 6, 2014	Feyse Tadese (ETH), 2:21:06, Apr. 7, 2013
Tokyo, Japan (D.)	35,308 Feb. 24, 2013	Dickson Chumba (KEN), 2:05:42, Feb. 23, 2014	Tirfi Tsegaye (ETH), 2:22:23, Feb. 23, 2014

Statistics correct as of Apr. 30, 2014. The IAAF rules the Boston course ineligible to set world records.

Most World Marathon Majors races won Female: Grete Waitz (NOR) won 12 Majors: nine in New York, two in London, and one World Championship between 1978 and 1987.

Male: Bill Rodgers (U.S.A.) won eight Majors: four in Boston and four in New York from 1975 to 1980.

Most ITU World Triathlon Series medals Female: Michellie Jones (AUS) won two gold, two silver, and four bronze medals at the International Triathlon Union World Championships. She won her eight medals in 1991–2003.

Male: Simon Lessing (UK) collected seven World Championship medals: four gold, two silver, and one bronze from 1992 to 1999. The record was equaled by Javier Gómez (ESP), with three golds, three silvers, and one bronze in 2007–13.

Fastest time to complete the Hawaiian Ironman Male: The Ironman World Championship, aka the "Hawaiian Ironman," was first held on Feb. 18, 1978 in Kailua-Kona, Hawaii, U.S.A. It was described as "Swim 2.4 miles! Bike 112 miles! Run 26.2 miles! Brag for the rest of your life!" Craig Alexander (AUS) holds the course record of 8 hr. 3 min. 56 sec., which he set on Oct. 8, 2011 with a 3.8-km swim in 51 min. 56 sec., a 180-km cycle in 4 hr. 24 min. 5 sec., and a marathon run in 2 hr. 44 min. 2 sec.

Female: On Oct. 12, 2013, Australia's Mirinda Carfrae recorded the fastest women's time, in 8 hr. 52 min. 14 sec. Her nearest rival was more than 5 min. behind.

The **oldest person to complete the Hawaiian Ironman** is Lew Hollander (U.S.A., b. Jun. 6, 1930), who was 82 years 129 days old when he crossed the finish line on Oct. 13, 2012.

Fastest time to run an ultramarathon on each continent Ziyad Tariq Rahim (PAK) ran seven 50-km (36.6-mi.) ultramarathons—one on each continent from Jan. 26 to Mar. 8, 2014. The timing for this record began when Ziyad started his first ultramarathon in Antarctica and ended when he crossed the line of his last ultramarathon in South Africa, with a total time of 41 days 3 hr. 23 min. 40 sec.

Andrei Rosu (ROM) set the **fastest time to run a marathon and an ultramarathon on each continent** in 1 year 217 days. He started with the Australian Outback Marathon on Jul. 31, 2010 and ended with the Supermaratona Cidade do Rio Grande ultramarathon in Brazil on Mar. 4, 2012.

Fastest time to complete 10 marathons in 10 days **Male:** Adam Holland (UK) ran the 2010 Brathay 10 in 10 challenge in Cumbria, UK, from May 7–16. His total time was 30 hr. 20 min. 54 sec.

Female: Sally Ford (UK) ran the same challenge two years later on May 11–20, taking 36 hr. 38 min. 53 sec.

Fastest marathon barefoot **Male:** Abebe Bikila (ETH) ran the 1960 Olympic marathon in his bare feet. He set a time of 2 hr. 15 min. 16.2 sec. in Rome, Italy, on Sep. 10, 1960.

Female: It took just 2 hr. 29 min. 45 sec. for barefooted Kenyan Tegla Loroupe to run the Olympic marathon in Sydney, Australia, on Sep. 24, 2000.

FASTEST OLYMPIC MARATHON **Female:** On Aug. 5, 2012, Tiki Gelana (ETH) clocked 2 hr. 23 min. 7 sec. to take gold in the women's marathon at the London 2012 Games. However, the Olympic record isn't her personal best. She ran the Rotterdam Marathon in the Netherlands in 2 hr. 18 min. 58 sec. on Apr. 15, 2012.

Male: Samuel Wanjiru (KEN) won the marathon in Beijing in 2 hr. 6 min. 32 sec. on Aug. 24, 2008.

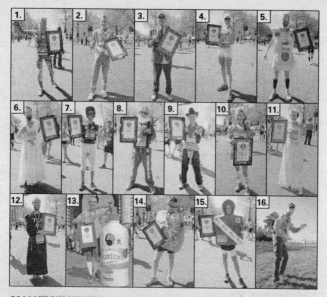

2014 VIRGIN MONEY LONDON MARATHON: NEW WORLD RECORDS

While marathon running is a serious business for elite athletes, such as those featured on pp. 522–25, for others it is a great excuse to have some fun and raise money for charity—and where better to have it than at the world's premier marathon event: the London Marathon! Pictured above are some of the colorful characters who took part this year, listed in order of their running times.

1. ANIMAL
Alex Collins (UK)
2 hr. 48 min. 29 sec.

2. TELEVISION CHARACTER
David Stone (UK)
2 hr. 49 min. 51 sec.

3. SCHOOLBOY
Steven Nimmo (UK)
2 hr. 50 min. 17 sec.

4. BABY
Ali King (UK)
2 hr. 51 min. 18 sec.

5. TOILET
Marcus Mumford (UK)
2 hr. 57 min. 28 sec.

6. BRIDE (MALE)
Lee Goodwin (UK)
3 hr. 0 min. 54 sec.

7. JOCKEY
Ross Birkett (UK)
3 hr. 8 min. 30 sec.

8. ASTRONAUT
Simon Couchman (UK)
3 hr. 8 min. 45 sec.

9. COWBOY
Rik Vercoe (UK)
3 hr. 9 min. 9 sec.

10. NURSE (FEMALE)
Caroline Pleasence (UK)
3 hr. 13 min. 58 sec.

11. BRIDE (FEMALE)
Sarah Dudgeon (UK)
3 hr. 16 min. 44 sec.

12. MONK
Tom Collins (UK)
3 hr. 29 min. 32 sec.

13. BOTTLE
Paul Simons (UK)
3 hr. 31 min. 57 sec.

14. ORGAN (MALE)
Adam Giangreco (UK)
3 hr. 36 min. 42 sec.

15. LOGO
Kevin Hunt (UK)
3 hr. 37 min. 14 sec.

16. MAILMAN
Pete Waumsley (UK)
3 hr. 47 min. 35 sec.

17. MASCOT
Francis Gilroy (UK)
3 hr. 51 min. 50 sec.

18. ORGAN (FEMALE)
Emma Denton (UK)
3 hr. 52 min. 2 sec.

19. FAUCET
Richard Quartermaine (UK)
3 hr. 52 min. 9 sec.

20. DOCTOR
Naomi Garrick (UK)
3 hr. 54 min. 6 sec.

21. CRUSTACEAN
Oliver Johnson (UK)
3 hr. 55 min. 13 sec.

22. PLAYING CARD
Lisa Wright (UK)
4 hr. 23 min. 57 sec.

23. NUT
Spenser Lane (UK)
4 hr. 29 min. 36 sec.

24. FIREMAN
James Dajlid (UK)
4 hr. 39 min. 13 sec.

25. CARRYING A 20-LB BACKPACK
Gill Begnor (UK)
5 hr. 7 min. 56 sec.

26. LONGEST CROCHET CHAIN WHILE RUNNING A MARATHON
Susie Hewer (UK)
139.4 m (time of 5 hr. 40 min. 47 sec.)

27. KNIGHT IN CHAINMAIL
Michael Dodd (UK)
5 hr. 49 min. 7 sec.

28. TELEPHONE BOOTH
Sid Keyte (UK)
5 hr. 54 min. 52 sec.

29. FOUR-PERSON COSTUME
Andy Newman (back) and, from front left, Earl Edwards, Adam James, and Stuart Bailey (all UK) 6 hr. 29 min. 44 sec.

30. MARCHING BAND
Huddersfield Marathon Band (UK)
6 hr. 56 min. 48 sec.

MOTOR SPORTS

BIKES

Most MotoGP championships won MotoGP is one of the three classes in the Road Racing World Championship Grand Prix, motorcycling's premier road-racing competition since it replaced the 500-cc class in 2002. The greatest number of victories in the MotoGP championships is six and was achieved by Valentino Rossi (ITA) in 2002–05 and 2008–09.

The **most wins of the MotoGP championships by a constructor** is seven, achieved by Honda (JPN) in 2002–04, 2006, and 2011–13.

Youngest rider to achieve a MotoGP pole position On Apr. 20, 2013, Marc Márquez (ESP, b. Feb. 17, 1993) took pole position at the 2013 Motorcycle Grand Prix of the Americas at the Circuit of the Americas in Austin, Texas, U.S.A., at the age of 20 years 62 days.

The next day, Márquez won the race, becoming the **youngest MotoGP race winner**, at the age of 20 years 63 days. He went on to win the 2013 MotoGP World Championship at Circuit Ricardo Tormo in Spain, becoming the **youngest MotoGP world champion**, at 20 years 266 days old on Nov. 10, 2013.

FASTEST LAP FOR A TT SUPERBIKE AT THE ISLE OF MAN TT In a TT Superbike-class race in Douglas, Isle of Man, UK, on Jun. 2, 2013, John McGuinness (UK) completed a lap on a Honda CBR1000RR in just 17 min 11.57 sec. McGuinness set the record with his sixth and final lap of the Mountain Course, during which he maintained an average speed of 131.67 mph (211.90 km/h).

There are approximately **80,000 components** in every Formula One car.

Fastest Isle of Man TT Superbike race Michael Dunlop (UK) set a time of 1 hr. 45 min. 29.98 sec. on his 1000-cc TT Legends Honda in a six-lap Isle of Man TT Superbike race in Douglas, Isle of Man, UK, on Jun. 2, 2013.

Most wins of the Motocross des Nations Staged on off-road circuits, the Motocross des Nations, also known as the "Olympics of Motocross," has been contested annually since 1947. The team with the most wins is the U.S.A., with 22 between 1981 and 2011.

CARS

Most F1 victories by a constructor The greatest number of Formula One (F1) Grand Prix wins by one manufacturer is 221, by Italian constructor Ferrari between 1951 and 2013. The team's first victory came at the 1951 British Grand Prix held at Silverstone, Northamptonshire, UK, which was won by Argentinian driver José Froilán González. Ferrari has also recorded the **most consecutive F1 Grand Prix points finishes by a constructor**. The team enjoyed 71 successive points finishes between the German Grand Prix staged on Jul. 25, 2010 and the Chinese Grand Prix on Apr. 20, 2014. Since 2010, a driver must finish in the top 10 to earn points for both themselves and their constructor.

MOST CONSECUTIVE NASCAR SPRINT CUP SERIES WINS Jimmie Johnson (U.S.A.) won five successive National Association for Stock Car Auto Racing (NASCAR) Sprint Cup Series championships between 2006 and 2010. His streak ended when Tony Stewart (U.S.A.) won in 2011, but Johnson regained the title in the 2013 series. This brings his total to six series titles overall in 2006–13.

MOST LEADERS IN AN INDIANAPOLIS 500 RACE There were 14 different leaders of the 2013 edition of the Indianapolis 500 race at Indianapolis Motor Speedway in Indiana, U.S.A., on May 26, 2013. In order, they were: Carpenter, Kanaan, Andretti, Hunter-Reay, Power, Jakes, Viso, Muñoz, Allmendinger, Tagliani, Bell, Hinchcliffe, Castroneves, and Dixon. The race was won by Tony Kanaan.

MOST WINS OF THE . . .

Competition	Wins	Champion
International Isle of Man TT (Tourist Trophy) Race	26	Joey Dunlop (UK) in 1977, 1980, 1983–88, 1992–98, and 2000
Motocross des Nations	22	U.S.A. in 1981–93, 1996, 2000, and 2005–11
Formula One World Constructors' Championship	16	Ferrari (ITA) in 1961, 1964, 1975–77, 1979, 1982–83, 1999–2004, and 2007–08
Road Racing World Championship Grand Prix	15	Giacomo Agostini (ITA) 500-cc in 1966–72 and 1975; and 350-cc in 1968–74
Motocross World Championship	10	Stefan Everts (DEU) 125-cc in 1991; 250-cc in 1995–97; 500-cc in 2001–02; MXGP in 2003; and MX1 in 2004–06
World Rally Championship	9	Sébastien Loeb (FRA) in 2004–12
Formula One World Drivers' Championship	7	Michael Schumacher (DEU) in 1994–95 and 2000–04
NASCAR Sprint Cup Series Drivers' Championship	7	Richard Petty (U.S.A.) in 1964, 1967, 1971–72, 1974–75, and 1979
		Dale Earnhardt, Sr. (U.S.A.) in 1980, 1986–87, 1990–91, and 1993–94
Karting World Championship	6	Mike Wilson (UK) in 1981–83, 1985, and 1988–89
MotoGP Championship	6	Valentino Rossi (ITA) in 2002–05 and 2008–09
Dakar Rally	5	Stéphane Peterhansel and Jean-Paul Cottret (both FRA) in 2004–05, 2007, and 2012–13
Superbike World Championship	4	Carl Fogarty (UK) in 1994–95 and 1998–99

Statistics correct as of Mar. 25, 2014

MOST FINISHERS IN THE BAJA 1000 OFF-ROAD RACE
The 620-mi. (1,000-km) Baja 1000 is staged on Mexico's Baja California peninsula. The off-road race allows motorcycles, cars, and trucks to compete together. Unmarked challenges include harsh desert conditions, wandering animals, and traps made by spectators for their own amusement. The most drivers to complete the race is 237, out of the 424 starters in 2007.

MOST WRC POINTS IN A SEASON BY A DRIVER Sébastien Ogier (FRA) scored 290 points driving for Volkswagen during the 2013 World Rally Championship (WRC) season. Ogier ended Sébastien Loeb's record run of nine consecutive championships by winning the 2013 season, and in the process scored 14 more points than Loeb amassed in 2010.

Most points by a driver in an F1 career

The greatest number of points in an F1 career is 1,647, by Fernando Alonso (ESP) between Mar. 9, 2003 and Apr. 20, 2014.

Most F1 Grand Prix wins by a driver in a season

Michael Schumacher (DEU) won 13 Grands Prix in the 2004 season. His feat was equaled by Sebastian Vettel (DEU) in 2013.

Most consecutive seasons to win an F1 Grand Prix from debut

British driver Lewis Hamilton made his F1 Grand Prix debut in 2007 and his first win was in Canada that year. He went on to win at least one Grand Prix in the eight successive seasons up to and including his victory at the Grand Prix in Sepang, Malaysia, on Mar. 30, 2014.

MOST CONSECUTIVE FORMULA ONE GRAND PRIX WINS Sebastian Vettel (DEU) won nine Formula One Grand Prix driving for Red Bull in the 2013 season from Aug. 25 to Nov. 24, 2013. Vettel also became the **youngest F1 world champion** when he won the 2010 Abu Dhabi Grand Prix at the age of 23 years 134 days on Nov. 14, 2010.

FIRST F1 DRIVER TO FINISH EVERY DEBUT SEASON GRAND PRIX Max Chilton (UK) (left) completed all 19 races during his debut season in 2013, driving for Marussia. True, he didn't secure a single point, but he became the first rookie in the 64-year history of the F1 championship to finish every race.

MOST NASCAR RACE VICTORIES IN A CAREER Richard Petty (U.S.A.) (right) enjoyed 200 wins during his NASCAR career from 1958 to 1992. He also had the **most NASCAR pole positions** (126) and **most NASCAR race wins from pole position** (61).

Most wins in a NASCAR Sprint Cup Series season In the 1967 season, Richard Petty (U.S.A.) recorded 27 wins in the NASCAR Sprint Cup Series. In the same year, he set the mark for the **most consecutive NASCAR race wins**, with 10 victories from Aug. 12 to Oct. 1, 1967.

RUGBY

LEAGUE

Fastest try Tim Spears (UK) scored for Featherstone Rovers just 7.75 sec. into a game against Wakefield Trinity Wildcats at Post Office Road in Featherstone, West Yorkshire, UK, on Jan. 12, 2014. This (just) beat the previous record of 7.9 sec. set by Rochdale Hornets' Danny Samuel (UK) in 2010.

Largest attendance at a World Cup final A crowd of 74,468 fans watched the Rugby League World Cup final between Australia and New Zealand at Old Trafford in Manchester, UK, on Nov. 30, 2013 (see p. 537).

Most siblings to play in the same NRL team Four brothers have played for the same National Rugby League (NRL) team twice in history. The first set of brothers to achieve this was Ray, Roy, Rex, and Bernard Norman (all AUS), playing for Annandale in the New South Wales Rugby League (the predecessor of the NRL) in the 1910 season. More than 100 years later, the feat was equaled by Sam, Luke, Tom, and George Burgess (all UK), who played for South Sydney Rabbitohs against Wests Tigers at the Allianz Stadium in Sydney, Australia, on Aug. 30, 2013.

Longest dropkick Joseph "Joe" Lydon (UK) scored a 183-ft. (56-m) dropkick for Wigan against Warrington in a Challenge Cup semifinal held at Maine Road in Manchester, UK, on Mar. 25, 1989.

Most points in an international career Between May 5, 2006 and Nov. 30, 2013, Australia's Johnathan Thurston scored 318 points in international rugby league matches. He finally surpassed Mick Cronin's long-standing record of 309 points when he kicked seven goals for 14 points in the 2013 World Cup final against New Zealand.

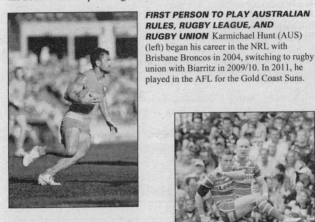

FIRST PERSON TO PLAY AUSTRALIAN RULES, RUGBY LEAGUE, AND RUGBY UNION Karmichael Hunt (AUS) (left) began his career in the NRL with Brisbane Broncos in 2004, switching to rugby union with Biarritz in 2009/10. In 2011, he played in the AFL for the Gold Coast Suns.

MOST POINTS SCORED IN A SUPER LEAGUE CAREER Kevin Sinfield (UK) (right) scored 3,498 points for Leeds Rhinos from Sep. 13, 1998 to Mar. 14, 2014. In 2012, the loose forward won the coveted *Rugby League World* Golden Boot Award, given to the player judged to be the best in the world.

Scotland beat England in the first international rugby match.

Oldest player with an international cap in union and league Tom Calnan (b. Oct. 22, 1976) is the oldest person to have won a "double cap" in international rugby, by playing in both codes. Calnan was 36 years 50 days old when he made his debut for the UAE rugby union side against Hong Kong in Dubai, UAE, on Dec. 11, 2012. He had previously represented the UAE rugby league side in a match on Mar. 30, 2012.

Youngest international player Gavin Gordon (b. Feb. 28, 1978) played for Ireland vs. Moldova on Oct. 16, 1995 at Spotland in Rochdale, UK, at the age of 17 years 229 days. He scored a hat-trick of tries in this debut game, which Ireland won 48–26.

UNION

Fastest try Just 7.24 sec into a game on Nov. 23, 2013, Tyson Lewis (UK) scored a try for Doncaster Knights vs. Old Albanians at Woollam Playing Fields in St. Albans, UK.

Fastest sending off in an English Premiership match London Scottish player Mike Watson (UK) was sent off after 42 sec. against Bath at the Recreation Ground in Bath, UK, on May 15, 1999.

Most consecutive international wins Cyprus had 21 successive victories from Nov. 29, 2008 to Nov. 30, 2013.

Most consecutive World Cup defeats Namibia suffered 15 Rugby Union World Cup losses in a row between Oct. 1, 1999 and Sep. 26, 2011.

Highest aggregate score in a World Cup match New Zealand beat Japan 145–17 on Jun. 4, 1995 at Bloemfontein in South Africa. During this match, the All Blacks scored 21 tries.

MOST INTERNATIONAL . . .

Rugby union		
Caps	141	Brian O'Driscoll (IRL, 1999–2014)
Points	1,442	Dan Carter (NZ, 2003–13)
Tries	69	Daisuke Ohata (JPN, 1996–2006)
Rugby league		
Caps	59	Darren Lockyer (AUS, 1998–2011)
Points	318	Johnathan Thurston (AUS, 2006–13)
Tries	41	Mick Sullivan (GB, 1954–63)

Statistics correct as of Mar. 15, 2014

MOST INTERNATIONAL APPEARANCES IN RUGBY UNION

Brian O'Driscoll (IRL, left with daughter Sadie) made 141 international appearances from Jun. 12, 1999 to Mar. 15, 2014, playing for Ireland 133 times and 8 times for the British and Irish Lions (2001, 2005, 2009, and 2013 tours). He scored 47 international tries and won 81 matches, ending with the 22–20 victory over France that secured the 2014 Six Nations trophy.

MOST TRIES SCORED IN RUGBY UNION WORLD CUP TOURNAMENTS BY A PLAYER

Jonah Lomu (NZ) scored 15 tries in the 1995 and 1999 Rugby Union World Cups. His top tally in a single match was four tries in a 45–29 win against England on Jun. 18, 1995. Right, Lomu is shown playing in the 1999 World Cup, in what proved to be a commanding 101–3 win over Italy.

MOST CONSECUTIVE INTERNATIONAL RUGBY UNION MATCHES UNBEATEN IN A CALENDAR YEAR

New Zealand's All Blacks remained unbeaten for 14 international matches during 2013, from Jun. 8 to Nov. 24. Not only was the team undefeated, but it also won all of the 14 matches played. In 2003, England won more games (16) but were not unbeaten, having lost one match.

Youngest World Cup player On Sep. 30, 2007, Thretton Palamo (b. Sep. 22, 1988) played for the U.S.A. vs. South Africa, at 19 years 8 days old, at Stade de la Mosson in Montpellier, France.

Most successive matches to score a try in the English Premiership Mark Cueto (UK) scored tries in eight consecutive games for Sale Sharks from Apr. 9 to Sep. 25, 2005.

Most Heineken Cup points scored by a player Ronan O'Gara (IRL) scored 1,365 points in Heineken Cup matches for Munster from Sep. 7, 1997 to Apr. 27, 2013.

The **most Heineken Cup tries scored by a player** is 35, by Vincent Clerc (FRA) for Stade Toulousain from Oct. 13, 2002 to Jan. 13, 2013.

Most tries in a Super Rugby career Doug Howlett (NZ) scored 59 tries for the Auckland Blues from 1999 to 2007.

Oldest international player Mark Spencer (b. May 21, 1954) was 57 years 340 days old when he played for Qatar in the Asian 5 Nations competition against Uzbekistan in Dubai, UAE, on Apr. 25, 2012. Mark was born in the U.S.A. but took up Qatari residency, allowing him to represent the national side.

MOST PENALTIES SCORED IN THE HEINEKEN CUP BY A PLAYER Owen Farrell (UK) (above) kicked 10 penalties for Saracens vs. Racing Métro 92 in the Heineken Cup match held at Stade de la Beaujoire in Nantes, France, on Jan. 12, 2013.

FACT: Farrell's debut, at the age of 17, for Saracens against the Llanelli Scarlets in 2008 made him the youngest player in English professional rugby at that time.

HIGHEST MARGIN OF VICTORY IN A WORLD CUP FINAL Australia's 32-point win over New Zealand in the 2013 Rugby League World Cup final on Nov. 30, 2013 represents the greatest victory margin ever recorded in this competition, which has been held since 1954.

CLUB SOCCER

Most valuable soccer club According to Forbes, as of Apr. 17, 2013, Real Madrid was valued at $3.3 bn. The Spanish side, who won a 32nd La Liga title in 2011/12, ended Manchester United's run at the top of the rich list.

Most red cards in a game In an Argentine Primera D match between Club Atlético Claypole and Victoriano Arenas on Feb. 27, 2011, 36 players (both sides and all substitutes) were sent off by Damián Rubino (ARG).

First player to hold four major continental trophies simultaneously When Chelsea won the Europa League on May 15, 2013, Fernando Torres and Juan Mata (both ESP) held four of soccer's most prestigious titles: the World Cup, European Championship, Champions League, and Europa League.

More than **265 million people** play soccer worldwide.

DOMESTIC

Most viewed domestic soccer league (global) In 2010/11, the English Premier League was viewed by 4.7 billion people across 212 territories. The total was boosted by its broadcast on terrestrial TV in China.

Most goals in a single national top-division season by an individual Archibald Stark (UK) scored 67 times for Bethlehem Steel in the American Soccer League between Sep. 15, 1924 and May 18, 1925.

Most consecutive top-division league titles Skonto FC, from capital city Riga, won the Latvian Higher League 14 consecutive times from 1991 to 2004.

Most hat-tricks in La Liga Telmo Zarra (ESP) scored 22 hat-tricks for Athletic Bilbao from 1940 to 1953. Alfredo Di Stéfano (ARG/ESP) matched the feat playing for Real Madrid and Espanyol from 1953 to 1966.

Most MLS championships Two teams have won the U.S.A.'s Major League Soccer Cup four times: Washington's DC United (1996–97, 1999, and 2004) and LA Galaxy from California (2002, 2005, and 2011–12).

Most consecutive losses A home defeat by Rothwell Corinthians saw Woodford United FC (UK) record 62 consecutive losses. The United Counties League match finished 6–2 at Byfield Road stadium in Woodford Halse, UK, on Oct. 26, 2013.

MOST APPEARANCES FOR THE SAME CLUB Rogério Ceni (BRA) appeared in 1,081 competitive matches for São Paulo Futebol Clube between Jul. 7, 1993 and Nov. 27, 2013. Keeper Ceni regularly takes free kicks and penalties, securing him the record for **most goals by a goalkeeper** (113) as of Nov. 13, 2013.

> **FACT:** The Copa Libertadores and Champions League are the most prestigious continental competitions in South America and Europe respectively.

FIRST PLAYER TO SCORE A HAT-TRICK IN THE COPA LIBERTADORES AND THE CHAMPIONS LEAGUE On Dec. 11, 2013, Barcelona's Neymar (BRA) scored a hat-trick in a Champions League game at the Nou Camp in Spain. Having previously achieved the feat in the Copa Libertadores on Mar. 7, 2012, for Brazilian side Santos, he became the first player to score hat-tricks in both contests.

Youngest man to play in all four English Football League divisions Jack Hobbs (UK, b. Aug. 18, 1988) made his debut for League One side Leicester City on Aug. 9, 2008, at the age of 19 years 357 days. Hobbs had previously played for Lincoln City in League Two, Liverpool in the Premier League, and Scunthorpe in the Championship.

MOST WINS OF A MAJOR CONTINENTAL TROPHY

Team	Country	Trophy	Wins
Real Madrid	Spain	European Cup/Champions League	9
Al Ahly	Egypt	African/CAF Champions League	8
AC Milan	Italy	European Cup/Champions League	7
Independiente	Argentina	Copa Libertadores	7
Boca Juniors	Argentina	Copa Libertadores	6
Cruz Azul	Mexico	CONCACAF Champions Cup/League	6
América	Mexico	CONCACAF Champions Cup/League	5
Auckland City	New Zealand	OFC Champions League	5
Bayern Munich	Germany	European Cup/Champions League	5
Liverpool	England	European Cup/Champions League	5
Peñarol	Uruguay	Copa Libertadores	5
Zamalek	Egypt	African/CAF Champions League	5

Statistics correct as of Apr. 25, 2014

Most appearances in the English top division Goalkeeper Peter Shilton (UK) recorded 848 appearances for Leicester City, Stoke City, Nottingham Forest, Southampton, and Derby County from May 3, 1966 to May 11, 1991.

EUROPEAN

Oldest player to make a Champions League debut Mark Schwarzer (AUS, b. Oct. 6, 1972) took to the pitch at the age of 41 years 66 days in his Champions League debut for Chelsea against Steaua Bucharest at Stamford Bridge in London, UK, on Dec. 11, 2013.

Tottenham keeper Brad Friedel (U.S.A., b. May 18, 1971) was 42 years 305 days old when he played against Benfica on Mar. 20, 2014, making him the **oldest player in the UEFA Europa League**.

Most appearances in the Champions League Ryan Giggs (UK) has racked up 151 appearances for Manchester United in the UEFA Champions League. His debut came in Sep. 1993, and more than 20 years later, on Apr. 1, 2014, he played in a quarter-final match against Bayern Munich.

Most Europa League appearances Ola Toivonen (SWE) appeared in 36 UEFA Europa League games for PSV Eindhoven between Jul. 30, 2009 and Dec. 12, 2013.

LONGEST GOAL SCORED On Nov. 2, 2013, when Stoke City's goalie Asmir Begović (BIH) cleared the ball 13 sec. into a Premier League game, something very unusual happened. The ball, caught by the wind, flew over the head of the Southampton keeper, scoring Begović a goal from 301 ft. 6 in. (91.9 m) away. Only Ledley King has scored faster in the Premier League, his goal coming after just 10 sec.

Most Champions League wins by an individual Spanish midfielder Xavi won 83 matches playing for Barcelona from Sep. 16, 1998 to Mar. 12, 2014.

Most consecutive Champions League matches with a goal Real Madrid scored in 35 consecutive Champions League games from May 3, 2011 to Apr. 2, 2014.

MOST CHAMPIONS LEAGUE GOALS IN A CALENDAR YEAR Cristiano Ronaldo (POR) found the back of the net 15 times for Real Madrid between Feb. 13 and Dec. 10, 2013, beating the record of 13 goals set by his Barcelona rival Lionel Messi in 2012.

FACT: Ronaldo is a record breaker off the pitch too. He has the **most Twitter followers for an athlete**, with 25,229,560 as of Apr. 1, 2014.

MOST CONSECUTIVE WEEKS LEADING LA LIGA Barcelona spent 59 weeks at the top of La Liga, the Spanish top division, from Aug. 19, 2012 to Jan. 27, 2014. Barcelona also holds the record for the **most consecutive La Liga victories**. They racked up 16 wins in a row between Oct. 16, 2010 and Feb. 5, 2011, outscoring their opponents by 60 goals to 6 during the streak.

Highest total score in a European Cup match A first-round European Cup match between Feyenoord (NLD) and KR Reykjavík (ISL) saw a total of 14 goals scored. The match, which took place on Sep. 17, 1969, saw a Dutch 12–2 victory.

The **most goals in a single Champions League match** is 11, and was achieved when Monaco (FRA) beat the Spanish side Deportivo La Coruña 8–3 at home on Nov. 5, 2003.

MOST EXPENSIVE PLAYER The transfer fee for winger Gareth Bale (UK) from Tottenham Hotspur (UK) to Real Madrid (ESP) on Sep. 1, 2013 was a reported £85.3 m ($132 m), eclipsing the £80 m ($132 m) Real Madrid paid for Cristiano Ronaldo on Jul. 1, 2009.

LONGEST UNBEATEN STREAK IN THE BUNDESLIGA Bayern Munich were unbeaten in the Bundesliga—the top division in German soccer—for 53 matches from Nov. 3, 2012 to Mar. 29, 2014. The run finally ended on Apr. 5, 2014 against Augsburg, who beat them 1–0. The previous record of 36 matches unbeaten had been set by Hamburg in 1983.

INTERNATIONAL SOCCER

Most international caps Kristine Lilly (U.S.A.) won 352 caps during her international career—more than any other man or woman. Her first cap came in 1987 and her last on Nov. 5, 2010.

The record for the **most international caps by a man** belongs to Ahmed Hassan (EGY), who won 184 caps between Dec. 29, 1995 and May 22, 2012.

Most international wins by a player Goalkeeper Iker Casillas racked up 112 wins playing in 153 games for Spain between Jun. 3, 2000 and Mar. 5, 2014.

Youngest player to reach 100 caps South Korea's Cha Bum-Kun (b. May 22, 1953) was 24 years 139 days old playing his 100th game on Oct. 9, 1977 against Kuwait.

LONGEST UNBEATEN RUN IN COMPETITIVE INTERNATIONALS Spain went unbeaten for 29 games between Jun. 21, 2010 and Jun. 27, 2013. Their winning streak came to an end at the hands of Brazil in the 2013 Confederations Cup final. If friendly matches were included, Spain and Brazil would share the record.

The average soccer player **runs 7 mi.** in a 90-min. match.

MOST INTERNATIONAL GOALS (MEN)
Ali Daei earned 149 caps for Iran in his career. He scored in more than half of the matches—109 goals in total—between Jun. 25, 1993 and Mar. 1, 2006. In second place is Hungarian Ferenc Puskás, who scored 84 goals in 85 matches.

Oldest international player
On Mar. 31, 2004, MacDonald Taylor Sr. (VIR, b. Aug. 27, 1957) played for the US Virgin Islands at the age of 46 years 217 days.

Most teams in UEFA European Championship qualifying
Following Gibraltar's addition to the Union of European Football Associations (UEFA) in 2013, a record 53 teams will try to qualify for the 2016 European Championship.

Most consecutive losses On Sep. 4, 2004, San Marino began a losing streak of 57 matches in a row. Their most recent match, on Oct. 15, 2013, saw an 8–0 hammering by Ukraine. Prior to Gibraltar joining UEFA, San Marino was the smallest side competing in European soccer, with a population of just 30,000.

Most hat-tricks in the Confederations Cup Fernando Torres (ESP) is the only player to have scored two hat-tricks in the FIFA (Fédération Internationale de Football Association) Confederations Cup. Torres scored them on Jun. 14, 2009 and Jun. 20, 2013.

OLDEST COACH TO WIN THE EUROPEAN CHAMPIONSHIP
Luis Aragonés (ESP, 1938–2014) was at the age of 69 years 337 days when he coached Spain to a UEFA European Championship title. The win came at the Ernst-Happel Stadium in Vienna, Austria, on Jun. 29, 2008.

MOST CONFEDERATION CHAMPIONSHIP WINS

Men's competition	No.	Country
Asian Football Confederation (AFC): Asian Cup	4	Japan
Confederation of African Football (CAF): African Cup of Nations	7	Egypt
Confederation of North, Central American and Caribbean Association Football (CONCACAF): Gold Cup	6	Mexico
Union of European Football Associations (UEFA): European Championship	3	Spain
		Germany
Confederación Sudamericana de Fútbol/Confederação Sul-Americana de Futebol (CONMEBOL): Copa América	15	Uruguay
Oceania Football Confederation (OFC): Nations Cup	4	New Zealand
		Australia
Women's competition	No.	Country
AFC: Asian Cup	8	China
CAF: African Women's Championship	8	Nigeria
CONCACAF: Gold Cup	4	U.S.A.
UEFA: European Championship	8	Germany
CONMEBOL: Sudamericano Femenino	5	Brazil
OFC: Oceania Cup	4	New Zealand

Statistics correct as of Mar 11, 2014

MOST INTERNATIONAL GOALS
No soccer player—male or female—has scored more international goals than American striker Abby Wambach (front left). As of Mar. 12, 2014, she had 167 goals to her name, scored since Sep. 9, 2001. Wambach surpassed her old teammate Mia Hamm's record of 158 goals, taking the record in Jun. 2013 with four goals against South Korea in Harrison, New Jersey, U.S.A.

FIFA WORLD CUP

Most tournaments won The Brazilian men's team have won five World Cups, taking the crown in 1958, 1962, 1970, 1994, and 2002.

The **most Women's World Cup wins** is two, first achieved by the U.S.A. in 1991 and 1999 and then matched by Germany in 2003 and 2007.

Highest goal average at a World Cup finals The 1954 World Cup in Switzerland saw an average of 5.38 goals scored per match. The **lowest goal average at a World Cup finals** was 2.21 per game in 1990.

Most goals scored Men: Brazilian striker Ronaldo, aka Ronaldo Luís Nazário de Lima, scored 15 goals across three World Cup tournaments in 1998–2006.

Women: Birgit Prinz (DEU) scored 14 goals at four World Cups between 1995 and 2007. Marta (BRA) matched the feat over three World Cups in 2003–11.

MOST WINS OF THE FIFA WORLD CUP BY A PLAYER
The only soccer player to have won the FIFA World Cup three times is Pelé (BRA), who won the 1958, 1962, and 1970 titles with Brazil.

From Sep. 7, 1956 to Oct. 1, 1977, Pelé scored 1,279 goals in 1,363 games—the **most career goals**.

MOST WINS OF THE CONFEDERATIONS CUP The Brazilians have won the FIFA Confederations Cup four times, in 1997, 2005, 2009, and 2013. They also have the **most consecutive Confederations Cup match wins**, with 12, from Jun. 25, 2005 to Jun. 30, 2013.

CUP COMPETITORS

The Confederations Cup is contested every four years by the winners of the six FIFA confederation championships (see table on p. 545), the FIFA World Cup holder, and the host nation.

HIGHEST MARGIN OF VICTORY IN A FIFA TOURNAMENT (MEN) A
Confederations Cup match on Jun. 20, 2013 saw Spain put 10 goals past Tahiti
at the Estádio do Maracanã in Rio de Janeiro, Brazil. Tahiti—a team of amateur
players—had been surprise qualifiers following their victory in the 2012 Oceania
Football Confederation Nations Cup.

Highest margin of victory

Women: The very first match at the Women's World Cup on Sep. 10, 2007 saw Germany put 11 goals past the Argentinian defense. Germany went on to lift the trophy, beating Brazil 2–0.

Men: On Jun. 17, 1954, five Hungarians scored in a 9–0 thrashing of South Korea. Subsequently, Yugoslavia defeated Zaire 9–0 in 1974 and Hungary beat El Salvador 10–1 in 1982.

Most players sent off in one finals match

Nicknamed "The Battle of Nuremberg," a match between the Netherlands and Portugal at the 2006 World Cup had four players seeing red, two from each side, in Nuremberg, Germany, on Jun. 25.

Most qualifiers played

Between Mar. 4, 1934 and Nov. 20, 2013, the Mexican men's team participated in 141 World Cup qualifying matches. Mexico won 92 of the games—the **most World Cup qualifiers won**.

West Germany recorded the **most consecutive World Cup qualifiers won**, with 16 between May 10, 1969 and Apr. 30, 1985.

MOST TEAMS REPRESENTED AT THE FIFA WORLD CUP FIFA rules
prohibit players from switching nationalities at senior level; however, Dejan
Stanković has represented three Balkan countries because political borders have
shifted. He played in three World Cups, representing Yugoslavia in 1998 (above
center), Serbia and Montenegro in 2006 (above left), and Serbia in 2010 (above
right).

TENNIS & RACKET SPORTS

BADMINTON

Most Sudirman Cup wins The Sudirman Cup—held every two years since 1989—is the mixed-team world championship. China accumulated nine wins between 1995 and 2013. The 2013 final (p. 549) also saw China record the **most consecutive Sudirman Cup wins**: five triumphs in a row (2005–13).

Most Thomas Cup wins Also known as the World Men's Team Championships, the Thomas Cup was won 13 times by Indonesia between 1958 and 2002.

Most singles BWF World Championships titles **Male:** When China's Dan Lin won the singles title at the Badminton World Federation (BWF) World Championships on Aug. 11, 2013, he did so for the fifth time.
   Female: Four Chinese women have won the singles title twice: Li Lingwei, Han Aiping, Ye Zhaoying, and, most recently, Xie Xingfang in 2005 and 2006.

Longest rally in competition On Mar. 18, 2010, during the third set of a Swiss Open match in Basel, 154 strokes were played by Petya Nedelcheva (BGR) and Anastasia Russkikh (RUS) vs. Shizuka Matsuo and Mami Naito (both JPN).

MOST IRF WORLD CHAMPIONSHIPS WON (MALE) Americans Rocky Carson (left) and Jack Huczek have each won the International Racquetball Federation (IRF) World Championships three consecutive times: Huczek in 2002–06, and Carson in 2008–12.

Wimbledon is the only tennis Grand Slam tournament still played on grass.

SQUASH

Most European Team Championships won England hold both the **male** and **female** records for this competition with 38 and 35 wins respectively.

Most World Open wins Male: Jansher Khan (PAK) won a record eight World Open titles: in 1987, 1989–90, and 1992–96.

    Female: The women's title has been won seven times by Nicol David (MYS), in 2005–06 and 2008–12.

Most World Series Finals Male: Jansher Khan has had the most wins of the World Series Finals, with four titles between 1993 and 1998.

    Female: The women's World Series Finals have been held twice. Nicol David won both times, in 2012 and 2013.

Longest singles marathon Guy Fotherby and Darren Withey (both UK) endured 31 hr. 35 min. 34 sec. playing squash singles at Racquets Fitness Centre in Thame, Oxfordshire, UK, on Jan. 13–14, 2012. Darren won 422 of 465 games.

***LONGEST UNBEATEN SQUASH RUN* Male:** The longest unbeaten run in men's squash is 555 games, by Jahangir Khan (PAK) from Nov. 1981 to Nov. 1986.

    Female: Heather McKay (AUS) was unbeaten in 1962–81, and lost just two matches in her career.

> **FACT:** Jahangir Khan and Jansher Khan were fierce rivals. However, they are not related.

MOST TENNIS GRAND SLAM SINGLES WINS

Australian Open

Female	11	Margaret Court (AUS, 1960–73)
Male	6	Roy Emerson (AUS, 1961–67)

French Open (Roland Garros)

Male	8	Rafael Nadal (ESP, 2005–13)
Female	7	Chris Evert (U.S.A., 1974–86)

Wimbledon

Female	9	Martina Navratilova (U.S.A., 1978–90)
Male	7	W. C. Renshaw (UK, 1881–89)
		Pete Sampras (U.S.A., 1993–2000)
		Roger Federer (CHE, 2003–12)

US Open

Female	8	Molla Mallory (NOR, 1915–26)
Male	7	Richard Sears (U.S.A., 1881–87)
		William Larned (U.S.A., 1901–11)
		Bill Tilden (U.S.A., 1920–29)

FIRST DUO TO WIN EACH GRAND SLAM TOGETHER Serena Williams (U.S.A.) and Rafael Nadal (ESP) are the only duo to win each tennis Grand Slam singles tournament together, both claiming titles at the 2009 Australian Open, Wimbledon in 2010, and Roland Garros in 2013. They completed their set at the U.S. Open on Sep. 8–9, 2013.

TENNIS

Most prize money for a Grand Slam Total prize money for the U.S. Open rose to $34.3 m for the 2013 tournament. The singles champions, Rafael Nadal and Serena Williams, each collected $2.6 m.

Most retirements in one day at a Grand Slam On Jun. 26, 2013, at the Wimbledon Championships in London, UK, seven players retired mid-match or withdrew before making it onto court. Dubbed "Wipeout Wednesday," the day saw injuries to one shoulder, one arm, one hamstring, and four knees.

Most singles titles won at one Grand Slam Female: No one, male or female, has won more open era (since 1968) singles titles at one Grand Slam than Martina Navratilova (U.S.A.). Between 1978 and 1990, she won Wimbledon nine times.

Male: Rafael Nadal won an eighth French Open title when he defeated David Ferrer in straight sets on Jun. 9, 2013.

Fastest serve On May 9, 2012, Samuel Groth (AUS) served an ace at 163.4 mph (263 km/h).

MOST "POWERFUL" ATHLETE Swiss sensation Roger Federer is the top sports star on Forbes' list of the world's most powerful celebrities, ranking No. 8 overall. Federer holds a wealth of men's tennis records, including **most Grand Slam singles titles** (17), **most Grand Slam matches won** (265), and **most weeks ranked world No. 1** (302). Forbes' list measures fame by considering earnings, TV and print exposure, strength of Internet presence, public opinion, and marketability.

> **FACT:** Federer earned an estimated $71 m from Jun. 2012 to Jun. 2013, according to Forbes.

> **FACT:** Graf won 22 Grand Slam singles titles, starting and ending with the French Open in 1987 and 1999.

FIRST TENNIS PLAYER TO WIN A "CAREER SUPER SLAM" A "Career Super Slam" involves winning all four Grand Slams, the Davis Cup (male)/Fed Cup (female), the ATP World Tour Finals (male)/WTA Tour Championships (female), and an Olympic gold medal. In 1988, Steffi Graf (DEU) became the **first tennis player to achieve this**. Her husband, Andre Agassi (U.S.A.), became the **first male tennis player to win a "Career Super Slam,"** doing so in 1999.

Most Grand Slams before first title win (female) Frenchwoman Marion Bartoli won her first Grand Slam title at her 47th attempt, defeating Germany's Sabine Lisicki in the Wimbledon final on Jul. 6, 2013. Her Grand Slam debut was at the 2001 French Open.

TABLE TENNIS

Most World Table Tennis Championships singles Female: Angelica Rozeanu (ROM) won six consecutive singles titles in 1950–55. **Male:** The men's singles crown was won five times by Viktor Barna (HUN), in 1930 and 1932–35.

Most ITTF World Tour Grand Finals singles titles Female: Zhang Yining (CHN) claimed four International Table Tennis Federation (ITTF) World Tours, taking the singles crown in 2000, 2002, and 2005–06.

 Male: Two Chinese men have won three ITTF singles titles: Wang Liqin (1998, 2000, and 2004) and Ma Long (2008–09 and 2011).

MOST CONSECUTIVE WINS OF THE ITTF WORLD TOUR GRAND FINALS Female: Liu Shiwen (CHN, left) won consecutively from 2011–13.

 Male: Two Chinese men have won two consecutive ITTF Grand Finals: Ma Long (2008–09) and Xu Xin (2012–13).

Most Olympic golds Male: Ma Lin (CHN) has won three table tennis golds, winning doubles in 2004, and singles and team in 2008.

Female: Three Chinese women have won four Olympic golds: Yaping Deng at the 1992 and 1996 Games; Nan Wang in 2000, 2004, and 2008; and Yining Zhang in 2004 and 2008.

Youngest Olympic table tennis gold medalist On Aug. 21, 2004, Chen Qi (CHN, b. Apr. 15, 1984)—one of the few top-ranked Chinese left-handers—won the men's doubles at the age of 20 years 128 days, with his partner Ma Lin (CHN).

WATER SPORTS

Most nations in a FINA World Championships The 15th FINA (Fédération Internationale de Natation) World Championships included participants from 181 nations. It was held in Barcelona, Spain, in 2013.

DIVING

Most consecutive FINA World Championships titles Guo Jingjing (CHN) won five 3-m diving titles in both individual and synchronized events from 2001 to 2009.

Youngest Summer Olympic medalist in an individual event Nils Skoglund (SWE, 1906–80) was just 14 years 11 days old when he won silver in the plain high-diving event at the 1920 Olympics.

Most Olympic medals Male: Dmitri Sautin (RUS) won eight Olympic medals, including two golds, in 1992–2008.

Female: Two Chinese divers have six Olympic medals: Guo Jingjing (2000–08) and Wu Minxia (2004–12).

MOST CONSECUTIVE GOLDS IN SYNCHRONIZED SWIMMING AT THE FINA WORLD CHAMPIONSHIPS From Jul. 23, 2009 to Jul. 27, 2013, Russia won 17 synchronized swimming golds at the FINA World Championships, with their latest clean sweep of seven golds in Barcelona, Spain. Russia hopes to add to their medal run on home soil at the 2015 Championships in Kazan.

MEN'S SWIMMING–FASTEST . . .

Event	Time	Name (Nationality)	Time	Name (Nationality)
Freestyle	**Short course**		**Long course**	
50 m	20.30	Roland Schoeman (ZAF)	20.91	Cesar Filho Cielo (BRA)
100 m	44.94	Amaury Leveaux (FRA)	46.91	Cesar Filho Cielo (BRA)
200 m	1:39.37	Paul Biedermann (DEU)	1:42.00	Paul Biedermann (DEU)
400 m	3:32.25	Yannick Agnel (FRA)	3:40.07	Paul Biedermann (DEU)
800 m	7:23.42	Grant Hackett (AUS)	7:32.12	Zhang Lin (CHN)
1,500 m	14:10.10	Grant Hackett (AUS)	14:31.02	Sun Yang (CHN)
4 x 100 m	3:03.30	U.S.A.	3:08.24	U.S.A.
4 x 200 m	6:49.04	Russia	6:58.55	U.S.A.
Butterfly	**Short course**		**Long course**	
50 m	21.80	Steffen Deibler (DEU)	22.43	Rafael Muñoz (ESP)
100 m	48.48	Evgeny Korotyshkin (RUS)	49.82	Michael Phelps (U.S.A.)
200 m	*1:48.56	Chad le Clos (ZAF)	1:51.51	Michael Phelps (U.S.A.)
Backstroke	**Short course**		**Long course**	
50 m	22.61	Peter Marshall (U.S.A.)	24.04	Liam Tancock (UK)
100 m	48.94	Nicholas Thoman (U.S.A.)	51.94	Aaron Peirsol (U.S.A.)
200 m	1:46.11	Arkady Vyatchanin (RUS)	1:51.92	Aaron Peirsol (U.S.A.)
Breaststroke	**Short course**		**Long course**	
50 m	25.25	Cameron van der Burgh (ZAF)	26.67	Cameron van der Burgh (ZAF)
100 m	55.61	Cameron van der Burgh (ZAF)	58.46	Cameron van der Burgh (ZAF)
200 m	2:00.67	Dániel Gyurta (HUN)	2:07.01	Akihiro Yamaguchi (JPN)

Medley	Short course		Long course	
200 m	1:49.63	Ryan Lochte (U.S.A.)	1:54.00	Ryan Lochte (U.S.A.)
400 m	3:55.50	Ryan Lochte (U.S.A.)	4:03.84	Michael Phelps (U.S.A.)
4 x 100 m	3:19.16	Russia	3:27.28	U.S.A.

As of Mar. 19, 2014 (*pending FINA approval)

SWIMMING

Most individual Olympic medals (male) Michael Phelps (U.S.A.) has won more individual medals than any other man across any discipline. He swam his way to 13 medals in individual events at Athens 2004, Beijing 2008, and London 2012. Only one athlete has won more individual medals than him: gymnast Larisa Latynina (USSR/UKR), who won 14.

Phelps also holds Olympic men's records for **most individual event golds** (11), **most golds** (18), and **most swimming medals** (22), as well as seven speed records (see table on pp. 554–55).

Most Olympic golds at one Games (female) Kristin Otto (GDR) won a sensational six swimming gold medals at the 1988 Olympic Games in Seoul.

FIRST OPEN-WATER SWIMMER TO WIN A WORLD CHAMPIONSHIPS GOLD IN EVERY DISCIPLINE (MALE) Thomas Lurz (DEU) was the first man to win a FINA World Championships gold in every open-water event, winning the 5, 10, and 25-km races between 2005 and 2013. The **first female** to achieve the same feat was Viola Valli (ITA), between 2001 and 2003.

Michael Phelps eats a mammoth **12,000 calories a day** during training.

WOMEN'S SWIMMING—FASTEST . . .

Event	Time	Name (Nationality)	Time	Name (Nationality)
Freestyle	**Short course**		**Long course**	
50 m	23.24	Ranomi Kromowidjojo (NLD)	23.73	Britta Steffen (DEU)
100 m	51.01	Lisbeth Trickett (AUS)	52.07	Britta Steffen (DEU)
200 m	1:51.17	Federica Pellegrini (ITA)	1:52.98	Federica Pellegrini (ITA)
400 m	3:54.52	Mireia Belmonte (ESP)	3:59.15	Federica Pellegrini (ITA)
800 m	7:59.34	Mireia Belmonte (ESP)	8:13.86	Katie Ledecky (U.S.A.)
1,500 m	*15:26.95	Mireia Belmonte (ESP)	15:36.53	Katie Ledecky (U.S.A.)
4 x 100 m	3:28.22	Netherlands	3:31.72	Netherlands
4 x 200 m	7:35.94	China	7:42.08	China
Butterfly	**Short course**		**Long course**	
50 m	24.38	Therese Alshammar (SWE)	25.07	Therese Alshammar (SWE)
100 m	55.05	Diane Bui Duyet (FRA)	55.98	Dana Vollmer (U.S.A.)
200 m	2:00.78	Liu Zige (CHN)	2:01.81	Liu Zige (CHN)
Backstroke	**Short course**		**Long course**	
50 m	25.70	Sanja Jovanović (CRO)	27.06	Zhao Jing (CHN)
100 m	55.23	Shiho Sakai (JPN)	58.12	Gemma Spofforth (UK)
200 m	2:00.03	"Missy" Franklin (U.S.A.)	2:04.06	"Missy" Franklin (U.S.A.)
Breaststroke	**Short course**		**Long course**	
50 m	*28.71	Yulia Efimova (RUS)	29.48	Rúta Meilutyté (LTU)
100 m	*1:02.36	Rúta Meilutyté (LTU)	1:04.35	Rúta Meilutyté (LTU)
200 m	2:14.57	Rebecca Soni (U.S.A.)	2:19.11	Rikke Moeller-Pederson (DNK)

Medley	Short course		Long course	
200 m	2:03.20	Katinka Hosszú (HUN)	2:06.15	Ariana Kukors (U.S.A.)
400 m	4:20.85	Katinka Hosszú (HUN)	4:28.43	Ye Shiwen (CHN)
4 x 100 m	3:45.56	U.S.A.	3:52.05	U.S.A.

*As of Mar. 19, 2014 (*pending FINA approval)*

FASTEST SHORT-COURSE 100-M MEDLEY (FEMALE)
Hungarian swimmer Katinka Hosszú completed the 100-m short-course medley in 57.45 sec. She set the record at the FINA Swimming World Cup in Berlin, Germany, on Aug. 11, 2013. Hosszú also holds two other short-course speed records (see table on pp. 556–57).

FASTEST SHORT-COURSE 800-M FREESTYLE (FEMALE)
On Aug. 10, 2013, Mireia Belmonte (ESP) finished the 800-m short-course freestyle in a time of 7 min. 59.34 sec.—the first woman to break the 8-min. barrier—in Berlin, Germany. Belmonte was awarded the title of Best Spanish Athlete of 2013, alongside tennis star Rafael Nadal.

WATER POLO

Most Olympic golds Hungary won gold on nine occasions, including consecutive wins in 2000, 2004, and 2008. Eleven men have recorded three Olympic water polo golds. Women's water polo was introduced into the Olympics in 2000, but no country has won gold more than once.

Most Water Polo World League wins Male: The Serbian national team have collected seven FINA Water Polo World League titles (two as Serbia and Montenegro), between 2005 and 2013. The competition was inaugurated in 2002.
   Female: The women's competition was added in 2004 and has seen the U.S.A. score seven titles in 2004, 2006–07, and 2009–12.

YOUNGEST ASP WORLD TOUR CHAMPION (FEMALE) Carissa Moore (U.S.A., b. Aug. 27, 1992) (above) became the youngest female ASP World Tour champion when she won the 2011 Tour at the age of 18 years 322 days on Jul. 15, 2011. Hawaiian-born Carissa won the title on her second attempt, having finished third in 2010. She broke the 27-year-old record held by Frieda Zamba (U.S.A.), who won the 1984 title as a teenager, at the age of 19 years 164 days.

SURFING

Most ASP World Tour event wins The surfer with the most ASP (Association of Surfing Professionals) World Tour event wins is Kelly Slater (U.S.A.), with 54 titles between 1992 and 2014.

Slater also boarded his way to the **most ASP World Championship Tour titles,** won by the surfer with the most points at the end of the year. Slater's 11 wins between 1992 and 2011 put him seven ahead of the man in second place: Mark Richards (AUS).

Layne Beachley (AUS) has the **most women's ASP World Championship Tour titles,** winning six consecutively from 1998 to 2003 and a seventh in 2006.

CANOEING

Most Olympic appearances (female) Josefa Idem (ITA, b. FRG) has participated in eight Olympic Games in the canoe sprint—the most for any female athlete. Idem competed for West Germany in 1984 to 1988 and Italy from 1992 to 2012. During her Olympic career, she won five medals, including gold in the K-1 500-m event at Sydney 2000.

Most individual canoe slalom Olympic medals Michal Martikán (SVK) won five Olympic canoe slalom medals. He picked up two gold, two silver, and a bronze between 1996 and 2012.

Most canoe slalom Olympic golds Tony Estanguet (FRA) claimed his third Olympic gold medal in canoe slalom on Jul. 31, 2012.

MOST AMERICA'S CUP WINS U.S. teams have won 30 of the 35 America's Cup sailing competitions held between 1851 and 2013. The America's Cup is a yacht race held between two clubs—the reigning champion and the challenger. The trophy was first won in 1851, making this the **oldest international yacht race**. The 2013 winners, Golden Gate Yacht Club, are pictured.

WINTER SPORTS

WINTER OLYMPICS

Most expensive Olympics (Winter or Summer) The 2014 Winter Olympics in Sochi, Russia, were widely reported to have cost $50 bn to stage, including all sports-related and infrastructure costs.

The Sochi Games also set the record for the **most participating countries at a Winter Olympics**: 87 National Olympic Committees entered athletes. Of these, the **largest Winter Olympics team** was the U.S.A., with 230 athletes.

Most medals won by a country By the close of the 2014 Sochi Games, Norway's all-time haul of Winter Olympics medals had grown to 329: 118 gold (the **most Winter Olympics gold medals won by a country**), 111 silver, and 100 bronze.

MOST APPEARANCES AT THE WINTER OLYMPICS Two athletes have competed in seven consecutive Winter Olympics: ski-jumper Noriaki Kasai (JPN) and luger Albert Demchenko (RUS, left) appeared in every Winter Games from Albertville 1992 to Sochi 2014.

MOST WINTER OLYMPICS MEDALS
Male: Ole Einar Bjørndalen (NOR) won 13 Olympic biathlon medals between 1998 and 2014.

Female: Three women have won 10 cross-country skiing medals: Raisa Smetanina (USSR/EUN), Stefania Belmondo (ITA), and Marit Bjørgen (NOR).

Downhill skiers can attain speeds of up to **155 mph**.

HIGHEST SCORE IN FREE DANCE FIGURE SKATING
US gold medalists Meryl Davis and Charlie White achieved a score of 116.63 at the XXII Winter Olympics in Sochi, Russia, on Feb. 17, 2014. Their high score was set in the free dance section of the ice dancing event, which they performed to Rimsky-Korsakov's "Scheherazade."

Most gold medals won by an individual Male: Two Norwegian Olympians have each won eight golds: Ole Einar Bjørndalen (see opposite page) in the biathlon in 1998–2014, and cross-country skier Bjørn Dæhlie in 1992–98.

Female: Three Olympians share this record with six gold medals apiece: speed skater Lydia Skoblikova (USSR) in 1960–64, and cross-country skiers Lyubov Yegorova (EUN/RUS) in 1992–94 and Marit Bjørgen (NOR) in 2010–14.

First women's Olympic curling team to win every first-round game The round-robin format was introduced to curling at the 1998 Winter Olympics in Nagano, Japan. Canada is the only women's team to have won every first-round game, with nine wins in Sochi from Feb. 10 to 18, 2014.

First shared gold medal in alpine skiing The women's downhill skiing event at the 2014 Games saw Tina Maze (SVN) and Dominique Gisin (CHE) record the exact same time, 41.57 sec., on Feb. 12.

FASTEST . . .

Ski-bob On Apr. 19, 2006, during the Pro Mondial speed skiing event at Les Arcs, Rhône-Alpes, France, Romuald Bonvin (CHE) attained a speed of 127.03 mph (204.43 km/h) on a ski-bob.

Speed skating 500 m Male: Jeremy Wotherspoon (CAN) skated 500 m in 34.03 sec. in Salt Lake City, Utah, U.S.A., on Nov. 9, 2007.

Female: Lee Sang-Hwa (KOR) took 36.36 sec. to skate 500 m, also in Salt Lake City, on Nov. 16, 2013.

Speed skating 1,000 m Male: On Mar. 7, 2009, multiple record holder Shani Davis (U.S.A.) skated 1,000 m in 1 min. 6.42 sec. in Salt Lake City, Utah, U.S.A.

Female: Brittany Bowe (U.S.A.) skated 1,000 m in 1 min. 12.58 sec., also in Salt Lake City on Nov. 17, 2013.

Bobsled skeleton Male: Alexander Tretyakov (RUS) and Sandro Stielicke (DEU) both reached 90.96 mph (146.4 km/h) during the Winter Olympics in British Columbia, Canada, on Feb. 19, 2010.

Female: Marion Trott (DEU) recorded a speed of 89.78 mph (144.5 km/h), also during the 2010 Winter Olympics competition at Whistler, on Feb. 19.

***MOST PARALYMPIC CROSS-COUNTRY SKIING GOLD MEDALS* Male:** Frank Höfle (DEU), Terje Loevaas (NOR), and Brian McKeever (CAN, left) have each won 10 golds in Paralympic cross-country skiing. McKeever added three golds to his tally in 2014.

Female: Norway's Ragnhild Myklebust won 16 Paralympic gold medals in cross-country skiing between 1988 and 2002.

PARALYMPIC WINTER GAMES

Most . . .	Total	Athlete	Dates
Medals (female)	27	Ragnhild Myklebust (NOR)	1988–2002
Medals (male)	22	Gerd Schönfelder (DEU)	1992–2010
Gold medals (female)	22	Ragnhild Myklebust (NOR)	1988–2002
Gold medals (male)	16	Gerd Schönfelder (DEU)	1992–2010
Most medals in . . .	**Total**	**Athlete**	
Alpine skiing (male)	22	Gerd Schönfelder (DEU)	1992–2010
Alpine skiing (female)	19	Reinhild Möller (DEU)	1980–98, 2006
Cross-country skiing (male)	17	Frank Höfle (DEU)	1988–2006
Cross-country skiing (female)	16	Ragnhild Myklebust (NOR)	1988–2002
Ice sled speed racing (male)	12	Knut Lundstrøm (NOR)	1988, 1994–98
Ice sled speed racing (female)	11	Brit Mjaasund Øjen (NOR)	1980–84, 1994
		Sylva Olsen (NOR)	1980–88
Biathlon (male)	7	Vitaliy Lukyanenko (UKR)	2002–14
Biathlon (female)	7	Olena Iurkovska (UKR)	2002–14

MOST . . .

Skiing Nations' Cup wins The skiing Nations' Cup is based on the combined men's and women's results at the Alpine Ski World Cup. It was won 35 times by Austria between 1969 and 2014.

WSOC medals Relay: Finland has won 38 World Ski Orienteering Championships (WSOC) medals across the three relay categories (men, women, and mixed).

    Individual (male): Eduard Khrennikov (RUS) has won 11 WSOC medals, including seven golds.

    Individual (female): Fellow Russian Tatiana Vlasova has taken 10 individual medals.

MOST POINTS IN A SINGLE END OF AN OLYMPIC CURLING MATCH An "end" in curling is complete when both teams have delivered all eight rocks. The most points scored by a team in a single end of an Olympic match is seven, by Great Britain against the U.S.A. in Sochi, Russia, on Feb. 11, 2014. Great Britain won the game 12–3, needing only 6 of the 10 possible ends to do so.

MOST OLYMPIC SHORT TRACK SPEED SKATING GOLDS (MALE) Viktor Ahn (KOR/RUS, b. Ahn Hyun-Soo) won three short track speed skating gold medals for South Korea at the 2006 Olympics in Turin, Italy, and another three golds for Russia at the 2014 Games in Sochi. Ahn represented South Korea at the 2006 Games, but in 2011 he became a Russian citizen and so represented Russia at the Sochi Olympics.

MOST CONSECUTIVE INDIVIDUAL OLYMPIC MEDALS Armin Zöggeler (ITA) won six consecutive individual Olympic medals from 1994 to 2014: two gold, one silver, and three bronze, all in the men's singles luge. The previous record was also held by a luger, Georg Hackl (DEU), who won five consecutive individual medals from 1988 to 2002.

Bobsled Skeleton World Cup race wins (male) Martins Dukurs (LVA) won 31 bobsled Skeleton World Cup races between Feb. 8, 2008 and Jan. 25, 2014.

YOUNGEST . . .

Curling rink (team) to win an Olympic medal (female) The Great Britain side of Eve Muirhead, Anna Sloan, Vicki Adams, Claire Hamilton, and Lauren Gray had an average age of 23 years 255 days when they won bronze in Sochi, Russia, on Feb. 20, 2014.

YOUNGEST OLYMPIC SNOWBOARD MEDALIST
Ayumu Hirano (JPN, b. Nov. 29, 1998) was just 15 years 74 days old when he won silver in the snowboard halfpipe in Sochi, Russia, on Feb. 11, 2014. The record for the **youngest Olympic freestyle skiing medalist (female)** was also set in Sochi, by Justine Dufour-Lapointe (CAN, b. Mar. 25, 1994), who won gold in the moguls event at 19 years 321 days old on Feb. 8, 2014.

FACT: Snowboarding was first included in the Winter Olympics in 1998.

World Women's Curling Championship winning skip Scottish skip Eve Muirhead (UK, b. Apr. 22, 1990) led her team to victory at the age of 22 years 336 days in Riga, Latvia, on Mar. 24, 2013.

OLDEST . . .

Individual Winter Olympics medalist Luge silver-medalist Albert Demchenko (RUS, b. Nov. 27, 1971) was 42 years 74 days old when he won in Sochi, Russia, on Feb. 9, 2014. The **oldest individual Winter Olympics gold medalist** is Ole Einar Bjørndalen (NOR, b. Jan. 27, 1974), who was 40 years 12 days old when he won the 10-km biathlon sprint on Feb. 8, 2014.

Skiing World Cup slalom race winner (male) Mario Matt (AUT, b. Apr. 9, 1979) finished first at the age of 34 years 250 days in Val d'Isère, France, on Dec. 15, 2013.

OLDEST SKI JUMP OLYMPIC MEDALIST Noriaki Kasai (JPN, b. Jun. 6, 1972) won bronze in the men's ski jump team event at 41 years 256 days old in Sochi, Russia, on Feb. 17, 2014. He's also the **oldest ski jump World Cup winner**, taking gold in the ski flying event at 41 years 219 days old in Tauplitz, Austria, on Jan. 11, 2014.

SPORTS ROUNDUP

Most competitive 147 breaks in snooker Ronnie O'Sullivan (UK) has racked up 12 maximum breaks in competitive snooker matches. He achieved his 147s from Apr. 21, 1997 to Mar. 2, 2014.

O'Sullivan has also made the **most century breaks at the World Snooker Championship** (144), from Apr. 15, 1995 to May 5, 2014.

In 1927, the first world snooker champion received **prize money of $10**.

MOST WINS OF THE INDIVIDUAL LONG-DISTANCE WORLD ORIENTEERING CHAMPIONSHIPS The World Orienteering Championships long-distance event has been contested annually since 1966. Simone Niggli-Luder (CHE) has taken the crown eight times, more than any other person—man or woman. Her wins came in 2001, 2003, 2005–06, 2009–10, and 2012–13.

First female snooker player to qualify for the final stages of a ranking event

Reanne Evans (UK)—10-time ladies' world champion—qualified for the televised stages of China's Wuxi Classic with a 5–4 victory over male snooker player Thepchaiya Un-Nooh (THA) in a qualifying match at the South West Snooker Academy in Gloucester, UK, on May 28, 2013.

Most century breaks in a season

Neil Robertson (AUS) made 103 century breaks in 22 tournaments in the 2013–14 season that ran from Jun. 7, 2013 to May 5, 2014. As of May 3, 2014, Robertson had made 361 century breaks as a professional. He is the fifth best all-time century maker, on a list that is headed by Stephen Hendry (UK) with 775.

Longest snooker ban On Sep. 25, 2013, an independent tribunal found professional snooker player Stephen Lee (UK) guilty of fixing seven matches in 2008 and 2009. Lee was banned from playing in any match sanctioned by the World Professional Billiards and Snooker Association for 12 years.

MOST RODEO WORLD CHAMPIONSHIPS Between 2002 and 2013, Trevor Brazile (U.S.A.) won 19 titles at the Professional Rodeo Cowboys Association World Championships. His titles were won across four events: All-Around, Tie-Down Roping (individual and team), and Steer Wrestling. Brazile also has the **most All-Around Rodeo World Championships titles**, with 11 wins in 12 years.

FACT: The All-Around title is awarded to the leading money winner in a single season in two or more events.

YOUNGEST WORLD ARTISTIC GYMNASTICS CHAMPIONSHIPS FLOOR GOLD MEDALIST (MALE) Kenzo Shirai (JPN, b. Aug. 24, 1996) won the floor event at the World Artistic Gymnastics Championships at the age of 17 years 43 days in Antwerp, Belgium, on Oct. 6, 2013. Shirai also became the **first person to perform a quadruple twist in a major final** (pictured above right).

Most Professional Bowlers Association tour event appearances

Between 1976 and 2013, Tom Baker (U.S.A.) competed in 840 Professional Bowlers Association (PBA) ten-pin bowling tour events.

Carmen Salvino (U.S.A., b. Nov. 23, 1933) is the **oldest ten-pin tour bowler**. He played in the 2014 PBA Tournament of Champions at the age of 80 years 58 days at Thunderbowl Lanes in Michigan, U.S.A., on Jan. 20. Walter Ray Williams, Jr. (U.S.A.) has the **most PBA ten-pin bowling titles**. His tally stands at 47 titles; the latest was won at the USBC Masters on Feb. 14, 2010.

PARALYMPIC (IPC) POWERLIFTING

Category	Weight	Name	Year
Male			
<49 kg	181 kg	Yakubu Adesokan (NGR)	2014
<59 kg	190 kg	Ali Jawad (UK, b. LBN)	2014
<80 kg	236 kg	Xiao Fei Gu (CHN)	2014
<97 kg	240 kg	Mohamed Eldib (EGY)	2013
107+ kg	285 kg	Siamand Rahman (IRN)	2014
Female			
<41 kg	103 kg	Nazmiye Muslu (TUR)	2014
<50 kg	122 kg	Olesya Lafina (RUS)	2014
<61 kg	135.5 kg	Fatma Omar (EGY)	2014
<73 kg	150 kg	Souhad Ghazouani (FRA)	2013
86+ kg	151 kg	Precious Orji (NGR)	2014

Statistics correct as of Apr. 21, 2014

Most players to score a televised nine-dart finish in one day The fewest throws needed to score 501 points in a game of darts is nine, aka the nine-dart finish. Two players achieved this feat during the televised 2014 PDC World Darts Championship in London, UK: Terry Jenkins (UK) and Kyle Anderson (AUS), in different matches, on Dec. 14, 2013.

First woman to win the Mongol Derby When Lara Prior-Palmer (UK, b. Jun. 24, 1994) won the Mongol Derby on Aug. 10, 2013, she became the first woman to do so. The competition takes place over a grueling 621-mi. (1,000-km) course and is the **longest multihorse race**. Lara's 2013 title also made her the youngest **Mongol Derby winner**, at the age of 19 years 47 days.

Most Grade 1 victories by a horse Hurricane Fly (IRL) won 19 Grade 1 races—the premium class of horse racing—from Nov. 30, 2008 to Jan. 26, 2014.

Most USASF Cheerleading Worlds international titles Cheer Athletics of Kentucky, U.S.A., had won 15 international All Star Federation Cheerleading Worlds titles as of the end of 2013. Their wins include both all-girl and co-ed, levels 5 and 6.

MOST ARCHERY WORLD CUP RECURVE WINS Female: Yun Ok-Hee (KOR) has won the women's recurve competition twice at the Archery World Cup. Ok-Hee's wins came in 2010 and 2013. The World Cup was instituted in 2006 and comprises four separate events in different locations before a final competition.

    Male: Brady Ellison (U.S.A.) has also scored two recurve World Cup wins, in 2010–11.

YOUNGEST X GAMES MEDALIST Alana Smith (U.S.A., b. Oct. 20, 2000) was 12 years 210 days old when she won a silver medal in the Women's Skateboard Park competition at the X Games in Barcelona, Spain, on May 18, 2013.

Tom Schaar (U.S.A., b. Sep. 14, 1999) is the **youngest X Games gold medalist**. He was 12 years 229 days old when he won the Mini Mega category on Apr. 30, 2012.

Fastest speed skating

- **200-m road (male):** On Dec. 9, 2012 in San Benedetto del Tronto, Italy, Ioseba Fernandez (ESP) finished the 200-m individual time trial in 15.879 sec.
- **200-m road (female):** Jersy Puello (COL) skated 200 m on the road in 17.677 sec. on Aug. 27, 2013 in Ostend, Belgium.
- **1,000-m track (male):** Bart Swings (BEL) skated 1,000 m on a track in 1 min. 20.923 sec. on Aug. 25, 2013 in Ostend, Belgium.
- **1,000-m track (female):** Barbara Fischer (DEU) set a track time of 1 min. 27.06 sec. in Inzell, Germany, on Aug. 27, 1988.
- **10,000-m track (male):** On Aug. 23, 2013, inline skating world champion Fabio Francolini (ITA) covered 10,000 m on a track in Ostend, Belgium, in just 14 min. 23.54 sec.
- **10,000-m track (female):** Yang Hochen (TWN) recorded a time of 15 min. 26.970 sec. in a 10,000-m track skate in Ostend, Belgium, on Aug. 24, 2013.

Most appearances in the World Equestrian Games

Anky van Grunsven (NLD) appeared in the Fédération Equestre Internationale (FEI) World Equestrian Games six times between 1990 and 2010. She is the only rider to have appeared in every edition of the tournament since its inception in 1990.

MOST JUMP RACING WINS Tony "AP" McCoy (UK) rode 4,106 jump racing winners in his career between Mar. 26, 1992 and Apr. 26, 2014. McCoy also has the **most jump racing wins in a season** (289 in 2001/02) and the **most jump racing Champion Jockey titles** (19, awarded from 1996 to 2014).

MOST 180S IN A WORLD DARTS CHAMPIONSHIP At the 2014 Professional Darts Corporation (PDC) World Championship, held at Alexandra Palace in London, UK, from Dec. 13, 2013 to Jan. 1, 2014, a total of 603 maximums (180s) were recorded, beating the 588 achieved in the 2012 competition. The title was eventually won by Michael van Gerwen (NLD, pictured), who hit 16 of the maximums.

Longest raft race The Great River Amazon Raft Race has been staged annually since 1999 between the Peruvian locations of Pescadores Island and the Club de Caza y Pesca in Bella Vista. The race, which covers some 112 mi. (180 km), was created by Mike Collis (UK). It challenges four-person teams to build a log raft and paddle the course in three stages over three days.

ACKNOWLEDGMENTS

Guinness World Records would like to thank the following for their help in compiling this edtion:

Across the Pond (Rob, Aaron, Julie, Karen, Katie, and all their colleagues); API Laminates Ltd (Simon Thompson); Asatsu-DK Inc. (Motonori Iwasaki, Shinsuke Sakuma); Charlotte Atkins; Eric Atkins; Freya Atkins; Simon Atkins; BAFTA; Alexander Balandin; Elle Bartlett; BBC; Oliver Beatson; Sarah Bebbington; Andrew Benson (Carnegie Institution for Science); BFI; Anisa Bhatti; Alexander Boatfield; Joseph Boatfield; Luke Boatfield; Bodyflight Bedford (Bryony Doughty, Ged Parker); Sam Borden; Chiara Bragato; Patrick Bragato; Veronica Bridges (Featherstone Rovers RLFC); Broadcast; Colin Burgess (Stoke City FC); Nicola Campbell (Camelot Group); Canton Classic Car Museum, Ohio, U.S.A.; Carousel Candies, California, U.S.A.; CCTV (Guo Tong, Wang Wei, and all their colleagues); Frank Chambers; Richard M. Christensen (Professor Research Emeritus, Stanford University); The Chunichi Shimbun (Tetsuya Okamura, Tadao Sawada); Adam Cloke; Collaboration Inc. Japan (Mr. Suzuki, Miho, Kyoto, and all their colleagues); Connexion Cars (Rob and Tracey); Ken Cook (Caboose Hobbies, Denver, Colorado, U.S.A.); Anne Cowne (Information Officer, Information Centre, Lloyd's Register); Pietro D'Angelo; Panos Datskos; Anastassia Davidzenka; Martyn Davis; Denmaur Independent Papers Limited (Julian Townsend); Frank Dimroth; Gemma Doherty; Emmys (Academy of Television Arts & Sciences); Europroduzione (Renato, Gabriela, Carlo, Paola, and all their colleagues); Toby and Amelia Ewen; Eyeworks/Warner Bros. Germany (Michael, Martin, Käthe, and all their colleagues); Benjamin Fall; Rebecca Fall; Daniel Fernandez; Jonathan de Ferranti; FJT Logistics Limited (Ray Harper, Gavin Hennessy); Forbes; Martin Fuechsle; Gemological Institute of America (Kristin Mahan, Shane McClure, Stephen Morisseau, Gwen Travis); Damien Gildea; Andrew Goodwin; Brandon Greenwood; Jordan Greenwood; Ryan Greenwood; Victoria Grimsell; GWRJ internship students (Jiani Xie, Natsumi Kawakami, Chisaki Iijima, Maho Miyamoto, Yumina Murata); Carmen Alfonzo de Hannah; Alexia Hannah Alfonzo; Amy Hannah Alfonzo; Rod Hansen (Museum of Idaho, Idaho Falls, Idaho, U.S.A.); Ellie Hayward; Dr. Haze (Circus of Horrors); Bob Headland; Matilda and Max Heaton; High Noon (Brad, Jim, Dana, and all their colleagues); The Himalayan Database; Hololens Technology Co., Ltd; Stephen J. Holroyd (U.S. Soccer Archives); Claire Holzman (Houghton Mifflin Harcourt); Marsha K. Hoover; Dora Howard; Tilly Howard; Colin Hughes; Cynthia Hunt; Sarah Icken (Camelot Group); Integrated Colour Editions Europe (Roger Hawkins, Susie Hawkins, Clare Merryfield); Richard Johnston, Barbara Jones (Information Centre Manager, Lloyd's Register); Stephanie Jones (Great British Racing); Raymond S. Jordan, Drogheda, Ireland; Justin Kazmark (Kickstarter); Harry Kikstra; Laleham Camping Club, UK; Orla Langton; Thea Langton; Sophie Lawrenson (Royal Collection Trust); Frederick Horace Lazell; Sydney Leleux; Lion Television (Simon, Jeremy, Tom, and all their colleagues); Lloyd's Insurance (Oonagh Bates, Jonathan Thomas); London Pet Show; London Wonderground; Rüdiger Lorenz; Luci Producciones (Maria, Shaun, Stefano); Ciara Mackey; Sarah & Martin Mackey; Theresa Mackey; Christian de Marliave; Missy Matilda; Dave McAleer; Chelsea McGuffin; Clare Merryfield; Metacritic; Jeremy Michell, Historic Photographs and Ships Plans Manager, Royal Museums Greenwich; Miditech (Niret, Nivedith, Nikhil, and all their colleagues); John Jackson Miller; Tamsin Mitchell; Harriet Molloy; Sophie, Joshua and Florence Molloy; Colin Monteath; Dan Morrison; Steven Munatones (Open Water Source); Museum of the Weird, Austin, Texas, U.S.A.; Anikó Németh-Móra (International Weightlifting Federation); James Ng; Jim Nicholls; David Oberlink; Caitlin Penny; Periscoop (Peri, Elsy, and all their colleagues); Karen Perkins (World Alternative Games); Tom Pierce; Sophie Procter (British Airways); Robert Pullar; Miriam Randall; John Reed (World Speed Sailing Records Council); Kevin Rochfort (FISB); Dan Roddick (World Flying Disc Association); Roller Coaster Database; Kate Rushworth (YouTube); Nick Ryan (Xpogo); Nick Ryuan (Xpogo); Eric Sakowski; Paolo Scarabaggio; Rob Schweitzer (Historic Hudson Valley); Nellie Scott (Brick Artist); Michael Serra (São Paulo Futebol Clube); Bill Sharp (Billabong XXL Big Wave Awards); Ang Tsering Sherpa; Dawa Sherpa; Patrice Simon; Athena Simpson; Chris Skone-Roberts; Katy Smith (John Wiley & Sons, Inc.); Spectratek Technologies, Inc. (Terry Conway, Mike Foster); Glenn Speer; Bill Spindler; St. Mary's University, UK; Ray Stevenson; Stephen Sutton; Charlie, Holly and Daisy Taylor; Terry and Jan Todd (H J Lutcher Stark Center for Physical Culture and Sports, University of Texas, U.S.A.); Matthew Tole; Anaelle Torres; Cliff Towne (Professional Disc Golf Association); truTV (Michael, Chris, Stephen, Angel, Marissa, and all their colleagues); Sheryl Twigg, Press & PR Manager, Royal Museums Greenwich; UPM Plattling, Germany; Kripa Varanasi; Variety; Virgin (Charmaine Clarke, Philippa Russ); Craig Walter; Lara and Sevgi White; Oli White; Robert White; Paul Winston (Zippos Circus); Robert Wood; Daniel Woods; Madeleine Wuschech; Hayley Wylie-Deacon; Rueben George Wylie-Deacon; Tobias Hugh Wylie-Deacon; Zodiak Clips (Sandra, David, Dom, Cath, and all their colleagues); Zodiak Kids (Karen, Gary, and all their colleagues); Zodiak Rights (Andreas, Tim, Barney, and all their colleagues)

PICTURE CREDITS

xi: Paul Michael Hughes/GWR **xii:** SYCO **xiii:** James Ellerker/GWR, Zef Nikolla **xiv:** Rick Kern/Bravo, Rich Pedroncelli/AP/PA **xvi:** Peter Kramer/NBC, Virginia Sherwood/NBC, Peter Kramer/NBC **xvi:** Ross Halfin **xvii:** Greg Lemaster, Greg Lemaster, Dan MacMedan/Chevrolet, Dan Mac-Medan/Chevrolet **xviii:** Kevin Scott Ramos/GWR **xxi:** Erik C. Pendzich/Rex **xxii:** Getty Images **xxiii:** Hilary Morgan/Alamy, V&A Images/Alamy, Getty Images, Lionel Cironneau/AP/PA, Lloyds of London/AP/PA, Lloyds of London/AP/PA **xxv:** Getty Images **xxvi:** Paul Michael Hughes/GWR, Getty Images, Photoshot **xxvii:** Clive Limpkin/Rex, Fox TV, ITV/Rex **xxviii:** John Wright/GWR **xxix:** Paul Michael Hughes/GWR **1:** NASA **3:** NASA, NASA, NASA, NASA/Science Photo Library, NASA, NASA **4:** NASA, NASA, NASA, NASA **5:** Reuters, Getty Images **6:** NASA, NASA, Getty Images, NASA, NASA, NASA **7:** NASA, NASA, NASA, Reuters **8:** NASA, ESA, NASA, NASA, Alamy, Alamy **9:** NASA, NASA, NASA, NASA, NASA, Mike Blake/Reuters, NASA, NASA **10:** NASA, NASA **11:** NASA, ESO **12:** ESO, ESO, NASA **13:** NASA, Alamy, Alamy **15:** NASA, NASA **16:** German Aerospace Center, NASA **17:** Mark A. Garlick/Science Photo Library **19:** Robert Matton/Alamy, Joongi Kim, Joongi Kim **20:** NASA/Alamy, NASA/Alamy, Science Photo Library, ESA **21:** NASA, Sci-Fi Photo Journal, MPIA **22:** NASA, Gavin Collins, NASA, NASA **23:** Denysov Dmytro/iStock, NASA **25:** Eberly College of Science, Zeit News **26:** NASA **28:** Alamy, Alamy, Alamy **29:** NASA **30:** NRAO/AUI, Large Binocular Telescope Observatory **31:** NRAO/AUI, Stefan Schwarzburg/H.E.S.S. Collaboration **32:** redOrbit.com, Alamy **34:** Pablo Bonet/IAC, Javier Larrea/Alamy, Alamy **35:** Alamy **37:** Thomas Senf/Mammut **38:** Getty Images, Getty Images, NASA, NOAA **39:** NASA, NASA, Kara Lavender, Argo Information Centre, University of Texas, NASA, ESA, NASA **40:** ESA, ESA, ESA, Curtin University of Technology, NASA, NASA **41:** University of California, Tomas Munita/Eyevine, Getty Images, Holger Leue/Corbis, NOAA, Alamy **42:** Ralph White/Corbis, Bill Waugh/Reuters, Dean Conger/Corbis, Alamy **43:** Roger Coulam/Alamy, NASA, AP/PA **44:** Alamy, Reuters, NASA/Reuters, NASA **45:** Reuters, NASA, Addi Bischoff, Stefan Ralew/sr-meteorites.de **46:** AP/PA, Australian Science **48:** NASA, NASA, NASA **49:** NASA, NASA, NASA, NASA, NASA **50:** NASA, NASA **51:** Getty Images **52:** Maps For Free, Dianne Blell/Getty Images **53:** Getty Images, Alamy **54:** Royal Geographical Society, Susanna Wikman, British Antarctic Survey **55:** Galen Rowell/Corbis **56:** Anderson Aerial Photography **57:** Andrew McLachlan/Superstock, Colorado State University, Doug Perrine/Corbis **58:** Massimo Brega/Science Photo Library, Massimo Brega/Science Photo Library **59:** Alamy, Gary Bell/Oceanwide Images, **60:** W. Robert Moore/National Geographic **62:** Carsten Peter/Getty Images **63:**

Alamy, Alamy, Robbie Shone/Alamy **64:** Stephen L Alvarez/National Geographic **65:** David Kilpatrick/Alamy, Dave Bunnell/Under Earth Images **66:** Getty Images, Getty Images **67:** Alamy **69:** Martin Strmiska/Alamy **70:** Alamy, Getty Images, Bio-Ken Snake Farm, Nurlan Kalchinov/Alamy **71:** Image Quest Marine, Image Quest Marine, Dirk Ercken/Alamy, Bruce Rasner/Nature PL, AP/PA, Daniel Heuclin/Nature PL **72:** Alamy, Sebastian Kennerknecht/FLPA, Miguel Rangel Jr, Jodi Rowley, Tilo Nadler, Richard Porter/Ardea **73:** Alamy, Nicole Dutra, Peter Kappeler, Public Library of Science, Knud Andreas Jønsson, Mahree-Dee White, Samuel Nienow **74:** Justin Hofman/Alamy **75:** Alamy, Alamy **76:** Martin Strmiska/Alamy, Alamy **77:** Human Dynamo Workshop, Steve Bloom/Alamy **79:** Thomas Marent/Corbis, H Lansdown/Alamy **80:** Denis Palanque/FLPA, Masahiro Iijima/Ardea **81:** Dave Watts/Alamy, Alamy, Alamy **82:** Corbis, FLPA, Anup Shah/Getty Images **83:** Getty Images **84:** Photoshot **85:** Barry Mansell/Nature PL, Corbis **86:** Alamy, Corbis, Donald M. Jones/FLPA **87:** Frans Lanting/Corbis, Eric Nathan/Photoshot **89:** Steven David Miller/Nature PL, Alamy, Photoshot, Cyril Laubscher/Getty Images **90:** Alamy, Jim Zipp/Ardea, Chris Howarth/Alamy, Kevin Elsby/Alamy **91:** Alamy **92:** Getty Images, M. Watson/Ardea **93:** Stan Osolinski/Getty Images **94:** Alamy, Milos Manojilovic/iStock, Chris Mattison/Alamy **95:** Danté Fenolio, Andrew Murray/Nature PL **96:** A & J Visage/Alamy, A & J Visage/Alamy, A & J Visage/Alamy, Alamy **98:** Doug Perrine/Nature PL, Zeb Hogan/WWF **99:** Catalina Island Marine Institute, Jesse Cancelmo/Alamy **100:** Steve Bloom Images/Alamy **101:** David Jenkins/Caters News **102:** Chris Radburn/PA **103:** Chris Skone-Roberts/GWR **104:** Getty Images, Reuters **105:** Koen G. H. Breedveld/Spring Rivers Ecological Sciences, Corbis, www.aphotomarine.com **106:** Alamy, creepyanimals.com, Corbis **108:** Louise Murray/Alamy, Maximilian Weinzierl/Alamy **109:** Csiro Ecosystem Sciences, Getty Images **110:** Dale Ward, Caters, Morley Read/Alamy **111:** The Natural History Museum, London **112:** Alamy, California Academy of Sciences **114:** SWNS, MMurphy/NPWS **115:** Seren/Bangor University **116:** Barry Durrant/Getty Images, snailworld.eu **117:** Alamy, Andrey Nekrasov/Alamy, Jeff Rotman/Getty Images, Andrey Nekrasov/Alamy **119:** Sophie Davidson/GWR, David Crump/Rex **120:** Kevin Scott Ramos/GWR **121:** James Ellerker/GWR, Ryan Schude/GWR, Ryan Schude/GWR **122:** Getty Images, Corbis, Elaine Thompson/AP/PA **123:** David Moir/Reuters, Ryan Schude/GWR **124:** Kevin Scott Ramos/GWR, Howard Burditt/Reuters, James Ellerker/GWR **125:** James Ellerker/GWR, Ranald Mackechnie/GWR, Kevin Scott Ramos/GWR **126:** Silvia Vignolini/PNAS, Frans Lanting/Corbis **127:** Redfern Natural History, Getty Images **128:** Alamy, Alamy, Alamy **129:** Jerry Lampen/Reuters, Paul Street/Alamy, Vinayaraj **131:** John Wright/GWR **133:** Paul Michael Hughes/GWR **134:** Ron Siddle/AP/PA, Corbis **135:** Buddhika Weerasinghe/Getty Images, Irish Independent, John Wright/GWR, Birmingham Mail **136:** Corbis, Getty Images, John Wright/GWR, The Burns Archive **137:** Getty Images, Paul Michael Hughes/GWR **138:** Alamy, Paul Michael Hughes/GWR **140:** Sam Green, Roslan Rahman/Getty Images **143:** Getty Images, Naturex **145:** Gary Wainwright **147:** Devon Steigerwald **148:** Reuters, Simon Pizzey/The Citizen **149:** Tyler Hicks/Evevine, Alamy, Reuters **150:** Drew Gardner/GWR **152:** Leon Schadeberg/Rex **153:** James Ellerker/GWR, Paul Michael Hughes/GWR, James Ellerker/GWR **154:** John Wright/GWR **155:** Kimberly Cook/GWR **156:** Rex, Hank Walker/Getty Images **157:** Tomas Bravo/Guinness World Records **158:** Paul Michael Hughes/GWR, Sean Sexton/Getty Images, Corbis **160:** D.L. Anderson **164:** Lakruwan Wannia-rachchi/Getty Images **166:** Corbis **168:** Alamy **169:** Getty Images, Well-come Images **170:** Rex Features, John A. Secoges/AP/PA **171:** Paul Michael Hughes/GWR **173:** Ranald Mackechnie/GWR **174:** Sam Christ-mas/GWR, Richard Howard/Getty Images, Tengku Bahar/Getty Images **179:** Richard Bradbury/GWR, Richard Bradbury/GWR **180:** Philip Robert-son/GWR, Shinsuke Kamioka/GWR **181:** Frank Espich/The Indianapolis Star **182:** Alamy, Mike Sonnenberg/iStock, Alamy **183:** Pete Jenkins/Alamy **184:** Peter Byrne/PA, Kevin Scott/Ramos **185:** David Cripps/Royal Collection, Steve Parsons/PA, Steve Parsons/PA **186:** Dan Kitwood/Getty Images, Ranald Mackechnie/GWR **189:** Ranald Mackechnie/GWR **190:** Ranald Mackechnie/GWR **193:** Fredrik Naumann/Felix Features, Fredrik Naumann/Felix Features, Ryan Schude/GWR **194:** Ranald Mackechnie/GWR, Ranald Mackechnie/GWR **195:** Richard Bradbury/GWR, Ranald Mackechnie/GWR, Paul Michael Hughes/GWR **196:** Kate Melton **197:** Ryan Schude/GWR **198:** Ryan Schude/GWR **199:** Ryan Schude/GWR **202:** Ryan Schude/GWR **204:** Dan Rowlands/Caters **206:** Reuters, David Parry/PA, David Parry/PA **207:** John Wright/GWR, Ryan Schude/GWR, Ranald Mackechnie/GWR **208:** Ryan Schude/GWR, Ryan Schude/GWR **209:** Ryan Schude/GWR, Rob Loud/Getty Images, Drew Gardner/GWR **210:** Ryan Schude/GWR **211:** Paul Michael Hughes, Ryan Schude/GWR **212:** Ranald Mackechnie/GWR **213:** Paul Michael Hughes/GWR **214:** Keith Heneghan/Phocus **216:** Richard Keith Wolff/Getty Images, Richard Keith Wolff/Getty Images **217:** Matt Crossick/GWR, Ryan Schude/GWR **218:** Ryan Schude/GWR **219:** John Wright/GWR, Ranald Mackechnie/GWR **220:** Ranald Mackechnie/GWR **221:** Paul Michael Hughes/GWR **222:** Paul Michael Hughes/GWR, Richard Birch, Paul Michael Hughes/GWR **223:** Ranald Mackechnie/GWR **224:** Nathan King/Alamy, Tomasz Rossa, Alex-ander Nemonov/Getty Images **226:** Aly Song/Reuters **228:** WSSA, WSSA, WSSA **230:** Marcel Wichert **231:** Andrew Schwartz/Corbis **234:** Paul Mi-chael Hughes/GWR **235:** Jeff Holmes, Alamy, The Strong **236:** Rick Belden, Christiane Kappes **237:** Mirja Geh/Red Bull **238:** Michael G Night-engale **239:** Capture The Moment Photography **241:** Anne Caroline/GWR **242:** Theo Cohen **243:** Rentsendorj Bazarsukh/Reuters **244:** Philip Robert-son/GWR, Ilya S. Savenok/Getty Images **245:** Daniel Berehulak/Getty Im-ages, Sanjay Kanojia/Getty Images **246:** Ruud van der Lubben/PA **247:** Paul Michael Hughes/GWR, Ryan Schude/GWR **248:** Paul Michael Hughes/GWR **249:** Mark Radford **250:** Paul Michael Hughes/GWR **251:** Alamy **253:** Ryan Schude/GWR **254:** Getty Images, Tim Rooke/Rex **255:** National Archives, Shel Hershorn/Getty Images, Alamy, Alamy, Corbis **256:** Alamy, Alamy, Corbis, Alamy, Nati Harnik/AP/PA **257:** Gus Ruelas/Reuters, Keith Dannemiller/Alamy **259:** Ahmad Masood/Reuters, Thomas Mukoya/Reuters, Ho New/Reuters **260:** Soe Zeya Tun/Reuters **261:** Getty

Images, Reuters **262:** Reuters **263:** Athar Hussain/Reuters, Ho New/Reuters, Reuters **264:** Christophe Simon/Getty Images, Evaristo Sa/Getty Images, Ezequiel Abiu Lopez/AP/PA **266:** Krishnendu Halder/Reuters, Global Times, Onur Coban/Getty Images **267:** Wim Scheire/Getty Images, Mahmoud Raouf Mahmoud/Reuters **268:** Kem McNair/Getty Images **269:** Ragnhild Gustad, Chaiwat Subprasom/Reuters **271:** United States Geological Survey **272:** Alamy, Pascal Ducept/Alamy, Oleksandr Rupeta/Alamy **273:** Manuel Silvestri/Reuters, Giorgio Marcoaldi/CVN, Reuters **274:** Kristijan Vuckovic **276:** National Center for Ecological Analysis and Synthesis, Michael Kooren/Reuters **277:** Jahre-Wallern, Aly Song/Reuters, Marine Traffic **278:** Reuters **279:** Cameron Laird/Rex **280:** Pablo Blazquez Dominguez/Getty Images **282:** Mark Bialek/Alamy **284:** Phil Mingo/Pinnacle **285:** Michael Urban/Getty Images, Paul Cooper/Rex **286:** Alamy **287:** Alamy, Alamy, Alamy **288:** RMN-Grand Palais/Musée du Louvre/Hervé Lewandowski, Roger Viollet/Getty Images **289:** Getty Images, Alamy **290:** Tina Hager/Getty Images, Chao-Yang Chan/Alamy **291:** George Nikitin/AP/PA, Craig Barritt/Getty Images **292:** Toru Hanai/Reuters, Alamy, Alamy **293:** Yorgos Karahalis/Reuters, Rebecca Cook/Reuters **294:** NASA **295:** Dove, Universal Pictures/Alamy, Facebook **296:** Google Maps, Alamy **297:** Instagram, Instagram, AP/PA, Lucy Nicholson/Reuters **298:** Andrew Kelly/Reuters, Laurence Mathieu/The Guardian **302:** Mike Goldwater/Alamy, Alamy **305:** Philip Temple **307:** Everest Media Productions **309:** Afanassi Makovnev **310:** Getty Images **311:** Jarek Jõepera/GWR **315:** Getty Images **316:** Paul Michael Hughes/GWR **319:** Will Wintercross **321:** James Ellerker/GWR **322:** Paul A. Souders/Corbis **323:** British Nanga Parbat 2012 Expedition, Philip Temple **324:** Frieder Blickle/Camera Press **326:** Paul Michael Hughes/GWR **328:** Felipe Souza **329:** Ben Duffy **330:** Daniel Deme/GWR, Torsten Blackwood/Getty Images **331:** Paul Michael Hughes/GWR **332:** Bas de Meijer **333:** Lars Stenholt Kirkegaard, Lupi_Spuma **334:** Shutterstock **335:** John Dickey, Claudia Marcelloni **336:** James Ellerker/GWR, James Ellerker/GWR **340:** Paul Michael Hughes/GWR, Paul Michael Hughes/GWR **343:** Twentieth Century Fox **345:** Lionsgate/Alamy **346:** Twentieth Century Fox, Universal/Alamy **347:** Walt Disney Pictures, Twentieth Century Fox/Alamy, MGM, Twentieth Century Fox **348:** Summit Entertainment, Universal, Walt Disney Productions, Twentieth Century Fox, Marvel **349:** MGM/Alamy, Lucasfilm, Hollywood Pictures, Warner Bros. **350:** MGM/Alamy, Walt Disney Productions, Paramount, Walt Disney Productions/Rex, MGM/Alamy, Twentieth Century Fox **351:** Warner Bros., MGM/Alamy, Lucasfilm, Universal, Twentieth Century Fox, Twentieth Century Fox **352:** Yash Raj Films **353:** Warner Bros., Paramount Pictures **355:** Warner Bros. **356:** Salty Features, Warner Bros. **357:** Yashraj Films, Twentieth Century Fox **358:** Alamy, Cross Creek Pictures, Alamy **359:** Alamy, Mario Anzuoni/Reuters **360:** Alamy, Walt Disney Pictures, Karen Ballard/Paramount Pictures **361:** Fred Prouser/Reuters **362:** Getty Images **363:** Brian Snyder/Reuters **364:** Lucy Nicholson/Reuters **365:** Steven Klein **366:** Terry Richardson, Isaac Brekken/Getty Images **367:** YouTube **368:** YouTube, YouTube, YouTube, YouTube, YouTube **369:** YouTube, YouTube **370:** YouTube, YouTube, YouTube **371:** YouTube,

Girlguiding North West, Matt Crossick/GWR **372:** Don Emmert/Getty Images **373:** Alamy, Marijan Murat/PA, Alamy, PA, Russell Cheyne/Reuters **374:** Rodrigo de Balbin Behrmann, WENN, WENN, Alain Perus/L'Oeil du Diaph **376:** Ryan Schude/GWR **378:** Alamy **379:** Olivia Harris/Reuters, Benjamin Pritzkuleit **381:** Rex Features **382:** Haut et Court **383:** Yogen Shah/Getty Images, Samir Hussein/Getty Images, Virginia Sherwood/Getty Images **385:** Bob D'Amico/Getty Images **386:** A & E Networks, BBC, Ryan Schude/GWR **387:** Kevin Scott Ramos/GWR, Ryan Schude/GWR, Paul Michael Hughes/GWR **388:** Richard Bradbury/GWR, Ryan Schude/GWR **389:** Ranald Mackechnie/GWR, Richard Bradbury/GWR, Ryan Schude/GWR **390:** Ranald Mackechnie/GWR **391:** Ho New/Reuters **393:** Kevin Scott Ramos/GWR **394:** NASA, Alcatel-Lucent, Topfoto **395:** HP Museum, Eric Risberg/AP/PA, Getty Images, Getty Images, AP/PA **396:** Gene J. Puskar/AP/PA, Science Photo Library, Elise Amendola/AP/PA, Getty Images, Getty Images **397:** Rebecca Cook/Reuters, Fabrizio Bensch/Reuters, Kimberly White/Reuters, Denis Closon/Rex **398:** Denis Closon/Rex, Reidar Hahn **399:** Mathew Imaging **400:** Justin Garvanovic/Coaster Club **401:** Iain Masterton/Alamy **402:** Stan Honda/Getty Images, Ho New/Reuters **403:** Craig T. Mathew/Mathew Imaging, Kazuhiro Nogi/Getty Images,**404:** Alamy, Alamy **405:** Alamy **406:** Alamy, Rex Features, Corbis, JS Callahan/Alamy **407:** Ray Roberts/Rex, Getty Images **409:** Canton Classic Car Museum, Alamy **410:** Max Earey/Newspress **411:** Damian Kramski, Chrysler Group LLC **412:** Alamy, Alamy **413:** Reuters, Kim Kyung Hoon/Reuters, Tobias Schwarz/Reuters **414:** Peter Brogden/Alamy, Robert Nickelsberg/Alamy **415:** Maciej Dakowicz/Alamy, iStock **417:** PA **420:** Alamy **421:** Shadow Fox, Andy Clark/Reuters **422:** Alison Thompson/Alamy, Mark L. Simpson/Electric Lemonade Photography, Colombia Travel **423:** Marcio Jose Sanchez/AP/PA, Rex **424:** Shinsuke Kamioka/GWR, Ranald Mackechnie/GWR, James Ellerker/GWR **425:** Kevin Scott Ramos/GWR, Paul Michael Hughes/GWR **426:** Paul Michael Hughes/GWR, Paul Michael Hughes/GWR, Paul Michael Hughes/GWR **427:** Richard Bradbury/GWR, Drew Gardner/GWR **428:** US Navy, USAF, Alamy **429:** Reuters, Solid Concepts **430:** US Navy **431:** USDA, USDA **432:** US Navy **433:** Rory Daniel **434:** Rex Features, Jianan Yu/Reuters **435:** Alamy, Alamy, Alamy, Sean Pavone/Alamy, Gustau Nacarino/Reuters **436:** iStock, Rex Features **439:** iStock, Postojna Cave **440:** Jorge Royan, Jim Zuckerman/Alamy **442:** Alamy, Alice Finch **444:** Dominique Debaralle/Corbis, Ed Jones/Getty Images, Chi Po-lin, Pichi Chuang/Reuters **445:** Khaled Al-Sayyed/Getty Images, Hans Blossey/Corbis **446:** David Cannon/Getty Images, David Cannon/Getty Images, Getty Images **447:** Christian Haugen, Joel Riner **448:** Reuters, Cor Mulder/EPA **449:** Sven Sturm/MPI for Nuclear Physics **450:** ESA, Long Hongtao/Rex, Long Hongtao/Rex **451:** Felipe Pedreros/IceCube/NSF, Jim Haugen/IceCube/NSF **452:** Alamy, Baxley/JILA, Baxley/JILA **454:** Kevin Ma and Pakpong Chirarattananon/Harvard Microrobotics Lab **455:** Alamy, Iberpress **456:** Harvard School of Engineering and Applied Sciences **457:** Boston Dynamics **459:** Seth Wenig/AP/PA, Peter Morgan/Reuters **461:** Kumar Sriskandan/Alamy, Alamy **462:** NASA, NASA **465:** John Thys/Getty Images **467:** Stephane Mahe/Reuters

COUNTRY CODES

ABW	Aruba	COM	Comoros
AFG	Afghanistan	CPV	Cape Verde
AGO	Angola	CRI	Costa Rica
AIA	Anguilla	CUB	Cuba
ALB	Albania	CXR	Christmas Island
AND	Andorra	CYM	Cayman Islands
ANT	Netherlands Antilles	CYP	Cyprus
ARG	Argentina	CZE	Czech Republic
ARM	Armenia	DEU	Germany
ASM	American Samoa	DJI	Djibouti
ATA	Antarctica	DMA	Dominica
ATF	French Southern Territories	DNK	Denmark
ATG	Antigua and Barbuda	DOM	Dominican Republic
AUS	Australia	DZA	Algeria
AUT	Austria	ECU	Ecuador
AZE	Azerbaijan	EGY	Egypt
BDI	Burundi	ERI	Eritrea
BEL	Belgium	ESH	Western Sahara
BEN	Benin	ESP	Spain
BFA	Burkina Faso	EST	Estonia
BGD	Bangladesh	ETH	Ethiopia
BGR	Bulgaria	FIN	Finland
BHR	Bahrain	FJI	Fiji
BHS	The Bahamas	FLK	Falkland Islands (Malvinas)
BIH	Bosnia and Herzegovina	FRA	France
BLR	Belarus	FRG	West Germany
BLZ	Belize	FRO	Faroe Islands
BMU	Bermuda	FSM	Micronesia, Federated States of
BOL	Bolivia	FXX	France, Metropolitan
BRA	Brazil	GAB	Gabon
BRB	Barbados	GEO	Georgia
BRN	Brunei Darussalam	GHA	Ghana
BTN	Bhutan	GIB	Gibraltar
BVT	Bouvet Island	GIN	Guinea
BWA	Botswana	GLP	Guadeloupe
CAF	Central African Republic	GMB	Gambia
CAN	Canada	GNB	Guinea-Bissau
CCK	Cocos (Keeling) Islands	GNQ	Equatorial Guinea
CHE	Switzerland	GRC	Greece
CHL	Chile	GRD	Grenada
CHN	China	GRL	Greenland
CIV	Côte d'Ivoire	GTM	Guatemala
CMR	Cameroon	GUF	French Guiana
COD	Congo, DR of	GUM	Guam
COG	Congo	GUY	Guyana
COK	Cook Islands	HKG	Hong Kong
COL	Colombia	HMD	Heard and McDonald Islands

HND	Honduras	MNP	Northern Mariana Islands
HRV	Croatia (Hrvatska)	MOZ	Mozambique
HTI	Haiti	MRT	Mauritania
HUN	Hungary	MSR	Montserrat
IDN	Indonesia	MTQ	Martinique
IND	India	MUS	Mauritius
IOT	British Indian Ocean Territory	MWI	Malawi
IRL	Ireland	MYS	Malaysia
IRN	Iran	MYT	Mayotte
IRQ	Iraq	NAM	Namibia
ISL	Iceland	NCL	New Caledonia
ISR	Israel	NER	Niger
ITA	Italy	NFK	Norfolk Island
JAM	Jamaica	NGA	Nigeria
JOR	Jordan	NIC	Nicaragua
JPN	Japan	NIU	Niue
KAZ	Kazakhstan	NLD	Netherlands
KEN	Kenya	NOR	Norway
KGZ	Kyrgyzstan	NPL	Nepal
KHM	Cambodia	NRU	Nauru
KIR	Kiribati	NZ	New Zealand
KNA	Saint Kitts and Nevis	OMN	Oman
KOR	Korea, Republic of	PAK	Pakistan
KWT	Kuwait	PAN	Panama
LAO	Laos	PCN	Pitcairn Islands
LBN	Lebanon	PER	Peru
LBR	Liberia	PHL	Philippines
LBY	Libyan Arab Jamahiriya	PLW	Palau
LCA	Saint Lucia	PNG	Papua New Guinea
LIE	Liechtenstein	POL	Poland
LKA	Sri Lanka	PRI	Puerto Rico
LSO	Lesotho	PRK	Korea, DPRO
LTU	Lithuania	PRT	Portugal
LUX	Luxembourg	PRY	Paraguay
LVA	Latvia	PYF	French Polynesia
MAC	Macau	QAT	Qatar
MAR	Morocco	REU	Réunion
MCO	Monaco	ROM	Romania
MDA	Moldova	RUS	Russian Federation
MDG	Madagascar	RWA	Rwanda
MDV	Maldives	SAU	Saudi Arabia
MEX	Mexico	SDN	Sudan
MHL	Marshall Islands	SEN	Senegal
MKD	Macedonia	SGP	Singapore
MLI	Mali	SGS	South Georgia and South SS
MLT	Malta	SHN	Saint Helena
MMR	Myanmar (Burma)	SJM	Svalbard and Jan Mayen Islands
MNE	Montenegro		
MNG	Mongolia	SLB	Solomon Islands

SLE	Sierra Leone	TUN	Tunisia
SLV	El Salvador	TUR	Turkey
SMR	San Marino	TUV	Tuvalu
SOM	Somalia	TZA	Tanzania
SPM	Saint Pierre and Miquelon	UAE	United Arab Emirates
SRB	Serbia	UGA	Uganda
SSD	South Sudan	UK	United Kingdom
STP	São Tomé and Príncipe	UKR	Ukraine
SUR	Suriname	UMI	U.S. Minor Islands
SVK	Slovakia	URY	Uruguay
SVN	Slovenia	U.S.A.	United States of America
SWE	Sweden	UZB	Uzbekistan
SWZ	Swaziland	VAT	Holy See (Vatican City)
SYC	Seychelles	VCT	Saint Vincent and the
SYR	Syrian Arab Republic		Grenadines
TCA	Turks and Caicos Islands	VEN	Venezuela
TCD	Chad	VGB	Virgin Islands (British)
TGO	Togo	VIR	Virgin Islands (U.S.)
THA	Thailand	VNM	Vietnam
TJK	Tajikistan	VUT	Vanuatu
TKL	Tokelau	WLF	Wallis and Futuna Islands
TKM	Turkmenistan	WSM	Samoa
TMP	East Timor	YEM	Yemen
TON	Tonga	ZAF	South Africa
TPE	Chinese Taipei	ZMB	Zambia
TTO	Trinidad and Tobago	ZWE	Zimbabwe

INDEX

Bold entries in the index indicate a main entry on a topic; **BOLD CAPITALS** indicate an entire chapter. The index does not list personal names.

STOP PRESS

Largest game of "What's the time, Mr. Wolf?" The playground favorite was played by 494 staff of Royal London (UK) at the EICC in Edinburgh, UK, on Feb. 6, 2014.

Largest charity walk Iglesia Ni Cristo (PHL) organized a walk with 175,509 people, starting at the Quirino Grandstand in Manila, Philippines, on Feb. 15, 2014. Money was raised for victims of 2013's Typhoon Haiyan.

Most southerly navigation On Jan. 27, 2014, the *Arctic P*, skippered by Russell Pugh and owned by the Packer family (both AUS), reached the Bay of Whales in the Ross Ice Shelf of Antarctica. An instrument on the bow recorded 78°43.042'S 163°42.069'W, the most southerly point. The latitude of the shelf is dynamic due to the ice calving—when ice melts and breaks off the shelf.

Most haikus about one town As of Apr. 29, 2014, 1,663 haikus had been written about Luton in Bedfordshire, UK, by the local *Clod Magazine*. The Luton Haiku team—Andrew Kingston, Tim Kingston, Andrew Whiting, and Stephen Whiting—began posting haikus online each weekday from Jan. 23, 2007.

LARGEST GARFIELD COLLECTION Cathy Kothe (U.S.A.) has 6,190 unique Garfield items, as listed by her official cataloger—husband Robert—and verified in Huntington Station, New York, U.S.A., on Apr. 10, 2014. The collection includes three slot machines and an inflatable measuring 25 ft. (7.6 m) tall—higher than the couple's house!

The **smallest parachute** measured 35 sq. ft. on Apr. 5, 2014.

TALLEST TEENAGER (FEMALE) Measuring 7 ft. 0.09 in. (213.6 cm) at full standing height, Rumeysa Gelgi (TUR, b. Jan. 1, 1997) is the tallest female under the age of 18. Rumeysa, pictured above with niece Zeynep Ravza Yakut, was diagnosed with Weaver syndrome, a rare genetic disorder that causes rapid growth. She was measured by Dr. Ömer Hakan Yavaşoğlu (left) in Karabük, Turkey, on Mar. 19, 2014.

RUMEYSA GELGI

The new record holder tells us: "I'm adapting everything to my height. It has good and bad sides but, anyway, I feel lucky myself."

LONGEST GROUP DRUM ROLL
To celebrate the 350th anniversary of the Royal Marines (founded in 1664), the Corps of Drums of Her Majesty's Royal Marines Band Service (UK) achieved a group drum roll lasting 64 hr. 27 min. 59 sec. Beginning on Apr. 30, 2014, 40 members of the Corps took it in turns to drum on the same snare drum at the Tower of London, London, UK, finishing on May 3, 2014.

FASTEST LAWN MOWER
The *Mean Mower* can cut grass while moving at a speed of 116.57 mph (187.61 km/h) and was constructed and raced by Honda and Team Dynamics (both UK) at Applus+ IDIADA's test track in Tarragona, Spain, on Mar. 8, 2014. *Top Gear* journalist Piers Ward drove the mower.

Most pubs visited As of Jan. 29, 2014, Bruce Masters (UK) had visited 46,495 pubs and drinking establishments, sampling local beers where available. He began his tour in 1960, and visited 936 pubs in 2013 alone. The most popular UK pub name so far, says Bruce, is the Red Lion.

Oldest boxing world champion Bernard Hopkins (U.S.A., b. Jan. 15, 1965) broke his own record when, at 49 years 94 days old, he outpointed Beibut Shumenov (KAZ) for the WBA (super) light heavyweight, IBA light heavyweight, and IBF light heavyweight titles on Apr. 19, 2014.

Largest greetings card A Mother's Day card measuring 33 ft. 5 in. (10.19 m) tall and 23 ft. 3 in. (7.09 m) wide was unveiled by Nestlé Middle East FZE (UAE) at Dubai Mall, United Arab Emirates, on Mar. 21, 2014.

TELMEX TRIPLE CERTIFICATION
Telmex (MEX) achieved a GWR treble at Aldea Digital in Mexico City, Mexico, from Apr. 11 to 27, 2014. CEO Héctor Slim (center) receives the certificate for **largest digital inclusion event**, (258,896 people), plus those for **most people trained in IT in one month** (177,517, at the same event) and for **most scans of an Augmented Reality app in eight hours** (49,273, on Apr. 26).

HIGHEST 2D MOVIE BOX-OFFICE GROSS (OPENING WEEKEND)

Shortly before we went to press, we were delighted to have the chance to present Tom Hardy (UK) with a GWR certificate. Tom played Batman's enemy Bane, who terrorizes the caped crusader and Gotham City in *The Dark Knight Rises* (U.S.A./UK, 2012). The hit movie grossed $160,887,295 from Jul. 20 to 22, 2012.

Most consecutive rolls by an aircraft

Kingsley Just (AUS) rolled his Pitts Special biplane 987 times at Lethbridge Airpark in Victoria, Australia, on Mar. 1, 2014. Kingsley rolled his aircraft continuously for just under an hour without any break.

Most siblings to celebrate diamond wedding anniversaries

Edward Thomas and Ellen Jane Howell (UK) had five children, all of whom had celebrated 60 years of marriage as of Mar. 4, 2014:
- Gwendoline Jean Howell and Douglas Derek Bennett: 61 years
- John Edward Howell and Sylvia Beryl (née Winter): 61 years
- Doris Winifred Howell and Donald Street: 66 years
- Stanley Frederick Howell and Margaret Elizabeth (née Sharpe): 65 years
- William George Howell and Hazel Pauline (née Freeman): 60 years.

MOST BUNGEE JUMPS IN 24 HOURS Fitness coach Colin Phillips (UK) recorded 151 bungee jumps from a 328-ft.-tall (100-m) crane in aid of charity Breast Cancer Arabia. His attempt was set with Gravity Zone at Dubai Autodrome in the United Arab Emirates on Mar. 21, 2014. He dislocated a finger and afterward admitted to feeling "a bit beaten up, to be honest."

MOST PEOPLE MAKING HEART-SHAPED HAND GESTURES Stephen Sutton (UK, 1994–2014) and 553 friends gathered to make a heart symbol with their hands on May 4, 2014 in Staffordshire, UK. Stephen, diagnosed with terminal cancer, made headlines in 2014 with his fund-raising efforts, and stated that one of his dreams was to secure a Guinness World Records title.

LARGEST OBSERVATION WHEEL The Las Vegas High Roller is 549 ft. 8 in. (167.5 m) tall. Opened on Mar. 31, 2014 in Las Vegas, Nevada, U.S.A., it has 28 cabins, each holding 40 people. One full revolution of the wheel takes 30 min.

Longest time ranked as chess world No. 1 (female)

As confirmed by the International Chess Federation, Judit Polgár (HUN) has been the world No. 1 female player since Feb. 1, 1989, and retains the spot as of Apr. 17, 2014.

Most valuable life-insurance policy

The identity of the Silicon Valley billionaire who holds an insurance policy worth $201 m remains anonymous, but with more than 100 billionaires resident in the famous strip of California, U.S.A., there is no shortage of candidates. The policy was brokered by Dovi Frances (ISR) of the advisory firm SG, LLC (U.S.A.), and certified by a public notary in Santa Barbara, California, U.S.A., on Feb. 28, 2014. This beats the long-standing record for a $100-m policy sold by Peter Rosengard (UK) for U.S. media mogul David Geffen back in 1990.

LARGEST UNDERWATER VIEWING DOME The whale shark tank at Chimelong Ocean Kingdom in Hengqin, Guangdong, China, has a dome with a diameter of 39 ft. 4 in. (12 m). The attraction opened on Jan. 28, 2014 and set five world records, including **largest underwater viewing dome** (left). It uses 12.87 million gal. (48.75 million liters) of salt and fresh water.

Most weight lifted by dumbbell rows in one minute with one arm

Strongman Robert Natoli (U.S.A.) set five records in an hour at the Pacific Health Club in Liverpool, New York, U.S.A., on Mar. 22, 2014, to raise money for the Patterson family, whose three children had been badly injured in a car crash that claimed the life of their mother. He lifted 4,356 lb. (1,975.85 kg) with dumbbell rows and recorded the **most pull-ups in one minute with a 40-lb. pack** (23); the **most step-ups in one minute with an 80-lb. pack** (41); the **most step-ups in one minute with a 100-lb. pack** (38); and the **most knuckle push-ups in one minute** (58).

In a separate charity event in Oswego, New York, U.S.A., on Apr. 4, 2013, Natoli achieved two further records: the **most step-ups in one minute with a 40-lb. pack** (52) and the **most step-ups in one minute with a 60-lb. pack** (47).